Interpersonal Communication

Relating to Others

Fifth Edition

Steven A. Beebe
Texas State University–San Marcos

Susan J. Beebe
Texas State University–San Marcos

Mark V. Redmond
Iowa State University

Boston New York San Francisco
Mexico City Montreal Toronto London Madrid Munich Paris
Hong Kong Singapore Tokyo Cape Town Sydney

Dedicated to our families

Mark and Matthew Beebe

Peggy, Nicholas, and Eric Redmond, and Beth Maroney

Editor-in-Chief: Karon Bowers
Series Editorial Assistant: Jenny Lupica
Development Editor: Judith Hauck
Associate Editor: Deb Hanlon
Marketing Manager: Suzan Czajkowski
Production Supervisor: Beth Houston
Editorial Production Service: Quica Ostrander, Lifland et al., Bookmakers
Composition Buyer: Linda Cox
Manufacturing Buyer: JoAnne Sweeney
Electronic Composition: Publishers' Design and Production Services, Inc.
Interior Design: Glenna Collett
Photo Researcher: PoYee Oster
Cover Administrator: Linda Knowles

For related titles and support materials, visit our online catalog at www.ablongman.com.

Library of Congress Cataloging-in-Publication Data

Beebe, Steven A., 1950-
Interpersonal communication : relating to others / Steven A. Beebe, Susan J. Beebe, Mark V. Redmond.—5th ed.
p. cm.
Includes bibliographical references and index.
ISBN 0-205-48879-X
1. Interpersonal communication—Textbooks. I. Beebe, Susan J. II. Redmond, Mark V., 1949-III. Title.

BF637.C45B43 2008
153.6—dc22

2006052638

Printed in the United States of America
10 9 8 7 6 5 4 3 2 1 11 10 09 08 07

Brief Contents

List of Features

Becoming Other-Oriented

Applying Theory and Research

Understanding Diversity

Building Your Skills

Interpersonal Communication and Emotion: Connecting Heart to Heart

Contents

Preface

This book is based on the premise that at the heart of quality interpersonal relationships is a focus on others. A focus on others rather than yourself remains the hallmark of most faith movements in the world. Yet this book is not about religion. It's about how you relate to others in interpersonal situations. To be other-oriented, you need not abandon your own thoughts, feelings, and behavior; an other-oriented person is self-aware as well as aware of others. Becoming other-oriented is instead the mindful process of considering the thoughts, needs, feelings, and values of others, rather than focusing exclusively on oneself. The importance of being other-oriented was the foundation of the first four editions of *Interpersonal Communication: Relating to Others*, and it continues as the central theme of the fifth edition.

This book is designed to be the primary text for college-level courses in interpersonal communication. We've written this book for college students from age 18 to 80 who are seeking research-based principles and skills to enhance their interpersonal relationships. We emphasize research because this edition, like our previous editions, is not merely a book of "how to" techniques to "win friends and influence people." Our ideas are based on decades of communication research and reflect the latest thinking about how human beings relate to each other. Our balance of principles and skills is designed to help students enhance their own command of communication skills and to give them insights into why people communicate as they do in interpersonal situations.

Our Approach to Interpersonal Communication

An Other-Oriented Approach

In a Peanuts cartoon reproduced on page 47 of this book, Linus says to Lucy, "The world does not revolve around you!" Lucy's astonished "You're kidding!" suggests that the idea is a startling revelation to her. Unlike Lucy, the rest of us may not be so startled to discover that considering others is central to improving our interpersonal communication.

Becoming other-oriented is not a single skill, but rather a collection of skills and principles that are designed to increase your sensitivity to and understanding of others. Being other-oriented doesn't mean abandoning your own ideas and feelings in order to please others; that would not only be unethical, it would be an ineffective approach to developing genuine, honest relationships with others. We repeatedly stress that true empathy, emotional intelligence, and sensitivity are possible only when we feel secure about our own identities.

Becoming other-oriented includes all of the classic skills and principles typically taught in interpersonal communication courses—such as listening, providing feedback, and using conflict management skills and verbal and nonverbal skills—and places additional emphasis on the importance of the perceptions, thoughts, attitudes, beliefs, values, and emotions of others. We also review how relationships are formed, main-

tained, redefined, and terminated. Toward the end of each chapter we include a feature called Becoming Other-Oriented, in which we identify a principle or skill to help you become more aware of others. We also use a margin icon, like the one in the margin here, to highlight other-oriented ideas and strategies throughout the book.

An Emphasis on Diversity

Inherent in our other-oriented approach is the theme that people differ in significant ways. It is because of those differences that we need skills and principles that allow us to develop links with others so that we can establish meaningful interpersonal relationships. The body of research about our differences in communication behavior has continued to grow; the last decade saw a significant leap in our understanding of the role of differences in culture, age, gender, sexual orientation, religion, political perspectives, and other points of view in people's ability to connect to others. In this book we do more, however, than just point to differences between human beings. Using a competency-based approach, we present practical, research-based strategies for increasing understanding when interacting with those who are different from us.

Communication occurs when people find commonalities in meaning that transcend their differences. In a revised and expanded Chapter 4, Interpersonal Communication and Cultural Diversity: Adapting to Others, we not only identify barriers to competent intercultural communication but also present strategies to bridge the chasm of differences that too often divide people. In addition, in the Understanding Diversity features in every chapter, we distill research conclusions and communication strategies for understanding differences. With examples, illustrations, and research conclusions liberally woven throughout each chapter in the book, we identify ways to become other-oriented despite differences we encounter in people of the opposite sex or of other cultures or ideologies.

An Emphasis on Relationships

As the book's subtitle, *Relating to Others*, suggests, we highlight the importance of cultivating relationships with others by developing an increased awareness of and sensitivity to those relationships. Our emphasis on relationships is reflected in the wide range of relationships we discuss, including relationships with friends, lovers, family members, and co-workers, as well as relationships formed and developed over the Internet. In this new edition, we not only discuss positive, affirming relationships but have augmented our discussion of the "dark side" of relationships—such issues as deception, hurtful messages, jealousy, and stalking. Whether emphasizing the positive nature of relationships or providing a glimpse into the challenges of relating to others, we rely on the latest communication research so that readers will have access to up-to-the-minute thinking about how relationships can be improved.

An Emphasis on Technology and Interpersonal Relationships

Contemporary technology profoundly influences how we relate to others, not just online but in person as well. In every chapter, we include the latest research findings about how electronic connections affect or even take the place of our face-to-face relationships.

A feature that we have retained in this edition is the Weblinks at the end of each chapter, which enrich and enliven chapter content with supplemental readings and activities. To make it even easier to connect to the vast resources of the Internet, students who are using MyCommunicationLab with their textbooks will find links to all of the

Web sites we reference. Although our primary focus remains on live, face-to-face communication, we believe we cannot and should not ignore the ever-increasing role of technology in interpersonal communication.

New Features of the Fifth Edition

We are continually grateful for the positive e-mail messages, comments, and endorsements we receive from both students and instructors who have used the previous four editions of this book. What readers seem to value most is our easily accessible style, our other-oriented approach, and our efforts to make the book a contemporary distillation of interpersonal communication research conclusions and classic skills. We also appreciate the suggestions that have further enhanced the book's value.

A new edition gives us the opportunity not only to include the latest research conclusions but also to polish every feature, activity, suggested skill, and principle that we discuss. A relationship is an ongoing connection we make with others. In this, our fifth edition, we have continued our ongoing relationship with students and instructors by carefully reviewing each word and feature to make this the best possible source of information about interpersonal communication. Here's a brief summary of the key revisions we've made to the fifth edition:

144 Part 2 Interpersonal Communication Skills

Interpersonal Communication and Emotion
Connecting Heart to Heart

How to Express Helpful and Empathic Social Support to Others

One of the ways you can communicate empathy to another person who is experiencing stress, pain, or a significant life problem is to provide what communication researchers call **social support**. You provide social support to another person when you sensitively and empathically listen and then offer messages of comfort or confirmation that let the other person know that he or she is both understood and valued.

One research study suggests that when we are experiencing stress we prefer what researchers called a mid-level amount of social support.[53] Most people don't need over-the-top, dramatic expressions of support; on the other hand, mild or timid expressions of support from others are not satisfying either. We seem to like a moderate level of positive, genuine supportive communication. The research also suggests that females prefer a bit higher level of comforting response than males.

An ability to listen empathically is important when you discern that someone needs positive, comforting social support. What do researchers suggest are the best ways to provide supportive, empathic, comforting messages to others? Although there are no magic words or phrases that will always ease someone's stress and anxiety, here's a summary of social support messages that seem to be appreciated by others.[54]

- Clearly express that you want to provide support. ("I would really like to help you.")
- Appropriately communicate that you have positive feelings for the other person; explicitly tell the other person that you are a friend, that you care about or love him or her. ("You mean a lot to me." "I really care about you.")
- Express your concern about the situation that the other person is in right now. ("I'm worried about you right now because I know you're feeling ____ [stressed, overwhelmed, sad, etc.].")
- Indicate that you are available to help, that you have time to support the person. ("I can be here for you when you need me.")
- Let the other person know how much you support her or him ("I'm completely with you on this." "I'm here for you, and I'll always be here for you because I care about you.")
- Acknowledge that the other person is in a difficult situation. ("This must be very difficult for you.")
- It may be appropriate to paraphrase what the other person has told you about the issue or problem that is causing stress. ("So you became upset when she told you she didn't want to see you again.")
- Consider asking open-ended questions to see if the other person wants to talk. ("How are you doing now?")
- Let the other person know that you are listening and supportive by providing conversational continuers such as "Yes, then what happened?" or "Oh, I see," or "Uh-huh."
- After expressing your compassion, empathy, and concern, just listen.

Some types of responses are less helpful when providing social support. Here are a few things *not* to do, based on the conclusions of communication researchers:

- Don't tell the other person that you know exactly how he or she feels.
- Don't criticize or negatively evaluate the other person; he or she needs support and validation, not judgmental comments.
- Don't tell the other person to stop feeling what he or she is feeling.
- Don't immediately offer advice. First, just listen.
- Don't tell the other person that "it's going to get better from here" or that "the worst is over."
- Don't tell the other person that there is really nothing to worry about or that "it's no big deal."
- Don't tell the other person that the problem can be solved easily. ("Oh, you can always find another girlfriend.")
- Don't blame the other person for the problem. ("Well, if you didn't always drive so fast, you wouldn't have had the accident.")
- Don't tell the other person that it is wrong to express feelings and emotions. ("Oh, you're just making yourself sick. Stop crying.")

New Boxed Feature: Interpersonal Communication and Emotion: Connecting Heart to Heart

This new feature, included in every chapter, emphasizes research conclusions and communication skills related to emotion and interpersonal communication. The new material emphasizes that the emotional connections we make with others are essential in developing an other-oriented perspective toward our interpersonal partners.

Expanded Discussion of Diversity

Chapter 4 begins with a significantly revised and expanded discussion of the multifaceted nature of human diversity by including new information about race, ethnicity, sexual orientation, gender, age, and social class. Chapter 4 also presents new information about how to become interculturally competent. New material about diversity and interpersonal communication is interwoven throughout every chapter of the book.

Expanded Discussion of Technology and Interpersonal Communication

From an augmented section in Chapter 1 to the addition of new research and applications throughout the book, there is an enhanced emphasis on the role of technology in the development and maintenance of interpersonal relationships. Chapter 12 includes an expanded section on computer-mediated communication and interpersonal relationships.

New Material on the "Dark Side" of Interpersonal Communication

The text discusses new research conclusions relating to such issues as jealousy, obsessive relational intrusion, relational violence, and stalking and points out the implications of such research for interpersonal relationships. Students will gain a realistic picture of how interpersonal relationships can be affected by and even result in aggression.

New Research Spotlighted in Applying Theory and Research Features

To help students see the link between theory, research, and application, several new research studies are highlighted in the Applying Theory and Research features. Students will learn practical applications of cutting-edge research to their daily living and relating to others.

New Weblinks on MyCommunicationLab

New Weblinks have been added to MyCommunicationLab that link the content of the book to a wealth of interpersonal communication resources available on the World Wide Web.

Expanded Coverage of Social Support

New material related to social support and listening in Chapter 5, as well as a new discussion of social support and relationship development in Chapter 10, augment the discussion of how social support skills can enhance relationships.

New Guidelines for Self Disclosure

Chapter 2 concludes with a new summary of practical tips and strategies for self disclosure, based on the latest research.

New Guidelines for Adapting to Others

Chapter 4 presents a new and revised summary of strategies and skills that help students adapt messages to those who are different from them.

New Discussion of Meta-Communication

Both in Chapter 1 and in Chapter 5, new material has been added that helps students understand the multifaceted nature of communication when relating to others.

New Material on Power and Language

Chapter 6 includes a discussion of research on interpersonal power and of how the words we use or don't use add to or diminish the power of interpersonal messages.

New Strategies for Enhancing Interpersonal Communication Skills

Some of the latest research findings about developing interpersonal skills, including new research-based strategies for using *I* language, provide the rationale for new tips on enhancing the quality of interpersonal communication.

New Suggestions for Managing Conflict

New tips and strategies have been added to Chapter 8 to help students work through interpersonal conflict.

Expanded and Revised Pedagogy

New cartoons, revised margin definitions, updated Recap features, and new Building Your Skills features have been added throughout the book to help students master the material. To streamline the book, we've moved some strategies for Building Your Skills to the end of the chapters.

Our Partnership with Instructors

Our partnership with educators is best explained using a musical analogy: We have provided the notes, but the instructor is the one who makes the music. In this fifth edition of *Interpersonal Communication: Relating to Others*, we continue our tradition of providing a wide array of instructional resources to help instructors teach and students learn principles and skills of interpersonal communication. Built into the book are a vast variety of pedagogical features:

- A chapter-opening quotation to provide a captivating focal point for each chapter.
- A list of chapter learning objectives.
- A comprehensive outline of key content.
- Understanding Diversity features that highlight the application of interpersonal communication in a diverse world.
- Building Your Skills features that help students see the connection between knowing and doing.
- Becoming Other-Oriented features that help students understand the signature theme of the book.
- New Interpersonal Communication and Emotion: Connecting Heart to Heart boxes in every chapter, which highlight the role of emotion in the development and maintenance of relationships.
- Highly praised Recap features to help students remember the essence of key concepts and terms.
- Margin definitions of all boldface terms in the text.
- Chapter-end questions that focus on critical thinking and ethics to spark thought and class discussion.
- Learning with Others, which are chapter-end collaborative learning activities and exercises.
- Updated Weblinks to steer readers to supplemental resources and activities.

In addition to the learning resources built into the book, we offer a wealth of instructor and student supplements.

Instructor's Supplements

Print Supplements

Instructor's Resource Manual, by Lauren L. Breslin of the University of Phoenix. This comprehensive guide provides a wealth of teaching tips, lecture outlines, sample syllabi, Internet exercises, class assignments, and student activities for each chapter of the text.

Test Bank. The *Test Bank*, by Katrina M. Eicher of Elizabethtown Community and Technical College, contains multiple-choice, true/false, matching, short answer, essay, midterm, and final exam questions.

The Blockbuster Approach: A Guide to Teaching Interpersonal Communication with Video, 3e. This guide, by Thomas E. Jewell of Bergen Community College, provides lists and descriptions of commercial videos that can be used in the classroom to illustrate concepts in interpersonal communication and complex interpersonal relationships. Sample activities are also included.

Electronic Supplements

MyCommuncationLab is an interactive and instructive online solution for interpersonal communication classes. Designed to be used either as a supplement to a traditional lecture course or as a complete online course, *MyCommunicationLab* combines multimedia, video, research support, tests, and quizzes to make teaching and learning fun! Students benefit from a wealth of video clips, many of which are accompanied by activities, questions to consider, and helpful tips—all geared to help students learn to communicate more effectively. Visit www.mycommunicationlab.com. (Access code required.)

Computerized Test Bank. The questions in the print *Test Bank* are also available electronically through our computerized testing system, TestGen EQ. The fully networkable test-generating software is now available on a multiplatform CD-ROM. The user-friendly interface enables instructors to view, edit, and add questions, transfer questions to tests, and print tests in a variety of fonts. Search and sort features allow instructors to locate questions quickly and arrange them in a preferred order.

PowerPoint Presentation™. This package consists of a collection of text-specific lecture outlines and graphic images keyed to every chapter in the text. It is available on the Web at www.ablongman.irc.

Allyn & Bacon provides a selection of video materials especially tailored for an interpersonal communication course.

Allyn & Bacon Interpersonal Communication Video. Interested adopters can receive Allyn & Bacon's interpersonal communication video, which contains scenarios that illustrate key concepts in the course. Some restrictions apply; please contact your Allyn & Bacon representative for details.

The Allyn & Bacon Communication Video Library is a collection of communication videos produced by Films for the Humanities and Social Sciences. Topics include, but are not limited to, Business Presentations, Great American Speeches, and Conflict Resolution. Contact your Allyn & Bacon sales representative for ordering information; some restrictions apply.

Allyn & Bacon's Digital Media Archive for Communication, Version 3.0. The Digital Media Archive CD-ROM contains electronic images of charts, graphs, maps, tables, and figures, along with media elements such as video, audio clips, and related Web links. These media assets are fully customizable for use with our pre-formatted PowerPoint™ outlines or to import into an instructor's own lectures. (Images are Windows and Mac compatible.)

VideoWorkshop for Interpersonal Communication, by Christine North of Ohio Northern University, is a new way to bring video into your course for maximum learning! This total teaching and learning system includes quality video footage on an easy-to-use CD-ROM, plus a *Student Learning Guide* and an *Instructor's Teaching Guide*—both with textbook-specific correlation grids. The result? A program that brings textbook concepts to life with ease and helps your students understand, analyze, and apply the objectives of the course. VideoWorkshop is available for your students as a value-pack option with this textbook.

Sandbox. With Sandbox Custom Publishing from Allyn & Bacon, you can build your own textbook—one designed specifically around the course you teach, with material relevant specifically to your course. Using texts from Allyn & Bacon, you can

- Develop a book with a single look and feel throughout.
- Update internal referencing, so that table of contents, index, glossary, and figure numbering all match.
- Revise and print on demand.
- Receive previews within two days.
- Receive a one-time downloadable, printable evaluation copy upon request.

Choose how your textbook looks both inside and out, with all the chapters you want, in the order you want them. With Sandbox, you can include your own class notes and remove chapters from one book and add chapters from another—and you can do it without having to sacrifice quality. Create a custom book as seamless as the original products used to construct it. Imagine the possibilities when you build your book in Sandbox! (Users of Sandbox must order a minimum of 25 copies of their custom book, which must have a minimum of 150 pages. Custom books are available in black and white only for adopters of fewer than 2,500 units.) For more information, contact your local Allyn & Bacon representative, or go to www.ablongmancustom.com.

Student Supplements

Print Supplements

Skillbuilder Workbook. This guide, by *Interpersonal Communication* co-author Mark V. Redmond, helps students reinforce and enhance their understanding of the principles and skills of interpersonal communication. Filled with exercises, activities, and study aids, it provides students with a wealth of opportunities to review and apply concepts introduced in the text.

ResearchNavigator.com Guide: Speech Communication. This updated booklet, by Steven L. Epstein of Suffolk County Community College, includes tips, resources, and URLs to aid students conducting research on Pearson Education's research Web site, www.researchnavigator.com. The guide contains a student access code for the Research Navigator database, offering students unlimited access to a collection of more than 25,000 discipline-specific articles from top-tier academic publications and peer-reviewed journals, as well as the *New York Times* and popular news publications. The guide introduces students to the basics of the Internet and the World Wide Web and includes tips for searching for articles on the site and a list of journals useful for research in their discipline. Also included are hundreds of Web resources for the discipline, as well as information on how to correctly cite research. The guide is available packaged with new copies of the text.

Study Card for Interpersonal Communication. Colorful, affordable, and packed with useful information, Allyn & Bacon's Study Cards make studying easier, more efficient, and more enjoyable. Course information is distilled down to the basics, helping you quickly master the fundamentals, review a subject, or prepare for an exam. Because they're laminated for durability, you can keep these Study Cards for years to come and pull them out whenever you need a quick review.

Pathways to Careers in Communication. The National Communication Association's booklet provides information about the discipline, its history and importance, information on career possibilities, and other available resources for investigating communication studies. Available value-packed with any Allyn & Bacon communication text.

Electronic Supplements

MyCommuncationLab is an interactive and instructive online solution for interpersonal communication classes. Designed to be used as a supplement to a traditional lecture course or as a complete online course, *MyCommunicationLab* combines multimedia, video, research support, tests, and quizzes to make teaching and learning fun! Students benefit from a wealth of video clips, many of which are accompanied by activities, questions to consider, and helpful tips—all geared to help students learn to communicate more effectively. Visit www.mycommunicationlab.com. (Access code required.)

VideoWorkshop for Interpersonal Communication: Student Learning Guide, by Christine North of Ohio Northern University, is more than just video footage you can watch. It's a total learning system. Our complete program includes quality video footage on an easy-to-use CD-ROM, plus a *Student Learning Guide* with textbook-specific correlation grids. The result? A program that brings textbook concepts to life with ease and helps you understand, analyze, and apply the objectives of the course.

Allyn &Bacon's Interpersonal Communication Study Site, accessed at http://www.abinterpersonal.com. This Web site features interpersonal communication study materials for students, including flashcards and a complete set of practice tests for all major topics. Students also will find links to other valuable Web sites.

Acknowledgments

This book is not only a collaboration among the three of us, but also a collaboration with a host of others. Without the research conclusions of the talented, creative scholars who have studied interpersonal communication and published their results, a book of this scope would not be possible. We also thank our students, who are a constant source of questions, ideas, inspiration, and challenges that enrich our teaching and writing.

We are especially thankful for the continuing outstanding editorial support and leadership that kept our multi-author team collaborating with aplomb. Editor-in-Chief Karon Bowers, who has worked with us for a decade, continues to be a source of inspiration and unwavering support. Our development editor Judy Hauck has skillfully guided us through every step of the revision process. We appreciate her fresh ideas and insights.

We also appreciate the dozens of gifted interpersonal communication instructors and scholars who read the manuscript and offered suggestions that have made this a better book. We thank the following people for sharing their information, ideas, and ingenuity with us throughout the life of our book.

Reviewers

Rebecca Anderson, *Johnson County Community College*

Leonard Barchak, *McNeese University*

Cameron Smith Basquiat, *Community College of Southern Nevada*

Judyth Betz-Gonzales, *Delta College*

Marion Boyer, *Kalamazoo Community College*

Scott E. Caplan, *University of Delaware*

Norman Clark, *Appalachian State University*
Carolyn P. DeLeCour, *Palo Alto College*
Carol Z. Dolphin, *University of Wisconsin–Waukesha*
Terrence Doyle, *Northern Virginia Community College*
Reginald E. Ecarma, *Campbellsville University*
David L. Edwards, *South Central Technical College*
Janie Harden Fritz, *Duquesne University*
Patricia M. Harris-Jenkinson, *Sacramento City College*
Sherry J. Holmen, *Albuquerque Technical Vocational Institute*
Adna G. Howell, *Delta College*
David D. Hudson, *Golden West College*
Diana K. Ivy, *Texas A&M University–Corpus Christi*
Thomas E. Jewell, *Bergen Community College*
Elizabeth R. Lamoureux, *Buena Vista University*
Heidi McGrew, *Sinclair Community College*
Charles R. McMahan, *Vincennes University*
Timothy P. Mottet, *Texas State University–San Marcos*
Lisa M. Orick, *Albuquerque Technical Vocational Institute*
James R. Pauff, *Bowling Green State University*
Nan Peck, *Northern Virginia Community College*
Terry Perkins, *Eastern Illinois University*
Narissra Punyanunt-Carter, *Texas Tech University*
Susan Richardson, *Prince George's Community College*
Michael Schliessman, *South Dakota State University*
Cheri Simonds, *Illinois State University*
Anntarie Lanita Sims, *Trenton State College*
Heather A. Smith, *Santa Monica College*
Vincent Scott Smithson, *Purdue University North Central*
Dickie Spurgeon, *Southern Illinois University*
Glen H. Stamp, *Ball State University*
Claire Sullivan, *University of Maine*
James J. Tolhuizen, *Indiana University Northwest*
Sally Vogl-Bauer, *University of Wisconsin–Whitewater*
Sheryl L. Williams, *University of Wisconsin–Whitewater*
Lori Wisdom-Whitley, *Everett Community College*
Richard L. Wiseman, *California State University–Fullerton*

We are blessed with the support and ideas of our colleagues and friends. Sue and Steve thank Thompson Biggers, a valued friend and colleague who helped conceptualize this book. Mary Jeanette Smythe and Tom Willett are long-time teachers and friends who provided seminal instruction about interpersonal communication. Phil Salem, Lee Williams, Tim Mottet, Cathy Fleuriet, and Maureen Keeley are friends and colleagues at Texas State University–San Marcos who have positively influenced our work. John Masterson, a valued friend and colleague, also greatly influenced our teaching and writing about interpersonal communication. We owe special thanks to the late Michael Argyle at Oxford University, Oxford, England, who sponsored Steve as a Visiting Scholar at Oxford's Wolfson College and generously shared his research findings. Thanks, too, to Peter Collett, friend and colleague from Oxford, for his assistance, support, and friendship. Thane McCollough, from Gonzaga University, also a colleague whom Steve met in Oxford, provided valuable support for this project.

Over the years Mark has had the opportunity to interact with a number of colleagues who have helped shape his views and understandings of interpersonal communication. Particularly, Mark thanks Kay Mueller, Denise Vrchota, and Todd Jenks; and Terry Pickett, David Waggoner, Judith Bunyi, and Steve Ralston for help in the earlier editions. Beth Lamoureux at Buena Vista University continues to be an extraordinary supporter of our text, as well as a supportive friend. Mark also acknowledges and thanks a group of colleagues he met years ago when they were all graduate students at the University of Denver and with whom he developed enduring and treasured friendships: Rich Arthur, at Slippery Rock University; John Masterson, Texas Lutheran University; Diane Ritzdorf, Arapahoe High School; Marc Routhier, Frostburg State University; Jim Tolhuizen, Indiana University Northwest; and especially Phil Backlund, Central Washington University.

We have outstanding support from many people. Sue Hall, senior administrative assistant in the Department of Communication Studies at Texas State, continues to be an invaluable assistant and friend. Sondra Howe and Bob Hanna are other valued colleagues and staff members who provided skilled support. We thank our former students and now good friends Kosta Tovstiadi and Rick Sabatino for their skillful assistance in helping us secure the most contemporary research we could find about interpersonal communication.

Finally, our families provide ongoing love and support to each of us. Mark thanks his parents, Jack and Alice Redmond; his brother, Jack; and his sisters, Ruthann, Mary Lynn, and Tina, who helped shape a family environment that planted the seeds for studying and appreciating interpersonal communication. Those seeds have been nurtured into a full-grown fascination with how communication shapes our lives and personal development by his wife, Peggy, his daughter Beth, and his sons, Nicholas and Eric. On a practical level, Mark owes a lot of his understanding of chat rooms and instant messaging to them.

Steve and Sue want especially to thank their parents, Russell and Muriel Beebe, who have recently celebrated their 65th wedding anniversary, and Herb and Jane Dye, who have been married for almost 60 years. These humble and dedicated mentors were our first and finest teachers of interpersonal communication. We also thank our son Mark, who continues to teach us that the power of love can overcomes life's challenges, and our son Matt, who teaches us about the importance of finding music in both days filled with sunshine and days filled with clouds.

Steven A. Beebe
Susan J. Beebe
San Marcos, Texas

Mark V. Redmond
Ames, Iowa

About the Authors

Steven A. Beebe is Professor and Chair of the Department of Communication Studies and Associate Dean of the College of Fine Arts and Communication at Texas State University–San Marcos. Steve is the author or co-author of eleven widely used communication books, most of which have been through multiple editions, as well as of numerous articles, book chapters, and conference presentations. He has been a Visiting Scholar at both Oxford University and Cambridge University in England, has traveled widely in Europe and Asia, and has played a leadership role in establishing new communication curricula in Russian universities. In 1996 he was named Outstanding Communication Professor by the National Speaker's Association. He has also received the President's Award for Research as well as the President's Award for Service at Texas State. His passions in life include his family and a life-long love of music; he is a pianist and organist and is currently struggling to learn the cello.

Susan J. Beebe's professional interests and expertise encompass both oral and written communication. Currently serving as Acting Director of Lower-Division Studies in the Department of English at Texas State University–San Marcos, Sue has co-authored three books and has published a number of articles and teaching materials in both English and communication studies. She has received both the Texas State Presidential Award for Excellence in Service and the College of Liberal Arts Award for Excellence in Scholarly/Creative Activities. An active volunteer in the community of San Marcos, Texas, Sue was the founding coordinator of the San Marcos Volunteers in Public Schools Program and has served on the San Marcos School Board and the Education Foundation Board. In 1993 she was named the statewide Friend of Education by the Texas Classroom Teachers' Association; in 2000 the San Marcos school district presented her with its Lifetime Achievement Award. Sue enjoys reading, traveling, and caring for the Beebe family pets, a Shih Tzu named Martin and a cat named Alice. Sue and Steve have two sons: Mark, a graduate of Rice University; and Matt, a graduate of Southwestern University.

Mark V. Redmond is an Associate Professor of Communication Studies at Iowa State University. Besides this book, Mark has authored an introductory text on communication theory and research, edited an upper-level text in interpersonal communication, and co-authored a public speaking text. His research focuses on social decentering (taking into account another person's thoughts, feelings, perspectives, etc.), one of the themes incorporated in this text. His studies have included an examination of initial interactions between strangers, adaptation in interpersonal interactions, interpersonal influence, and intercultural communication competence. He is a Cyclone sports fan with an avocation for playing basketball at least three times a week (despite an aging hook shot). An unaccomplished piano and guitar player, he loves composing and writing songs and vows to someday complete the musical he's been working on for twenty years. Mark and his wife Peggy have three children: Beth, completing her nursing degree; Nicholas, a graduate of Iowa State University; and Eric, a student at Iowa State.

Part One

Interpersonal Communication Foundations

The first four chapters present fundamental concepts that frame our study of interpersonal communication. In Chapter 1, you will learn answers to these questions: What is interpersonal communication? What is the connection between interpersonal communication and interpersonal relationships? Why is it important to study relationships? What can I do to improve my relationships with others? Chapter 2 offers concepts and skills to help you understand more about who you are and how your self-concept and sense of self-worth influence your relationships, as well as how you reveal yourself to others. In Chapter 3, you will learn that perception plays a key role in effective interpersonal communication. By recognizing the factors that influence your perceptions and actively analyzing the meaning of perceptual information, you can become more adept at sharing your sense of the world with others. Chapter 4 explores principles to help you better understand people who are different from you and explains how developing an other-oriented perspective helps bridge cultural differences.

CHAPTER 1

Introduction to Interpersonal Communication

OBJECTIVES

1. Compare and contrast definitions of communication, human communication, and interpersonal communication.
2. Explain why it is useful to study interpersonal communication.
3. Compare and contrast communication as action, interaction, and transaction.
4. Describe the key components of the communication process.
5. Discuss the Internet's role in developing and maintaining interpersonal relationships.
6. Discuss five principles of interpersonal communication.
7. Describe four interpersonal communication myths.
8. Identify strategies that can improve your communication competence.

OUTLINE

Communication is to a relationship what breathing is to maintaining life.

Virginia Satir

Interpersonal communication is like breathing; it is a requirement for life. And, like breathing, interpersonal communication is inescapable. Unless you live in isolation, you communicate interpersonally every day. Listening to your roommate, talking to a teacher, meeting for lunch with a friend, and talking to your parents or your spouse are all examples of interpersonal communication.

It is impossible *not* to communicate with others. Even before we are born, we respond to movement and sound. With our first cry, we announce to others that we are here. Once we make contact with others, we communicate, and we continue to do so until we draw our last breath. Even though many of our messages are not verbalized, we nonetheless send messages to others—intentionally and sometimes unintentionally. Whatever our intentions, people draw conclusions from our behavior. Without interpersonal communication, a special form of human communication that occurs as we manage our relationships, people suffer and even die. Recluses, hermits, and people isolated in solitary confinement dream and hallucinate about talking with others face to face.

Human communication is at the core of our existence. Think of the number of times you communicated with someone today, as you worked, ate, studied, shopped, or went about your other daily activities. Most people spend between 80 and 90 percent of their waking hours communicating with others.[1] It is through these interactions with others that we develop interpersonal relationships.[2]

Because these relationships are so important to our lives, later chapters will focus on the communication skills and principles that explain and predict how we develop, sustain, and sometimes end relationships. We'll explore such questions as the following: Why do we like some people and not others? How can we interpret other people's unspoken messages with greater accuracy? Why do some relationships blossom and others deteriorate? How can we better manage disagreements with others? How can we better understand our relationships with our family, friends, and coworkers?

This chapter charts the course ahead, addressing key questions about what interpersonal communication is and why it is important. We will begin by seeing how our understanding of the interpersonal communication process has evolved. And we will conclude by examining how we initiate and sustain relationships through interpersonal communication.

Defining Interpersonal Communication

To understand interpersonal communication, we must begin by understanding how it relates to two broader categories: communication in general and human communication. Scholars have attempted to arrive at a general definition of communication for decades, yet experts cannot agree on a single one. One research team counted more than 126 published definitions;[3] however, in the broadest sense, **communication** is the process of acting on information.[4] Someone does or says something, and others think or do something in response to the action or the words as they understand them.

To refine our broad definition, we can say that **human communication** is the process of making sense out of the world and sharing that sense with others by creating meaning through the use of verbal and nonverbal messages.[5] We learn about the world by listening, observing, tasting, touching, and smelling; then we share our conclusions with others. Human communication encompasses many media: speeches, e-mail, songs, radio and television broadcasts, online discussion groups, letters, books, articles, poems, and advertisements.

Interpersonal communication is a distinctive, transactional form of human communication involving mutual influence, usually for the purpose of managing relationships. The three essential elements of this definition distinguish the unique nature of interpersonal communication from other forms of human communication.[6]

Interpersonal Communication Is a Distinctive Form of Communication

For years, many scholars defined interpersonal communication simply as communication that occurs when two people interact face to face. This limited definition suggests that if two people are interacting, then they are engaging in interpersonal communication. Today, interpersonal communication is defined not just by the number of people who communicate, but also by the quality of the communication. Interpersonal communication occurs not simply when you interact with someone, but when you treat the other person as a unique human being.[7]

Think of all human communication as ranging on a continuum from impersonal to interpersonal communication. **Impersonal communication** occurs when you treat people as objects, or when you respond to their roles rather than to who they are as unique people. Philosopher Martin Buber influenced our thinking about human communication when he presented the concept of honest dialogue as the essence of true, authentic communication.[8] He described communication as consisting of two different qualities of relationships. He discussed an "I–It" relationship as an impersonal one; the other person is viewed as an "It" rather than as an authentic, genuine person. When you buy a pair of socks at a clothing store, you have a two-person, face-to-face, relatively brief interaction with someone. You communicate. Yet that interchange could hardly be described as intimate or personal. When you ask a server in a restaurant for a glass of water, you are interacting with the role, not necessarily with the individual. You know nothing personal about this individual, and he or she knows nothing personal about you (unless this person eavesdrops on your conversation).

Interpersonal communication occurs when you interact with another person as a unique, authentic individual rather than as an object or an "It." Buber calls this kind of relationship an "I–Thou" relationship. In this kind of relationship, there is true dialogue. An "I–Thou" relationship is not self-centered. The communicators have developed an attitude toward each other that is honest, open, spontaneous, nonjudgmental, and based on equality rather than superiority.[9]

communication. Process of acting on information.

human communication. Process of making sense out of the world and sharing that sense with others by creating meaning through the use of verbal and nonverbal messages.

interpersonal communication. A distinctive, transactional form of human communication involving mutual influence, usually for the purpose of managing relationships.

impersonal communication. Process that occurs when we treat others as objects or respond to their roles rather than to who they are as unique persons.

We're not suggesting that the goal of every communication transaction is to develop a personal, intimate dialogue. That would be unrealistic and inappropriate. It's possible to go through an entire day communicating with others but not be involved in interpersonal communication. As we noted earlier, interpersonal communication is a distinctive form of communication; it does not occur just because two people are communicating.

Additionally, although interpersonal communication is more intimate and reveals more about the people involved than does impersonal communication, not all interpersonal communication involves sharing closely guarded personal information. As we discuss later in the book, there are degrees of intimacy when interacting with others.

The Continuum Between Interpersonal Communication and Impersonal Communication

Interpersonal Communication	Impersonal Communication
• People are treated as unique individuals.	• People are treated as objects.
• People communicate in an "I-Thou" relationship. Each person is special.	• People communicate in an "I-It" relationship. Each person has a role to perform.
• People communicate in an "I-It" relationship. There is true dialogue and honest sharing of self with others.	• There is mechanical, stilted interaction, rather than honest sharing of feelings.
• Interpersonal communication often involves communicating with someone you care about, such as a good friend or cherished family member.	• Impersonal communication involves communicating with people such as sales clerks and servers—you have no history with them, and you expect no future with them.

Interpersonal Communication Involves Mutual Influence Between Individuals

Mutual influence means that *all* partners in the communication are affected by a transaction. Interpersonal communication may or may not involve words. The degree of mutual influence varies a great deal from transaction to transaction. You probably would not be affected a great deal by a brief smile that you received from a traveling companion on a bus, but you would be greatly affected by your lover telling you he or she was leaving you. Every interpersonal communication transaction influences us. Sometimes it changes our lives dramatically, sometimes in small ways. Long-lasting interpersonal relationships are sustained not by one person giving and another taking, but by a spirit of mutual equality. Both you and your partner listen and respond with respect for each other. There is no attempt to manipulate others. True dialogue, says researcher Daniel Yankelovich, involves a collaborative climate. It's not about winning or losing an argument. It's about being understood and accepted.[10]

Buber's concept of an "I–Thou" relationship includes the quality of being fully "present" when communicating with another person.[11] To be present is to give your full attention to the other person. The quality of interpersonal communication is enhanced when both you and your partner are simultaneously present and focused on each other.

In face-to-face encounters, we simultaneously exchange both verbal and nonverbal messages that result in shared meanings. Through this kind of interrelation, we build relationships with others.

Interpersonal Communication Helps Individuals Manage Their Relationships

A **relationship** is a connection established when you communicate with another person. When two individuals are in a relationship, what one person says or does influences the other person. As in dancing, people in relationships are affected by the beat of the music (that is, the situation in which they are communicating), their ability to interpret the music and move accordingly (the personal skills they possess), and the moves and counter-moves of their partner.

You initiate and form relationships by communicating with others whom you find attractive in some way. You seek to increase your interactions with people with whom you wish to develop relationships, and you continually communicate interpersonally to maintain the relationship. You also use interpersonal communication to end or redefine relationships that you have decided are no longer viable or need to be changed. In summary, to relate to someone is to "dance" with them. We dance with them in a specific time and place, with certain perceptions and expectations. Over time, this dance becomes an ongoing interpersonal relationship.

In this book, we define interpersonal communication as a unique form of human communication. There are other forms of communication, as well. **Mass communication** occurs when someone communicates the same message to many people at once, but the creator of the message is usually not physically present, and listeners have virtually no opportunity to respond immediately to the speaker. Messages communicated via radio and TV are examples of mass communication. **Public communication** occurs when a speaker addresses an audience in person. **Small group communication** occurs when a group of from three to fifteen people meet to interact with a common purpose and mutually influence one another. The purpose of the gathering could be to solve a problem, make a decision, learn, or just have fun. While communicating with others in a small group, it is also possible to communicate with others interpersonally—to communicate to manage a relationship with one or more individuals in the group. Finally, **intrapersonal communication** is communication with yourself. Thinking is perhaps the best example of intrapersonal communication. In our discussion of self and communication in Chapter 2, we discuss the relationships between your thoughts and your interpersonal communication with others.

relationship. Connection established with another person through communication.

mass communication. Process that occurs when one person issues the same message to many people at once; the creator of the message is usually not physically present, and there is virtually no opportunity for listeners to respond immediately to the speaker.

public communication. Process that occurs when a speaker addresses an audience in person.

small group communication. Process that occurs when a group of from three to fifteen people meet to interact with a common purpose and mutually influence one another.

intrapersonal communication. Communication with yourself; thinking.

The Importance of Interpersonal Communication

Why learn about interpersonal communication? Because it touches every aspect of our lives. It is not only pleasant or desirable to develop quality interpersonal relationships with others, it is vital for our well-being. We have a strong need to communicate interpersonally with others. Learning how to understand and improve interpersonal communication can improve relationships with family, loved ones, friends, and colleagues and can enhance the quality of physical and emotional health.

Understanding Interpersonal Communication Can Improve Relationships with Family

Relating to family members can be a challenge. The divorce statistics in the United States document the difficulties that can occur when people live in relationships with others: About half of all marriages end in divorce. We don't claim that you will avoid all family conflicts or that your family relationships will always be harmonious if you learn principles and skills of interpersonal communication. You can, however, develop more options for responding when family communication challenges come your way. You will be more likely to develop creative, constructive solutions to family conflict if you understand what's happening and can promote true dialogue with your spouse, partner, parent, brother, or sister. Furthermore, family relationships play a major role in determining how you interact with others. Family communication author Virginia Satir calls family communication "the largest single factor determining the kinds of relationships [people make] with others."[12] Being able to have conversations with family members and loved ones is the fundamental way of establishing close, personal relationships with them.

Research shows that effective interpersonal skills can be beneficial to our emotional and physical well-being.

Understanding Interpersonal Communication Can Improve Relationships with Friends and Lovers

For unmarried people, developing friendships and falling in love are the top-rated sources of satisfaction and happiness in life.[13] Conversely, losing a relationship is among life's most stressful events. Most people between the ages of 19 and 24 report that they have had from five to six romantic relationships and have been "in love" once or twice.[14] Studying interpersonal communication may not unravel all the mysteries of romantic love and friendship, but it can offer insight into behaviors.

Understanding Interpersonal Communication Can Improve Relationships with Colleagues

In many ways, colleagues at work are like family members. Although you choose your friends and lovers, you don't always have the same flexibility in choosing those with whom or for whom you work. Understanding how relationships develop on the job can help you avoid conflict and stress and increase your sense of satisfaction. In addition, your success or failure in a job often hinges on how well you get along with supervisors and peers.

Several surveys document the importance of quality interpersonal relationships in contributing to success at work.[15] The abilities to listen to others, manage conflict, and develop quality interpersonal relationships with others are usually at the top of the list of the skills employers seek in today's job applicants.[16]

Understanding Interpersonal Communication Can Improve Physical and Emotional Health

Research has shown that the lack or loss of a close relationship can lead to ill health and even death. Physicians have long observed that patients who are widowed or divorced experience more medical problems such as heart disease, cancer, pneumonia, and diabetes than do married people.[17] Grief-stricken spouses are more likely than others to die prematurely, especially around the time of the departed spouse's birthday or near their wedding anniversary.[18] Being childless can also shorten one's life. One study found that middle-aged, childless wives were almost two-and-one-half times more likely to die in a given year than those who had at least one child.[19] Terminally ill patients with a limited number of friends or no social support die sooner than those with stronger ties.[20] Without companions and close friends, opportunities for intimacy and stress-minimizing interpersonal communication are diminished. Although being involved in intimate interpersonal relationships can lead to conflict and feelings of anger and frustration, researchers suggest that when all is said and done, having close relationships with others is a major source of personal happiness.[21] Studying how to enhance the quality of your communication with others can make life more enjoyable and enhance your overall well-being.

Comparing Key Definitions

Term	Definition
Communication	The process of acting on information
Human communication	The process of making sense out of the world and sharing that sense with others by creating meaning through verbal and nonverbal messages
Interpersonal communication	A distinctive, transactional form of human communication involving mutual influence, usually for the purpose of managing relationships

An Evolving Model for Human and Interpersonal Communication

Interpersonal communication involves more than simply transferring or exchanging messages; it is a complex process of creating meaning in the context of an interpersonal relationship. So that we can understand this process more fully, it is useful to see how perspectives on the human communication process have evolved over the past half century.[22] We will begin with the simplest and oldest model of the human communication process and then discuss more contemporary models.

Human Communication as Action: Message Transfer

"Did you get my message?" This simple sentence summarizes the communication-as-action approach to human communication. Communication takes place when a message is sent and received. Period. It is a way of transferring meaning from sender to receiver.

Figure 1.1 shows a basic model that depicts communication as a linear input/output process. Today, although they view the process as more complicated, researchers still define most of the key components in this model in basically the same way.

source. Originator of a thought or emotion, who puts it into a code that can be understood by a receiver.

encode. To translate ideas, feelings, and thoughts into a code.

Source

The **source** for communication is the originator of a thought or an emotion, who expresses ideas and feelings as a code that can be understood by a receiver. Translating ideas, feelings, and thoughts into a code is called **encoding.** Vocalizing a word, gesturing, and establishing eye contact are signals that we use to encode our thoughts into

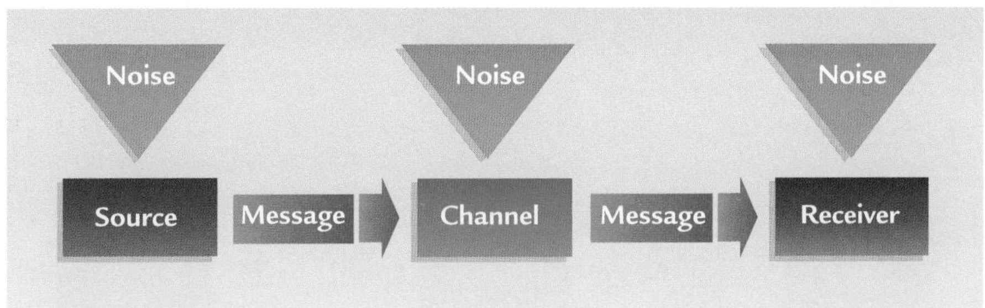

FIGURE 1.1

A Simple Model of Human Communication as Action

a message that can be decoded by someone. **Decoding,** the opposite process of encoding, occurs when the words or unspoken signals are interpreted by the receiver.

Message

Messages are the written, spoken, and unspoken elements of communication to which people assign meaning. You can send a message intentionally (talking to a professor before class) or unintentionally (falling asleep during class); verbally ("Hi. How are you?"), nonverbally (a smile and a handshake), or in written form (this book).

Channel

A message is communicated from sender to receiver via some pathway called a **channel.** Channels correspond to your senses. When you call your mother on the telephone, the channel is an auditory one. When you talk with your mother face to face, the channels are many. You see her: the visual channel. You hear her: the auditory channel. You may smell her perfume: the olfactory channel. You may hug her: the tactile channel.

Receiver

The **receiver** is the person who decodes and attempts to make sense of what the source encoded. Think of a radio station as a source broadcasting to a receiver that picks up the station's signal. In human communication, however, there is something in between the source and the receiver: People filter messages through past experiences, attitudes, beliefs, values, prejudices, and biases.

Noise

Noise is anything that interferes with a message and keeps it from being understood and achieving its intended effect. Without noise, all messages would be communicated with sublime accuracy. But noise is always present. It can be literal (the obnoxious roar of a neighbor's lawn mower), or it can be psychological (instead of concentrating on your teacher's lecture, you may start thinking about the chores you need to finish before the end of the day). Whichever kind it is, noise gets in the way of the message and may even distort it. Communicating accurate messages involves minimizing both external and psychological noise.

The action approach is simple and straightforward, but it has a key flaw: Human communication rarely, if ever, is as simple and efficient as "what we put in is what we get out." Others cannot automatically know what you mean just because you think you know what you mean. Although by the early 1940s, when the action approach was formulated, communication scholars had already begun identifying an array of key elements in the communication process, the action approach overlooked the complexity of those elements.

decode. To interpret ideas, feelings, and thoughts that have been translated into a code.

message. Written, spoken, and unspoken elements of communication to which people assign meaning.

channel. Pathway through which messages are sent.

receiver. Person who decodes a message and attempts to make sense of what the source has encoded.

noise. Anything literal or psychological that interferes with accurate reception of a message.

FIGURE 1.2

A Model for Communication as Interaction
Interaction models of communication include feedback as a response to a message sent by the communication source and context as the environment for communication.

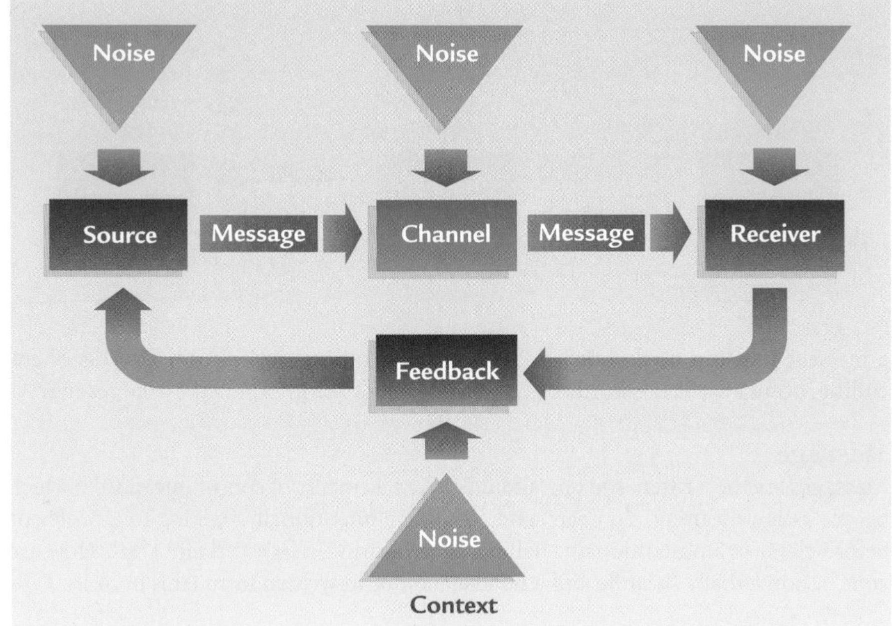

Human Communication as Interaction: Message Exchange

The communication-as-interaction perspective used the same elements as the action models but added two new ones: feedback and context.

Feedback is the response to the message. Think of a Ping-Pong game. Like a Ping-Pong ball, messages bounce back and forth. We talk; someone listens and responds; we listen and respond to this response. This perspective can be summarized using a physical principle: For every action, there is a reaction.

Without feedback, communication is rarely effective. When you order a black olive pizza and the server says in response, "That's a black olive pizza, right?" he has provided feedback to ensure that he decoded the message correctly. Like other messages, feedback can be intentional (your mother gives you a hug when you announce your engagement) or unintentional (you yawn as you listen to your uncle tell his story about bears again), verbal ("That's a black olive pizza, right?") or nonverbal (blushing after being asked to dance).

A second component recognized by the interaction perspective is **context**, the physical and psychological environment for communication. All communication takes place in some context. As the cliche goes, "Everyone has to be somewhere." A conversation with your good friend on the beach would likely differ from a conversation the two of you might have in a funeral home. Context encompasses not only the physical environment but also the number of people present and their relationships with the communicators, the communication goal, and the culture of which the communicators are a part.[23]

The communication-as-interaction perspective, as shown in Figure 1.2, is more realistic than the action perspective, but it still has limitations. Although it emphasizes feedback and context, it does not quite capture the complexity of interpersonal communication, which typically takes place simultaneously. The interaction model of communication still views communication as a linear, step-by-step process. But in interpersonal situations, both the source and the receiver send and receive messages at the same time.

feedback. Response to a message.

context. Physical and psychological environment for communication.

Recap: Components of the Human Communication Process

Term	Definition
Source	Originator of a thought or emotion who encodes it for a receiver
Receiver	Person who decodes a message from a source and attempts to make sense of it
Message	Written, spoken, and unspoken elements of communication to which people assign meaning
Channel	Pathway through which messages are sent
Noise	Anything literal or psychological that interferes with the clear reception and interpretation of a message
Encode	To translate ideas, feelings, and thoughts into a code
Decode	To interpret ideas, feelings, and thoughts that have been translated into a code
Context	Physical and psychological environment for communication
Feedback	Verbal and nonverbal responses to a message

Human Communication as Transaction: Message Creation

The communication-as-transaction perspective acknowledges that when you talk to another person face to face, you are constantly reacting to your partner's responses. Most scholars today view the transaction perspective as the most realistic model for interpersonal communication. Like action and interaction, transaction uses various components to describe communication. However, in this model, all the components are simultaneous. As Figure 1.3 indicates, you send and receive messages concurrently. Even as you talk, you are also interpreting your partner's nonverbal and verbal responses.

The transactional approach to communication is based on **systems theory.** A system is a set of interconnected elements in which a change in one element affects all of the other elements. Your body is an example of a system. Key aspects of any system include *inputs* (all of the variables that go in to the system), *throughputs* (which are all of the things that make communication a process), and *outputs* (what the system produces). Systems theory, from a communication perspective, helps us to understand the transactional nature of communication, in that a change in any aspect of the communication system (source, message, channel, receiver, context, feedback, etc.) has a potential influence on all of the other elements of the system. Viewing communication

systems theory. Theory that describes the interconnected elements of a system in which a change in one element affects all of the other elements.

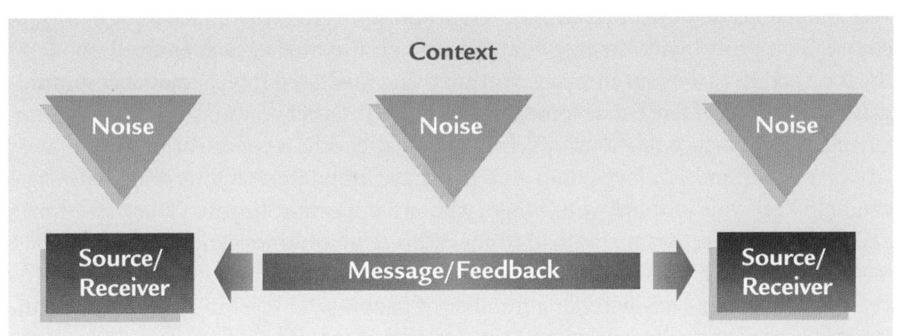

FIGURE 1.3

A Model for Communication as Mutual Transaction

The source and receiver of a message experience communication simultaneously.

as action or interaction does not quite capture the complexity of the communication process as a systems or transactional process does. From a systems theory point of view, all of the elements of communication are connected to every other element of communication.

A transactional approach to communication suggests that no single cause explains why you interpret messages the way you do. In fact, it is inappropriate to point to a single factor to explain how you are making sense of the messages of others; communication is messier than that. The meaning of messages in interpersonal relationships evolves from the past, is influenced by the present, and is affected by visions of the future.

One researcher says that interpersonal communication is "the coordinated management of meaning" through **episodes**, sequence of interactions between individuals during which the message of one person influences the message of another.[24] Technically, only the sender and receiver of those messages can determine where one episode ends and another begins.

An Evolving Model for Interpersonal Communication

Human Communication as Action 	Human communication is linear, with meaning sent or transferred from source to receiver.
Human Communication as Interaction 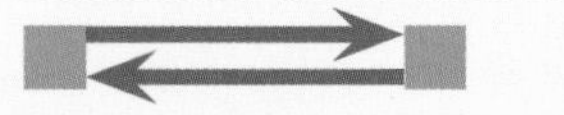	Human communication occurs as the receiver of the message responds to the source through feedback. This interactive model views communication as a linear action–reaction sequence of events within a specific context.
Human Communication as Transaction 	Human communication is mutually interactive. Meaning is created based on a concurrent sharing of ideas and feelings. This transaction model most accurately describes human communication.

Mediated Interpersonal Communication: Relating to Others Online

Can you really communicate *interpersonally* with someone on the Internet? Can relationships be developed with others without meeting them face to face? Yes, of course. You probably do so every day. When you use media, such as a cell phone or the Internet, to carry your message, you are using **mediated interpersonal communication**. There is evidence that some long-distance Internet relationships can be as satisfying as face-to-face relationships.[25] If you are attending a college or university away from family, friends, or loved ones, you may have found that sending e-mail messages can help keep you in touch with others who are important to you. College freshmen and their parents report that e-mail connections reduce homesickness for the students and the sadness parents often feel as their son or daughter leaves home. The past few years have seen an ever-increasing number of people who meet in chat rooms on the Internet and eventually develop real-time relationships.

episode. Sequence of interactions between individuals, during which the message of one person influences the message of another.

mediated interpersonal communication. Communication with others established or maintained through media (such as e-mail, telephones, or faxes) rather than through face-to-face encounters.

DILBERT: © Scott Adams/Dist. by United Feature Syndicate, Inc.

Of course, people have been communicating without being face to face for centuries; sending letters and other written messages to others is an established human practice. What's new today is that there are so many different ways of *immediately* connecting with someone, such as using a cell phone, e-mail, instant messaging, or a host of other Internet-based ways of developing interpersonal relationships. Research has found that immediately after the terrorist attacks on September 11, 2001, not only the telephone, but also the Internet was a prime means of spreading the news of the attacks.[26] People used e-mail not only to share the shocking news, but also to seek support and reassurance from friends that their loved ones were safe. Other research suggests that we are increasingly using online communication channels to seek emotional support from others.[27] We use the Internet to share information that ranges from the dramatic to the routine, as well as relationship-enriching messages.

How is mediated interpersonal communication different from live, face-to-face conversation? There are four key differences:[28]

1. *Anonymity:* You may not always know precisely with whom you are communicating when you receive an e-mail message.
2. *Physical Appearance:* There is typically less emphasis on a person's physical appearance online. Yes, we are curious about what our online partner may look like, and there are computers with cameras that let you see the person with whom you're communicating, but the majority of Internet communication occurs with people we don't see.
3. *Distance:* Although we certainly can and do send e-mail messages to people who live and work in the same building we're in, there is typically greater physical distance between people who are communicating online. Via the Internet, we can just as easily send a message to someone on the other side of the globe as we can to someone who is on the other side of town.
4. *Time:* You have greater control over the timing and pacing of the messages you send and receive. You can decide, for example, when to retrieve e-mail messages or when to respond to a message you receive. Your interaction with others can be **asynchronous**—which means your messages are not necessarily read, heard, or seen at the time you send them; there may be a time delay between when you send and receive a message.

asynchronous interaction. Process in which messages are not necessarily read, heard, or seen at the time you send them; there may be a time delay between when you send a message and when it is received.

Do people who spend a lot of time online generally have more or less personal contact with other people? A team of researchers led by Robert Kraut and Sara Kiesler made headlines when they published the results of their study, which concluded that

Applying Theory and Research

Communicating Online: Social Information-Processing Theory

Social information-processing theory helps to explain how we process information communicated via e-mail and other online methods. According to this theory, a key difference between face-to-face and computer-mediated communication is the *rate* at which information reaches you. During a live, in-person communication, you process a lot of information quickly; you process the words you hear as well as the many nonverbal cues you see (facial expression, gestures, and body posture) and hear (tone of voice and the use of pauses). During e-mail interactions, there is less information to process (no audio cues or visual nonverbal expressions), so it takes a bit longer for the relationship to develop—but it does develop as you learn more about your e-mail partner's likes, dislikes, and feelings. Social information-processing theory also suggests that if you expect to communicate with your electronic communication partner again, you will likely pay more attention to the relationship cues—expressions of emotions that are communicated directly (such as someone writing, "I'm feeling bored today") or indirectly (such as when you write a long e-mail message and your e-mail partner writes back only a sentence, which suggests he or she may not want to spend much time "talking" today).

In one study, communication researchers Joseph Walther and Judee Burgoon found that the kinds of relationships that developed between people who met face to face differed little from those between people who had computer-mediated interactions.[29] The general stages and patterns of communication were evident in both face-to-face and e-mail relationships. But, over time, the researchers found that the computer-mediated group actually developed *more* socially rich relationships than the face-to-face group; this suggests that relationship cues are present in computer-mediated communication—it just may take longer for the relationship cues to be expressed. So, even though it may take more time for a relationship to develop online, it does indeed develop and can be just as satisfying as a face-to-face conversation.

A study by Lisa Tidwell and Joseph Walther investigated how computer-mediated communication affects how much and how quickly people reveal information about themselves and the overall impressions people form of one another.[30] In comparing computer-mediated exchanges with face-to-face conversations, Tidwell and Walther found that people in computer-mediated conversations asked more direct questions, which resulted in people's revealing more information about themselves when online. The pattern of differences between computer-mediated communication and face-to-face communication is still being explored as computer-mediated communication becomes an even more significant part of contemporary life.

APPLYING the Research to Your Life

So what are the implications of the online relationship-development process compared with that of face-to-face interpersonal relationships? The research indicates that there are several implications:

- You can develop rich, satisfying interpersonal relationships with people online as well as during face-to-face conversations. However, it may take a bit longer to develop the online relationship. Even though e-mail does not allow the communication of facial expressions and tone of voice, relationship cues are nonetheless present and influential.
- Although you may not be able to see or hear the person when communicating online, you can detect relationship cues. The more time you spend communicating with someone via the Internet, the more you will be likely to pick up on the sometimes subtle relationship cues embedded in a message, such as the length of a message, the time of day or night your partner communicates with you, or how quickly he or she responds to your message.
- In online communication, you can take greater care in what you express. Joseph Walther has introduced the idea of **hyperpersonal communication**, which is a certain type of interpersonal communication that is facilitated by using a computer to establish relationships with others.[31] Composing and responding to e-mail messages or using instant messaging are examples of hyperpersonal communication. Because you are writing rather than spontaneously speaking your message, you are able to be more mindful of what you are expressing—you have the ability to write something and then edit or revise it before you send it. This gives you the ability to more consciously manipulate what you say about yourself. In contrast, when you communicate face to face with someone, once you've spoken an idea, it's been expressed. When we talk to people in person, we don't thoughtfully compose our message and then push the Send key. So when you communicate online, you have the potential to be more thoughtful about what you communicate.

the more people use the Internet, the less they will interact with people in person.[32] The researchers also found a correlation between people who said they were lonely and those who used the Internet. Yet two follow-up studies found that people who use the Internet are *more* likely to have an increased number of friends; they are more involved with community activities and overall have greater levels of trust in other people. The follow-up research seems to suggest that for some people—those who are already prone to being shy or introverted—there may be a link between Internet use and loneliness or feelings of social isolation. However, their isolation may not be because of their use of the Internet, but simply because they are less likely to make contact with others.[33] For those who are generally outgoing and who like to interact with others, the Internet is just another tool to reach out and make contact.

One early theory of communication via the Internet was called **cues-filtered-out theory.** This theory suggested that emotional expression is severely restricted when we communicate online because sending text messages via the Internet filters out nonverbal cues such as facial expression, gestures, and tone of voice. The assumption was that e-mail and other text messages were best used for more task-oriented work, such as sharing large amounts of information; text messages were assumed to be less effective in helping people establish meaningful relationships with one another.[34]

Another more recent theory, called **social information-processing theory**, suggests that we *can* communicate relational and emotional messages via the Internet, but it just may take longer to express messages that are typically communicated with facial expressions and tone of voice. We discuss social information-processing theory in the Applying Theory and Research box.

Because of technology, some electronic interpersonal exchanges may not be simultaneous. Nonetheless, there can be mutual understanding, and the communication can be truly personal rather than impersonal. We suggest that these electronic, or hyperpersonal, communication exchanges, even though not as rich in nonverbal and relational information, can mirror characteristics of face-to-face interpersonal communication in the sense that you are developing or maintaining a unique relationship with someone. In addition, electronically mediated relationships can involve mutual influence. And whether you're e-mailing someone that you'd like to marry or just to get together with for a cup of coffee, e-messages can alter both lives and relationships. Clearly, not all e-mail correspondence is interpersonal communication; today's technology, however, sometimes makes it possible to emulate in cyberspace the characteristics of interpersonal transactions.

One research team has developed a theory called **media richness theory** that describes the richness of a communication channel using four criteria: (1) the amount of feedback that the communicators can receive, (2) the number of cues that the channel can convey and that can be interpreted by a receiver, (3) the variety of language that communicators use, and (4) the potential for expressing emotions and feelings.[35] Using these four criteria, researchers have developed a continuum of communication channels, from communication-rich to communication-lean. Figure 1.4 illustrates this continuum.

There is some evidence that those wishing to communicate a negative message to someone, such as a message ending a relationship, may select a less-rich communication message—they may be more likely to send a letter or an e-mail rather than share the bad news face to face.[36] Similarly, people usually want to share good news in person, when they can enjoy the positive reaction to the message.

In summary, we believe this new frontier of electronic communication makes it possible for people to develop interpersonal relationships with others who are miles away. We agree with Walther and Tidwell that the "Information Superhighway" is

hyperpersonal communication. A certain type of interpersonal communication that is facilitated by using a computer to establish relationships with others.

cues-filtered-out theory. Theory that suggests that communication of emotions is restricted when people send messages to others via e-mail because nonverbal cues such as facial expression and tone of voice are filtered out.

social information-processing theory. Theory that suggests people can communicate relational and emotional messages via the Internet, although such messages take longer to express without nonverbal cues.

media richness theory. Theory that identifies the richness of a communication medium based on the amount of information, including emotional expression, it communicates.

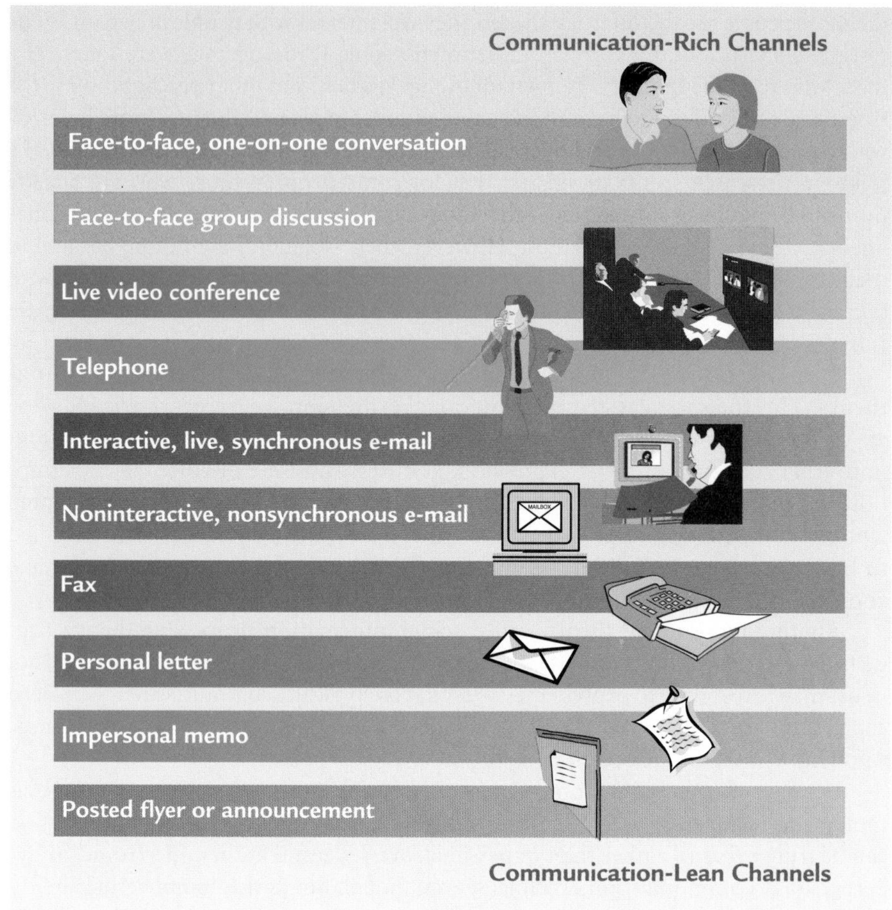

FIGURE 1.4

A Continuum of Communication-Rich and Communication-Lean Channels

Adapted from L. K. Trevino, R. L. Draft, and R. H. Lengel, "Understanding Managers' Media Choices: A Symbolic Interactionist Perspective." In *Organizations and Communication Technology,* edited by J. Fulk and C. Steinfield (Newbury Park, CA: Sage, 1990), 71–94. Reprinted by permission of Sage Publications, Inc.

clearly not just a road for moving data from one place to another, but a roadside where people pass each other, occasionally meet, and decide to travel together. You can't see very much of other drivers at first, unless you do travel together for some time. There are highway bandits, to be sure, who are not as they appear to be—one must drive defensively—and there are conflicts and disagreements online as there are off-road, too.[37]

Principles of Interpersonal Communication

As we introduce the study of interpersonal communication in this chapter, it is useful to present fundamental principles that help explain its nature. Underlying our current understanding of interpersonal communication are five principles: Interpersonal communication connects us to others, is irreversible, is complicated, is governed by rules, and involves both content and relationship dimensions.

Interpersonal Communication Connects Us to Others

Unless you are a living in a cave or have become a cloistered monk, you interact with others every day. Even if you work at home in front of a glowing computer screen, you encounter other people in the course of living your life. The opportunities for inter-

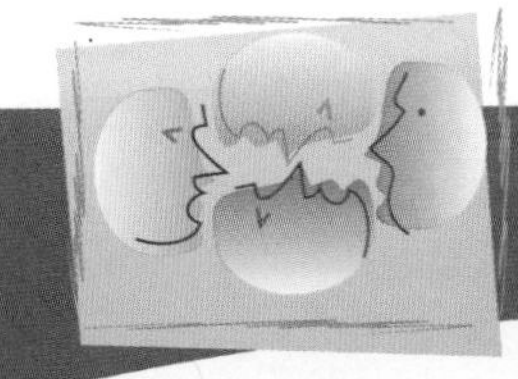

Understanding Diversity

The World Is Here

One of our most visionary politicians said that he envisioned a time when the United States could become the brain of the world, by which he meant the repository of all the latest advanced information systems. I thought of that remark when an enterprising poet friend of mine called to say that he had just sold a poem to a computer magazine and that the editors were delighted to get it because they didn't carry fiction or poetry. Is that the kind of world we desire? A humdrum homogenous world of all brains but no heart, no fiction, no poetry; a world of robots with human attendants, bereft of imagination or culture. Or does North America deserve a more exciting destiny? To become a place where the cultures of the world crisscross. This is possible because the United States is unique in the world: The world is here.[38]

These words from Ishmael Reed's essay "The World Is Here" remind us that America is not a one-dimensional culture. You need not travel to far-off places to develop interpersonal relationships with people from other cultures, races, or ethnic backgrounds. America has long been known as a melting pot—a place where people from a variety of cultures and traditions have come together to seek their fortunes. Others think America is more like a tossed salad than a melting pot—in a salad, each ingredient retains its essential character rather than melting together to form a united whole. Focusing on communication and diversity means much more than focusing on cultural differences. Culture consists of the learned values, behaviors, and expectations shared by a group of people. You need skill and sensitivity to develop quality interpersonal relationships with others whose religion, race, ethnicity, age, gender, or sexual orientation differs from your own. Throughout the text, we include boxes like this one to help you develop your sensitivity to important issues related to cultural diversity. As you embark on your study of interpersonal communication, consider these questions, either individually or with a group of your classmates:

1. What are the implications of this melting pot or tossed salad culture for your study of interpersonal communication?
2. Is there too much emphasis on being politically correct on college campuses today? Support your answer.
3. What specific interpersonal skills will help you communicate effectively with others from different cultural and ethnic traditions?

personal communication are ubiquitous—they are everywhere. It is through inescapable interpersonal communication with others that we affect and are affected by other human beings.

We agree with author H. D. Duncan, who said, "We do not relate and then talk, but relate in talk." Fundamental to an understanding of interpersonal communication is the assumption that the quality of interpersonal relationships stems from the quality of communication with others. It's been said—and we noted earlier—that people can't *not* communicate. Because people often don't intend to express ideas or feelings, this perspective is debated among communication scholars. However, there is no question that interpersonal communication is inescapable in the twenty-first century.

The ever-present nature of interpersonal communication doesn't mean others will *accurately* decode your message; it does mean that others draw inferences about you and your behavior—inferences that may be right or may be wrong. Even as you silently stand in a crowded elevator, your lack of eye contact with others communicates your unwillingness to interact with fellow passengers. Your unspoken messages, even when you are asleep, provide cues that others interpret. Remember: *People judge you by your behavior, not your intent.* Your interpersonal communication is how you develop connections to others. Even in well-established interpersonal relationships, you may be evoking an unintended response by your behavior.

FIGURE **1.5**

Interpersonal Communication Is Irreversible

This helical model shows that interpersonal communication never loops back on itself. Once it begins, it expands infinitely as the communication partners contribute their thoughts and experiences to the exchange. Copyright © F. E. X. Dance in *Human Communication Theory* (Holt, Rinehart and Winston, 1967), 294. Reprinted with permission.

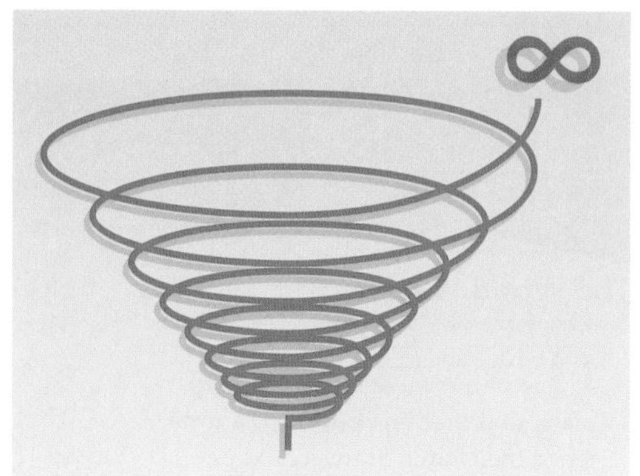

Interpersonal Communication Is Irreversible

"Disregard that last statement made by the witness," instructs the judge. Yet the clever lawyer knows that once her client has told the jury that her husband gave her a black eye during an argument, the client cannot really "take it back." This principle applies to all forms of communication. We may try to modify the meaning of a spoken message by saying something like "Oh, I really didn't mean it." But in most cases, the damage has been done. Once created, communication has the physical property of matter; it can't be uncreated. As the helical model in Figure 1.5 suggests, once interpersonal communication begins, it never loops back on itself. Instead, it continues to be shaped by the events, experiences, and thoughts of the communication partners. A Russian proverb nicely summarizes the point: "Once a word goes out of your mouth, you can never swallow it again."

Interpersonal Communication Is Complicated

No form of communication is simple. If any were, we would know how to reduce the number of misunderstandings and conflicts in our world. Because of the variables involved in interpersonal exchanges, even simple requests are extremely complex. Life holds much uncertainty; there are many things we do not know. One of the purposes of communication, according to communication theorists, is to reduce our uncertainty.[39] The process of sharing information and asking questions helps us reduce our uncertainty about what is happening at any given moment. Communication theorists have noted that whenever you communicate with another person, there are really at least six "people" involved: (1) who you think you are; (2) who you think the other per-

son is; (3) who you think the other person thinks you are; (4) who the other person thinks he or she is; (5) who the other person thinks you are; and (6) who the other person thinks you think he or she is.[40] Whew! And when you add more people to the interaction, it becomes even more involved.

Moreover, when humans communicate, they interpret information from others as symbols. A **symbol** is a word, sound, or visual image that represents something else, such as a thought, concept, or object; it can have various meanings and interpretations. Language is a system of symbols. In English, symbols do not resemble the objects they represent. The word (symbol) for *cow* does not look at all like a cow; someone, somewhere, decided that *cow* should mean a beast that chews its cud and gives milk. The reliance on symbols to communicate poses a communication challenge; you are often misinterpreted. Sometimes you don't know the code. Only if you are up to date on contemporary slang will you know that "homeskillet" means a good friend, "circle of death" means a lousy pizza, and "papaflage" is strategy for hiding something from your father.

Messages are not always interpreted as we intend them. Osmo Wiio, a Scandinavian communication scholar, points out the messiness of communicating with others when he suggests the following maxims:

THE FAR SIDE® By GARY LARSON

"I'm afraid you misunderstood. ... I said I'd like a mango."

> If communication can fail, it will.
>
> If a message can be understood in different ways, it will be understood in just that way which does the most harm.
>
> There is always somebody who knows better than you what you meant by your message.
>
> The more communication there is, the more difficult it is for communication to succeed.[41]

Although we are not as pessimistic as Professor Wiio, we do suggest that the task of understanding each other is challenging.

Interpersonal Communication Is Governed by Rules

According to communication researcher Susan Shimanoff, a **rule** is a "followable prescription that indicates what behavior is obligated, preferred, or prohibited in certain contexts."[42] The rules that help define appropriate and inappropriate communication in any given situation may be *explicit* or *implicit.* For your interpersonal communication class, explicit rules are probably spelled out in your syllabus. But your instructor has other rules that are more implicit. They are not written or verbalized, because you learned them long ago: Only one person speaks at a time, you raise your hand to be called on, you do not pass notes.

Interpersonal communication rules are developed by the people involved in the interaction and by the culture in which the individuals are communicating. Many times, we learn communication rules from experience, by observing and interacting with others.

British researcher Michael Argyle and his colleagues asked people to identify general rules for relationship development and maintenance and then rate their importance. The study yielded the following most important rules:[43]

> Respect each other's privacy.
>
> Don't reveal each other's secrets.

symbol. Word, sound, or visual image that represents something else, such as a thought, concept, or object.

rule. Followable prescription that indicates what behavior is obligated, preferred, or prohibited in certain contexts.

For many of us, friendships are vital to our personal well-being. By improving our interpersonal communication skills, we can learn how to improve our friendships.

Look the other person in the eye during conversation.

Don't criticize the other person publicly.

Although we may modify rules to achieve the goals of our relationships, and although there may be cultural differences, these general rules remain fairly constant. In interpersonal relationships, the rules of a relationship are mutually defined and agreed on. Most of us don't like to be told what to do or how to behave all the time. The expectations and rules are continually renegotiated as the relationship unfolds. Few of us learn relationship rules by copying them from a book. Most of us learn these rules from experience, through observing and interacting with family members and friends. Individuals who grow up in environments in which these rules are not observed may not know how to behave in close relationships.

Interpersonal Communication Involves Both Content and Relationship Dimensions

What you say (your words) and how you say it (your tone of voice, amount of eye contact, facial expression, and posture) can reveal much about the true meaning of your message. If one of your roommates loudly and abruptly bellows, "HEY, DORK! CLEAN THIS ROOM!" and another roommate uses the same verbal message but more gently and playfully says, "Hey, dork. Clean this room," both are communicating a message aimed at achieving the same outcome. But the two messages have different relationship cues. The shouted message suggests that roommate number one may be frustrated that the room is still full of leftovers from last night's pizza party, whereas roommate number two's teasing request suggests he or she may be fondly amused by your untidiness.

The **content** of a communication message consists of the information, ideas, or suggested actions that the speaker wishes to share. The **relationship dimension** of a communication message is usually more implied; it offers cues about the emotions, attitudes, and amount of power and control the speaker feels toward the other person.[44]

content. Information, ideas, or suggested actions that a speaker wishes to share.

relationship dimension. The implied aspect of a communication message, which conveys information about emotions, attitudes, power, and control.

metacommunication. Verbal or nonverbal communication about communication.

emotional response theory. Theory that suggests any human emotion experienced can be interpreted along three dimensions: (1) pleasure–displeasure, (2) arousal–nonarousal, and (3) dominance–submissiveness. Our emotional response to what we experience helps determine whether we ultimately approach or avoid what we are experiencing.

Another way of distinguishing between the content and the relationship dimensions of communication is to consider that the content of a message refers to *what* is said. Relationship cues refer to *how* it is communicated. This distinction explains why reading a transcript of what someone says can reveal a quite different meaning from actually hearing the person say the message.

Given these two dimensions of communication, one dimension can modify or contradict the other dimension. Communication theorists have a word that describes how we can communicate about our communication: metacommunication. Stated in the simplest way, **metacommunication** is communication about communication; it can be nonverbal or verbal. Accurately decoding these unspoken or even verbalized metamessages helps you understand what people really mean.

You can express an idea nonverbally (for example, by smiling to communicate that you are pleased), and you can also express your positive feeling verbally (for example, by saying, "I'm happy to be here"). But sometimes your nonverbal communication can contradict your verbal message. You can say "Oh, that's just great" and use your voice to provide relational cues that express just the opposite of what the verbal content of

Interpersonal Communication and Emotion Connecting Heart to Heart

The Role of Emotions in Our Relationships with Others

Emotions don't literally come from our hearts, yet for thousands of years poets, authors, and songwriters in Western culture have identified the heart as a metaphor for the source of human emotions. (In some cultures, it's the liver rather than the heart that serves as a metaphorical source of emotions. But connecting liver to liver just doesn't sound right, does it?) Perhaps it's because the human heart is vital for survival that it has become an important metaphor for our emotions: If it stops beating, we die. Similarly, without experiencing emotions, we are not truly alive. And our emotions are related to everything—from how fast our heart beats to the intensity of our blood pressure and our breathing. Throughout this book we highlight the importance of emotion in a feature called Interpersonal Communication and Emotion: Connecting Heart to Heart.

What is emotion? How do emotions work? Precisely what causes us to experience emotions? There are various theories, but scholars don't agree on any one specific answer to each of these questions. One researcher described an emotion as a biological, cognitive, behavioral, and subjective affective reaction to an event.[45] A closer look at that definition suggests that an emotional reaction includes four things: biological or physiological reactions (heart rate increases, changes in breathing); cognitive responses (angry thoughts, happy thoughts); behavioral reactions to our thoughts and feelings (frowning, laughing); and subjective affective responses (either mild or strong experiences of joy, panic, anger, pleasure, and the like).[46]

Emotional response theory suggests that any human emotion experience can be interpreted along three dimensions: (1) pleasure-displeasure, (2) arousal-nonarousal, and (2) dominance-submissiveness.[47] At any given moment, including while you are reading this book, you are experiencing some degree of pleasure (happiness, joy) or displeasure (sadness, disgust). Or you could be at a midpoint—somewhere between pleasure and displeasure. Similarly, on the second dimension of this theory, you are experiencing a degree of emotional arousal (wide awake) or nonarousal (asleep). Or you could be somewhere on a continuum between being awake and asleep. Finally, at any given moment, according to emotional response theory, you are feeling a level of dominance (powerful, in control) or submissiveness (weak, not in control); there is a midpoint between these feelings as well. The theory suggests that these three dimensions make up all your emotional responses to what you experience.[48] We defined *communication* as the process of making sense of the world and sharing that sense with others through the creation of meaning using verbal and nonverbal messages. According to emotional response theory, our emotional responses along the three dimensions of pleasure-displeasure, arousal-nonarousal, and dominance-submissiveness are among the ways we attempt to make emotional sense out of what we experience.

Several general principles describe how we experience and express emotions in the context of our relationships with others. To provide an introduction to the role emotions play in our relationships, we offer the following principles:

We are more likely to discuss our emotions in an *interpersonal* relationship than in an *impersonal* relationship. Research supports our common intuition: We are more likely to talk about our personal feelings with people we know, care about, and feel a unique relationship with (like friends, lovers, and family members) than people we don't know or don't particularly care about.[49]

We express our emotions both verbally and nonverbally, yet our nonverbal messages often communicate our emotions more honestly. We sometimes explicitly tell people how we are feeling ("I'm feeling sad," "I'm angry with you," or "I love you"). But it's often through our nonverbal expressions (facial expression, tone of voice, or body posture) that our true feelings are communicated to others. We'll explore the role of nonverbal communication and emotion in greater detail in Chapter 7.

Our culture influences our emotional expression. It may seem that we express our feelings of happiness, joy, or sadness spontaneously, yet there is evidence that we often learn what is and is not appropriate in expressing emotions.[50] The culture in which we were raised has a major influence on how we learn to both express and respond to emotions expressed by others. In Western cultures, for example, males are sometimes encouraged not to express emotions ("Boys don't cry"). One study found that Japanese students express fewer negative emotions than American students.[51]

In summary, emotions include four things: biological/physiological reactions, cognitive responses, behavioral reactions to our thoughts and feelings, and subjective affective responses. To experience emotion—to sense feelings of pleasure-displeasure, arousal-nonarousal, and dominance-submissiveness—is to experience life.

the message means. The sarcasm communicated by the tone of your voice (a relationship cue) modifies the meaning of your verbal message (the content of your message).

In addition to nonverbal cues, which provide communication about communication, you can also use words, to explicitly talk about your message. For example, you can ask, "Is what I'm saying bothering you?" Your question is seeking information about the communication. We use metacommunication to check on how our message is being understood or to make sure we understand what someone else is saying. When you say, "I'm not sure what you said is clear to me," you are using a metamessage to help you better understand the communication; it's a metamessage because you are talking about your talk. Here's another example of verbal metacommunication: "I'd like to talk with you about the way we argue." Again, you are using communication to talk about communication. Taking time to talk about the way you talk can help clarify misunderstandings. Being aware of the metamessage, in both its verbal and its nonverbal forms, can help improve the accuracy of your interpretations of the meaning of message content as well as enhance the quality of your relationships with others.

Interpersonal Communication Myths

Several common misconceptions about interpersonal communication can undermine the quality of your interpersonal relationships with others. As we embark on our study of interpersonal communication, it's just as important to unlearn some commonly held misconceptions as it is to learn research conclusions and time-tested principles of interpersonal communication. Don't believe the following myths.

Myth: "More Words Will Make the Meaning Clearer"

More is not necessarily better. Just as there is a time to talk, there is a time to be silent. Piling on more words when your interpersonal communication partner is already baffled by what you are talking about can make matters worse. If someone is confused, hurt, or angry, continuing to add verbiage may hurt, not help. Maybe you just need to stop and listen rather than talk. Or ask a question, and then just silently wait for an answer. Or perhaps, rather than words, your friend needs a nonverbal message of reassurance—a hug, a smile, or a nod of your head in agreement. And just as a picture can be worth a thousand words, so can demonstrating to someone what you mean be more powerful than continuing to pile on the words. When you communicate feelings and attitudes, your nonverbal, unspoken expressions are where the action is.

Are we suggesting that more communication is always bad? No. Just don't fall into the trap of believing that more words will solve all problems, enhance the quality of interpersonal relationships, and make the meaning clearer. There is a time to stop talking and listen.

Myth: "Meanings Are in Words"

In and of itself, spoken or written, a word has no meaning. It's just a sound, marks on paper, or characters on a computer screen. Our definition of human communication says that meaning is created. It is created in our own and others' minds and hearts when we communicate. Meaning resides in people, not in words. Others provide the meaning to "connect the dots" between the words you've spoken and the meaning you

Instead of focusing entirely on the message we want to convey, we can sometimes communicate even more effectively when we take the time to be other-oriented—to listen to what others are saying.

intend to create. But sometimes people connect the dots in a way you had not intended. Words are, simply, symbols we use to communicate with others. Remember, meanings are in people, not in words.

Myth: "Information Equals Communication"

"How many times do I have to tell you not to use the copy machine?" "Can't you read? It's in the syllabus." "It's in the policy and procedure manual." "Are you deaf? I've told you that I love you several times." Each of these exasperated communicators seems to have thought that information is the same thing as communication. It's not. Information is not communication. This simple, yet powerful, principle helps combat the myth that if you say it or write it, then communication has taken place.

Earlier in the chapter, we defined communication at the most basic level as acting on information. If you say it, but no one hears it—does that mean there has been communication? Like the proverbial tree that falls silently in the forest because no one is there to hear it, the message you thought you sent is not necessarily communication just because you've put your thoughts into a code. Encoding does not always ensure decoding. And as we already discussed, even if someone has decoded the message, his or her interpretation could be different from the one you intended. Information is not communication.

Myth: "Interpersonal Relationship Problems Are Always Communication Problems"

"You don't understand me!" shouts Paul to his exasperated partner, Pat. "We just can't communicate anymore!" Paul seems to think the problem he and Pat are having is a communication problem. But Paul and Pat may understand each other perfectly; they may simply disagree. Although it's certainly true that conflict and discord in interpersonal relationships can occur because of misunderstandings, not *all* conflict and bumpy relationships stem from misunderstandings. There could be several explanations for why a relationship is experiencing turbulence. Perhaps the communication partners are very clear when communicating but are so self-centered or self-absorbed that the quality of the relationship suffers. Or perhaps the communication partners just don't like each other; or, if they do like and understand each other, they just disagree. Their messages are understood but rejected. Although missed meaning may be a contributing factor in interpersonal conflict, it's a myth that all relational discord stems from misunderstanding.

Even though one purpose of this course is to help you enhance the quality of your relationships by becoming a better communicator, we don't claim that *all* interpersonal conflict stems from the misunderstanding of messages. Nor are we claiming that learning principles and skills of interpersonal communication will solve all your interpersonal relationship problems. One of this book's three authors was approached by a potential client, who said, "I understand you are a communication consultant. I need help with my communication skills. *Do something to me* to make me a better communicator." But communication skill development does not work like Harry Potter's magic wand; there's not something that can be "done to" someone to enhance his or her communication ability. And even if there were a wizard's wand to make others perfectly understand all your communications, and you theirs, your interpersonal relationships would undoubtedly still experience stress and conflict.

How to Improve Your Own Interpersonal Communication Competence

Now that we have previewed the study of interpersonal communication, you may be saying to yourself, "Well, that's all well and good, but is it possible to improve my own interpersonal communication? Aren't some people just born with better interpersonal skills than others?" Just as some people have more musical talent or greater skill at throwing a football, evidence does suggest that some people may have an inborn, biological talent for communicating with others.[52]

A growing body of research on what is called the **communibiological approach** to communication suggests that some people inherit certain traits or characteristics that affect the way they communicate with others. There may be a genetic basis for why people communicate as they do. For example, perhaps someone you know may be a born introvert, always shy, and thus have more stage fright or anxiety when communicating with others.[53] And some people may not be as comfortable interacting in interpersonal situations as others are.

So what are the implications of the communibiological approach to communication? Does it mean you can't improve your interpersonal communication? *Absolutely not!* Some researchers and teachers believe that the communibiological approach puts too much emphasis on biology and not enough on how we can learn to compensate for what nature did not give us.[54] The underlying premise of our study of interpersonal communication is that you can learn ways to enhance your interpersonal communication competence.

Social learning theory suggests that we can learn how to adapt and adjust our behavior toward others; how we behave is not solely dependent on our genetic makeup. By observing and interacting with others (hence the term *social* learning), we discover that we can adapt and adjust our behavior.[55] Although biology unquestionably plays a key role in how we behave, we can't blame biology for all aspects of our behavior. We believe that people can learn how to enhance their communication competence.

communibiological approach. Theoretical perspective that suggests communication behavior can be predicted based on personal traits and characteristics that result from people's genetic or biological background.

social learning theory. Theory of human behavior that suggests we can learn how to adapt and adjust our behavior toward others; how we behave is not solely dependent on our genetic or biological makeup.

To be a competent communicator is to communicate in ways that are perceived to be both *effective* and *appropriate*.[56] You communicate effectively when your message is understood by others and achieves its intended effect. For example, if you want your roommate to stop using your hair dryer, and after you talk to your roommate, he stops using your hair dryer, your message has been effective.

Competent communication should also be appropriate. By *appropriate,* we mean that the communicator should consider the time, place, and overall context of the message and should be sensitive to the feelings and attitudes of the listener. Who determines what is appropriate? Communication scholar Mary Jane Collier suggests that competence is a concept based on privilege; to label someone as competent means that another person has made a judgment as to what is appropriate or inappropriate behavior. Collier asks the following questions: ". . . competence and acceptance for whom? Who decides the criteria? Who doesn't? Competent or acceptable on the basis of what social and historical context?"[57] What Collier points out is that we have to be careful not to insist on one approach (our own approach) to interpersonal communication competence. *There is no single best way to communicate with others.* There are, however, avenues that can help you become both more effective and more appropriate when communicating with others.[58] We suggest a six-part strategy for becoming a more competent communicator.

Become Knowledgeable

By reading this chapter, you have already begun improving your interpersonal communication competence. Effective communicators are knowledgeable. They know how communication works. They understand the components, principles, and rules of the communication process. As you read further in this book, you will learn theories, principles, concepts, and rules that will help you explain and predict how humans communicate interpersonally.

Understanding these things is a necessary prerequisite for enhancing your interpersonal effectiveness, but this kind of knowledge alone does not make you an effective communicator. You would not let someone fix your car's carburetor if he or she had only read a book. Knowledge must be coupled with skill. And we acquire skill through practice.

Become Skilled

Effective communicators know how to translate knowledge into action.[59] You can memorize the characteristics of a good listener but still not listen well. To develop skill requires practice and helpful feedback from others who can confirm the appropriateness of your actions.

It has been suggested that learning a social skill is not much different from learning how to drive a car or operate a computer.[60] To learn any skill, you must break it down into subskills that you can learn and practice. "Hear it, see it, do it, correct it" is the formula that seems to work best for learning any new behaviors. In this book, we examine the elements of complex skills (such as listening), offer activities that let you practice the skills, and provide opportunities for you to receive feedback and correct your application of the skills.

Become Motivated

Practicing skills requires work. You need to be motivated to use your knowledge and skill. You must want to improve, and you must have a genuine desire to connect with

Ethical communicators are sensitive to the needs of others

others if you wish to become a competent communicator. You may know people who understand how to drive a car and have the skill to drive, yet hesitate to get behind the wheel. Or maybe you know someone who took a course in public speaking but is reluctant to stand in front of a crowd. Similarly, someone may pass a test about interpersonal communication principles with flying colors, but unless that person is motivated to use those newfound skills, his or her interactions with others may not improve.

Become Adaptable

Effective communicators appropriately adapt their messages to others; they are flexible. In this book, we do not identify tidy lists of sure-fire strategies that you can use to win friends and influence people. The same set of skills is not effective in every situation, so competent communicators do not assume that "one size fits all." Rather, they assess each unique situation and adapt their behavior to achieve the desired outcome. They examine the context, the situation, and the needs, goals, and messages of others to establish and maintain relationships.

Become Ethical

ethics. Beliefs, values, and moral principles by which people determine what is right or wrong.

other-oriented communicator. One who considers the thoughts, feelings, and perspectives of communication partners while maintaining his or her own integrity.

Ethics are the beliefs, values, and moral principles by which we determine what is right or wrong. Ethics and ethical behavior have always been critical components of human interactions. Effective interpersonal communicators are ethical. To be an ethical communicator means to be sensitive to the needs of others, to give people choices rather than forcing them to act a certain way. Unethical communicators believe that they know what other people need, even without asking them for their preferences. As we discuss in Chapter 6, being manipulative and forcing opinions on others usually results in a climate of defensiveness. Effective communicators seek to establish trust and reduce interpersonal barriers, rather than erect them. Ethical communicators keep confidences; they keep private information that others wish to be kept private. They also do not intentionally decrease others' feelings of self-worth. Another key element in being an ethical communicator is honesty. If you intentionally lie or distort the truth, then you are not communicating ethically or effectively. Ethical communicators also don't tell people only what they want to hear. At the end of each chapter, we offer a section called Focus on Ethics, in which we pose ethical questions to help you explore the ethics of interpersonal relationships.

Become Other-Oriented

The signature concept for our study of interpersonal communication is the goal of becoming other-oriented in relationships. To be an **other-oriented communicator** is to consider the thoughts, needs, experiences, personality, feelings, motives, desires, culture, and goals of your communication partners, while still maintaining your own integrity. The choices we make in forming our messages, in deciding how best to express those messages, and in deciding when and where to deliver those messages will be more effective when we consider the other person's thoughts and feelings. *To emphasize the importance of being an other-oriented communicator, throughout this book we'll use this margin icon to highlight discussions of being other-oriented.*

Being other-oriented involves a conscious effort to consider the world from the point of view of those with whom you interact.[61] This effort occurs almost automatically when you are communicating with those you like or who are similar to you. Thinking about the thoughts and feelings of those you dislike or who are different from you is more difficult and requires more effort and commitment.

Think about a person you dislike. Do you truly understand the factors in his or her life that have had an impact on the way he or she behaves? Do you appreciate the emotions he or she feels? If you're not confident that you can accurately understand the thoughts and feelings of a person you dislike, it probably signals the need to work on your ability to be other-oriented.

Sometimes, we are **egocentric communicators;** we create messages without giving much thought to the person who is listening. To be egocentric is to be self-focused and self-absorbed. Scholars of evolution might argue that our tendency to look out for Number One ensures the continuation of the human species and is therefore a good thing. Yet, it is difficult to communicate effectively when we focus exclusively on ourselves. Research suggests that being egocentric is detrimental to developing a healthy relationship with others.[62] If we fail to adapt our message to our listener, we may not be successful in achieving our intended communication goal. Other people can often perceive whether we're self-focused or other-oriented (especially if the person we're talking with is a sensitive, other-oriented communicator).

Are people more self-focused today than in the past? Sociologist Jean Twenge suggests that people today are increasingly more narcissistic (self-focused) than they have been in previous generations—she dubs today's narcissistic generation the "me generation." Her research found that "in the early 1950s, only 12% of teens aged 14 to 16 agreed with the statement 'I am an important person.' By the late 1980s, an incredible 80%—almost seven times as many—claimed they were important."[63] Using the Narcissistic Personality Inventory, an instrument designed to assess egocentrism and self-focus, Twenge and two of her colleagues found corroborating evidence for an increased self-focus among contemporary students.[64]

We may find ourselves speaking without considering the thoughts and feelings of our listener when we have a need to purge ourselves emotionally or to confirm our sense of self-importance, but doing so usually undermines our relationships with others. A self-focused communicator often alienates others. Fortunately, research suggests that, almost by necessity, we adapt to our partner in order to carry on a conversation.[65] Adaptation includes such things as simply asking questions in response to our partner's disclosures, finding topics of mutual interest to discuss, selecting words and

egocentric communicator. Person who creates messages without giving much thought to the person who is listening; a communicator who is self-focused and self-absorbed.

Becoming Other-Oriented

Consider Others' Needs and Perspectives Without Abandoning Your Integrity

At the heart of our study of interpersonal communication is the principle of becoming other-oriented. To be other-oriented means that you are aware of others' thoughts, feelings, goals, and needs and respond appropriately in ways that offer personal support. It does not mean that you abandon your own needs and interests or that you diminish your self-respect. To have integrity is to behave in a thoughtful, integrated way toward others while being true to your core beliefs and values. To be other-oriented is to have integrity; you don't just agree with others or give in to the demands of others in encounters with them.

Do you know a sycophant? A *sycophant* is a person who praises others only to manipulate emotions so that his or her needs are met. Sycophants may look as though they are focused on others, but their behavior is merely self-serving. A sycophant is not other-oriented. A person who is truly other-oriented is aware of the thoughts, feelings, and needs of others and then mindfully and honestly chooses to respond to those needs. To enhance your other-oriented awareness and skill takes practice. Throughout the book, we offer both principles and opportunities to practice the skill and mindset of being other-oriented.

To develop an awareness of being other-oriented with a communication partner, role-play the following interpersonal situations in two ways. First, role-play the scene as a communicator who is not other-oriented but rather self-focused. Then reenact the same scene as a communicator who is other-oriented—someone who considers the thoughts and feelings of the other person while maintaining his or her own integrity.

Suggested situations:

- Return a broken DVD player to a department store salesperson
- Correct a grocery store cashier who has scanned an item at the wrong price
- Meet with a teacher who gave your son or daughter a failing grade
- Ask your professor for a one-day extension on a paper that is due tomorrow
- Ask someone for a donation to a worthy cause
- Ask a professor for permission to get into a class that has reached its maximum enrollment
- Accept an unappealing CD as a gift from a friend
- Remind your son or daughter that he or she needs to practice the cello

examples that are meaningful to our partner, and avoiding topics that we don't feel comfortable discussing with another person.

Adapting messages to others does *not* mean that we tell them only what they want to hear; that would be unethical. Nor does being considerate of others mean abandoning all concern for our own interests; that would be unwise. Other-oriented communicators maintain their own personal integrity while simultaneously being aware of the thoughts and feelings of others. Being other-oriented is more than just being "nice."[66] It involves being principled enough to be considerate of others, but making mindful choices about how and when to adapt interpersonal messages to others.

How do you become other-oriented? Being other-oriented is really a collection of skills rather than a single skill. We devote considerable discussion throughout the book to developing this collection of essential communication skills.[67]

Focusing on others begins with an accurate understanding of your self-concept and self-esteem; we discuss these foundation principles in the next chapter. As you will learn in Chapter 3, developing an accurate perception of both yourself and others is an important element of relating to others effectively.

Becoming other-oriented also involves adapting to those who may be considerably different from you. Your communication partner may have a different cultural background, be of the opposite sex, or be older or younger than you. In Chapter 4, we explore some of these differences, especially cultural differences, that can sometimes challenge effective and appropriate communication with others; we also suggest specific strategies to help you adapt to others who differ from you.

Being other-oriented is more than just having a set of skills or behaviors. It also includes developing positive, healthy attitudes about others. In 1951, Carl Rogers wrote a pioneering book called *Client-Centered Therapy,* which transformed the field of psychotherapy. In it, Rogers explains how genuine positive regard for another person and an open and supportive communication climate lay the foundation for trusting relationships. Rogers emphasizes the importance of listening in forging a connection to another human being. We explore this topic in depth in Chapter 5.

People gain insight into others' feelings by being sensitive to nonverbal messages as well as the explicit verbal statements they make. We discuss verbal communication skills in Chapter 6 and nonverbal communication skills in Chapter 7. The skills and principles of managing conflict presented in Chapter 8 provide tools and ideas for understanding others when you disagree.

Chapters 9, 10, 11, and 12 build on the principles of interpersonal relationships introduced in this chapter to help you understand how relationships evolve, are maintained, and sometimes end. The final chapter applies our discussion of other-oriented interpersonal communication to various contexts such as families, friends, and colleagues. Our goals are to help you understand better how you relate to others and to help you develop enhanced interpersonal skills.

How Can You Improve Your Communication Competence?

Become Knowledgeable	Learn principles, concepts, and ideas.
Become Skilled	Translate knowledge into action.
Become Motivated	Resolve to use your knowledge and skill.
Become Adaptable	Select the right behavior; one size does not fit all.
Become Ethical	Offer choices, establish trust, and be honest.
Become Other-Oriented	Focus on others' thoughts and feelings rather than only on your own.

Summary

At the most basic level, communication is the process of acting on information. Human communication is the process of making sense of the world and sharing that sense with others. Interpersonal communication is the process of developing a unique relationship with another person by interacting and sharing mutual influence. Early models of human communication viewed it as a simple message-transfer process. Later models viewed communication as interaction and then as transaction. Contemporary approaches to interpersonal communication emphasize the simultaneous nature of the process. They identify seven key components in the interpersonal communication process:

source, receiver, message, channel, noise, context, and feedback. Electronic media may encourage further evolution of our models for interpersonal communication.

The goal of this book is to help you improve your interpersonal skills and relationships. Interpersonal relationships range from impersonal to intimate, are governed by rules, and involve both content and relationship dimensions. The most effective interpersonal communicators are not swayed by common myths about communication. Rather, they are knowledgeable, skilled, motivated, adaptable, ethical, and other-oriented. Learning to connect with others is the key to establishing satisfying relationships.

For Discussion and Review

Focus on Critical Thinking

1. Analyze a recent interpersonal exchange that did not go well. Write down some of the dialogue. Did the other person understand you? Did your communication have the intended effect? Was your message ethical?
2. Make a relationship scale on a piece of paper, and label it "impersonal" at one end and "intimate" at the other. Place your family members and closest friends on the scale; then compare and discuss your entries with your classmates.
3. What rules govern your relationship with your mother? Your father? Your communication teacher? Your roommate? Your spouse?

Focus on Ethics

4. Think about your primary goal for this course. Is it to develop strategies to achieve your own personal goals? Is it to develop sensitivity to the needs of others? What is behind your desire to achieve your goal? Is your purpose ethical?
5. Your parents want you to visit them for the holidays. You would rather spend the time with a friend. You don't want to hurt your parents' feelings, so you tell them that you have an important project that you are working on; you won't be able to come home for the holidays. Your message is understood. It achieves the intended effect: Your parents don't seem to have hurt feelings, and you don't go home. Explain whether your message is ethical or unethical.

Learning with Others

1. Working with a group of your classmates, develop a five-minute lesson to teach one of the following concepts to your class:
   a. How interpersonal relationships range from impersonal to intimate
   b. Human communication as action
   c. Human communication as interaction
   d. Human communication as transaction
   e. How interpersonal relationships are governed by rules
   f. How to improve communication effectiveness
2. Working with a group of your classmates, develop your own model of interpersonal communication. Include all of the components that are necessary to describe how communication between people works. Your model could be a drawing or an object (such as a Slinky toy) that symbolizes the communication process. Share your model with the class, describing the decisions your group made in developing it. Illustrate your model with a conversation between two people, pointing out how elements of the conversation relate to the model.

Weblinks

Go to *www.mycommunicationlab.com* (access code required) to find Web resources for your text that supplement the material in Chapter 1, including links to information on the following topics:

The National Communication Association
Interpersonal Communication Skills Test
Publications about communibiology
E-mail communication tips
Information about relationships between interpersonal communication and health

CHAPTER 2

Interpersonal Communication and Self

OBJECTIVES

1. Define, compare, and contrast self-concept and self-esteem.
2. Identify factors that shape the development of your self-concept.
3. List and describe strategies for improving your self-esteem.
4. Describe how your self-concept affects your relationships with others.
5. Describe the process of appropriate self-disclosure, including two models of self-disclosure.

OUTLINE

People tell themselves stories and then pour their lives into the stories they tell.

Anonymous

Philosophers suggest that there are three basic questions to which all people seek answers: (1) "Who am I?" (2) "Why am I here?" and (3) "Who are all these others?" In this chapter, we focus on these essential questions about the self. We view them as progressive. Grappling with the question of who you are and seeking to define a purpose for your life are essential to understanding others and becoming other-oriented in your interpersonal communication and relationships.

Fundamentally, all your communication starts or ends with you. When you are the communicator, you intentionally or unintentionally code your thoughts and emotions to be interpreted by another. When you receive a message, you interpret the information through your own frame of reference. Your self-image and self-worth, as well as your needs, values, beliefs, and attitudes, serve as filters for your communication with others. As you establish and develop relationships, you may become more aware of these filters, and perhaps want to alter them. A close relationship often provides the impetus for change.

To understand the role that self-concept plays in interpersonal communication, we will explore the first two basic questions—"Who am I?" and "Why am I here?"—in an effort to discover the meaning of self. We will examine the multifaceted dimensions of self-concept, learn how it develops, and compare self-concept to self-esteem. Then we will move to the third basic question, "Who are all these others?" What you

choose to tell and not tell others about yourself reveals important clues about who you are, what you value, and how you relate to another person. We will explore the process of self-disclosure—purposefully revealing information about yourself—later in this chapter.

Self-Concept: Who Are You?

You can begin your journey of self-discovery by doing the exercise in Building Your Skills: Who Are You?

How did you answer the question "Who are you?" Perhaps you listed activities in which you participate, or groups and organizations to which you belong. You may have listed some of the roles you assume, such as student, child, or parent. All these things are indeed a part of your self, the sum total of who you are. Psychologist Karen Horney defines **self** as "that central inner force, common to all human beings and yet unique in each, which is the deep source of growth."[1]

Your answers are also part of your **self-concept.** Your self-concept is your subjective description of who you *think* you are—it is filtered through your own perceptions. For example, you may have great musical talent, but you may not believe in it enough to think of yourself as a musician. You can view self-concept as the labels you consistently use to describe yourself to others.

Who you are is also reflected in the attitudes, beliefs, and values that you hold. These are learned constructs that shape your behavior and self-image. An **attitude** is a learned predisposition to respond to a person, object, or idea in a favorable or unfavorable way. Attitudes reflect what you like and what you don't like. If you like school, butter pecan ice cream, and your brother, you hold positive attitudes toward these things. You were not born with a fondness for butter pecan ice cream; you learned to like it, just as some people learn to enjoy the taste of snails, raw fish, or pureed turnips.

self. Sum total of who a person is; a person's central inner force.

self-concept. Person's subjective description of who he or she is.

attitude. Learned predisposition to respond to a person, object, or idea in a favorable or unfavorable way.

Building Your Skills

Who Are You?

Consider this question: Who are you? More specifically, ask yourself this question ten times. Write your responses in the spaces provided here or on a separate piece of paper. It may be challenging to identify ten aspects of yourself. The Spanish writer Cervantes said, "To know thyself . . . is the most difficult lesson in the world." Your answers will help you begin to explore your self-concept and self-esteem in this chapter.

I am ______________________ I am ______________________

I am ______________________ I am ______________________

I am ______________________ I am ______________________

I am ______________________ I am ______________________

I am ______________________ I am ______________________

Beliefs are the way in which you structure your understanding of reality—what is true and what is false for you. Most of your beliefs are based on previous experience. You believe that the sun will rise in the morning and that you will get burned if you put your hand on a hot stove.

How are attitudes and beliefs related? They often function quite independently of each other. You may have a favorable attitude toward something and still believe negative things about it. You may believe, for example, that your school football team will not win the national championship this year, although you may be a big fan. Or you may believe that God exists, yet not always like what you think God does or does not do. Beliefs have to do with what is true or not true, whereas attitudes reflect likes and dislikes.

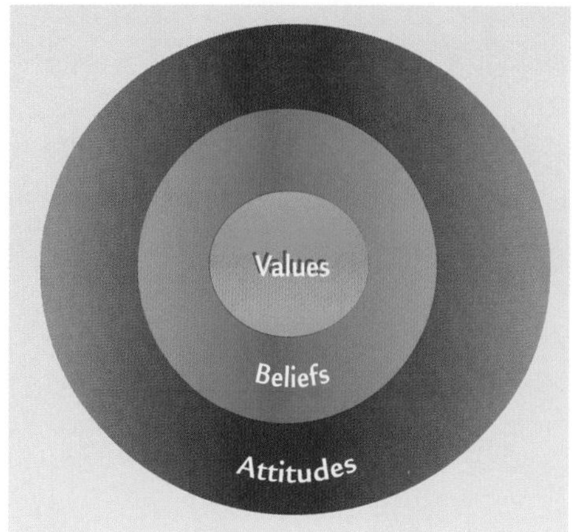

FIGURE **2.1**

Values, Beliefs, and Attitudes in Relation to Self

Values are enduring concepts of good and bad, right and wrong. Your values are more resistant to change than either your attitudes or your beliefs. They are also more difficult for most people to identify. Values are so central to who you are that it is difficult to isolate them. For example, when you go to the supermarket, you may spend a few minutes deciding whether to buy regular or cream-style corn, but you probably do not spend much time deciding whether you will steal the corn or pay for it. Our values are instilled in us by our earliest interpersonal relationships; for almost all of us, our parents shape our values.

The model in Figure 2.1 illustrates that values are central to our behavior and concept of self and that what we believe to be true or false stems from our values; that's why values are in the center of the model. Attitudes are at the outer edge of the circle because they are the most likely to change. You may like your coworker today but not tomorrow, even though you *believe* the person will come to work every day and you still *value* the concept of friendship. Beliefs are between attitudes and values in the model because they are more likely to change than our core values but don't change as much as our attitudes (likes and dislikes).

Who You Are Is Reflected in Your Attitudes, Beliefs, and Values

	Definition	Dimensions	Example
Attitude	Learned predisposition to respond favorably or unfavorably to something	Likes–Dislikes	You like ice cream, incense, and cats.
Belief	The way in which you structure reality	True–False	You believe your parents love you.
Value	Enduring concepts of what is right and wrong	Good–Bad	You value honesty and truth.

Are You Conscious of Who You Are?

Do you know what you're doing right now? "Of course," you may think, "I'm reading this textbook." But are you *really* aware of all of the fleeting thoughts bouncing in your head, whether you're truly happy or sad, or even whether you may be twiddling a pencil, jiggling your leg, or in need of a snack? To be aware of who you are and what you may be thinking about is a more involved process than you may think. Researchers have

belief. Way in which you structure your understanding of reality—what is true and what is false for you.

value. Enduring concept of good and bad, right and wrong.

Peter Blake sought to explore his self-dimensions by painting his self-portrait. What qualities does this self-portrait reveal about the artist?

described three ways of being self-aware—conscious of who you are and what you are doing: subjective self-awareness, objective self-awareness, and symbolic self-awareness.[2]

Subjective Self-Awareness

Subjective self-awareness is the ability that people have to differentiate themselves from their environment. You are a separate being apart from your surroundings. It is so basic an awareness that it may even seem not worth talking about. You know, for example, that you're not physically attached to the chair you may be sitting in. You are a separate entity from all that is around you.

Objective Self-Awareness

Objective self-awareness is the ability to be the object of our own thoughts and attention. You (and based on research, some primates) have the ability to think about your own thoughts as you are thinking about them. Not only are you aware that you're separate from your environment (subjective self-awareness), but you can also ponder the distinct thoughts you are thinking. Of course, objective self-awareness, like subjective self-awareness, can be "turned on" and "turned off." Sometimes you are aware of what you are thinking, sometimes you're unaware of what you are thinking or on what you are focusing.

Symbolic Self-Awareness

Symbolic self-awareness, unique to humans, is our ability not only to think about ourselves, but to use language (symbols) to represent ourselves to others. For example, you have the ability to think about how to make a good impression on others. In an effort to make a positive impression on someone, you may say, "Good evening, Mrs. Cleaver. You look nice this evening" rather than just saying, "Hi ya." You make conscious attempts to use symbols to influence the way you want to be perceived by others.

A four-stage model of how aware or unaware we are of what we are doing at any given moment has been attributed to psychologist Abraham Maslow. This framework has also been used to explain how individuals develop communication skills.

Stage 1: *Unconscious incompetence.* You are unaware of your own incompetence. You don't know what you don't know. For example, at one point in your life you didn't know how to ride a bicycle and you didn't even realize that you were missing this skill. You were unconsciously incompetent about bicycle-riding skills.

Stage 2: *Conscious incompetence.* At this level, you become aware or conscious that you are not competent: You know what you don't know. Continuing our example, at some point you realized that others could ride a bike and you could not. You became conscious of your incompetent bicycle-riding skills.

Stage 3: *Conscious competence.* You are aware that you know something, but applying it has not yet become a habit. When you first learned to ride a bike, if you're like most people, you had to concentrate on keeping your balance and focus on riding forward without falling over.

Stage 4: *Unconscious competence.* At this level, your skills become second nature to you. Now you don't have to mentally review how to ride a bike every time you hop on it. You are unconsciously competent of how to ride a bicycle; you

subjective self-awareness. Ability to differentiate the self from the social and physical environment.

objective self-awareness. Ability to be the object of one's own thoughts and attention—to be aware of one's state of mind and that one is thinking.

symbolic self-awareness. Uniquely human ability to think about oneself and use language (symbols) to represent oneself to others.

just get on and automatically start pedaling. The same could be said about tying your shoes; you don't have to think about how to tie your shoes; you just do it without thinking about each step. These same four stages explain how you learn any skill, from riding a bike to enhancing the interpersonal communication skills we discuss in this book.

One or Many Selves?

Shakespeare's famous line "To thine own self be true" suggests that you have a single self to which you can be true. But do you have just one self? Or is there a more "real you" buried somewhere within? Most scholars conclude that each of us has a core set of behaviors, attitudes, beliefs, and values that constitutes our self—the sum total of who we are. But our *concept* of self can and does change, depending on circumstances and influences.

In addition, our self-concepts are often different from the way others see us. We almost always behave differently in public than we do in private. Sociologist Erving Goffman suggests that, like actors and actresses, we have "on-stage" behaviors when others are watching and "backstage" behaviors when they are not.[3] Goffman writes that "often what talkers undertake to do is not to provide information to a recipient but to present dramas to an audience. Indeed, it seems that we spend most of our time not engaged in giving information but in giving shows."[4] With an audience present, whether it's one person or several, you adapt and "perform."

Perhaps the most enduring and widely accepted framework for describing who we are was developed by the philosopher William James. He identified three classic components of the self: the material self, the social self, and the spiritual self.[5] We will continue our exploration by examining these components.

The Material Self

Perhaps you've heard the statement "You are what you eat." The concept of the **material self** goes a step further by suggesting that "You are what you have." The material self is a total of all the tangible things you own: your body, your possessions, your home. As you examine your list of responses to the question "Who are you?" note whether any of your statements refer to one of your physical attributes or something you own.

One element of the material self gets considerable attention in this culture: the body. Do you like the way you look? Most of us, if we're honest, would like to change something about our appearance. When there is a discrepancy between our desired material self and our self-concept, we may respond to eliminate the discrepancy. We may try to lose weight, develop our muscles, or acquire more hair. The multibillion-dollar diet industry is just one of many that profit from our collective desire to change our appearance.

The Social Self

Look at your "Who are you?" list once more. How many of your responses relate to your **social self,** the part of you that interacts with others? William James believed that you have many social selves—that, depending on the friend, family member, colleague, or acquaintance with whom you are interacting, you change the way you are. A person has, said James, as many social selves as there are people who recognize him or her. For example, when you talk to your best friend, you are willing to "let down your hair" and reveal more thoughts and feelings than you would in a conversation with your communication professor, or even your parents.

material self. Concept of self as reflected in a total of all the tangible things you own.

social self. Concept of self as reflected in social interactions with others.

We discuss this process of self-disclosure later in the chapter. Each relationship that you have with another person is unique because you bring to it a unique social self.

The Spiritual Self

Your **spiritual self** consists of all your thoughts and introspections about your values and moral standards. It does not depend on what you own or with whom you talk; it is the essence of who you *think* you are and your *feelings* about yourself, apart from external evaluations. It is an amalgam of your religious beliefs and your sense of who you are in relationship to other forces in the universe. Whether you believe in intelligent design or Darwinian evolution (or both), your beliefs about the ultimate origins of the world (and about your own origins and ultimate destination) are embedded in your spiritual self. Your spiritual self is the part of you that answers the question "Why am I here?"

William James's Dimensions of Self

	Definition	Examples
Material Self	All the physical elements that reflect who you are	Body, clothes, car, home
Social Self	The self as reflected through your interactions with others; actually, a variety of selves that respond to changes in situations and roles	Your informal self interacting with your best friend; your formal self interacting with your professors
Spiritual Self	Introspections about values, morals, and beliefs	Belief or disbelief in God; regard for life in all its forms

How Your Self-Concept Develops

Some psychologists and sociologists have advanced theories that suggest you learn who you are through five basic means: (1) interactions with other individuals, (2) associations with groups, (3) roles you assume, (4) self-labels, and (5) your personality. Like James's framework, this one does not cover every base in the study of self, but its constructs can provide some clues about how your own self-concept develops.

Interaction with Individuals

In 1902, Charles Horton Cooley first advanced the concept of the **looking-glass self,** which was his term for the notion that we form our self-concepts by seeing ourselves in a kind of figurative looking glass: We learn who we are by interacting with others, much as we look into a mirror and see our reflection.[6] Like Cooley, George Herbert Mead also believed that our sense of who we are is a consequence of our relationships with others.[7] And Harry Stack Sullivan theorized that from birth to death our selves change primarily because of how people respond to us.[8] One sage noted, "We are not only our brother's keeper; we are our brother's maker."

The process begins at birth. Our names, one of the primary ways we identify ourselves, are given to us by someone else. During the early years of our lives, our parents are the key individuals who reflect who we are. If our parents encouraged us to play the piano, we probably play now. As we become less dependent on our parents, our friends become highly influential in shaping our attitudes, beliefs, and values. And

spiritual self. Concept of self based on thoughts and introspections about personal values, moral standards, and beliefs.

looking-glass self. Concept that suggests you learn who you are based on your interactions with others, who reflect your self back to you.

friends continue to provide feedback on how well we perform certain tasks. This, in turn, helps us shape our sense of identity as adults—we must acknowledge our talents in math, language, or art in our own minds before we say that we are mathematicians, linguists, or artists.

Fortunately, not *every* comment affects our sense of who we think we are. We are likely to incorporate the comments of others into our self-concept under three conditions.

First, we are more likely to believe another's statement if he or she repeats something we have heard several times. If one person casually tells you that you have a good singing voice, you are not likely to launch a search for an agent and a recording contract. But if several individuals tell you on many different occasions that you have a talent for singing, you may decide to do something about it.

Second, we are more likely to value another's statements if we perceive him or her to be credible. If we believe the individual is competent, trustworthy, and qualified to make a judgment about us, then we are more likely to believe the person's assessment.

Third, we are likely to incorporate another's comments into our own concept of self if the comments are consistent with other comments and our own experience. If your boss tells you that you work too slowly, but for years people have been urging you to slow down, then your previous experience will probably encourage you to challenge your boss's evaluation.

Associations with Groups

Reflect once more on your responses to the "Who are you?" question. How many responses associate you with a group? Religious groups, political groups, ethnic groups, social groups, study groups, and occupational and professional groups play important roles in determining your self-concept. Some of these groups you are born into; others you choose on your own. Either way, these group associations are significant parts of your identity.

Associating with groups is especially important for people who are not part of the dominant culture. Gays and lesbians, for example, find the support provided by associating with other gays and lesbians to be beneficial to their well-being. The groups you associate with not only provide information about your identity, but also provide needed social support.

Roles You Assume

Look again at your answers to the "Who are you?" question. Perhaps you see words or phrases that signify a role you often assume. Father, aunt, sister, uncle, manager, sales-

Applying Theory and Research

Symbolic Interaction Theory

We defined human communication as the way we make sense of the world and share that sense with others by creating meaning through verbal and nonverbal messages. **Symbolic interaction theory** is based on the assumption that we each make sense of the world based on our interactions with others. We interpret what a word or symbol means based, in part, on how other people react to our use of that word or symbol. Even our own understanding of who we think we are (our self-concept) is influenced by who others tell us we are. Central to understanding ourselves is understanding the importance of other people in shaping our self-understanding. Symbolic interaction theory has had a major influence on communication theory because of the pervasive way our communication with others influences our attitudes, beliefs, values, and self-concept.

George Herbert Mead is credited with the development of symbolic interaction theory, although Mead did not write extensively about his theory.[9] One of Mead's students, Herbert Blumer, actually coined the term *symbolic interaction* to describe the process through which our interactions with others influence our thoughts about others, our life experiences, and ourselves. Mead believed that we cannot have a concept of our own self-identity without interactions with other people.

APPLYING the Research to Your Life

Symbolic interaction theory suggests that you make sense out of your world and your life experiences based on the influence of your family, friends, and other people with whom you communicate. Because of the far-reaching influence of others on your life, it's sometimes hard to be consciously aware of how other people shape your thoughts about yourself and others. Consider the following questions to explore how other people have shaped your understanding of your self-concept and attitudes you hold.

1. How have other people helped shape your own sense of your skills and talents? Identify specific people, and recall things they have said to you that have either reinforced or contradicted your understanding of your own abilities and skills.
2. How do you and your friends and family members talk about your attitudes toward the college or university you now attend? How do other people, especially your family and friends, describe your school, either positively or negatively? How do their comments influence your own attitudes about your school?
3. Has your own concept of who you are undergone dramatic changes? What role did the comments and expressed attitudes of your family, friends, and co-workers play in how you changed your self-concept?

Source: George Herbert Mead, *Mind, Self, and Society* (Chicago: University of Chicago Press, 1934).

person, teacher, and student are labels that imply certain expectations for behavior, and they are important in shaping self-concept. Couples who live together before they marry often report that marriage alters their relationship. Before, they may have shared domestic duties such as doing dishes and laundry. But when they assume the labels of "husband" and "wife," they slip into traditional roles. Husbands don't do laundry. Wives don't mow the grass. These stereotypical role expectations that they learned long ago may require extensive discussion and negotiation. Couples who report the highest satisfaction with marriage agree on their expectations regarding roles ("We agree that I'll do laundry and you'll mow the grass").[10]

symbolic interaction theory. Theory that people make sense of the world on the basis of their interactions with other people.

One reason we assume traditional roles automatically is that our gender group asserts a powerful influence from birth on. As soon as parents know the sex of their children, many begin placing them in that gender group by following cultural rules. They paint the nursery pink for a girl, blue for a boy. Boys get catcher's mitts, train sets, or footballs for their birthdays; girls get dolls, frilly dresses, and tea sets. These cultural conventions and expectations play a major role in shaping our self-concept and our behavior.

Although it is changing, American culture is still male-dominated. What we consider appropriate and inappropriate behavior is often different for males and for females. For example, in group and team meetings, task-oriented, male-dominated roles are valued more than relationship-building roles.[11] Some may applaud fathers who work sixty hours a week as diligent and hard-working but criticize mothers who do the same as neglectful and selfish.

Although our culture defines certain roles as masculine or feminine, we still exercise individual choices about our gender roles. One researcher developed an inventory designed to assess whether we play traditional masculine, feminine, or androgynous roles.[12] Because an **androgynous role** is both masculine and feminine, such a role encompasses a greater repertoire of actions and behaviors.

In American culture, behavior among girls is in many ways quite distinct from that among boys.

Self-Labels

Although our self-concept is deeply affected by others, we are not blank slates for them to write on. The labels we use to describe our own attitudes, beliefs, values, and actions also play a role in shaping our self-concept.

Where do our labels come from? We interpret what we experience; we are self-reflexive. **Self-reflexiveness** is the human ability to think about what we are doing while we are doing it. We talk to ourselves about ourselves. We are both participants and observers in all that we do. This dual role encourages us to use labels to describe who we are.

When you were younger, perhaps you dreamed of becoming an all-star basketball player. Your coach may have told you that you were a great player, but as you matured, you probably began observing yourself more critically. You scored no points. So you self-reflexively decided that you were not, deep down, a basketball player, even though others may have labeled you as "talented." But sometimes, through this self-observation, people discover strengths that encourage them to assume new labels. One woman we know never thought of herself as "heroic" until she went through seventy-two hours of labor before giving birth!

Your Personality

The concept of personality is central to **psychology,** the study of how your thinking influences how you behave. According to psychologist Lester Lefton, your **personality** consists of a set of enduring internal predispositions and behavioral characteristics that describe how you react to your environment.[13] Understanding the forces that shape your personality is central to increasing your awareness of your self-concept and how you relate to others.

Does nature or nurture play the predominant role in your personality? As we noted in Chapter 1, the **communibiological approach** to communication suggests that a major factor affecting how people communicate with others is genetic makeup.[14] Others argue that although it's true that communication behavior is influenced by genes, we should not forget that humans can learn to adjust and adapt.[15]

One personality characteristic that communication researchers have spent considerable time studying is the level of comfort or discomfort individuals experience when interacting with other people. Some people just don't like to talk with others.[16] We may say such a person is shy. **Shyness** is the behavioral tendency not to talk with

androgynous role. Gender role that includes both masculine and feminine qualities.

self-reflexiveness. Ability to think about what you are doing while you are doing it.

psychology. Study of how thinking influences behavior.

personality. Set of enduring internal predispositions and behavioral characteristics that describe how people react to their environment.

communibiological approach. Perspective that suggests that genetic and biological influences play a major role in influencing communication behavior.

shyness. Behavioral tendency not to talk or interact with other people.

others. One study found that about 40 percent of adults reported they were shy.[17] In public-speaking situations, we say a person has stage fright; a better term to describe this feeling is *communication apprehension.* **Communication apprehension,** according to communication experts James McCroskey and Virginia Richmond, is "the fear or anxiety associated with either real or anticipated communication with another person or persons."[18] One study found that up to 80 percent of the population experiences some degree of nervousness or apprehension when they speak in public.[19] Another study found that about 20 percent of people are considerably anxious when they give a speech.[20] What makes some people apprehensive about communicating with others? Again, we get back to the nature–nurture issue. Heredity plays an important role in whether you are going to feel nervous or anxious when communicating with someone else. But so does whether you were reinforced for talking with

Interpersonal Communication and Emotion *Connecting Heart to Heart*

Self and Emotion: How We Influence How We Feel

In Chapter 1, we defined an emotion as a biological, cognitive, behavioral, and subjective affective reaction to an event. Emotions are reactions to what we experience. What continues to be debated is the specific sequence of events that results in an emotional response. Are we in control of our emotions, or do our emotions control us? We present three different theories that describe the chain of events that cause us to experience emotions.

Commonsense Theory of Emotion: Emotions Happen
The commonsense approach is so named because it seems to be a description of the way many people would describe how emotions occur. The commonsense theory, shown in Figure 2.2, suggests the following order of emotional experience: (1) Something happens, (2) you have an affective (that is, an emotional) reaction to the event (you feel sad or happy), and finally, (3) you respond physiologically by blushing, experiencing an increased heart rate, or having another biological reaction to your emotion.[21] Here's an example: (1) You meet your new boss for the first time, (2) you feel nervous, and (3) your heart rate increases and you begin to perspire. This sequence is typically the way many people think about emotions occurring—emotions just happen, and we really have no choice in how we feel. But there are other theories about what causes emotions.

James-Lange Theory of Emotion: Physiological Response Determines Emotional Response
Another theory of emotion, developed by psychologists William James and

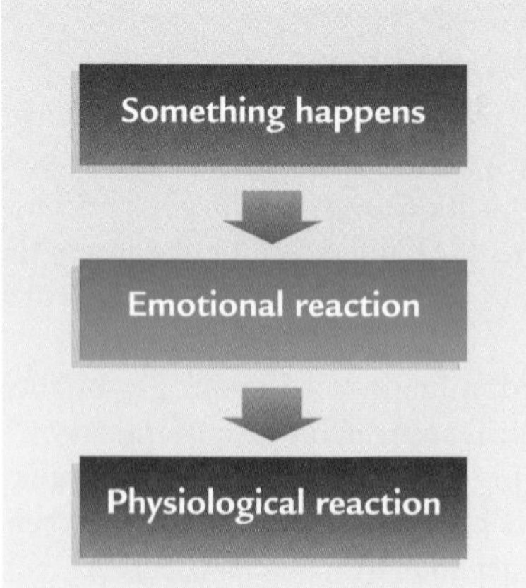

FIGURE **2.2**
Commonsense Theory of Emotion

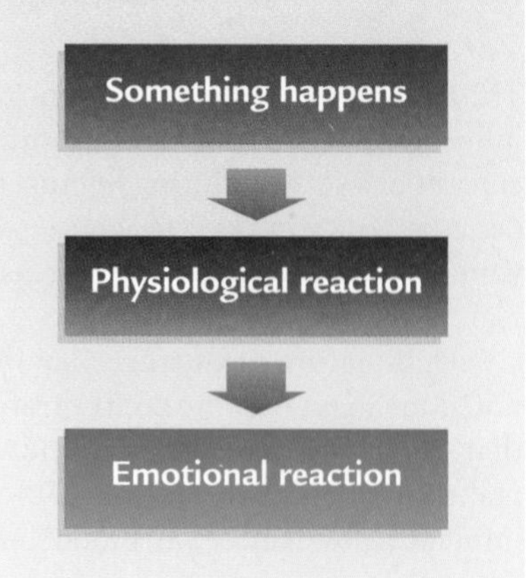

FIGURE **2.3**
James-Lange Theory of Emotion

others as a child, as well as other experiences that are part of your culture and learning.

Your overall **willingness to communicate** with others is a general way of summarizing the likelihood that you will talk with others in a variety of situations, including interpersonal conversations. If you are unwilling to communicate with others, you will be less comfortable in a career that forces you to interact with other people.

Understanding the factors that influence your self-concept—such as your interactions with individuals and groups, the roles you assume, your self-labels, and your personality, including your overall comfort level in communicating with others—can help you understand who you are and why you interact (or don't interact) with others. But it's not only who you are that influences your communication; it's also your overall sense of self-esteem or self-worth that affects how you express yourself and respond to others.

communication apprehension. Fear or anxiety associated with either real or anticipated communication with other people.

willingness to communicate. General term for the likelihood that an individual will communicate with others in certain situations.

Carl Lange, is called the James-Lange theory of emotions.[22] Note the difference in the sequence of events in this theory in Figure 2.3: (1) Something happens, (2) you respond physiologically, and then (3) you experience an emotion. This theory suggests that we respond physiologically *before* we experience an emotion. The physiological responses tell us whether or not to experience an emotion. When you meet your new boss, you begin to perspire, and your heart starts beating more rapidly; this, in turn, *causes* you to feel nervous.

Appraisal Theory of Emotions: Labels Determine What Emotions Are Experienced

Yet a third view suggests that you are more in control of your emotions than you might think. You can change the emotion you are feeling by the way you decide to label or describe your experiences to yourself. This theory is called the appraisal theory, which means we appraise and label what we feel; the labels we use to describe what we experience have a major effect on what we feel as an emotional response.[23] Here's the suspected sequence in this theory: (1) Something happens, (2) you respond physiologically, (3) you decide how you will react to what is happening to you, and then (4) you experience the emotion. (See Figure 2.4.) Do you see the difference in this last approach? *It suggests that you have control over how you feel, based in part on what you tell yourself about what you are experiencing.*

According to the appraisal theory of emotions, you actively participate in determining what emotion you experience by labeling your experiences. For example, (1) you meet your new boss, (2) your heart rate increases and you start to perspire, (3) you tell yourself that this is an important and fear-inducing event, so (4) you feel nervous and anxious. Or you could tell yourself, "This is no big deal" and not feel nervous but look forward to meeting your new boss.

Although researchers continue to debate precisely how events trigger our emotions, we know that our emotional reaction to what we experience has a profound impact on how we relate to others.

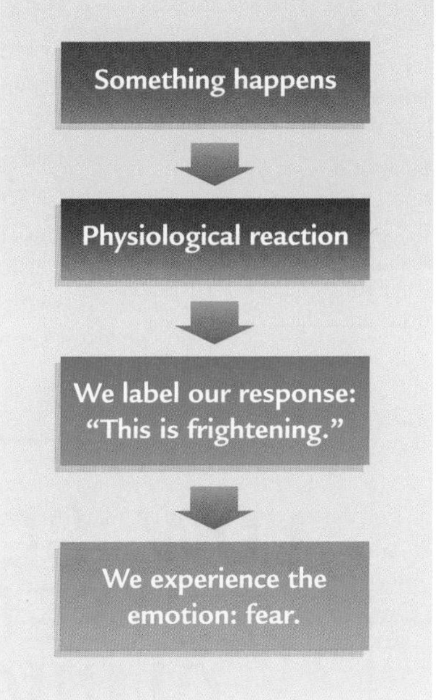

FIGURE 2.4
Appraisal Theory of Emotion

Self-Esteem: Your Self-Worth

Your self-esteem is closely related to your self-concept. Your self-concept is a *description* of who you are. Your self-esteem is an *evaluation* of who you are. The term **self-worth** is often used interchangeably with *self-esteem.* There is evidence that your overall feeling of self-worth is related to feeling and expressing positive messages toward others as well as being supportive of other people.[24] You feel better about yourself if you behave in ways that researchers call being *prosocial,* which means your behaviors benefit others.

People derive their sense of self-worth from comparing themselves to others, a process called *social comparison.* **Social comparison** helps people measure how well they think they are doing compared to others. I'm good at playing soccer (because I beat others); I can't cook (because others cook better than I do); I'm not good at meeting people (most people I know seem to be more comfortable interacting with others); I'm not handy (but my brothers and sisters can fix a leaky faucet). Each of these statements implies a judgment about how well or badly you can perform certain tasks, with implied references to how well others perform the same tasks. A belief that you cannot fix a leaky faucet or cook like a chef may not in itself lower your self-esteem. But if there are *several* things you can't do well or *many* important tasks that you cannot seem to master, these shortcomings may begin to color your overall sense of worth.

self-worth (self-esteem). Your evaluation of your worth or value based on your perception of such things as your skills, abilities, talents, and appearance.

social comparison. Process of comparing yourself to others who are similar to you to measure your worth and value.

life position. Feelings of regard for yourself and others, as reflected in your sense of worth and self-esteem.

face. Person's positive perception of himself or herself in interactions with others.

facework. Using communication to maintain your own positive self-perception (self-face) or to support, reinforce, or challenge someone else's self-perception (other-face).

In the 1960s, psychologist Eric Berne developed the concept of a **life position** to describe people's overall sense of their own worth and that of others.[25] He identified four life positions: (1) "I'm OK, you're OK," or positive regard for self and others; (2) "I'm OK, you're not OK," or positive regard for self and low regard for others; (3) "I'm not OK, you're OK," or low self-regard and positive regard for others; and (4) "I'm not OK, you're not OK," or low regard for both self and others. Your life position is a driving force in your relationships with others. People in the "I'm OK, you're OK" position have the best chance for healthy relationships because they have discovered their own talents and also recognize that others have been given talents different from their own.

Another way communication researchers talk about being "OK" is by referring to what is called *face.* **Face** is a person's positive perception of himself or herself in interactions with others.[26] **Facework** is the use of communication to maintain one's own positive self-perception (self-face) or to support, reinforce, or even challenge someone else's self-perception (other-face).[27] You are involved in facework, for example, when you announce to your parents that you made the dean's list during your most recent semester in college. By telling them the good news about your academic success, you're

using communication to maintain your parents' positive image of you and thus reinforce your own positive self-image. The effort you expend to save face (protect your positive image) reflects the kind of perception you want others to have of you.

Although positive self-talk will never be able to make all of us become champion cyclists like Lance Armstrong, it can help us focus on our own goals and improve our performance levels.

How to Improve Your Self-Esteem

We have mentioned that low self-esteem can affect our own communications and interactions. In recent years, teachers, psychologists, ministers, rabbis, social workers, and even politicians have suggested that many societal problems also stem from collective feelings of low self-esteem. Feelings of low self-worth may contribute to choosing the wrong partners; to becoming dependent on drugs, alcohol, or other substances; or to experiencing problems with eating or other vital activities. So people owe it to society, as well as to themselves, to maintain or develop a healthy sense of self-esteem.

Although no simple list of tricks can easily transform low self-esteem into feelings of being valued and appreciated, you can improve how you think about yourself and interact with others. We'll explore seven proven techniques that have helped others.

Engage in Self-Talk

Cycling champion Lance Armstrong is also a cancer survivor. When he got sick, he told a friend, "Cancer picked the wrong guy. When it looked around for a body to hang out in, it made a big mistake when it chose mine. Big mistake."[28] The positive self-talk reflected in his words undoubtedly helped Armstrong to overcome the challenge of cancer and go on to win the Tour de France seven times.

Intrapersonal communication is communication within yourself—self-talk. Realistic, positive self-talk can have a reassuring effect on your level of self-worth and on your interactions with others.[29] Conversely, repeating negative messages about your lack of skill and ability can keep you from trying and achieving.

Of course, blind faith without hard work won't succeed. Self-talk is not a substitute for effort; it can, however, keep you on track and help you ultimately to achieve your goal.

Visualize a Positive Image of Yourself

Visualization takes the notion of self-talk one step further. Besides just telling yourself that you can achieve your goal, you can actually try to "see" yourself conversing effectively with others, performing well on a project, or exhibiting some other desirable behavior. Being able to visualize completing a goal (thinking positively rather than thinking you won't achieve your goals) adds to your overall sense of happiness and well-being.[30] Recent research suggests that an apprehensive public speaker can manage his or her fears not only by developing skill in public speaking, but also by visualizing positive results when speaking to an audience.[31] The same technique can be used to boost your sense of self-worth about other tasks or skills. If, for example, you tend

intrapersonal communication. Communication within yourself; self-talk.

visualization. Technique of imagining that you are performing a particular task in a certain way; positive visualization can enhance self-esteem.

Michael continually measures himself against others.

to get nervous when meeting people at a party, imagine yourself in a room full of people, glibly introducing yourself to others with ease. Visualizing yourself performing well can yield positive results in changing long-standing feelings of inadequacy. Of course, your visualization should be realistic and coupled with a plan to achieve your goal.

Avoid Comparing Yourself with Others

Even before we were born, we were compared with others. The latest medical technology lets us see sonograms of fetuses still in the womb, so parents may begin comparing children with other babies before birth. For the rest of our lives, we are compared with others, and rather than celebrating our uniqueness, comparisons usually point up who is stronger, brighter, on more beautiful. Many of us have had the experience of being chosen last to play on a sports team, passed over for promotion, or standing unchosen against the wall at a dance.

In North American culture, we may be tempted to judge our self-worth by our material possessions and personal appearance. If we know someone who has a newer car (or simply a car, if we rely on public transportation), a smaller waistline, or a higher grade point average, we may feel diminished. Comparisons such as "He has more money than I have" or "She looks better than I look" are likely to deflate our self-worth.

Rather than finding others who seemingly are better off, focus on the unique attributes that make you who you are. Avoid judging your own value by comparing yourself with others. A healthy, positive self-concept is fueled not by judgments of others, but by a genuine sense of worth that you recognize in yourself.

Reframe Appropriately

Reframing is the process of redefining events and experiences from a different point of view. Just as reframing a work of art can give the picture a whole new look, reframing events that cause you to devalue your self-worth can change your perspective. For example, if you get a report from your supervisor that says you should improve one area of your performance, instead of listening to the self-talk that says you're bad at your job, reframe the event within a larger context: Tell yourself that one negative comment does not mean you are hopeless as a worker.

Of course, not all negative experiences should be lightly tossed off and left unexamined, because you can learn and profit from your mistakes. But it is important to remember that your worth as a human being does not depend on a single exam grade, a single response from a prospective employer, or a single play in a football game.

Develop Honest Relationships

Having at least one other person who can help you objectively and honestly reflect on your virtues and vices can be extremely beneficial in fostering a healthy, positive self-image. As we noted earlier, other people play a major role in shaping your self-concept and self-esteem. The more credible the source of information, the more likely you

reframing. Process of redefining events and experiences from a different point of view.

are to believe it. Later in the chapter, we discuss how honest relationships are developed through the process of self-disclosure. Honest, positive support can provide encouragement for a lifetime.

Let Go of the Past

Your self-concept is not a fixed construct. It was not implanted at birth to remain constant for the rest of your life. Things change. You change. Others change. Individuals with low self-esteem may be locking on to events and experiences that happened years ago and tenaciously refusing to let go of them. Perhaps you've heard religious and spiritual leaders suggest that it's important to forgive others who have hurt you in the past. There is research evidence that suggests it's important to your own mental health and sense of well-being to let go of old wounds and forgive others.[32] Someone once wrote, "The lightning bug is brilliant, but it hasn't much of a mind; it blunders through existence with its headlight on behind." Looking back at what we can't change only reinforces a sense of helplessness. Constantly replaying negative experiences with our mental DVD player only serves to make our sense of worth more difficult to change. Becoming aware of the changes that have occurred and can occur in your life can help you develop a more realistic assessment of your value.

Seek Support

You provide **social support** when you express care and concern as well as listen and empathize with others. Perhaps you just call it "talking with a friend." Having someone be socially supportive is especially important to us when we experience stress and anxiety or are faced with a vexing personal problem.[33]

Social support from a friend or family member can be helpful, but some of your self-image problems may be so ingrained that you need professional help. A trained counselor, clergy member, or therapist can help you sort through them. The technique of having a trained person listen as you verbalize your fears, hopes, and concerns is called **talk therapy.** You talk, and a skilled listener helps you sort out your feelings and problems. There is power in being able to put your thoughts, especially your negative thoughts and emotions, into words. By saying things out loud to an open, honest, empathic listener, we gain insight and can sometimes figure out why we experience the hurts and difficulties that we do. If you are not sure to whom to turn for a referral, you can start with your school counseling services. Or, if you are near a medical-school teaching hospital, you can contact the counseling or psychotherapy office there for a referral.

social support. Expression of empathy and concern for others that is communicated while listening to them and offering positive and encouraging words.

talk therapy. Technique in which a person describes his or her problems and concerns to a skilled listener in order to better understand the emotions and issues that are creating the problems.

Because you have spent your whole lifetime developing your self-esteem, it is not easy to make big changes. But talking through problems can make a difference. As communication researchers Frank E. X. Dance and Carl Larson see it, "Speech communication empowers each of us to share in the development of our own self-concept and the fulfillment of that self-concept."[34]

Strategies for Improving Your Self-Esteem

Engage in Self-Talk	If you're having a bad hair day, tell yourself that you have beautiful eyes and lots of friends who like you anyway.
Visualize	If you feel nervous before a meeting, visualize everyone in the room congratulating you on your great ideas.
Avoid Comparison	Focus on your positive qualities and on what you can do to enhance your own talents and abilities.
Reframe Appropriately	If you experience one failure, keep the larger picture in mind, rather than focusing on that isolated incident.
Develop Honest Relationships	Cultivate friends in whom you can confide and who will give you honest feedback for improving your skills and abilities.
Let Go of the Past	Talk yourself out of your old issues; focus on ways to enhance your abilities in the future.
Seek Support	Talk with professional counselors who can help you identify your gifts and talents.

How Self-Concept and Self-Esteem Affect Interpersonal Communication and Relationships

Your self-concept and self-esteem filter every interaction with others. They determine how you approach, respond to, and interpret messages. Specifically, your self-concept and self-esteem affect your ability to be sensitive to others, your self-fulfilling prophecies, your interpretation of messages, your own social needs, and your typical communication style.

Self and Others

BE OTHER-ORIENTED 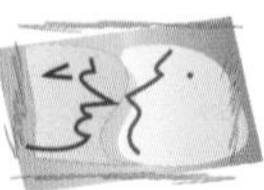

We have suggested the importance of becoming other-oriented—being sensitive to the thoughts and feelings of others—as a requisite for developing quality interpersonal relationships with others. Becoming other-oriented involves recognizing that your "self" is different from others. As the Peanuts cartoon on the previous page reminds us, the world does not revolve around our solitary selves. Others influence our actions and our self-image. Mead suggests that we develop an "I," which is based on our own perspective of ourselves, and a "Me," which is an image of ourselves based on the collective responses we receive and interpret from others. Being aware of how your concept of self ("I") differs from the perceptions others have of you ("Me") is an important first step in developing an other-orientation.

When you begin the **social decentering** process—taking into account what others may be thinking and feeling—you often interpret your assumptions about others using your own self as a frame of reference, especially if you do not know the other person well.[35] For example, if you are nervous and frightened when you have to take a test, you might assume that your friend will react the same way. You may need to remind yourself that the other person is separate from you and may have a different set of responses.

When you use a **specific-other perspective,** you rely on information that you have observed or that you can imagine about a particular person to predict his or her reactions. For example, if you know firsthand that your sister hates to have someone take food from her plate during dinner, you may use that experience to conclude that she would dislike sharing a bag of popcorn at the movies.

Sometimes, a **generalized-other perspective** will be more useful. When you think about and respond to others, you can apply knowledge and personal theories that you have about people in general or about specific subgroups to the person with whom you are interacting. For example, you might think that your economics professor, who holds a Ph.D., would prefer to be addressed as "Doctor" rather than as "Mister" because almost all your other professors with doctorates prefer to be called "Doctor."

Your ability to predict how others will respond to you is based on your ability to understand how your sense of the world is similar to and different from theirs. First, you must know yourself well. Then you can know and understand others. One of the best ways to improve your ability to be other-oriented is to notice how others respond when you act on the predictions and assumptions you have made about them. You may discover that you have not moved out of your own frame of reference enough to make an accurate prediction about another person.

Self-Fulfilling Prophecy

What people believe about themselves often comes true because they expect it to come true. Their expectations become a **self-fulfilling prophecy.** If you think you will fail the math quiz because you have labeled yourself inept at math, then you must overcome not only your math deficiency, but also your low expectations of yourself. The theme of George Bernard Shaw's *Pygmalion* is "If you treat a girl like a flower girl, that's all she will ever be. If you treat her like a princess, she may be one." Research suggests that you can create your own obstacles to achieving your goals by being too critical of yourself.[36] Or you can increase your chances for success by having a more positive mindset.[37] Your attitudes, beliefs, and general expectations about your performance have a powerful and profound effect on your behavior.

The medical profession is learning the power that attitudes and expectations have over healing. Physician Howard Brody's research suggests that in many instances, just giving patients a placebo—a pill with no medicine in it—or telling patients that they have been operated on when they haven't had an operation can yield positive medical results. In his book *The Placebo Response,* Brody tells of a woman with debilitating Parkinson's disease who made a miraculous recovery; her only treatment was the doctors' telling her that they had completed a medical procedure.[38] They hadn't. Yet before the "treatment," she could barely walk; now she can easily pace around the room. There is a clear link, suggests Dr. Brody, between mental state and physical health. Patients who believe they will improve are more likely to improve.

social decentering. Cognitive process in which you take into account another person's thoughts, feelings, values, background, and perspective.

specific-other perspective. Perspective that uses information that one can observe or imagine about another person to predict that person's behavior.

generalized-other perspective. Perspective that uses observed or imagined information about many people, or people in general, to predict a person's behavior.

self-fulfilling prophecy. Prediction about future actions that is likely to come true because the person believes that it will come true.

Self and Interpretation of Messages

Although it may have been several years since you've read A. A. Milne's classic children's stories about Winnie-the-Pooh, you probably remember Eeyore, the donkey friend of Winnie-the-Pooh and his friends. Eeyore lives in the gloomiest part of the Hundred Acre Wood and has a self-image to match. In one story, all the animals congregate on a stormy night to check on Eeyore:

> . . . they all came to the part of the forest known as Eeyore's gloomy place. On this stormy night it was terribly gloomy indeed—or it would have been were it not for Christopher Robin. He was there with a big umbrella.
>
> "I've invited Eeyore to come and stay with me until the storm is over," said Christopher Robin.
>
> "If it ever is," said Eeyore, "which doesn't seem likely. Not that anybody asked me, you understand. But then, they hardly ever do."[39]

Perhaps you know or have known an Eeyore—someone whose low self-esteem colors how he or she interprets messages and interacts with others. According to research, such people are more likely to

- Be more sensitive to criticism and negative feedback from others.
- Be more critical of others.
- Believe they are not popular or respected by others.
- Expect to be rejected by others.
- Prefer not to be observed while performing.
- Feel threatened by people who they feel are superior.
- Expect to lose when competing with others.
- Be overly responsive to praise and compliments.
- Evaluate their overall behavior as inferior to that of others.[40]

The Pooh stories offer an antidote to Eeyore's gloom in the character of the optimistic Tigger, who assumes that everyone shares his exuberance for life:

> . . . when Owl reached Piglet's house, Tigger was there. He was bouncing on his tail, as Tiggers do, and shouting to Piglet. "Come on," he cried. "You can do it! It's fun!"[41]

If, like Tigger, your sense of self-worth is high, research suggests you will

- Have higher expectations for solving problems.
- Think more highly of others.
- Be more likely to accept praise and accolades from others without feeling embarrassed.
- Be more comfortable having others observe you when you perform.
- Be more likely to admit you have both strengths and weaknesses.
- Prefer to interact with others who view themselves as highly competent.
- Expect other people to accept you for who you are.
- Be more likely to seek opportunities to improve skills that need improving.
- Evaluate your overall behavior more positively than would people with lower self-esteem.[42]

Self and Interpersonal Needs

According to social psychologist Will Schutz, our concept of who we are, coupled with our need to interact with others, profoundly influences how we communicate with others. Schutz identifies three primary social needs that affect the degree of communication we have with others: the need for inclusion, the need for control, and the need for affection.[43]

Although assertiveness is often thought of as a masculine trait, anyone can use an assertive communication style.

Inclusion

Each of us has a **need for inclusion**—the need to be included in the activities of others and to experience human contact and fellowship. We need to be invited to join others, and perhaps we need to invite others to join us. Of course, the level and intensity of this need differ from person to person, but even loners desire some social contact. Our need to include others and be included in activities may stem, in part, from our concept of ourselves as either a "party person" or a loner.

Control

We also have a **need for control:** We need some degree of influence over the relationships we establish with others. We may also have a need to *be* controlled because we desire some level of stability and comfort in our interactions with others. If we view ourselves as people who are comfortable being in charge, we are more likely to give orders to others rather than take orders from them.

Affection

Finally, we each have a **need for affection.** We need to give and receive love, support, warmth, and intimacy, although the amounts we need vary enormously from person to person. The greater our needs for inclusion, control, and affection, the more likely it is that we will actively seek others as friends and initiate communication with them.

Self and Communication Style

Our self-concept and self-esteem ultimately affect how we treat other people. One dimension of the self that is particularly relevant to our interactions with others is communication style. Each of us has a **communication style,** sometimes called *social style,* that is identifiable by the habitual ways we behave toward others. The style we adopt helps others interpret our messages and predict how we will behave. As they get to know us, other people begin to expect us to communicate in a certain way, based on previous associations with us.

How do we develop our communication style? Many communication researchers, sociologists, and psychologists believe that we have certain underlying genetic traits or personality characteristics that influence how we interact with others.[44] Others emphasize the social learning approach—we communicate with other people as we do because of our interactions with others such as our parents and friends. The truth is that researchers cannot yet explain exactly how we come to communicate as we do.

Even though we don't know the precise role of nature or nurture in determining how we communicate, most inventories of personality or communication style focus on two primary dimensions that underlie how we interact with others—assertiveness and responsiveness.[45] **Assertiveness** is the tendency to make requests, ask for information, and generally pursue our own rights and best interests. An assertive style is sometimes called a "masculine" style. By masculine, we don't mean that only males can be assertive, but that in many cultures being assertive is synonymous with being masculine. You are assertive when you seek information if you are confused or direct others to help you get what you need.

Responsiveness is the tendency to be sensitive to the needs of others. Being other-oriented and sympathetic to the feelings of others, and placing others' feelings above your own are examples of being responsive. Researchers sometimes label responsiveness a "feminine" quality. Again, this does not mean only women are or should be re-

need for inclusion. Interpersonal need to be included and to include others in social activities.

need for control. Interpersonal need for some degree of influence in our relationships, as well as the need to be controlled.

need for affection. Interpersonal need to give and receive love, support, warmth, and intimacy.

communication style. Style that is identifiable by habitual ways in which you communicate with other people.

assertiveness. Tendency to make requests, ask for information, and generally pursue your own rights and best interests.

responsiveness. Tendency to be sensitive to the needs of others, including being sympathetic to others' feelings and placing the feelings of others above your own feelings.

Sociocommunicative Orientation

Directions: The following questionnaire lists 20 personality characteristics. Please indicate the degree to which you believe each of these characteristics applies to you, as you normally communicate with others, by marking whether you (5) strongly agree that it applies, (4) agree that it applies, (3) are undecided, (2) disagree that it applies, or (1) strongly disagree that it applies. There are no right or wrong answers. Work quickly; record your first impression.

_____ 1. helpful
_____ 2. defends own beliefs
_____ 3. independent
_____ 4. responsive to others
_____ 5. forceful
_____ 6. has strong personality
_____ 7. sympathetic
_____ 8. compassionate
_____ 9. assertive
_____ 10. sensitive to the needs of others
_____ 11. dominant
_____ 12. sincere
_____ 13. gentle
_____ 14. willing to take a stand
_____ 15. warm
_____ 16. tender
_____ 17. friendly
_____ 18. acts as a leader
_____ 19. aggressive
_____ 20. competitive

Scoring: Items 2, 3, 5, 6, 9, 11, 14, 18, 19, and 20 measure assertiveness. Add the scores on these items to get your assertiveness score. Items 1, 4, 7, 8, 10, 12, 13, 15, 16, and 17 measure responsiveness. Add the scores on these items to get your responsiveness score. Scores range from 50 to 10. The higher your score, the higher your orientation as assertive and responsive.

Source: James C. McCroskey and Virginia P. Richmond, *Fundamentals of Human Communication: An Interpersonal Perspective* (Prospect Heights, IL: Waveland Press, 1996), 91. Reprinted with permission of James C. McCroskey and Virginia P. Richmond.

sponsive, only that many cultures stereotype being responsive as a traditional behavior of females.

What is your communication style? To assess your style of communication on the assertiveness and responsiveness dimensions, take the "Sociocommunicative Orientation" test by James McCroskey and Virginia Richmond in the Building Your Skills box. You may discover that you test higher on one dimension than on others. It's also possible to be high on both or low on both. Assertiveness and responsiveness are two different dimensions; you need not have just one or the other.

What many people want to know is, "What's the best communication style? Should I be assertive or responsive?" The truth is, there is no one best style for every situation. Sometimes, the appropriate thing to do is to assert yourself—to ask or even demand that you receive what you need and have a right to receive. In other situations, it may be more appropriate to be less confrontational. Maintaining the quality of the relationship by simply listening and being thoughtfully responsive to others may be best.

BE OTHER-ORIENTED

Although we're not recommending any one communication style as the best in *every* situation, being perceived as both appropriately assertive and appropriately responsive reflects positively on your relationships with others. One research team led by Virginia Richmond found that physicians who were perceived to have high levels of both assertiveness and responsiveness had more credibility than physicians who had lower levels of these two communication dimensions.[46] And not only did patients find the physicians with appropriate assertiveness and responsiveness more credible, patients were also more satisfied with their medical care. The appropriateness of a specific communication style involves issues we will discuss in future chapters, such as how individuals adapt to culture and gender differences, their needs, the needs and rights of others, and the goal of their communication.

Recap

How Self-Concept and Self-Esteem Affect Interpersonal Communication and Relationships

Term	Definition	Example
Self-Fulfilling Prophecy	What you believe about yourself will come true because you expect it to come true.	You expect to have a rotten time at a party so you behave in ways that guarantee you won't enjoy the party.
Message Interpretation and Interaction	Feelings of high or low self-esteem affect how you understand and react to messages.	If you have high self-esteem, you are more likely to accept praise without embarrassment.
Communication Style	Your self-concept and self-esteem contribute to habitual ways of responding to others.	Your image of yourself influences your responsive or assertive behavior toward others.

Self-Disclosure: Connecting Self to Others Through Talk

One important way people develop and revise their self-concept is through other people's reactions to their self-disclosure. **Self-disclosure** occurs when you purposefully provide information to others about yourself that they would not learn if you did not tell them. Self-disclosure ranges from revealing innocuous information about who you are to admitting your deepest fears and most private fantasies. Disclosing personal information not only provides a basis for another person to understand you better, it also conveys your level of trust and acceptance of the other person. Because others self-disclose, you are able to learn information about them and deepen your interpersonal relationships with them.[47] To help explore the relationships among self-concept, self-esteem, and self-disclosure, we will describe how self-disclosure occurs, note how people become aware of who they are through self-disclosure, and identify general characteristics of self-disclosure.

Interpersonal relationships cannot achieve intimacy without self-disclosure. Without true self-disclosure, you form only superficial relationships. You can confirm another person's self-concept, and have your own self-concept confirmed, only if both you and your partner have revealed yourselves to each other.

Understanding the Depth and Breadth of Self-Disclosure: The Social Penetration Model of Self-Disclosure

self-disclosure. Purposefully providing information about yourself to others that they would not learn if you did not tell them.

What makes your best friend your best friend? Undoubtedly, one characteristic is that you have shared your most personal information with him or her. You share more

FIGURE 2.5

Social Penetration Model

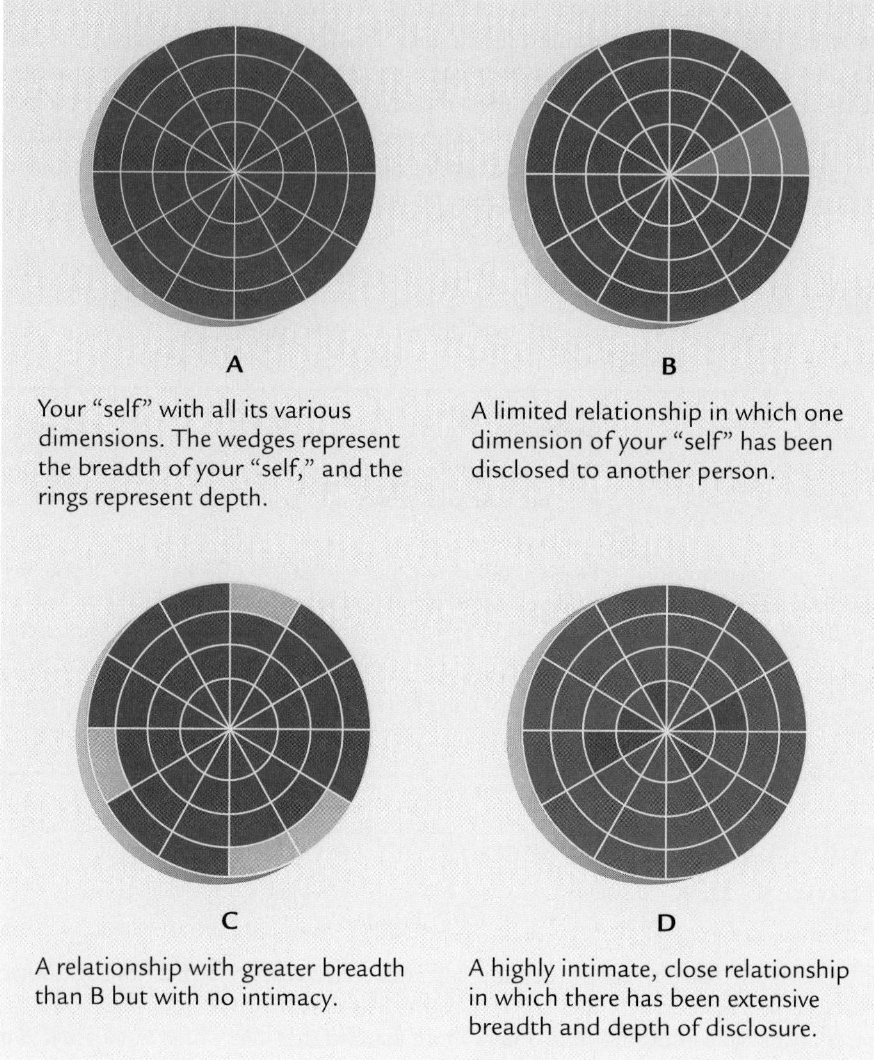

personal information over a broader range of topics with people you know well and who know you, than you do with people you know only superficially. Researchers Irwin Altman and Dalmas Taylor developed the **social penetration model** that illustrates how much and what kinds of information people reveal in various stages of a relationship.[48] Their model starts with a circle that represents all the potential information about yourself that you could disclose to someone (see Figure 2.5, circle A). This circle is divided into many pieces like a pie, with each piece of pie representing a particular aspect of yourself. For instance, some pieces in your pie might relate to athletic activities, religious beliefs, family, school, recreational activities, political interests, and fears. These pieces of pie represent the breadth of topics or information available about you.

social penetration model. Model of self-disclosure and relational development that reflects both depth and breadth of shared information.

In addition, the concentric circles in the pie represent the depth of information you could disclose. By depth, we mean how personal or intimate the information is; telling your friend about your fear of elevators is more intimate than telling someone that your favorite ice cream is homemade vanilla. The smallest circle represents the most personal information. Each of your relationships represents a degree of social

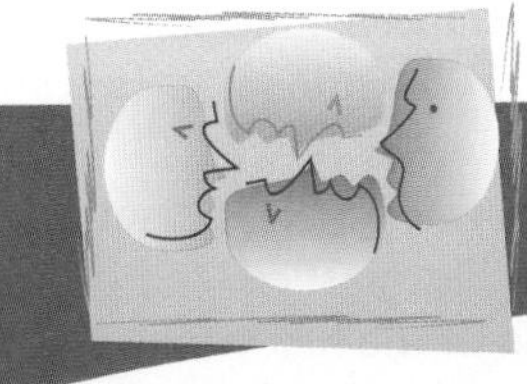

Understanding Diversity

Cultural Differences in Self-Disclosure

The social penetration model of self-disclosure suggests that self-disclosure can be described by both breadth—the number of topics we discuss—and depth—the level of intimacy we establish with others. Do cultural differences affect how much we disclose to one another? Several researchers suggest that the answer is yes. People's cultural backgrounds affect both the kinds of things they reveal and the intimacy of the information about themselves they share with others. Intercultural communication scholar William Gudykunst found that North Americans are more likely than Japanese to reveal more personal and intimate information about themselves to people whom they consider to be close friends.[49] Self-disclosure researcher Mie Kito found the same thing; Japanese students disclosed less about themselves than did students from North America.[50] Both Japanese and American students disclosed more about themselves in romantic relationships than with their friends. Americans were more likely than the Japanese to talk about their sex lives, dating patterns, and love interests and to reveal their emotions. A researcher investigating Korean communication patterns found that North Americans tended to disclose more than Koreans about their marital status, sexual morality, and use of birth control.[51] But Koreans were more likely than Americans to talk about issues related to education and family rules. What are the larger implications of these studies? Simply this: The amount of self-disclosure that is considered appropriate is learned; the level of self-disclosure with which we are comfortable varies from culture to culture. Cultural norms influence how much we reveal about ourselves.

penetration, or the extent to which the other person has penetrated your concentric circles (depth) and shared pieces of your pie (breadth). For example, the shading on circle B shows a relationship that involves a high degree of penetration, but of only one aspect of yourself. Perhaps you have a good friend with whom you study and go to the library, but you don't spend much time socializing with your friend; it's all work and no play with this friend. You might have disclosed some personal or intimate information to your friend about your study skills and weaknesses, but little about your family, hobbies, political views, religious beliefs, or other aspects of who you are.

Your relationships with your instructors probably look a little like circle B, with its limited breadth. In circle C, more pieces of the pie are shaded, but the information is all fairly safe, superficial information about yourself, such as where you went to school, your hometown, or your major. These would be the kind of disclosures associated with a new friendship. Circle D represents almost complete social penetration, the kind achieved in an intimate, well-developed relationship in which a large amount of self-disclosure has occurred.

Understanding How We Learn About Ourselves from Others: The Johari Window Model of Self-Disclosure

To disclose personal information to others, you must first be aware of who you are. Your **self-awareness** is your understanding of who you are. In addition to just thinking about who you are, asking others for information about yourself and then listening to what they tell you can enhance your self-awareness. A variety of personality tests, such as the Myers-Briggs personality inventory, may give you additional insight into your interests, style, and ways of relating to others. Most colleges and universities have a career services office where you can take vocational aptitude tests to help you identify careers that fit who you are.

self-awareness. Person's conscious understanding of who he or she is.

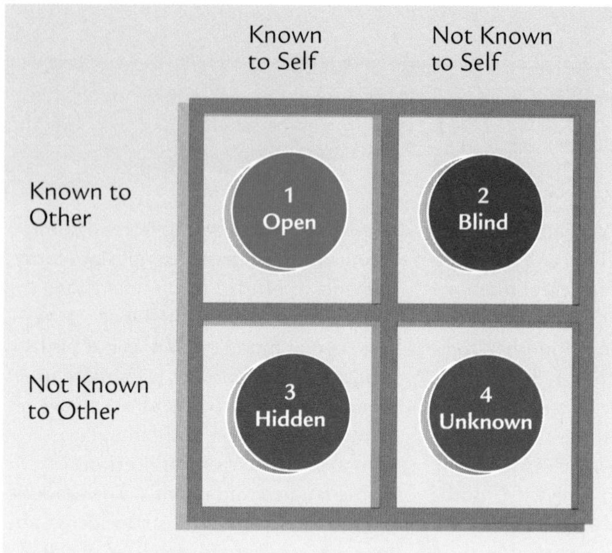

FIGURE **2.6**

Johari Window of Self-Disclosure

The **Johari Window model** nicely summarizes how your awareness of who you are is influenced by your own level of disclosure, as well as by how much information others share *about* you *with* you. (The name "Johari Window" sounds somewhat mystical and exotic, but it is simply a combination of the first names of the creators of the model, Joseph Luft and Harry Ingham.[52]) As Figure 2.6 shows, the model looks like a window. Like the circles in the social penetration model, the window represents your self. This self includes everything about you, including things even you don't yet see or realize. One axis is divided into what you have come to know about yourself and what you don't yet know about who you are. The other axis represents what someone else may know about you and not know about you. The intersection of these categories creates a four-panel, or four-quadrant, window.

Open: Known to Self and Known to Others

Quadrant 1 is an *open area.* The open area contains information that others know about you and that you are also aware of—such as your age, your occupation, and other things you might mention about yourself. At first glance, all four quadrants in the window appear to be the same size. But that may not be the case (in fact, it probably isn't). In the case of quadrant 1, the more information that you reveal about yourself, the larger this quadrant will be. Put another way, the more you open up to others, the larger the open area will be.

Blind: Not Known to Self but Known to Others

Quadrant 2 is a *blind area.* This part of the window contains information that other people know about you, but that you do not know. Perhaps when you were in grade school, as a joke someone put a sign on your back that said, "Kick me." Everyone was aware of the sign but you. The blind area of the Johari Window represents much the same situation. For example, you may see yourself as generous, but others may see you as a tightwad. As you learn how others see you, the blind area of the Johari Window gets smaller. Generally, the more accurately you know yourself and perceive how others see you, the better your chances to establish open and honest relationships with others.

Hidden: Known to Self but Not Known to Others

Quadrant 3 is a *hidden area.* This area contains information that you know about yourself, but that others do not know about you. You can probably think of many facts, thoughts, feelings, and fantasies that you would not want anyone else to know. They may be feelings you have about another person or something you've done privately in the past that you'd be embarrassed to share with others. The point here is not to suggest you should share all information in the hidden area with others. It is useful to know, however, that part of who you are is known by some people, but remains hidden from others.

Johari Window model. Model of self-disclosure that summarizes how self-awareness is influenced by self-disclosure and information about yourself from others.

Unknown: Not Known to Self or Others

Quadrant 4 is an *unknown area.* This area contains information that is unknown to both you and others. These are things you do not know about yourself *yet.* Perhaps you do not know how you will react under certain stressful situations. Maybe you are

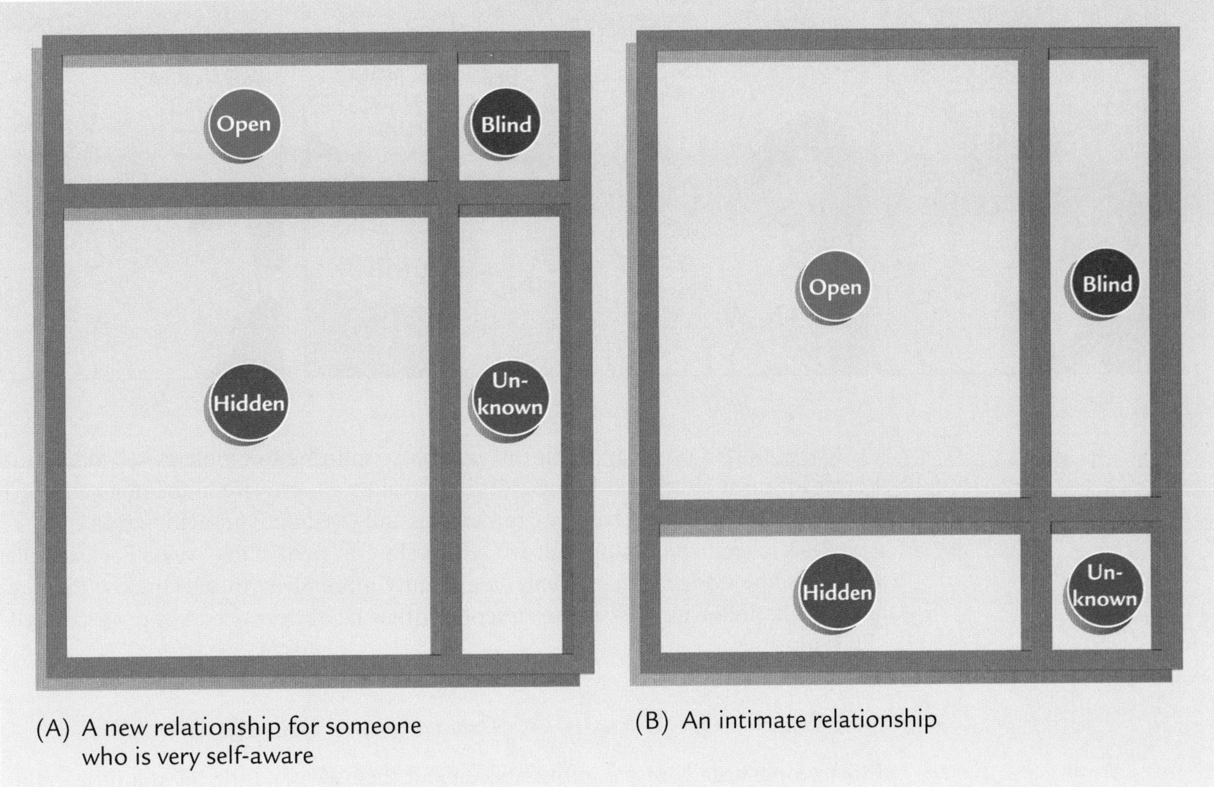

(A) A new relationship for someone who is very self-aware

(B) An intimate relationship

FIGURE 2.7

Variations on the Johari Window

not sure what stand you will take on a certain issue next year or even next week. Other people may also not be aware of how you would respond or behave under certain conditions. Your personal potential, your untapped physical and mental resources, are unknown. You can assume that this area exists, because eventually some (though not necessarily all) of these things will become known to you, to others, or to both you and others. Because you can never know yourself completely, the unknown quadrant will always exist; you can only guess at its current size, because the information it contains is unavailable to you.

As we did with the social penetration model, we can draw Johari Windows to represent each of our relationships (see Figure 2.7). Window A shows a new or restricted relationship for someone who knows himself or herself very well. The open and blind quadrants are small, but the unknown quadrant is also small. Window B shows a very intimate relationship, in which both individuals are open and disclosing.

We've discussed what self-disclosure is and described two models that explain how self-disclosure works and affects your understanding of who you think you are. Next, we will describe characteristics of self-disclosure and discuss how disclosure, both appropriate and inappropriate, can affect our interpersonal relationships with others.

Characteristics of Self-Disclosure

Have you had the experience of meeting someone who told you more than you wanted to know about himself or herself? Although self-disclosure is a means of establishing relationships with others, revealing too much too soon or making the

disclosure only a one-way stream of revelatory information violates self-disclosure norms for most North Americans. It is by revealing who we are in the normal course of conversations that others come to know us and (we hope) grow to like us.[53]

Researchers have found that we self-disclose in predictable ways. For example, there is some evidence that women are slightly more likely to self-disclose than are men.[54] The following discussion describes other characteristics of appropriate self-disclosure.

Self-Disclosure Usually Occurs in Small Increments

Most people usually reveal information about themselves a little bit at a time, rather than delivering a condensed version of their autobiography all at once. Monitor your own self-disclosure. Are you revealing information at a greater depth sooner than you should? If you do, others may find your disclosure disquieting. Appropriate self-disclosure should be well timed to suit the occasion and the expectations of the individuals involved.

Communication privacy management theory suggests that each of us has our own boundaries and rules for sharing personal information—that is, we manage our own degree of privacy.[55] We typically don't share all that we know about ourselves to most people when we first meet them. And when we do start sharing information, we offer smaller bits and pieces, rather than revealing our entire life story to someone. Communication privacy management theory suggests that we each have individual rules about how much private information we share and with whom we share that information. What determines how much information we share with others? According to communication privacy management theory, our cultural background, our need to connect to others, and the amount of risk involved in sharing information (whether the information would embarrass us or others) are factors that determine how much and how quickly we share information about our personal lives with others.[56]

Self-Disclosure Moves from Less Personal to More Personal Information

communication privacy management theory. Theory that suggests that we each manage our own degree of privacy by means of personal boundaries and rules for sharing information.

As the social penetration model (Figure 2.5) illustrates, we can describe the depth of our self-disclosure by the intimacy level of the information we share. If we move too quickly to more intimate information before we've developed a history with someone, we violate social norms or expectations our partner may have. John Powell, author of *Why Am I Afraid to Tell You Who I Am?*, notes that the information we reveal about ourselves often progresses through the following predictable levels.[57]

Level 5: *Cliché communication.* We first establish verbal contact with others by saying something that lets the other person know we acknowledge his or her presence. Standard phrases such as "Hello" or the more contemporary "What's up?" signal the desire to initiate a relationship, even if it is a brief, superficial one.

Level 4: *Facts and biographical information.* After using cliché phrases and responses to establish contact, we typically next reveal nonthreatening information about ourselves, such as our names, hometowns, or majors.

Level 3: *Attitudes and personal ideas.* After noting our name and other basic information, we often begin talking about more personal information, such as our attitudes about work or school or other relatively safe topics. At this level, the information is not too threatening or revealing, but we do begin to talk about our likes and dislikes or about what we assume are noncontroversial topics.

Level 2: *Personal feelings.* At this level, we discuss topics and issues that are exceedingly more personal. After we've developed rapport with someone, we then share more intimate fears, secrets, and attitudes. Increasingly, we take risks when we share this information. It requires trust to share these personal feelings.

Level 1: *Peak communication.* Powell calls this the ultimate level of self-disclosure that is seldom reached; his other name for level 1 communication is "gut level" communication. Only with our most intimate friends do we reveal such personal information. And it's possible, says Powell, that we may not reach this level of intimacy with our life partners, parents, or children. Peak communication is rare because of the risk and trust involved in being so open and revealing.

Self-Disclosure Is Reciprocal

In mainstream U.S. culture, when people share information about themselves, they expect the other person to share similar information about herself or himself. If you introduce yourself by name to someone, you expect that person to respond by telling you his or her name. This cultural rule allows people to use self-disclosure as a strategy for gaining information and reducing uncertainty. The reciprocal nature of self-disclosure is called the **dyadic effect:** You disclose to me, and I'll disclose to you.

Self-Disclosure Involves Risk

Although self-disclosure is a building block for establishing intimacy with others, it can be risky. Once you disclose something to someone, that person can now share that information with others; that person has additional power if the information is something you'd rather not have others know.

There is also the risk of rejection when you tell someone something that is personal. As Powell comments, "If I tell you who I am, and you do not like who I am, that is all that I have."[58] Once you reveal what you believe is your true nature or personal feeling and you are rejected or rebuffed, you can't explain your rejection away by saying, "Oh, they don't know the real me."

Self-Disclosure Online Is Different from Face-to-Face Disclosure

Communication researchers Lisa Tidwell and Joseph Walther wanted to know whether there are differences between face-to-face conversations and e-mail conversations in

dyadic effect. The reciprocal nature of self-disclosure: "You disclose to me, and I'll disclose to you."

amount of self-disclosure, perceptions of confidence, and effectiveness of communication. They found that when people communicate via e-mail, they exchange information more directly with each other and perceive themselves and others to be more "conversationally effective" because they are more direct. E-mail conversation partners also reported that they were more confident when communicating online than they were in their face-to-face encounters.[59]

In addition to the tendency for people to self-disclose more information about themselves via e-mail, they may be less truthful in what they say about themselves when they are online compared with face-to-face communication. Two Internet researchers found strong evidence that people are much more likely to misrepresent themselves in cyberspace than in "realspace" relationships.[60] These researchers also found that people reported their face-to-face realspace relationships were more serious. And even though there were greater feelings of commitment to realspace relationships than to cyberspace relationships, the participants reported about the same levels of satisfaction with both types of relationships and similar potential for emotional growth in their romantic relationships, whether in realspace or cyberspace.

Self-Disclosure Involves Trust

As we have already noted, to know something personal about someone is to have power over that person. Using personal information against others to manipulate and control is a misuse of the trust that was placed in you.[61] According to British social psychologists Michael Argyle, Monica Henderson, and Adrian Furnham, one of the most fundamental expectations people have of their friends is that they will not reveal confidences. When you say, "Oh, I won't tell anyone. Your secret's safe with me," mean it.

Perhaps the most intimate secrets are known by family members; our parents and siblings know quite a few things about us that we'd rather others not know. Interpersonal communication researchers Anita Vangelisti, John Caughlin, and Lindsay Timmerman found several factors that may help predict whether we do or don't disclose family secrets. For example, we would be *more* likely to share a family secret under certain conditions:

- If, during an intimate conversation with another person, we found out that this person had a similar problem or we thought revealing the secret would help the other person.
- If we thought the secret would eventually come to light even if we didn't reveal the secret.
- If there was some urgency or importance in revealing the secret; if we didn't reveal the secret, the concealment would create more problems than revealing the secret would cause.
- If we thought the family member would not mind if the secret were told; the family member would still accept us.
- If it seemed like a normal and natural thing to reveal, given the topic of conversation; if the topic came up, we might disclose the secret.[62]

As we develop a relationship, we reveal more of ourselves, removing the masks that we routinely use with strangers.

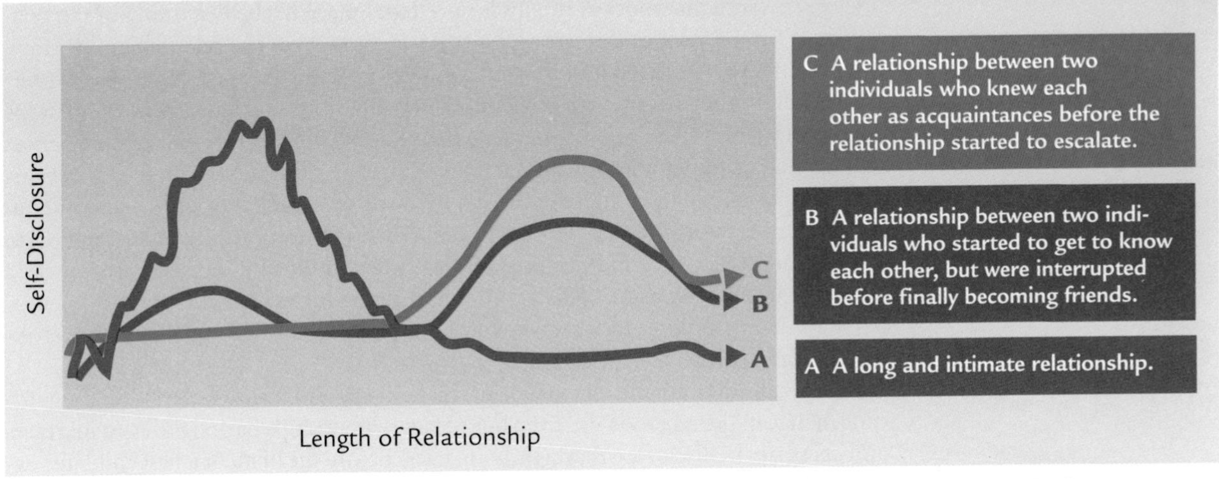

FIGURE 2.8

Self-Disclosure and Relational Development

You might read this list and become worried that your family members might tell things they know about you that you'd rather others not know. Don't worry (too much). If sharing the secret with others would hurt the person sharing the secret, then there is less likelihood that the secret will be shared.[63] The researchers also found that there were some secrets that people would never disclose.

Self-Disclosure Over Time: Enhancing Intimacy

Self-disclosure is often associated with relationship development, because it is through the process of revealing information about yourself that it becomes possible for relationships to become more intimate. However, simply disclosing information about yourself is no guarantee that your relationship will become intimate.[64] (Note that when we talk about intimacy and self-disclosure, we're not just talking about sex; rather, we're talking about both greater depth and greater breadth of self-disclosure.) In an intimate friendship, we become aware of things about our friend that few if any other people may know. Intimacy occurs through the process of self-disclosure.

As relationships move toward intimacy, they typically include periods of high self-disclosure early in the relationship. However, the *amount* of information that is disclosed decreases as the relationship becomes more and more intimate. In other words, there is generally more self-disclosing activity earlier in a relationship than later. As a relationship proceeds, we begin sharing low-risk information fairly rapidly, move on to share higher-risk information, and then finally, to share our most personal disclosures. The more intimate the relationship becomes, the more intimate the information that is disclosed. The sculpture in the photo on the facing page represents the way we reveal ourselves when we are with close friends; with our best friends, we may reveal what is behind our "masks." Holding back from sharing intimate information signals a reluctance to escalate the relationship. The amount of information that we have to share about ourselves is finite, so we slow down as we have less left to disclose.

Graph A in Figure 2.8 illustrates a typical disclosure pattern over the course of a long and intimate relationship. The peaks and valleys represent periods of variable disclosure. Note that most of the disclosure takes place in the beginning of the relationship. Not all relationships progress this way, however. The relationship in graph B represents two individuals who started to get to know each other but were interrupted before they became close friends. They might have stopped because of some conflict, indecisiveness about pursuing the relationship, or external circumstances that limited opportunities for interacting. When the disclosure resumed, it became more intense. Graph C represents two individuals who probably knew each other as acquaintances for some time but never really had the opportunity or inclination to self-disclose. Once they did begin to escalate the relationship, however, there was a steep rise in self-disclosure. This graph might represent two coworkers who eventually start dating, or two students who have shared a class or two together before striking up a friendship.

Generally, a dramatic increase or decrease in self-disclosure reflects some significant change in the relationship. Even long-term relationships have significant increases and decreases in disclosure that signify changes. Before the birth of a first child, for example, both parents might disclose their fears and expectations about child rearing, and the information might have a profound effect on the relationship.

Interpersonal relationships cannot achieve intimacy without self-disclosure. Without true self-disclosure, we form only superficial relationships. You can confirm another person's self-concept, and have your self-concept confirmed, only if both you and your partner have revealed yourselves to each other.

BE OTHER-ORIENTED

Future chapters will discuss the essential other-oriented skills of perceiving others accurately, using and understanding verbal and nonverbal messages, and listening empathetically.

Self-Disclosure Reflects Perceptions About the Nature of Your Relationships

What you reveal about yourself to others and what others reveal to you about themselves provide important information about how each of you perceives the nature, quality, and intimacy of your relationship.

The tricky part of interpreting the level of intimacy you have with another person, however, is to consider that what someone else thinks is very intimate and personal information you may perceive as not intimate and personal at all. For example, as a relationship becomes more intimate, a friend might say, "I've never told anyone this before, but when I was in high school, I had a crush on my English teacher." Your friend may share this information because he or she feels comfortable sharing intimate information with you and may think, "I'm being quite intimate in sharing this information." You, on the other hand, may think it's no big deal to have had a crush on a high school teacher. It is difficult to know precisely what others think about a particular relationship, because we don't all view the same self-disclosing information as being equally intimate or risky. It is possible to send the wrong signal about how you regard the relationship or to misperceive your partner's perception about the quality and nature of the relationship.

As you disclose information to another person, consider how the other person may perceive the level of intimacy and trust that you are implying when you reveal personal information. Being other-oriented means being aware that what *you* perceive as intimate and personally revealing may not be perceived as intimate information by your partner. Briefly stated, intimacy is in the mind of the listener. So, although the depth and breadth of self-disclosure provides important information about the quality of the interpersonal relationship you have with another person, ultimately each person determines whether the information is actually intimate.

Self-Disclosure Guidelines

Here are some guidelines for helping you appropriately self-disclose and respond to the disclosures of others.

When self-disclosing to others:

- Be other-oriented when you self-disclose; think about how the information you share will affect the other person. Are you self-disclosing only to meet your own needs (which is sometimes appropriate)? Will your disclosure make your communication partner unnecessarily uncomfortable?

BE OTHER-ORIENTED

- Monitor the nonverbal responses others have when you disclose to them; these will help you determine if you are giving someone too much personal, intimate information. If the other person has little eye contact with you or is fidgeting, shifting in his or her seat, or making facial expressions that suggest he or she is uncomfortable, limit your self-disclosure. Or check your perceptions: Ask the other person if the information you are sharing is making him or her uncomfortable.
- Be careful not to disclose too much information about yourself too soon in a relationship. Self-disclosure usually occurs in smaller bits and pieces.
- Decrease self-disclosure if you are sharing information about yourself and your communication partner is not sharing information about himself or herself.

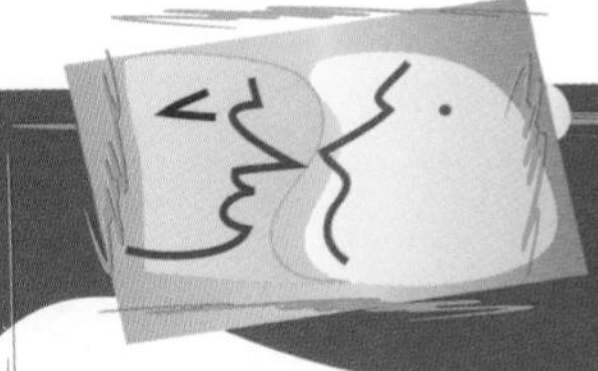

Becoming Other-Oriented

A World View

It is sometimes a challenge to avoid becoming self-absorbed—focusing exclusively on yourself and not others. There is evidence that the challenge of becoming other-oriented rather than self-absorbed is not new. Most world religions emphasize a common spiritual theme, known in Christianity as the Golden Rule: Do unto others as you would have others do unto you. This "rule" is the basis for most ethical codes throughout the world and has been the foundation of ideas about how we should treat others for centuries. The following excerpts from various religious traditions emphasize the importance of becoming other-oriented.

Hinduism	This is the sum of duty: Do nothing to others that would cause pain if done to you.
Buddhism	One should seek for others the happiness one desires for one self.
Taoism	Regard your neighbor's gain as your own gain, and your neighbor's loss as your loss.
Confucianism	Is there one principle that ought to be acted on throughout one's whole life? Surely it is the principle of loving-kindness: do not unto others what you would not have them do unto you.
Zoroastrianism	The nature alone is good that refrains from doing unto another whatsoever is not good for itself.
Judaism	What is hateful to you, do not do to others. That is the entire law: all the rest is but commentary.
Islam	No one of you is a believer until he desires for his brother that which he desires for himself.
Christianity	Do unto others as you would have others do unto you.

Source: Adapted from Wayne Ham, *Man's Living Religions* (Independence, MO: Herald Publishing House, 1966), 39–40. By permission of Herald Publishing House.

- Don't expect that each time you're with your communication partner there will be the same amount of self-disclosure. It's normal for the amount of self-disclosure to decrease over time as a relationship matures.

When listening to others' self-disclosure:

- Keep confidences. Don't reveal information another person tells you without his or her permission.
- Provide appropriate social support when another person shares information about problems, stress, and anxiety. Respond with appropriate positive verbal and nonverbal expressions to communicate that you are listening and responsive to what he or she is saying.
- Although self-disclosure is meant to be reciprocal (the dyadic effect), don't feel pressured to reveal personal information to another person just because he or she is sharing intimate information with you. Be mindful of what you are sharing with others.
- Sometimes the best response when hearing personal, intimate information is simply to listen and appropriately paraphrase key pieces of information. Don't worry about providing advice or recommendations; just be supportive through your listening.

Summary

We all seek answers to three questions: "Who am I?" "Why am I here?" "Who are all these others?" William James answered the first question by dividing the self into three parts. The material self includes our bodies and those tangible possessions that give us identity. The social self is the part that engages in interaction with others. The spiritual self consists of thoughts and assumptions about values and moral standards and beliefs about forces that influence our lives. Other theorists conclude that our self-concept develops through interaction with other people. The groups we belong to also give us identity. Our roles as sisters, brothers, students, and parents are important in how we view who we are; the roles we assume provide labels for who we are. We also make our own observations about ourselves apart from others and about groups or roles we assume. Our gender plays a key part in affecting our view of who we are in relationship to others.

Given the importance of developing a positive sense of self-esteem, we identified strategies that can enhance your self-worth. Those strategies include engaging in self-talk, using positive visualization, avoiding comparisons with others, reframing, developing honest relationships, letting go of the past, and seeking support when needed.

Our sense of self relates to self-disclosure. Self-disclosure occurs when we purposefully provide information to others that they would not learn if we did not tell them. The social penetration model of self-disclosure describes how the depth and breadth of our disclosure can affect our relationships. The Johari Window model of self-disclosure provides an explanation of the relationship between our self-awareness and self-disclosure. The four quadrants in the Johari Window (Open, Hidden, Unknown, and Blind) reflect how much information we and others know about ourselves. As we develop relationships, the sizes of these windows change relative to one another. Appropriate self-disclosure occurs in small increments, moves from less to more personal information, is reciprocal, involves risk, involves trust, has the potential to enhance the quality of our interpersonal relationships, and reflects perceptions about the nature of our relationships.

The amount of information we disclose decreases as a relationship becomes more intimate. We first are likely to share low-risk information; as the relationship matures, we typically disclose more personal, high-risk information.

For Discussion and Review

Focus on Critical Thinking

1. Joel, who is 30 years old, married, and the father of two children, suffers from feelings of low self-esteem. Although he has many friends and a wife who loves him, he feels that others perform much better than he does at work. What strategies would help Joel enhance his self-esteem?
2. Make a list of all the groups, clubs, and organizations to which you belong. Rank them from most important to least important. What does your ranking tell you about these groups in reference to your self-concept?
3. Provide an original example of how visualization might help you enhance your self-esteem. Describe the positive scene.
4. Provide an example from your own experiences that illustrates the Johari Window model of self-disclosure.

Focus on Ethics

5. Discuss the ethical implications of using untrue flattery to enhance a friend's self-esteem.
6. Many self-help books on the market claim to enrich your social life by providing sure-fire techniques for enhancing self-esteem. Do you think these claims are ethical? Why or why not?
7. Aelish has long planned to attend a top-notch Ivy League college. Her grades, however, are only in the C and B range. Her SAT scores are average. Should she try to reframe this factual information or deal with her problem in another way?
8. Carmelita would like to become better friends with Hector. She decides to disclose some personal information to Hector, hoping that this self-disclosure will increase feelings of intimacy between them. Is it ethical to self-disclose to others as a strategy to enhance intimacy in a relationship?

Learning with Others

1. Rank the following list of values from 1 to 12. In a group with other students, compare your answers. Discuss how your personal ranking of these values influences your interaction with others.

_____ Honesty	_____ Justice
_____ Salvation	_____ Wealth
_____ Comfort	_____ Beauty
_____ Good health	_____ Equality
_____ Human rights	_____ Freedom
_____ Peace	_____ Mercy

2. Make a shield of your life (like a coat of arms): Draw a large outline of a shield that fills up an entire sheet of paper. Divide your shield into four equal sections. In the upper right-hand section of your shield, draw or symbolize something for which you have skill or talent. In the upper left-hand section, draw or symbolize something you are trying to improve or a new skill you are learning. In the lower right-hand section, draw or symbolize your most prized material possession. Finally, in the lower left-hand section, write three words that you hope someone would use to describe you.

   Share your shield with your classmates, explaining why you drew what you did. Discuss how your shield reflects your attitudes, beliefs, and values.
3. Go through your personal music library of tapes or CDs, and identify a selection that best symbolizes you. Your selection may be based on either the lyrics or the music. Bring your selection to class and play it for your classmates. (Your instructor will bring a tape or CD player.) Tell why this music symbolizes you. Discuss with classmates how your choice of music provides a glimpse of your culture and a vehicle for self-expression.

Weblinks

Go to *www.mycommunicationlab.com* (access code required) to find Web resources for your text that supplement the material in Chapter 2, including links to information on the following topics:

Self-esteem test
Self-disclosure quiz
Works of William James
Theory of symbolic interactionism
Personality tests

CHAPTER 3

Interpersonal Communication and Perception

OBJECTIVES

1. Define perception and interpersonal perception.
2. Identify and explain the three stages of interpersonal perception.
3. Describe the relationship between interpersonal communication and interpersonal perception.
4. Explain how we form impressions of others, describe others, and interpret others' behavior.
5. Identify the eight factors that distort the accuracy of our interpersonal perceptions.
6. Offer five suggestions for improving interpersonal perceptions.

OUTLINE

What you see and what you hear depends a good deal on where you are standing. It also depends on what sort of person you are.

C. S. Lewis

Look at the Norman Rockwell painting. What is happening, and what has happened? What is the relationship among the individuals in the painting? You probably have deduced that the boy was running away from home, the policeman found him, and then he took the boy into the local coffee shop for ice cream or some other treat. Perhaps you think that the man behind the counter is wistfully recalling his own days of running away as a child. What are your feelings about the policeman? Do you see him as a friendly and caring person who has a good understanding of kids?

Saturday Evening Post cover, September 20, 1958. Old Corner House Collection, Stockbridge, Massachusetts.

In Chapter 1, we defined human communication as the process of making sense of the world and sharing that sense with others by creating meaning through the use of verbal and nonverbal messages. In this chapter, we discuss the first half of that definition—the process of making sense of our world. How we make sense out of what we experience is the starting point for what we share with others. As human beings, we interpret and attribute meaning to what we observe or experience, particularly if what we are observing is other people. We tend to make inferences about their motives, personalities, and other traits based on their physical qualities and behaviors. Those who are skilled at making observations and interpretations have a head start in developing effective interpersonal relationships. Those who are other-oriented, who are aware of and sensitive to the communication behaviors of others, will likely be better at accurately perceiving others.

Before we turn to the role that perception plays in interpersonal communication, let's first take a closer look at the interpersonal perception process itself.

Understanding Interpersonal Perception

What is perception? **Perception** is the process of experiencing your world and then making sense out of what you experience. You experience your world through your five senses. For example, a sound travels through the air and causes your eardrum to vibrate, which activates the nerves and sends a signal to the brain. A similar sequence of events takes place when you see, smell, feel, or taste something. The process of perception also includes organizing and interpreting information provided by the senses. You come out of a building and see wet pavement and puddles of water, hear thunder, smell a distinct odor caused by ions, and observe drops of water falling in front of you. You integrate all those bits of information and conclude that it is raining and has been for a while.

Your perceptions of people, however, include analysis and interpretation that go beyond simple interpretation of sensory information. **Interpersonal perception** is the process by which you decide what people are like and give meaning to their actions. It includes making judgments about personality and drawing inferences from what you observe.[1] When you meet someone new, you *select* certain information to attend to: For example, you note whether the person is male or female, has an accent, smiles, and uses a friendly tone of voice, as well as particular personal information (she is from Boone, Iowa). You then *organize* the information under some category that is recognizable to you, such as "a friendly Midwesterner." Then you *interpret* the organized perceptions: This person is trustworthy, honest, hardworking, and likable.

In our discussion, we focus on this kind of interpersonal perception, which relates to understanding our observations of other people. We begin by examining the three stages of the interpersonal perception process that we have already described: selecting, organizing, and interpreting what we observe.

Stage 1: Selecting

Sit for a minute after you read this passage and tune in to all the sensory input you are receiving: Consider the feel of your socks against your feet, the pressure of the floor on your heels, the pressure of the piece of furniture against your body as you sit, the buzzing sounds from various sources around you—"white noise" from a refrigerator, personal computer, fluorescent lights, water in pipes, voices, passing traffic, or your own heartbeat or churning stomach. What do you smell? What do you see? Without moving your eyes, turn your awareness to the images you see in the corner of your vision. What colors do you see? What shapes? What taste is in your mouth? How do the pages of this book feel against your fingertips? Now stop reading and consider all these sensations. Try to focus on all of them at the same time. You can't.

You are selective as you attempt to make sense out of the world around you. The number of sensations you can attend to at any given time is limited. Perhaps you close your eyes or sit in the dark as you listen to music. This allows you to select more auditory sensations because you have eliminated visual cues.

perception. Process of experiencing the world and making sense out of what you experience.

interpersonal perception. Process of selecting, organizing, and interpreting your observations of other people.

selective perception. Process of seeing, hearing, or making sense of the world around us based on such factors as our personality, beliefs, attitudes, hopes, fears, and culture, as well as what we like and don't like.

Principles of Selection

Why do we select certain sounds, images, and sensations and not others? Four principles of selection frame the process of how we select what we see, hear, and experience: selective perception, selective attention, selective exposure, and selective recall.

Selective perception occurs when we see, hear, or make sense of the world around us based on a host of factors such as our personality, beliefs, attitudes, hopes, fears, and culture, as well as what we like and don't like. We literally see and don't see things because of our tendency to perceive selectively. Your eyes and your brain do not work like a camera, which records everything in the picture. When you develop film, you capture what was in the viewfinder. Your brain doesn't necessarily process everything you see through your viewfinder. Similarly, your ear is not a microphone that consciously picks up every sound.

In a court of law, eyewitness testimony often determines whether someone is innocent or guilty of a crime. Recent research suggests, however, that a witness's powers of observation are not flawless. In fact, researchers have discovered several perceptual errors in eyewitness testimony. Many innocent people have been convicted because of what a witness thought he or she saw or heard. As this evidence documents, our eyes are not cameras; our ears are not microphones. We perceive selectively.

Selective attention is the process of focusing on specific stimuli; we selectively lock on to some things in our environment and ignore others. As in the selective perception process, we have a tendency to attend to those things around us that relate to our needs and wants. When you're hungry, for example, and you're looking for a place to grab a quick bite of lunch, you'll probably be more attentive to fast-food advertising and less focused on ads for cars. We also attend to information that is moving, blinking, flashing, interesting, novel, or noisy. Web page designers, for example, give a lot of thought to ways of catching our attention with advertisements on the Internet.

Selective exposure is our tendency to put ourselves in situations that reinforce our attitudes, beliefs, values, or behaviors. The fact that we're selective about what we expose ourselves to means that we are more likely to be in places that make us feel comfortable and support the way we see the world than to be in places that make us uncomfortable. Whom do you usually find at a Baptist church on Sunday mornings? Baptists. Who attends a Democratic Party convention? Democrats. If you perceive yourself to be a good student who does everything possible to get high grades, you will do your best to attend class. We expose ourselves to situations that reinforce how we make sense out of the world.

Selective recall occurs when we remember things we want to remember and forget or repress things that are unpleasant, uncomfortable, or unimportant to us. Because our brains don't operate like cameras or microphones, not all that we see or hear is recorded in our memories so that we can easily retrieve it. Some experiences may simply be too painful to remember. Or we just don't remember some information because it's not relevant or needed (like the address of the Web page you clicked on yesterday).

selective attention. Process of focusing on specific stimuli, locking on to some things in the environment and ignoring others.

selective exposure. Tendency to put ourselves in situations that reinforce our attitudes, beliefs, values, or behaviors.

selective recall. Process that occurs when we remember things we want to remember and forget or repress things that are unpleasant, uncomfortable, or unimportant to us.

thin slicing. Observing a small sample of someone's behavior and then making a generalization about what the person is like, based on the sample.

Thin Slicing: Making a Judgment Based on a Small Sample of Behavior

Have you ever gone to a grocery store and enjoyed the free samples that are sometimes offered to get you to buy various products? The grocer hopes that if you like the small sample, you'll want to purchase more. Perhaps after tasting a thin slice of cheese, you'll buy a pound of it. The concept of **thin slicing** in the perception process works the same way. You sample a little bit of someone's behavior and then generalize as to what the person may be like, based on the brief information you have observed. Journalist Malcolm Gladwell wrote a popular book called *Blink: The Power of Thinking Without Thinking,* in which he pointed to several examples of how people thin slice to make judgments of others.[2] For example, Gladwell reviewed research that found that a patient was less likely to sue a physician for malpractice if the doctor had effective "people skills." Doctors who took the time to listen, respond positively, empathize, and, in short, be other-oriented were less likely to be sued than doctors who were not other-oriented. As patients, we thin slice when we make a judgment about the overall credibility of a doctor based on just one aspect of the doctor's behavior—his or her bedside manner. Later in the book, we'll review the research of John Gottman, another researcher who has evidence of the accuracy of thin slicing; he has done extensive research about marriage and divorce. Gottman has been able to thin slice behaviors in marriage to be able to predict with 94 percent accuracy whether a couple will divorce.[3] He has found that when he watches videotapes of couples having conversations and discussing real issues and problems in their marriage, he can make very accurate guesses as to whether the couple will stay together. Gottman has developed a way of thin slicing these marriage relationships. The four behaviors that predict divorce if all are present are defensiveness, stonewalling (not responding), criticism, and contempt—with contempt being the most corrosive.

Some people are better at thin slicing than others. There is evidence, for example, that women are better than men in interpreting nonverbal cues. Can you improve your ability to thin slice with accuracy? Yes, but it takes time and skill practice. It took marriage researcher John Gottman many years and a significant amount of research to be able to know what to look for in order to predict a successful or unsuccessful marriage. Learning how to be more perceptive and being more other-oriented, the focus of this book, can improve your ability to thin slice accurately.

BE OTHER-ORIENTED

Stage 2: Organizing

Look at the four items in Figure 3.1. What does each of them mean to you? If you are like most people, you will perceive item A as a rabbit, item B as a telephone number, item C as the word *interpersonal,* and item D as a circle. Strictly speaking, none of those perceptions is correct. We discuss why after we explore the second stage of perception, organizing.

We organize our world by creating categories, linking together the categories we've created, and then seeking closure by filling in any missing gaps in what we perceive. Let's examine each of these in greater detail.

We Create Categories

After we perceive certain stimuli, we organize them into convenient, understandable, and efficient categories that let us make sense of what we have observed. Organizing, or chunking, what we perceive makes it easier to process complex information because it lets us impose the familiar on the unfamiliar, and because we can more easily store and recall simple patterns.

One of the ways we create categories is by **superimposing** a familiar structure on information we select. To superimpose is to use a framework we're already familiar with to interpret information that may, at first, look formless. We look for the familiar in the unfamiliar. For example, when you looked at item A in Figure 3.1, you saw the pattern of dots as a rabbit because *rabbit* is a concept you know and to which you attach various meanings. The set of dots would not have meaning for you in and of itself, nor would it be meaningful to you to attend to each particular dot or to the dots' relationships to one another. It would be possible to create a mathematical model of the dots indicating their placement on the *x-y* grid, but such a model would be extremely complex and difficult to observe and remember. It's much easier to organize the dots by superimposing something that is stored in your memory: a rabbit. For similar reasons, people have organized patterns of stars in the sky into the various constellations and have given them names that reflect their shapes, like the Bear, the Crab, and the Big and Little Dippers.

superimpose. To place a familiar structure on information you select.

People also search for and apply patterns to their perceptions of other people. You might have a friend who jogs and works out at a gym. You put these together to create a pattern and label the friend as "athletic." That label represents a pattern of qualities you use in relating to your friend, a pattern that we discuss later in the chapter.

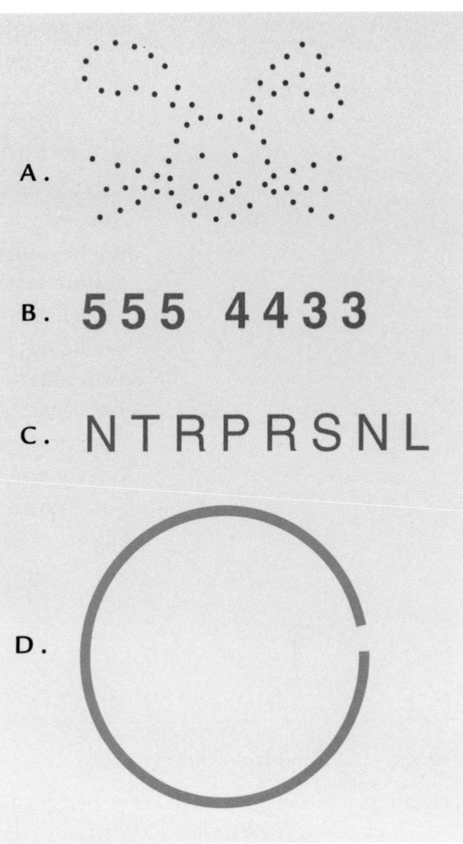

FIGURE 3.1

What Do You See?

We Link Categories

Once we have created categories, we link them together as a way of further making sense of how we have chunked what we experience. We link the categories though a process called *punctuation.* **Punctuation** is the process of making sense out of stimuli by grouping, dividing, organizing, separating, and further categorizing information.[4]

Just as punctuation marks on this page tell you when a sentence ends, punctuation in the perception process makes it possible for you to see patterns in information. To many Americans, item B in Figure 3.1 looks like a telephone number because it has three numbers followed by four numbers. However, the digits could just as easily represent two totally independent numbers: five hundred fifty-five followed by the number four thousand, four hundred thirty-three. How we interpret the numbers depends on how we punctuate or separate them. When we record information, we use commas, periods, dashes, and colons to signal meanings and interpretations. In our minds, we sometimes impose punctuation marks where we believe they should be. For example, perhaps you mentally put a dash between 555 and 4433, even though no dash appears there.

When it comes to punctuating relational events and behaviors, people develop their own separate sets of standards. You will sometimes experience difficulties and disagreements because of differences in how you and your communication partner choose to punctuate a conversational exchange or a shared sequence of events.[5] One classic example of relational problems resulting from differences in punctuation involves a husband who withdraws and a wife who nags.[6] The husband punctuates their interactions in such a way that he sees his withdrawing as a reaction to her nagging. The wife, in contrast, sees herself as nagging her husband because he keeps withdrawing. The husband and wife punctuate their perceptions differently because they each perceive different starting points for their interactions. Resolving such conflicts involves having the parties describe how they have punctuated the event and agree on a common punctuation.

We Seek Closure

Another way we organize information is by seeking closure. **Closure** is the process of filling in missing information or gaps in what we perceive. Looking again at Figure 3.1, you can understand people's inclination to label the figure in item D a circle, even though circles are continuous lines without gaps. We apply the same principles in our interactions with people. When we have an incomplete picture of another human being, we impose a pattern or structure, classify the person on the basis of the information we do have, and fill in any missing information. For example, when meeting someone for the first time who looks and acts like someone you already know, you may make assumptions about your new acquaintance, based on the characteristics of the person you already know. You close the gaps in the missing information about your new acquaintance, based on the characteristics of the person well known to you. Many

punctuation. Process of making sense out of stimuli by grouping, dividing, organizing, separating, and categorizing information.

closure. Process of filling in missing information or gaps in what we perceive.

of us are uncomfortable with uncertainty; creating closure is a way of helping us make better sense out of what is new and unfamiliar.

Stage 3: Interpreting

Once you have selected and organized stimuli, you next typically interpret the stimuli. You see your best friend across a crowded room at a party. He waves to you, and you say to yourself, "He wants to talk with me." Or you nervously wait as your British literature teacher hands back the results of the last exam. When the professor calls your name, she frowns ever so slightly; your heart sinks. You think, "I must have bombed on the test." Or, while you are out, your administrative assistant leaves you a note that your sister called. You're worried. You reflect, "My tightwad sister never uses her daytime cell phone minutes to call during the day. There must be something wrong." In each of these situations, you're trying to make sense out of the information you hear or see. You're attempting to interpret the meaning of the verbal and nonverbal cues you experience. We'll discuss how the process of selecting, organizing, and interpreting affects our perceptions of others and influences our interpersonal relationships.

The Interpersonal Perception Process

Term	Explanation	Example
Selecting	The first stage in the perceptual process, in which we select certain sensations to focus awareness on	Sitting in your apartment where you hear lots of traffic sounds and car horns, but attending to a particular rhythmic car honking that seems to be right outside your door
Organizing	The second stage in the perceptual process, in which we assemble stimuli into convenient and efficient patterns	Putting together the car honking with your anticipation of a friend's arrival to pick you up in her car to drive to a movie that starts in five minutes
Interpreting	The final stage in perception, in which we assign meaning to what we have observed	Deciding the car honking must be your friend signaling you to come out to the car quickly because she's running late

Perceiving Others

Our perceptions of others affect the ways in which we communicate with them, and their perceptions of us affect the way they communicate with us. We continually modify the topics, the language, and the manner in which we communicate, according to the perceptions we have of others.

As we collect information about others, we organize and interpret that information in various ways. Interpersonal perception involves three processes: First, we form initial impressions of others; second, we describe others based on what we see and hear; and finally, we interpret their behavior—we attribute meaning and intention to what we see and hear others do.

How much we notice about another person's communication behavior relates to our level of interest and need. Perception can be either a passive or an active process. **Passive perception** occurs simply because our senses are in operation. We see, hear, smell, taste, and feel things around us without any conscious attempt to do so.

passive perception. Perception that occurs without conscious effort, but simply because your senses are in operation.

Active perception is the process of seeking out specific information by intentionally observing and questioning; we make a conscious effort to figure out what we are experiencing. We actively perceive information when we are uncertain about what we are seeing or hearing. We've all heard noises that startle us and make us wonder, "What was that?" We then try to recall the sound and identify it, or we might investigate—seek out additional information.

If you can gain information and reduce your uncertainty about others, then you can predict their reactions and behaviors, adapt your behaviors and strategies, and therefore maximize the likelihood of fulfilling your social needs.[7] Although this might sound calculating, it really isn't. If you enjoy outdoor activities such as camping and hiking, one of your goals in establishing social relationships is probably to find others who share your interest. So observing, questioning, and processing information to determine a potential friend's interests can help you assess whether the relationship will meet your goals. In Chapter 5, we discuss ways to improve your ability to gain information through more effective listening.

How We Form Impressions of Others

Impressions are collections of perceptions about others that we maintain and use to interpret their behaviors. Impressions tend to be very general: "She seemed nice," "He was very friendly," or "What a nerd!" According to **impression formation theory,** we form these impressions through perceptions of physical qualities and behavior, information people disclose about themselves, and information that third parties tell us. We tend to form these impressions readily and part with them reluctantly. When we first meet someone, we form a first impression without having much information, and we often hold on to this impression throughout the relationship.

Primacy Effect: We Emphasize What Comes First

There is evidence that when we form impressions of others, we pay more attention to our first impressions. The process of attending to the first pieces of information that we observe about another person is called the **primacy effect**. The primacy effect was documented in a famous study conducted by Solomon Asch.[8] Individuals were asked to evaluate two people based on two lists of adjectives. The list for the first person had the following adjectives: *intelligent, industrious, impulsive, critical, stubborn,* and *envious.* The list for the other person had the same adjectives, but in reverse order. Although the content was identical, respondents gave the first person a more positive evaluation than the second. One explanation for this is that the first words in each list created a first impression that respondents used to interpret the remaining adjectives. In a similar manner, the first impressions we form about someone often affect our interpretation of subsequent perceptions of that person.

Recency Effect: We Emphasize What Comes Last

Not only do we give more weight to our first impressions, we also give considerable attention to our most recent experiences and impressions. The tendency to put a lot of stock in the last thing we observe is called the **recency effect.**[9] For example, if you have thought for years that your friend is honest, but today you discover that she lied to you about something important, that lie will have a greater impact on your impression of her than the honest behavior she has displayed for years. Similarly, if, during a job interview, you skillfully answered all of the interviewer's questions yet your last answer to a question was not the answer the interviewer was looking for, you may not get the job. If you're going to make mistakes in an interview, it's best not to do it at the beginning of the interview (primacy effect) or at the end of the conversation (recency effect).

active perception. Perception that occurs because you seek out specific information through intentional observation and questioning.

impression. Collection of perceptions about others that you maintain and use to interpret their behaviors.

impression formation theory. Theory that explains how you develop perceptions about people and how you maintain and use those perceptions to interpret their behaviors.

primacy effect. Tendency to attend to the first pieces of information observed about another person in order to form an impression.

recency effect. Tendency to attend to the most recent information observed about another person in order to form or modify an impression.

People watching can give us the information we need to understand others.

How We Describe Others

Do you like to "people watch"? If you have some time on your hands while waiting for a friend, you may just start looking at people and making guesses about what these strangers do for a living, or whether they are friendly or grumpy, peaceful or petulant, kind or mean. You make assumptions about their personalities. Even when we know people well, we don't know everything about them. Most of us have developed an **implicit personality theory,** a pattern of associated qualities that we attribute to people, which allows us to understand them—whether we've met them 10 minutes ago or 10 years ago. We make guesses about who they are, based on the information we already have about them. Implicit personality theory provides a way of organizing the vast array of information we have about people's personalities.[10] Implicit personality theories are essentially stereotypes that we apply to people in general. We accomplish perceptual closure through the use of implicit personality theory; that is, we are able to fill in the blanks about a person's personality without actually having to observe additional qualities. Once you have determined that someone is a "warm" person, you automatically associate other related terms. Your implicit personality theory may be similar to that held by others in your culture, but each person forms his or her own individual theory. There is more consistency between the personality frameworks you would use to judge two strangers than there is between the personality framework you use and the one another person uses to describe the same stranger.

Although implicit personality theory describes how we organize and interpret our perceptions of people's personalities in general, we develop categories for people, called *constructs,* that help us explain our perceptions of a specific person. According to psychologist George Kelly, a **construct** is a bipolar quality (that is, a quality with two opposite categories) that we use to classify people.[11] We may pronounce someone as good or bad, athletic or nonathletic, warm or cold, funny or humorless, selfish or generous, and so on.

Halo Effect: Generalizing Positive Qualities to Others

One feature common to most of our implicit personality theories is the tendency to put people into one of two categories: people we like and people we don't like. Categorizing people as those we "like" often creates a **halo effect,** in which we attribute a variety of positive qualities to them without personally confirming the existence of these qualities. If you like me, you will put a halo around your impression of me and then apply those qualities from your implicit personality theory that apply to people you like, such as being considerate of other people, warm, caring, and fun to be with and having a great sense of humor.

implicit personality theory. Your unique set of beliefs and hypotheses about what people are like.

construct. Bipolar quality used to classify people.

halo effect. Attributing a variety of positive qualities to those you like.

horn effect. Attributing a variety of negative qualities to those you dislike.

Horn Effect: Generalizing Negative Qualities to Others

Just as we can use the halo effect to generalize about someone's positive qualities, the opposite can also happen. We sometimes make many negative assumptions about a person because of one unflattering perception. This is called the **horn effect**, named for the horns associated with medieval images of a devil. If you don't like the way someone looks, you might also decide that person is selfish or stingy and attribute a variety of negative qualities to that individual, using your implicit personality theory. As evidence of the horn effect, research suggests that during periods of conflict in our relationships, we are more likely to attribute negative behaviors to our feuding partner than we are to ourselves.[12] A little bit of negative information can affect how we perceive other attributes of a person.

In support of the premise underlying the horn effect, researchers Dominic Infante and Andrew Rancer observed that some people have a tendency to see the worst in others, which causes them to lash out and be verbally aggressive.[13] There is also evidence that some people interpret any negative feedback they receive as a personal attack, no matter how carefully the feedback is worded.[14] For many people, there is no such thing as "constructive criticism." Like a sunburned sunbather, such people perceive even a mild suggestion presented with a light touch as a stinging rebuke.

To help us understand the people we know, we develop a set of constructs for each person. A highly perceptive person may see a whole array of constructs for this woman: whimsical, warm, dependable, friendly, generous, and kind. A person with a less developed set of constructs may see only her whimsical side.

How We Interpret the Behavior of Others

"I know why Alice didn't come to our meeting. She just doesn't like me," says Cathy. "She also just wants people to think she's too busy to be bothered with our little group." Cathy seems not only to have formed a negative impression of Alice, but also to harbor a hunch as to why Alice didn't come to the meeting. Cathy is attributing meaning to Alice's behavior. Even though Alice could have just forgotten about the meeting, Cathy thinks Alice's absence is caused by feelings of superiority and contempt. Cathy's assumptions about Alice can be explained by attribution theory.

Attribution theory explains how we ascribe specific motives and causes to the behaviors of others. It helps us interpret what people do. For example, suppose the student sitting next to you in class gets up in the middle of the lecture and walks out. Why did the student leave? Did the student become angry at something the instructor said? No, the lecturer was simply describing types of cloud formations. Was the student sick? You remember noticing that the student looked a little flushed and occasionally winced. Maybe the student has an upset stomach. Or maybe the student is just a bit of a rebel and often does strange things like leaving in the middle of a class.

Social psychologist Fritz Heider says that we are "naive psychologists,"[15] because we all seek to explain people's motives for their actions. We are naive because we do not create these explanations in a systematic or scientific manner, but rather by applying common sense to our observations. Developing the most credible explanation for the behavior of others is the goal of the attribution process.

Causal attribution theory identifies three potential causes for any person's action: circumstance, a stimulus, or the person herself or himself.[16] Attributing behavior to

attribution theory. Theory that explains how you generate explanations for people's behaviors.

causal attribution theory. Theory of attribution that identifies the cause of a person's actions as circumstance, a stimulus, or the person himself or herself.

circumstance means that you believe a person acts in a certain way because the situation leaves no choice. This way of thinking places responsibility for the action outside of the person. There is interesting research that suggests that during times when you feel lonely and isolated from others, you are more likely to attribute your feelings of loneliness to your specific circumstance rather than to any flaws in your personality.[17]

You would be attributing to circumstance if you believed the student quickly left the classroom because of an upset stomach. Concluding that the student left because the instructor said something inappropriate would be attributing the student's action to the *stimulus* (the instructor). But if you knew the instructor hadn't said anything out of line and that the student was perfectly healthy, you would place the responsibility for the action on the student. Attributing to the *person* means that you believe there is some quality about the person that caused the observed behavior.

To explore how attributions to a person affect us, interpersonal communication researchers Anita Vangelisti and Stacy Young wanted to know whether intentionally hurtful words inflict more pain than unintentionally hurtful comments.[18] As you might suspect, if we think someone intends to hurt us, spiteful words have more sting and bite than if we believe someone does not intend to hurt our feelings. Our attributions are factors in our impressions.

Standpoint theory is yet another framework that seeks to explain how we interpret the behavior of others. The theory is relatively simple: We each see the world differently because we're each viewing it from a different position. Some people have positions of power, and others do not; the resources that we have to help us make our way through life provide a lens through which we view the world and the people in it.

standpoint theory. Theory that a person's social position, power, or cultural background influences how the person perceives the behavior of others.

Standpoint theory explains why people with differing cultural backgrounds have different perceptions of others' behavior. In the early nineteenth century, German philosopher Georg Hegel noted this simple but powerful explanation of why people

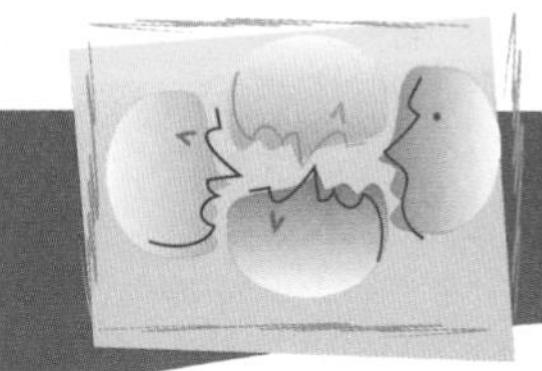

Understanding Diversity

The Power of Perspective

As noted in our discussion of standpoint theory, where you stand makes a difference in what you see and how you interpret human behavior. Following the September 11, 2001, terrorist attacks on the United States, discussions about the perceptions of the power and influence of different cultural groups and countries became more common.

Men and women, blacks and whites, Jews and Christians, Muslims and Hindus, Hispanics and Asians, gay and straight individuals, all experience life from their own cultural standpoint, which means they all have perceptions about their influence on others. To become more other-oriented is to become aware of your own perceived place in society and to be more sensitive to how that position of power or lack of power affects how you perceive others with a different standpoint.

To explore applications of standpoint theory in your life, consider the following questions:

1. How would you describe your standpoint in terms of power and influence in your school or at work, or in your family? Have you ever experienced rejection, alienation, or discrimination based on how others perceived you?
2. How would other people in your life (parents, siblings, children, co-workers, employer, or friends) describe your power and influence on them?
3. How does your standpoint influence your relationship with others? Identify a specific relationship with a teacher, co-worker, or family member in which different standpoints influence the quality of the relationship in either positive or negative ways.
4. What can you do to become more aware of how your standpoint influences your interactions with others? How can your increased awareness enhance the quality of your interpersonal communication with others?

see and experience the world differently.[19] Hegel was especially interested in how one's standpoint was determined in part by one's power and influence. For example, people who have greater power and more influence in a particular culture may not be aware of their power and influence and how this power affects their perceptions of others. A person with less power (which in many cultures includes women and people of color) may be acutely aware of the power he or she doesn't have.

As evidence of standpoint theory, one team of researchers found that people who perceived that they were the victims of someone's lying to them or cheating them had an overall more negative view of the communication with their lying or cheating communication partner than with someone who they perceived did not lie or cheat.[20] This makes sense, doesn't it? If our point of view is that a certain person can't be trusted in one situation, we are less likely to trust the person in other situations. C. S. Lewis was right: What we see and hear depends a good deal on where we are standing.

How We Organize and Interpret Interpersonal Perceptions

Theory	Description	Example
Impression Formation Theory	We form general impressions of others based on general physical qualities, behaviors, and disclosed information.	Categorizing people as nice, friendly, shy, or handsome
Implicit Personality Theory	We draw specific conclusions about someone's personality.	"If she is intelligent, then she must be caring, too."
Attribution Theory	We develop reasons to explain the behaviors of others.	"I guess she didn't return my call because she doesn't like me." "He's just letting off steam because he had a bad week of exams."
Causal Attribution Theory	We ascribe a person's actions to circumstance, a stimulus, or the person himself or herself.	"He didn't go to class because his alarm didn't go off." "He didn't go to class because it was a makeup session." "He didn't go to class because he is bored by it."
Standpoint Theory	We interpret the behavior of others through the lens of our own social position, power, or cultural background.	"He won't join the fraternity because he doesn't understand how important that network can be to his professional career."

Barriers to Accurate Interpersonal Perception

Think about the most recent interaction you had with a stranger. Do you remember the person's age, sex, race, or body size? Did the person have any distinguishing features, such as a beard, tattoos, or a loud voice? The qualities you recall will most likely serve as the basis for attributions you make about that person's behavior. But these attributions, based on your first impressions, might be wrong. Each person sees the world from his or her own unique perspective. That perspective is clouded by a number of distortions and barriers that contribute to inaccurate interpersonal perception. We'll examine these barriers next.

Ignoring Information

People sometimes don't focus on important information, because they give too much weight to information that is obvious and superficial.[21] Why do we ignore important information that may be staring us in the face? It's because, as you learned in the discussion about attribution theory, we tend to explain the motives for a person's actions on the basis of the most obvious information rather than on in-depth information we might have. When meeting someone new, we perceive his or her physical qualities first: color of skin, body size and shape, age, sex, and other obvious characteristics. We overattribute to these qualities, because they are so vivid and available, and ignore other details. We have all been victims of these kinds of attributions, some of us more than others. Often, we are unaware that others are making biased attributions, because they do not express them openly. But sometimes we can tell by the way others react to us and treat us.

Overgeneralizing

People treat small amounts of information as if they were highly representative.[22] This tendency also leads people to draw inaccurate, prejudicial conclusions.[23] For example, a professor may talk to two students and then generalize the impression he or she develops of those two students to the entire student population. In a similar way, most people tend to assume that the small sampling of another person's behavior is a valid representation of who that person is. As you saw in Figure 3.1, you might create a rabbit even when you have only a few dots on which to base your perception.

To overgeneralize is similar to the concept of thin slicing that we discussed earlier in the chapter. Although we each thin slice—use a small sample of information to reach a conclusion—a problem occurs when the conclusion we reach from a brief observation is inaccurate. Overgeneralization occurs when the thin sliced information we use to reach a conclusion is wrong. When making snap judgments from only bits of information, realize the potential for making an inaccurate conclusion.

Oversimplifying

People prefer simple explanations to complex ones. When Imelda picks you up late to go to a movie, she says, "Sorry, I lost track of the time." The next day, Mary also picks you up late to go to a movie. She says, "Sorry. You wouldn't believe how busy I've been. I ran out of hot water when I was showering, and my hair dryer must be busted. It kept shutting off. Then I stopped to get something to eat, and it took forever to get my order. And then it turned out they had it all messed up and had to redo it." Whose explanation can you accept more easily, Imelda's or Mary's?

Usually, people prefer simple explanations; they tend to be more believable and easier to use in making sense of another's actions. But in reality, our behaviors are affected by a multitude of factors, as Mary's explanation indicates. Unfortunately, it takes a lot of effort to understand what makes another person do what he or she does—more effort than we are typically willing to give.

Stereotyping

stereotype. To attribute a set of qualities to a person because of the person's membership in some category.

Preconceived notions about what they expect to find may keep people from seeing what's before their eyes and ears. We see what we want to see, hear what we want to hear. We stereotype others. To **stereotype** someone is to attribute a set of qualities to the person because of his or her membership in some category. The word *stereotype* was originally a printing term, referring to a metal plate that was cast from type set by a printer.

The plate would print the same page of type over and over again. When we stereotype people, we place them into inflexible, all-compassing categories. We "print" the same judgments on anyone placed in a given category. We may even choose to ignore contradictory information that we receive directly from the other person. Instead of adjusting our conception of that person, we adjust our perception.[24] The halo and horn effects discussed earlier reflect this tendency. For example, if an instructor gets an excellent paper from a student who the instructor has concluded is not particularly bright or motivated, she may tend to find errors and shortcomings that are not really there, or she may even accuse the student of plagiarism.

Stereotypes can help us make sense out of the wide range of stimuli we encounter every day. But we also need to be sure that we don't overuse stereotypes and thus fail to see people as individuals.

Stereotyping others is apparently widespread. It's not limited to one cultural group. In a study investigating whether people from a variety of cultural backgrounds make stereotypical judgments of others, researchers found that stereotyping is rampant in many cultures.[25] In this study, participants from Australia, Botswana, Canada, Kenya, Nigeria, South Africa, Zambia, Zimbabwe, and the United States all consistently formed stereotypes of others.

Categorizing individuals is not an inherently bad thing to do, but it is harmful to hang on to an inflexible image of another person in the face of contradictory information. For example, not all mothers are responsible or loving. But because American culture typically reveres motherhood, we may not easily process our perceptions of a mother who is abusive or negligent.

Imposing Consistency

People overestimate the consistency and constancy of others' behaviors. When we organize our perceptions, we also tend to ignore fluctuation in people's behaviors and instead see them as consistent. We believe that if someone acted a certain way one day, he or she will continue to act that way in the future. Perhaps you have embarrassed yourself in front of a new acquaintance by acting foolish and silly. At another encounter with this new acquaintance, you realize that the person is continuing to see your behavior as foolish, even though you don't intend it to be seen that way. The other person is imposing consistency on your inconsistent behavior.

In fact, everyone's behavior varies from day to day. Some days, we are in a bad mood, and our behavior on those days does not represent what we are generally like. As intimacy develops in relationships, we interact with our partners in a variety of activities that provide a more complete picture of our true nature.

Focusing on the Negative

People give more weight to negative information than to positive information.[26] Job interviewers often ask you to describe your strengths and weaknesses. If you describe five great strengths and one weakness, it is likely that the interviewer will attend more to the one weakness you mention than to the strengths. We seem to recognize this bias and compensate for it when we first meet someone by sharing only positive information about ourselves.

In another of Solomon Asch's experiments on impression formation, participants heard one of the following two lists of terms to describe a person: (1) *intelligent, skillful, industrious, warm, determined, practical, cautious;* or (2) *intelligent, skillful, indus-*

trious, cold, determined, practical, cautious.[27] The only difference in these two lists is the use of *warm* in the first list and *cold* in the second. Despite the presence of six other terms, those with the "cold" list had a much more negative impression of the person than those with the "warm" list. One piece of negative information can have a disproportionate effect on our impressions and negate the effect of several positive pieces of information. Perhaps you've noticed that following a near-flawless Olympic ice skating performance, the TV commentator, rather than focusing on the best executed leaps, twists, and turns, will first replay the one small error the skater made in the performance. In our own lives, we may have a tendency to do the same thing; we may focus on what we didn't do well rather than emphasizing what we've done skillfully.

Blaming: Assuming That Others Have Control

People are more likely to believe that others are to blame when things go wrong than to believe that the problem was beyond their control. Your parents were looking forward to celebrating their twenty-fifth wedding anniversary. They planned a quiet family celebration at a restaurant. You set your personal digital assistant to remind you one week before the anniversary dinner to buy them a present to give to them at the dinner. You hadn't anticipated, however, that you'd lose your PDA. When the phone rang and your mom asked, "Where are you?" it all came jarringly back to you: Today was their anniversary, and you'd forgotten it! Not only did you forget to buy them a present, you forgot to attend the dinner. Your parents were hurt. Your mother's quivering "How could you forget?" still sears your conscience. Your parents' hurt feelings evolved into anger. They think you just didn't care enough about them to remember such an important day. Rather than thinking that there might be an explanation for why you forgot their important day, they blame you for your thoughtlessness. Although they certainly have a right to be upset, their assuming that you don't care about them is an example of what researchers call a fundamental attribution error.

A **fundamental attribution error** occurs when a person blames a problem on something that is personally controllable (such as forgetting an important date because you don't care about your parents) rather than something uncontrollable (losing your personal digital assistant and having no back-up system to remind you of the event).[28] As summarized by communication researcher Kory Floyd, the fundamental attribution error "predicts that, all other things being equal, people are more likely to attribute others' behavior to internal, controllable causes than to external, uncontrollable causes."[29] For example, the fundamental attribution error would predict that you're more likely to assume that the person who cuts you off in traffic is a jerk rather than that he's trying to get out of the way of the truck that's tailgating him. If you assume another person made a conscious choice to hurt you instead of considering that there may be other reasons for the person's behavior that are beyond the person's control, you've made a fundamental attribution error. You can avoid making a fundamental attribution error by honestly examining your role in the communication process. When you've made a mistake about a person's behavior, admit it. You can enhance the quality of your relationships when you own up to making perceptual errors.

fundamental attribution error. Error that arises from attributing another person's behavior to internal, controllable causes rather than to external, uncontrollable causes.

Avoiding Responsibility

People are more likely to save face by believing that they are not the cause of a problem; people assume that other people or events are more than likely the source of problems or events that may put them in an unfavorable light. In one classic episode of *The Simpsons,* Bart Simpson created a popular catch phrase by saying, "I didn't do it" when he

Applying Theory and Research

Politeness Theory

Social psychologists Penelope Brown and Stephen Levinson suggest that people from all cultures have a universal need to be treated with politeness.[30] Politeness theory makes inituitive sense. The theory predicts that we will have a positive perception of people who treat us politely and respectfully. Although people from different cultures have varying levels of need to be treated politely, what seems clear is that everyone needs to be valued and appreciated.

A concept related to politeness theory is the need to project a positive image or to have a positive face. Sociologist Erving Goffman suggests that saving face is important for most people.[31] As we discussed in Chapter 2, by "face" we mean more than just our physical face; we're talking about an overall projection of a positive image to other people. Because of our need to be treated politely, our perceptions of others are affected when people violate our expectations and do or say things that are impolite or cause us to lose face. It is polite to help others save face and protect their positive self-image. We behave in ways to help us present the best possible image of ourselves to others.

To have a positive face is to be approved of and liked by others. When people treat us with politeness, they help contribute to a positive face. Providing compliments, behaving respectfully, and showing concern for others are all ways of using positive politeness to help others project a positive face.

All would be well and good if we could always provide positive, confirming comments to others, but that simply is not realistic or possible. We engage in face-threatening acts when we communicate in a way that undermines someone's positive face. According to politeness theory, people can communicate in a variety of ways that are face-threatening. The following list is arranged from most to least face-threatening.

1. Bluntly communicate a negative message. ("Your office is a mess.")
2. Deliver the negative message but also communicate a positive face-saving message. ("Your office is a mess, but perhaps messy is the look you want.")
3. Deliver the negative message but offer a counter-explanation to help the person save face. ("Your office is a mess, but that's understandable given how much work you do around here.")
4. Communicate the negative message but do so "off the record" or in such an indirect way that the other person saves face. ("I'm not supposed to tell you this, but even though your office is a mess, the boss is impressed with how well you seem to find everything.")
5. Don't communicate any message that would cause someone to lose face.

Applying the Research to Your Life

How is politeness theory of value to you? By being aware of people's need for politeness to help them save face, you can try to be more aware of how you communicate negative messages to others. You can help others maintain a positive face by consciously trying to be more indirect or to offer a counter-explanation when you deliver a negative message.

Consider the following questions as you apply politeness theory to your own relationships:

1. If you have a face-threatening message for a friend or loved one, what would be a way of expressing yourself while also letting the other person save face?
2. How are your perceptions of others influenced by the manner in which they help you save face? Provide an example of when someone helped you save face and that effort had a positive effect on how you perceived the person.
3. Is being polite and trying to help someone save face merely a way to manipulate others so that they perceive you in a favorable way?

Source: P. Brown and S. Levinson, *Politeness: Some Universals in Language Usage* (Cambridge, England: Cambridge University Press, 1987).

clearly was the cause of a calamity. Whether it was lighting Lisa's hair on fire, calling Moe's tavern asking for Al Coholic, or putting baby Maggie on the roof, Bart would simply say, "I didn't do it." We chuckle at Bart's antics and would never stoop to such juvenile pranks. Yet there is evidence that when we do cause a problem or make a mistake, we are more likely to blame someone else rather than ourselves. Bart's "I didn't do it" approach to life represents self-serving bias.

When we avoid taking responsibility for our own errors and mistakes, we are guilty of what researchers call the self-serving bias. **Self-serving bias** is the tendency to perceive our own behavior as more positive than others' behavior. Sociologist Erving Goffman was one of the first to note this tendency when he wrote his classic book *The Preservation of Self in Everyday Life.*[32] As the title of Goffman's book reveals, we work hard to preserve our own selves. We strive to preserve not only our physical existence, but our psychological health as well. We sometimes may try to preserve a positive image of ourselves by not taking responsibility for our mistakes and by telling ourselves that we are skilled and effective. We are likely, for example, to attribute our own personal success to our hard work and effort rather than any to external, uncontrollable causes. You get an A on your anthropology paper because, you think, "I'm smart." When you get an F on your history paper, it's because your neighbor's loud party kept you up all night and you couldn't study. Self-serving bias is the tendency to take credit for the good things that happen to you and to say "I didn't do it" or "It's not my fault" when bad things happen to you.[33] Simply being aware of the self-serving bias may help you become more objective and accurate in identifying the cause of calamities in your own life.

Barriers to Accurate Interpersonal Perception

Ignoring information	We don't focus on important information because we give too much weight to obvious and superficial information.
Overgeneralizing	We treat small amounts of information as if they were highly representative.
Oversimplifying	We prefer simple explanations to complex ones.
Stereotyping	We allow our pre-existing rigid expectations about others to influence our perceptions.
Imposing consistency	We overestimate the consistency and constancy of others' behavior.
Focusing on the negative	We give more weight to negative information than to positive information.
Blaming others by assuming they have control	We are more likely to believe that others are to blame when things go wrong than to assume that the cause of the problem was beyond their control.
Avoiding responsibility	We save face by believing that other people, not ourselves, are the cause of problems; when things go right, it's because of our own skills and abilities rather than help from others.

Improving Your Perception Skills

With so many barriers to perceiving and interpreting other people's behavior accurately, what can you do to improve your perception skills? Increasing your awareness of the factors that lead to inaccuracy will help initially, and you will find further suggestions in this section. Ultimately, your improvement will depend on your willingness to expand your experiences, to communicate about your perceptions with others, and to seek out and consider others' perceptions of you. Realize that you have had a lifetime to develop these barriers and that it will take time, commitment, and effort to overcome their effects.

self-serving bias. Tendency to perceive our own behavior as more positive than others' behavior.

And just by reading this chapter, you've gained greater understanding of how the perception process affects your relationships with others. Use your knowledge of the perceptual process to sharpen your own perceptions and conclusions. Here are additional strategies to help you become a more accurate perceiver.

Link Details with the Big Picture

Any skilled detective knows how to take a small piece of information or evidence and use it to reach a broader conclusion. Skilled perceivers keep the big picture in mind as they look for clues about a person. Just because someone may dress differently from you, or have a pronounced accent, don't rush to judgment about the person's competence based on such few snatches of information. Look and listen for other cues about your new acquaintance that can help you develop a more accurate understanding of who that person is. Try not to use early information to form a quick or rigid judgment that may be inaccurate. Look at all the details you've gathered.

Become Aware of Others' Perceptions of You

The best athletes don't avoid hearing criticisms and observations from their coaches. Instead, they seek out as much feedback as they can about what they are doing right and wrong. It is difficult to be objective about our own behavior, so feedback from others can help us with our self-perceptions. The strongest relationships are those in which the partners are willing both to share their perceptions and to be receptive of the perceptions of the other.

BE OTHER-ORIENTED

Increase Your Conscious Awareness

Your senses are constantly bombarding you with information, much of which you ignore. You can increase the amount of information you process from your senses by consciously attending to the input. To increase your conscious awareness of others is to be **mindful**—conscious of what you are doing, thinking, and sensing at any given moment. The opposite of being mindful is to be mindless—to be not attuned to what is happening to you. Have you ever walked into a room and then forgotten why you were going there? (Trust us: If this hasn't happened to you, it will happen as you get older.) Or have you ever misplaced your keys, even though you just had them in your hand minutes earlier? How could you forget what you were directly experiencing just moments ago? The answer is, you were mindless rather than mindful. We sometimes aren't paying attention to what we are doing. When you interact with others, try to

mindful. Conscious of what you are doing, thinking, and sensing at any given moment.

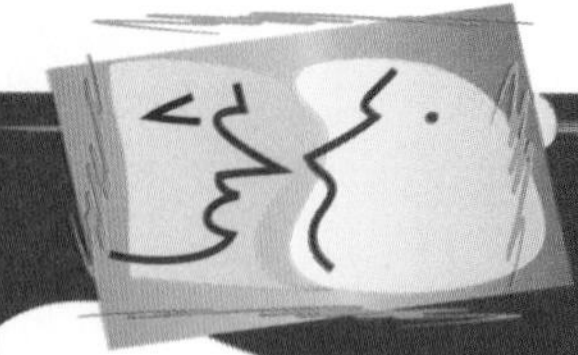

Becoming Other-Oriented

Ten Questions That Can Help You Become Other-Oriented

1. What factors or circumstances are affecting the person?
2. How can I determine whether there are factors I don't know about or don't fully understand?
3. What do I know about this person that explains his or her behaviors and feelings?
4. What is going through the other person's mind at this time?
5. What are the other person's feelings at this time?
6. What other explanations could there be for the person's actions?
7. What would I think if I were in the same situation?
8. How would I feel if I were in the same situation?
9. What would other people think if they were in that situation?
10. How would other people feel if they were in that situation?

identify one new thing to focus on and observe each time. Watch gestures, eyes, the wrinkles around eyes, foot movements; listen to tone of voice. Try to notice as much detail as possible, but keep the entire picture in view.

Become Other-Oriented

BE OTHER-ORIENTED

Do you think these people are using direct perception checking, indirect perception checking, or a combination of the two?

Effective interpersonal perception depends on the ability to understand where others are coming from, to get inside their heads, to see things from their perspectives.

Becoming other-oriented involves a two-step process: social decentering (consciously *thinking* about another's thoughts and feelings) and empathizing (*responding emotionally* to another's feelings).[34] What does your boss think and feel when you arrive late for work? What would your spouse think and feel if you brought a dog home as a surprise gift? Throughout this book we offer suggestions for becoming other-oriented, for reminding yourself that the world does not revolve around you. Being other-oriented enables you to increase your understanding of others and improve your ability to predict and adapt to what others do and say.

To improve your ability to socially decenter and to empathize, strive for two key goals: (1) Gather as much information as possible about the circumstances that are affecting the other person; and (2) gather as much information as possible about the other person.

Check Your Perceptions

Throughout this chapter we've encouraged you to be more perceptive of communication with others. It may seem like we're expecting you to be a mind reader—to just look at someone and know precisely what he or she is thinking. Mind reading may be a good circus act, but it's not a well-documented way of enhancing your perception of others. What does seem to work is to check your perceptions of others.

You can check out the accuracy of your perceptions and attributions in two ways: indirectly and directly. **Indirect perception checking** involves seeking additional information through passive perception, either to confirm or to refute your interpretations. If you suspect someone is angry at you but is not admitting it, for example, you could look for more cues in his or her tone of voice, eye contact, and body movements to confirm your suspicion. You could also listen more intently to the person's words and language.

Direct perception checking involves asking straight out whether your interpretations of a perception are correct. Asking someone to confirm a perception shows that you are committed to understanding his or her behavior. If your friend's voice sounds weary and her posture is sagging, you may assume that she is depressed or upset. If you ask, "I get the feeling from your tone of voice and the way you're acting that you are kind of down and depressed; what's wrong?" your friend can then either provide another interpretation: "I'm just tired; I had a busy week"; or expand on your interpretation: "Yeah, things haven't been going very well. . . ." Your observation might also trigger a revelation: "Really? I didn't realize I was acting that way. I guess I am a little down."

indirect perception checking. Seeking additional information to confirm or refute interpretations you are making through passive perception such as observing and listening.

direct perception checking. Asking for confirmation from the observed person of an interpretation or a perception about him or her.

Interpersonal Communication and Emotion
Connecting Heart to Heart

How to More Accurately Perceive the Emotions of Others

One barrier to effective interpersonal communication is inaccurately perceiving the emotional expressions of others. Misreading someone's emotional response can impede effective and appropriate communication with that person. If, for example, you think your friend is angry with you because of something that you did, when in reality, he is upset because of his poor performance on a test, your misattribution of your friend's emotion could create relational turbulence between you and your friend. Inaccurately jumping to conclusions, either about what emotion someone may be experiencing or about the cause of that emotion, reduces communication effectiveness.

In this chapter we've discussed the role of attribution theory as a framework for understanding how we interpret the behavior of others, including emotional expression. Attribution theory explains why we may think someone is angry, upset, frustrated, or delighted because of something we said or did.

How can we improve our ability to accurately perceive what others may feel or express? One way is to use the perception checking skills we've presented. You can try the indirect perception checking approach by simply withholding your interpretation until you spend more time observing your partner. Or you can use direct perception checking. Rather than trying to read someone's mind and make an assumption about what the person may be feeling, you can directly check your perceptions by asking that person what she or he is feeling.

- Step one is to observe what someone is expressing nonverbally (the person's facial expression, tone of voice, movement, posture, and gestures).
- Step two is to make a mindful guess as to what the person may be feeling. But don't stop there.
- Step three is to ask a perception checking question to check whether your impression was accurate or not.

Besides using perception checking, it's useful to keep the following principles in mind when trying to accurately perceive others' emotions.

- Seek to interpret someone's emotion by considering the overall context of the communication.
- Don't consider just one bit of behavior, such as only your partner's facial expression or only his or her tone of voice; look for a variety of cues, both spoken and unspoken, to increase your accurate perception of another person's emotions.
- Consider how your partner has responded to information and events in the past to help you interpret emotional responses.

Being conscious of attribution theory, effectively using perception checking skills, and being mindful of general strategies for accurately interpreting emotions can help enhance the quality of your interpretations of the emotional expressions of others.

Summary

Interpersonal perception is a fundamental element of interpersonal communication. Our communication and interpersonal relationships are affected by the ways we perceive those with whom we interact. Interpersonal perception involves more than just the arousal of the senses; it also involves selecting, organizing, and interpreting what we observe in order to decide what people are like and to give meaning to their actions.

Our perceptions of others affect how we communicate, and how others perceive us affects how they communicate with us. Interpersonal perception can be a passive or an active process. It is passive when only our senses are in operation; it is active when we feel a need for information and intentionally seek it. We are motivated to seek information in situations that have high amounts of uncertainty. Perception of information helps reduce uncertainty and provides us with more control of the situation.

Interpersonal perception affects and is affected by the development of impressions, our own implicit personality theories, and attributions. Our general impressions of individuals are often affected by primacy and recency effects; we pay particular attention to the first things we notice and the most recent things we notice about others. In our interactions with others, we all seem to operate as "naive psychologists," developing and applying our own implicit personality theories. These implicit personality theories represent the general way we believe people behave. We develop specific personal constructs that represent the qualities we associate with specific people we know. Finally, we try to explain the actions and behaviors of others through the process of attribution. According to attribution theorists, we seek to find out the intent and cause of a person's action; for example, we see a person's action as a response to a given circumstance, a particular stimulus, or the person's own personality. To make rational and accurate attributions, we must overcome perceptual barriers. A number of tendencies distort the accuracy of our attributions, such as focusing on obvious or negative information.

The following suggestions can help you to improve your interpersonal perception: (1) link details with the big picture; (2) increase your awareness skills; (3) increase your awareness of others' perceptions of you; (4) become other-oriented; and (5) check your perceptions.

For Discussion and Review

Focus on Critical Thinking

1. Think about some of your recent interpersonal conflicts. How would you describe your perception of the problem in each conflict? How do you think the others would describe their perceptions of it? What role did perception play in contributing to or resolving the conflict?
2. What do you think contributes to the development of the tendency to perceive others inaccurately? How might the effects of those factors be minimized or eliminated?

Focus on Ethics

3. Do you have a right in an intimate relationship to expect your partner to share his or her perceptions of you, whether those perceptions are positive or negative? Explain your reasoning.
4. If you are aware of how you are distorting your own perceptions and attributions, should you try to change them? Is it a moral obligation? Explain your reasoning.

Learning with Others

1. Choose a magazine ad or illustration, a photograph, or a painting that shows a group of people, and bring it to class. In groups of four or five, pass around the pictures. For each picture, write down a few words to describe your perceptions of what you see. What are the people doing? What is their relationship to one another? What is each one like? How is each one feeling? Why are they doing what they are doing? After you have finished, share with one another what you wrote down. Try to determine why there were differences. What factors influenced your perceptions?

2. Pair up with someone in class whom you do not know and have not interacted with before. Without saying anything to each other, write down the words from the following list that you think apply to the other person. Now chat together for five minutes. In a separate section of your paper, write down any additional words

that you believe apply to the person; you can also go back and put a line through any of the words in the first list that you now think are inaccurate. Share with your partner what words you put down before and during the conversation, and what words you changed. Have your partner share his or her perceptions of you. Discuss, as best you can, the reasons you chose each word.

intelligent	athletic	artistic	studious
nice	funny	conceited	friendly
introvert	extrovert	hard worker	shy
talented	popular	inquisitive	moody
emotional	happy	brave	responsible
leader	follower	uncertain	confused

3. Think about your own preconceptions about cause–effect relationships. For each of the following, think about what your first explanation of the cause would be.

- A person not calling back after a first date
- A waitress giving you lousy service
- Your car not being repaired after you paid a high service fee
- A teacher being late for class
- A child beating up other kids
- A student copying test answers from the student next to him
- A mother refusing to let her teenage son drive the car on Friday nights

Now go back and generate as many alternative explanations for each behavior as you can. How can you be sure which explanation is correct?

Weblinks

Go to *www.mycommunicationlab.com* (access code required) to find Web resources for your text that supplement the material in Chapter 3, including links to information on the following topics:

The perception process
Attribution theory
Brain research and perception
Optical illusions
Stereotypes: How we stereotype others

Interpersonal Communication and Cultural Diversity: Adapting to Others

OBJECTIVES

1. Describe five human differences that influence communication.
2. Define *culture*.
3. Identify cultural elements, values, and contexts.
4. Discuss barriers that inhibit effective intercultural communication.
5. Identify strategies for developing knowledge, motivation, and skills that can improve intercultural competence.

OUTLINE

Strangers, people different from us, stir up fear, discomfort, suspicion, and hostility. They make us lose our sense of security just by being "other."

Henri J. M. Nouwen

Perhaps you've heard the saying, "Everyone is a little bit strange except for me and you, and I'm not so sure about you." Each of us is unique. There is no one exactly like you. But because of our uniqueness, we can sometimes seem strange to others. In their book *Communicating with Strangers,* intercultural communication researchers William Gudykunst and Young Yun Kim point out that strangers are "people who are different and unknown."[1] Although as human beings we share many things in common, our interpersonal interactions with others also make us aware of how people look and communicate in ways that are different from ours.

In the first three chapters, we acknowledged the influence of diversity on interpersonal relationships. In this chapter, we examine in more detail the impact that people's differences have on their lives and suggest some communication strategies for bridging those differences in our interpersonal relationships. Our premise for this discussion of diversity is that in order to live comfortably in the 21st century, people must learn ways to appreciate and understand our differences instead of ignoring them, suffering because of them, or wishing that they would disappear.

A goal of studying interpersonal communication is to learn how to put aside differences in age, gender, race, or ability that might cause barriers to effective communication.

Some people may be weary of what they perceive as an overemphasis on diversity. One student overheard a classmate say, "I've had it with all this diversity stuff. It seems like every textbook in every class is obsessed with it. I'm tired of all this politically correct nonsense. I mean, we're all Americans. We're not all going off to live in China. Why don't they just teach us what we need to know and cut all of this diversity garbage?" Perhaps you've encountered this kind of "diversity backlash" among some of your classmates (or maybe you hold this attitude yourself). It may seem unsettling to some that textbooks are changing and emphasizing cultural diversity. But these changes are not motivated by an irrational desire to be politically correct. They are taking place because the United States and other countries are becoming increasingly diverse.[2]

Journalist Thomas Friedman argues that **globalization,** the integration of economics and technology that is contributing to a worldwide, interconnected business environment, is changing the way we work and relate to people around the world.[3] The world is "flat" rather than round, says Friedman, because if you have a computer connected to the Internet or own a cell phone, you can connect with anyone else in the

globalization. The integration of economics and technology that is contributing to a worldwide, interconnected business environment.

world who also has those technologies. Describing the world as flat is a metaphor Friedman uses to convey the interconnectedness of people throughout the world. Our point is not to debate the advantages or disadvantages of globalization, but only to suggest that one key implication of a "flat" world is that you will increasingly communicate with people who are different from you and who may be strangers to you.

As further suggested by the statistics in *Understanding Diversity: A Diversity Almanac,* the United States is becoming increasingly diverse. With this diversity comes a growing awareness that learning about differences, especially cultural differences, can affect every aspect of people's lives in positive ways. You need not travel the world to interact with people who may seem strange to you; the world is traveling to you.

BE OTHER-ORIENTED

A central goal of your study of interpersonal communication is to learn how better to relate to others. Some of the differences that contribute to diversity and may interfere with developing relationships include differences in age, learning style, gender, religion, race and ethnicity, sexual orientation, social class, and culture. We will emphasize the role of cultural differences and how those differences affect our interpersonal communication while also noting a variety of ways in which we may seem strange to one another.

Understanding Diversity

A Diversity Almanac

1. Two-thirds of the immigrants on this planet come to the United States.[4]
2. In the United States, there are "minority majorities" (where minorities outnumber traditional European Americans) in Miami; Laredo, Texas; Gary, Indiana; Detroit; Washington, DC; Oakland, California; Atlanta; San Antonio; Los Angeles; Chicago; Baltimore; Houston; New York; Memphis; San Francisco; Fresno, California; and San Jose, California.[5]
3. It is estimated that more than forty million U.S. residents have a non-English first language, including eighteen million people whose first language is Spanish.[6]
4. Almost one-third of U.S. residents under age thirty-five are members of minority groups, compared with one-fifth of those age thirty-five or older. According to U.S. Bureau of the Census population projections, by the year 2025 nearly half of all young adults in this country will come from minority groups.[7]
5. If the current trend continues, by the year 2050 the percentage of the U.S. population that is white will decrease to 53 percent, down from a current 79 percent. Asians will increase to 16 percent, up from 1.6 percent; Hispanics will more than triple their numbers to over 25 percent, up from just over 7.5 percent; and African Americans will increase their proportion slightly from the current 12 percent.[8]
6. It is estimated that during the first ten years of the twenty-first century, Vermont's Asian population will grow by 80 percent, Arizona's will increase by 52 percent, and that of the state of Delaware will grow by 56 percent.[9]
7. At the end of the twentieth century, one in ten U.S. residents was born outside the country.[10]
8. One out of every eight U.S. residents speaks a language other than English at home, and one-third of children in urban U.S. public schools speak a first language other than English.[11]
9. During the past decade, the combined population of African Americans, Native Americans, Asians, Pacific Islanders, and Hispanics grew thirteen times faster than the non-Hispanic white population.[12]
10. In 2004, for the first time since the 1850s when California was seized from Mexico, a majority of the babies born in California were Hispanic.[13]
11. Non-Hispanic whites constitute a minority of the population in Texas, New Mexico, and California.[14]
12. Sixty percent of the residents of Miami, Florida, are foreign-born.[15]

Understanding Diversity: Describing Our Differences

How are we different? Let us count the ways. No, let's not—that would take up too much space! There are an infinite number of ways in which we are different from one another. Unless you have an identical twin, you look different from everybody else, although you may have some things in common with a larger group of people (such as skin color, hair style, or clothing choice). Communication researchers have, however, studied several major differences that affect the way we interact with one another. To frame our discussion of diversity and communication, we'll note differences in gender, sexual orientation, race and ethnicity, age, and social class. Each of these differences—some learned, some based on biology, economic status, or simply on how long someone has lived—has an effect on how we perceive others and interact with them. Following our discussion of some classic ways in which we are diverse, we'll turn our attention to cultural differences and then note the barriers that cultural differences can create. We'll conclude the chapter by identifying strategies to enhance the quality of interpersonal communication with others, despite our differences.

Gender

Perhaps the most obvious form of human diversity is the existence of female and male human beings.[16] A person's *sex* is determined by biology; only men can impregnate; only women can menstruate, gestate, and lactate. In contrast to sex differences, *gender differences* focus on learned behavior that is culturally associated with being a man or a woman. Gender role definitions are flexible: A man can adopt behavior associated with a female role in a given culture, and vice versa. **Gender** refers to psychological and emotional characteristics that cause people to assume masculine, feminine, or androgynous (having a combination of both feminine and masculine traits) roles. Your gender is learned and socially reinforced by others, as well as by your life experiences and genetics. Some researchers prefer to study gender as a sub-culture (a subset of the larger cultural group). We view gender as one of many basic elements of culture.

In the predominant culture of the United States, someone's gender is an important thing to know. Yet how different are men and women? John Gray, author of the popular book *Men Are from Mars, Women Are from Venus,* would have us believe that the sexes are so different from each other that we approach life as if we lived on two different planets.[17] Communication researchers have challenged many of Gray's stereotypical conclusions.[18] Although researchers have noted some differences in the way men and women interact, to label *all* men and *all* women as acting in prototypical ways may cause us to assume differences that aren't really there.

Deborah Tannen, author of several books on the behavior of the sexes, views men and women as belonging to different cultural groups.[19] She suggests that female–male communication is cross-cultural communication, with all of the challenges of communicating with people who are different from us.

Research conclusions can result in uncertainty about sex and gender differences. Are there really fundamental differences in the way men and women communicate? Yes, some differences have been documented by researchers. But the differences may have more to do with *why* we communicate than *how.* There is evidence that men tend to talk to accomplish something or to complete a task. Women are often more likely to use conversation to establish and maintain relationships. There is a short way of summarizing this difference: *Men often communicate to report; women often communicate to establish rapport.*[20] Research suggests that many men tend to approach communication from a content orientation, meaning that they view the purpose of

gender. Socially learned and reinforced characteristics that include one's biological sex and psychological characteristics (femininity, masculinity, androgyny).

communication as primarily information exchange. You talk when you have something to say. Women, research suggests, tend to use communication for the purpose of relating or connecting to others. So the point of difference isn't in the way the sexes actually communicate but in their motivations or reasons for communicating.

Sexual Orientation

During the past two decades, gays and lesbians have become more assertive in expressing their rights within American society. Questions of whether gays should participate in the military, the clergy, and the teaching profession have stirred the passions of many. Being gay has become a source of pride for some, but it is still a social stigma for others. The incidence of suicide among gay teenagers is significantly higher than among non-gay teens.[21] Although gay people are gaining legal rights and protections, they are still subject to discriminatory laws and social intolerance. Yet the gay and lesbian communities are important sub-cultures within the larger U.S. culture.

There is evidence that gay and lesbian individuals continue to be judged negatively based solely on their sexual orientation.[22] Research further suggests that heterosexuals who have negative perceptions of gays and lesbians are more likely to have rigid views about gender roles and to assume that their peers also hold such rigid views and negative impressions of gays and lesbians.[23] In addition, those who hold negative attitudes toward gays and lesbians are less likely to have interpersonal communication with gays or lesbians.[24] It is because of the existence of these negative attitudes as well as anti-gay violence and harassment, that some gays and lesbians continue to conceal their sexual orientation.

An effective and appropriate interpersonal communicator is aware of and sensitive to issues and attitudes about sexual orientation in contemporary society. Homophobia, the irrational fear of, aversion to, or discrimination against homosexuality and gays or lesbians, continues to exist among many people. Just as you have been taught to avoid biased expressions that degrade someone's race or ethnicity, it is equally important to avoid using language that demeans a person's sexual orientation. Telling stories and jokes whose points or punch lines rely on cruelly ridiculing a person because of his or her sexual orientation lowers perceptions of your credibility not only among gay and lesbian people, but also among people who dislike any show of bias against gays and lesbians.

Although we may not intend anything negative, sometimes we unintentionally offend someone through more subtle use and misuse of language.[25] For example usually gays and lesbians typically prefer to be referred to as "gay" or "lesbian" rather than "homosexual." In addition, the term *sexual orientation* is preferred over *sexual preference* when describing a person's sexual orientation. Our language should reflect and acknowledge the range of human relationships that exist. Our key point is this: Be sensitively other-oriented as you interact with those whose sexual orientation is different from your own.

Race and Ethnicity

Racial and ethnic differences among people are often discussed and sometimes debated. According to *Random House Webster's Unabridged Dictionary,* **race** is based on the genetically transmitted physical characteristics of a group of people who are also classified together because of a common history, nationality, or geographical location.[26] A person's racial classification is typically based on visible physiological attributes—*phenotypes*—which include skin color, body type, hair color and texture, and facial attributes. Skin color and other physical characteristics affect our responses and influence the way people of different races interact.

race. Genetically transmitted physical characteristics of a group of people.

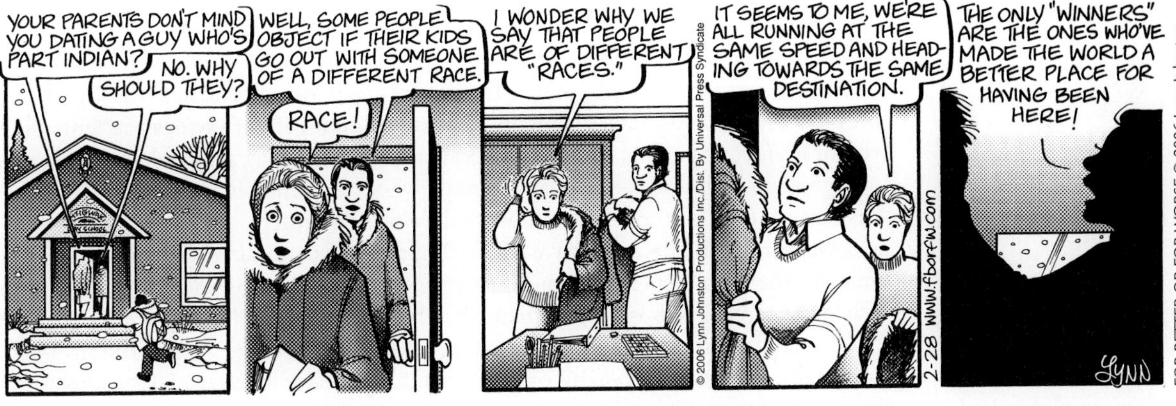

Although it may seem neat and tidy to classify individuals genetically as belonging to one race or another, it's not quite that simple. One geneticist has concluded that there is much more genetic variation *within* a given racial category than *between* one race and another.[27] There really aren't vast genetic differences among people who have been assigned to racial categories. That's why many scholars suggest that we think of race as a category that not only emphasizes biological or genetic characteristics, but also includes cultural, economic, social, geographic, and historical elements.[28] The term *race,* therefore, is a fuzzy, somewhat controversial way of classifying people.

Ethnicity is a related term, yet scholars suggest it is different from race. **Ethnicity** is a *social classification* based on a variety of factors, such as nationality, religion, language, and ancestral heritage (race), that are shared by a group of people who also share a common geographic origin. Simply stated, an ethnic group is a group of people who have self-labeled themselves an ethnic group based on a variety of factors that may or may not include race. In making distinctions between race and ethnicity, Brenda Allen suggests that ethnicity refers to "a common origin or culture based on shared activities and identity related to some mixture of race, religion, language and/or ancestry."[29] She suggests that while ethnicity may include race, race is a separate category that is based on genetic or biological factors. But research has found those genetic or biological distinctions are not clear-cut. A key distinction between race and ethnicity is that one's ethnicity is a *socially constructed* category that emphasizes culture and a host of other factors other than one's racial or genetic background. Not all Asians (race), for example, have the same cultural background (ethnicity).[30] Nationality and geographical location are especially important in defining an ethnic group. Those of Irish ancestry are usually referred to as an ethnic group rather than as a race. The same could be said of Britons, Norwegians, and Spaniards.

Ethnicity, like race, fosters common bonds that affect communication patterns. On the positive side, ethnic groups bring vitality and variety to American society. On the negative side, members of these groups may experience persecution or rejection by members of other groups in society.

One of the most significant problems that stem from attempts to classify people by racial or ethnic type is the tendency to discriminate and unfairly, inaccurately, or inappropriately ascribe stereotypes to racial or ethnic groups. **Discrimination** is the unfair or inappropriate treatment of other people based on their group membership.[31] One of the goals of learning about diversity and becoming aware of both differences and similarities among groups is to eliminate discrimination and stereotypes that cause people to rigidly and inappropriately pre-judge others.

ethnicity. Social classification based on nationality, religion, language, and ancestral heritage, shared by a group of people who also share a common geographical origin.

discrimination. Unfair or inappropriate treatment of people based on their group membership.

Age

Different generations, because they have experienced different cultural and historical events, tend to view life differently. If your grandparents experienced the Great Depression of the 1930s, they may have different attitudes about savings accounts than you or even your parents do. Today's explicit song lyrics may shock older Americans who grew up with such racy lyrics as "makin' whoopee." The generation gap is real and has implications for the relationships we develop with others.

Generational differences have an effect not just on communication with your parents or other family members, but on a variety of relationships, including those with teachers, merchants, bosses, and mentors. There is considerable evidence that people hold stereotypical views of others based on others' perceived age.[32] In addition, a person's age has an influence on his or her communications with others. For example, one study found that older adults have greater difficulty in accurately interpreting the nonverbal messages of others than younger people do.[33] Older adults also don't like to be patronized or talked down to (who does?).[34] And younger people seem to value social support, empathic listening, and being mentored more than older people do.[35]

Authors Neil Howe and William Strauss, two researchers who have investigated the role of age and generation on society, define a generation as "a society-wide peer group, born over a period roughly the same length as the passage from youth to adulthood, who collectively possess a common persona."[36] Baby boomers is the label for one such generation, people born between 1943 and 1960. Perhaps your parents or grandparents are Boomers. *Generation X* is the term used for people born between 1961 and 1981. If you were born between 1982 and 2002, you and your generation have been labeled *millennials.*[37] Researchers Howe and Strauss suggest that, as a group, "Millennials are unlike any other youth generation in living memory. They are more numerous, more affluent, better educated, and more ethnically diverse. More importantly, they are beginning to manifest a wide array of positive social habits that older Americans no longer associate with youth, including a focus on teamwork, achievement, modesty, and good conduct."[38] Table 4.1 summarizes labels for and common characteristics and values of several generational groups.

Your generation of origin has important implications for communication, especially as you relate to others in both family and work situations. Each generation has developed its own set of values, which are anchored in social, economic, and cultural factors stemming from the times in which the generation has lived. Our values, core conceptualizations of what is fundamentally good or bad, right or wrong, color our way of thinking about and responding to what we experience. Generational and age differences may create barriers and increase the potential for conflict and misunderstanding.[39] For example, one team of researchers who investigated the role of generations in the workforce suggests that Generation X workers are paradoxically both more individualistic (self-reliant) and more team-oriented than Boomers are.[40] In contrast, Boomers are more likely to have a sense of loyalty to their employers, expect long-term employment, value a pension plan, and experience job burnout from overwork. Generation Xers, on the other hand, seek a more balanced approach between work and personal life, expect to have more than one job or career, value good working conditions over other job factors, and have a greater need to feel appreciated.[41] Of course, these are broad generalizations and do not apply to all people in these categories.

Social Class

The Constitution of the United States declares that all people are created equal, but there is dramatic evidence that class differences exist and affect communication patterns. Social psychologist Michael Argyle reports that the cues we use to identify class

TABLE 4.1 Summary of Generational Characteristics

Generation Name	Birth Years	Typical Characteristics
Matures	1925–1942	• Work hard • Have a sense of duty • Are willing to sacrifice • Have a sense of what is right • Work quickly
Baby Boomers	1943–1960	• Value personal fulfillment and optimism • Crusade for causes • Buy now, pay later • Support equal rights for all • Work efficiently
Generation X	1961–1981	• Live with uncertainty • Consider balance important • Live for today • Save • Consider every job as a contract
Millennials	1982–2002	• Are close to their parents • Feel "special" • Are goal-oriented • Are team-oriented • Focus on achievement

Source: Information summarized from N. Howe and W. Strauss, *Millennials Rising: The Next Great Generation* (New York: Vintage Books, 2000).

distinctions are (1) way of life, (2) family, (3) job, (4) money, and (5) education.[42] Brenda Allen suggests, "Social class encompasses a socially constructed category of identity that involves more than just economic factors; it includes an entire socialization process."[43] Such a socialization process influences the nature and quality of the interpersonal relationships we have with others. Although sociologists are the primary academic group of scholars who study social class, psychologists, business professionals, marketing specialists, and communication scholars also are interested in how a person's social class has an effect on his or her thoughts and behavior. Class differences influence whom we talk with, whether we are likely to invite our neighbors over for coffee, and whom we choose as our friends and lovers. And research suggests that social class is used by advertisers to target sales pitches to specific types of people.[44]

Some principles that describe how social classes emerge from society include the following:[45]

1. Virtually every organization or group develops a hierarchy that makes status distinctions.
2. We are more likely to interact with people from our own social class. There seems to be some truth to the maxim "Birds of a feather flock together." Most of us must make a conscious effort if we want to expand beyond our class boundaries.
3. People who interact with one another over time tend to communicate in similar ways; they develop similar speech patterns and use similar expressions.

4. Members of a social class develop ways of communicating class differences to others by the way they dress, cars they drive, homes they live in, schools they attend, and other visible symbols of social class.

5. It is possible to change one's social class through education, employment, and income.

Differences in social class and the attendant differences in education and lifestyle affect whom we talk with and even what we talk about.[46] These differences influence our overall cultural standpoint, from which we perceive the world.

Understanding Culture: Describing Our Mental Software

We have noted a few of the fundamental ways people differ. Differences in gender, sexual orientation, race and ethnicity, age, and social class contribute to an overall cultural perspective that influences on a fundamental level how we relate to others. **Culture** is a learned system of knowledge, behaviors, attitudes, beliefs, values, and norms that is shared by a group of people. In the broadest sense, culture includes how people think, what they do, and how they use things to sustain their lives. Researcher Geert Hofstede describes culture as the "mental software" that touches every aspect of how we make sense out of the world and share that sense with others.[47] Just like software in a computer, our culture influences how we process information. To interact with other people is to be touched by the influence of culture and cultural differences.

Sometimes when we speak of culture, we may be referring to a sub-culture. A **sub-culture** is a distinct culture within a larger culture. The differences of gender, sexual orientation, race and ethnicity, age, and social class that we discussed earlier are sub-cultures within the predominate culture. For example, about 80 percent of the population of the United States is classified as white, European, American, or Caucasian. Members of minority groups such as African Americans, Latinos, and Asians develop a sub-culture, or what is sometimes called a *microculture.* The Amish, Mennonite, Mormon, Islamic, and Jewish religious groups are additional examples of important religious sub-cultures.

Cultural Elements

Categories of things and ideas that identify the most profound aspects of cultural influence are known as **cultural elements.** According to one research team, cultural elements include the following:[48]

- *Material culture:* housing, clothing, automobiles
- *Social institutions:* schools, governments, religious organizations
- *Belief systems:* ideas about individuals and the universe
- *Aesthetics:* music, theater, art, dance
- *Language:* verbal and nonverbal communication system

Cultural elements are not only things we can see and hear, but also the ideas and values that are reflected in our topics of conversation.

culture. Learned system of knowledge, behavior, attitudes, beliefs, values, and norms that is shared by a group of people.

sub-culture. A microculture; a distinct culture within a larger culture (such as the gay and lesbian sub-culture).

cultural elements. Categories of things and ideas that identify the most profound aspects of cultural influence (such as schools, governments, music, theater, language).

How We Learn Our Culture

As we grow and develop, we learn to value the elements of our culture. We are not born with a certain taste in music, food, and automobiles. We learn to like or dislike the elements that make up our culture. We learn to adopt and appreciate the elements of our culture just as we learn anything: through role models and positive reinforcement. The process of communicating a group's culture from generation to generation is called **enculturation**. Your friends, colleagues, the media, and, most importantly, your family communicate information about these elements and advocate choices for you to make. How you celebrate holidays, your taste in clothing styles, and your religious beliefs are learned through the enculturation process.

Cultures are not static; they change as new information and new influences penetrate their stores of knowledge. We no longer believe that bathing is unhealthy, or that we can safely use makeup containing lead. These changes resulted from scientific discoveries. But other changes take place through **acculturation;** we acquire other approaches, beliefs, and values by coming into contact with other cultures. Today, acupuncturists and yoga, t'ai chi, and karate studios are commonplace in most cities across America. Taco shells are available in every supermarket, salsa sales now surpass ketchup sales, and Dunkin' Donuts sells bagels. In less obvious ways, "new" perspectives from other cultures have also influenced our thoughts, actions, and relationships.

Cultural Values

Identifying what a given group of people values or appreciates can provide insight into the behavior of an individual raised within that group. Although there are great differences among the world's **cultural values,** Geert Hofstede identifies four variables for measuring values that are significant in almost every culture[49] (see Table 4.2 on page 98). According to Hofstede, each culture places varying degrees of value on

- Masculine and feminine perspectives
- Avoidance of uncertainty
- Distribution of power
- Individualism

Though now dated, Hofstede's research remains one of the most comprehensive, data-based studies of cultural values.[50] He surveyed more than 100,000 employees of IBM in more than 50 countries; his research effort has yet to be duplicated or surpassed.

Masculine versus Feminine Perspectives

Some cultures emphasize traditional male values, whereas others place greater value on female perspectives. These values are not really about biological sex differences but about overarching approaches to interacting with others.

People from **masculine cultures** tend to value more traditional roles for both men and women. Masculine cultures also value achievement, assertiveness, heroism, and material wealth. Research reveals that men tend to approach communication from a content orientation, meaning that they view communication as functioning primarily for information exchange. Men talk when they have something to say. This is also consistent with the tendency of men to base their relationships, especially their male friendships, on sharing activities rather than talking.

Men and women from **feminine cultures** tend to value such things as caring for the less fortunate, being sensitive toward others, and enhancing the overall quality of life.[51] Women, as research suggests, tend to approach communication for the purpose of relating or connecting to others, of extending themselves to other people in order

enculturation. Process of communicating a group's culture from generation to generation.

acculturation. Process through which an individual acquires new approaches, beliefs, and values by coming into contact with other cultures.

cultural values. What a given group of people values or appreciates.

masculine culture. Culture that emphasizes achievement, assertiveness, heroism, and material wealth.

feminine culture. Culture that emphasizes relationships, caring for the less fortunate, and overall quality of life.

TABLE 4.2 Examples of Countries That Illustrate Four Cultural Values

Cultural Value	Examples of Countries That Scored Higher on This Cultural Value	Examples of Countries That Scored Lower on This Cultural Value
Masculinity: People from countries with higher masculinity scores prefer high achievement, men being in more assertive roles, and more clearly differentiated sex roles than do people from countries with lower scores on this cultural dimension.	Japan, Australia, Venezuela, Italy, Switzerland, Mexico, Ireland, Jamaica, Great Britain	Sweden, Norway, Netherlands, Denmark, Yugoslavia, Costa Rica, Finland, Chile, Portugal, Thailand
Uncertainty Avoidance: People from countries with higher uncertainty avoidance scores generally prefer to avoid uncertainty; they like to know what will happen next. People from countries with lower scores are more comfortable with uncertainty.	Greece, Portugal, Guatemala, Uruguay, Belgium, Japan, Yugoslavia, Peru, France, Argentina, Chile	Singapore, Jamaica, Denmark, Sweden, Hong Kong, Ireland, Great Britain, Malaysia, India, Philippines, United States, Canada
Power Distribution: People from countries with higher power distribution scores generally prefer greater power differences between people; they are generally more accepting of someone having authority and power than are people from countries with lower scores on this cultural dimension.	Malaysia, Guatemala, Panama, Philippines, Mexico, Venezuela, Arab countries, Ecuador, Indonesia, India	Austria, Israel, Denmark, New Zealand, Ireland, Sweden, Norway, Finland, Switzerland, Great Britain
Individualism: People from countries with higher individualism scores generally prefer individual accomplishment rather than collective or collaborative achievement.	United States, Australia, Great Britain, Canada, Netherlands, New Zealand, Italy, Belgium, Denmark, Sweden, France	Guatemala, Ecuador, Panama, Venezuela, Colombia, Indonesia, Pakistan, Costa Rica, Peru, Taiwan, South Korea

Source: Adapted from Geert Hofstede, *Cultures and Organizations: Software of the Mind* (London: McGraw-Hill, 1991).

to know them and be known by them.[52] What women talk about is less important than the fact that they're talking, because talking implies relationship.

Of course, rarely is a culture on the extreme end of the continuum; many are somewhere in between. For centuries, most countries in Europe, Asia, and the Americas have had masculine cultures. Men and their conquests dominate history books; men have been more prominent in leadership and decision making than women. But today many of these cultures are moving slowly toward the middle—legal and social rules are encouraging more gender balance and greater equality between masculine and feminine roles.

Tolerance of Uncertainty versus Avoidance of Uncertainty

Some cultures tolerate more ambiguity and uncertainty than others. Cultures in which people need certainty to feel secure are more likely to have and enforce rigid rules for

Applying Theory and Research

Uncertainty Reduction Theory

Uncertainty reduction theory, developed by Charles Berger and Richard Calabrese, helps explain how we seek to reduce our uncertainty during an initial meeting with strangers or when we find ourselves in a new situation.[53] In some respects, each of us is different from everyone else. The more different we are from others and the less we know about them, the more uncertainty and sometimes anxiety and fear we may have about other people.

Uncertainty reduction theory describes how we strategically interact with others to enhance our understanding of others so that strangers seem less strange to us. The theory predicts that high levels of uncertainty will increase information-seeking behavior, such as asking questions or doing research about a new place we may be visiting. As we become less uncertain and more certain, we use fewer information-seeking strategies because we have a better understanding of how to predict what will happen to us.[54]

When we are uncertain about someone else, we could use a passive strategy: observe the person to see if we can learn more about him or her and thus reduce our uncertainty. Another strategy to reduce our uncertainty of others is more active: We could ask others for information about the person who is unfamiliar to us. Or we could use an interactive strategy to try to reduce our uncertainty about someone by asking questions, self-disclosing, and listening for self-disclosures from the other person.

As we noted in Table 4.2, people in some cultures (such as people from Argentina, Chile, and Peru) prefer to avoid uncertainty. They would rather have straight answers and know whom they are talking to; they are uncomfortable with uncertainty. People in other cultures (like Canadians, the British, and Jamaicans) are typically more comfortable with uncertainty. They feel that eventually things will get sorted out and they can be patient and wait for things to be resolved. Although we caution that these are broad generalizations and are not true in each situation, we can nonetheless use such generalizations to test our assumptions and help unravel our uncertainty. Geert Hofstede suggests that people who dodge uncertainty by avoiding people who are different from themselves, and who are also more likely to visit places that are in their comfort zone rather than to seek new places to visit, operate from the framework that "What is different is dangerous."[55] Hofstede suspects that people in cultures with a low need to avoid uncertainty—that is, people who are more comfortable with uncertainty—would agree with the phrase, "What is different is interesting."

Applying the Research to Your Life

Your comfort level with strangers and people who are different from you may stem from your personal tolerance for uncertainty. If you generally prefer to avoid new places, especially places that are different from your current surroundings, you may also be someone who likes certainty and dislikes uncertainty. If you prefer certainty and you don't prefer ambiguity, you may be more likely to use communication strategies to manage the uncertainty or to avoid situations that create uncertainty. You'll be less likely to strike up a conversation with people who are different from yourself. If you are comfortable with uncertainty, you will be not quite as anxious, nervous, or upset if you don't have all of the answers; you'll likely be more patient finding out information about a stranger. The goal of inviting you to consider your own approach to uncertainty is not to change your tolerance for uncertainty, but to help you understand why and how you behave toward others who are different from you. Consider the following questions to help you apply uncertainty reduction theory to your interactions with others:

1. On a scale of 1 to 10 (with 10 being very comfortable with uncertainty and 1 being very uncomfortable with uncertainty), how would you rate your own level of comfort with uncertainty about others?
2. Do you actively try to reduce your uncertainty level, or do you just live with not knowing information about others, especially others who are different from you?
3. What strategies do you use to learn about others who are different from you? Do you prefer to use passive, active, or interactive strategies to reduce your uncertainty?
4. Do you actively avoid people who are different from you?
5. Would you rather visit new places or return to surroundings that are comfortable and familiar?

Source: C. R. Berger and R. J. Calabrese, "Some Explorations in Initial Interactions and Beyond: Toward a Developmental Theory of Interpersonal Communication," *Human Communication Research,* 1 (1975): 99–112.

Many cultures have traditionally put a high value on masculine domination of women, but today there is a gradual trend toward greater equality between male and female roles.

behavior and develop more elaborate codes of conduct. People from cultures with a greater tolerance for uncertainty have more relaxed, informal expectations for others. "Go with the flow" and "It will sort itself out" are phrases that describe their attitudes. Research suggests that people from Portugal, Greece, Peru, Belgium, and Japan have high certainty needs, but people from Scandinavian countries tend to tolerate uncertainty.[56]

Centralized versus Decentralized Distribution of Power

Some cultures value an equal or decentralized distribution of power, whereas others accept a concentration of hierarchical power in a centralized government and other organizations. In cultures in which people prefer a more centralized approach to power, hierarchical bureaucracies are common, and people expect some individuals to have more power than others. Russia, France, and China are all high on the concentrated power scale. Those that often strive for greater equality and distribution of power and control include many (but not all) citizens of Australia, Denmark, New Zealand, and Israel. People from these latter countries tend to minimize differences in power between people.

Individual versus Group Achievement

Traditionally, North Americans champion individual accomplishments and achievements. People from Asian backgrounds often value collective or group achievement more highly. One researcher summed up the American goal system this way:

> Chief among the virtues claimed . . . is self-realization. Each person is viewed as having a unique set of talents and potentials. The translation of these potentials into actuality considered the highest purpose to which one can devote one's life.[57]

Conversely, in a collectivistic culture, people strive to attain goals for all members of the family, group, or community. In Kenyan tribes, for example,

Recap: Cultural Values

Masculine and Feminine	• Masculine cultures value achievement, assertiveness, heroism, material wealth, and more traditional sex roles. • Feminine cultures value relationships, caring for the less fortunate, overall quality of life, and less traditional distinctions between sex roles.
Uncertainty and Certainty	• Cultures that value certainty do not like ambiguity and value feeling secure. • Cultures that value uncertainty are comfortable with ambiguity and less information.
Decentralized and Centralized Power	• Centralized power cultures value having power in the hands of a small number of people. • Decentralized power cultures favor equality and an even distribution of power in government and organizations.
Individualistic and Collectivistic	• Individualistic cultures value individual achievement and accomplishments. • Collectivistic cultures value group and team collaboration.

> [N]obody is an isolated individual. Rather, his [or her] uniqueness is a secondary fact. . . . In this new system group activities are dominant, responsibility is shared, and accountability is collective. . . . Because of the emphasis on collectivity, harmony and cooperation among the group tends to be emphasized more than individual function and responsibility.[58]

Individualistic cultures tend to be more loosely knit socially; individuals feel responsible for taking care of themselves and their immediate families.[59] In collectivistic cultures, individuals expect more support from others; they also experience more loyalty to and from the community. Because collectivistic cultures place more value on "we" than "I," teamwork approaches usually succeed better in their workplaces. U.S. businesses have tried to adopt some of Japan's successful team strategies for achieving high productivity.

cultural context. Information not explicitly communicated through language but through environmental or nonverbal cues.

high-context culture. Culture that derives much information from nonverbal and environmental cues.

Cultural Contexts

Individuals from different cultures use cues from the **cultural context** to varying degrees to enhance messages and meaning. This insight led anthropologist Edward T. Hall to categorize cultures as either high- or low-context.[60] As shown in Figure 4.1, in **high-context cultures,** nonverbal cues are extremely important in interpreting

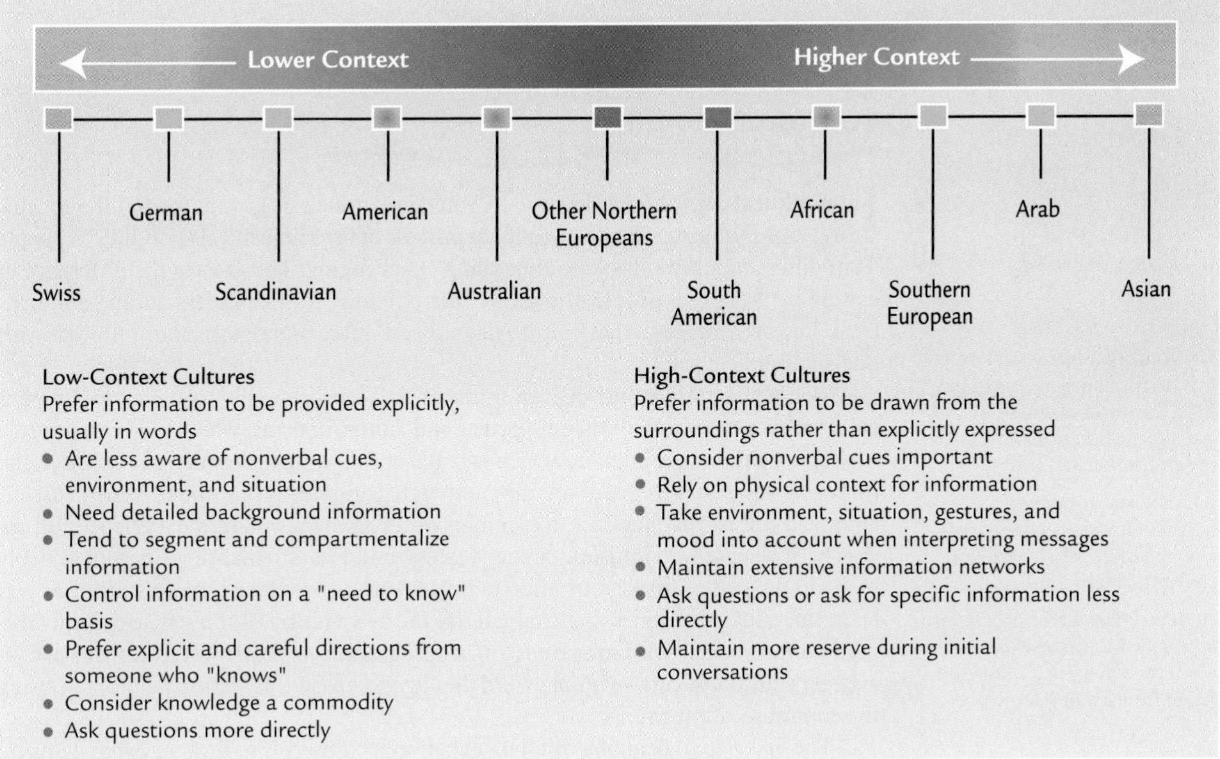

FIGURE 4.1

High/Low Contexts: Where Different Cultures Fall on the Context Scale

Source: From *Beyond Culture* by Edward T. Hall, copyright © 1976, 1981 by Edward T. Hall. Used by permission of Doubleday, a division of Random House, Inc.

messages. **Low-context cultures** rely more explicitly on language and use fewer contextual cues to send and interpret information. Individuals from high-context cultures may perceive people from low-context cultures as less attractive, knowledgeable, and trustworthy, because they violate unspoken rules of dress, conduct, and communication. Individuals from low-context cultures often are not skilled in interpreting unspoken, contextual messages.[61]

The Nature of Culture

Cultural Elements	Things and ideas that represent profound aspects of cultural influence, such as art, music, schools, and belief systems
Cultural Values	What a culture reveres and holds important
Cultural Contexts	Information not explicitly communicated through language but gleaned from environmental or nonverbal cues. High-context cultures (such as Japanese, Chinese, Korean) derive much information from these cues. Low-context cultures (such as North American, Western European) rely more heavily on words.

Barriers to Effective Intercultural Communication

Intercultural communication occurs when individuals or groups from different cultures communicate. The transactional process of listening and responding to people from different cultural backgrounds can be challenging. The greater the difference in culture between two people, the greater the potential for misunderstanding and mistrust. Research suggests that culture has a direct effect on how we communicate with one another.[62]

Misunderstanding and miscommunication occur between people from different cultures because of different coding rules and cultural norms, which play a major role in shaping patterns of interaction. The greater the difference between the cultures, the more likely it is that they will use different verbal and nonverbal codes. When you encounter a culture that has little in common with your own, you may experience **culture shock,** or a sense of confusion, anxiety, stress, and loss. If you are visiting or actually living in the new culture, your uncertainty and stress may take time to subside as you learn the values and codes that characterize the new culture. But if you are simply trying to communicate with someone from a background very different from your own—even on your home turf—you may find the suggestions in this section helpful in closing the communication gap.[63]

The first step to bridging differences between cultures is to find out what hampers effective communication. What keeps people from connecting with others from other cultures? Sometimes, it is different meanings created by different languages or by different interpretations of nonverbal messages. Sometimes, it is the inability to stop focusing on oneself and begin focusing on the other. We'll examine some of these barriers first, then discuss strategies and skills for overcoming them.

low-context culture. Culture that derives much information from the words of a message and less information from nonverbal and environmental cues.

intercultural communication. Communication between or among people who have different cultural traditions.

culture shock. Feelings of stress and anxiety a person experiences when encountering a culture different from his or her own.

Ethnocentrism

Marilyn had always been intrigued by Russia. Her dream was to travel the country by train, spending time in small villages as well as exploring the cultural riches of Moscow, Pyatigorsk, and St. Petersburg. Her first day in Russia was a disappointment, however. When she arrived in Moscow, she joined a tour touting the cultural traditions of Russia. When the tour bus stopped at Sparrow Hills, affording the visitors a breathtaking hilltop view of the Moscow skyline, she was perplexed and mildly shocked to see a woman dressed in an elegant wedding gown mounted on horseback and galloping through the parking lot. Men in suits were cheering her on as a crowd of tipsy revelers set off fireworks and danced wildly to a brass band. "What kind of people are these?" sniffed Marilyn.

"Oh," said the tour guide, "it is our custom to come here to celebrate immediately following the wedding ceremony."

"But in public with such raucousness?" queried Marilyn.

"It is our tradition," said the guide.

"What a backward culture. They're nothing but a bunch of peasants!" pronounced Marilyn, who was used to more refined nuptial celebrations at a country club or an exclusive hotel.

For the rest of the tour, Marilyn judged every Russian behavior as inferior to that of Westerners. That first experience colored her perceptions, and her ethnocentric view served as a barrier to effective interpersonal communication with the Russian people she met.

Colorful celebrations like this local festival in Bali can reinforce healthy ethnic pride. But if ethnic pride is taken to extremes, the resulting ethnocentrism may act as a barrier between groups.

Ethnocentrism stems from a conviction that our own cultural traditions and assumptions are superior to those of others. It is the opposite of an other-orientation that embraces and appreciates the elements that give another culture meaning. This kind of cultural snobbism is one of the fastest ways to create a barrier that inhibits rather than enhances communication.

The concept of ethnocentrism is not new. One hundred years ago, W. G. Sumner defined it as "the technical name of this view of things in which one's own group is the center of everything and all others are scaled and rated with reference to it."[64] Many scholars have found that virtually all cultural groups are ethnocentric to some degree.[65] Some even argue that it's not always bad to see one's own cultural group as superior; ethnocentric tendency enhances group pride and patriotism and encourages cultural traditions.[66] A problem occurs, however, when a group views its own preferences as *always* the best way. Extreme ethnocentrism creates a barrier between the group and others.

Different Communication Codes

You are on your first trip to Los Angeles. As you step off the bus and look around for Hollywood Boulevard, you realize you have gotten off at the wrong stop. You see what looks like an old-fashioned corner grocery store with "Bodega" painted on a red sign. So you walk in and ask the man behind the counter, "How do I get to Hollywood Boulevard, please?"

"*No hablo inglés,*" says the man, smiling and shrugging his shoulders. But he points to a transit map pasted on the wall behind the counter.

ethnocentrism. Belief that your cultural traditions and assumptions are superior to those of others.

Understanding Diversity

Ethnocentric Thinking

All good people agree,
And all good people say,
All nice people like Us, are We,
And everyone else is They.

In a few short lines, Rudyard Kipling captured the essence of what sociologists and anthropologists call ethnocentric thinking. Members of all societies tend to believe that "All nice people like Us, are We. . . ." They find comfort in the familiar and often denigrate or distrust others. Of course, with training and experience in other climes, they may learn to transcend their provincialism, placing themselves in others' shoes. Or, as Kipling put it,

. . . if you cross over the sea,
Instead of over the way,
You may end by (think of it!)
looking on We
As only a sort of They.

In a real sense, a main lesson of the sociology of intergroup relations is to begin to "cross over the sea," to learn to understand why other people think and act as they do and to be able to empathize with their perspectives.

Source: Adapted from Faun B. Evans, Barbara Gleason, and Mark Wiley, *Cultural Tapestry: Readings for a Pluralistic Society* (New York: HarperCollins, 1992).

Today, even when you travel within the United States, you are likely to encounter people who do not speak your language. Obviously, this kind of intercultural difference poses a formidable communication challenge. And even when you do speak the same language as someone else, he or she may come from a place where the words and gestures have different meanings. Research has found that your culture and ethnic background have a direct effect on the way you listen to information from others.[67] Ultimately, your ability to communicate effectively and appropriately depends on whether you can understand each other's verbal and nonverbal codes.

In the preceding example, although the man behind the counter did not understand your exact words, he noted the cut of your clothing, your backpack, and your anxiety, and he deduced that you were asking directions. And you could understand what his gesture toward the transit map meant. Unfortunately, not every communication between speakers of two different languages is this successful.

Even when language is translated, meaning can be missed or mangled. Note the following examples of mistranslated advertisements:

- "Body by Fisher" in a General Motors auto ad became "Corpse by Fisher" in Flemish.
- A Colgate-Palmolive toothpaste named "Cue" was advertised in France before anyone realized that *Cue* also happened to be the name of a widely circulated pornographic book about oral sex.
- Pepsi-Cola's "Come Alive with Pepsi" campaign, when it was translated for the Taiwanese market, conveyed the unsettling news that "Pepsi brings your ancestors back from the grave."
- Parker Pen could not advertise its famous "Jotter" ballpoint pen in some languages because the translation sounded like "jockstrap" pen.
- One American airline operating in Brazil advertised that it had plush "rendezvous lounges" on its jets, unaware that in Portuguese (the language of Brazil), *rendezvous* implies a special room for making love.[68]

Building Your Skills

Assessing Your Ethnocentrism

The following measure of ethnocentrism was developed by communication researchers James Neuliep and James McCroskey. Answer the following questions honestly.

Directions: This instrument is composed of twenty-four statements concerning your feelings about your culture and other cultures. In the space provided to the left of each item, indicate the degree to which the statement applies to you by marking whether you (5) strongly agree, (4) agree, (3) are neutral, (2) disagree, or (1) strongly disagree with the statement. There are no right or wrong answers. Work quickly and record your first response.

____ 1. Most other cultures are backward compared with my culture.

____ 2. People in other cultures have a better lifestyle than we do in my culture.

____ 3. Most people would be happier if they didn't live like people do in my culture.

____ 4. My culture should be the role model for other cultures.

____ 5. Lifestyles in other cultures are just as valid as those in my culture.

____ 6. Other cultures should try to be more like my culture.

____ 7. I'm not interested in the values and customs of other cultures.

____ 8. It is not wise for other cultures to look up to my culture.

____ 9. People in my culture could learn a lot from people in other cultures.

____ 10. Most people from other cultures just don't know what's good for them.

____ 11. People from my culture act strange and unusual when they go into other cultures.

____ 12. I have little respect for the values and customs of other cultures.

____ 13. Most people would be happier if they lived like people in my culture.

____ 14. People in my culture have just about the best lifestyles of anywhere.

____ 15. My culture is backward compared with most other cultures.

____ 16. My culture is a poor role model for other cultures.

____ 17. Lifestyles in other cultures are not as valid as those in my culture.

____ 18. My culture should try to be more like other cultures.

____ 19. I'm very interested in the values and customs of other cultures.

____ 20. Most people in my culture just don't know what is good for them.

____ 21. People in other cultures could learn a lot from people in my culture.

____ 22. Other cultures are smart to look up to my culture.

____ 23. I respect the values and customs of other cultures.

____ 24. People from other cultures act strange and unusual when they come into my culture.

Scoring: To determine your ethnocentrism, *reverse* your score for items 2, 3, 5, 8, 9, 11, 15, 16, 18, 19, 20, and 23. For these items, 5 = 1, 4 = 2, 3 = 3, 2 = 4, and 1 = 5. That is, if your original score was a 5, change it to a 1. If your original score was a 4, change it to a 2, and so forth. Once you have reversed your score for these twelve items, add up all twenty-four scores. This is your generalized ethnocentrism score. Scores greater than 80 indicate high ethnocentrism. Scores of 50 and below indicate low ethnocentrism.

Source: J. W. Neuliep and J. C. McCroskey, "The Development of a U.S. and Generalized Ethnocentrism Scale," *Communication Research Reports,* 14 (1997): 393.

Stereotyping and Prejudice

All Europeans dress fashionably.

All Asians are good at math.

All Americans like to drive big cars.

These statements are stereotypes. They are all inaccurate. As we discussed in Chapter 3, to **stereotype** someone is to push him or her into an inflexible, all-encompassing category. Our tendency to simplify sensory stimuli can lead us to adopt stereotypes as we interpret and label the behavior of others.[69] As we also noted in Chapter 3, there is evidence that we thin slice—make judgments about others in just seconds based on nonverbal cues. One study found that after viewing just 20 seconds of silent videotape, subjects made stereotypical, biased racial judgments of others.[70] Stereotypes become a barrier to effective intercultural communication when we fail to consider the uniqueness of individuals, groups, or events. Two anthropologists suggest that every person is, in some respects, (1) like all other people, (2) like some other people, and (3) like no other people.[71] The challenge when meeting others is to sort out how they are alike and how they are unique.

Can stereotypes play any useful role in interpersonal communication? It may sometimes be appropriate to draw on stereotypes, or generalizations drawn from limited instances. If, for example, you are alone and lost in a large city at two o'clock in the morning and another car aggressively taps your rear bumper, it would be prudent to try to drive away as quickly as possible, rather than to hop out of your car to make a new acquaintance. You would be wise to pre-judge that the other driver might have some malicious intent. In most situations, however, **prejudice**—a judgment or opinion of someone formed on the basis of stereotypes or before you know all the facts—inhibits effective communication, especially if your labels are inaccurate or assume superiority on your part.[72]

Certain prejudices are widespread. Although there are slightly more females than males in the world, one study found that even when a male and a female hold the same type of job, the male's job is considered more prestigious than the female's.[73] Today, gender and racial discrimination in hiring and promotion is illegal in the United States. But some people's opinions have not kept pace with the law.

stereotype. To place a person or group of persons into an inflexible, all-encompassing category.

prejudice. A judgment or opinion of someone formed before you know all of the facts or the background of that person.

Assuming Similarities

Just as it is inaccurate to assume that all people who belong to another social group or class are worlds apart from you, it is usually erroneous to assume that others act and think just as you do. Cultural differences *do* exist. Research and our own observations support the commonsense conclusion that people from different cultural and ethnic backgrounds do speak and behave differently.[74] Even if they appear to be like you, all people are not alike. Although this statement is not profound, it has profound implications. People often make the mistake of assuming that others value the same things they do, maintaining a self-focused perspective instead of an other-oriented one. As you saw in Chapter 3, focusing on superficial factors such as appearance, clothing, and even a person's occupation can lead to false impressions. Instead, you must take the time to explore a person's background and cultural values before you can determine what you really have in common.

Assuming Differences

Although it may seem to contradict what we just noted about assuming similarities, another barrier to intercultural communication is to automatically assume that another person is different from you. It can be just as detrimental to communication to assume someone is different from you as it is to assume that others are similar to you. The fact is, human beings *do* share common experiences, while at the same time there are differences.

The point of noting that humans have similarities as well as differences is not to diminish the role of culture as a key element that influences communication, but to recognize that despite cultural differences, we are all members of the human family. The words *communication* and *common* resemble one another. We communicate effectively and appropriately when we can connect to others based on what we hold in common. Identifying common cultural issues and similarities can also help us establish common ground with others.

BE OTHER-ORIENTED

How are we all alike? Cultural anthropologist Donald Brown has compiled a list of hundreds of "surface" universals of behavior and language use that have been identified. According to Brown, people in all cultures[75]

- Have beliefs about death.
- Have a childhood fear of strangers.
- Divide labor on the basis of sex.
- Experience envy, pain, jealousy, shame, and pride.
- Use facial expressions to express emotions.
- Have rules for etiquette.
- Experience empathy.
- Value some degree of collaboration or cooperation.
- Experience conflict and seek to manage or mediate conflict.

Of course, all cultures do not have the same beliefs about death, or divide labor according to sex in the same ways, but all cultures address these issues. Communication researcher David Kale believes that all humans seek to protect the dignity and worth of other people.[76] Thus, he suggests, all people can identify with the struggle to enhance their own dignity and worth, although different cultures express that in different ways. A second common value that Kale notes is the search for a world at peace. Intercultural communication scholars Larry Samovar and Richard Porter suggest that there are other elements that cultures share.[77] They note that people from all cultures seek physical pleasure as well as emotional and psychological pleasure and avoid personal harm. It's true that each culture and each person decide what is pleasurable or painful; nonetheless, Samovar and Porter argue, all people operate within this pleasure–pain continuum.

BE OTHER-ORIENTED

What are the practical implications of trying to identify common human values or characteristics? Here's one implication: If you are speaking about an issue on which you and another person fundamentally differ, identifying a larger common value—such as the value of peace, prosperity, or the importance of family—can help you find a foothold so that the other person will at least listen to your ideas. It's useful, we believe, not just to categorize our differences but also to explore how human beings are similar to one another. Discovering how we are alike can provide a starting point for human understanding. Yes, we are all different, but we share things in common as well. Communication effectiveness is diminished when we assume we're all different from one another in *every* aspect, just as communication is affected negatively if we assume we're all alike.[78] We're more complicated than that.

Recap
Barriers to Effective Intercultural Communication

Ethnocentricism	Assuming that one's own culture and cultural traditions are superior to those of others
Different Communication Codes	Allowing differences in language and the interpretation of nonverbal cues to lead to misunderstanding
Stereotyping and Prejudice	Rigidly categorizing and prejudging others based on limited information
Assuming Similarity	Assuming that other people respond to situations as we do; failing to acknowledge and consider differences in culture and background
Assuming Differences	Assuming that other people are always different from and have nothing in common with us; failing to explore common values and experiences that can serve as bridges to better understanding

Improving Intercultural Competence

Eleanor Roosevelt once said, "We have to face the fact that either all of us are going to die together or we are going to live together, and if we are to live together we have to talk."[79] In essence, she was saying that to overcome differences people need effective communication skills. It is not enough just to point to the barriers to effective intercultural communication and say, "Don't do that." Although identifying the causes of misunderstanding is a good first step to becoming interculturally competent, most people need help with specific strategies to help them overcome these barriers. In this book and in this chapter, we want to focus attention on the interpersonal communication strategies that can lead to intercultural communication competence.

intercultural communication competence. Ability to adapt one's behavior toward another in ways that are appropriate to the other person's culture.

Intercultural communication competence is the ability to adapt your behavior toward another in ways that are appropriate to the other person's culture.[80] To be in-

Interpersonal Communication and Emotion Connecting Heart to Heart

Are There Universal Emotions?

Do all of us experience and express emotions in the same way? The question of whether there are universal emotions or universal ways of expressing emotions has been studied and debated by scholars for decades.

One widely debated analysis, developed by psychologist Robert Plutchik and shown in Figure 4.2, suggests that there are eight primary human emotions: joy, acceptance, fear, surprise, sadness, disgust, anger, and anticipation.[81] These eight primary emotions can combine to produce eight secondary emotions. Although not all researchers agree that the eight primary emotions are the definitive set of human emotions, a host of scholars argue that yes, there is a set of basic emotions that all humans experience.[82] They believe that through the biological process of evolution, all humans have a core set of emotional experiences. The debate about whether there are universal emotions boils down to whether you believe that nature (biology) or nurture (culture) determines common, core emotions. Those who think we are "wired" or programmed for common emotions believe that biology is the predominant influence in determining how we both interpret emotional expression and respond emotionally.

Researcher Paul Ekman has spent many years working with several colleagues to determine if people from a wide variety of cultures all interpret facial expressions of emotion in the same way. His conclusion: "Our evidence, and that of others, shows only that when people are experiencing strong emotions, are not making any attempt to mask their expressions, the expression will be the same regardless of age, race, culture, sex and education. That is a powerful finding."[83]

Other researchers have reached a different conclusion.[84] When critically examining the evidence of Paul Ekman and others, they have found that culture does play an important role in determining how facial expressions are displayed and interpreted.[85] There is some evidence, for example, that people from collectivistic cultures are socialized to not express emotions that would disrupt harmony in the group. Specifically, people with collectivist values may work harder at regulating how they express such emotions as anger, contempt, and disgust—emotions that would hinder group peace.[86] And people from individualistic cultures may feel that they have greater cultural license to express these emotions more freely.

Why is it important to know whether emotional expression and interpretation are common to all humans or are learned, just as other elements of culture are learned? If there are indeed universal human attributes common to all people, their existence provides powerful additional evidence for the theory of evolution. It also has implications for the development of a truly human theory of communication.

So are there universal expressions and interpretations of human emotions? Among experts, consensus is emerging that all humans have in common a biologically based tendency to express emotions, while cultural differences exist in how some emotions are interpreted. As one team of emotion research experts put it, "It is clear that emotional-relevant faces are interpreted with some consistency across cultures, suggesting a universal link between facial position and at least some aspect or correlate of emotion. However, it is also apparent that variations exist both within and across societies in the extent of this consistency."[87]

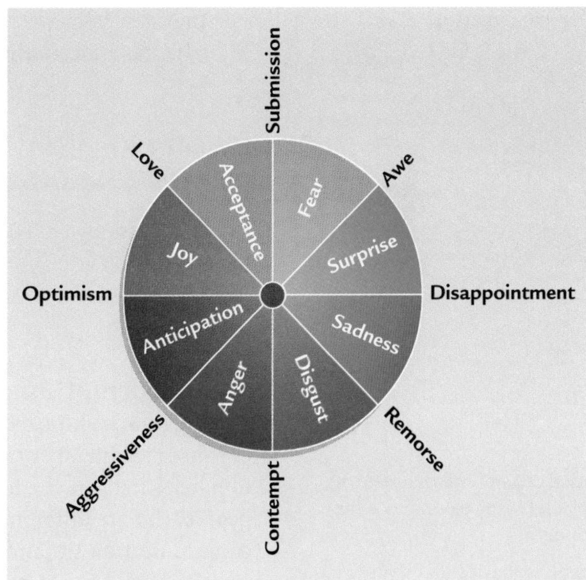

FIGURE **4.2**

Robert Plutchik's Model of Emotions From Robert Plutchik, *Emotion: A Psychoevolutionary Synthesis,* © 1980. Published by Allyn & Bacon, Boston, MA. Copyright © by Pearson Education. By permission of the publisher.

terculturally competent is to be more than merely aware of what is appropriate or simply sensitive to cultural differences. To be interculturally competent is to *behave* toward others in ways that are appropriate. But prior to behaving appropriately, an individual needs to have knowledge about another culture and the motivation to adapt or modify his or her behavior.

Developing Bridging Strategies

Three strategy sets to help you bridge differences between yourself and people from different cultural backgrounds—developing appropriate knowledge, developing motivation, and developing skill—are based on our understanding of how to be a competent communicator.[88]

- *Develop Appropriate Knowledge.* One of the barriers to effective intercultural communication is having different communication codes. Improving your knowledge of how others communicate can reduce the impact of this barrier. We offer strategies to help you learn more about other cultures by actively pursuing information about others.
- *Develop Motivation.* **Motivation** is an internal state of readiness to respond to something. A competent communicator wants to learn and improve. Developing strategies to appreciate others who are different from you may help you appreciate different cultural approaches to communication and relationships. We suggest you endeavor to be tolerant of uncertainty and to avoid knee-jerk negative evaluations of others.
- *Develop Skill.* Developing **skill** in adapting to others focuses on specific behaviors that can help overcome barriers and cultural differences. As we discussed in Chapter 1, becoming other-oriented is critical to the process of relating to others.

BE OTHER-ORIENTED

Developing Knowledge: Strategies to Understand Others Who Differ from Us

Knowledge is power. To increase your knowledge of others who are different from you, we suggest that you actively seek information about others, ask questions and listen for the answers, and establish common ground. Let's discuss these strategies in more detail.

Seek Information

Seeking information about a culture or even about a specific communication situation enhances the quality of intercultural communication. Why? Because seeking information helps manage the uncertainty and anxiety that we may feel when we interact with people who are different from us.[89] Sometimes we feel uncomfortable in intercultural communication situations because we just don't know how to behave. We aren't sure what our role should be; we can't quite predict what will happen when we communicate with others because we're in a new or strange situation. Seeking new information can help counter inaccurate information and prejudice.

Every person has a **world view** based on cultural beliefs about the universe and key issues such as death, God, and the meaning of life.[90] According to communication scholar Carley Dodd, "A culture's world view involves finding out how the culture perceives the role of various forces in explaining why events occur as they do in a social setting."[91] These beliefs shape our thoughts, language, and behavior. Only through intercultural communication can we hope to understand how each individual views the

motivation. Internal state of readiness to respond to something.

skill. Behavior that improves the effectiveness or quality of communication with others.

world view. Individual perceptions or perceptions by a culture or group of people about key beliefs and issues, such as death, God, and the meaning of life, which influence interaction with others.

world. As you speak to a person from another culture, think of yourself as a detective watching for implied, often unspoken messages that provide information about the values, norms, roles, and rules of that person's culture.

You can also prepare yourself by studying the culture. If you are going to another country, courses in the history, anthropology, art, or geography of that place can give you a head start on communicating with understanding. Learn not only from books and magazines, but also from individuals whenever possible.

Given the inextricable link between language and culture, the more you learn about another language, the more you will understand the traditions and customs of the culture. Politicians have long known the value of using even a few words of their constituents' language. President Kennedy impressed and excited a crowd in Berlin by proclaiming, "Ich bin ein Berliner" ("I am a Berliner"). Even though his diction was less than perfect, he conveyed the message that he identified with his listeners. Speaking even a few words can signify your interest in learning about the language and culture of others.

Ask Questions and Listen Effectively

When you encounter a person from another background, asking questions and then pausing to listen is a simple technique for gathering information and also for confirming the accuracy of your expectations and assumptions. For example, some cultures, such as the Japanese culture, have clear expectations regarding gift giving. It is better to ask what these expectations are than to assume that your good old down-home manners will see you through.

When you ask questions, be prepared to share information about yourself, too. Otherwise, your partner may feel that you are interrogating him or her as a way to gain power and dominance rather than from a sincere desire to learn about cultural rules and norms.

Communication helps to reduce the uncertainty that is present in any relationship.[92] When you meet people for the first time, you may be uncertain about who they are and what they like and dislike. When you communicate with someone from another culture, the uncertainty level is particularly high. As you begin to interact, you exchange information that helps you develop greater understanding. If you continue to ask questions, eventually you will feel less uncertain about how the person is likely to behave.

Just asking questions and sharing information about yourself are not sufficient to bridge differences in culture and background. It is equally important to listen to what others share. In the next chapter, we provide specific strategies for improving your listening skills.

Develop a "Third Culture"

Several researchers suggest that one of the best ways to enhance understanding when communicating over a period of time with someone from a different cultural background is to develop a **third culture.** This is created when the communication partners join aspects of separate cultures to create a third, "new" culture that is more comprehensive and inclusive than either of the two separate cultures.[93]

According to one intercultural communication researcher, F. L. Casmir, a third-culture approach to enhancing the quality of intercultural communication occurs when the people involved in the conversation construct "a mutually beneficial interactive environment in which individuals from two different cultures can function in a way beneficial to all involved."[94]

How do you go about developing a third culture? In a word: talk. Developing a third culture does not just happen all at once; it evolves from dialogue. The communicators construct a third culture *together.* After they realize that cultural differences may divide them, they may develop a third culture by making a conscious effort to develop common assumptions and common perspectives for the relationship. Dialogue,

third culture. Common ground established when people from separate cultures create a third, "new," more comprehensive and inclusive culture.

In families with members from different cultures, creating a third culture that is more inclusive than the separate cultures of the family members can eliminate some communication barriers.

negotiation, conversation, interaction, and a willingness to let go of old ways and experiment with new frameworks are the keys to developing a third culture as a basis for a new relationship.

Developing a third-culture mentality can reduce our tendency to approach cultural differences from an "us-versus-them" point of view. Rather than trying to eliminate communication barriers stemming from two different sets of experiences, adopting a third-culture framework creates a new understanding of the other on the part of both participants.[95]

Consider the example of Marsha, a businesswoman from Lincoln, Nebraska, and Tomiko, a businesswoman from Tokyo, Japan. In the context of their business relationship, it would be difficult for them to develop a comprehensive understanding of each other's cultural traditions. However, if they openly acknowledged the most significant of these differences and sought to create a third culture by identifying explicit rules and norms for their interaction, they might be able to develop a more comfortable relationship with each other.

As described by communication researcher Benjamin Broome, the third culture "is characterized by unique values and norms that may not have existed prior to the dyadic [two-person] relationship."[96] Broome labels the essence of this new relationship **relational empathy,** which permits varying degrees of understanding, rather than requiring complete comprehension of another's culture or emotions.

relational empathy. Essence of a relationship that permits varying degrees of understanding, rather than requiring complete comprehension of another's culture or emotions.

The cultural context includes all the elements of the culture (learned behaviors and rules, or "mental software") that affect the interaction. Do you come from a culture that takes a tea break each afternoon at 4 P.M.? Does your culture value hard work and achievement, or relaxation and enjoyment? Creating a third culture acknowledges the different cultural contexts and interactions participants have experienced and seeks to develop a new context for future interaction.

Improving Intercultural Competence: Developing Knowledge to Enhance Understanding

Seek Information About the Culture	Learn about a culture's world view.
Ask Questions and Listen	Reduce uncertainty by asking for clarification and listening to the answer.
Develop a Third Culture	Create common ground.

Developing Motivation: Strategies to Accept Others

Competent communicators want to learn and improve. They are motivated to enhance their ability to relate to others and to accept others as they are. A key to accepting others is to develop a positive attitude of tolerance and acceptance of those who are different from you. We suggest three strategies to help improve your acceptance and appreciation of others who differ from you: Tolerate ambiguity, develop mindfulness, and avoid negative judgments of others.

Tolerate Ambiguity

Communicating with someone from another culture produces uncertainty. It may take time and several exchanges to clarify a message. Be patient and try to expand your capacity to tolerate ambiguity if you are speaking to someone with a markedly different world view.

When Ken and Rita visited Miami from Peoria, they asked their hotel concierge to direct them to a church of their faith, and they wound up at one with a predominantly Haitian congregation. They were not prepared for the exuberant chanting and verbal interchanges with the minister during the sermon. They weren't certain whether they should join in or simply sit quietly and observe. Ken whispered to Rita, "I'm not sure what to do. Let's just watch and see what is expected of us." In the end, they chose to sit and clap along with the chanting rather than to become actively involved in the worship. Rita felt uncomfortable and conspicuous, though, and had to fight the urge to bolt. But after the service, several members of the congregation came up to greet Ken and Rita, invited them to lunch, and expressed great happiness in their visit. "You know," said Rita later in the day, "I'm so grateful that we sat through our discomfort. We might never have met those terrific people. Now I understand why their worship is so noisy—they're just brimming with joy."

Develop Mindfulness

"Our life is what our thoughts make it," said Marcus Aurelius in *Meditations.* As we noted in Chapter 3, to be mindful is to be consciously aware of what you are doing, thinking, and sensing. With regard to cultural differences, to be **mindful** is to acknowledge that there is a connection between thoughts and deeds when you interact with a person from a background different from your own. William Gudykunst suggests that being mindful is one of the best ways to approach any new cultural encounter.[97] Remember that there are and will be cultural differences, and try to keep them in your consciousness. Also try to consider the other individual's frame of reference or world view and to use his or her cultural priorities and assumptions when you are communicating.[98] Adapt your behavior to minimize cultural noise and distortion.

You can become more mindful through self-talk, something we discussed in Chapter 2. Self-talk consists of rational messages you tell yourself to help you manage your emotions or discomfort with a certain situation. Imagine that you are working on a group project with several of your classmates. One classmate, Suji, was born in Iran. When interacting with you, he consistently stands about a foot away from you, whereas you are more comfortable with three or four feet between you. When Suji encroaches on your space, you could be mindful of the reason for this behavior by mentally noting, "Suji sure likes to get close to people when he talks to them. This may represent a practice in his culture." This self-talk message makes you consciously aware that there may be a difference in your interaction styles. If you still feel uncomfortable, instead of blurting out, "Hey, man, why so close?" you could express your own preferences with an "I" message: "Suji, I'd prefer a bit more space between us when we talk."

mindful. Aware of cultural differences and the connection between thoughts and deeds in one's interactions with someone from a background different from one's own.

Avoid Negative Judgments About Another Culture

American tourist on her first visit to France:	Can you believe it? How repulsive! These people actually eat horse meat and think it's a delicacy.

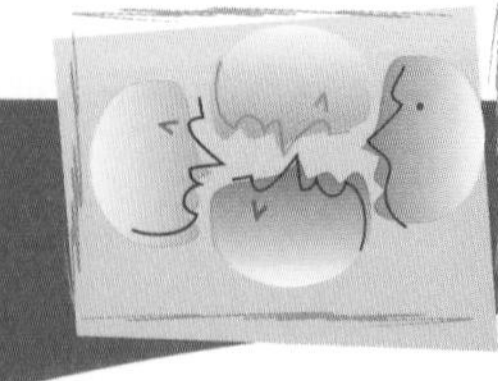

Understanding Diversity

Tao: A Universal Moral Code

It's clear that there are cultural differences among the world's people and that these differences have existed since there have been people. Anthropologists and communication scholars who study intercultural communication teach us the value of adapting to cultural differences in order to understand others better. But are there any universal values that are or have been embraced by all humans? The question is not a new one; scholars, theologians, and many others have debated for millennia whether there are any universal underpinnings for all human societies. In Chapter 3 we noted that social psychologists Penelope Brown and Stephen Levinson suggest that people from all cultures have a universal need to be treated with politeness.[99] Are there other needs and values that all humans share? To uncover such commonalities is to develop a truly human communication theory rather than a theory that applies to a specific cultural context.

C. S. Lewis, a British scholar, author, and educator who taught at both Oxford University and Cambridge University, argued that there are universal ethical and moral principles that undergird all societies of civilized people, regardless of their religious beliefs, cultural background, or government structure. He suggested that the existence of Natural Laws, or what he called a *Tao*—a universal moral code—informs human ethical decisions. In his book *The Abolition of Man,* Lewis presented eight universal principles, or laws.[100] He did not claim that all societies have followed these laws—many of them have been clearly violated and continue to be violated today—but he did suggest they provide a bedrock of values against which all societies may be measured. Here are his eight laws:

1. The Law of General Beneficence: Do not murder, be dishonest, or take from others what does not belong to us.
2. The Law of Special Beneficence: Value your family members.
3. Duties to Parents, Elders, and Ancestors: Especially hold your parents, those who are a generation older than you, and your ancestors with special honor and esteem.
4. Duties to Children and Posterity: We have a special obligation to respect the rights of the young and to value those who will come after us.
5. The Law of Justice: Honor the basic human rights of others; each person is of worth.
6. The Law of Good Faith and Veracity: Keep your promises, and do not lie.
7. The Law of Mercy: Be compassionate to those less fortunate than you are.
8. The Law of Magnanimity: Avoid unnecessary violence against other people.

To support his argument that these are universal values, Lewis offered quotations from several well-known sources, including religious, historical, and political writings, both contemporary and centuries-old. Lewis implied that these eight laws may be viewed as a universal Bill of Rights, and that they constitute an underlying set of principles that either implicitly or explicitly guide all civilized society. Do you agree? Is it useful to search for underlying principles of humanness? Despite cultural differences, are there underlying values or principles that should inform our interactions with others? Is there truly a universal human theory of communication? Or might it do more harm than good to suggest that universal principles underlie what it means to behave and communicate appropriately and effectively?

Black teenager watching his white classmates dance:	Man, they don't know anything about good music! And those dances are so dumb. I don't call this a party.
Japanese businessperson visiting Argentina:	These people are never on time. No wonder they can never catch up to us.
German student, after watching a documentary about life in Japan:	No wonder they work so hard. They have dinky little houses. I'd work long hours too if I had to live like that.

The kind of ethnocentrism that underlies judgments like these is a communication barrier. It is also an underlying cause of suspicion and mistrust and, in extreme cases, a spark that ignites violence. Instead of making judgments about another culture, try simply to acknowledge differences and to view them as interesting challenges rather than as obstacles to be eradicated.

Improving Intercultural Competence: Developing Motivation to Accept Others

Tolerate Ambiguity	Take your time, and expect some uncertainty.
Develop Mindfulness	Be conscious of cultural differences, rather than ignoring the differences.
Avoid Negative Judgments	Resist thinking that your culture has all the answers.

Developing Skill: Strategies to Adapt to Others

To be skilled is to be capable of putting into action what you know and want to achieve. The underlying skill in being interculturally competent is the ability to be flexible, to be other-oriented, and to adapt your communication to others. We discuss these crucial skills as an introduction to the communication skills that we present in the next four chapters.

Develop Flexibility

When you interact with someone from another background, your responding skills are crucial. You can only learn so much from books; you must be willing to learn as you communicate. Every individual is unique, so cultural generalizations that you learn from research will not always apply. It is not accurate to assume, for example, that *all* French people are preoccupied with food and fashion. Many members of minority groups in the United States find it draining to correct these generalizations in their encounters with others. Pay close attention to the other person's nonverbal cues when you begin conversing; then adjust your communication style and language, if necessary, to put the person at ease. And avoid asking questions or making statements based on generalizations.

Become Other-Oriented

Throughout the book, we have emphasized the importance of becoming other-oriented—focusing on others rather than yourself—as an important way to enhance your interpersonal competence.[101] We have also discussed the problems ethnocentrism can create when you attempt to communicate with others, especially with people whose culture differs from yours. We now offer two specific ways to increase your other-orientedness: social decentering and empathy.

Although our focus in this discussion is on how to increase other-orientation in intercultural interactions, the principles apply to *all* interpersonal interactions. The major difference between intercultural interactions and those that occur within your own culture is primarily the obviousness of the differences between you and the other person.

1. *Social Decentering.* **Social decentering,** the first strategy, is a *cognitive process* in which you take into account the other person's thoughts, feelings, values, background, and perspectives. This process involves viewing the world from the other person's point of view. The greater the difference between you and the other person, the more difficult it is to accomplish social decentering. In doing the exercise in Building Your Skills: Predicting How Others Feel, you may find it easier to predict the reaction of your close friend than that of any of the other people described. The rest of your rankings will depend on the various experiences you have had.

social decentering. Cognitive process in which we take into account another person's thoughts, feelings, values, background, and perspectives.

Grief for the loss of a loved one is a universal emotion experienced by people in all cultures.

There are three ways to socially decenter, or take another's perspective: (1) Develop an understanding of another, based on how you have responded when something similar has happened to you, (2) base your understanding of others on the knowledge you have about a specific person, or (3) make generalizations about someone, based on your understanding of how you think most people would feel or behave.[102]

First, when you draw on your direct experience, you use your knowledge of what happened to you in the past to help you guess how someone else may feel. To the degree that the other person is similar to you, your reactions and his or hers will match. For example, suppose you are talking to a student who has just failed a midterm exam in an important course. You have also had this experience. Your reaction was to discount it because you had confidence you could still earn a passing grade. You might use this self-understanding to predict your classmate's reactions. To the degree that you are similar to the classmate, your prediction will be accurate. But suppose your classmate comes from a culture with high expectations for success. Your classmate might feel upset over having dishonored his family by his poor performance. In this situation, your understanding of your own reaction needs to be tempered by your awareness of how similar or dissimilar the other person is to you. Recognition of differences should lead you to recognize the need to socially decenter in another way.

The second way we socially decenter—or take the perspective of another—is based on the specific knowledge we have of the person with whom we are interacting. Drawing on your memory of how your classmate reacted to a previous failed midterm gives you a basis to more accurately predict his reaction. Even if you have not observed your classmate's reaction to the same situation, you project how you think he would feel based on similar instances. As relationships become more intimate, you gain more information to allow you to socially decenter more readily. Your accuracy in predicting and understanding your partners usually increases as relationships become more intimate. In intercultural interactions, the more opportunity you have to interact with the same person and learn more about the person and his or her culture, the more your ability to socially decenter will increase.

The third way to socially decenter is to apply your understanding of people in general, or of categories of people from whom you have gained some knowledge. Each of us develops implicit personality theories, constructs, and attributions of how people act. You might have a general theory to explain the behavior of men and another for that of women. You might have general theories about Mexicans, Japanese, Canadians, Slovenians, Texans, or Iowans. As you meet someone who falls into one of your categories, you draw on that conceptualization to socially decenter. The more you can learn about a given culture, the stronger your general theories can be, and the more effectively you can use this method of socially decentering. The key, however, is to avoid developing inaccurate, inflexible stereotypes of others and basing your perceptions of others only on those generalizations.

2. *Empathy.* Besides *thinking* about how another may feel (socially decentering), you can have an *emotional* reaction to what others do or tell you. A second skill for becoming other-oriented is learning to feel empathy for another. **Empathy** is an *emotional reaction* that is similar to the one being experienced by another person (as compared to social decentering, which is a *cognitive reaction*). Empathizing is feeling what another person feels. Our emotional reaction may or may not be of the same intensity as the emotions the other person

empathy. Emotional reaction that is similar to the reaction being experienced by another person; empathizing is feeling what another person is feeling.

is experiencing. You may experience mild pity for your classmate who has failed the midterm, in contrast to his stronger feeling of anguish and dishonor. Or you may share his same feelings of anguish and dishonor.

Some emotional reactions are almost universal and cut across cultural boundaries. You may experience empathy when seeing photos or videos depicting emotional scenes occurring in other countries. Seeing a mother crying while holding her sick or dying child in a refugee camp might move you to cry and feel a deep sense of sadness or loss. You empathize with the woman. Tears come to your eyes, and you grieve with her. Empathy can enhance interpersonal interactions in a number of ways: It can provide a bond between you and the other person, it is confirming, it is comforting and supportive, it can increase your understanding of others, and it can strengthen the relationship. People can empathize most easily with those who are similar, and in situations in which they have had a similar emotional experience.

Developing empathy is different from sympathizing with others. When you offer **sympathy,** you tell someone you are sorry he or she feels what he or she is feeling: "I'm sorry your Uncle Joe died" or "I'm sorry to hear you failed your test." When you sympathize with others, you acknowledge their feelings. But when you empathize, you experience an emotional reaction that is similar to that of the other person; you, too, feel grief or sadness. Can people be taught to be more empathic? Research suggests that the answer is a clear yes.[103] One goal of this book is to enhance your skill in being other-oriented; empathy is at the heart of being other-oriented. We discuss strategies for developing empathic listening skills in the next chapter.

Appropriately Adapt Your Communication to Others

The logical extension of being flexible and becoming other-oriented is to adapt your communication to enhance the quality and effectiveness of your interpersonal communication. To **adapt** means to adjust your behavior to others to accommodate differences and expectations. Appropriate adaptation occurs in the context of the relationship you have with the other person and what is happening in the communication environment. **Communication accommodation theory** suggests that all people adapt their behavior to others to some extent. Those who adapt to others appropriately and sensitively are more likely to experience more positive communication.[104] Adapting to others doesn't mean you only tell others what they want to hear and do what others want you to do. Such spineless, placating behavior is not wise, effective, or ethical. Nor are we suggesting that you adapt your behavior only so that you can get your way; the goal is effective communication, not manipulation. We are suggesting, however, that you be aware of what your communication partner is doing and saying, especially if there are cultural differences between you, so that your message is understood and you don't unwittingly offend others. Although it may seem to be common sense, being sensitive to others and adapting behaviors to others are not as common as you might think.

Sometimes people adapt their behavior based on what they think someone will like. At other times, they adapt their communication after realizing they have done something wrong. When you modify your behavior in anticipation of an event, you **adapt predictively.** For example, you might decide to buy a friend flowers to soften the news about breaking a date because you know how much your friend likes flowers. When you modify your behavior after an event, you **adapt reactively.** For example, you might buy your friend flowers to apologize after a fight.

You often adapt your messages to enhance message clarity. There are at least four reasons that explain why you may adapt your communication with another person.

sympathy. Acknowledgment that someone may be feeling bad; compassion toward someone.

adapt. To adjust one's behavior in accord with what someone else does. We can adapt based on the individual, the relationship, and the situation.

communication accommodation theory. Theory that all people adapt their behavior to others to some extent.

adapt predictively. To modify or change behavior in anticipation of an event.

adapt reactively. To modify or change behavior after an event.

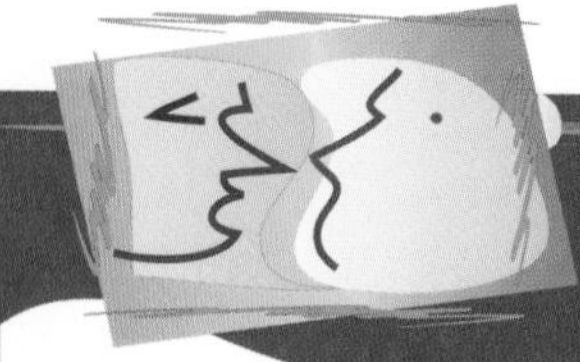

Becoming Other-Oriented

The Platinum Rule

The ultimate goal of becoming other-oriented goes beyond having sympathy for others. Being other-oriented may even go beyond what is typically labeled as the "Golden Rule": Do to others as you would have them do to you. Or, as stated by the Buddha: Consider others as yourself. In Chapter 2 (page 63), we identified additional interpretations of the same principle from a variety of religious traditions. Communication researcher Milton Bennett calls the ultimate other-oriented principle the "Platinum Rule": *Do to others as they themselves would like to be treated.*[105] Rather than treating people as *you* would like to be treated, interact with others the way you think and feel *they* would like to be treated. For example, when ordering a pizza for your friends, the Golden Rule would suggest you order a pizza with toppings you would like; the Platinum Rule is to order what you think your dining partners would like. Or, if you've decided to buy your friend a book for her birthday, buy a book not because you like it, but because you think your friend will like it. According to Bennett, at its essence, empathy is "the imaginative, intellectual and emotional participation in another person's experience."[106] The goal, according to Bennett, is to attempt to think and feel what another person thinks and feels and to go beyond that by taking positive action toward others in response to your empathic feelings.

As you ponder the virtues and challenges of becoming other-oriented, consider the following questions:

1. Is the Platinum Rule always useful, desirable, or even possible? Explain your answer.
2. What are some of the obstacles to applying the Platinum Rule during your everyday interactions with others?
3. How can the Platinum Rule be useful when you are having a disagreement or conflict with another person?
4. Think about a time when you used the Platinum Rule. What was the effect on the person with whom you were communicating?

- *Information:* You adapt your message in response to specific information that you already know about your partner, such as what he or she may like or dislike, or information that your partner has shared with you.
- *Perceived Behavior:* You adapt your communication in response to what you think the other person is thinking, what you see the person doing, and your observations of the person's emotional expressions and moods.
- *History:* You adapt your messages to others based on previous conversations, past shared experiences, and personal information that others have shared with you.
- *Communication Context:* You adapt your message depending on where you are; you may whisper a brief comment to someone during a movie, yet shout a comment to someone when attending a loud rock concert.

BE OTHER-ORIENTED

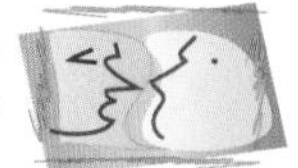

In intercultural interactions, people frequently adapt communication in response to the feedback or reactions they are receiving during a conversation. An other-oriented communicator is constantly looking and listening to the other person in order to appropriately adapt his or her communication behavior. Table 4.3 describes how we adapt our verbal messages to others and provides some examples.

People in conversations also adapt to nonverbal cues. Many times, they raise or lower voice volume in response to the volume of a partner, or lean toward people in response to their leaning toward the speaker. We talk more about such nonverbal cues in Chapter 7.

Adaptation across intercultural contexts is usually more difficult than adaptation within your own culture. Imagine shaking hands with a stranger and having the stranger hold on to your hand as you continue to talk. In the United States, hand holding between strangers violates nonverbal norms. But in some cultures, maintaining physical contact while talking is expected. Pulling your hand away from this person would be rude. What may be mannerly in one culture is not always acceptable in another. Adapting to these cultural differences means developing that "third culture" that we talked about earlier in the chapter.

Taking an other-oriented approach to communication means considering the thoughts, feelings, background, perspectives, attitudes, and values of your partners and adjusting your interaction with them accordingly. Other-orientation leads to more effective interpersonal communication, regardless of whether you are dealing with someone in your family or a person from another country.

BE OTHER-ORIENTED

TABLE 4.3 How Do We Adapt to Others?

Type of Adaptation	Examples
Topical Adaptation (including self-disclosures): Choosing topics of conversation because of interests or things you have in common with your partner, including sharing information about yourself	• Talking about a class you both attend • Mentioning an article you read about a TV show your partner really likes • Telling someone about your depression because you believe he or she cares
Explanatory or Elaborated Adaptation: Providing additional information or detail because you recognize that your communication partner has certain gaps in his or her information	• Telling a story about Ike, whom your partner doesn't know, and explaining that Ike is your uncle • Describing Facebook to your grandparent, who doesn't know what the Internet is • Telling someone, "I know my behavior might seem a little erratic, but I'm under a lot of pressure at work right now and my parents are on my case"
Adaptation Through Withholding or Avoiding Information: Not providing explanations of something your partner already knows; not providing information to avoid an anticipated undesired reaction from your partner, or not providing information because of a fear of how your partner might potentially use the information (such as sharing the information with other people)	• Not elaborating on the parts of an auto engine when describing a car problem because you know your partner is knowledgeable about cars • Not telling someone you saw his or her lover with another because he or she would be hurt • Not mentioning your interest in a mutual friend because you know the listener would blab about it to the mutual friend
Adaptation Through Examples, Comparisons, and Analogies: Choosing messages you believe your partner will find relevant	• Describing a person who is not known by your partner by comparing the person to someone your partner knows • Explaining roller-blading by comparing it to ice skating because your partner is an avid ice skater
Adaptation Through Language Choice: Choosing or avoiding specific words because of the anticipated effect on your partner; consciously selecting words that you believe are understandable to your partner; or using words that have a unique meaning to you and your partner	• Using formal address in response to status differences: "Thank you, Professor Smith" • Using slang when the relationship is perceived as informal • Using nicknames, inside jokes, or teasing comments with close friends

Source: © Mark V. Redmond, 2005. Used by permission.

In an effective interpersonal relationship, your partner is also orienting himself or herself to you. A competent communicator has knowledge of others, is motivated to enhance the quality of communication, and possesses the skill of being other-oriented.

If you learn the skills and principles we have presented here, will it really make a difference in your ability to relate to others? Recent evidence suggests the answer is yes. A study by communication researcher Lori Carrell found that students who had been exposed to lessons in empathy linked to a study of interpersonal and intercultural communication improved their ability to empathize with others.[107] There is evidence that if you master these principles and skills, you will be rewarded with greater insight and ability to relate to others who are different from you.

Recap

Improving Intercultural Competence: Developing Skill to Adapt to Others

Develop flexibility	Learn to "go with the flow."
Become other-oriented	Put yourself in the other person's mental and emotional mindset; listen and respond appropriately.
Adapt your communication to others	Adjust your behavior to others to accommodate differences and expectations.

Summary

There are many ways in which we are different from one another. Gender, sexual orientation, age, social class, and race and ethnicity are some of the characteristics by which people group themselves to develop a specific culture.

A culture is a system of knowledge that is shared by a group of people. It includes cultural elements, values, goals, and contexts. Cultural elements are categories of things and ideas that identify key aspects of cultural influence. Cultural values reflect how individuals regard masculine and feminine behaviors and individual and collective achievements. They also reflect whether individuals can tolerate ambiguity or need a high degree of certainty, and whether they prefer concentrated or decentralized power structures. The goals of a culture depend on the way it values individual versus group achievement. In high-context cultures, the meaning of messages depends heavily on nonverbal information; people in low-context cultures rely more heavily on words than on context for deriving meaning.

Intercultural communication occurs when individuals or groups from different cultures communicate. Several barriers inhibit effective intercultural communication. Ethnocentrism is the belief that one's own cultural traditions and assumptions are superior to those of others. Differences in language and the way people interpret nonverbal messages also interfere with effective intercultural communication. People stereotype by placing a group or a person into an inflexible, all-encompassing category. A related barrier is prejudice—people often pre-judge someone before they know all the facts. Stereotyping and prejudice can keep people from viewing others as unique individuals and therefore hamper effective, honest communication. Assuming that one is similar to others can be a barrier to intercultural communication. Finally, assuming that we are *always* different from one another can also hinder communication.

Although it is reasonably easy to identify cultural differences, it is more challenging to bridge those differences. To enhance understanding between cultures, we suggest the following: Develop knowledge by seeking information about the culture, ask questions and listen, and develop a "third culture." Increase your motivation to appreciate others who are different from you by tolerating ambiguity, developing mindfulness, and avoiding negative judgments about another culture. Finally, enhance your skill by becoming flexible. Be other-oriented by socially decentering and becoming more empathic. And adapt your verbal and nonverbal communication to others.

For Discussion and Review

Focus on Critical Thinking

1. Jonna, an American, has just been accepted as a foreign exchange student in Germany. What potential cultural barriers may she face? How should she manage these potential barriers?
2. What's the problem in assuming that other people are like us? How does this create a barrier to effective intercultural communication?
3. If you were to design a lesson plan for elementary age students about how to deal with racial and ethnic stereotypes, what would you include?
4. What are appropriate ways to deal with someone who consistently utters racial slurs and evidences prejudice toward racial or ethnic groups?

Focus on Ethics

5. Marla is the director of the campus multicultural studies program. She wants to require all students in a four-year degree program to take at least four courses that focus on multicultural issues. Is it appropriate to force students to take such a concentration of courses?
6. When Wayne, a Catholic Polish American, went to visit Dave, who was from an old Southern Baptist family, Dave's dad made a bigoted statement about African Americans. This upset Wayne, and he wondered whether Dave's father was prejudiced against Catholics, too. Should Wayne have spoken up and told Dave's dad that he did not like the remark?
7. Is it ethical or appropriate for someone from one culture to attempt to change the cultural values of someone from a different culture? For example, culture A practices polygamy: One husband can be married to several wives. Culture B practices monogamy: One husband can be married to only one wife. Should a person from culture B attempt to make someone from culture A change his or her ways?

Learning with Others

1. How well do you think you could predict someone's reactions to finding out his or her mother or other close relative had just died? Rank-order each of the following from 1 (the person whose reaction you could predict most confidently) to 6 (the person whose reaction you'd be least confident about predicting).

   a. _____ A close friend of the same sex, age, race, and culture
   b. _____ A sixty-year-old male Chinese farmer
   c. _____ A college student who is twenty years older than you but of the same race, sex, and culture
   d. _____ A ten-year-old California girl who is the child of Asian and Latino parents
   e. _____ A college student of a different race but the same age, culture, and sex as you
   f. _____ A college student of the opposite sex but of the same age, race, and culture

   What qualities do you feel provide you the best information on which to base your judgments? Why? What would you need to know about each person to feel comfortable in making a prediction? How can you get that information?
2. Bring to class a fable, folktale, or children's story from a culture other than your own. As a group, analyze the cultural values implied by the story or characters in the story.
3. In small groups, identify examples from your own experiences for each barrier to effective intercultural communication discussed in the text. Use one of the examples to develop a skit to perform for the rest of the class. See whether the class can identify which intercultural barrier your group is depicting. Also suggest how the skills and principles discussed in the chapter might have improved the communication in the situation you role-play.

Weblinks

Go to *www.mycommunicationlab.com* (access code required) to find Web resources for your text that supplement the material in Chapter 4, including links to information on the following topics:

Gender and communication styles
National Forum on People's Differences
The Human Diversity Resource Page
Egoism/Altruism Test
U.S. Census Bureau and minority statistics

Parts Equal the Whole I. Diana Ong (b. 1940 Chinese-American). Computer graphics. © Diana Ong/SuperStock.

Part Two

Interpersonal Communication Skills

People judge you by your behavior, not by your intentions. The following four chapters focus on research-based communication skills that can help you monitor and shape your behavior to improve the quality of your relationships. Chapter 5 offers tips and strategies for listening to others and confirming your understanding of what you hear. Chapter 6 explores how the words people use and misuse affect interpersonal relationships. Becoming other-oriented involves both listening to the words and reading the behavior cues of others. Chapter 7 focuses on the scope and importance of unspoken messages. We will explore the implications of the adage "Actions speak louder than words." Chapter 8 presents principles and skills to help you manage conflict and disagreements with others.

CHAPTER 5

Listening and Responding Skills

OBJECTIVES

1. Describe five elements of the listening process.
2. Identify characteristics of four listening styles.
3. Understand why we listen, and list several important barriers to effective listening.
4. Identify ways to improve your other-orientation and listening skills.
5. Identify responding skills and understand strategies for improving them.

OUTLINE

Listening Defined

Listening Styles

Listening Barriers

Improving Listening, Comprehension, and Responding Skills

Improving Empathic Listening and Responding Skills

Responding to Confirm or Disconfirm Others

Improving Critical Listening Skills

Improving Your Responding Skills

I never learned anything while I was talking.

Larry King

Think about your best friend. What are some of the qualities you most admire in your friend? Many people would respond that one of the most valued qualities in a friend is his or her just being there—supporting, comforting, and listening. As theologian Henri Nouwen so eloquently put it,

> Listening is much more than allowing another to talk while waiting for a chance to respond. Listening is paying full attention to others and welcoming them into our very beings. . . . Listening is a form of spiritual hospitality by which you invite strangers to become friends, to get to know their inner selves more fully, and even dare to be silent with you.[1]

Simply stated, friends listen. They listen even if we sometimes say foolish things. Again, Nouwen describes it well: "True listeners no longer have an inner need to make their presence known. They are free to receive, to welcome, to accept."[2] As we consider the essential skills of interpersonal communication, the skill of listening to others would be at or near the top of the list in terms of importance.[3] Skilled communicators do more than impassively listen—they appropriately respond to what we say. They confirm that they understand and care for us by providing both verbal and nonverbal feedback. There is also evidence that listening is the quintessential skill of being an effective leader.[4]

Listening and responding skills are important for several reasons. Some researchers suggest that because listening is the first communication skill that we learn (because we respond to sounds even while in our mother's womb), it's also the most important skill. Listening plays a key role in helping us learn to speak.

Another reason listening is important: You spend more time listening than participating in any other communication activity. In fact, you spend more time listening to others than doing almost anything else. Typical Americans spend more than 80 percent of an average day communicating with other people, and, as the pie chart in Figure 5.1 on page 126 shows, they spend 45 percent of that communication time listening to others.[5] Ironically, most people's formal communication training focuses on writing, the activity to which they devote the least amount of communication time. Chances are that until now you have had no formal training in listening.

Listening may be an even more important skill in the twenty-first century than in the past.[6] Why? Communication researcher Sheila Bently suggests that because of

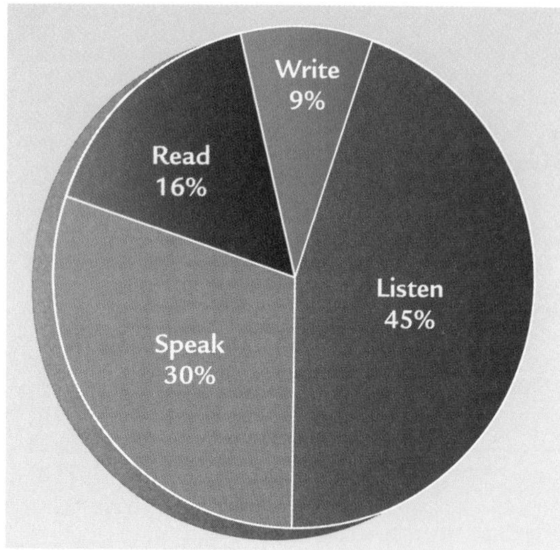

FIGURE 5.1

What You Do with Your Communication Time

globalization and today's technology, listening skills are essential for professional and personal success.[7] The world is shrinking. No longer do vast distances keep us from communicating with people from around the globe. Cultural differences make listening an essential skill in relating to others who may have a different cultural perspective than our own. In addition, today's technological tools make it possible for us to listen to others anytime and anywhere.[8]

There is an increase in **asynchronous listening**, which is listening to someone's recorded message on an answering machine, via voicemail, or retrieved from your cell phone; you listen after the message has been created, when no person is able to respond to your feedback. Without immediate feedback or the ability to ask for clarification, there is significant potential to misunderstand the message. It's easy to understand why listening is becoming increasingly important and challenging. In this chapter, we focus on this often neglected, yet quintessential, skill for developing quality interpersonal relationships. Listening is the process by which people learn the most about others. In addition, we explore ways to respond appropriately to others.

Listening Defined

"Did you hear what I said?" demanded a father who had been lecturing his teenage son on the importance of hanging up his clothes. In fact, his son did *hear* him, but he may not have been *listening.* **Listening** is a complex process of selecting, attending to, constructing meaning from, remembering, and responding to verbal and nonverbal messages.[9] When we listen, we hear words and try to make sense out of what we hear. The essence of being a good listener is being able to accurately interpret the messages expressed by others.[10] **Hearing** is the physiological process of decoding sounds. You hear when sound vibrations reach your eardrum and cause the middle ear bones—the hammer, anvil, and stirrup—to move. Eventually, these sound vibrations are translated into electrical impulses that reach the brain. In order to listen to something, you must first select that sound from competing sounds. Then you must attend to it, understand it, and remember it. A fifth activity—responding—confirms that listening has occurred.[11]

asynchronous listening. Listening to someone's recorded message (on an answering machine, via voicemail, or on a cell phone) without the person being present.

listening. Process of selecting, attending to, creating meaning from, remembering, and responding to verbal and nonverbal messages.

hearing. Physiological process of decoding sounds.

selecting. Process of choosing one sound while sorting through various sounds competing for your attention.

Selecting

Selecting a sound is the process of choosing one sound as you sort through the various sounds competing for your attention. As you listen to someone in an interpersonal context, you focus on the words and nonverbal messages of your partner. Even now, as you

are reading this book, there are undoubtedly countless noises within earshot. Stop reading for a moment and sort through the various sounds around you. Do you hear music? Is there noise from outside? How about the murmur of voices, the tick of a clock, the hum of a computer, the whoosh of an air conditioner or furnace? To listen, you must select which of these sounds will receive your attention.

Healthy family relations result when parents and children are able to develop people-oriented listening styles.

Attending

After selecting a sound, you then **attend** to or focus on it. Attention can be fleeting. You may attend to the sound for a moment and then move on or return to other thoughts or other sounds. As we discussed in Chapter 3, your attention is sometimes selective. Either consciously or unconsciously, you are more likely to attend to those messages that meet your needs and are consistent with your attitudes or interests. Information that is novel or intense, or that somehow relates to you, may capture your attention. And conflict, humor, new ideas, and real or concrete things command your attention more easily than abstract theories that do not relate to your interests or needs.

Understanding

Whereas hearing is a physiological phenomenon, **understanding** is the process of assigning meaning to the sounds you select and to which you attend; to understand a message is to construct meaning from what you hear and see. There are several theories about how you assign meaning to words you hear, but there is no universally accepted notion of how this process works. We know that people understand best if they can relate what they are hearing to something they already know.

A second basic principle about how people understand others is this: The greater the similarity between individuals, the greater the likelihood for more accurate understanding. Individuals from different cultures who have substantially different religions, family lifestyles, values, and attitudes often have difficulty understanding each other, particularly in the early phases of a relationship.

You understand best that which you also experience. Perhaps you have heard the Montessori school philosophy: I hear, I forget; I see, I remember; I experience, I understand. Hearing alone does not create understanding. People hear over one billion words each year, but understand only a fraction of that number. They may not be attending to the words coming their way, or they may simply not know what some words mean. A key to establishing relationships with others is trying to understand those differences in experience in order to arrive at a common meaning for the messages exchanged.

Remembering

Remembering is the process of recalling information. Some researchers theorize that you store every detail you have ever heard or witnessed; your mind operates like a hard drive on a computer. But you cannot retrieve or remember all the information. Sometimes you were present, yet have no recollection of what occurred.

Human brains have both short-term and long-term memory storage systems. Short-term memory is where you store almost all the information you hear. You look

attending. Process of focusing on a particular sound or message.

understanding. Process of assigning meaning to sounds.

remembering. Process of recalling information.

up a phone number in the telephone book, mumble the number to yourself, then dial the number, only to discover that the line is busy. Three minutes later, you have to look up the number again because it did not get stored in your long-term memory. Short-term storage is very limited. Just as airports have just a few short-term parking spaces, but lots of spaces for long-term parking, brains can accommodate only a few things of fleeting significance, but acres of important information. Most of us forget hundreds of bits of insignificant information that pass through our brains each day.

The information stored in long-term memory includes events, conversations, and other data that are significant. People tend to remember dramatic and vital information, as well as seemingly inconsequential details connected with such information. Most people over the age of fifty-five today know exactly where they were on November 22, 1963, the day President Kennedy was assassinated. Many over the age of seventy-five can also recall where they were on December 7, 1941, when Japanese bombers attacked Pearl Harbor. Do you recall the day in April 1999, when students were indiscriminately shot at Columbine High School in Colorado? What were you doing on the morning of September 11, 2001, when you first heard that a plane had flown into the World Trade Center in New York? Information makes it to long-term memory because of its significance to us.

Responding

Interpersonal communication is transactive; it involves both talking and responding. You are **responding** to people when you let them know you understand their messages. Responses can be nonverbal; direct eye contact and head nods let your partner know you're tuned in. Or you can respond verbally by asking questions to confirm the content of the message: "Are you saying you don't want us to spend as much time together as we once did?" or by making statements that reflect the feelings of the speaker: "So you are frustrated that you have to wait for someone to drive you where you want to go." We discuss responding skills in more detail later in the chapter.

What Is Listening?

Selecting	Sorting through various sounds that compete for your attention
Attending to	Focusing on a particular sound or message
Understanding	Assigning meaning to sounds
Remembering	Recalling information
Responding	Confirming your understanding of a message

responding. Process of confirming your understanding of a message.

listening style. Preferred way of making sense out of spoken messages.

Listening Styles

What's your listening style? Do you focus more on the content of the message than on the feelings being expressed by the speaker? Or do you prefer brief sound bites of information that you can hear quickly? Your **listening style** is your preferred way of making sense out of the spoken messages you hear. Listening researchers Kitty Watson, Larry Barker, and James Weaver found that listeners tend to fall into one of four listening styles: people-oriented, action-oriented, content-oriented, or time-oriented.[12] There are a variety of factors that influence your listening style.[13] Researchers Randy Dillon and Nelya McKenzie suggest that your culture and ethnicity are powerful forces that affect how you listen to others.[14]

"Are you listening to me?"

People-Oriented Listeners

As you might suspect from the label, **people-oriented listeners** tend to be comfortable with and skilled at listening to people's feelings and emotions. They are likely to empathize and search for common areas of interest. People-oriented listeners embody many of the attributes of being other-oriented that we've discussed throughout the book—they seek strong interpersonal connections when listening to others. Research suggests that those who strongly prefer the people-oriented listening style will be less anxious or apprehensive about listening to other people, especially when listening to just one other person.[15] There is also evidence that people-oriented listeners may be more empathic; they have greater skill in understanding the thoughts and feelings of others.[16] One study also found that jurors who are people-oriented listeners tend to find the plaintiffs less at fault in civil court trials.[17]

Action-Oriented Listeners

An **action-oriented listener** prefers information that is well organized, brief, and error-free. An action-oriented listener doesn't like the speaker to tell lengthy stories and digress. The action-oriented listener may think "Get to the point" or "What am I supposed to do with this information?" when hearing a message filled with too many anecdotes or rambling, disorganized bits of information. Whereas a people-oriented listener would be more likely to focus on the feelings of the person telling the story, the action-oriented listener wants to know the point or the punch line. There is new evidence to suggest that action-oriented listeners are more likely to be more skeptical when listening to information. Researchers call this skepticism **second-guessing**—questioning the ideas and assumptions underlying a message. Rather than taking the information they hear at face value, action-oriented listeners are more likely to reinterpret or evaluate the literal message to determine whether it is true or false—they make another guess (hence the term *second-guessing*) as to whether the information they are listening to is accurate.[18]

Content-Oriented Listeners

If you are a **content-oriented listener**, you are more comfortable listening to complex, detailed information than are people with other listening styles. A content-oriented listener homes in on the facts, details, and evidence in a message. In fact, if a message does not include ample supporting evidence and specific details, the content-oriented listener is more likely to reject the message. Like the action-oriented listener, content-oriented listeners are likely to make second guesses about the messages they hear. Content-oriented listeners are also less apprehensive when communicating with others in group and interpersonal situations.[19] People who have listening style preferences for both high content and high action are more likely to have a precise and attentive style of arguing with others; they leave a strong impression on others when trying to per-

people-oriented listener. Listener who is comfortable with and skilled at listening to people's feelings and emotions.

action-oriented listener. Listener who prefers information that is well-organized, brief, and error-free.

second-guessing. Questioning the ideas and assumptions underlying a message; assessing whether the message is true or false.

content-oriented listener. Listener who is more comfortable listening to complex, detailed information than are those with other listening styles.

suade them.[20] Content-oriented listeners would make good judges or lawyers; they focus on issues and arguments and listen to see whether a speaker's conclusion is accurate or credible.

Time-Oriented Listeners

You're a **time-oriented listener** if you like your messages delivered succinctly. Time-oriented listeners are keenly aware of how much time they have to listen. They have many things on their "to-do" list; their "in basket" often overflows, so they want messages delivered quickly and briefly. Whereas a people-oriented listener might enjoy spending time over a cup of coffee catching up on the day's activities, a time-oriented listener is more like a drive-by listener—a time-oriented listener may think, "Give me what I need so I can keep on moving to my next task or hear my next message. Don't ramble, don't digress, just get to the point quickly."

Understanding Your Listening Style

Now that we've identified the four listening styles, you may wonder, "Do I have just one listening style, or do I have more than one style?" According to Watson and Barker, about 40 percent of all listeners use one primary listening style, especially if they are under stress.[21] Another 40 percent of listeners prefer to use more than one style—for example, sometimes they may prefer to listen to content and may also want the information delivered in a short amount of time (content- and time-oriented listening styles). And about 20 percent of people do not have a specific listening style preference; these individuals may just want to avoid listening altogether, either because they are shy and don't like to be around others in social situations, they have listener apprehension, or they are simply weary of listening to other people.

Knowing your listening style can help you better understand how to adapt to various listening situations. If, for example, you know that you are a time-oriented or action-oriented listener and your friend or companion is a people-oriented listener, you and your friend will need to adjust your speaking and listening styles. When speaking to an action-oriented listener, give the listener a brief preview of what you will be talking about. You could say, "Phil, there are three things I'd like to share with you." Stick to that structure. When speaking to a people-oriented listener, realize that he or she will feel rushed or hurried if you skip information about feelings or relationships. A people-oriented listener prefers to spend more time talking about emotions than do those with other listening styles. A time-oriented listener would like information summarized as in a concisely written business memo punctuated with bullets and lists of essential information.

What is the best listening style? It depends on the listening situation and the communication context and objectives. In a high-pressure, fast-paced job such as stock trading, you don't have time to listen to stories about clients' families or the latest TV show; you need information delivered quickly and efficiently. A father listening to a daughter talk about her rotten day at school would find a people-oriented listening style better for listening to his daughter pour her heart out. Being aware of your own preferred listening style and the needs of your communication partner can help you adopt a listening style that best suits the situation.

BE OTHER-ORIENTED

Listening Barriers

time-oriented listener. Listener who likes messages delivered succinctly.

Even though people spend so much of their communication time listening, most don't listen as well as they should. Twenty-four hours after you hear a speech, a class lecture, or a sermon, you have forgotten more than half of what was said. And it gets worse. In another twenty-four hours, you have forgotten half of what you remembered, so you really remember only a quarter of the lecture.

Interpersonal listening skills may be even worse. When you listen to a speech or lecture, you have a clearly defined listening role; one person talks, and you are expected to listen. But in interpersonal situations, you may have to alternate quickly between speaking and listening. This takes considerable skill and concentration. Often you are thinking of what you want to say next, rather than listening.

One surprising study found that we sometimes listen better to strangers than to intimate friends or partners. Married couples in the study tended to interrupt each other more often and were generally less polite to each other than were strangers involved in a decision-making task.[22] Apparently, we take listening shortcuts when communicating with others in close relationships. As Understanding Diversity: Who Listens Better, Men or Women? suggests, the problem may be gender-related.

Inattentive listening is a bit like channel surfing when we watch TV—pushing the remote control button to switch from channel to channel, avoiding commercials and focusing for brief periods on attention-grabbing programs. When we listen to others, we may fleetingly tune in to the conversation for a moment, decide that the content is uninteresting, and then focus on a personal thought. These thoughts are barriers to communication, and they come in a variety of forms.

Are we more attentive listeners to TV? Apparently not. One research team phoned TV viewers as soon as the evening news program was over. On average, most people remembered only about 17 percent of what they heard. And even when they were reminded of some of the news coverage, most averaged no better than 25 percent recall.[23] Even though more highly educated viewers did a little better, the overall conclusion is not good: We often don't "catch" what we hear, even a few moments after hearing it. Let's explore several listening barriers that keep us from catching others' meaning.

Being Self-Absorbed

You're in your local grocery store during "rush hour." It appears that most of your community has also decided to forage for food at the same time. You are trying to get in and out of the store quickly, but many of the shoppers are oblivious to those around them. They stop in the aisle, blocking the path for others (including you). They elbow their way into crowded checkout stands. And the "express lane" that limits customers to ten items or fewer is backed up because some shoppers have difficulty counting to ten. You find yourself becoming tense—not just because you are hungry, but because it seems the grocery store is filled with people who are self-absorbed; they are focused on getting their needs met and are oblivious to the needs of others.

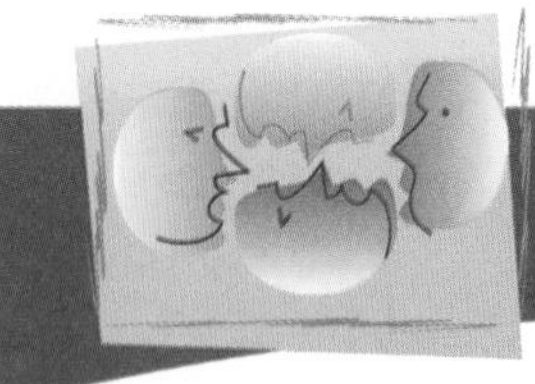

Understanding Diversity

Who Listens Better, Men or Women?

Research provides no definitive answer to the question "Who listens better, men or women?" There is evidence that men and women listen somewhat differently and have different expectations about the roles of listening and talking. Deborah Tannen suggests that one of the most common complaints wives have about their husbands is "He doesn't listen to me anymore," along with "He doesn't talk to me anymore." Another scholar noted that complaints about lack of communication were usually at the top of women's lists of reasons for divorce but were mentioned much less often by men. Why are women more often dissatisfied with the listening and talking process than men are? Tannen's explanation: Women expect different things from conversations than men expect.

One researcher suggests that men and women may have different attention styles. When men listen, they may be looking for a new structure or organizational pattern, or trying to separate bits of information they hear. They continually shape, form, observe, inquire, and direct energy toward a chosen goal. Men's attention style is sometimes reported to be more emotionally controlled than women's attention style. Women have sometimes been described as more subjective, empathic, and emotionally involved as they listen. They are perceived as more likely to search for relationships among parts of a pattern and to rely on more intuitive perceptions of feelings. They are also more easily distracted by competing details. Females may hear more of the message because they reject less of it. These differences in attention styles and the way men and women may process information can potentially affect listening, even though we have no direct evidence linking attention style to listening skill.

Another researcher suggests that when men listen, they listen to solve a problem; men are more instrumental and task-oriented. Women listen to seek new information to enhance understanding.

What are the implications of these research studies? They may mean that men and women focus on different parts of messages and have different listening objectives. These differences can affect relationship development. Males may need to recognize that while they are attending to a message and looking for new structure to solve a problem or achieve a goal, they may hear less of the message and therefore listen less effectively. And even though many females may hear more of the message, they may need to make connections between the parts of the information they hear to look for major ideas, rather than just focusing on the details. In any case, gender-based differences in attention style and information processing may account for some of the relational problems that husbands and wives, lovers, siblings, and male and female friends experience.[24]

Although it may seem that men and women have somewhat different approaches to listening, it is still not clear whether men and women are really that different when it comes to relating to one another. Communication researchers Stephanie Sargent and James Weaver suggest that pop psychology conclusions, which erroneously promote dramatic differences between the way men and women listen, may simply be perpetuating stereotypes of the way men and women *think* they are supposed to listen.[25] Although there is research that suggests men and women may differ somewhat in the way they respond to information, the difference may not be based in a person's biological sex; it is more likely a reflection of gender differences (socially constructed, cultural or co-cultural, learned approaches). Listening differences may, in fact, show up in the research because men and women *think* they are supposed to have different approaches to listening. When it comes to enhancing communication and listening to one another, it is best to start not from the position that men and women are from different planets, but rather from the position that they share common needs.[26]

Self-absorbed listeners are focused on their needs rather than yours; the message is about *them*, not *you*. During conversations with a self-absorbed communicator, you have difficulty sustaining the conversation about anything except your self-absorbed partner's ideas, experiences, and stories. This problem is also called **conversational narcissism.** To be narcissistic is to be in love with oneself, like the mythical Greek character Narcissus, who became enamored with his reflection in a pool of water.[27]

conversational narcissism. Focus on personal agendas and self-absorption rather than a focus on the needs and ideas of others.

The self-absorbed listener is actively involved in doing several things other than listening. The self-absorbed person is much more likely to interrupt others in midsentence, as he or she is seeking ways to focus the attention on himself or herself. The

self-absorbed listener is also not focusing on his or her partner's message but thinking about what he or she is going to say next. This focus on an internal message can keep a listener from selecting and attending to the other person's message.

How do you short-circuit this listening problem in yourself? First, diagnose it. Note consciously when you find yourself drifting off, thinking about your agenda rather than concentrating on the speaker. Second, throttle up your powers of concentration when you find your internal messages are distracting you from listening well.

BE OTHER-ORIENTED

Unchecked Emotions

Words are powerful symbols that affect people's attitudes, behavior, and even blood pressure. Words arouse people emotionally, and your emotional state can affect how well you listen. **Emotional noise** occurs when emotional arousal interferes with communication effectiveness. If you grew up in a home in which R-rated language was never used, then four-letter words may be distracting to you. Words that insult your religious or ethnic heritage can be fighting words. Most people respond to certain trigger words like a bull to a waving cape; they want to charge in to correct the speaker or perhaps even do battle with him or her.

Sometimes, it is not specific words but rather concepts or ideas that cause an emotional eruption. Some talk-radio hosts try to boost their ratings by purposely using demagogic language that elicits passionate responses. Although listening to such conflict can be interesting and entertaining, when your own emotions become aroused, you may lose your ability to converse effectively. Unchecked emotions can interfere with focusing on the message of another.

If you are listening to someone who is emotionally distraught, you will be more likely to focus on his or her emotions than on the content of the message.[28] Communication author R. G. Owens advises that when you are communicating with someone who is emotionally excited, you should remain calm and focused and try simply to communicate your interest in the other person.[29]

BE OTHER-ORIENTED

Your listening challenge is to avoid emotional sidetracks and keep your attention focused on what others are saying. When you find yourself distracted by emotional noise brought on by objectionable words or concepts, or by an emotional speaker, make an effort to quiet the noise and steer back to the subject at hand.

Criticizing the Speaker

The late Mother Teresa once said, "If you judge people, you have no time to love them." Being critical of the speaker may distract a listener from focusing on the

emotional noise. Form of communication interference caused by emotional arousal.

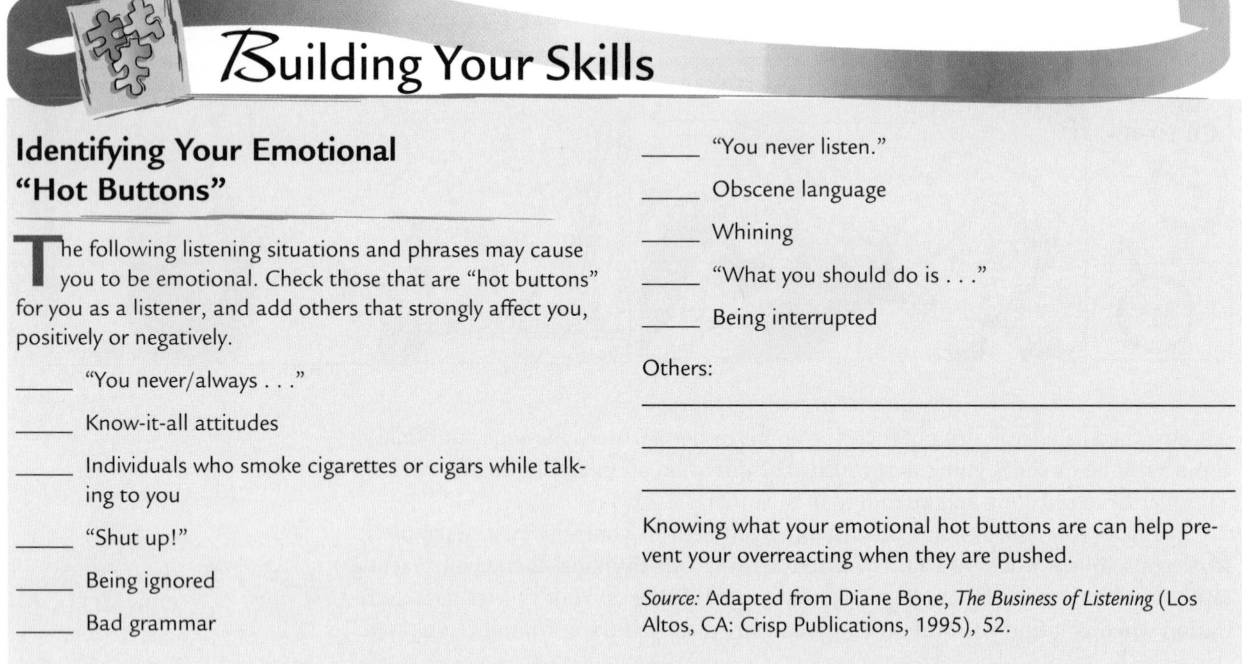

Building Your Skills

Identifying Your Emotional "Hot Buttons"

The following listening situations and phrases may cause you to be emotional. Check those that are "hot buttons" for you as a listener, and add others that strongly affect you, positively or negatively.

_____ "You never/always . . ."

_____ Know-it-all attitudes

_____ Individuals who smoke cigarettes or cigars while talking to you

_____ "Shut up!"

_____ Being ignored

_____ Bad grammar

_____ "You never listen."

_____ Obscene language

_____ Whining

_____ "What you should do is . . ."

_____ Being interrupted

Others:

____

____

____

Knowing what your emotional hot buttons are can help prevent your overreacting when they are pushed.

Source: Adapted from Diane Bone, *The Business of Listening* (Los Altos, CA: Crisp Publications, 1995), 52.

message. Do you remember seeing villains in movies about the Old West, waiting in the bushes, ready to jump out and ambush an unsuspecting passerby? Perhaps you know someone who is an **ambush listener**. This is a person who eagerly pounces on the speaker to argue, criticize, or find fault with what the other person has said. Although the ambush listener may look as if she or he is listening, in reality this type of listener is just waiting to critique the speaker for a variety of reasons.

Superficial factors such as clothing, body size and shape, age, and ethnicity all affect our interpretation of a message. In his essay "Black Men and Public Space," journalist Brent Staples provides this account of an incident that made communication impossible because of the way a woman reacted to his appearance:

> On assignment for a local paper and killing time before an interview, I entered a jewelry store on the city's affluent Near North Side. The proprietor excused herself and returned with an enormous red Doberman pinscher straining at the end of a leash. She stood, the dog extended toward me, silent to my questions, her eyes bulging nearly out of her head.[30]

Again, it is important to monitor your internal dialogue to make sure you are focusing on the message rather than on judging the messenger. Good listeners say to themselves, "While it may be distracting, I am simply not going to let the appearance of this speaker keep my attention from the message."

Differing Speech Rate and Thought Rate

ambush listener. Person who is overly critical and judgmental when listening to others.

Your ability to think faster than people speak is another listening pitfall. The average person speaks at a rate of 125 words a minute. Some folks talk a bit faster, others more slowly. In contrast, you have the ability to process up to 600 or 800 words a minute. The difference between your mental ability to handle words and the speed at which

they arrive at your cortical centers can cause trouble, giving you time to daydream and to tune the speaker in and out and giving you the illusion that you are concentrating more attentively than you actually are.[31]

You can turn your listening speed into an advantage if you use the extra time instead to summarize what a speaker is saying. By periodically sprinkling in mental summaries during a conversation, you can dramatically increase your listening ability and make the speech-rate/thought-rate difference work to your advantage.

Shifting Attention

Some people can do two things at once, and some people can't. To be able to multitask—work on several tasks simultaneously—is a valued skill for administrative assistants, but some people have more difficulty multitasking than others. When it comes to listening to more than one message at a time, research suggests that men are more likely to have difficulty attending to multiple messages; when they are focused on a message, they may have more difficulty than women in carrying on a conversation with another person.[32] Men have a tendency to lock on to a message, while women seem more adept at shifting between two or more simultaneous messages. Sometimes, when men watch a TV program, they may seem lost in their video world—oblivious to other voices around them. Women, on the other hand, are more likely to be carrying on a conversation with one person and also focusing on a message they may hear nearby. No, this difference doesn't mean that women are more likely to eavesdrop intentionally—simply that some women have greater potential to listen to two things at once.

What are the implications of this research? It may be especially important for women to stop and focus on the message of others, rather than on either internal or external competing messages. And men may need to be sensitive to others who may want to speak to them, rather than becoming oblivious to their surroundings and fixated on their own internal message or on a single external message such as sports, news, opera, or a movie on TV. Being able to stop competing thoughts and focus on a single message can enhance comprehension of the message on which you are focused.[33] It's useful, however, to make sure this message is the most important one to which you should be attending.

Information Overload

We live in an information-rich age. We are all constantly bombarded with sights and sounds, and experts suggest that the volume of information competing for our attention is likely to become even greater in the future. Fax machines, satellite radio, cell phones, audio features on computers, and other technological devices can interrupt conversations and distract us from listening to others.

Information overload can prevent us from being able to communicate effectively with people around us.

Be on the alert for these information interruptions when you are talking with others. Don't assume that because you are ready to talk, the other person is ready to listen. If your message is particularly sensitive or important, you may want to ask your listening partner, "Is this a good time to talk?" Even if he or she says yes, look for eye contact and a responsive facial expression to make sure the positive response is genuine.

External Noise

As you will recall, all the communication models in Chapter 1 include the element of noise—distractions that take your focus away from the message. Many households seem to be addicted to noise. Often, there is a TV on (sometimes more than one), a computer game beeping, and music emanating from another room. These and other sounds compete for your attention when you are listening to others.

Besides literal noise, there are other potential distractors. A headline in your evening paper about a lurid sex scandal may "shout" for your attention just when your son wants to talk with you about his latest science fiction story. A desire to listen to your new compact disk of "Pacific Overtures" may drown out your spouse's overtures to have a heart-to-heart talk about your family's budget problems. The lure of music, TV, books, or your computer can all distract you from your listening task.

Distractions make it difficult to sustain attention to a message. You have a choice to make. You can attempt to listen through the competing distractions, or you can modify the environment to reduce them. Turning off the stereo, setting down the paper, and establishing eye contact with the speaker can help minimize the noise barrier.

Listener Apprehension

Not only do some people become nervous and apprehensive about speaking to others, but some are anxious about listening to others. Listener apprehension is the fear of misunderstanding or misinterpreting, or of not being able to adjust psychologically to messages spoken by others.[34] Because some people are nervous or worried about missing the message, they *do* misunderstand the message; their fear and apprehension keep them from absorbing it.[35] President Franklin Roosevelt's admonition that "The only thing we have to fear is fear itself" implies correctly that fear can become "noise" and keep people from listening to messages accurately. If you are one of those people who are nervous when listening, you may experience difficulty understanding all you hear.

If you're an apprehensive listener, you will have to work harder when you listen to others. When listening to a public speech, it may be acceptable to use a tape or digital recorder or to start taking notes; it's not appropriate or even always possible to have a recorder or paper and pencil to take notes during interpersonal conversations. If you're on the phone, you can take notes when you listen to help you remember the message content, but taping phone conversations without the other speaker's consent is not ethical. Whether you're face-to-face with the speaker or on the phone, what you can do is try to mentally summarize the message as you're listening to it. Concentrating on the message by mentally summarizing what you hear can help take your mind off your anxiety and help you focus on the message.

Listening Barriers

Listening Barrier	To Overcome the Barrier
Being Self-Absorbed	Consciously become aware of the self-focus and shift attention.
Unchecked Emotions	Use self-talk to manage emotions.
Criticizing the Speaker	Focus on the message, not the messenger.
Differing Speech and Thought Rate	Use the time difference between speech rate and thought rate to mentally summarize the message.
Shifting Attention	Focus on the most important message vying for your attention.
Information Overload	Realize when you or your partner is tired or distracted and not ready to listen.
External Noise	Take charge of the listening environment by eliminating distractions.
Listener Apprehension	Concentrate on the message as you mentally summarize what you hear.

Improving Listening, Comprehension, and Responding Skills

Many of the listening problems that we have identified stem from focusing on one's self rather than on the messages of others. Dale Carnegie, in his classic book *How to Win Friends and Influence People,* offered this tip to enhance interpersonal relationships: "Focus first on being interested, not interesting."[36] In essence, he was affirming the importance of being other-oriented when listening to others.

You can become a more other-oriented listener by following three steps you probably first encountered in elementary school: (1) stop, (2) look, and (3) listen; then (4) ask questions, and (5) reflect content by paraphrasing. Although these steps may seem simplistic and just common sense, they are not always common practice. They can provide the necessary structure to help you refocus your mental energies and improve your listening power. These steps to improved listening are supported by a considerable body of listening research. Let's consider each step separately.

Stop

Stop what? What should you *not* do in order to be a better listener? You should not be attending to "self-talk." Your internal, self-generated messages may distract you from giving your undivided attention to what others are saying.

Most interpersonal listening problems can be traced to a single source—ourselves. While listening to others, we also "talk" to ourselves. Our internal thoughts are like a play-by-play sportscast. We mentally comment on the words and sights that we select and to which we attend. If we keep those comments focused on the message, they may be useful. But we often attend to our own internal dialogues instead of others' messages. Then our listening effectiveness plummets.

Two listening researchers conducted a study to identify the specific behaviors that good listeners perform when listening. What they discovered supports our admonition that the first thing you have to do be a better listener is to stop focusing on your own mental messages and be other-oriented. Specifically, you should take the following actions during what the researchers called the "pre-interaction phase" of listening.

In a noisy environment, listeners must carefully select the sounds of a conversation from an array of other sounds they are hearing.

- Put your own thoughts aside.
- Be there mentally as well as physically.
- Make a conscious, mindful effort to listen.
- Take adequate time to listen; don't rush the speaker; be patient.
- Be open-minded.[37]

It boils down to this: When you listen, you are either on task or off task. When you are on task, you are concentrating on the message; when you're off task, your mind may be a thousand miles away. What's important is to be mindful of what you are doing. Research suggests that you can increase your motivation to listen by reminding yourself why listening is important; sprinkling in a few "self-talk" reminders of why the information you are listening to is important can enhance your listening skill.[38]

Two researchers studied how to enhance the performance of "professional listeners" who work in call centers, places where customers call to order products, make product suggestions, or even offer complaints.[39] They found that customers preferred listeners who were focused and communicated that they were devoting their full attention to the caller. Training listeners to avoid distractions, home in on the essence of a caller's message, and stop and focus on what the callers were telling them increased customers' confidence and satisfaction in the speaker–listener relationship. The researchers also concluded that the ability to stop and focus on the comments of others can be taught. People who learn how to stop mental distractions can improve their listening comprehension.

BE OTHER-ORIENTED 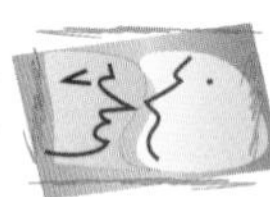

Look

Nonverbal messages are powerful. As the primary ways we communicate feelings, emotions, and attitudes, they play a major role in the total communication process, particularly in the development of relationships. Facial expressions and vocal cues, as well as eye contact, posture, and use of gestures and movement, can dramatically color the meaning of a message. When the nonverbal message contradicts the verbal message, people almost always believe the nonverbal message. In listening to others, it is vital that you focus not only on the words, but also on the nonverbal messages.

Accurately interpreting nonverbal messages can help you "listen between the lines" by noting what someone is not saying verbally but expressing nonverbally. By attending to your partner's unspoken message, you are looking for the **meta-message**—the message about the message. Meta-communication, as you learned in Chapter 1, is communication about communication. The nonverbal meta-message provides a source of information about the emotional and relational impact of what a speaker may be expressing with the verbal message. For example, a friend may not explicitly say that he or she is angry, upset, or irritated, but his or her nonverbal cues let you know that your friend is not happy. The essence of the "look" step is to listen with your eyes as well as your ears.

meta-message. A message about a message; the message a person is expressing via nonverbal means (such as by facial expression, eye contact, and posture) about the message articulated with words.

Another reason to look at another person is to establish eye contact, which signals that you are focusing your interest and attention on him or her. If your eyes are darting over your partner's head, looking for someone else, or if you are constantly peeking at your watch, your partner will rightly get the message that you're not really listening. Researcher J. Harrigan found that people telegraph desire to change roles from listener to speaker by increasing eye contact, using gestures such as a raised finger, and shifting posture.[40] So it is important to maintain eye contact and monitor your partner's nonverbal signals when you are listening as well as when you are speaking.

It is important, however, not to be distracted by nonverbal cues that may prevent you from interpreting the message correctly. A research team asked one group of college students to listen to a counselor, and another group both to watch the counselor and to listen.[41] The students then rated the counselor's effectiveness. Students who both saw and heard the counselor perceived him as *less* effective, because his distracting nonverbal behaviors affected their evaluations.

Listen

After making a concerted effort to stop distracting internal dialogue and to look for nonverbal cues, you will be in a better position to understand the verbal messages of others. To listen is to do more than focus on facts and message details; it is to search for the essence of the speaker's thoughts.

Research suggests that effective listeners are active rather than passive when listening. Precisely what are some of the behaviors involved in active listening? Here's a summary of what two listening researchers found that listeners do during the normal course of actively listening to another person:[42]

- Just listen—do not interrupt.
- Respond appropriately and provide feedback; provide both appropriate verbal feedback ("yes, I see," "I understand") as well as nonverbal feedback (eye contact, nodding, appropriate facial expressions).
- Appropriately contribute to the conversation.

Effective listeners are not only goal-oriented (listening to the point of the message) but are also people-oriented (listening to appropriately affirm the person). To maximize your listening effectiveness, we offer several more specific strategies and tips.

Determine Your Listening Goal

You listen to other people for several reasons—to learn, to enjoy yourself, to evaluate, or to provide empathic support. With so many potential listening goals and options, it is useful to decide consciously what your listening objective is.

If you are listening to someone give you directions to the city park, then your mental summaries should focus on the details of when to turn left and how many streets past the courthouse you go before you turn right. The details are crucial to achieving your objective. If, in contrast, your neighbor is telling you about her father's triple bypass operation, then your goal is to empathize. It is probably not important that you be able to recall when her father checked into the hospital or other details. Your job is to listen patiently and to provide emotional support. Clarifying your listening objective in your own mind can help you use appropriate skills to maximize your listening effectiveness.

Transform Listening Barriers into Listening Goals

If you can transform into listening goals the listening barriers you read about earlier, you will be well on your way to improving your listening skill. Make it a goal not to focus on your personal agenda. Make it a goal to use self-talk to manage emotional noise. Set a goal not to criticize the speaker. Remind yourself before each conversation to create mental summaries that capitalize on the differences between your information processing rate and the speaker's verbal delivery rate.[43] And make it your business to choose a communication environment that is free of distraction from other incoming information or noise.

When Your Listening Goal Is to Remember a Message, Mentally Summarize the Details of the Message

This suggestion may seem to contradict the suggestion to avoid focusing only on facts; but if your goal is to be able to recall information, it is important to grasp the details that your partner provides. As we noted earlier, you can process words much more quickly than a person speaks. So periodically summarize the names, dates, and locations in the message. Organize the speaker's factual information into appropriate categories or try to place events in chronological order. Without a full understanding of the details, you will likely miss the speaker's major point.

Mentally Weave These Summaries into a Focused Major Point or a Series of Major Ideas

Facts usually make the most sense when you can use them to help support an idea or major point. So, as you summarize, try to link the facts you have organized in your mind with key ideas and principles. Use facts to enhance your critical thinking as you analyze, synthesize, evaluate, and finally summarize the key points or ideas your listening partner is making.[44]

Practice Listening to Challenging Material

To improve or even maintain any skill, you need to practice it. Listening experts suggest that listening skills deteriorate if people do not practice what they know. Listening to difficult, challenging material can sharpen listening skills, so good listeners practice by listening to documentaries, debates, and other challenging material.

Ask Questions

Sometimes when someone has something momentous to share, the story tumbles out in a rambling, disorganized way. You can help sort through the story if you ask questions to identify the sequence of events. "What happened first?" and "Then what happened?" can help both you and your partner clarify what happened.

If your partner is using words or phrases that you don't understand, ask for definitions. "He's just so lackadaisical!" moans Mariko. "What do you mean by lackadaisical? Could you give me an example?" asks Reggie. Sometimes asking for an example helps the speaker sort through the events as well.

Of course, if you are trying to understand another's feelings, you can ask how he or she is feeling, or how the event or situation made him or her feel. Often, however, nonverbal cues are more revealing than a verbal disclosure about feelings and emotions.

Reflect Content by Paraphrasing

BE OTHER-ORIENTED

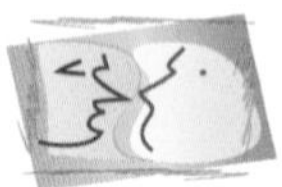

The only way to know whether you understand another person's message is to check your understanding of the facts and ideas by paraphrasing your understanding. Verbally reflecting what you understood the speaker to say can dramatically minimize misunderstanding. Respond with a statement such as

"Are you saying . . ."

"You seem to be describing . . ."

"So the point you are making seems to be . . ."

"Here is what I understand you to mean . . ."

"So here's what seems to have happened . . ."

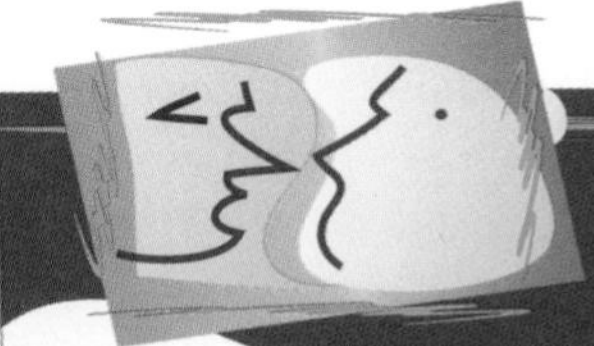

Becoming Other-Oriented

Identifying Message Details and Major Ideas

How skilled are you at noting both the details of a message and its major ideas? To become a skilled listener, you must know how to identify both of these aspects of what someone is telling you. Here's a chance to practice your skill in identifying and remembering bits of information, as well as the main meaning of a message.

Read each of the following statements. After you have read each statement, cover it with your hand or a piece of paper. First, list as many of the details as you can recall from the message. Second, summarize your understanding of the major idea or key point of the message. As a variation on this activity, rather than reading the statement, have someone read the statement to you and then identify the details and major idea.

Statement 1: "I'm very confused. I reserved our conference room for 1 P.M. today for an important meeting. We all know that conference space is tight. I reserved the room last week with the administrative assistant. Now I learn that you are planning to use the conference room at noon for a two-hour meeting. It's now 11 a.m. We need to solve this problem soon. I have no other option for holding my meeting. And if I don't hold my meeting today, the boss is going to be upset."

Statement 2: "Hello, Marcia? I'm calling on my cell phone. Where are you? I thought you were supposed to meet me at the circle drive 45 minutes ago. You know I can't be late for my seminar this evening. What do you mean, you're waiting at the circle drive? I don't see you. No, I'm at Switzler Hall circle drive. You're where? No, that's not the circle drive I meant. I thought you'd know where I meant. Don't you ever listen? If you hurry, I can just make it to the seminar."

Statement 3: "Oh, Mary, I just don't know what to do. My daughter announced that when she turns 18 next week she's going to shave her head, get a large tattoo, and put a ring in her nose and eyebrow. She said it's something she's always wanted to do and now she can do it without my permission. She's always been such a sweet, compliant girl, but she seems to have turned wacky. I've tried talking with her. And her father isn't much help. He thinks it may look 'cool.' I just don't want her to look like a freak when she has her senior picture taken next month."

Then summarize the events, details, or key points you think the speaker is trying to convey. Your summary need not be a word-for-word repetition of what the speaker has said, nor do you need to summarize the content of *each* phrase or minor detail. Rather, you will **paraphrase** to check the accuracy of your understanding. Here is an example:

Juan: This week I have so much extra work to do. I'm sorry if I haven't been able to help keep this place clean. I know it's my turn to do the dishes tonight, but I have to get back to work. Could you do the dishes tonight?

Brigid: So you want me to do the dishes tonight and for the rest of the week. Right?

Juan: Well, I'd like you to help with the dishes tonight. But I think I can handle it for the rest of the week.

Brigid: OK. So I'll do them tonight and you take over tomorrow.

Juan: Yes.

Research conducted in clinical counseling settings found that when a listener paraphrases the content and feelings of a speaker, the speaker is more likely to trust and

paraphrase. Verbal summary of the key ideas of your partner's message that helps you check the accuracy of your understanding.

value the listener.[45] Paraphrasing to check understanding is also a vital skill to use when you are trying to reconcile a difference of opinion. Chapter 8 shows you how to use it in that context.

Recap: How to Improve Your Listening Skills

Step	Listening Skill	Action
Stop	Tune out distracting competing messages.	Become conscious of being distracted; use self-talk to remain focused.
Look	Become aware of the speaker's nonverbal cues; monitor your own nonverbal cues to communicate your interest in the speaker.	Establish eye contact; avoid fidgeting or performing other tasks when someone is speaking to you; listen with your eyes.
Listen	Create meaning from your partner's verbal and nonverbal messages.	Mentally summarize details; link these details with main ideas.
Ask questions	Clarify the message by questioning the speaker.	Ask for definitions and examples; clarify feelings and sequences of events.
Reflect content by paraphrasing when appropriate	Briefly state the essence of what the speaker has said, to ensure the accuracy of your understanding.	Summarize the key details or points of what the speaker has said.

Improving Empathic Listening and Responding Skills

When your friends have "one of those days," perhaps they seek you out to talk about it. They may not have any real problems to solve—perhaps it was just a day filled with miscommunication and squabbles with their partners or co-workers. But they want to tell you the details. Your friends are seeking a listener who focuses attention on them and understands what they are saying. As we discussed in Chapter 4, at the heart of being other-oriented is cultivating **empathy**—feeling what someone else is feeling.[46] The word *empathy* comes from a Greek word for "passion" and is related to the German word *einfülung,* which means "to feel with."

BE OTHER-ORIENTED

Developing empathy is not a single skill but a collection of skills that help you predict how others will respond. There is clear evidence that being empathic is linked to being a better listener.[47] Daniel Goleman's book *Emotional Intelligence* is an outstanding resource that discusses the role and importance of our emotions in developing empathy with others.[48] Goleman has found evidence that people who are emotionally intelligent—sensitive to others, empathic, and other-oriented—have better interpersonal relationships. Goleman summarizes the centrality of emotions in developing empathy by quoting Antoine de Saint-Exupery: "It is with the heart that one sees rightly; what is essential is invisible to the eye."[49]

empathy. Feeling what others are feeling, rather than just acknowledging that they are feeling a certain way.

active listening. Interactive process of responding mentally, verbally, and nonverbally to a speaker's message.

Good listening, especially listening to empathize with another, is active, not passive. To listen passively is to sit with a blank stare or a frozen facial expression. A passive listener's thoughts and feelings could be anywhere, for all the speaker knows.[50] Those who engage in **active listening,** in contrast, respond mentally, verbally, and nonverbally to a speaker's message. Responding serves several specific functions. First, it can be a measure of how accurately you understood the message. If you burst out laughing as your friend tells you about losing his house in a flood, he'll know you misunderstood what he was saying. Second, your responses indicate whether you agree or disagree with the comments others make. If you tell your friend that you do not approve of her comments on abortion, she'll know your position on the information she shared. Finally, your responses tell speakers how they are affecting you. When you get tears in your eyes as you listen to your friend describe how lonely he has felt since his father died, he will know that you are affected by the pain he is feeling. Like radar that guides high-tech rockets, your feedback provides information to help others decide whether or not to correct the course of their messages.

Of course, listening to empathize is only one of the possible listening goals you may have. We are not suggesting that ferreting out someone's emotions is the goal of every listening encounter. That would be tedious for both you and your listening partners. But when you do want to listen empathically and respond, you must shift the focus to your partner and try to understand the message from his or her perspective.[51] Psychologist and counselor Carl Rogers summarized the value of empathy when he said, "A high degree of empathy in a relationship is possibly the most potent factor in bringing about change and learning."[52]

The quiz in Building Your Skills: Test Your Empathy can help you determine how effectively you empathize with others. We then discuss strategies you can use to enhance your empathy skills.

Building Your Skills

Test Your Empathy

Empathy is an emotional capability that often grows out of a conscious decentering process. It is the ability to move away from yourself enough to "feel with" another person. But feeling empathy does not mean abandoning your own self. On the contrary, empathic people often have a strong self-concept and high self-esteem, which enable them to be generous with others. Take this short test to assess your empathy. Respond to each statement by indicating the degree to which the statement reflects how you typically communicate with others. Is the statement (1) Always false, (2) Usually false, (3) Sometimes false and sometimes true, (4) Usually true, or (5) Always true?

_____ 1. I try to understand others' experiences from their perspectives.

_____ 2. I follow the Golden Rule ("Do unto others as you would have them do unto you") when communicating with others.

_____ 3. I can "tune in" to emotions others are experiencing when we communicate.

_____ 4. When trying to understand how others feel, I imagine how I would feel in their situation.

_____ 5. I am able to tell what others are feeling without being told.

_____ 6. Others experience the same feelings I do in any given situation.

_____ 7. When others are having problems, I can imagine how they feel.

_____ 8. I find it hard to understand the emotions others experience.

_____ 9. I try to see others as they want me to.

_____ 10. I never seem to know what others are thinking when we communicate.

To find your score, first reverse the responses for the even-numbered items (if you wrote 1, make it 5; if you wrote 2, make it 4; if you wrote 3, leave it as 3; if you wrote 4, make it 2; if you wrote 5, make it 1). Next, add the numbers next to each statement. Scores range from ten to fifty. The higher your score, the more you are able to empathize.

Source: William Gudykunst, *Bridging Differences,* 3rd ed. (Thousand Oaks, CA: Sage, 1998), 234. Reprinted by permission of Sage Publications, Inc.

Interpersonal Communication and Emotion: Connecting Heart to Heart

How to Express Helpful and Empathic Social Support to Others

One of the ways you can communicate empathy to another person who is experiencing stress, pain, or a significant life problem is to provide what communication researchers call **social support**. You provide social support to another person when you sensitively and empathically listen and then offer messages of comfort or confirmation that let the other person know that he or she is both understood and valued.

One research study suggests that when we are experiencing stress we prefer what researchers called a mid-level amount of social support.[53] Most people don't need over-the-top, dramatic expressions of support; on the other hand, mild or timid expressions of support from others are not satisfying either. We seem to like a moderate level of positive, genuine supportive communication. The research also suggests that females prefer a bit higher level of comforting response than males.

An ability to listen empathically is important when you discern that someone needs positive, comforting social support. What do researchers suggest are the best ways to provide supportive, empathic, comforting messages to others? Although there are no magic words or phrases that will always ease someone's stress and anxiety, here's a summary of social support messages that seem to be appreciated by others.[54]

- Clearly express that you want to provide support. ("I would really like to help you.")
- Appropriately communicate that you have positive feelings for the other person; explicitly tell the other person that you are a friend, that you care about or love him or her. ("You mean a lot to me." "I really care about you.")
- Express your concern about the situation that the other person is in right now. ("I'm worried about you right now because I know you're feeling _____ [stressed, overwhelmed, sad, etc.].")
- Indicate that you are available to help, that you have time to support the person. ("I can be here for you when you need me.")
- Let the other person know how much you support her or him ("I'm completely with you on this." "I'm here for you, and I'll always be here for you because I care about you.")
- Acknowledge that the other person is in a difficult situation. ("This must be very difficult for you.")
- It may be appropriate to paraphrase what the other person has told you about the issue or problem that is causing stress. ("So you became upset when she told you she didn't want to see you again.")
- Consider asking open-ended questions to see if the other person wants to talk. ("How are you doing now?")
- Let the other person know that you are listening and supportive by providing conversational continuers such as "Yes, then what happened?" or "Oh, I see," or "Uh-huh."
- After expressing your compassion, empathy, and concern, just listen.

Some types of responses are less helpful when providing social support. Here are a few things *not* to do, based on the conclusions of communication researchers:

- Don't tell the other person that you know exactly how he or she feels.
- Don't criticize or negatively evaluate the other person; he or she needs support and validation, not judgmental comments.
- Don't tell the other person to stop feeling what he or she is feeling.
- Don't immediately offer advice. First, just listen.
- Don't tell the other person that "it's going to get better from here" or that "the worst is over."
- Don't tell the other person that there is really nothing to worry about or that "it's no big deal."
- Don't tell the other person that the problem can be solved easily. ("Oh, you can always find another girlfriend.")
- Don't blame the other person for the problem. ("Well, if you didn't always drive so fast, you wouldn't have had the accident.")
- Don't tell the other person that it is wrong to express feelings and emotions. ("Oh, you're just making yourself sick. Stop crying.")

PEARLS BEFORE SWINE: © Stephan Pastis/Dist. by United Features Syndicate, Inc.

Understand Your Partner's Feelings: Imagine How You Would Feel

When your goal is to empathize with your partner, you might begin by imagining how you would feel under the same circumstances. If your spouse comes home dejected from being hassled at work, try to recall how you felt when that happened to you. If a friend calls to tell you his mother is ill, try to imagine how you would feel if the situation were reversed. Of course, your reaction to these events might be different from your spouse's or your friend's. You may need to decenter and remember how your partner felt in other similar situations, to understand how he or she is feeling now.

BE OTHER-ORIENTED

Paraphrase Emotions

The bottom line in empathic responding is to make certain that you accurately understand how the other person is feeling. You can paraphrase, beginning with such phrases as

"So you are feeling . . ."

"You must feel . . ."

"So now you feel . . ."

In the following example of empathic responding, the listener asks questions, summarizes content, and summarizes feelings.

David: I think I'm in over my head. My boss gave me a job to do, and I just don't know how to do it. I'm afraid I've bitten off more than I can chew.

Mike: (Thinks how he would feel if he were given an important task at work but did not know how to complete the task, then asks for more information.) What job did she ask you to do?

David: I'm supposed to do an inventory of all the items in the warehouse on the new computer system and have it finished by the end of the week. I don't have the foggiest notion of how to start. I've never even used that system.

Mike: (Summarizes feelings.) So you feel panicked because you may not have enough time to learn the system *and* do the inventory.

David: Well, I'm not only panicked; I'm afraid I may be fired.

Mike: (Summarizes feelings.) So your fear that you might lose your job is getting in the way of just focusing on the task and seeing what you can get done. It's making you feel like you made a mistake in taking this job.

David: That's exactly how I feel.

Note that toward the end of the dialogue, Mike has to make a couple of tries to summarize David's feelings accurately. Also note that Mike does a good job of listening and responding without giving advice. Just by being an active listener, you can help your partner clarify a problem.

BE OTHER-ORIENTED

Researcher John Gottman summarizes several specific ways to make listening active rather than passive:[55]

- Start by asking questions.
- Ask questions about people's goals and visions of the future.

social support. Positive, sincere, supportive messages, both verbal and nonverbal, offered to help others deal with stress, anxiety, or uncertainty.

- Look for commonalities.
- Tune in with all your attention.
- Respond with an occasional brief nod or sound.
- From time to time, paraphrase what the speaker says.
- Maintain the right amount of eye contact.
- Let go of your own agenda.

sympathy. Acknowledgment that someone is feeling bad; offer of support

We have discussed responding and active listening using a tidy step-by-step textbook approach. In practice, you may have to back up and clarify content, ask more questions, and rethink how you would feel before you attempt to summarize how someone else feels. Conversely, you may be able to summarize feelings *without* asking questions or summarizing content if the message is clear and it relates to a situation with which you are very familiar. Overusing paraphrasing can slow down a conversation and make the other person uncomfortable or irritated. But if you use it judiciously,

Building Your Skills

Sympathy versus Empathy

Most card shops have a sympathy card section. Such cards let people know you realize they are feeling bad about something—perhaps the death of someone close to them. To offer **sympathy** is to offer your support and acknowledge that someone is feeling bad. *Empathy* goes one step further than sympathy. Empathy means that you try to perceive the world from another's perspective; you attempt to feel what someone else feels.

Respond to these sample situations with sympathy and with empathy.

1. A good friend just phoned to tell you that her well-loved fourteen-year-old dog has just died.

   Respond with sympathy: ____________________

   Respond with empathy: ____________________

2. Your older brother comes to visit you and tells you that he and his wife are getting a divorce after twenty years of marriage.

   Respond with sympathy: ____________________

   Respond with empathy: ____________________

Source: Adapted from William Gudykunst, *Bridging Differences,* 3rd ed. (Thousand Oaks, CA: Sage, 1998). Reprinted by permission of Sage Publications, Inc.

paraphrasing can help both you and your partner keep focused on the issues and ideas at hand.

Reflecting content or feeling through paraphrasing can be especially useful in the following situations:

- Before you take an important action
- Before you argue or criticize
- When your partner has strong feelings or wants to talk over a problem
- When your partner is speaking "in code" or using unclear abbreviations

Applying Theory and Research

Listening to Others' Stories as Co-Storyteller

A study conducted by communication researchers Janet Bavelas, Linda Coates, and Trudy Johnson sought to investigate what kinds of responses listeners make when listening to a personal story and how those responses affect the speaker. To investigate the effect of listeners' responses to a storyteller, they had one person listen and another person tell a story about a time when she or he had experienced a close call—such as narrowly missing being hurt or injured. In one condition, the listener was just to listen and make no comments. In the second condition, the listener was to listen and summarize the gist of what the speaker was saying in a sentence or two. The third condition had the listener actively paraphrase what the speaker was saying. For the fourth condition, the listeners were to listen while mentally counting how many days it was until Christmas. Although this last condition sounds like a bizarre task, the purpose was to explore the effects of having a listener supposedly listening but not paying attention to what the speaker was saying. The researchers wanted to know whether how a listener responded to what a speaker was saying had an impact on how the speaker told the story.

APPLYING the Research to Your Life

The researchers found that when the listener made no responses to the speaker, the speaker told the story less effectively. When speakers had a listener who made specific responses and responded in meaningful ways, the speakers were better at telling their story. The researchers also discovered that listeners are more likely to make specific rather than general comments later in the narrative. This observation makes sense; more specific comments are more likely to occur later in a story because the listener has had time to learn about the major elements in the story he or she is listening to. The results suggest that an effective listener is really a "co-narrator," or active participant in the communication process, rather than merely a passive listener. It's not that specific comments are better than general comments; what's important is that the responses the listener makes should be appropriate—comments that fit the story can actually help the speaker gauge how effectively he or she is telling the story. And without any responses, the speaker may think the listener isn't really interested in the story. The kinds of responses a listener makes during an effective conversation are different than those a listener makes if a speaker is delivering a monologue. Because communication is transactive, a dynamic process in which meaning is created between speaker and listener, the kinds of responses a listener makes should be authentic, not "canned" or stilted.

What do these results mean to you? If, while your friend is pouring her heart out about the exasperating experience of having a flat tire in the rain, you respond with a vacant look and periodically grunt, "Uh-uh," or "OK," or "Ah," your mumbles may lead your friend to believe you aren't really listening all that closely. And if your friend thinks you aren't interested or listening to her story, she may either cut the story short or try to throttle up the drama of the story to get your attention. On the other hand, if you appropriately paraphrase the worst parts of her experience, or provide well-timed responses that fit with what she is saying, she's more likely to believe that you are really listening and that you care about her ordeal.

A good listener can help bring out the best in a speaker.

Source: J. B. Bavelas, L. Coates, and T. Johnson, "Listeners as Co-Narrators," *Journal of Personality and Social Psychology,* 79(6) (2000): 941–52.

- When your partner wants to understand your feelings and thoughts
- When you are talking to yourself
- When you encounter new ideas[56]

Sometimes, however, you truly don't understand how another person really feels. At times like this, be cautious of telling others, "I know just how you feel." It may be more important simply to let others know that you care about them than to grill them about their feelings.

If you do decide to use paraphrasing skills, keep the following guidelines in mind:

- Use your own words.
- Don't go beyond the information communicated by the speaker.
- Be concise.
- Be specific.
- Be accurate.

Do *not* use paraphrasing skills if you aren't able to be open and accepting, if you do not trust the other person to find his or her own solution, if you are using these skills as a way of hiding yourself from another, or if you feel pressured, hassled, or tired. And as we have already discussed, overuse of paraphrasing can be distracting and unnatural.

BE OTHER-ORIENTED 

Don't be discouraged if your initial attempts to use these skills seem awkward and uncomfortable. Any new skill takes time to learn and use well. The instructions and samples you have read should serve as guides, rather than as hard-and-fast prescriptions to follow during each conversation.

Listen

When I ask you to listen to me and you start giving advice,
you have not done what I asked.
When I ask you to listen to me and you begin to tell me why I shouldn't feel that way,
you are trampling on my feelings.
When I ask you to listen to me and you feel you have to do something
to solve my problems, you have failed me, strange as that may seem.
Listen! All I asked, was that you listen. Not talk or do—just hear me.
Advice is cheap: 50 cents will get you both Dear Abby and Billy Graham
in the same newspaper.
And I can do for myself; I'm not helpless. Maybe discouraged and faltering,
but not helpless.
When you do something for me that I can and need to do for myself,
you contribute to my fear and weakness.
But when you accept as a simple fact that I do feel what I feel,
no matter how irrational, then I quit trying to convince you and
can get about the business of understanding what's behind this irrational feeling.
And when that's clear, the answers are obvious and I don't need advice.
Irrational feelings make sense when we understand what's behind them.
Perhaps that's why prayer works, sometimes, for some people—
because God is mute, and doesn't give advice or try to fix things,
God just listens and lets you work it out for yourself.
So, please listen and just hear me, and, if you want to talk,
wait a minute for your turn, and I'll listen to you.

Anonymous

Responding to Confirm or Disconfirm Others

Couple A:

Wife to husband: "I just don't feel appreciated any more."

Husband to wife: "Margaret, I'm so very sorry. I love you. You're the most important person in the world to me."

Couple B:

Wife to husband: "I just don't feel appreciated any more."

Husband to wife: "Well, what about my feelings? Don't my feelings count? You'll have to do what you have to do. What's for dinner?"

It doesn't take an expert in interpersonal communication to know that Couple B's relationship is not warm and confirming. Researchers have studied the specific kinds of responses people offer to others.[57] Some responses are confirming; other responses are disconfirming. A **confirming response** is an other-oriented statement that causes others to value themselves more; Wife A is likely to value herself more after her husband's confirming response. A **disconfirming response** is a statement that causes others to value themselves less. Wife B knows firsthand what it's like to have her feelings ignored and disconfirmed. Are you aware of whether your responses to others confirm them or disconfirm them? To help you be more aware of the kinds of responses you make to others, we'll review the results of studies that identify both confirming and disconfirming responses.[58]

BE OTHER-ORIENTED

Provide Confirming Responses

The adage "People judge us by our words and behavior rather than by our intent" summarizes the underlying principle of confirming responses. Those who receive your messages determine whether they have the effect you intended. Formulating confirming responses requires careful listening and attention to the other person. Does it really matter whether we confirm others? Marriage researcher John Gottman used video cameras and microphones to observe couples interacting in an apartment over an extended period of time. He found that a significant predictor of divorce was neglecting to confirm or affirm one's marriage partner during typical, everyday conversation—even though couples who were less likely to divorce spent only a few seconds more confirming their partner than couples who eventually did divorce. His research conclusion has powerful implications: Long-lasting relationships are characterized by supportive, confirming messages.[59] The everyday kinds of confirmation and support we offer need not be excessive—sincere moderate, heart-felt support is evaluated as the most positive and desirable kind of support.[60] We will describe several kinds of confirming responses in this section.

Direct Acknowledgment

When you respond directly to something another person says to you, you are acknowledging not only the statement, but also that the person is worth responding to.

Joan: It certainly is a nice day for a canoe trip.

Mariko: Yes, Joan, it's a great day to be outside.

confirming response. Statement that causes another person to value himself or herself more.

disconfirming response. Statement that causes another person to value himself or herself less.

Agreement About Judgments

When you confirm someone's evaluation of something, you are also affirming that person's sense of taste and judgment.

Nancy: I think the steel guitar player's riff was fantastic.

Victor: Yes, I think it was the best part of the performance.

Supportive Response

When you express reassurance and understanding, you are confirming a person's right to his or her feelings.

Lionel: I'm disappointed that I only scored 60 on my interpersonal communication test.

Sarah: I'm sorry to see you so frustrated, Lionel. I know that test was important to you.

Clarifying Response

When you seek greater understanding of another person's message, you are confirming that he or she is worth your time and trouble. Clarifying responses also encourage the other person to talk in order to explore his or her feelings.

Larry: I'm not feeling very good about my family situation these days.

Tyrone: Is it tough with you and Margo working different shifts?

Expression of Positive Feeling

We feel confirmed or valued when someone else agrees with our expression of joy or excitement.

Lorraine: I'm so excited! I was just promoted to associate professor.

Dorette: Congratulations! I'm so proud of you! Heaven knows you deserve it.

Compliment

When you tell people you like what they have done or said, what they are wearing, or how they look, you are confirming their sense of worth.

Jean-Christophe: Did you get the invitation to my party?

Manny: Yes! It looked so professional. I didn't know you could do calligraphy. You're a talented guy.

In each of these examples, note how the responder provides comments that confirm the worth or value of the other person. But keep in mind that confirming responses should be sincere. Offering false praise is manipulative, and your communication partner will probably sniff out your phoniness.

Avoid Disconfirming Responses

Some statements and responses can undermine another person's self-worth. We offer these categories so that you can avoid using them and also recognize them when someone uses them to chip away at your self-image and self-esteem.

Impervious Response

When a person fails to acknowledge your statement or attempt to communicate, even though you know he or she heard you, you may feel a sense of awkwardness or embarrassment.

Rosa: I loved your speech, Harvey.

Harvey: (No response, verbal or nonverbal.)

Interrupting Response

Interrupting another person is one of the most corrosive, disconfirming responses you can make. Why is it so irritating to be interrupted? Because when you interrupt someone, you are implying that what you have to say is more important than what the other person has to say. In effect, your behavior communicates that *you* are more important than the other person is. You may simply be enthusiastic or excited when the words tumble out of your mouth, interrupting your communication partner. Nonetheless, be especially mindful of not interrupting others. An interrupting response is a powerful disconfirming behavior, whether you are aware of its power or not.

Anna: I just heard on the news that . . .

Sharon: Oh yes. The stock market just went down 100 points.

Irrelevant Response

An irrelevant response is one that has nothing at all to do with what you were saying. Chances are your partner is not listening to you at all.

Arnold: First we're flying down to Rio, and then to Quito. I can hardly wait to . . .

Peter: They're predicting a hard freeze tonight.

The real message Peter is sending is "I have more important things on my mind."

Tangential Response

A tangential response is one that acknowledges you, but that is only minimally related to what you are talking about. Again, it indicates that the other person isn't really attending to your message.

Richard: This new program will help us stay within our budget.

Samantha: Yeah. I think I'll save some bucks and send this letter by regular mail.

Impersonal Response

A response that intellectualizes and uses the third person distances the other person from you and has the effect of trivializing what you say.

Diana: Hey, Bill. I'd like to talk with you for a minute about getting your permission to take my vacation in July.

Bill: One tends to become interested in recreational pursuits about this time of year, doesn't one?

Incoherent Response

When a speaker mumbles, rambles, or makes some unintelligible effort to respond, you may end up wondering if what you said was of any value or use to the listener.

Paolo: George, here's my suggestion for the merger deal with Techstar. Let's make them an offer of forty-eight dollars a share and see how they respond.

George: Huh? Well . . . so . . . well . . . hmmm . . . I'm not sure.

Incongruous Response

When a verbal message is inconsistent with nonverbal behavior, people usually believe the nonverbal message, but they usually feel confused as well. An incongruous response is like a malfunctioning traffic light with red and green lights flashing simultaneously—you're just not sure whether the speaker wants you to go or stay.

Sue: Honey, do you want me to go grocery shopping with you?

Steve: (Shouting) OF COURSE I DO! WHY ARE YOU ASKING?

Although it may be impossible to eliminate all disconfirming responses from your repertoire, becoming aware of the power of your words and monitoring your conversation for offensive phrases may help you avoid unexpected and perhaps devastating consequences.

How to Respond with Empathy

Responding with Empathy	Action
Understand Your Partner's Feelings	Ask yourself how you would feel if you had experienced a similar situation, or recall how you did feel under similar circumstances. Or recall how your partner felt under similar circumstances.
Paraphrase Emotions	When appropriate, try to summarize what you think your partner may be feeling.
Provide Confirming Responses	Acknowledge what others say to you, confirm others' judgments, offer supportive responses, seek to clarify others' messages, affirm others' positive feelings, and pay sincere compliments.
Avoid Disconfirming Responses	Provide some acknowledgment of others' attempts to communicate; do not interrupt; avoid irrelevant, tangential, impersonal, incoherent, or incongruous responses.

Improving Critical Listening Skills

After putting it off for several months, you've decided to buy a cell phone. As you begin to talk to your friends, you're surprised to find a bewildering number of factors to consider: Do you want a prepaid plan? A plan that includes text messaging? Do you want your phone to take photos? Receive TV signals? How many weekend minutes, evening minutes, or daily minutes of calling time do you need? You decide to head to a store to see if a salesperson can help you sort through the maze of options. The salesperson is friendly enough, but you become even more overwhelmed with the number of options, bells, and whistles to consider. As you try to make this decision, your listening goal is not to empathize with those who extol the virtues of cell phones. Nor do you need to take a multiple-choice test on the information they share. To sort through the information, you need to listen critically.

Effective critical listening skills are crucial in a business environment.

Critical listening involves listening to evaluate the quality, appropriateness, value, or importance of the information you hear. *The goal of a critical listener is to use information to make a choice.* Whether you're selecting a new phone, deciding whom to vote for, choosing a potential date, or evaluating a new business plan, you will be faced with many opportunities to use your critical listening skills in interpersonal situations.

Identify Useful and Flawed Information

A critical listener does not necessarily offer negative comments. A critical listener seeks to identify both good information and information that is flawed or less helpful. We call this process *information triage. Triage* is a French term that usually describes the process used by emergency medical personnel to determine which of several patients is the most severely ill or injured and needs immediate medical attention. **Information triage** is a process of evaluating and sorting out information. An effective critical listener performs information triage; he or she is able to distinguish useful and accurate information and conclusions from information that is less useful, as well as conclusions that are inaccurate or invalid.

How do you develop the ability to perform information triage? Initially, listening critically involves the same strategies as listening to comprehend, which we discussed earlier. Before you evaluate information, it's vital that you first *understand* the information. Second, examine the logic or reasoning used in the message. And finally, be mindful of whether you are basing your evaluations on facts (something observed or verifiable) or inference (a conclusion based on partial information). Although courses in logic, argumentation, and public speaking often present skills to help you evaluate information, it's also important to listen critically during interpersonal conversations.

Avoid Jumping to Conclusions

Imagine that you are a detective investigating a death. You are given the following information: (1) Leo and Moshia are found lying together on the floor; (2) Leo and Moshia are both dead; (3) Leo and Moshia are surrounded by water and broken glass; (4) on the sofa near Leo and Moshia is a cat with its back arched, apparently ready to defend itself.

Given these sketchy details, do you, the detective assigned to the case, have any theories about the cause of Leo and Moshia's demise? Perhaps they slipped on the

critical listening. Listening to evaluate and assess the quality, appropriateness, value, or importance of information.

information triage. Process of evaluating information to sort good information from less useful or valid information.

water, crashed into a table, broke a vase, and died (that would explain the water and broken glass). Or maybe their attacker recently left the scene, and the cat is still distressed by the commotion. Clearly, you could make several inferences (conclusions based on partial information) as to the probable cause of death. Oh yes, there is one detail we forgot to mention: Leo and Moshia are fish. Does that help?

People often spin grand explanations and hypotheses based on sketchy details. Making inferences, people may believe the "facts" clearly point to a specific conclusion. Determining the difference between a fact and an inference can help you more accurately use language to reach valid conclusions about what you see and experience.

What makes a fact a fact? Most students, when asked this question, respond by saying, "A fact is something that has been proven true." If that is the case, *how* has something been proven true? In a court of law, a **fact** is something that has been observed or witnessed. Anything else is speculation or inference.

"Did you see my client in your house, taking your jewelry?" asks the defendant's clever attorney.

"No," says the plaintiff.

"Then you do not know for a fact that my client is a thief."

"I guess not," the plaintiff admits.

Problems occur when we respond to something as if it were a fact (something observed), when in reality it is an **inference** (a conclusion based on speculation):

"It's a fact that you will be poor all of your life."

"It's a fact that you will fail this course."

Both of these statements, although they may very well be true, misuse the term *fact*. If you cannot recognize when you are making an inference instead of stating a fact, you may give your judgments more credibility than they deserve. Being sensitive to the differences between facts and inferences can improve both critical listening and responding skills.

Improving Your Responding Skills

We've offered several strategies for responding to others when your goal is to comprehend information, empathize with others, or evaluate messages. Regardless of your communication goal, you can use several additional strategies to enhance your skill in responding to others. The timing of the response, usefulness of the information, amount of detail, and descriptiveness of the response are important to consider when responding to others.

BE OTHER-ORIENTED

Provide Well-Timed Responses

Feedback is usually most effective when you offer it at the earliest opportunity, particularly if your objective is to teach someone a skill. For example, if you are teaching your friend how to make your famous egg rolls, you provide a step-by-step commentary as you watch your pupil. If he makes a mistake, you don't wait until the egg rolls are finished to tell him that he left out the cabbage. He needs immediate feedback to finish the rest of the sequence successfully.

fact. Something that has been directly observed to be true and thus has been proven to be true.

inference. Conclusion based on speculation.

Sometimes, however, if a person is already sensitive and upset about something, delaying feedback can be wise. Use your critical thinking skills to analyze when feedback will do the most good. Rather than automatically offering immediate correction, use the just-in-time (JIT) approach and provide feedback just before the person might make another mistake. If, for example, your daughter typically rushes through math tests and fails to check her work, remind her right before her next test to double-check her answers, not immediately after the one she just failed. To provide feedback about a relationship, select a mutually agreeable place and time when both of you are rested and relaxed; avoid hurling feedback at someone "for his own good" immediately after he offends you.

When you are teaching someone a new skill, it is important to provide useful information. Here, an experienced DJ reminds a novice to spin the record with the tips of his fingers only.

Provide Usable Information

Perhaps you've heard this advice: Never try to teach a pig to sing. It wastes your time. It doesn't sound pretty. And it annoys the pig. When you provide information to someone, be certain that it is useful and relevant. How can you make sure your partner can use the information you share? Try to understand your partner's mindset. Ask yourself, "If I were this person, how would I respond to this information? Is it information I can act on? Or is it information that may make matters worse?" Under the guise of providing effective feedback, you may be tempted to tell others your complete range of feelings and emotions. But research suggests that selective feedback is best. In one study, married couples who practiced selective self-disclosure were more satisfied than couples who told everything they knew or were feeling.[61] Immersing your partner in information that is irrelevant or that may be damaging to the relationship may be cathartic, but it may not enhance the quality of your relationship or improve understanding.

Avoid Unnecessary Details

When you are selecting meaningful information, also try to cut down on the volume of information. Don't overwhelm your listener with details that obscure the key point of your feedback. Hit only the high points that will benefit the listener. Be brief.

Be Descriptive Rather Than Evaluative

"You're an awful driver!" shouts Doris to her husband, Frank. Although Doris may feel she has provided simple feedback to her spouse about his skills, Frank will probably not respond warmly or even listen closely to her feedback. If Doris were to be more descriptive and less evaluative, then he might be inclined to listen: "Frank, you are traveling 70 miles an hour in a 50 miles an hour zone," or "Frank, I get very nervous when you zigzag so fast through the freeway traffic" is a less offensive comment. It describes Frank's behavior rather than rendering judgments about him that are likely to trigger a defensive response.

Recap
Suggestions for Improving Responding Skills

Provide Well-Timed Responses	Sometimes immediate feedback is best; at other times, provide a just-in-time (JIT) response when it will do the most good.
Provide Meaningful Information	Select information that your partner can act on, rather than making vague comments or suggestions that are beyond his or her capabilities.
Avoid Unnecessary Details	Avoid information overload; be brief.
Be Descriptive	Don't evaluate your listening partner; focus on behavior rather than on personality.

Summary

Listening effectively to others is the quintessential skill required for establishing other-oriented relationships. Listening—a complex process of receiving, constructing meaning from, and responding to verbal and nonverbal messages—involves selecting, attending, understanding, remembering, and responding. Preferred listening styles vary. Some of us are people-oriented listeners; some are action-oriented; others are content-oriented; and still others are time-oriented.

Most of us don't listen effectively because we are self-oriented instead of other-oriented. Barriers to effective listening include being self-absorbed, being distracted by unchecked emotions, criticizing the speaker, not taking advantage of the difference between speech rate and thought rate, shifting attention, being distracted by information overload and external noise, and experiencing listener apprehension.

To become better listeners, we can pursue three seemingly simple steps: Stop, look, and listen. To stop means to avoid tuning in to our own distracting messages and to become mindful of what others are saying. To look is to observe and interpret unspoken messages. After stopping and looking, we can then listen more effectively to others by focusing on details and the speaker's key ideas. Being other-oriented does not mean that we should abandon our own convictions or values, but that we should make a conscious effort to pay attention to the needs and concerns of others. After we complete these three steps, we should ask questions and reflect content by paraphrasing.

We can further improve our ability to listen and respond empathically by seeking to understand our partner's feelings, paraphrasing his or her emotions, and providing confirming responses. We can further improve our ability to listen and respond critically by looking for faulty logic and becoming competent at distinguishing facts from inferences. And we can improve our responding skills regardless of the communication objective, by providing well-timed responses, providing usable information, avoiding unnecessary details, and being descriptive rather than evaluative.

For Discussion and Review

Focus on Critical Thinking

1. Identify two situations during the past twenty-four hours in which you were an effective or ineffective listener. What factors contributed to your listening skill (or lack of skill)?

2. Miranda and Salvador often disagree about who should handle some of the child-rearing tasks in their home. When they have discussions about these issues, what are some effective listening skills and strategies that they could use to make sure they understand each other?

3. Jason and Chris are roommates. They both work hard each day and come home exhausted. What suggestions would you offer to help them listen effectively, even when they are tired?

Focus on Ethics

4. Is it possible for paraphrasing and active listening to become a way to manipulate others? Support your answer.

5. Your friend asks you how you like her new dress. You really feel it is a bit too revealing and may embarrass her. But it is time to leave for an appointment. Should you respond honestly, even though it may mean that you and your friend will be late for important engagements?

6. Your roommate wants to tell you about his day. You are tired and really don't want to hear all the details. Should you fake attention so that you won't hurt his feelings, or simply tell your roommate you are tired and would rather not hear the details?

Learning with Others

1. Charting Your Listening Cycle
   Are you a morning person or an evening person? Use the chart shown here to plot your listening energy cycle. Draw a line starting at 6 A.M. showing the highs and lows of your potential listening effectiveness. For example, if you are usually still asleep at 6 A.M., your line will be at 0 and start upward when you awake. If you are a morning person, your line will peak in the morning. Or perhaps your line will indicate that you listen best in the evening.

   After you have charted your typical daily listening cycle, gather in small groups with your classmates to compare listening cycles. Identify listening strategies that can help you capitalize on your listening "up" periods. Also, based on the chapter and your own experiences, identify ways to enhance your listening when you traditionally have low listening energy.

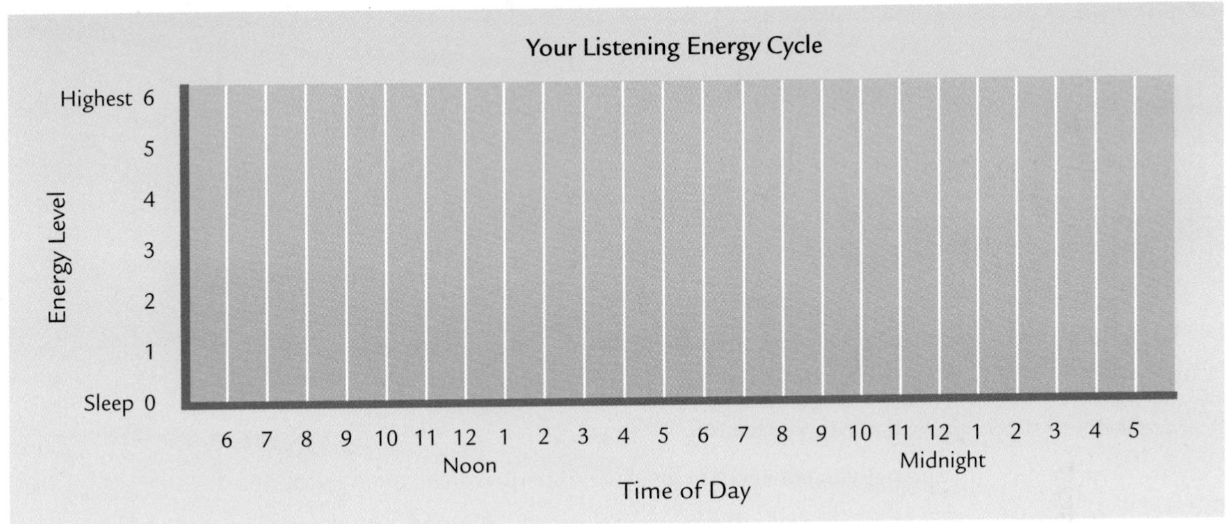

2. Assign one student from your group to speak very slowly on a difficult subject. The other members of the group should write down short summaries during pauses in the speech. Compare summaries with others in the group.
3. Make a list of "red-flag" words that have derailed your listening ability in the past. Ask another student to make up a paragraph about an important issue, using these words, and read it aloud to you. Monitor your reactions to the words and see whether you can steer your internal conversations back to the issue. Also, notice how you begin to feel about the speaker and what you do about those feelings.

Weblinks

Go to *www.mycommunicationlab.com* (access code required) to find Web resources for your text that supplement the material in Chapter 5, including links to information on the following topics:

Emotional intelligence
International Listening Association
Identifying poor listening habits

CHAPTER 6

Verbal Communication Skills

OBJECTIVES

1. Describe the relationship between words and meaning.
2. Understand how words influence us and our culture.
3. Identify word barriers and know how to manage them.
4. Discuss how the words we use affect our relationships with others.
5. Describe supportive approaches to relating to others.
6. Describe how an apology can enhance the quality of interpersonal communication.
7. Use appropriate assertiveness skills to enhance the quality of interpersonal communication.

OUTLINE

Words can destroy. What we call each other ultimately becomes what we think of each other, and it matters.

Jeanne J. Kirkpatrick

Words are powerful. Those who use them skillfully can exert great influence with just a few of them. Consider these notable achievements:

Lincoln set the course for a nation in a 267-word speech: the Gettysburg Address.

Shakespeare expressed the quintessence of the human condition in Hamlet's famous "To be, or not to be" soliloquy—363 words long.

Two billion people accept a comprehensive moral code expressed in a mere 297 words: the Ten Commandments.

Words have great power in private life as well. In this chapter, we will examine ways to use them more effectively in interpersonal relationships. We'll investigate how to harness the power that words have to affect emotions, thoughts, and actions, and we'll describe links between language and culture. We will also identify communication barriers that may keep you from using words effectively and note strategies and skills for managing those barriers. Finally, we will examine the role of speech in establishing supportive relationships with others.

According to one study, a person's ability to use words—more specifically, to participate in conversation with others—is one of the best predictors of communication competence.[1] People who simply didn't talk much were perceived as being less interpersonally skilled than people who spent an appropriate amount of time engaged in conversation with others.[2] This chapter is designed to help you better understand the power of words and to use them with greater skill and confidence.

Throughout our discussion of the power of verbal messages, we invite you to keep one important idea in mind: *You are not in charge of the meaning others derive from your messages.* Meaning is created in others. You don't determine what other people think. That is, words don't have meaning; people create meaning.

Understanding How Words Work

As you read the printed words on this page, how are you able to make sense out of these black marks? When you hear words spoken by others, how are you able to interpret those sounds? Although several theories attempt to explain how people learn language and ascribe meaning to both printed and uttered words, there is no single universally held view that neatly clarifies the mystery.

Words Are Symbols

As we noted in Chapter 1, words are **symbols** that represent something else. A printed or spoken word triggers an image, sound, concept, or experience. Take the word *cat*, for instance. The word may conjure up in your mind's eye a hissing creature with bared claws and fangs. Or perhaps you envision a cherished pet curled up by a fireplace.

The classic model in Figure 6.1 was developed by Charles Ogden and Ivor Richards to explain the relationships between *referents, thought,* and *symbols.*[3] **Referents** are the things the symbols (words) represent. **Thought** is the mental process of creating an image, sound, concept, or experience triggered by the referent or the symbol. So the three elements—referents, thought, and symbols—are inextricably linked. Although some scholars find this model too simplistic to explain how people link all words to meaning, it does illustrate the process for most concepts, people, and tangible things.

Words Are Arbitrary

American linguist (a person who studies the origin and nature of language) Charles Hockett suggested that words are, for the most part, arbitrary.[4] There's not an obvious reason many words represent what they refer to. The word *dog,* for example, does not look like a dog or sound like a dog. Yet there is a clear connection in your mind between your pet pooch and the symbol *dog.* The words we use have agreed-on general meanings, but there is not typically a logical connection between a word and what it represents. Yes, some words, such as *buzz, hum, snort,* and *giggle,* do recreate the sounds they represent. And many words can trace their origin to other languages.[5] But most of the time words have an arbitrary meaning. A linguistic group, such as all the people who speak the English language, has agreed that the word *tree,* for example, will represent the thing with bark, branches, and leaves growing in your yard or a nearby park. The arbitrary nature of most words means that there is no inherent meaning in

symbol. Word, sound, or visual device that represents an image, sound, concept, or experience.

referent. Thing that a symbol represents.

thought. Mental process of creating an image, sound, concept, or experience triggered by a referent or symbol.

FIGURE 6.1

Triangle of Meaning

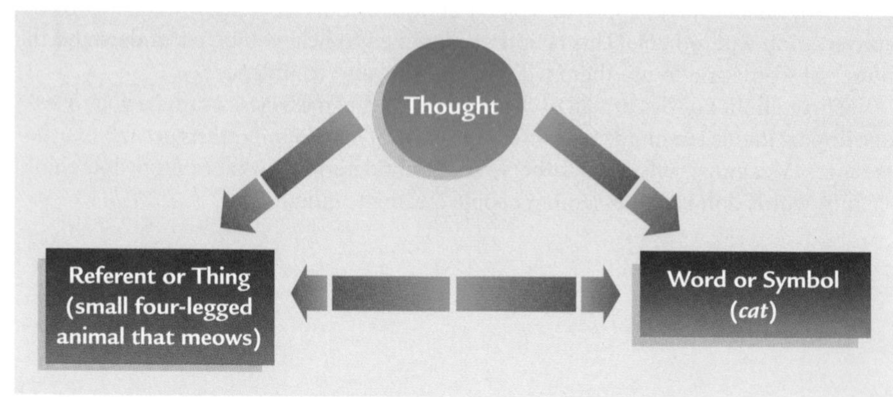

a word. Therefore, unless we develop a common meaning for a word, misunderstanding and miscommunication may occur.

Words Are Context-Bound

Your English or communication teacher has undoubtedly cautioned you that taking something out of context partially changes its meaning. Symbols derive their meaning from the situation in which they are used. The phrase *old man* could refer to a male over the age of seventy, your father, your teacher, your principal, or your boss. You need to know the context of the phrase in order to decipher its specific meaning. The transactional nature of communication emphasizes how meaning is created through discussion.

Words Are Culture-Bound

As you learned in Chapter 4, culture consists of the rules, norms, values, and mores of a group of people, which have been learned and shaped by successive generations. The meaning of a symbol such as a word can change from culture to culture. To a European, for example, a "Yankee" is someone from the United States; to a player on the Boston Red Sox, a "Yankee" is an opponent; and to someone from the American South, a "Yankee" is someone from the American North. A few years ago, General Motors sold a car called a Nova. In English, *nova* means bright star—an appropriate name for a car. In Spanish, however, the spoken word *nova* sounds like the words "no va," which translate, "It does not go." As you can imagine, this name was not a great sales tool for the Spanish-speaking market.

One way to measure how words reflect culture is to consider the new words that become new entries in dictionaries. Here are some of the recent additions to *Webster's New World College Dictionary,* published at the start of the twenty-first century.

bubba: A slang term that means *brother*

pumped: Enthusiastic, confident

viewbook: Richly illustrated booklet produced by a college or university for prospective students

slamming: Switching someone's long-distance phone service without the person's knowledge

face time: Time spent in the presence of someone

hat head: Hair that is matted from wearing a hat

The study of words and meaning is called *semantics.* One important semantic theory known as **symbolic interaction theory** suggests that a society is bound together by the common use of symbols. Originally developed by sociologists as a way of making sense out of how societies and groups are linked together,[6] the theory of symbolic interaction also illuminates how we use our common understanding of symbols to form interpersonal relationships. Common symbols foster links in understanding and therefore lead to satisfying relationships. Of course, even within a given culture people misunderstand each other's messages. But the more similar the cultures of the communication partners, the greater the chance for a meeting of meanings.

Some researchers, such as linguist Deborah Tannen, suggest that gender plays a major role in how we interpret certain verbal messages.[7] Women tend to interpret messages based on how personally supportive they perceive the message to be. Men, according to Tannen, are more likely to interpret messages based on issues related to

symbolic interaction theory. Theory that members of a society are bound together through common use of symbols.

dominance and power. Research confirms that psychological gender is a better predictor than biological sex of the general framework we use to interpret messages.[8] Clearly, our life experiences help us interpret the words we hear.

Words Communicate Denotative and Connotative Meaning

Language creates meaning on two levels: the denotative and the connotative.

Denotative Meaning

The **denotative meaning** of a word creates content. The denotation of a word is its restrictive or literal meaning. For example, here is one dictionary definition for the word *school:*

> An institution for the instruction of children; an institution for instruction in a skill or business; a college or a university.[9]

This definition is the literal, or denotative, definition of the word *school;* it describes what the word means in American culture.

Connotative Meaning

The **connotative meaning** of a word creates feelings. Words have personal and subjective meanings. To you, the word *school* might mean a wonderful, exciting place where you meet your friends, have a good time, and occasionally take tests and perform other tasks that keep you from enjoying your social life. To others, *school* could be a restrictive, burdensome obligation that stands in the way of making money and getting on with life. The connotative meaning of a word is more individualized. Whereas the denotative, or objective, meaning of the word *school* can be found in any dictionary, your subjective, personal response to the word is probably not contained there.

Denotative and Connotative Meaning

Meaning	Definition	Examples
Denotative	Literal, restrictive definition of a word	Mother: the female person who gave birth to you
Connotative	Personal, subjective reaction to a word	Mother: the warm, caring woman who nurtured and loved you; or the cold, distant woman who always implied that you were not measuring up to her standards

Words Communicate Concrete or Abstract Meaning

Words can be placed along a continuum from abstract to concrete. People call a word *concrete* if they can experience its referent with one of their senses; if you can see it, touch it, smell it, taste it, or hear it, then it's concrete. If you cannot do these things with the referent, then the word is abstract. You can visualize the continuum from abstract to concrete as a ladder.

In the example that follows, the bottom, most abstract term, *transportation,* is quite a broad, general term that could mean a variety of things. As you move up the

denotative meaning. Restrictive or literal meaning of a word.

connotative meaning. Personal and subjective meaning of a word.

abstraction ladder, the images that come to mind are more concrete and specific; they can be more precisely visualized.

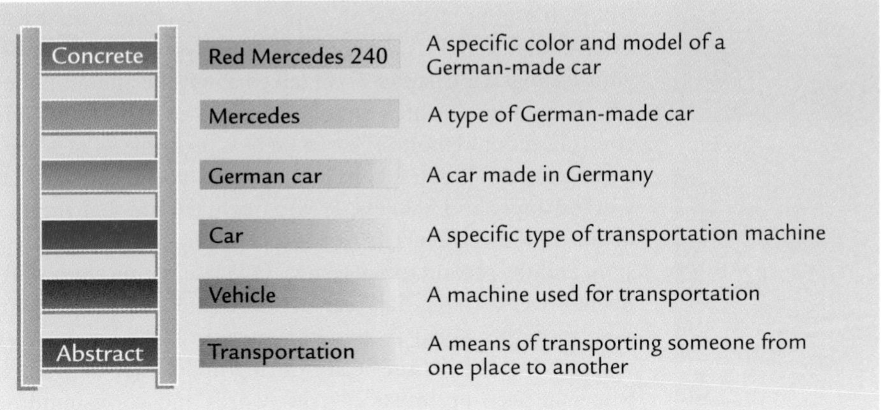

In general, the more concrete the language, the more likely the precise meaning of a word will be communicated to a listener.

Recognizing the Power of Words

Sticks and stones may break my bones,
But words can never hurt me.

This old schoolyard chant may provide a ready retort for the desperate victim of name-calling, but it is hardly convincing. With more insight, the poet Robert Browning wrote, "Words break no bones; hearts though sometimes." And in his book *Science and Sanity,* mathematician and engineer Alfred Korzybski argued that the words we use (and misuse) have tremendous effects on our thoughts and actions.[10] Browning and Korzybski were right. As we said at the beginning of this chapter, words have power.

Words Have Power to Create

"To name is to call into existence—to call out of nothingness," wrote French philosopher Georges Gusdorff.[11] Words give you a tool to create the world by naming and labeling what you experience. You undoubtedly learned in your elementary science class that Sir Isaac Newton discovered gravity. It would be more accurate to say that he *labeled* rather than discovered it. His use of the word *gravity* gave us a cognitive category; we now converse about the pull of the earth's forces that keeps us from flying into space. Words give us the symbolic vehicles to communicate our creations and discoveries to others.

When you label something as "good" or "bad," you are using language to create your own vision of how you experience the world. If you tell a friend that the movie you saw last night was vulgar and obscene, you are not only providing your friend with a critique of the movie; you are also communicating your sense of what is appropriate and inappropriate.

You create your self-worth largely with self-talk and with the labels you apply to yourself. Psychologist Albert Ellis believes that you also create your moods and

Most of us can agree on the denotative meaning of the word *school.* But the connotative meaning will be different for each person.

emotional state with the words you use to label your feelings.[12] Although emotions may sometimes seem to wash over you like ocean waves, there is evidence that you have the ability to control your emotions based on your ability to control what you think about, as well as the choice of words you use to describe, your feelings. In Chapter 2, we talked about the appraisal theory of emotions, which suggests that we exert considerable control over our emotions based on how we frame what is happening to us.[13] If you get fired from a job, you might say that you feel angry and helpless, or you might declare that you feel liberated and excited. The first response might lead to depression, and the second to happiness. One fascinating study conducted over a thirty-five-year period found that people who described the world in pessimistic terms when they were younger were in poorer health during middle age than those who had been optimistic.[14] Your words and corresponding outlook have the power to affect your health. The concept of reframing, discussed in Chapter 2 as a way to improve self-concept, is based on the power of words to "call into existence" whatever we describe with them.

Words Have Power to Affect Thoughts and Actions

How about some horse meat for supper tonight? Most of us find such a question disgusting. Why? Horse meat is not something we typically eat. Perhaps the reason horse meat is not a featured delicacy at the local supermarket is simply that we have no other word for it. Your butcher does not advertise pig meat or cow meat; labeling the meat as pork chops, ham, and sausage, or as steak and ribs, makes it sound more appetizing. Advertisers have long known that the way a product is labeled affects our propensity to purchase it.

In the late 1960s, a California sociology professor conducted an experiment to demonstrate that words have the power to affect behavior.[15] He divided his class into two groups. To one group, he distributed a bumper sticker that boldly displayed the words "I support the Black Panthers." At that time, many members of the students' local community thought the Panthers were using unnecessary force to promote their agenda. Students in this first group had to drive around for a week with the stickers on their cars. The other group drove around as usual, without stickers.

It took only a few hours to demonstrate the professor's point: Words do affect attitudes and behavior. Students who had the stickers were harassed by other motorists and issued traffic tickets at an alarming rate. The other group experienced no increase in hassles. By the end of the study, seventeen days later, the "Panther" group had received thirty-three traffic citations.

Research suggests that the very way we use language can communicate the amount of power we have in a conversation with others.[16] We use language in ways that are both powerful and powerless. When we use powerless speech, we are less persuasive and have less influence on others. Powerless speech is characterized by more frequent use of hesitations and pauses, which may be filled with "umm," "ahhh," and "ehh." We also express our lack of power by using more hesitation and unnecessary verbal fillers like "you know," and "I mean." We communicate our low power when we hedge our conclusions by saying "I guess" and "sort of." Another way of communicating a lack of power is by tacking on a question at the end of a statement, such as "I'm right, aren't I?" or "This is what I think, OK?" So, the very way in which you speak can influence the thoughts and actions of others.[17]

Words Have Power to Affect and Reflect Culture

Surfers have created their own special language as part of the culture they share.

In the early part of the twentieth century, anthropologists Edward Sapir and his student Benjamin Whorf worked simultaneously to refine a theory called **linguistic determinism.**[18] The essence of linguistic determinism is that language shapes the way we think. Our words also reflect our thoughts and our culture. A related principle, called **linguistic relativity**, states that each language has unique elements embedded within it. Together these two principles form the underlying elements in the **Sapir–Whorf hypothesis**, which suggests that language shapes our culture and culture shapes our language. To support the theory, Benjamin Whorf studied the languages of several cultures, particularly that of Hopi Native Americans. He discovered that in Hopi, one word (the word *masa'ytaka*) is used for every creature that flies, except for birds. While this seems odd to an English speaker, because the English language has many different words for different flying creatures (and things such as airplanes, balloons, and rockets), for the Hopi, flying creatures (or objects) constitute a single category. Whorf saw this as support of his hypothesis that the words we use reflect our culture and our culture influences our words. Similarly, today's highly developed technological culture has given rise to many new words that reflect the importance we place on technology; terms such as *PC, hard drive,* and *gigabytes* weren't part of your grandparents' language. And the fact that a certain type of behavior is now labeled attention-deficit/ hyperactivity disorder (ADHD) is an example of how words can create a reality in a culture. Grandpa might argue that there weren't any ADHD kids in his day—some kids were just "rowdy."[19]

Words not only reflect your culture; there is evidence that they mold it. When Wendell Johnson, a speech therapist, noticed that very few Native Americans in a certain tribe stuttered, he also found that their language had no word for stuttering.[20] He concluded that few people had this affliction because it never entered their minds as a possibility. Perhaps you've heard that Eskimos have forty-nine different words for snow. Even though they really don't have quite that many, there is evidence that they have more words for snow than does someone native to Miami, Florida.[21]

These examples also show that the words people use affect their **world view**—how they interpret what they experience. The words you use to describe your view of the world, including those you use in your everyday interpersonal conversations with your friends, reflect and further shape your perspective.[22] And you, in turn, help to shape your culture's collective world view through your use of language.

linguistic determinism. Theory that describes how use of language determines or influences thoughts and perceptions.

linguistic relativity. Theory that each language includes some unique features that are not found in other languages.

Sapir–Whorf hypothesis. Based on the principles of linguistic determinism and linguistic relativity, the hypothesis that language shapes our thoughts and culture, and our culture and thoughts affect the language we use to describe our world.

world view. Culturally acquired perspective for interpreting experiences.

Words Have Power to Affect the Quality of Our Interpersonal Relationships

What you say and how you say it have a strong impact on how you relate to others. Relationships are the connections we make with others. As we noted in Chapter 1, to relate to another person is like dancing with the person. When you dance with a partner, your moves and counter-moves respond to the rhythm of the music and the moves your partner makes. In our interpersonal relationships with others, we "dance" as we relate to our communication partners with both language and nonverbal cues (something we'll discuss in more detail in the next chapter). A good conversation has a rhythm, created by both communicators as they listen and respond to each other. Even our "small talk," which is our everyday, sometimes brief, responses and exchanges with others

("Nice weather we're having" or, simply, "Oh, that's nice"), is important in establishing how we feel about others.[23] The words we use, especially in our daily conversations, are directly related to the quality of the relationships we have with others.

Interpersonal communication researcher Steve Duck suggests that we literally talk a relationship into being.[24] It is through our talk that we establish our relationships with other people. And what do we talk about? One research team simply looked at what satisfied couples talked about with each other during the course of a week. The team found that the most frequent topic was the couples themselves—what they did during the day and how they were feeling—followed by general observations, and then responses to each other such as, "Yes, I see," and "Uh huh"—what researchers call *backchannel talk.* The researchers also found we're more likely to have conflict with our partners on the weekend, as well as to use humor, to talk about household tasks, and to make general plans about the future.[25] Couples were least satisfied with their partners on Saturdays and Wednesdays; Monday was the day they were most satisfied. What this means is that what we talk about and the way we talk to others form the basis of how we relate to others.

Avoiding Word Barriers

According to theologian and educator Ruel Howe, a communication barrier is "something that keeps meaning from meeting."[26] Words have the power to create monumental misunderstandings as well as deep connections.[27] Although it is true that meanings are in people, not in words, sometimes assumptions or inaccurate use of words hinders understanding. Let's identify some of the specific barriers to understanding that people sometimes create through language.

Bypassing: One Word, Two Thoughts

A student pilot was on his first solo flight. When he called the tower for flight instructions, the control tower asked, "Would you please give us your altitude and position?" The pilot replied, "I'm five feet ten inches, and I'm sitting up front."

Bypassing occurs when the same words mean different things to different people. Meaning is fragile. And the English language is imprecise in many areas. One researcher estimated that the 500 words used most often in daily conversations have more than 14,000 different dictionary definitions. And this number does not take into account personal connotations. So it is no wonder that bypassing is a common communication problem. Consider the unsubstantiated story about a young FBI employee who was put in charge of the supply department. In an effort to save money, he reduced the size of memo paper. One of the smaller sheets ended up on J. Edgar Hoover's

bypassing. Confusion caused by the same words' meaning different things to different people.

desk. The director didn't like the small size and wrote on the narrow margin of the paper, "Watch the borders." For the next six weeks, it was extremely difficult to enter the United States from Canada or Mexico.

Pavlov's dog salivated when he heard the bell that he had learned to associate with food. Sometimes we respond to symbols the way Pavlov's dog did to the bell, forgetting that symbols (words) can have more than one meaning.

How do you avoid bypassing and missing someone's meaning? Using the listening and responding skills we talked about in the previous chapter is key to enhancing communication accuracy. Ask questions if you're uncertain of the meaning. Listen and paraphrase your understanding of the message.

THE FAR SIDE® By GARY LARSON

Ha ha ha, Biff. Guess what? After we go to the drugstore and the post office, I'm going to the vet's to get tutored.

Lack of Precision: Uncertain Meaning

Alice Roosevelt Longworth writes about a merchant seaman who was being investigated under the McCarran Act. "Do you," asked the interrogator, "have any pornographic literature?"

"Pornographic literature!" the sailor burst out indignantly. "I don't even have a pornograph!"

At a ceremony in the Princeton University chapel, an old lady buttonholed an usher and commanded, "Be sure you get me a seat up front, young man. I understand they've always had trouble with the agnostics in the chapel!"

Each of these examples, along with the Far Side cartoon above, illustrates a **malapropism,** a confusion of one word or phrase for another that sounds similar to it. You have probably heard people confuse such word pairs as *construction* and *instruction,* and *subscription* and *prescription.* Although this confusion may at times be humorous, it may also result in failure to communicate clearly. So, too, can using words out of context, using inappropriate grammar, or putting words in the wrong order. Confusion is the inevitable result, as illustrated by these notes written to landlords:

> The toilet is blocked and we cannot bathe the children until it is cleared.
>
> Will you please send someone to mend our cracked sidewalk? Yesterday my wife tripped on it and is now pregnant.

These are funny examples, but in fact, incorrect or unclear language can launch a war or sink a ship. We give symbols meaning; we do not receive inherent meaning *from* symbols. If you are other-oriented, you will assess how someone else will respond to your message and try to select those symbols that he or she is most likely to interpret as you intend.

BE OTHER-ORIENTED

For most communication, the object is to be as correct, specific, and concrete as possible. Vague language creates confusion and frustration. Consider this example:

Derrick: Where's the aluminum foil?

Pam: In the drawer.

Derrick: What drawer?

Pam: In the kitchen.

Derrick: But where in the kitchen?

Pam: By the fridge.

malapropism. Confusion of one word or phrase for another that sounds similar to it.

Derrick: But which one? There are five drawers.

Pam: Oh, the second one from the top.

Derrick: Why didn't you say so in the first place?

But is it possible to be too precise? It is if you use a restricted code that has a meaning your listener does not know. A **restricted code** is a set of words that have a particular meaning to a subgroup or culture. Sometimes, we develop abbreviations or specialized terms that make sense and save time when we speak to others in our group. Musicians, for example, use special terms that relate to reading and performing music. Most computer users know that "a screamer" is someone who sends e-mail messages typed in ALL CAPITAL LETTERS. Ham radio operators use codes to communicate over the airwaves. Yet, in each instance, this shorthand language would make little sense to an outsider. In fact, groups that rely on restricted codes may have greater cohesiveness because of this shared "secret" language, or **jargon.** Whatever your line of work, guard against lapsing into phrases that can only be interpreted by a few.

Dot Mobile is a British cell phone service for students that uses a restricted code to summarize classic literary phrases in a text-message format. Can you break the code of the following phrases from literature?[28]

1. 2B?NTB? = ????
2. Ahors, m'kindom 4 Ahors
3. 2morrow &"&"
4. WenevalUFeelLykDissinNel,jstMembaDatADaOoubDaWrldHvntHdDaVantg-stU vAd
5. IfURlyWnt2HrBoutit,Da1stFingUlProbWnt2NolsWhereIWsBorn&WotMy Lousy ChldhdWsLyk&HwMyRetsWerOcupyd&AlB4TheyHdMe&ThtDave CopafieldKi ndaCr"p,BtIDnFeelLykGolnintaltifUWannaNoDaTruf

Here are the answers:

1. "To be or not to be? That is the question."(William Shakespeare, *Hamlet*)
2. "A horse, a horse, my kingdom for a horse." (William Shakespeare, *Richard III*)
3. Tomorrow and tomorrow and tomorrow." (William Shakespeare, *Macbeth*)
4. "Whenever you feel like criticizing anyone . . . just remember that all the people in this world haven't had the advantages that you've had." (F. Scott Fitzgerald, *The Great Gatsby*)
5. "If you really want to hear about it, the first thing you'll probably want to know is where I was born, and what my lousy childhood was like, and how my parents were occupied and all before they had me, and all that David Copperfield kind of crap, but I don't feel like going into it, if you want to know the truth." (J. D. Salinger, *The Catcher in the Rye*)

restricted code. Set of words that have particular meaning to a person, group, or culture.

jargon. Another name for restricted code; specialized terms or abbreviations whose meanings are known only to members of a specific group.

When people have known one another for a long time, they may also use restricted codes for their exchanges. Often married couples communicate using shorthand speech that no outsider could ever interpret. To enhance the clarity of your messages with others, especially people who don't know you well, be as clear as you can to reduce uncertainty. For example, rather than saying, "I may go to town today," one research team suggests you should be more specific by saying, "There's a 50 percent chance I may go to town today."[29] Be precise to be clear.

Allness: The Language of Generalization

The tendency to use language to make unqualified, often untrue generalizations is called **allness.** Allness statements deny individual differences or variations. Statements such as "All women are poor drivers" and "People from the South love iced tea" are generalizations that imply that the person making the pronouncement has examined all the information and has reached a definitive conclusion. Although the world would be much simpler if we *could* make such statements, reality rarely, if ever, provides evidence to support sweeping generalizations.

One way to avoid untrue generalizations is to remind yourself that your use and interpretation of a word are unique. Saying the words "to me" either to yourself or out loud before you offer an opinion or make a pronouncement can help communicate to others (and remind yourself) that your view is uniquely yours. Rather than announcing, "Curfews for teenagers are ridiculous," you could say, "To me, curfews for teenagers are ridiculous."

Indexing your comments and remarks is another way to avoid generalizing. To index is to acknowledge that each individual, each situation, or each example is unique. Rather than announcing that all doctors are abrupt, you could say, "My child's pediatrician spends a lot of time with me, but my internist never answers my questions." This helps you remember that doctor number one is not the same as doctor number two.

Static Evaluation: The Language of Rigidity

You change. Your world changes. An ancient Greek philosopher said it best: "You can never step in the same river twice." A **static evaluation** is a statement that fails to recognize change; labels in particular have a tendency to freeze-frame our awareness.

allness. Tendency to use language to make unqualified, often untrue generalizations.

indexing. Avoiding generalizations by using statements that separate one situation, person, or example from another.

static evaluation. Pronouncement that does not take the possibility of change into consideration.

Ruby, known as the class nerd in high school, is today a successful and polished businessperson; the old label does not fit.

In addition, some people suffer from "hardening of the categories." Their world view is so rigid that they can never change or expand their perspective. But the world is a technicolor moving target. Just about the time you think you have things neatly figured out and categorized, something moves. Your labels may not reflect the buzzing, booming, zipping process of change. It is important to acknowledge that perception is a process, and to avoid trying to nail things down permanently into all-inclusive categories.

General semanticists use the metaphorical expression "the map is not the territory" to illustrate the concept of static evaluation. Like a word, a map symbolizes or represents reality. Yet the road system is constantly changing. New roads are built, old ones are closed. If you were to use a 1949 map to guide you on your cross-country trip from Washington, D.C., to Kansas City, Missouri, you would probably lose your way because the interstate highway system would not even be on it. Similarly, if you use old labels and do not adjust your thinking to accommodate change, you will get lost semantically.

To avoid static evaluation yourself, try dating your observations and indicate to others the time period from which you are drawing your conclusion. For example, if your second cousin comes to town for a visit, say, "When I last saw you, you loved to listen to The Dixie Chicks." This allows for the possibility that your cousin's tastes may have changed during the last few years. But most importantly, try to observe and acknowledge changes in others. If you are practicing what you know about becoming other-oriented, you are unlikely to erect this barrier.

Polarization: The Language of Extremes

Describing and evaluating what you observe in terms of extremes, such as good or bad, old or new, beautiful or ugly, brilliant or stupid, is known as **polarization**. General semanticists remind us that the world is not black and white but comes in a variety of colors, hues, and shades. If you describe things in extremes, leaving out the middle ground, then your language does not accurately reflect reality. And because of the power of words to create, you may believe your own pronouncements.

"You either love me or don't love me," says Jerome.

"You're either for me or against me," replies Lisa.

Both people are overstating the case, using language to polarize their perceptions of the experience.

Family counselors who listen to family feuds find that the tendency to see things from an either/or point of view is a classic symptom of a troubled relationship. Placing the entire blame on your partner for a problem in your relationship is an example of polarizing. Few relational difficulties are exclusively one-sided.

Biased Language: Insensitivity Toward Others

Using words that reflect your biases toward other cultures or ethnic groups, the other gender, people with a different sexual orientation, or people who are different from you in some other way can create a barrier for your listeners. Because words, including the words used to describe people, have power to create and affect thoughts and behavior, they can affect the quality of relationships with others. Although TV and radio shows and magazine articles may debate the merits of political correctness, there is no doubt that sexist or racially stereotypical language can offend others. We'll address three is-

polarization. Description and evaluation of what you observe in terms of extremes such as good or bad, old or new, beautiful or ugly.

sues in language use that can reflect poorly on the speaker and affect interpersonal relationships with others: sexist language, ethnic or racially biased language, and elitist language—language that assumes superiority.

The term *policeman* fails to accurately describe the person shown here. A more inclusive term would be *police officer.*

Avoid Sexist Language

Sexist language is the use of words that reflect stereotypical attitudes or that describe roles in exclusively male or female terms.

Words such as congress*man,* mail*man,* and *man*kind ignore the fact that women are part of the workforce and the human race. Contrast these with *member of Congress, letter carrier,* and *humankind,* which are gender-neutral and allow for the inclusion of both men and women. Or, rather than eliminating the word *man* from your vocabulary, try to use appropriate labels when you know the gender of the subject. A male police officer is a *policeman;* a female police officer is a *policewoman.* Rather than *salesperson,* you could say *salesman* or *saleswoman,* depending on the gender of the seller.

H. S. O'Donnell found that even dictionaries fall into the trap of describing men and women with discriminatory language.[30] Included in the *Oxford English Dictionary* definition of *woman* are (1) an adult female being, (2) a female servant, (3) a lady-love or mistress, and (4) a wife. Men are described in more positive and distinguished terms: (1) a human being, (2) the human creation regarded abstractly, (3) an adult male endowed with many qualities, and (4) a person of importance of position.

Many of our social conventions also diminish or ignore the importance of women:

Sexist	Unbiased
I'd like you to meet Dr. and Mrs. John Chao.	I'd like you to meet Dr. Sue Ho and Dr. John Chao. They are husband and wife.
	or
	I'd like you to meet John Chao and Sue Ho. They're both doctors at Mercy Hospital.
Let me introduce Mr. Tom Bertolone and his wife, Beverly.	Let me introduce Beverly and Tom Bertolone.

Language has, however, made more substantial progress in reflecting changes and changed attitudes toward women in the professional arena. Compare the terms used to describe workers now with those used in the 1950s:

Terms Used Today	Terms Used in 1950s
Flight attendant	Stewardess
Firefighter	Fireman
Police officer	Policeman
Physician	Female doctor
Women at the office	Girls at work
Ms.	Miss/Mrs.
People/humans	Mankind

Consciously remembering to use nonsexist language will result in several benefits.[31] First, nonsexist language reflects nonsexist attitudes. Your attitudes are reflected in your speech, and your speech affects your attitudes. Monitoring your speech for sexist remarks can help you monitor your attitudes about sexist assumptions you may hold. Second, using nonsexist language will help you become more other-oriented. Monitoring your language for sexist remarks will reflect your sensitivity to others. Third, nonsexist language will make your speech more contemporary and unambiguous. By substituting the word *humankind* for *mankind,* for example, you can communicate that you are including all people, not just men, in your observation or statement. And finally, your nonsexist language will empower others. By eliminating sexist bias from your speech, you will help confirm the value of all the individuals with whom you interact.

BE OTHER-ORIENTED

In addition to the debate over language that refers to gender, there is considerable discussion about the way people talk about sexual orientation. The principle of being other-oriented suggests that you can be sensitive in the way you speak of someone's sexual orientation. Labeling someone a *fag, queer,* or *dyke* not only may be offensive and hurtful to the person being labeled but also reflects on the sensitivity of the person doing the labeling. We're not suggesting that certain words be expunged from dictionaries or never uttered; we are suggesting that when describing others, people should be sensitive to how the others wish to be addressed and discussed.

Avoid Ethnically or Racially Biased Language

In addition to monitoring your language for sexual stereotypes, avoid racial and ethnic stereotypes. Using phrases such as "She's an Indian giver," or "I jewed him down on the price," or "He doesn't have a Chinaman's chance" demonstrates an insensitivity to members of other cultural groups. Monitor your speech so that you are not, even unconsciously, using phrases that depict a racial group or ethnic group in a negative, stereotypical fashion.

Is Supreme Court Justice Clarence Thomas black or African American? Is labor leader Dolores Huerta Hispanic or Latina? Given the power of words, the terms we use to label ethnic groups reflect perceptions of culture and identity. Using the wrong word can result in your being labeled "politically incorrect," or worse, a "bigot." In 1995, the U.S. Bureau of Labor Statistics surveyed 60,000 households, asking what ethnic label they liked best. More than 44 percent of households then called "black" by the government preferred the term "black," and 28 percent preferred "African American." Twelve percent preferred "Afro-American" and a little more than 9 percent had no preference. In another ethnic category, "Hispanic" was the choice of 58 percent of those currently labeled "Hispanics," rather than terms such as "Latino/Latina" or the generic "of Spanish origin." More than 10 percent had no preference. The survey also reported that the label "American Indian" was the term of choice for slightly fewer than half of the respondents, whereas 37 percent preferred "Native American." Most of those currently designated "white" preferred that term, although 16 percent liked the term "Caucasian" and a very small percentage liked the term "European American."[32] Some of these preferences may surprise you, in that they may have changed since this survey was conducted. A sensitive, other-oriented communicator keeps abreast of such changes and adopts the designations currently preferred by members of the ethnic groups themselves.

BE OTHER-ORIENTED

Avoid Demeaning Language

Language barriers are created not only when a speaker uses sexist or racially biased language, but also when a speaker disparages a person's age, mental or physical ability, or social standing. Calling someone a "geezer," "retard," or "trailer trash" is disparaging.[33]

Discrimination based on age is a growing problem in the workplace. In some occupations, as a worker moves into his or her fifties, it may be difficult to change jobs or find work. Despite laws designed to guard against age discrimination, such discrimination clearly exists. As we have noted, the language that people use has power to affect attitudes and behavior. That's why using negative terms to describe the elderly can be a subtle—or sometimes not-so-subtle—way of expressing disrespect toward the older generation.

Similarly, the way someone describes people with disabilities can negatively affect how they may be perceived. A study by researcher John Seiter and his colleagues found that when people with a disability were called demeaning or disparaging names, they were perceived as less trustworthy, competent, persuasive, and sociable than when the same people were described in more positive or heroic terms.[34] At the end of their

Word Barriers and How to Overcome Them

Barrier	Definition	Example
Bypassing	Confusion caused by the fact that the same word may evoke different meanings for different people	*W.C.* might mean "wayside chapel" to a Swiss person and "water closet" to a British person.

When speaking, provide specific examples; when listening, ask questions to clarify the meaning.

Barrier	Definition	Example
Lack of clarity	Inappropriate or imprecise use of words	Sign in Acapulco hotel: "The manager has personally passed all the water served here."

When speaking, use more precise language. Provide short, specific examples or indicate the probability of something happening: "There's a 40 percent chance I won't go shopping today." When listening, paraphrase the message to ensure you understand it accurately.

Barrier	Definition	Example
Allness	Tendency to lump things or people into all-encompassing categories	"All Texans drive pickup trucks and hang a rifle in their back windows."

When speaking, say "To me" before you offer a generalization to indicate that the idea or perception is your own. Index a generalized statement by using phrases that separate one situation, person, or example from another. When listening, ask the speaker whether he or she intends to mean that *all* or *every* situation or person fits the generalization presented.

Barrier	Definition	Example
Static evaluation	Statement labeling people, objects, or events without considering change	You still call your twenty-eight-year-old nephew a juvenile delinquent because he spray-painted your fence when he was eleven.

When speaking, put a date on your observation: "In 1989 I thought he was a difficult child to manage." When listening, ask the speaker whether the observation remains true today or if the same generalization applies now.

Barrier	Definition	Example
Polarization	Use of either/or terms—good or bad, right or wrong	"You're either for me or against me."

When speaking, avoid either/or terms and blaming something on a specific cause. When listening, ask the speaker whether a statement really reflects an all-or-nothing, either/or proposition.

Barrier	Definition	Example
Biased language	Language that reflects gender, racial, ethnic, age, ability, or class biases	"His mom is a mailman."

When speaking, be mindful of how insensitive language can hurt someone. Avoid using labels or derogatory terms. When listening, try to keep your emotions in check when others use inappropriate words or insensitive, derogatory phrases. You can't control what others do or say, only what you do and say and how you react. Consider appropriately but assertively communicating that a word, label, or phrase offends you.

study, the authors note, "communicators who want to be effective should avoid using derogatory language." Guard against calling attention to someone as a "cripple," "retarded," "dim-witted," or "mental"; these terms are offensive. As suggested by communication researcher Dawn Braithwaite, the preferred terms are "disabled people" or "people with disabilities."[35]

Also monitor the way you talk about someone's social class. Although some societies and cultures make considerable distinctions among classes, it is nonetheless offensive today to use words that are intended to demean someone's social class. Terms such as "welfare recipient," "manual laborer," and "blue-collar worker" are often used derogatorily. Avoid labeling someone in a way that shows disrespect toward the person's social standing, education, or socioeconomic status.

Using Words to Establish Supportive Relationships

"I'm going to win this argument."
"You're wrong and I'm right. It's as simple as that."
"You're going to do it my way or else!"

None of these statements is likely to result in a positive communication climate. All three are likely to lead to debate rather than true dialogue. The words you hear and use are central to your establishing a quality or positive relationship with others. Author and researcher Daniel Yankelovich suggests that the goal of conversations with others should be to establish a genuine dialogue rather than to verbally arm-wrestle a partner in order to win the argument.[36] A true dialogue involves establishing a climate of equality, listening with empathy, and trying to bring underlying assumptions into the open. Expressing equality, empathy, and openness is more likely to occur if you approach conversations as dialogue rather than debate. As shown in Table 6.1, in true dialogue people look for common ground rather than using a war of words to defend a position.

TABLE 6.1 **Debate and Dialogue Compared**

Debate	Dialogue
There is one right answer, and you assume that you have it.	Many people have pieces of the answer; together, you can find the best solution.
The goal is to win.	The goal is to seek common ground and agreement.
The focus is on combat; you try to prove that you are right and the other person is wrong.	The focus is on collaboration and seeking common understanding.
You search for weaknesses and errors in others' positions.	You search for strengths and value the truth in what others say.
You defend your views.	You use the contributions of others to improve your thinking.

Source: Adapted from Daniel Yankelovich, *The Magic of Dialogue: Transforming Conflict into Cooperation* (New York: Simon & Schuster, 1999), 39–40. Reprinted with the permission of Simon & Schuster Adult Publishing Group.

For more than three decades, Jack Gibb's observational research has been used as a framework for both describing and prescribing verbal behaviors that contribute to feelings of either supportiveness or defensiveness. His research, one of the most cited studies in communication textbooks in the past century, is so popular because he's identified practical strategies for developing supportive relationships with others—dialogue rather than debate—through the way we talk to each other.[37] Gibb spent several years listening to and observing groups of people in meetings and conversations, noting that some exchanges seem to create a supportive climate, whereas others create a defensive one. Words and actions, he concluded, are tools we use to let someone know whether we support them or not. And an emotional response in one person is likely to trigger an emotional response in another.[38] Now let's consider how you can use words to create a supportive climate rather than an antagonistic or defensive one.

BE OTHER-ORIENTED

Describe Your Own Feelings, Rather Than Evaluate the Behavior of Others

Most people don't like to be judged or evaluated. Criticizing and name calling obviously can create relational problems, but so can attempts to diagnose others' problems or win their affection with insincere praise. In fact, any form of evaluation creates a climate of defensiveness. As British statesman Winston Churchill declared, "I am always ready to learn, although I do not always like being taught." Correcting others, even when we are doing it "for their own good," can raise their hackles.

One way to avoid evaluating others is to eliminate the accusatory *you* from your language. Statements such as "You always come in late for supper" or "You never pick up the dirty clothes in your room" attack a person's sense of self-worth and usually result in a defensive reaction.

Instead, use the word *I* to describe your own feelings and thoughts about a situation or event:[39] "I find it hard to keep your supper warm when you're late," or "I don't enjoy the extra work of picking up your dirty clothes." When you describe your own feelings instead of berating the receiver of the message, you are, in essence, taking ownership of the problem. This approach leads to greater openness and trust because your listener is less likely to feel rejected or as if you were trying to control him or her. Also, when you express your emotions, make sure you choose the right words to communicate your feelings.

Although we've discussed the importance of using *I* messages, interpersonal communication researchers Amy Bippus and Stacy Young found that simply prefacing an emotionally charged piece of feedback with the word *I* instead of *you* doesn't always melt away relational tension.[40] These researchers had subjects in their research read hypothetical examples in which people used either *I* messages or *you* messages. The researchers found no significant difference in how people thought others would respond to the messages. In other words, an *I* message was not found to be better than a *you* message in all instances. (Of course, the fact that the subjects were reading a message rather than actually involved in their own conversation with a partner may have affected the results.) The researchers concluded that regardless of whether a message is prefaced with *I* or *you*, people don't like hearing negative expressions of emotion directed toward them.

A climate of defensiveness can stall communication. Long before your interaction passes from defensiveness to stony silence, try using "I" language.

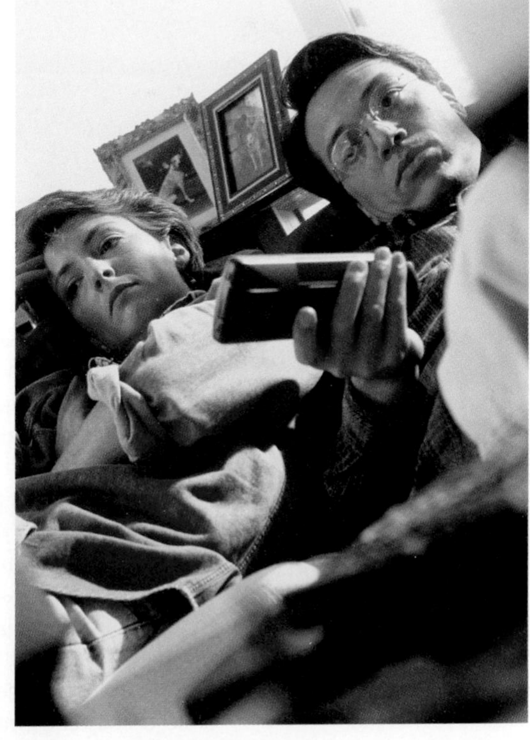

Practice Using "I" Language and Extended "I" Language

An essential skill in being supportive rather than creating defensiveness is describing what you want with "I" language or extended "I" language rather than "you" language. Rephrase the following "you" statements into "I" statements and extended "I" statements.

"You" Language	"I" Language	Extended "I" Language
You are messy when you cook.	______	______
Your driving is terrible.	______	______
You never listen to me.	______	______
You just lie on the couch and never offer to help me.	______	______
You always decide what we watch on TV.	______	______

Sometimes simply using an *I* message may be too subtle to take the sting out of the negative message you want to express. You may need to add a longer justification when you provide negative, emotional information to another. We call this using **extended *I* language**, which is a brief preface to a feedback statement, intended to communicate that you don't want the person to think that you don't value or care about him or her even though you have a negative message to share. Saying something like, "I don't want you to misinterpret what I'm about to say, because I really do care about you," or "I don't think it's entirely your fault, but I'm feeling frustrated when I experience . . ." may have a better chance of enhancing communication than simply beginning a sentence with the word *I* instead of *You.* Remember, *there are no magic words for enhancing communication.* However, strategies of being other-oriented do seem to enhance the quality of communication. See Building Your Skills: Practice Using *I* Language and Extended *I* Language, which will help you practice expressing your feelings accurately and effectively.

extended *I* language. Brief preface to a feedback statement, intended to communicate that you don't want your listener to take your message in an overly critical way.

Applying Theory and Research

The Pros and Cons of Expressing Your Affection to Your Friends

It makes intuitive sense that telling a friend that you care about him or her may increase intimacy and enhance your relationship with your friend. But does expressing your affection for a friend also have potential negative relational consequences? A study by communication researchers Larry Erbert and Kory Floyd explored the implications of directly and clearly expressing your affection for your friends.

Erbert and Floyd developed a study to test a theory suggesting that explicitly expressing your affection for a friend can both enhance intimacy and possibly make the other person feel that his or her freedom and autonomy are threatened. They used a survey to help them determine the effects of someone's directly expressing love and affection toward another person. The researchers first asked the participants to think about a platonic friend (not a former, current, or potential romantic partner). They then presented one of three different situations to the survey participants, who were asked to consider the situation with this friend in mind. Researchers asked one group of participants how they would react if the friend said, "I want you to know I really care about you. You're very important to me, and I will always value our friendship. I feel very close to you right now, and I just wanted you to know that." A second group was asked to imagine what their response would be if the friend said, "I don't mean this in a romantic way, but I want you to know I really care about you. You don't have to say anything back—but you're very important to me, and I will always value our friendship. I'm not trying to get anything back here, but I feel very close to you right now, and I just wanted you to know that." This second message was designed to be less intimate than the first message. A third group was asked how they would respond if their friend simply smiled, nudged them, and jokingly said "You're pretty cool. I guess I'll keep you around!"

What the researchers discovered is that a very positive expression of affection from a friend (the first scenario) did two things at the same time. First, it enhanced the participants' feeling of being accepted and liked—but it also somewhat threatened their sense of freedom. A strong expression of affection made the participants feel uncomfortable because they thought that their friend might want a more exclusive relationship with them than they would prefer.

APPLYING the Research to Your Life

Erbert and Floyd's research confirms that our relationships with others are complicated. These researchers found that the words we use to express our affection for our friends may be interpreted in multiple ways *at the same time.* We emphasize "at the same time" to stress that our expressions of affection for others apparently result in multiple meanings and interpretations. When we tell friends that we like them, it may make our friends feel positively about themselves because someone cares for them. But at the same time, it may make them feel that their freedom may be restricted; perhaps they are thinking that we want a more exclusive relationship with them.

Previous research has confirmed that there are times when expressing your affection toward others may have negative consequences for a relationship.[41] What are those negative consequences? Perhaps you've picked the wrong time and place to express your affection, and you end up making your friend feel embarassed or ill at ease rather than valued. Or, if the other person thinks that your relationship is nonromantic yet perceives your expression of affection as a ploy to initiate a sexual relationship, the friend is likely to have a negative response to your declaration of affection. Negative consequences for expressing your love for another person also may occur when the other person simply doesn't expect it, or when the affection is not mutual. Finally, expressing your affection may also lead to your friend's feeling that you want something from and are trying to manipulate him or her.

The point of this research is not to prescribe whether to tell your friends that you like them. The research simply confirms that people may interpret what we say to them with multiple meanings at the same time. When you express your affection for a good friend, he or she may feel flattered and affirmed; your friend may also believe that you want something from him or her or may want more of his or her time than your friend would like to give. Ultimately, the meaning and interpretation of messages resides in the mind of the receiver. The ultimate interpretation of your message depends on the timing of your message and the quality of the relationship you have with your friend, as well as the overall context—when and where you express your affection.

Source: L. A. Erbert and K. Floyd, "Affectionate Expressions as Face-Threatening Acts: Receiver Assessments," *Communication Studies,* 55(2) (Summer 2004): 254–70.

Solve Problems Rather Than Try to Control Others

Most of us don't like others' attempts to control us. Someone who presumes to tell us what's good for us, instead of helping us puzzle through issues and problems, is likely to engender defensiveness. Open-ended questions, such as "What seems to be the problem?" or "How can we deal with the issue?" create a more supportive climate than critical comments, such as "Here's where you are wrong" or commands such as "Don't do that!"

Be Genuine Rather Than Manipulative

To be genuine means that you honestly seek to be yourself rather than someone you are not. It also means taking an honest interest in others and considering the unique-

Interpersonal Communication and Emotion Connecting Heart to Heart

Expressing Your Emotions

Communication is enhanced if you can clearly express the emotions you are feeling. One way to communicate your emotions is to describe how you are feeling with a well-chosen word or phrase. The following list gives you several options for expressing your feelings in positive, neutral, or negative terms. Categorizing these terms as positive, neutral, or negative doesn't mean that you should only use positive or neutral terms and avoid negative terms. What's important is that you select a word that accurately helps you communicate your emotions to others.

Positive		Neutral	Negative	
calm	hopeful	amazed	afraid	helpless
cheerful	interested	ambivalent	alone	horrible
comfortable	joyful	apathetic	angry	humiliated
confident	loving	bashful	annoyed	hysterical
content	optimistic	bored	bitter	intimidated
delighted	passionate	detached	confused	listless
ecstatic	peaceful	hurried	defeated	mad
elated	playful	lukewarm	defensive	mean
enthusiastic	pleased	numb	depressed	miserable
excited	refreshed	possessive	devastated	paranoid
flattered	romantic	sentimental	disappointed	rebellious
free	sexy	vulnerable	disgusted	regretful
friendly	tender		disturbed	resentful
glad	warm		empty	restless
grateful	willing		exhausted	sad
happy	wonderful		fearful	shocked
high			frustrated	suspicious
			furious	terrified
			guilty	ugly

ness of each individual and situation, avoiding generalizations or strategies that focus only on your own needs and desires. A manipulative person has hidden agendas; a genuine person discusses issues and problems openly and honestly.

Carl Rogers, the founder of person-centered counseling, suggests that true understanding and dialogue occur when people adopt a genuine or honest positive regard for others.[42] If your goal is to look out only for your own interests, your language will reflect your self-focus. At the heart of being genuine is being other-oriented—being sincerely interested in those with whom you communicate. Although it's unrealistic to assume you will become best friends with everyone you meet, Rogers suggests that you can work to develop an unselfish interest, or what he called an unconditional positive regard for others. That's hard to do. But the effort will be rewarded with a more positive communication climate.

word picture. Short statement or story that illustrates or describes an emotion; word pictures often use a simile (a comparison using the word *like* or *as*) to clarify the image.

To practice expressing your emotions, imagine yourself in each of the following situations, and use some of the words listed here to write a response for each situation. Describe your response using either a single word or a short phrase, such as "I feel angry," or express your feelings in terms of what you'd like to do, such as "I'd be so embarrassed I would sink through the floor" or "I would feel like leaving and never coming back to this house."

- You have several thousand dollars charged to your credit cards, and you get fired from your job.
- Your best friend, with whom you spend a lot of time, is moving to another country.
- You have just learned that your adored aunt has died and left you a $35,000 inheritance.
- Even though you do your best to keep your room clean, your roommate is complaining again that you are a slob.
- You have brought your two-year-old son to a worship service, but he talks and runs around during the service and will not sit still. Other worshipers are looking at you with disapproval.
- You arrive at your vacation hotel only to discover that they do not have a reservation for you, and you do not have your room confirmation number.

Another skill to help you accurately and appropriately express your emotions is to use a word picture. A **word picture** is a short statement or story that dramatizes an emotion you have experienced. Using a visual image can add extra power in expressing your feelings when a simple descriptive word may not suffice. Word pictures can be used to clarify how you feel, to offer praise or correction, and to create greater intimacy. A key goal of a word picture is to communicate your feelings and emotions. An effective way to express your emotions through a word picture is to use a simile. A simile, as you may remember from your English class, is a comparison that uses the word *like* or *as* to clarify the image you want to communicate. "When you forgot my birthday, I felt like crumbs swept from the table," exclaimed Marge to her forgetful husband. Or, after a hard day's work, Jeff told his family, "I feel like a worn-out punching bag—I've been pounded time and time again, and now I feel torn and scuffed. I need a few minutes of peace and quiet before I join in the family conversation." His visual image helped communicate how exhausted he really felt. The best word pictures use an image to which the listener can relate. To practice your skill, try to develop word pictures to express in a powerful and memorable way the feelings you might have in the following situations.

- You have just learned that a cherished family pet has died.
- You want to tell your friends how happy you are when you learn you received an A in a difficult course.
- You've asked your sister not to leave empty milk cartons in the refrigerator, but you discover another empty carton in the fridge.
- Your family is planning a vacation but didn't ask you to be involved in the planning.

Empathize Rather Than Remain Detached from Others

Empathy is one of the hallmarks of supportive relationships. As you learned earlier, empathy is the ability to understand the feelings of others and to predict the emotional responses they will have to different situations. Being empathic is the essence of being other-oriented. The opposite of empathy is neutrality. To be neutral is to be indifferent or apathetic toward another. Even when you express anger or irritation toward another, you are investing some energy in the relationship.

Research suggests that one of the most important things we can do to be empathic and supportive is simply what we have been suggesting throughout this book: Be other-oriented. Interpersonal communication researcher Amy Bippus determined that what most people want from others during times of stress are messages of empathy and sensitivity to their feelings, followed by problem solving, relating, refraining from general negativity, and offering a different perspective. The positive interpersonal outcomes that resulted from providing other-oriented messages were a more upbeat mood, feelings of empowerment, and more focused, calmer thoughts.[43]

BE OTHER-ORIENTED

Be Flexible Rather Than Rigid Toward Others

Most people don't like someone who always seems certain that he or she is right. A "you're wrong, I'm right" attitude creates a defensive climate. This does not mean that you should have no opinions and go through life blithely agreeing to everything. And it doesn't mean that there is *never* one answer that is right and others that are wrong. But instead of making rigid pronouncements, you can use phrases such as "I may be wrong, but it seems to me . . ." or "Here's one way to look at this problem." This manner of speaking gives your opinions a softer edge that allows room for others to express a point of view.

Present Yourself as Equal Rather Than Superior

You can antagonize others by letting them know that you view yourself as better than they are. You may be gifted and intelligent, but it's not necessary to announce it. And although some people have the responsibility and authority to manage others, "pulling rank" does not usually produce a cooperative climate. With phrases such as "Let's work on this together" or "We each have a valid perspective," you can avoid erecting walls of resentment and suspicion.

Also, avoid using abstract language or professional jargon to impress others. Keep your messages short and clear, and use informal language. When you communicate with someone from another culture, you may need to use an **elaborated code** to get your message across. This means that your messages will have to be more explicit, but they should not be condescending. For example, two of this book's authors vividly remember trying to explain to a French exchange student what a fire ant was. First, we had to translate *ant* into French, and then we had to provide scientific, descriptive, and narrative evidence to help the student understand how these tiny biting insects terrorize people in the southern part of the United States.

Underlying the goal of creating a supportive rather than a defensive communication climate is the importance of providing social and emotional support when communicating with others. A basic principle of all healthy interpersonal relationships is the importance of communicating positive, supportive messages that impart liking or affection.[44] Several researchers have documented that providing verbal messages of comfort and support, not surprisingly, enhances the quality of a relationship.[45] As a relationship develops over time and the communication partners gain more credibility

elaborated code. Conversation that uses many words and various ways of describing an idea or concept to communicate its meaning.

and influence, messages of comfort play an even more important role in maintaining the quality of the interpersonal relationship.[46] We use not only words of comfort but, as you will learn in Chapter 7, nonverbal expressions of comfort as well.[47]

Communication researchers have documented the power of humor in helping to turn a tense, potentially conflict-producing confrontation into a more supportive, positive conversation. Research by communication scholar Amy Bippus found that most people report using humor as a way of providing comfort to others.[48] Humor also was perceived as a productive way to help a distressed person better cope with problems and stress.

Recap: Using Supportive Communication and Avoiding Defensive Communication

Supportive Communication Is . . .

Descriptive: Use "I" language that describes your own feelings and ideas.

Problem Oriented: Aim communication at solving problems and generating multiple options.

Spontaneously Genuine: Develop a here-and-now orientation. Be honest and authentic rather than fake and phony.

Empathic: Be emotionally involved in the conversation; attempt to understand what your partner is thinking and feeling.

Provisionally Flexible: Be open to receive new information; demonstrate flexibility in the positions you take.

Equal: Adopt a communication style based on mutual respect, and assume each person has a right to express ideas and share information.

Defensive Communication Is . . .

Evaluative: Avoid using "You" language that attacks the worth of another person.

Controlling: Don't attempt to get others to do *only* what you want them to do in order to control the outcome.

Strategically Manipulative: Avoid planning your conversation in advance to get what you want. Don't develop a script to manipulate and accomplish your goal.

Neutrally Detached: Avoid being emotionally indifferent or creating the impression that you don't care how another person is feeling.

Certain and Rigid: Don't take a dogmatic, entrenched, or rigid position on issues; be willing to listen to others.

Superior: Avoid assuming an attitude or mindset that your ideas are better than those of others.

When You've Not Been Other-Oriented: The Power of an Apology

In this chapter, we've talked about the power of words and how communication sometimes can create problems and bruise a relationship. There are times, if we're honest with ourselves, that we aren't as other-oriented as we should be, and we may say and do things that we shouldn't. We're human; we make mistakes. Words, however, not only inflict pain but also have power to repair relational damage.

One of the ways to mend a relational rift when we have made a mistake is to offer an **apology**—to explicitly admit that we made an error and to ask the person we offended to forgive us. An apology helps us save face and can repair relational stress. One research team found that people who received an apology felt less anger, were less likely to be aggressive, and had a better overall impression of the offender.[49] In addition, research has found that when we apologize to someone, the person we initially offended

apology. Explicit admission of an error, along with a request for forgiveness.

has greater empathy toward us and is less likely to avoid us or seek revenge.[50] An apology can calm a turbulent relationship.

Communication researchers Janet Meyer and Kyra Rothenberg found that the seriousness of the offense and the quality of the relationship we have with another person determines whether we are likely to apologize and the kind of apology we should offer.[51] Committing a serious blunder or error is more likely to result in an apology than committing a mild offense—especially if we believe we've hurt someone. We're also more likely to apologize to someone if we feel guilty or embarrassed by something we've said or done.[52] And the more interpersonally intimate we are with someone, the more likely we are to apologize.[53]

What kind of apologies are most effective? One of the most effective ways to apologize is simply to honestly and sincerely admit that you were wrong. It's not enough just to say, "I'm sorry I hurt you." A true apology acknowledges that the offending individual was wrong. Thus, it's better to say it explicitly: "I was wrong." Assuming responsibility for the error and offering to do something to repair the damage are specific

Building Your Skills

How to Assert Yourself If You Are Sexually Harassed

What Is Sexual Harassment?

Any unwelcome sexual advances, requests for sexual favors, or other inappropriate verbal or physical behavior of a sexual nature may be classified as sexual harassment. Examples include

- Repeated and unwanted requests for dates, sexual flirtations, or propositions of a sexual nature
- Unwanted sexual remarks or questions about a person's clothing, body, or sexual activity
- Unnecessary touching, patting, hugging, or brushing against a person's body
- Direct or implied threats that failure to submit to sexual advances will affect employment, work status, grades, letters of recommendation, or residential choice
- Physical assault
- A pattern of conduct that causes humiliation or discomfort, such as inappropriate terms of greeting; sexually explicit or sexist comments, questions, or jokes; or leering at a person's body

What to Do If You Are Sexually Harassed

- Be direct and candid with the person.
- Use "I" messages (for example, "I don't like those kinds of jokes made about me").
- Avoid being overly dramatic; remain confident that the incident will be dealt with.
- If the incident happens at school or work, use the grievance procedure.
- Report the harasser to your supervisor, department chair, or dean.
- If the harasser is your supervisor or an administrative official, report the incident to his or her supervisor.
- Report the harassment immediately after it occurs. The longer you wait, the less credible your story will be.
- When the harassment occurs, write down important facts.
- Report the incident as if you were a journalist: Give the who, what, when, where, and how; keep to the facts.
- Be prepared to give the interviewer names of witnesses.
- Put aside your anger and embarassment and be thorough when telling the story.

Source: Information adapted from Texas State University policy and procedure statement on sexual harassment and Vicki West, "Sexual Harassment: Identify, Stop, and Prevent" seminar.

kinds of behaviors that enhance the effectiveness of an apology. Researchers Cynthia McPherson Frantz and Courtney Bennigson found that it may not be best to apologize immediately after you make a mistake; their results indicated that it may be better to wait a short time before apologizing.[54] Your apology will be perceived as more sincere and heartfelt if the other person believes you truly understand how your mistake hurt him or her and that you want to repair the damage. An apology given too quickly may be perceived as insincere—the offended person may think that you're just trying to quickly dismiss the error. Being perceived as sincerely remorseful is one of the keys to an effective apology.

The words we use can hurt others. We can also use words to repair the damage we have done by offering an apology expressing that we were wrong (not simply sorry), we are sincerely remorseful, we want to do something to repair the damage, we understand how much we may have hurt our communication partner. The Book of Proverbs says, "Words fitly spoken are like apples of gold in pictures of silver." A well-worded apology can help restore luster to a relationship that may have become tarnished. Words have power—to hurt and to heal.

Using Words to Be Appropriately Assertive

At times, you run across people who are verbally aggressive, obnoxious, or worse—they may try to coerce or intimidate you into doing things you'd rather not do. Should the other-oriented person just politely accept obnoxious verbal assaults? No—being other-oriented doesn't mean you should ignore such boorish behavior. Nor do you have to respond in the same way you were treated. Rather than return mean-spirited aggressiveness with an equally inappropriate stream of aggressive words or rude behavior, consider using your verbal skills to be appropriately assertive. To be **assertive** is to make requests, ask for information, stand up for your rights, and generally pursue your own best interests without denying your partner's rights.

Each individual has rights. You have the right to refuse a request someone makes of you, the right to express your feelings as long as you don't trample on the feelings of others, and the right to have your needs met if this doesn't infringe on the rights of others. Assertive people let their communication partners know when a message or behavior is infringing on their rights.

Some people confuse the terms *assertive* and *aggressive.* Being **aggressive** means pursuing your interests by denying the rights of others. Being appropriately assertive is being other-oriented; aggressiveness is exclusively self-oriented. Aggressive people blame, judge, and evaluate to get what they want. We'll expand on our discussion of aggressive behavior when we discuss relationship challenges in Chapter 11. Aggressive communicators use defensive communication tactics, including such intimidating nonverbal cues as steely stares, a bombastic voice, and flailing gestures. Assertive people can ask for what they want without judging or evaluating their partners.

When presenting the dos and don'ts of appropriate verbal communication in this chapter, we've often emphasized strategies for initiating communication with others. Sometimes what's most challenging is to respond appropriately when another person (someone who has not taken a course in interpersonal communication) comes at you with an inappropriately aggressive, argumentative, or defensive message, especially if the inappropriate message that's hurled at you takes you by surprise. You do not have to be passive when you are on the receiving end of such messages. We suggest instead that an effective communicator is appropriately assertive.

assertive. Able to pursue one's own best interests without denying a partner's rights.

aggressive. Expressing one's interests while denying the rights of others by blaming, judging, and evaluating other people.

Recap
Assertiveness versus Aggressiveness

Assertiveness . . .	Aggressiveness . . .
Expresses your interests without denying the rights of others.	Expresses your interests and denies the rights of others.
Is other-oriented.	Is self-oriented.
Describes what you want.	Evaluates the other person.
Discloses your needs using "I" messages.	Discloses your needs using "you" messages.

Behaving Assertively: Five Steps

Many people have a tendency to withdraw in the face of controversy, even when their rights are being violated or denied. But you can develop skill in asserting yourself by practicing five key suggestions.[55]

Describe

Describe how you view the situation. To assert your position, you first need to describe how you view the situation. You need to be assertive because the other person has not been other-oriented. For example, Doug is growing increasingly frustrated with Maria's tardiness for weekly staff meetings. He approaches the problem by first describing his observation: "I have noticed that you are usually fifteen minutes late to our weekly staff meetings." A key to communicating your assertive message is to monitor your nonverbal message, especially your voice. Avoid sarcasm or excessive vocal intensity. Calmly yet confidently describe the problem.

Disclose

Disclose your feelings. After describing the situation from your perspective, let the other person know how you feel.[56] Disclosing your feelings will help to build empathy and avoid lengthy harangues about the other person's unjust treatment. "I feel you don't take our weekly meetings seriously," continues Doug as he asserts his desire for Maria to be on time to the meeting. Note that Doug does not talk about how others are feeling ("Every member of our group is tired of your coming in late"); he describes how *he* feels.

Becoming Other-Oriented

Bumper Sticker Slogans

The key to shared understanding is to focus on the needs, goals, and mindset of your communication partner. Throughout this chapter, we have emphasized how to develop an other-oriented approach when communicating verbally. To help you remember some of the essential principles of being other-oriented, consider the following "bumper sticker" slogans:

Meanings are in people, not in words.

Words are arbitrary, contextually and culturally bound symbols that can have denotative and connotative, concrete or abstract meaning. Focus on what the words may mean to your partner.

Think before you speak.

Words have tremendous power in our lives. They create and affect people's emotions and actions, as well as affecting and reflecting culture. Before you speak, consider the impact your words will have on others. Remember that words can hurt—and once spoken, words cannot be taken back.

SAY WHAT YOU MEAN; MEAN WHAT YOU SAY

Choose your words with care. Be mindful of the potential for miscommunication and misunderstanding. The spoken word belongs half to the person who speaks and half to the person who understands.

Speak to others as you think they'd like to be spoken to.

Words can engender a supportive communication climate or create defensiveness, which can lead to misunderstandings. Try to put yourself in your partner's place when you're conversing with others.

Identify Effects

Identify the effects of the behavior. Next, you can identify the effects of the other person's behavior on you or others. "When you are late, it disrupts our meeting," says Doug.

Be Silent

Be silent and wait. After taking the first three steps, simply wait for a response. Some people find this step hard. Again, be sure to monitor your nonverbal cues. Make sure your facial expression does not contradict your verbal message. Delivering an assertive message with a broad grin might create a double bind for your listener, who may not be sure what the primary message is—the verbal one or the nonverbal one.

Paraphrase

Paraphrase content and feelings. After the other person responds, paraphrase both the content and the feelings of the message. Suppose Maria says, "Oh, I'm sorry. I didn't realize I was creating a problem. I have another meeting that usually goes overtime. It's difficult for me to arrive at the start of our meeting on time." Doug could respond, "So the key problem is a time conflict with another meeting. It must make you feel frustrated to try to do two things at once."

If the other person is evasive, unresponsive, or aggressive, you'll need to cycle through the steps again: Clearly describe what the other person is doing that is not acceptable; disclose how you feel; identify the effects; wait; then paraphrase and clarify as needed. A key goal of an assertive response is to seek an empathic connection between you and your partner. Paraphrasing feelings is a way of ensuring that both parties are connecting.

If you tend to withdraw from conflict, how can you become assertive? Visualizing can help. Think of a past situation in which you wished you had been more assertive and then mentally replay the situation, imagining what you might have said. Also practice verbalizing assertive statements. When you are able to be appropriately assertive, consciously congratulate yourself for sticking up for your rights. To sharpen your assertiveness skills, try Building Your Skills: Assertiveness.

Building Your Skills

Assertiveness

Practice

Working with a partner, describe a situation in which you could have been more assertive. Ask your partner to assume the role of the person toward whom you should have been more assertive. Now replay the situation, using the following skills:

1. *Describe:* Tell the other person that what he or she is doing bothers you. Describe rather than evaluate.
2. *Disclose:* Then tell the other person how you feel. For example, "I feel *X*, when you do *Y*."
3. *Identify effects:* Tell the other person the effects of his or her behavior on you or your group. Be as clear and descriptive as you can.
4. *Wait:* After you have described, disclosed, and identified the effects, wait for a response.
5. *Paraphrase:* Use reflective listening skills: Question, paraphrase content, paraphrase feelings.

Observe

Ask your classmates to observe your role play and provide feedback, using the following checklist. When you have finished asserting your point of view, reverse roles with your partner.

_____ Clearly describes what the problem was

_____ Effectively discloses how he or she felt

_____ Clearly describes the effects of the behavior

_____ Pauses or waits after describing the effects

_____ Uses effective questions to promote understanding

_____ Accurately paraphrases content

_____ Accurately paraphrases feelings

_____ Has good eye contact

_____ Leans forward while speaking

_____ Has an open body posture

_____ Has appropriate voice tone and quality

How to Assert Yourself

Step	Example
1. Describe.	"I see you haven't completed the report yet."
2. Disclose.	"I feel the work I ask you to do is not a priority with you."
3. Identify effects.	"Without that report, our team will not achieve our goal."
4. Wait.	Be silent, and wait for a response.
5. Use reflective listening skills:	
Question.	"Do you understand how I feel?"
Paraphrase content.	"So you were not aware the report was late."
Paraphrase feelings.	"Perhaps you feel embarrassed."

Summary

The words we use have great power to affect our self-image and to influence the relationships we establish with others. Words are symbols that refer to objects, events, people, and ideas. They are arbitrary. We interpret their meaning through the context and culture to which they belong. Communication is complex because most words create both denotative (literal) meanings and connotative (subjective) meanings, and because words range from concrete to abstract.

The power of words stems from their ability to create images and to influence our thoughts, feelings, and actions. There is also an important link between the words we use and our culture. Language shapes culture, and culture shapes language. Our view of the world is influenced by our vocabulary and the categories we have created with words.

Several word barriers can contribute to misunderstanding in interpersonal communication. Bypassing occurs when a word means one thing to one person and another to someone else. Our verbal expressions may lack clarity, either because we make language errors or because the meaning we want to convey is not clear to us. Allness statements can mislead and alienate listeners because the speaker falsely implies that he or she knows all there is to know about something. Another barrier, static evaluation, fails to take changes into account and uses outdated labels and categories. Polarization is the language of extremes; when someone thinks in black and white, many shades of meaning disappear. Finally, biased language that is insensitive to others creates noise that interferes with the meaning of a message.

The words you use can ultimately enhance or detract from the quality of relationships you establish with others. Supportive communication is descriptive rather than evaluative, problem-oriented rather than control-oriented, genuine rather than contrived or strategically manipulative, empathic rather than neutral, and flexible rather than rigid. It also assumes equality rather than superiority.

When you become the victim of inappropriate, non–other-oriented verbal attacks or intimidating behavior, we suggest that you respond assertively. Being assertive involves five steps: describe, disclose, identify effects, silently wait, then paraphrase what your communication partner has said. Being a competent communicator involves listening and then appropriately responding to enhance, rather than detract from, the quality of interpersonal communication.

For Discussion and Review

Focus on Critical Thinking

1. Marge and Paul are having an argument. Paul shouts, "You're constantly criticizing me! You don't let me make any important decisions!" How could Paul communicate how he feels in a more supportive way?
2. Alan asked Jessie to pick him up after work at the parking garage at 5:30 P.M. Jessie waited patiently at the parking garage on the other side of campus and finally went home at 6:30 P.M., having seen no sign of Alan. Alan was waiting at the parking garage behind his office rather than at the one on the other side of the campus. What word barriers do you think led to this misunderstanding?
3. Rephrase the following statements to use less biased language:
   a. I'd like to introduce Mr. Russell Browne and his wife, Muriel.
   b. In an office memo: "Several gals have been leaving their purses at their desks."
4. Rephrase the following statements, using the skill of indexing.
   a. All politicians want power and control over others.
   b. All teachers are underpaid.
   c. All Texans like to brag about how great their state is.

Focus on Ethics

5. If you really don't want to listen to your co-worker go into detail about her latest vacation trip or provide details about the recent escapades of her children or grandchildren, is it appropriate to tell her that you'd rather not hear her "news"? Support your response.
6. Is it ethical to correct someone when he or she uses sexist language or makes a stereotyping remark about someone's race, gender, or sexual orientation? What if that person is your boss or your teacher? Explain your answer.
7. Is it ethical to mask your true feelings of anger and irritation with someone by using supportive statements or confirming statements when what you really want to do is tell him or her "the truth" in no uncertain terms?

Learning with Others

1. Think of a bypass miscommunication that you've experienced. Share your recollection with a small group, and compare your feelings and responses with those of others.
2. In your group, choose one person to play someone who is recently divorced and whose spouse is not abiding by a child custody agreement and insists on seeing the children at odd hours. Another person should play the role of a trusted friend who only listens and responds. Ask the trusted friend to use the skills he or she learned in this chapter along with effective listening skills presented in Chapter 4. Then do a group evaluation of his or her response.
3. Divide into groups of two to four people. Each team or group should prepare a short play depicting one of the supportive or defensive communication responses described in this chapter. Perform your play for the class or another team to see whether they can identify the type of supportive or defensive communication behavior your team is portraying. Consider one of the following situations or develop one of your own:

   Speaking with a professor about a grade
   Returning a broken item to a store
   Talking with your child about his or her grades
   Responding to a telemarketer who calls you during dinner
   Talking with one of your employees who made a work-related mistake
   Rebooking a flight because your flight was canceled by the airline
   Taking an order from a customer at a fast-food restaurant
   Receiving a complaint from a customer about poor service
   Talking with someone who has knocked on your door to invite you to his or her church
   Asking someone to turn down the stereo or TV while you are trying to study

Variation: Instead of illustrating supportive and defensive communication, role-play an example of one of the confirming or disconfirming communication behaviors discussed in Chapter 5.

Weblinks

Go to *www.mycommunicationlab.com* (access code required) to find Web resources for your text that supplement the material in Chapter 6, including links to information on the following topics:

Symbols and communication
The Sapir–Whorf Hypothesis
Avoiding gender bias
Assertive communication
Conversation skills

CHAPTER 7

Nonverbal Communication Skills

OBJECTIVES

1. Explain why nonverbal communication is an important and challenging area of study.
2. Describe the functions of nonverbal communication in interpersonal relationships.
3. Summarize research findings that describe codes of nonverbal communication behavior.
4. Describe three bases for interpreting nonverbal behavior.
5. Formulate a strategy for improving your ability to interpret nonverbal messages accurately.

OUTLINE

What you are speaks so loudly that I cannot hear what you say.

Ralph Waldo Emerson

Do you like to "people watch"? When you are sitting in a public place such as a shopping mall, an airport, or a bus stop, do you sometimes make assumptions about what other people might be like as you observe their comings and goings? Most of us are people watchers from time to time—we rely on nonverbal communication to help us make predictions about others. **Nonverbal communication** is behavior other than written or spoken language that creates meaning for us. A person's tone of voice, eye contact, facial expressions, posture, movement, general appearance, use of personal space, manipulation of the communication environment, and a host of other nonverbal clues reveal how that person feels about others. All communication has both a content and a relationship dimension. Our nonverbal communication is a primary source of relationship cues.

In this chapter, we focus on how nonverbal communication affects the quality of our interpersonal relationships. Being able to interpret others' unspoken messages and appropriately express our own feelings through nonverbal communication are key components of being other-oriented. To help you become more skilled in both expressing and interpreting nonverbal messages, we'll discuss why nonverbal communication is important in establishing interpersonal relationships with others. We'll also note challenges in trying to accurately interpret the unspoken messages of others. After we discuss several nonverbal communication codes, we'll offer tips for helping you more accurately interpret nonverbal communication.

Why Learn About Nonverbal Communication?

Wherever You Go, There You Are is the title of a popular book about Zen meditation.[1] The title could easily refer to nonverbal communication: Wherever you go, nonverbal communication is there. Nonverbal communication is an ever-present form of human expression. If you are alive, chances are that people are making inferences about you based on your nonverbal behavior. But are our people-watching guesses about others accurate? Sometimes yes, and sometimes no. This chapter is designed to help you increase your accuracy in evaluating the nonverbal messages of others. And just as you may inaccurately interpret the nonverbal messages of others, other people

nonverbal communication. Behavior other than written or spoken language that creates meaning for someone.

may misjudge your nonverbal cues. Because much of our nonverbal communication behavior is unconscious, most of us have only a limited awareness or understanding of it. We begin our examination of nonverbal communication by looking at the multiple reasons that nonverbal communication is so important in the total communication process.

Nonverbal Messages Are the Primary Way We Communicate Our Feelings and Attitudes

Daryl knew that he was in trouble the moment he walked into the room. His wife, Sandra, gave him a steely stare. Her brow was furrowed and her arms were crossed. On the table was a dish of cold lobster Newburg, extinguished candles burnt to nubs, and dirty dishes in all but one spot: his. Daryl was in the doghouse for forgetting the special meal his wife had prepared, and he needed no words to sense the depth of her displeasure. Although Daryl was momentarily in trouble for his forgetfulness, his ability to quickly read the nonverbal message in that situation will serve him well in the long run. Marriage partners who are skilled at interpreting the emotional meaning of a message are typically more satisfied in their marriages.[2] Nonverbal communication is the primary way in which we communicate feelings, attitudes, and emotions.

BE OTHER-ORIENTED 

Psychologist Albert Mehrabian concluded that as little as 7 percent of the emotional meaning of a message is communicated through explicit verbal channels.[3] The most significant source of emotional communication is our face—according to Mehrabian's study, it channels as much as 55 percent of our meaning. Vocal cues such as volume, pitch, and intensity communicate another 38 percent of our emotional meaning. In all, we communicate approximately 93 percent of the emotional meaning of our messages nonverbally. Although these percentages do not apply to every communication situation, the results of Mehrabian's investigation do illustrate the potential power of nonverbal cues in communicating emotion.[4] Researchers are continuing to find new ways to measure the impact and power of nonverbal messages in the communication of emotions.[5]

Nonverbal Messages Are Usually More Believable Than Verbal Messages

"Honey, do you love me?" asks Brenda.

"OF COURSE I LOVE YOU! HAVEN'T I ALWAYS TOLD YOU THAT I LOVE YOU? I LOVE YOU!" shouts Jim, keeping his eyes glued to his morning newspaper.

Brenda will probably not be totally reassured by Jim's pledge of affection. The contradiction between his spoken message of love and his nonverbal message of irritation and disinterest will leave her wondering about his true feelings.

Actions speak louder than words. This cliché became a cliché because nonverbal communication is more believable than verbal communication. Nonverbal messages are more difficult to fake. One research team concluded that North Americans use the following cues, listed in order from most to least important, to help them discern when a person is lying.[6]

- Greater time lag in response to a question
- Reduced eye contact
- Increased shifts in posture
- Unfilled pauses
- Less smiling

- Slower speech
- Higher pitch in voice
- More deliberate pronunciation and articulation of words

BE OTHER-ORIENTED

Because it is difficult to manipulate an array of nonverbal cues, a skilled other-oriented observer can see when a person's true feelings leak out. Social psychologists Paul Ekman and Wallace Friesen have identified the face, hands, and feet as key sources of nonverbal cues.[7] Are you aware of what your fingers and toes are doing as you are reading this book? Even if you become expert at masking and manipulating your face, you may first signal lack of interest or boredom with another person by finger wiggling or toe wagging. Or you may twiddle a pen or pencil. When you become emotionally aroused, the pupils of your eyes dilate, and you may blush, sweat, or change breathing patterns.[8] Lie detectors (polygraphs) rely on these unconscious clues. A polygraph measures a person's heart and breathing rate, as well as the electrical resistance of the skin (called *galvanic skin response*), to determine whether he or she is giving truthful verbal responses.

Nonverbal Messages Work with Verbal Messages to Create Meaning

Although we rely heavily on nonverbal messages, they do not operate independently of spoken messages in our relationships. Instead, verbal and nonverbal cues work together in two primary ways to help us make sense of others' messages: They help us manage the verbal message, and they augment the emotional meaning of what we say.

1. *Nonverbal cues help us manage verbal messages.* Specifically, our nonverbal cues can substitute for verbal messages, as well as repeat, contradict, or regulate what we say. An extended thumb signals that a hitchhiker would like a ride. A circle formed by the thumb and index finger can either signal that everything is A-OK or convey an obscene message. When someone asks, "Which way did he go?" you can silently point to the back door. In these instances, you are substituting nonverbal cues for a verbal message.

   You can also use nonverbal cues to repeat or reinforce your words. "Where is the personnel department?" asks a job applicant.

   "Three flights up. Take the elevator," says the security guard, pointing to the elevator. The guard's pointing gesture repeats her verbal instruction and clarifies the message.

   "Sure, this is a good time to talk about the Henrikson merger," says the business executive, nervously looking at her watch, stuffing papers into her attaché case, and avoiding eye contact with her co-worker. In this instance, the nonverbal cues contradict the verbal ones. And as you learned earlier, the nonverbal message is almost always the one we believe.

   We also use nonverbal cues to regulate our participation in verbal exchanges. In most informal meetings, it is not appropriate or necessary to signal your desire to speak by raising your hand. Yet somehow you are able to signal to others when you'd like to speak and when you'd rather not talk. How does this happen? You use eye contact, raised eyebrows, an open mouth, or perhaps a single raised index finger to signal that you would like to make a point. If your colleagues do not see these signals, especially the eye contact, they may think you are not interested in talking.[9]

Portrait artists pay close attention to nonverbal cues such as posture, facial expression, and gesture to capture their subjects' personalities. What do the nonverbal cues reveal about this woman?

2. *Nonverbal cues augment the emotional meaning of verbal messages.* Our unspoken cues accent and complement verbal messages to increase or decrease the emotional impact of what we say. "Unless we vote to increase our tax base," bellows Mr. Coddlington, "we will not have enough classroom space to educate our children." While delivering his impassioned plea to the school board, Mr. Coddlington also loudly slaps the lectern to accent his message and reinforce its intensity. A scolding mother's wagging finger and an angry supervisor's raised voice are other nonverbal cues that accent verbal messages.

   Simultaneous and complementary verbal and nonverbal messages can also help to color the emotion we are expressing or the attitude we are conveying. The length of a hug while you tell your son you are proud of him provides additional information about the intensity of your pride. The firmness of your handshake when you greet a job interviewer can confirm your verbal claim that you are eager for employment.

People Respond and Adapt to Others Through Nonverbal Messages

You sense that your best friend is upset. Even though she doesn't tell you she's angry, you sense her mood by observing her grimacing facial expression and lack of direct eye contact with you. To help lighten the mood, you tell a joke. Many times every day, you "read" the nonverbal cues of others, even before they utter a word, to gain a clue about what to say or how to react. Interpreting others' nonverbal messages helps us appropriately adapt our communication as we interact with them. **Interaction adaptation theory** describes how people adapt to the communication behavior of others.[10]

The theory suggests that we respond not only to what people say, but also to their nonverbal expressions to help us navigate through our interpersonal conversations each day.[11] If, for example, your friend leans forward to tell a story, you may lean forward to listen. Or if during a meeting you sit with folded arms, unconvinced of what you are hearing, you may look around the conference table and find others with similarly folded arms. As if we were part of an intricate dance, when we communicate, we relate to others by responding to their movements, eye contact, gestures, and other nonverbal cues.

Sometimes, we relate by mirroring the posture or behavior of others. Or we may find ourselves gesturing in sync with someone's vocal pattern. At times, you are conscious of such mirroring of behavior, which is called **interactional synchrony.** At other times, you may not be aware that when your friend folds her arms while talking with you, you also fold your arms across your chest in a similar way. One researcher found that people evaluate such synchrony as positive; somewhat synchronized behavior (but not so synchronized that it feels as though someone is purposefully imitating you) communicates partners' mutual interest and positive regard.[12]

interaction adaptation theory. Theory suggesting that people interact with others by adapting to their communication behaviors.

interactional synchrony. Mirroring of each other's nonverbal behavior by communication partners.

Nonverbal Messages Play a Major Role in Interpersonal Relationships

As you learned in Chapter 1, because of the ubiquitous nature of nonverbal communication, you cannot *not* communicate; psychologist Raymond Birdwhistell suggests that as much as 65 percent of the social, or relational, meaning in messages is based on nonverbal communication.[13] Of course, the meaning that others interpret from your behavior may not be the one you intended, and the inferences they draw based on nonverbal information may be right or wrong.

Applying Theory and Research

Are Happily Married Couples Better at Interpreting Their Partners' Nonverbal Messages?

The divorce rate in the United States continues to be about 50 percent. And there is evidence that another 25 percent of marriages are under stress. Because of the challenges of being in a sustained, committed marriage, researchers have been interested in identifying the warning signs of a troubled marriage. One of the suspected predictors of the health of a marriage relationship is the skill with which each marriage partner communicates with the other.[14] Communication researchers have been especially interested in how accurately spouses interpret the nonverbal cues of their partners.[15] It seems reasonable to conclude that happily married couples tend to more accurately interpret the emotions communicated by their partners and have better ability to express or encode nonverbal messages.

Research conducted by communication scholars Ascan Koerner and Mary Anne Fitzpatrick asked the question "Are happily married couples able to both accurately express their own nonverbal messages and interpret nonverbal messages from their marriage partner?" To answer this question, the researchers invited married couples to participate in a research study. First, couples were given a questionnaire to determine whether the partners were satisfied with their marriage. They were then asked to take turns expressing and interpreting certain emotions such as affection, pleasure, depression, or a neutral expression. They were videotaped so that the researchers could validate that the participants were, in fact, accurately expressing the emotions and interpreting the nonverbal cues correctly.

Besides studying the accuracy of expressing and interpreting emotions, the researchers also wanted to know whether unhappily married couples were more likely to attribute a negative emotional expression to problems that occurred in the relationship. If, for example, a wife was not satisfied with the marriage, the researchers wanted to know whether she would interpret a negative nonverbal emotional expression by her husband as being about her or the marriage. So spouses were asked to express emotions related to something that happened in the relationship between the husband and wife. For example, one person might frown in response to being asked to take out the garbage. At other times spouses were asked just to express an emotion but not link their emotional expression to something that occurred in the relationship.

Here's what the researchers found. The more satisfied a person was with his or her marriage, the more accurately he or she was able to interpret the nonverbal emotional expressions of the partner. The ability to *express* an emotion was not found to be related to the quality of the marriage, but the ability to accurately *interpret* an emotional expression was better in marriages that were more satisfying to the couple. In addition, a happily married spouse was less likely to assume that a negative emotional expression was specifically directed toward him or her.

APPLYING the Research to Your Life

The research results have important implications for your relationships with others, especially in a married relationship.

- There is a strong relationship between a spouse's ability to accurately interpret nonverbal messages and overall satisfaction with the marriage. This does not mean that accurately interpreting nonverbal messages *causes* a marriage to be happier, only that being able to accurately decode nonverbal cues seems to be one component of marital satisfaction.
- A happily married spouse is less likely to suspect that a negative emotional expression is directed toward him or her personally—it is just a negative expression of emotion. In unhappy marriages, a negative emotional expression is more likely to be perceived as being specifically directed toward the other person.
- A husband's accurate interpretation of the nonverbal expressions of his wife is a good predictor of marital satisfaction, more so than a wife's accurate interpretation of her husbands' emotional expression. Research generally supports the assumption that women are better than men in interpreting nonverbal messages. So a man's ability to accurately interpret his wife's nonverbal messages is a good indicator of a satisfied marital relationship.
- In general, a spouse's ability to interpret nonverbal messages is more highly related to marital satisfaction than his or her ability to express nonverbal messages.

Source: Ascan F. Koerner and Mary Anne Fitzpatrick, "Nonverbal Communication and Marital Adjustment and Satisfaction: The Role of Decoding Relationship Relevant and Relationship Irrelevant Affect," *Communication Monographs,* 69 (2002): 33–51.

You learned in Chapter 3 that people begin making judgments about strangers just a fraction of a second after meeting them, based on nonverbal information. Within the first four minutes of interaction, you scope the other person out and draw conclusions about him or her.[16] Another research team found that you may decide whether a date is going to be pleasant or dull during the first thirty seconds of meeting your partner, before your partner has had time to utter more than "Hello."[17] Nonverbal cues, accurate or not, affect first impressions.

Nonverbal expressions of support also are important when providing comforting messages to others during times of stress and anxiety. Communication researchers Susanne Jones and Laura Guerrero found that being nonverbally expressive and supportive is important in helping people cope with stress.[18] Providing empathic, supportive facial expressions and vocal cues, hugs, and positive touch helps to reduce stress and enhance a person's overall well-being.

BE OTHER-ORIENTED

Nonverbal cues are important not only when people initiate relationships, but also as they maintain and develop mature relationships with others. In fact, the more intimate the relationship, the more people use and understand the nonverbal cues of their partners.

Long-married couples spend less time verbalizing their feelings and emotions to each other than they did when they were first dating; each learns how to interpret the other's subtle nonverbal cues.[19] If your spouse is silent during dinner, you may know that her day was a tough one and you should give her a wide berth. And if, when you put on your new Kelly green pants, your husband grimaces as he asks, "New pants?" you may understand that he does not love them. In fact, all of us are more likely to use nonverbal cues to convey negative messages than to announce explicitly our dislike of something or someone. People also use nonverbal cues to signal changes in the level of satisfaction with a relationship.[20] When we want to cool things off, we may start using a less vibrant tone of voice and cut back on eye contact and physical contact with our partner.

Why Learn About Nonverbal Communication?

1. Nonverbal messages communicate our feelings and attitudes.
2. Nonverbal messages are usually more believable than verbal messages.
3. Nonverbal messages work with verbal messages to create meaning.
   - Nonverbal cues substitute for, repeat, contradict, or regulate verbal messages.
   - Nonverbal cues accent and complement emotional messages.
4. People respond and adapt to others through nonverbal messages.
5. Nonverbal messages play a major role in initiating, maintaining, and developing interpersonal relationships.

The Challenge of Interpreting Nonverbal Messages

Even though we have made great claims for the value of studying nonverbal behaviors, it is not always easy to decipher unspoken messages.[21] You have dictionaries to help interpret words, but there is no handy reference book to help decode nonver-

bal cues. Although the phrase *body language* is often used in casual conversation, there is no universal or agreed-on interpretation for body movements or gestures. To help you with the decoding process, we will classify some common types of nonverbal behaviors. But first you should be aware of some of the difficulties that hinder classification.

Nonverbal Messages Are Often Ambiguous

Most words carry a meaning that everyone who speaks the same language can recognize. But the meaning of nonverbal messages may be known only to the person displaying them. Perhaps even more importantly, that person may not intend for the behavior to have any meaning at all. And some people have difficulty expressing their emotions nonverbally. They may have a frozen facial expression or a monotone voice. Or they may be teasing you, but their deadpan expressions lead you to believe that their negative comments are heartfelt. Often, it is difficult to draw meaningful conclusions about another person's behavior, even if you know him or her quite well.

Nonverbal Messages Are Continuous

Words are discrete entities; they have a beginning and an end. You can circle the first word in this sentence and underline the last one. Nonverbal behaviors are not as easily dissected. Like the sweep of a second hand on a watch, nonverbal behaviors are continuous. Some, such as a slap or a hand clap, have definite beginnings and endings. But more often than not, nonverbal behavior unfolds without clearly defined starting and stopping points. Gestures, facial expressions, and even eye contact can flow from one situation to the next with seamless ease. Researchers have difficulty studying nonverbal cues because of this continuous stream, so trying to categorize and interpret them will be challenging for us as well.

Nonverbal Cues Are Multichanneled

Have you ever tried to watch two or more TV programs at once? Some televisions let you see as many as eight programs simultaneously so that you can keep up with three ball games and two soap operas and view commercials on the three other channels. Like the programs on a multichannel TV, nonverbal cues come at us from a variety of sources simultaneously. And just as you can really only pay attention to one channel at a time on your multichannel television—although you can move among them very rapidly—so, too, can you actually attend to only one nonverbal cue at a time.[22] Social psychologist Michael Argyle suspects that negative nonverbal messages (frowns,

Understanding Diversity

Cultural Differences in Interpreting Nonverbal Messages

Research investigating nonverbal communication in a variety of cultures confirms that individuals interpret nonverbal messages from their unique cultural perspective. Note the following conclusions:[23]

Facial Expressions
One research team found that some facial expressions, such as those conveying happiness, sadness, anger, disgust, and surprise, were the same in 68 to 92 percent of the cultures examined.[24] All humans probably share the same neurophysiological basis for expressing emotions, but learn different rules for displaying and interpreting the expressions. For example, the Japanese culture does not reinforce the show of negative emotions; it is important for Japanese to "save face" and to help others save face as well.

Eye Contact
There seems to be more eye contact in interpersonal interactions between Arabs, South Americans, and Greeks than between people from other cultures. There is evidence that some African Americans look at others less than whites do when sending and receiving messages. One of the most universal expressions appears to be the eyebrow flash (the sudden raising of the eyebrows when meeting someone or interacting with others).

Gestures
Hand and body gestures with the most shared meaning among Africans, North Americans, and South Americans include pointing, shrugging, nodding the head, clapping, pointing the thumb down, waving hello, and beckoning. There are, however, regional variations within cultures; it is not wise to assume that all people in a given culture share the same meaning for certain gestures. The "okay" gesture made by forming a circle with the thumb and finger has sexual connotations for some South American and Caribbean countries. In France, the "okay" sign means "worthless."

Space
Arabs, Latin Americans, and Southern Europeans seem to stand closer to others than do people from Asia, India, Pakistan, and northern Europe. If you have been to Britain, you know that people queue or wait for buses in orderly straight lines. In France, however, queuing is less orderly, and individuals are more likely to push forward to be the next customer or to get the next seat on the bus. As with gestures, however, there are regional variations in spatial preferences.

grimaces, lack of eye contact) command attention before positive messages when the two compete.[25] Moreover, if the nonverbal message contradicts the verbal message, then you may have trouble interpreting either one correctly.[26]

Nonverbal Interpretation Is Culture-Based

There is some evidence that humans from every culture smile when they are happy and frown when they are unhappy.[27] We also all raise, or flash, our eyebrows when meeting or greeting others, and young children in many cultures wave to signal that they want their mothers, raise their arms to be picked up, and suck their thumbs for comfort.[28] All this suggests that there is some underlying basis for expressing emotion. Yet each culture may develop unique rules for displaying and interpreting these gestures and expressions.

For example, unless you grew up there, you might be startled when on a visit to New Orleans you stumble on a handkerchief-waving, dancing, exuberantly singing crowd and discover that it is an African American jazz funeral. What to the uninformed may seem like disrespect for the dead, others recognize as a joyous send-off to a better world.

Understanding Nonverbal Communication Codes

Keeping in mind all the challenges to our understanding that we've just discussed, we can begin looking at the categories of nonverbal information that researchers have studied: movement and gestures, eye contact, facial expressions, use of space and territory, touch, and personal appearance. Although we will concentrate on the codes that fall within these categories in mainstream Western culture, we will also look at codes for other cultures and subcultures.

Body Movement, Posture, and Gestures

In 1771, when English explorer Captain Cook arrived in the New Hebrides, he didn't speak the language of the natives. His only way of communicating was sign language. Through gestures, pointing, and hand waving, he established contact with the natives. There is evidence that people have used gestures to communicate since ancient times—especially to bridge cultural and language differences. The first record of the use of sign language to communicate is found in Xenophon's *The March Up Country,* in which he describes unspoken gestures used to help the Greeks cross Asia Minor around 400 B.C. Even when we do speak the same language as others, we use gestures to help us make our point.[29]

Kinesics is the study of human movement and gesture. Francis Bacon once noted, "As the tongue speaketh to the ear, so the hand speaketh to the eye." People have long recognized that movement and gestures provide valuable information to others. Various scholars and researchers have proposed paradigms for analyzing and coding these movements and gestures, just as grammarians have codified spoken or written language.[30]

kinesics. Study of human movement and gesture.

One paradigm identifies four stages of "quasi-courtship behavior."[31] The first stage is *courtship readiness.* When you are attracted to someone, you may suck in your stomach, tense your muscles, and stand up straight. The second stage includes *preening behaviors:* You manipulate your appearance by combing your hair, applying makeup, straightening your tie, pulling up your socks, and double-checking your appearance in the mirror. In stage three, you demonstrate *positional cues,* using your posture and body orientation to ensure that you will be seen and noticed by others.

One researcher found 52 gestures and nonverbal behaviors that women use to signal an interest in men. Among the top unspoken flirting cues were smiling and surveying a crowded room with the eyes, and moving closer to the object of affection.[32] People intensify these cues in the fourth stage, *appeals to invitation,* using close proximity, exposed skin, open body positions (uncrossed arms and legs), and eye contact to signal availability and interest. The classic Norman Rockwell painting here shows teenagers illustrating typical appeals to invitation. Subjects in one study reported that they were aware of using all these techniques to promote an intimate relationship. In fact,

Can you identify the quasi-courtship behavior in this painting?

people use these quasi-courtship behaviors to some extent in almost any situation in which they are trying to gain favorable attention from another.

Another team of researchers focused on nonverbal behaviors that prompt people to label someone warm and friendly, or cold and distant.[33] The team found that "warm" people face their communication partners directly, smile more, make more direct eye contact, fidget less, and generally make fewer unnecessary hand movements. "Cold" people make less eye contact, smile less, fidget more, and turn away from their partners.

Albert Mehrabian has identified the nonverbal cues that contribute to perceptions of liking.[34] He found that an open body and arm position, a forward lean, and a relaxed posture communicate liking. When you are attempting to persuade someone, you typically have more eye contact and a more face-to-face body orientation; you are more likely to lean forward and closer to others.

Ekman and Friesen classified movement and gestures according to their function. They identified five categories: emblems, illustrators, affect displays, regulators, and adaptors.[35]

Emblems

Nonverbal cues that have specific, generally understood meanings in a given culture and may actually substitute for a word or phrase are called **emblems.** When you are busy typing a report that is due tomorrow and your young son bounces in to ask for permission to buy a new computer game, you turn from your computer and hold up an open palm to indicate your desire for uninterrupted quiet. To communicate your enthusiastic enjoyment of a violin soloist at a concert, you applaud wildly. You want your children to stop talking in the library, so you put an index finger up to your pursed lips.

Illustrators

People frequently accompany a verbal message with **illustrators** that either contradict, accent, or complement the message. Slamming a book closed while announcing, "I don't want to read this anymore" or pounding a lectern while proclaiming, "This point is important!" are two examples of nonverbal behaviors that illustrate the verbal message. Typically, English speakers use nonverbal illustrators at the beginning of clauses or phrases.[36] TV newscasters, for example, turn a page to signal that they are moving to a new story or topic. Most of us use illustrators to help us communicate information about the size, shape, and spatial relationships of objects. You probably even use them when you talk on the phone, although probably not as many as you use in face-to-face conversation.[37]

Affect Displays

Nonverbal movements and postures used to communicate emotion are called **affect displays.** As early as 1872, when Charles Darwin systematically studied the expression of emotion in both humans and animals,[38] people recognized that nonverbal cues are the primary ways to communicate emotion. Facial expressions, vocal cues, posture, and gestures convey the intensity of your emotions.[39] If you are happy, for example, your face will telegraph your joy to others. The movement of your hands, the openness of your posture, and the speed with which you move will tell others *how* happy you are. Similarly, if you are feeling depressed, your face will probably reveal your sadness or dejection, while your slumped shoulders and lowered head will indicate the intensity of your despair. When you are feeling friendly, you use a soft tone of voice, an open smile, and a relaxed posture.[40] When you feel neutral about an issue, you signal it by putting little expression on your face or in your voice. When you feel hostile, you use a harsh voice, frown with your teeth showing, and keep your posture tense and rigid.

emblems. Nonverbal cues that have specific, generally understood meanings in a given culture and may substitute for a word or phrase.

illustrators. Nonverbal behaviors that accompany a verbal message and either contradict, accent, or complement it.

affect display. Nonverbal behavior that communicates emotions.

Regulators

People use **regulators** to control the interaction or flow of communication between themselves and another person. When you are eager to respond to a message, you make eye contact, raise your eyebrows, open your mouth, raise an index finger, and lean forward slightly. In a classroom, you may raise your hand to signal overtly that you want to talk. When you do not want to be part of the conversation, you do the opposite: avert your eyes, close your mouth, cross your arms, and lean back in your seat or away from the verbal action as attempts to regulate the interaction.

Adaptors

When you are cold, you reach for a sweater or wrap your arms around your chest to keep warm. When it's 102 degrees Fahrenheit in the shade without a breeze, you may reach for a fan to make your own breeze. These behaviors are examples of **adaptors**—nonverbal behaviors that help you satisfy a personal need and adapt to the immediate situation. When you adjust your glasses, scratch a mosquito bite, or comb your hair, you are using movement to help you manage your personal needs and adapt to your surroundings—and you're communicating something about yourself to whoever may be present.

Understanding these five categories of nonverbal behavior can help you understand interpersonal communication by giving you a new and more precise way to think about your own behavior. By noting how often you use emblems instead of words to communicate a message, you can recognize how important emblems are in your relationships with others. The more you rely on emblems that have unique meanings for you and your partner, the more intimate the interpersonal relationship. Also, start to notice whether your nonverbal behavior contradicts what you say. Monitoring your use of illustrators can help you determine whether you are sending mixed signals to others. Be aware of how you display affect. Knowing that your face and voice communicate emotion, and that posture and gesture indicate the intensity of your feelings, can help you understand how others make inferences about your feelings and attitudes. If other people have difficulty interpreting your emotional state, you may not be projecting your feelings nonverbally.

Since nonverbal cues are ambiguous, it may not be a good idea to use them to achieve a specific objective. But as you have seen, people are more likely to respond in predictable ways if you use behaviors they can recognize and interpret easily.

regulators. Nonverbal messages that help to control the interaction or flow of communication between two people.

adaptors. Nonverbal behaviors that satisfy a personal need and help a person adapt or respond to the immediate situation.

Categories of Movement and Gestures

Category	Definition	Example
Emblems	Behaviors that have specific, generally understood meaning	Raising a hitchhiking thumb
Illustrators	Cues that accompany verbal messages and add meaning to the message	Pounding the lectern to emphasize a point
Affect displays	Expressions of emotion	Hugging someone to express love
Regulators	Cues that control and manage the flow of communication between two people	Looking at someone when you wish to speak
Adaptors	Behaviors that help you adapt to your environment	Scratching; combing your hair

Eye Contact

Whether you choose to look at someone or avert your gaze has an enormous impact on your relationship with that person.[41] Researcher Adam Kendon has identified four functions of eye contact in interpersonal interactions.[42]

First, eye contact serves a *cognitive* function because it gives you information about another person's thought processes. For example, if your partner breaks eye contact after you ask him or her a question, you will know that he or she is probably thinking of something to say.

Second, people use eye contact to *monitor* the behavior of others. You receive a major portion of the information you obtain through your eyes. You look at others to determine whether they are receptive to your messages.

Third, eye contact is one of the most powerful *regulatory* cues you use to signal when you want to talk and when you don't. We have noticed that when we ask questions such as "Who can tell me the four functions of eye contact?" students quickly yet unobtrusively avert their eyes to signal "Don't call on me." When you do want to communicate with others, you make eye contact—as, for example, when standing in line at the bakery, you fix your eyes on the clerk to signal, "My turn next. Please wait on me."

Finally, the area around your eyes serves an *expressive* function. The eyes have been called the "mirror of the soul" because they reveal emotions to others. You may cry, blink, and widen or narrow your gaze to express your feelings.

As shown in Table 7.1, researchers Mark Knapp and Judith Hall have summarized conclusions on nonverbal communication that predict when you are most and least likely to have eye contact with someone.[43]

When people do establish eye contact with others, it may seem that their gaze is constant. Yet research suggests that they actually spend the majority of their time looking at something other than the person's eyes. One research team found that people focus on something else, including their partner's mouth, 57 percent of the time.[44] Not surprisingly then, facial expressions are another rich source of information in your communication with others.

Facial Expression

The Palo Alto, California, city council may well have the distinction of being the first legislative body to try to regulate facial expression. They proposed a code of conduct banning facial expressions that show "disagreement or disgust."[45] The controversy generated by the proposal attests to the importance of facial expressions in the communication process. So, too, does our reliance on *emoticons,* the "smiley faces" and other symbols created with combinations of keyboard characters to communicate facial expression via e-mail. The face is the exhibit gallery for emotional displays.

TABLE 7.1 When Are You Most and Least Likely to Make Eye Contact with Someone?

You are more likely to make eye contact when you . . .	You are less likely to make eye contact when you . . .
• Like or love your partner.	• Do not like your partner.
• Are physically distant from him or her.	• Are physically near your partner.
• Are discussing easy, impersonal topics.	• Are discussing difficult, intimate topics.
• Have nothing else to look at.	• Have other things to look at.
• Are interested in your partner's reactions.	• Are not interested in your partner's reactions.
• Are trying to dominate or persuade your partner.	• Are not trying to dominate or persuade your partner.
• Are from a culture that emphasizes eye contact.	• Are from a culture that de-emphasizes eye contact.
• Are an extrovert.	• Are an introvert.
• Have a high need to affiliate or to be included.	• Have a low need to affiliate or to be included.
• Are dependent on your partner (and your partner is not responsive).	• Are more independent of your partner (and your partner is responsive to you).
• Are listening rather than talking.	• Are talking rather than listening.
• Are female.	• Are male.

Source: Adapted from *Nonverbal Communication in Human Interaction*, 4th edition, by Mark L. Knapp and Judith A. Hall, 1997. Reprinted with permission of Wadsworth, a division of Thomson Learning.

BE OTHER-ORIENTED

To interpret a partner's facial expressions accurately, you need to put your other-orientation skills to work, focusing on what the other person may be thinking or feeling. It helps if you know the person well, can see his or her whole face, have plenty of time to watch it, and understand the situation that prompted the emotion.[46] But it is also helpful to know the cues for "reading" facial expressions.

Your face is versatile. According to Ekman and Friesen, it is capable of producing over 250,000 different expressions.[47] Research suggests that women have greater variety in their emotional expressions and spend more time smiling than men.[48] But all facial expression can be grouped in six primary emotional categories; the following list describes the changes that occur on your face for each one.[49]

Surprise: Wide-open eyes; raised and wrinkled brow; open mouth

Fear: Open mouth; tense skin under the eyes; wrinkles in the center of the forehead

Disgust: Raised or curled upper lip; wrinkled nose; raised cheeks; lowered brow; lowered upper eyelid

Anger: Tensed lower eyelid; either pursed lips or open mouth; lowered and wrinkled brow; staring eyes

Happiness: Smiling; mouth may be open or closed; raised cheeks; wrinkles around lower eyelids.

Sadness: Lip may tremble; corners of the lips turn downward; corners of the upper eyelid may be raised.

The face can shift between the six categories rapidly, as is evident on the NASA videotape of activity inside Mission Control at the Johnson Space Center during the final minutes of the doomed flight of the space shuttle *Columbia* in February 2003. *New York Times* reporter John Schwartz describes how

> though the voices of the mission controllers remained steady, their faces and body language showed a marked transition from the cool professionalism to wide-eyed alertness to dread and, finally, tears.[50]

How accurately do people interpret emotions expressed on the face? Several studies have attempted to measure subjects' skill in identifying emotional expressions of others. They have found that reading facial expression is a tricky business. According to Ekman and Friesen, even though faces provide a great deal of information about emotions, people have learned how to control facial expressions.[51] In addition, facial expressions seem to be contagious. One researcher who showed his subjects video clips of President Reagan giving speeches discovered that they were likely to smile when Reagan smiled and frown when Reagan appeared angry or threatening.[52] Another study found that people were better able to judge the accuracy of facial expressions when the expressions were more complex.[53] The distinctiveness of a facial expression with compound meanings may be what makes it easier to interpret. It is also probable that people have more practice interpreting facial expressions with compound meanings than they do those that communicate a single emotion such as sadness or happiness. Yet despite the complexity of some facial expressions, we seem to be able to determine whether someone is really happy or merely offering a phony smile. One research team found that a genuine smile is more fleeting than a forced smile, which tends to last a bit too long.[54]

At the opposite end of the spectrum from complex facial expressions are what Ekman calls "microexpressions," fleeting facial expressions that may last only .05 of a second. Most of Ekman's test groups, including policemen and judges, have difficulty detecting microexpressions. On the other hand, Buddhists, whom Ekman calls "gymnasts of the mind," were surprisingly sensitive to microexpressions.[55]

Vocal Cues

Vocal cues are another category of nonverbal code that we respond to. Vocal cues communicate emotions and help us manage conversations. And even the lack of vocal cues communicates information.

Our Vocal Cues Communicate Emotions

Whether you are an infant or an adult, your voice is a major vehicle for communicating your emotions and a primary tool for communicating information about the nature of relationships between you and others.[56] As an adult, you use your voice to present one message on the surface (with words) and usually a more accurate expression of your feelings with your vocal quality. Say the following sentence out loud, as if you really mean it: "This looks great." Now say it sarcastically, as if you really don't think it looks great. Clearly, your vocal cues provide the real meaning.

One team of nonverbal communication researchers concluded that it's primarily your voice that communicates your level of intimacy with others when you express your ideas.[57] The words you use may communicate explicit ideas and information, but it is your vocal cues that provide the primary relational cues, which truly indicate the degree of liking and trust that you feel toward others.

Some vocal expressions of emotion are easier to identify than others. Expressions of joy and anger are obvious ones, whereas shame and love are the most difficult emotions to identify based on vocal cues alone.[58] People are also likely to confuse fear with nervousness, love with sadness, and pride with satisfaction.

Laughter is another vocal cue that you probably express every day; your laugh not only reflects your emotional state but, according to research, has a strong impact on the emotions of others. Laughter is contagious.[59] When you laugh, you are not only expressing your emotions but you also increase the likelihood that others will laugh as well.

Your voice also provides information about your self-confidence and your knowledge of the subject matter in your messages. Most of us would conclude that a speaker who mumbles, speaks slowly, consistently mispronounces words, and uses "uhs" and "ums" is less credible and persuasive than one who speaks clearly, rapidly, and fluently.[60] Even though mispronunciations and vocalized pauses ("ums" and "ahs") seem to have a negative effect on credibility, they do not seem to be a major impediment to attitude change. People may, for example, think that you are less knowledgeable if you stammer, but you may still be able to get your persuasive message across.

Not only "ums" and "ahs" but also speaking rate influences our perception of others. One team of researchers found that North Americans evaluated speakers with a moderate to slightly faster speaking rate as more "socially attractive" than speakers who had a slow rate of speech.[61] North American listeners also seem to prefer a speaking rate that is equal to or slightly faster than their own speaking rate.

Vocal Cues Help Us Manage Conversations

In addition to providing information about emotions, self-confidence, and knowledge, vocal cues, known as **backchannel cues,** can serve a regulatory function in interpersonal situations, signaling when we want to talk and when we don't. When we are finished talking, we may lower the pitch of our final word. When we want to talk, we may start by interjecting sounds such as "I . . . I . . . I . . ." or "Ah . . . Ah . . . Ah . . ." to interrupt the speaker and grab the verbal ball. We also may use such cues as "Sure," "I understand," "Uh-huh," or "Okay" to signal that we understand the message of the other person and now we want to talk or end the conversation. These backchannel cues are particularly useful in telephone conversations when we have no other nonverbal cues to help us signal that we would like to get off the phone.

Our Use of Silence Speaks Volumes

Sometimes it is not what we say, or even how we say it, that communicates our feelings. Being silent may communicate volumes. One researcher, in commenting about the importance of silence in speech, said, "Silence is to speech as white paper is to this print. . . . The entire system of spoken language would fail without [people's] ability to both tolerate and create sign sequences of silence–sound–silence units."[62]

Would you be comfortable just sitting silently with a good friend? Sidney Baker's theory of silence suggests that the more at ease you are when you share a silence with a close friend, the more comfortable you are with just being together and enjoying each other's companionship. People need to talk until there is nothing left to say; by that point, the uncertainty has been managed. In most long-term relationships, partners may not feel a need to fill the air with sound. Just being together to enjoy each other's company may be most fulfilling. Baker calls such moments "positive silence."[63] While watching a sunset with a close friend, for example, there may be no need to narrate what you are seeing—it's enough just to experience it.

Personal Space

Imagine that you are sitting alone in a booth at your local pizza parlor. As you sit munching your thin-and-crispy pepperoni pizza, you are startled when a complete

backchannel cues. Vocal cues that signal your wish to speak or not to speak.

Interpersonal Communication and Emotion
Connecting Heart to Heart

How to Accurately Interpret the Nonverbal Expression of Emotions

Are you skilled at accurately interpreting the emotions others are expressing? Since emotions are primarily communicated via nonverbal cues, the more skilled you are at interpreting nonverbal messages in general, the more likely it is that you will be able to accurately interpret the emotions other people are expressing. And there is evidence that if you are skilled in accurately interpreting the emotional expressions of others, then you will generally have more positive interpersonal relationships with others. People who are more sensitive in interpreting emotions expressed nonverbally tend to be more popular, to have a wider circle of friends, and to be less likely to experience relationship anxiety. The following research conclusions may help you enhance both your ability and your confidence in interpreting the emotional expression of others.[64]

Facial Expression

- You are more likely to be skilled at interpreting positive emotional expressions (happiness) than negative emotional expressions (sadness, anger, disgust).[65]
- You are more likely to confuse the expression of fear with surprise or anger because of the similar position of the eyes and especially the area around the brow.
- Because facial expressions can be grouped based on the dimensions of activity, intensity, and pleasantness, similar expressions are more likely to be confused. The more dramatically different the emotions being expressed, the more likely you are to accurately identify the emotions based on facial expression alone.
- The presence of other people seems to have an effect on how emotions are expressed; you are, for example, more likely to smile when others are present than when you are alone.

Vocal Cues

- It's generally easier to interpret anger, sadness, happiness, and nervousness from vocal cues alone and harder to identify disgust, shame, fear, jealousy, love, satisfaction, and sympathy.[66]
- People sometimes have difficulty distinguishing love from sympathy, fear from sadness, and interest from happiness.[67]
- Knowing more about the context or reason for someone's nonverbal communication helps you interpret what emotion is being expressed by vocal cues.

General Principles of Interpreting Emotions

- How you interpret emotions in others is strongly influenced by your culture; although there is some common basis for expressing emotions, there are cultural variations in how emotions are interpreted.[68]
- You are more likely to accurately interpret emotions expressed by people who are from your own cultural background.
- You are more likely to accurately interpret emotional expression in someone from a culture other than your own if the emotional expression is static (for example, a photograph of a facial expression) rather than dynamic (an in-person expression or a video of the expression).
- You are more likely to accurately interpret someone's emotional expression if it is genuine than if it is fake.
- Your ability to interpret emotions improves as you get older; your skill declines as age begins to have an effect on your ability to accurately see and hear others.[69]
- A person's facial expression and vocal cues communicate a specific emotional response; his or her posture and gestures communicate the *intensity* of the emotion expressed.
- In general, women are more likely to accurately interpret emotions in others than are men.
- Research suggests that women are typically more nonverbally expressive than are men in social situations.[70]
- Your ability to accurately interpret emotions is a skill that does not appear to be related to race, education, or cognitive intelligence level.
- People who more accurately interpret the emotional expressions of others tend to work at people-oriented jobs more than people who do not have such skill.[71]

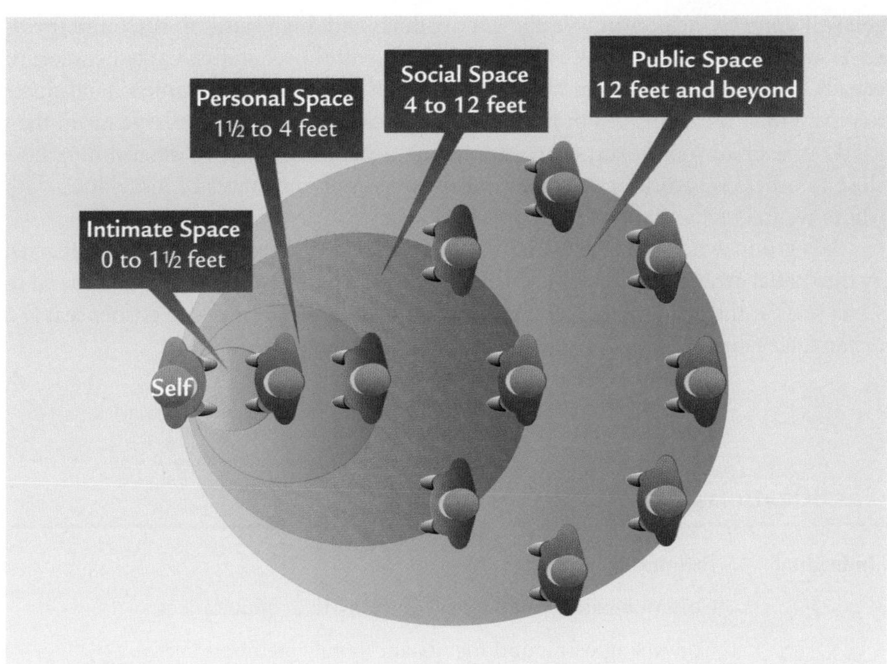

FIGURE **7.1**

Edward T. Hall's Four Zones of Space

stranger sits down in your booth directly across from you. With several empty tables and booths in the restaurant, you feel very uncomfortable that this unknown individual has invaded "your" area.

Normally, people do not think much about the rules of personal space, but in fact every culture has fairly rigid ways of regulating space in social interactions. Violations of these rules can be alarming and, as in the preceding scenario, even threatening. How close you are willing to get to others relates to how well you know them and to considerations of power and status.

One pioneer in helping people understand the silent language of personal space was Edward T. Hall. His study of **proxemics** investigated how close or how far away from people and things we arrange ourselves.[72] Hall identified four spatial zones that speakers in Western cultures sometimes define for themselves unconsciously, as shown in Figure 7.1. When we are between 0 and 1½ feet from someone, we are occupying **intimate space.** This is the zone in which the most intimate interpersonal communication occurs. It is open only to those with whom we are well acquainted, unless we are forced to stand in an elevator, a fast-food line, or some other crowded space.

The second zone, which ranges from 1½ to 4 feet from each person, is called **personal space.** Most conversations with family and friends occur in this zone. If someone you don't know well invades this space on purpose, you may feel uncomfortable.

Zone three, called **social space,** ranges from 4 to 12 feet from a person. Most group interaction, as well as many professional relationships, takes place in this zone. The interaction tends to be more formal than that in the first two zones.

Public space, the fourth zone, begins 12 feet from a person. Interpersonal communication does not usually occur in this zone, and many public speakers and teachers position themselves even more than 12 feet from their audience.

Don't get the idea that these special zones described by Hall *always* occur precisely in the measurements that we've described. They don't. The specific space that you and others choose depends on several variables.[73] The more you like someone, the closer

proxemics. Study of how close or far away from people and objects people position themselves.

intimate space. Zone of space most often used for very personal or intimate interactions, ranging from 0 to 1½ feet from the individual.

personal space. Zone of space most often used for conversations with family and friends, ranging from 1½ to 4 feet from the individual.

social space. Zone of space most often used for group interactions, ranging from 4 to 12 feet from the individual.

public space. Zone of space most often used by public speakers or anyone speaking to many people, ranging beyond 12 feet from the individual.

you will stand to the person. We allow individuals with high status to surround themselves with more space than we allow for people with lower status. Large people also usually have more space around them than smaller people do, and women stand closer to others than men do.[74] All of us tend to stand closer to others in a large room than we do in a small room. And our culture plays a significant role in determining how close to others we work or stand, as well as the power and status of individuals with whom we interact.

In a group, who's in charge, who's important, and who talks to whom are reflected by the spatial arrangement people select. The more dominant group members tend to select seats at the head of a table, while shyer individuals often select a corner seat at a rectangular table.[75]

Edward T. Hall's Classification of Spatial Zones

	Distance from the Individual	Examples
Zone One	0 to 1½ feet	Communicating with our most intimate acquaintances
Zone Two	1½ feet to 4 feet	Conversing with good friends and family members
Zone Three	4 feet to 12 feet	Working with others in small groups and in professional situations
Zone Four	12 feet and beyond	Public speaking situations

Territory

Territoriality is the study of how animals (including humans) use space and objects to communicate occupancy or ownership of space. Earlier, we gave the example of a stranger sitting down with you in a pizza parlor. In that case, you had assumed "ownership" of the booth in the pizza parlor and the accompanying "right" to determine who sat with you, because you and your pizza were occupying the booth. In addition to invading your personal space, the intrusive stranger broke the rules that govern territoriality.

People announce ownership of space with **territorial markers**—things that signify the area has been claimed—much as explorers once planted flags claiming uncharted land for their kings. When you are studying at the library, for example, and need to hop up and check a reference at the computerized card catalog, you might leave behind a notebook or a pencil. In rural areas, landowners post signs at the borders of their property to keep hunters off their territory. Signs, locks, electronic security systems, and other devices secure home and office territories.

You also use markers to indicate where your space stops and someone else's starts. "Good fences make good neighbors," wrote the poet Robert Frost. When someone sits too close, you may try to erect a physical barrier, such as a stack of books or a napkin holder, or you might use your body as a shield by turning away. If the intruder does not get the hint that "this land is my land," you may ultimately resort to words to announce that the space is occupied.

territoriality. Study of how animals and humans use space and objects to communicate occupancy or ownership of space.

territorial markers. Tangible objects that are used to signify that someone has claimed an area or space.

Touch

Standing elbow to elbow in a crowded elevator, you may find yourself in physical contact with total strangers. As you stiffen your body and avert your eyes, a baffling sense of shame floods over you. If you are sitting at a conference table and you accidentally brush the toes of your shoes against your colleague's ankle, you may jerk away and even blush or apologize. Why do people react this way to unpremeditated touching? Normally, you touch to express intimacy. When intimacy is not your intended message, you instinctively react to modify the impression.

When you find a spot for sunbathing in a public park, how much of the space around you do you consider to be "your" territory? How close does someone else have to be before you feel he or she is invading your space?

Countless studies have shown that intimate touching is vital to your personal development and well-being.[76] Infants and children need to be touched to confirm that they are valued and loved. Many hospitals invite volunteers in to hold and rock newborns whose mothers cannot do it themselves. Advocates of breastfeeding argue that the intimate touching it entails strengthens the bond between mother and child.[77]

The amount of touch you need, tolerate, receive, and initiate depends on many factors. The amount and kind of touching you receive in your family is one big influence. If your mom or dad greets you with hugs, caresses, and kisses, then you probably do this to others. If your family is less demonstrative, you may be restrained yourself. Studies by researcher Nancy Henley show that most of us are more likely to touch people when we are feeling friendly or happy, or under some of the following specific circumstances:[78]

- When we ask someone to do something for us
- When we share rather than ask for information
- When we try to persuade someone to do something
- When we are talking about intimate topics
- When we are in social settings that we choose rather than in professional settings that are part of our job
- When we are thrilled and excited to share good news
- When we listen to a troubled or worried friend

Research has identified differences in the amount of touch men and women prefer to give and receive.[79] In general, women have less positive attitudes about being touched by members of the opposite sex than do men. Men are more likely than women to initiate touch in casual romantic heterosexual relationships, yet women are more likely to reach out and touch their spouses than are men. As a general rule, men are more likely to initiate touch with a woman before they are married than after they

Does your experience reflect research that shows that attractive people are more credible, happier, more popular, and more sociable than less attractive people?

are married. North American men are also more uncomfortable with being touched by other men than women are with being touched by other women. In addition to one's sex, personal preferences determine how much touch a person prefers to initiate or receive. Some people just don't like to be touched; they are what researchers call high-touch-avoidance individuals; to be touched by anyone simply makes them feel uncomfortable.

Appearance

In all interactions with others, appearance counts. American culture places a high value on how much you weigh, the style of your hair, and the clothes you wear; these things are particularly important in the early stages of relationship development. Attractive females have an easier time persuading others than do those who are perceived as less attractive. In general, Americans think attractive people are more credible, happier, more popular, more sociable, and even more prosperous than less attractive people.[80] There is also evidence that if you believe that others think a person is attractive, you'll be more likely to evaluate that person as attractive as well.[81]

The shape and size of your body also affects how others perceive you. Heavier and rounder individuals are often perceived to be older, more old-fashioned, less good-looking, more talkative, and more good-natured than thin people, who are perceived to be more ambitious, more suspicious of others, more uptight and tense, more negative, and less talkative. Muscular and athletically fit folks are seen as better looking, taller, and more adventurous. These perceptions are, in fact, so common that they have become easily recognizable stereotypes on which casting directors for movies, TV shows, and plays rely in selecting actors and actresses.

Aside from keeping you warm and within the legal bounds of decency, your clothes also affect how others perceive you. The clothes you wear are a way of communicating to others how you want to be treated. One classic study found that a man who jaywalked while dressed in nice clothes attracted more fellow violators than he could when he was shabbily attired.[82] Although studies have attempted to identify a "power" look, and magazines are constantly giving prescriptions for ways to be attractive and stylish, there is no formula for dressing for success.[83]

Recap: Codes of Nonverbal Communication

Movements and Gestures	Communicate information, status, warmth, credibility, interest in others, attitudes, liking
Eye Contact	Serves cognitive, monitoring, regulatory, and expressive functions
Facial Expressions	Express emotions
Vocal Cues	Communicate emotion through pitch, rate, volume, and quality; modify the meaning of messages
Personal Space	Provides information about status, power, and intimacy
Territoriality	Provides cues to use, ownership, or occupancy of space
Touch	Communicates intimacy, affection, or rejection
Appearance	Influences perceptions of credibility and attraction

Interpreting Nonverbal Communication

So what does it all mean? How do you make sense out of the postures, movements, gestures, eye contact, facial expressions, uses of space and territory, touch, and appearance of others? Albert Mehrabian has found that people synthesize and interpret nonverbal cues along three primary dimensions: *immediacy, arousal,* and *dominance.*[84] These three dimensions provide a useful way to summarize how nonverbal cues may be interpreted.

Immediacy: Communicating Liking

Sometimes, we cannot put a finger on the precise reason we find a person likable or unlikable. Mehrabian believes that immediacy cues are a likely explanation. Immediacy cues are behaviors that communicate liking and engender feelings of pleasure. The principle underlying the communication of our feelings of **immediacy** is simple: We move toward persons and things we like and avoid or move away from those we dislike. Immediacy cues increase our sensory awareness of others. Use of space and territory is not the only cue that contributes to positive or negative feelings. Mehrabian has noted several other nonverbal cues that increase immediacy. One of the most powerful is touch; others include a forward lean, increased eye contact, and an open body orientation. The meaning of these behaviors is usually implied rather than explicitly spelled out in words.

Not surprisingly, communication researcher Lois Hinkle found that spouses who reported high feelings of affection for their mates reported that their mates responded by expressing more immediacy cues toward them.[85] There is also evidence that when someone expresses immediate or pleasant nonverbal messages toward us, we reciprocate by responding in a pleasant manner. Researchers Judee Burgoon and Beth Le Poire found that people adapt their nonverbal messages to others.[86] When people express immediacy or liking toward you, you are more likely to reciprocate and express a similar sentiment toward them. Immediacy is contagious. Yet another research study found that expressions of nonverbal immediacy on the part of someone trying to offer support and comfort to another person, such as closer personal distance, touching, and forward lean, helped reduce the other person's stress and tension.[87]

In brief, we use the following cues to communicate that we like someone:[88]

Proximity: Close, forward lean

Body orientation: Typically face to face, but could be side by side

Eye contact: Mutual eye contact

Facial expression: Smiling

Gestures: Head nods, movement

Posture: Open, arms oriented toward others

Touch: Cultural- and context-appropriate touch

Voice: Higher pitch, upward pitch

immediacy. Feelings of liking, pleasure, and closeness communicated by such nonverbal cues as increased eye contact, forward lean, touch, and open body orientation.

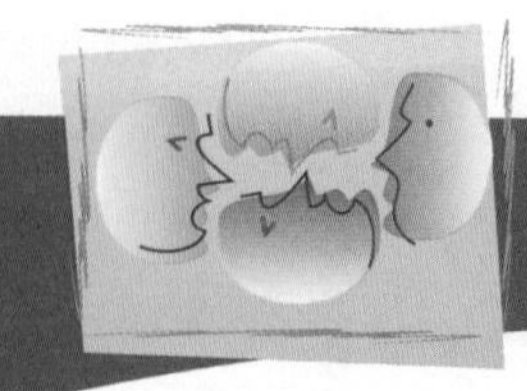

Understanding Diversity

Gender Differences and Nonverbal Communication

There is evidence that men and women display and interpret nonverbal cues differently.[89]

Eye Contact
Women usually use a more prolonged gaze than do men. Women, however, are less likely just to stare at someone; they break eye contact more frequently than men. In general, women receive more eye contact from others than do men.

Space
Men tend to require more space around them than do women. Women both approach and are approached more closely than men. And when conversing with others, women seem to prefer side-by-side interactions.

Facial Expression
Research suggests that women smile more than men. It is also reported that women tend to be more emotionally expressive with their faces than men; this is perhaps related to the conclusion that women are more skilled at both displaying and interpreting facial expressions.

Gesture and Posture
Overall, women appear to use fewer and less expansive gestures than men. Women are more likely, for example, to rest their hands on the arms of a chair while seated; men are more likely to gesture. Men and women cross their legs differently: women cross their legs at the knees or ankles while men are more likely to sit with their legs apart.

Touch
Men are more likely to initiate touch with others than are women. Women are touched more than men. Men and women also attribute different meaning to touch; women are more likely to associate touch with warmth and expressiveness than are men.

Vocal Cues
Vocal patterns may be more related to biological differences in the vocal register than other nonverbal behaviors. Women speak in both higher and softer tones than do men. Women use their voices to communicate a greater range of emotions than do men. Women are also more likely to raise their pitch when making statements; some people interpret the rising pattern (as in asking a question) as an indication of greater uncertainty.

Arousal: Communicating Responsiveness

The face, voice, and movement are primary indicators of **arousal.** If we sense arousal cues, we conclude that another person is responsive to and interested in us. If the person acts passive or dull, we conclude that he or she is uninterested.

When you approach someone and ask whether he or she has a minute or two to talk, that person may signal interest with a change in facial expression and more animated vocal cues. People who are aroused and interested in you show animation in their face, voice, and gestures. Forward lean, a flash of the eyebrows, and a nod of the head are other cues that implicitly communicate arousal. Someone who says, "Sure, I have time to talk with you" in a monotone and with a flat, expressionless face is communicating the opposite. Think of arousal as an on-off switch. Sleeping is the ultimate switched-off state.

arousal. Feelings of interest and excitement communicated by such nonverbal cues as vocal expression, facial expressions, and gestures.

dominance. Power, status, and control communicated by such nonverbal cues as a relaxed posture, greater personal space, and protected personal space.

Dominance: Communicating Power

The third dimension of Mehrabian's framework for implicit cues communicates the balance of power in a relationship. **Dominance** cues communicate power, status, position, and importance.[90] A person of high status tends to have a relaxed body posture when interacting with a person of lower status.[91] When you talk to a professor, he may lean back in his chair, put his feet on the desk, and fold his hands behind his head during the conversation. But unless your professor is a colleague or a friend, you will maintain a relatively formal posture during your interaction in his office.

Shaking hands is a centuries-old greeting or farewell ritual that communicates power or lack of it. Alan and Barbara Pease report that people in leadership positions are more likely to be the ones who initiate a handshake than are non-leaders.[92] The person who feels the most power in a relationship is more likely to shake hands with his or her palm facing down; a submissive handshake, reports nonverbal communication researcher Peter Collett, is offered with the palm facing up. Collett has meticulously analyzed handshakes of politicians and other leaders to reveal that the person who feels the most power literally takes the upper hand when shaking hands.[93]

Another dominance cue is the use of space. High-status individuals usually have more space around them; they have bigger offices and more "barriers" protecting them. A receptionist in an office is usually easily accessible, but to reach the president of the company, you may have to navigate through several corridors, past several secretaries and administrative assistants who are "guarding" the door.

Are most people aware of the power cues they express or receive from others? Your ability to detect nonverbal expressions of power may relate to whether you think you are powerful or not. One research team found that subordinates were better at interpreting power cues from their supervisors than supervisors were at interpreting power cues from their subordinates.[94] What this means is that if you think you have less power in a relationship, you are more likely to be aware of the more dominant power of others' nonverbal cues. If you think you do have power, you may be less sensitive to nonverbal expressions of power.

Other power cues that communicate dominance include use of furniture, clothing, and locations. You study with others at a table in the library; the college president has a large private desk. You may wear jeans and a T-shirt to class; the head of the university wears a business suit. Your dorm may be surrounded by other dorms; the president's residence may be a large house surrounded by a lush, landscaped garden in a prestigious neighborhood. People use space, territory, posture, and artifacts such as clothing and furniture to signal feelings of dominance or submissiveness in the presence of others.

Research confirms that we have certain expectations about how people who are perceived to have power will behave nonverbally.[95] People who are thought to have more power, for example, are thought to more freely express their anger and disgust than are people who have less power and status. British social psychologist Michael Argyle summarizes the nonverbal cues that communicate dominance:[96]

Use of space: Height (on a platform or standing)
Facing a group
More space surrounding a person

Eye contact:	More when initially establishing dominance More when staring to establish power More when talking
Face:	Frown, no smile
Touch:	Initiating touch
Voice:	Loud, low pitch, greater pitch range Slow, more interruptions, more talk Slight hesitation before speaking
Gesture:	Pointing at the other or at his or her property
Posture:	Standing, hands on hips, expanded chest, more relaxed

Dimensions for Interpreting Nonverbal Behavior

Dimension	Definition	Nonverbal Cues
Immediacy	Cues that communicate liking and pleasure	Eye contact, touch, forward lean, closeness to partner
Arousal	Cues that communicate active interest and emotional involvement	Eye contact, varied vocal cues, animated facial expressions, forward lean, movement
Dominance	Cues that communicate status and power	Protected space, relaxed posture, status symbols

Improving Your Ability to Interpret Nonverbal Messages

As we have already cautioned, there are no dictionaries to which you can turn for help in interpreting specific nonverbal behaviors. People interpret the messages of others based on their own experiences and cultural perspective. One theory that helps explain how to interpret nonverbal messages is called **expectancy violation theory.** Developed by Burgoon and several of her colleagues, this theory suggests that each of us enters a relationship with certain preconceived expectations for others' behavior.[97] For example, when meeting a business colleague for the first time, most North Americans would expect someone to smile, extend his or her hand, and say, "Hello, I'm Steve Beebe" (or whatever the name is). If, instead, the person clasps two hands together and bows demurely without uttering a word, the nonverbal behavior is not what we expect. This violation of our expectation would result in our thinking about what the "violator" of our expectations might mean by bowing instead of offering to shake our hand. When our expectations are violated, we may feel uncomfortable. Communication researchers Beth Le Poire and Stephen Yoshimura found that people tend to adapt to the behavior of others, even when the behavior of others is not what they expected.[98] If someone behaves in a pleasant way by smiling, establishing eye contact, and main-

expectancy violation theory. Theory that you interpret the messages of others based on how you expect others to behave.

taining an open body posture, we are more likely to reciprocate by displaying equally pleasant nonverbal messages. We interpret the messages of others by considering how we *expect* others to behave and by adapting to others.

Some people are simply better at interpreting nonverbal cues than others. The ability to interpret nonverbal cues is *not* related to a person's race, amount of education, or intelligence, but it *is* related to certain personality traits. Research offers some clues as to who is most skilled at encoding nonverbal messages.[99]

1. People who are better at accurately expressing their feelings and emotions are also better able to interpret nonverbal expressions from others.
2. People who are skilled in interpreting one channel of information (for example, facial expression or vocal cues) are likely to be more accurate at interpreting nonverbal messages from other channels (such as posture or use of space).
3. People with certain personality characteristics have been found to interpret nonverbal messages more accurately. For instance, people who are extroverted, have high self-esteem, are nondogmatic, are not shy, and are expressive typically do a better job of interpreting nonverbal messages than do people who do not have these personality characteristics.
4. People who select such people-oriented jobs as teachers, salespersons, and nurses often have more skill in interpreting nonverbal messages.

Even if you don't have a natural talent for interpreting nonverbal cues, with training and practice, you can enhance your sensitivity to and accuracy in interpreting them. Several principles and key skills can help you to interpret others' nonverbal messages.

Consider Nonverbal Cues in Context

Just as quoting someone out of context can change the meaning of a statement, trying to draw conclusions from an isolated snatch of behavior or a single cue can lead to misinterpretations. Beware of looking at someone's folded arms and concluding that he or she does not like you or is not interested in what you are saying. It could be that the air conditioner is set too low and the person is just trying to keep warm.

Look for Clusters of Nonverbal Cues

Instead of focusing on a specific cue, look for corroborating cues that can lead you to a more accurate conclusion about the meaning of a behavior. Is the person making eye contact? Is he or she facing you? How far away is he or she standing from you? Always consider nonverbal behaviors in conjunction with other nonverbal cues, the environment, and the person's verbal message.

Consider Past Experiences When Interpreting Nonverbal Cues

It may be that "familiarity breeds contempt," as the old saying goes, but familiarity with another person also increases your ability to interpret his or her nonverbal behavior. You may have learned, for example, that when your mother started crying when you played the piano, it signaled pride, not melancholy. Family members can probably interpret each other's nonverbal cues more accurately than can those from outside the family. But after knowing someone over a period of time, you begin to increase your sensitivity to certain glances, silences, movements, and vocal cues that might be overlooked or misunderstood by others.

Check Your Perceptions with Others

A key skill called **perception checking** was discussed in Chapter 3. You can follow three steps to check your perception of someone's nonverbal behavior. First, observe the nonverbal cues, making a point to note such variables as eye contact, posture, use of gestures, facial expression, and tone of voice. Second, try to interpret what the individual is expressing through his or her nonverbal behavior. Finally, check your perception by asking him or her if it is accurate. Of course, we are not suggesting that you need to go through life constantly checking everyone's nonverbal cues. Overusing this skill would be irritating to most people. We are suggesting, however, that when you are uncertain of how someone feels, and it is important to know, a perception check may be in order. Consider this example:

Deonna: Hi, Mom. I'm sorry Erik and I missed the family reunion last week. It's been a hectic week. The kids had something going on every night, and we just needed to rest.

Muriel: (Frowns, makes little eye contact, folds her arms, and uses a flat voice.) Oh, don't worry about it.

perception checking. Asking someone whether your interpretation of his or her nonverbal behavior is accurate.

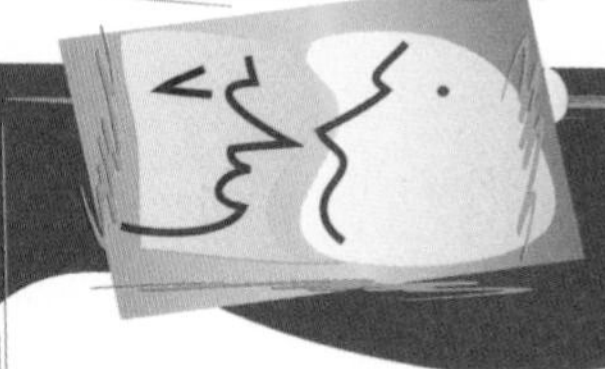

Becoming Other-Oriented

Checking Perceptions

We have identified several strategies to improve your skill at interpreting the nonverbal messages of others, including being able to check your perceptions of others. Accurately perceiving others gets to the heart of becoming other-oriented.

Look at the photographs. First, note the nonverbal behavior of the target person in the picture. Next, form a mental impression of what you think the person is thinking and feeling. Finally, compose a perception-checking question that the other person in the photo could ask to confirm the target person's thoughts and feelings.

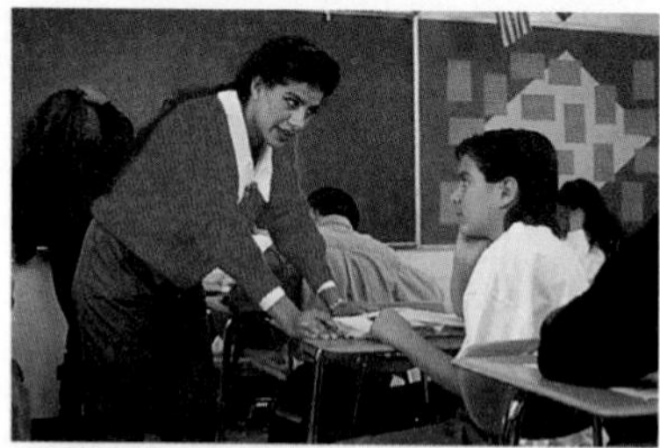

Photo 1

A. Describe the student's nonverbal behavior.

B. What do you think the student is thinking and feeling?

C. What is a perception-checking question the teacher could ask her student?

Photo 2

A. Describe the customer's nonverbal behavior.

B. What do you think the customer is thinking and feeling?

C. What is a perception-checking question the salesman could ask the customer?

Deonna: I know you said don't worry about it, Mom, but it looks like you are still upset. I know that look of yours. I also hear in your voice that you are not really pleased. Is it really OK, or are you still a little miffed?

Muriel: Well, yes, to be honest, Dad and I were really looking forward to getting all the kids together.

Deonna: I'm sorry, Mom. We will make an effort to be at the next one. Thanks for admitting how you really feel.

Asking about a specific nonverbal cue will help you interpret your partner's behavior in future interactions as well. As we noted earlier, evidence suggests that the longer couples are married, the more they rely on nonverbal behavior to communicate. One study claims that most couples spend less than eleven minutes a week in sustained conversation.[100] Even in marriages of fifty years, however, conversation is still required occasionally to clarify nonverbal responses.

Recap: How to Check Your Perceptions of Others' Nonverbal Cues

Steps	Consider . . .
1. Observe their nonverbal behavior	Are they frowning?
	Do they make eye contact?
	Are their arms crossed?
	What is their tone of voice?
	What is their posture?
2. Form a mental impression of what you think they mean.	Are they happy, sad, angry?
	Is the nonverbal message contradicting the verbal message?
3. Ask questions to check whether your perception is accurate.	"Are you upset? You look angry."
	"Your expression and your voice suggest you don't believe me. Do you think I'm lying?"
	"The look on your face tells me you really like it. Do you?"

Be Aware That the Nonverbal Expression of Emotion Is Contagious

Have you ever noticed that when you watch a funny movie, you are more likely to laugh out loud if other people around you are laughing? That when you are around people who are sad or remorseful, you are more likely to feel and express sadness? There's a reason this happens. Nonverbal emotional expressions are contagious. People often display the same emotions that a communication partner is displaying. **Emotional contagion theory** suggests that people tend to "catch" the emotions of others.[101] Interpersonal interactions with others can affect your nonverbal expression of

emotional contagion theory. Theory that emotional expression is contagious; people can "catch" emotions just by observing others' emotional expressions.

emotions.[102] The ancient Roman orator Cicero knew this when he gave advice to public speakers. He said if you want your audience to experience joy, you must be a joyful speaker. Or, if you want to communicate fear, then you should express fear when you speak.

Look for Cues That May Communicate Lying

"Look at me, young man. I know you're not telling the truth." Sometimes parents just seem to know whether kids are telling the truth or lying. How do they know? It may not be the "story" but the nonverbal message that gives the kids away. Several researchers have been interested in identifying those nonverbal cues that indicate deceit.[103] Remember not to place too much emphasis on a single cue. As we've just noted, look for clusters of cues rather than pointing your finger when someone has less eye contact and saying, "Ah ha! Now I know you're a liar!" Table 7.2 summarizes research conclusions about nonverbal messages, comparing liars and those who are telling the truth.[104]

It would be easier to detect deception if people had noses like Pinocchio's, which would grow just a bit whenever they told a lie. But they don't. Apparently, among the best ways to detect whether someone is telling the truth is to (1) look for nonverbal clues, (2) listen to the content of what the person says, and (3) measure such physiological responses as heart rate, breathing and other factors.[105] Although nonverbal cues (such as hand and finger movements, pauses, and increased use of illustrators) can be important in helping judges sort out truth-tellers from liars, ultimately it's better to

TABLE 7.2 Who's Telling the Truth? Differences Between Honest and Dishonest Communicators

Nonverbal Cue	Honest Communicators . . .	Dishonest Communicators . . .
Voice	Use fewer pauses when they talk.	Pause more; they are thinking about what "story" they want to give.
	Speak fluently, smoothly.	Use more nonfluencies ("ah," "er," "um").
	Speak at a normal speaking rate.	Speak a bit faster than normal.
Facial Expression	Smile genuinely and sincerely.	Display a plastered-on, phony smile.
		May smile a bit too long.
Gestures	Are less likely to play with objects as they speak.	Are more likely to play with objects (for example, twiddle a pencil).
	Use fewer gestures.	Use more gestures, more self-adaptors, touching their face and body, shrugging their shoulders.
	Are not likely to shift body weight.	Are more likely to shift their posture.
	Generally display less nervousness.	Display increased nervousness.
Eye Contact	Maintain normal eye contact—a steady, natural gaze.	May look away, maintain less direct eye contact.
	Have a normal eye-blink rate.	Have an increased eye-blink rate, a sign of increased anxiety.

listen to the message and monitor physiological responses (which, of course, may not always be practical).

Unless you have a portable lie detector, which measures physiological responses such as heart rate, blood pressure, and breathing rate, the best approach may be to ask other people for corroborating information.[106] Or you can do your own investigation to ferret out whether someone is really telling the truth. Nonverbal cues may be important in giving us an *initial* hunch as to whether someone is telling the truth, but personal detective work may be the real way we ultimately confirm our hunches.

Summary

Unspoken messages have a major effect on interpersonal relationships. The primary way in which you communicate feelings, emotions, and attitudes is through nonverbal cues. When there is a contradiction between your verbal and nonverbal messages, others almost always believe the nonverbal one. But nonverbal messages usually work with verbal messages to create meaning. It is primarily through nonverbal messages that people respond and adapt to others and initiate, maintain, and develop interpersonal relationships. Important as they are, nonverbal messages can also be challenging. They are usually more ambiguous than verbal messages. Although some nonverbal messages have a definite beginning and ending, most are part of a seamless flow of movement, gestures, glances, and inflections. Also, there are culture-based differences in the way people express and interpret unspoken messages.

Nonverbal cues can be categorized and studied to reveal the codes to our unspoken communication. Movement, posture, and gestures communicate both content and expressive information when we use them as emblems, illustrators, affect displays, regulators, and adaptors. Eye contact is an important code for regulating interaction in interpersonal exchanges. Facial expressions and vocal cues provide a wealth of information about our emotions. Our use of personal space and territory communicates a variety of messages relating to power, status, and other relational concerns. Touch is one of the most powerful cues to communicate liking; and our appearance telegraphs to others how we wish to be treated and how we perceive our role in relation to them.

One of the most fascinating aspects of nonverbal messages is the potential to reveal hidden meaning communicated through unspoken codes. It is not as easy to read nonverbal cues as it is to read the words on this page, but there is a general framework that can help you assess the nonverbal messages of others, as well as your own nonverbal expressions. Researchers have identified three primary dimensions for interpreting nonverbal messages: Immediacy cues provide information about liking and disliking. Arousal cues tip others off as to your interest and level of engagement with them. And position, power, and status are often communicated through dominance cues.

To enhance your skill in interpreting nonverbal messages, always consider the context in which you observed the cues, and look for clusters of nonverbal behaviors. The longer you have known someone, the easier it is to interpret his or her unspoken messages. But to verify whether you understand someone's nonverbal behavior, ask whether your interpretation is accurate, or do your own investigation into the truth.

For Discussion and Review

Focus on Critical Thinking

1. Sasha has had difficulty getting hired as a manager. One of her best friends suggests that she ought to pay more attention to her nonverbal behavior when she is interviewed for a job. What advice would you give Sasha to help her monitor her nonverbal interview behavior?

2. Greg has been told that he sometimes comes across as cold, aloof, and standoffish. What could Greg do to communicate his sincere desire to be warm and approachable?

Focus on Ethics

3. Donald really wants to be hired as a salesperson. He hires a fashion consultant to recommend what he should wear and determine how he should look when he interviews for a job. In general, is it ethical to manipulate your appearance so that you can impress others?

4. Is it appropriate to draw definitive conclusions about another's personality and attitudes based only on a "reading" of his or her other nonverbal cues? Support your answer.

5. Is it ethical for salespeople, politicians, and others who wish to make favorable impressions to alter their nonverbal messages to get you to like them, vote for them, or buy their products? Explain your answer.

Learning with Others

1. Go on a nonverbal communication scavenger hunt. Your instructor will ask you to observe your family members and friends to find one or more of the following sets of nonverbal communicators:
    a. Examples of emblems, illustrators, affect displays, regulators, and adaptors.
    b. Examples of how people use the four zones of personal space.
    c. Examples of immediacy, arousal, and dominance cues.
    d. Examples of the cognitive, monitoring, regulatory, and expressive functions of eye contact.
    e. Examples of clothing that reveals intentions or personality traits.
2. Spend some time observing people in a public place, such as a restaurant, airport terminal, student center, or bar, and note examples of quasi-courtship behavior as discussed in this chapter on pages 199–200. List the four phases we described (courtship readiness, preening, positional cues, appeals to invitation) on a sheet of paper, and describe several examples to illustrate each of these phases.
3. Nonverbally play the roles of both a good listener and a bad listener. First, imagine that you are listening to someone talk. As a good listener, how would you communicate your interest in what the person is saying, without uttering a word? Note your posture, eye contact, presence or lack of hand movement. Are your arms and legs crossed?

    Now role-play a poor listener—someone who appears to be bored or even irritated by what a speaker is saying. What are the differences in the cues you use?

Weblinks

Go to *www.mycommunicationlab.com* (access code required) to find Web resources for your text that supplement the material in Chapter 7, including links to information on the following topics:

Interpreting nonverbal messages
Using emoticons to communicate feelings and emotions
Information about proxemics
Office culture and nonverbal communication

CHAPTER 8

Conflict Management Skills

OBJECTIVES

1. Define interpersonal conflict.
2. Identify commonly held myths about interpersonal conflict.
3. Compare and contrast three types of interpersonal conflict.
4. List and describe five stages of conflict.
5. Describe differences between destructive and constructive approaches to managing conflict.
6. Describe five conflict management styles.
7. Identify and use conflict management skills to help manage emotions, information, goals, and problems when attempting to resolve interpersonal differences.

OUTLINE

Outside noisy, inside empty.

Chinese Proverb

"This house stinks," says Paolo, wrinkling up his nose. "It smells like day-old garbage."

"Take it out yourself. It's your job," retorts Anya, turning her back on him to scrub furiously at an imaginary morsel of food on a frying pan that was already polished clean.

"Hey, hey," says Paolo, holding up both hands in front of him, "I wasn't accusing you. I just said it smelled bad in here. Don't be so touchy."

"Oh, no? Well, you're always criticizing me. You think just because you have a big important job that you can come in here and say anything you like. And I come home from work feeling tired, too, you know, but you don't do anything to help, not even the things you agree to!" shouts Anya, turning around to confront her mate, planting her soapy hands on her hips.

"Well, you're always getting on my case for no reason. I'm not putting up with this stuff from you anymore," snarls Paolo. As he turns on his heel to stalk out of the kitchen, Anya bursts into tears.

Why have Paolo and Anya reached an impasse in their attempt to communicate? Paolo and Anya's exchange is complicated, seething with conflicting goals and underlying resentments. Eventually, all relationships experience conflict. It's been estimated that people in a stable, romantic relationship experience a conflict episode about twice a week.[1] And the longer you know someone, the greater the likelihood that you'll experience conflict with that person, simply because you spend time together and know more about each other.[2] The key question of this chapter is, How can you best manage the inevitable conflict that occurs in your relationships with others?

Conflict management is not a single skill, but a set of skills. But to manage conflict effectively involves more than learning simple techniques. The best route to success in resolving conflict effectively is acquiring knowledge about what conflict is, what makes it happen, and what we can do about it. We will begin by defining conflict, then examine some of the myths about it and focus on some of its constructive functions. We will also discuss the relationship among conflict, power, and conflict management styles.

In addition, we will discuss how learning about your typical style of managing conflict can give you insight into managing interpersonal differences. And finally, we will build on our discussions of listening skills and verbal and nonverbal communication in the previous chapters to help you learn to manage the inevitable interpersonal conflicts that arise in the best of relationships.

Of course, if Wile E. Coyote and Roadrunner ever found a way to resolve their conflicts, we'd stop watching their cartoons. But humans are better off finding ways to resolve their conflicts.

What Is Conflict?

Interpersonal conflict is an expressed struggle that occurs when people cannot agree on a way to meet their needs and achieve their goals. If the needs are incompatible, if there are too few resources to accomplish the goals, or if the individuals opt to compete rather than to cooperate to meet needs and achieve goals, then interpersonal conflict occurs. People involved in such a conflict are **interdependent;** this means that what one person does or says affects the other.[3] Unresolved and poorly managed interpersonal conflict is a significant predictor of an unsatisfactory relationship, and the opposite is also true: Partners in relationships with effectively managed conflict report being more satisfied with the relationship.[4]

You typically don't know that someone is upset with you until conflict is expressed by a remark or by nonverbal behavior such as a glare, steely facial expression, or emotion-laden tone of voice. The intensity level of a conflict (conveyed through the intensity of nonverbal expressions of emotion) usually relates to the intensity of the unmet needs or goals. Conflict sometimes escalates into physical abuse. One research team estimated that 50–60 percent of U.S. households have experienced at least minor forms of violence; there's evidence that in one out of every six romantic relationships, one partner has stalked the other.[5] Experts surmise that one reason violence is so prevalent in many relationships is that people don't have the skills to manage conflict and disagreement.[6] Sam Keltner developed the "struggle spectrum," shown in Figure 8.1, to describe conflicts ranging from mild differences to fights.[7] At the bedrock of all conflict are differences—in goals, needs, and experiences.

interpersonal conflict. Expressed struggle that occurs when people cannot agree on a way to meet their needs or goals.

interdependent. Dependent on each other; one person's actions affect the other person.

FIGURE **8.1**

The Struggle Spectrum
Used by permission of the National Communication Association.

Mild Differences	Disagreement	Dispute	Campaign	Litigation	Fight

Myths About Conflict

Although not all conflict is destructive to relationships, many cultures have taboos against displaying it in public. The prime experiences in life that shape how we learn to express and manage conflict occur in the families in which we grew up. It's in our families that we learn life lessons about relationships that remain with us throughout our days.[8] According to one researcher, many of us were raised with four myths that contribute to our negative feelings about conflict.[9] As you read the following sections, you may shake your head and say, "That's not where I came from." In some American families, conflict is expressed openly and often. But even if your experience has been different, reading about these prevailing myths may help you understand your or your partner's emotional responses to conflict.

Myth 1: "Conflict Is Always a Sign of a Poor Interpersonal Relationship"

It is an oversimplification to assume that all conflict is rooted in underlying relational problems. Conflict is a normal part of any interpersonal relationship.[10] Although it is true that constant bickering and sniping can be symptomatic of deeper problems, disagreements do not necessarily signal that the relationship is on the rocks. All relationships experience conflict. In fact, overly polite, stilted conversation is more likely to signal a problem than periodic disagreements.[11] The free expression of honest disagreement is often a hallmark of healthy relationships. Assertively and honestly expressing ideas may mean that a person feels safe and comfortable enough with his or her partner to disagree. As we will discuss later, conflict in interpersonal relationships can play a constructive role in leading people to focus on issues that may need attention. The ebb and flow of interpersonal psychological intimacy and separation inevitably lead to some degree of conflict in any relationship. When conflict happens in your relationships, don't immediately assume that the relationship is doomed.

Myth 2: "Conflict Can Always Be Avoided"

"If you can't say anything nice, don't say anything at all." Many of us were taught early in our lives that conflict is undesirable and that we should eliminate it from our conversations and relationships. Yet evidence suggests that conflict arises in virtually every relationship.[12] Because each of us has a unique perspective on our world, it would be extraordinary for us *always* to see eye-to-eye with another person. One study found that most romantic couples have some kind of disagreement or conflict, on average, about twice a week. Although such conflicts may not be intense, many differences of opinion punctuate our relationships with people we care about.[13]

Research suggests that contentment in marriage relates not to the amount of conflict, but to the way in which partners manage it.[14] Conflict is also a normal and productive part of interaction in group deliberations.[15] It is a myth that conflict is inherently unproductive and something to be avoided. It happens, even in the best of relationships.

Myth 3: "Conflict Always Occurs Because of Misunderstandings"

"You just don't understand what my days are like. I need to go to sleep!" shouts Janice as she scoops up a pillow and blanket and stalks off to the living room. "Oh, yeah? Well, you don't understand what will happen if I don't get this budget in!" responds Ron, who is hunched over the desk in their bedroom. It is clear that Ron and Janice are having a conflict. They have identified the cause of their problem as a lack of understanding between them, but in reality they *do* understand each other. Ron knows that Janice wants to sleep; Janice knows he wants to stay up and work. Their problem is that they disagree about whose goal is more important. This disagreement, not lack of understanding, is the source of the conflict.

Myth 4: "Conflict Can Always Be Resolved"

Consultants, corporate training experts, and authors of self-help books often offer advice about how to resolve conflicts so that all will be well and harmony will prevail. Some people claim that with the application of a few skills and how-to techniques, conflicts can disappear like a stain from a shirt laundered with the right kind of detergent. This is simply not true. Not all differences can be resolved by listening harder or paraphrasing your partner's message. Some disagreements are so intense and the perceptions so fixed that individuals may have to agree to disagree and live with it.

Conflict Myths

Myth 1: "Conflict is always a sign of a poor interpersonal relationship."

Myth 2: "Conflict can always be avoided."

Myth 3: "Conflict always occurs because of misunderstandings."

Myth 4: "Conflict can always be resolved."

Types of Conflict

At some time or another, many close relationships go through a conflict phase. "We're always fighting," complains a newlywed. But if she were to analyze these fights, she would discover important differences among them. According to communication researchers Gerald Miller and Mark Steinberg, most conflicts fit into one of three different categories: (1) **pseudoconflict**—triggered by a lack of understanding; (2) **simple conflict**—stemming from different ideas, definitions, perceptions, or goals and (3) **ego conflict**—which occurs when conflict gets personal.[16]

pseudoconflict. Conflict triggered by a lack of understanding and miscommunication.

simple conflict. Conflict that stems from different ideas, definitions, perceptions, or goals.

ego conflict. Conflict in which the original issue is ignored as partners attack each other's self-esteem.

Pseudoconflict: Misunderstandings

Will: Let's walk to the store.

Sean: No, it's too far. Let's drive.

Will: But the store is close.

Sean: No, it's not.

Will: Yes, it is. It's just off Market Street.

Sean: Oh, you mean the convenience store.

Will: Sure, that's exactly what I mean.

Sean: Oh, no problem. I thought you meant the supermarket.

Pseudo means false or fake. Pseudoconflict occurs when we simply miss the meaning in a message. But unless we clear up the misunderstanding by asking for more information, a real conflict might ensue. Note that in this example, Will offers helpful information ("It's just off Market Street"), and Sean checks it with feedback ("Oh, you mean the convenience store").

How can you avoid pseudoconflict? A key strategy is to clarify the meaning of words and expressions that you don't understand. Keep the following strategies in mind to minimize misunderstandings before they occur:

- *Check your perceptions:* Ask for clarification of anything you don't understand; seek to determine whether your interpretation is the same as your partner's.
- *Listen between the lines:* Look for puzzled or quizzical facial expressions from your partner. People may not voice their misunderstanding but express their uncertainty nonverbally.
- *Establish a supportive rather than a defensive climate for conversation:* Avoid evaluating, controlling, using manipulative strategies, being aloof, acting superior, or rigidly asserting that you're always right. These classic behaviors are like pushing the button to increase defensiveness and misunderstanding.

Pseudoconflict is simply a misunderstanding. Your partner may communicate confusion by facial expressions or other nonverbal behavior. Pseudoconflict can be resolved if partners ask for clarification, listen between the lines, and work to establish a supportive climate.

Simple Conflict: Different Stands on the Issues

Simple conflict stems from differences in ideas, definitions, perceptions, or goals. You want to go to Disney World for your vacation; your spouse wants to go to Washington, D.C. Your spouse wants to fly; you would rather take the train. You understand each other, but you disagree.

A key to unraveling a simple conflict is to keep the conversation focused on the issues at hand so that the expression of differences does not deteriorate into a battle focusing on personalities.

The following exchange between Jason and Nick illustrates a conflict over a simple difference of opinion; notice how both partners stick to the issues and figure out a way to resolve their differences.

Jason: I want to watch *The Simpsons* tonight. It's their Christmas show.

Nick: No way, man. I have to watch a documentary about textiles for my history class. It's an assignment.

Jason: But I've worked all weekend. I'm beat. The last thing I want to watch is some stuffy old documentary on the history of weaving.

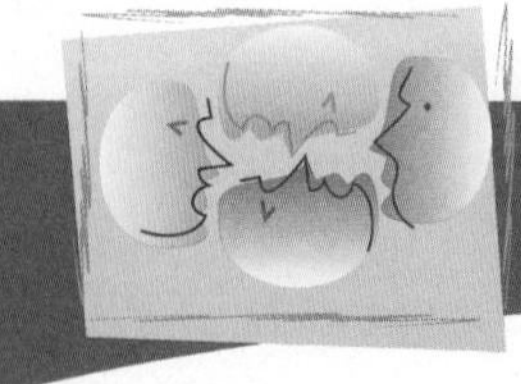

Understanding Diversity

Gender, Culture, and Conflict

Some research suggests that there are distinctions between feminine and masculine styles of responding to conflict. The feminine style is more likely to focus on relationship issues, whereas the masculine style typically focuses on tasks.[17] People with a feminine style often interact with others to achieve intimacy and closeness, but people with a masculine style interact to get something done or to accomplish something apart from the relationship. People employing a masculine style are often more aggressive and assertive than those employing a feminine style when pursuing a goal.[18] The following list summarizes key differences that researchers have observed between feminine and masculine styles of responding to conflict. Note that individuals of either sex may employ some characteristics of both feminine and masculine gender styles.

Perceived Gender Differences in Responding to Conflict[19]

People with Feminine Styles . . .	People with Masculine Styles . . .
Are concerned with equity and caring; connect with and feel responsible to others.	Are concerned with equality of rights and fairness; adhere to abstract principles, rules.
Interact to achieve closeness and interdependence.	Interact to achieve specific goals; seek autonomy and distance.
Attend to interpersonal dynamics to assess relationship's health.	Are less aware of interpersonal dynamics.
Encourage mutual involvement.	Protect self-interest.
Attribute crises to problems in the relationship.	Attribute crises to problems external to the relationship.
Are concerned with the impact of the relationship on personal identity.	Are neither self- nor relationship-centered.
Respond to conflict by often focusing mainly on the relationship.	Respond to conflict by often focusing on rules and being evasive until a unilateral decision is reached.

Nick: Tell you what. Go ahead and watch *The Simpsons.* I'll record the documentary and watch it later. Deal?

Jason: Okay. Thanks. And I'll grill some burgers so we can have supper together first.

This next exchange between Sue and Nadiya is a bumpier one. What starts as a simple conflict deteriorates into a series of personal attacks.

Nadiya: Sue, can I borrow your skirt? I have a date tonight. It would look great with my new jacket.

Sue: Sorry, Nadiya. I'm going to wear it tonight. I've got to give a presentation to the school board about our new mentor program.

Nadiya: In case you don't remember, when you brought it home, you said I could borrow it any time. Besides, you haven't paid back the twenty bucks I loaned you to buy it.

Sue: Yes, but I bought the skirt especially for this occasion.

Nadiya: Well, don't ask to borrow anything from me ever again. You're just plain selfish.

Although research has identified some gender-based differences in the way we manage conflict, some research studies suggest that the differences can, at times, be quite small. The context for the argument or the specific conflict trigger may be a more important factor than gender in shaping how we respond to and manage interpersonal conflict.[20]

The most recent perspective on analyzing gender differences is called the *partnership perspective.* This perspective suggests that men and women are not locked into particular styles or approaches.[21] The partnership approach emphasizes the importance of keeping channels open and avoiding the tendency to stereotype communication styles by gender.

An individual's culturally learned assumptions influence his or her conflict behavior. In some cultures, most conflict is **expressive;** it focuses on the quality of relationships and on managing interpersonal tension and hostility. In other cultures, conflict is more **instrumental.** It centers less on relationships and more on achieving a specific goal or objective.[22] One researcher noted that for people from low-context cultures (those who derive more meaning from words than from the surrounding context), conflicts are most often instrumental.[23] Most North Americans come from low-context cultures. Many Asian cultures, in contrast, are high-context cultures. They are also collectivist: they value group effort over individual achievement. For people from these cultures, conflicts often center on expressive, relational concerns. Keeping peace in the group or saving face is often a higher priority than achieving a goal.

Yet don't think that everyone in a given culture manages conflict the same way. For example, one research team found that there are differences in the way older and younger Chinese adults seek to manage conflict.[24] Older Chinese people tended to favor more accommodating approaches to managing differences, while younger Chinese adults used a problem-solving approach.

Managing culture-based conflict requires a strong other-orientation. One research team suggests that Anglo-Americans of European descent receive little training in how to develop solutions to problems that are acceptable to an entire group.[25] They are often socialized to stick up for their own rights at any cost, and they approach conflict as a win–lose situation. In contrast, people from collectivist cultures approach conflict management situations from a win–win perspective; it is important that both sides save face and avoid ridicule. Such differences in approaches provide a double challenge. In addition to disagreeing over the issue at hand, people from different cultures may also have different strategies for reaching agreement.

Sue: Oh, yeah? Well *you're* the one who hogs all the space in the refrigerator. Talk about someone who's selfish. If that's not the pot calling the kettle black!

Nadiya: All right, now that we're being honest about who hogs what, *you're* the one who monopolizes the bathroom in the morning.

And so it escalates. The original disagreement about the skirt is forgotten, and egos become attacked and bruised.

To keep simple conflict from escalating into personal vendettas, consider the following strategies:

- *Clarify your and your partner's understanding* of the issues and your partner's understanding of the source of the disagreement.
- *Keep the discussion focused* on facts and the issue at hand, rather than drifting back to past battles and unrelated personal grievances.
- *Look for more than just the initial solutions* that you and your partner bring to the discussion; generate many options.
- *Don't try to tackle too many issues at once.* Perform "issue triage"—identify the important issues, and work on those.

expressive conflict. Conflict that focuses on issues about the quality of the relationship and managing interpersonal tension and hostility.

instrumental conflict. Conflict that centers on achieving a particular goal or task and less on relational issues.

- *Find the kernel of truth in what your partner is saying.* Find agreement where you can.
- *If tempers begin to flare and conflict is escalating, cool off.* Come back to the discussion when you and your partner are fresh.

Ego Conflict: Conflict Gets Personal

As you can see from the preceding exchange between Sue and Nadiya, a personal attack puts your partner on the defensive, and many people behave according to the adage "The best defense is a good offense." When you launch a personal attack, you are "picking a fight." And as Sue and Nadiya's exchange illustrates, fights that begin as pseudo- or simple conflicts can easily lapse into more vicious ego conflicts. And as each person in the conflict becomes more defensive about his or her position, the issues become more tangled.

Remember Paolo and Anya's argument about taking out the garbage at the beginning of this chapter? It started with what was probably an offhand remark and escalated into a major argument because both participants began attacking each other and bringing up other sensitive issues instead of focusing on the original comment.

If you find yourself involved in ego conflict, try to refrain from hurling personal attacks and emotional epithets back and forth. Instead, take turns expressing your feelings without interrupting each other, then take time to cool off.[26] It is difficult to use effective listening skills when your emotions are at a high pitch.

Here are additional strategies to consider when conflict becomes personal:

- *Try to steer the ego conflict back to simple conflict:* Stay focused on issues rather than personalities.
- Make the issue a problem to be solved rather than a battle to be won.
- *Write down what you want to say:* It may help you clarify your point, and you and your partner can develop your ideas without interruption. A note of caution: Don't put angry personal attacks in writing. Make your written summary rational, logical, and brief rather than emotion-laden.
- *When things get personal, make a vow not to reciprocate:* Use *I* messages that we talked about in Chapter 5 ("I feel uncomfortable and threatened when we yell at each other" rather than *You* messages ("You're such a creep. You never listen.") to express how you are feeling.

Our focus has been on de-escalating conflict when it occurs in face-to-face situations. But simple conflict can become ego conflict when communicating online, just as it can when communicating in person. When communicating in cyberspace, you can turn an exchange of differing opinions into a personal attack on someone when you use flaming in your communication.[27] **Flaming** occurs when someone sends an overly negative message that personally attacks another person. The flamer can further augment the intensity of the negative message by "shouting" the message in ALL CAPITAL LETTERS. Flaming can also include calling someone a nasty name or using foul language. There is evidence that people are more likely to use flaming language online than when talking in person.

Our recommendation: Don't flame; it makes conflict more difficult to manage. When you are the recipient of a flaming message, first recognize that your impulse will be to reciprocate. Without resorting to flaming, let the other person know that the flaming makes it less likely for you to respond in a calm and rational manner. Or simply take some time to cool off before typing a return message that you'll later regret.

Types of Conflict

	Pseudoconflict	Simple Conflict	Ego Conflict
What It Is	Individuals misunderstand each other.	Individuals disagree over which action to pursue to achieve their goals.	Individuals feel personally attacked.
What to Do	Check your perceptions.	Clarify understanding.	Return to issues rather than personal attacks.
	Listen between the lines; look for nonverbal expressions of puzzlement.	Stay focused on facts and issues.	Talk about a problem to be solved rather than a fight to be won.
	Be supportive rather than defensive.	Generate many options rather than arguing over one or two options.	Write down rational arguments to support your position.
	Listen actively.	Find the kernel of truth in what your partner is saying; emphasize where you agree.	Use "I" messages rather than "You" messages.

Conflict as a Process

Cathy was reading the Sunday paper, enjoying a second cup of coffee, and listening to her favorite classical music station. All seemed well. Suddenly, for no apparent reason, her roommate Barb brusquely stormed into the room and shouted, "I can't stand it anymore! We have to talk about who does what around here." Cathy was taken completely off guard. She had no idea her roommate was upset about the division of household chores. To her, this outburst seemed to come out of the blue; in reality, however, several events had led up to it.

Most relational disagreements have a source, a beginning, a middle, an end, and an aftermath.[28] Let's find out about these stages.

flaming. Sending an overly negative online message that personally attacks another person.

Source: Prior Conditions

The first phase in the conflict process is the one that sets the stage for disagreement; it begins when you become aware that there are differences between you and another person. The differences may stem from role expectations, perceptions, goals, or resources. In the previous example, Barb perceived that she and Cathy played different roles in caring for the household.

In interpersonal relationships, *many* potential sources of conflict may be smoldering below the surface. It may take some time before they flare up into overt conflict. Moreover, they may be compounded with other concerns, making them difficult to sort out. And it may not be just one conversation or issue that triggers conflict; multiple conflict "trip wires" may contribute to a conflict episode.[29]

Beginning: Frustration Awareness

At this stage, at least one of you becomes aware that the differences in the relationship are increasingly problematic. You may begin to engage in self-talk, noting that something is wrong and creating frustration. Perhaps you realize that you won't be able to achieve an important goal or that someone else has resources you need to achieve it. Or you may become aware of differences in perceptions. Barb knew that Cathy's family always spent their weekends relaxing. All the members of Barb's family, in contrast, pitched in on weekends to get household chores done for the week. Barb may have recognized that difference, even as her frustration level rose.

Becoming aware of differences in perception does not always lead to increased frustration. But when the differences interfere with something you want to accomplish, your frustration level rises. Barb wanted to get the house clean so that she could turn her attention to studying for a test she had the next day. Cathy's apparent indifference to helping Barb achieve that goal was a conflict trigger.

Middle: Active Conflict

When you bring your frustration to the attention of others, a conflict becomes an active, *expressed struggle.*[30] If frustrations remain only as thoughts, the conflict is passive, not active. Active conflict does not necessarily mean that the differences are expressed with shouting or emotional intensity. An expression of disagreement may be either verbal or nonverbal. Calmly asking someone to change an attitude or behavior to help you achieve your goal is a form of active conflict; so is kicking your brother under the table when he starts to reveal your secret to the rest of the family.

Cathy was not aware of the division of labor problem until Barb stormed into the room demanding a renegotiation of roles. Barb had been aware of her frustration for some time, yet had not acted on it. Many experts advocate not waiting until your frustration level escalates to peak intensity before you approach someone with your conflict. Unexpressed frustration tends to erupt like soda in a can that has just been shaken. Intense emotions can add to the difficulty of managing a conflict.

End: Resolution

When you begin to try to manage the conflict, it has progressed to the resolution stage. Of course, not all conflicts can be neatly resolved. Couples who divorce, business partners who dissolve their corporation, or roommates who go their separate ways have all found solutions, even though they may not be amicable ones.

After Barb's outburst, she and Cathy were able to reach a workable compromise about the division of their household labor. Cathy agreed to clean the house every other week; Barb promised not to expect her to do it on weekends.

Aftermath: Follow-Up

As Yogi Berra once said, "It ain't over 'til it's over." After a conflict has been resolved, the follow-up stage involves dealing with hurt feelings or managing simmering grudges, and checking with the other person to confirm that the conflict has not retreated into the frustration awareness stage.[31] As we noted in Chapter 1, interpersonal relationships operate as transactive processes rather than as linear, step-by-step ones. Conflict does progress in stages, but you may need to resolve the same conflict again unless you confirm your understanding of the issues with your partner.

The Friday after their discussion, Cathy proudly showed off a spotless apartment to Barb when she came home from class. Barb responded with a grin and a quick hug and privately resolved to get up early on Sunday morning so that she could go out to get Cathy pastries and the Sunday papers before she awoke. This kind of mutual thoughtfulness exemplifies a successful follow-up in a conflict.

Understanding Conflict as a Process

Prior Conditions Stage	The stage is set for conflict because of differences in the individuals' actions or attitudes.
Frustration Awareness Stage	One individual becomes aware that the differences are problematic and becomes frustrated and angry.
Active Conflict Stage	The individuals communicate with each other about the differences; the conflict becomes an expressed struggle.
Resolution Stage	The individuals begin seeking ways to manage the conflict.
Follow-Up Stage	The individuals examine their own feelings and check with each other to monitor whether both are satisfied with the resolution.

Understanding the stages of conflict can help you better manage the process. You'll also be in a better position to make the conflict a constructive rather than a destructive experience. Conflict is **constructive** if it helps build new insights and establishes new patterns in a relationship. Airing differences can lead to a more satisfying relationship in the long run. David W. Johnson lists the following as benefits of conflict in interpersonal relationships. Interpersonal conflict

- Focuses attention on problems that may have to be solved.
- Clarifies what may need to be changed.
- Focuses attention on what is important to you and your partner.
- Clarifies who you are and what your values are.
- Helps you learn more about your partner.

constructive conflict. Conflict that helps build new insights and establishes new patterns in a relationship.

By focusing on the problem at hand rather than assuming a defensive attitude, this machinist and his foreman may reach a constructive solution to their conflict.

- Keeps relationships interesting.
- Strengthens relationships by increasing your confidence that you can manage disagreements.[32]

Although conflict can be constructive, we don't want to oversell the value or function of conflict in relationships with others. Conflict can also be **destructive.** The hallmark of destructive conflict is a lack of flexibility in responding to others.[33] Conflict can become destructive when people view their differences from a win–lose perspective, rather than looking for solutions that allow both individuals to gain.

Conflict Management Styles

What's your approach to managing interpersonal conflict: fight or flight? Do you tackle conflict head-on or seek ways to remove yourself from it? Most of us do not have a single way of dealing with differences, but we do have a tendency to manage conflict by following patterns that we have used before. The pattern we choose depends on several factors: our personality, the individuals with whom we are in conflict, the time and place of the confrontation, and other situational factors. For example, if your boss gives you an order, you respond differently from the way you do if your spouse gives you an order. Virginia Satir, author of *Peoplemaking,* a book about family communication, suggests that we learn conflict response patterns early in life.[34] Ample research evidence supports Satir's conclusion.[35] How we manage conflict with others is related to how our family of origin dealt with conflict.

One of several classifications of **conflict styles** is a five-style model based on the work of K. W. Thomas and R. H. Kilmann that includes two primary dimensions: concern for others and concern for self.[36] These two dimensions result in five conflict management styles, shown in Figure 8.2. The five styles are (1) avoidance, (2) accommodation, (3) competition, (4) compromise, and (5) collaboration.

destructive conflict. Conflict that dismantles rather than strengthens relationships.

conflict style. Consistent pattern or approach you use to manage disagreement with others.

Avoidance

Concern for Self

Competition

Collaboration

Compromise

Avoidance

Accommodation

Concern for Others

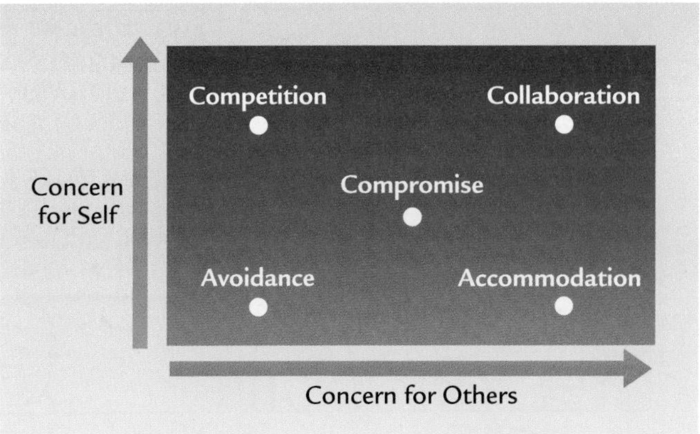

FIGURE 8.2

Conflict Management Styles The five conflict management styles in relation to concern for others and concern for self.

One approach to managing conflict is to back off and try to side-step the conflict. Typical responses from someone who uses this style are "I don't want to talk about it," "It's not my problem," "Don't bother me with that now," or "I'm not interested in that." The **avoidance** style might indicate that a person has low concern for others as well as for himself or herself. This is sometimes called the "lose–lose" approach to conflict. The person using the avoidance conflict style wishes the problem or conflict would go away by itself and appears uninterested in managing the conflict or in meeting the needs of the other person involved in the disagreement. People who avoid conflict may also just not like the hassle of dealing with a difficult, uncomfortable situation. Not dealing directly with conflict may also stem from being unassertive and unable to stand up for one's own rights.

Other times, people avoid conflict because they don't want to hurt the feelings of others. There may be times when avoiding a major blowup with someone is a wise strategy, but hoping the conflict will go away on its own may not always be the best plan.

Evidence suggests that husbands are more likely to avoid confrontation as a way of managing conflict with their wives. One research team argues that males are likely to avoid conflict because of the way they process information, especially emotions.[37] Husbands may implicitly reason that it's better to keep quiet and avoid conflict than to speak up and try to sort things out; for them, the dissonance that results from speaking up is not worth the effort.

Research that looked at how parents and teenagers managed their conflict found that one of the least satisfying approaches to conflict management is the **demand-withdrawal pattern**; either the parent or the teenager makes a demand and the other person avoids conflict by changing the subject or walking away.[38] Researchers have found that making repeated demands that aren't directly addressed, while also hurling put-downs at one another, results in a more distressed parent–teenager relationship. If you see that you're in a demand-withdrawal pattern of conflict, try to change the tone of the interaction so that it becomes a conversation rather than a shouting match or a standoff in which you both just stop talking. Make it a goal to keep the conversation going rather than making a demand that results in the other person just walking away.

In some respects, avoiding conflict could be perceived as uncooperative. However, although it may not be cooperative, there are some advantages to avoiding conflict. Doing so provides time for each person in the conflict to think about the issues, cool down, and ponder other approaches to dealing with the issues. If the conflict issue really is trivial or silly, it may also be advantageous not to throttle up the tension to make a mountain out of a molehill.

Avoiding conflict can also de-escalate the tension and allow each person to save face. One of the ways people avoid conflict and try to de-escalate emotional tension is by being deliberately vague or ambiguous about what is causing the conflict. They provide general rather than specific feedback. Yet there is also evidence that in certain situations people find a direct response more honest and competent than a vague one.[39] The trick is accurately reading a situation to know when to be vague and when to be specific.

avoidance. Conflict management style that involves backing off and trying to side-step conflict.

demand-withdrawal pattern of conflict management. Pattern in which one person makes a demand and the other person avoids conflict by changing the subject or walking away.

PEARLS BEFORE SWINE: © Stephan Pastis/Dist. by United Feature Syndicate, Inc.

There are also several disadvantages of avoiding conflict. If you avoid the conflict, you may be sending a message that you really don't care about the other person's feelings; you're more concerned about your own needs. Avoiding the conflict may also just make things worse. A conflict that was simply simmering may boil over if it's not tended to. And, of course, another disadvantage is that the issue remains unresolved. Like a lump in the throat, the conflict just sits there.

Accommodation

To accommodate is to give in to the demands of others. Someone who accommodates believes it's OK if the other person gets what he or she wants. People may sometimes adopt an **accommodation** style because they fear rejection if they rock the boat. Sometimes, people who accommodate don't seem to get angry or upset; they just do what others want them to do. But, in reality, they also accommodate to serve their own interests—to get people to like them. This conflict management style is sometimes called the "lose–win" approach. If you consistently accommodate, you sacrifice your own needs so that someone else can win the argument.

Using the accommodation style has several advantages. For one thing, it shows that you're reasonable and you want to help. If the issue is a minor or trivial one, you may gain some credibility by just letting it slide. Of course, if you are wrong or have made a mistake, accommodation is an appropriate response.

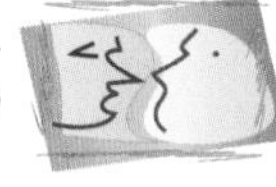

BE OTHER-ORIENTED

There are disadvantages to accommodating, just as there are disadvantages to any conflict style. Throughout this book, we've stressed the importance of becoming other-oriented. But we've also noted that being other-oriented means considering the needs and position of the other person, without necessarily doing what the other person wants. Sometimes, a person may accommodate for self-protection rather than because he or she is genuinely interested in others. In the following exchange, note Luke's accommodation response to Martin:

Martin: Luke, I'm not in agreement with you on the QCN merger. I think the merger should be called off.

Luke: OK. Whatever you think is best. I just want you to feel good about your decision.

To accommodate can give the accommodator a false sense of security by producing a "pseudosolution"—one that doesn't really solve anything but just postpones the effort of seeking a solution to the problem. Also, if you consistently accommodate, you may diminish your power to the extent that others take advantage of you; the next time a conflict arises, the expectation may be that you'll give in and the other person will

accommodation. Conflict management style that involves giving in to the demands of others.

get his or her way again. In addition, if you accommodate too quickly, you short-circuit the possibility of finding a creative solution that is to everyone's liking.

Competition

"You're wrong!" shouts Ed. "Here's how to get our project in on time. We can't waste time in the library. We just have to write up what we have."

"But Ed," suggests Derrick, "the assignment calls for us to have three library sources."

"No. We don't have time. Just do it," Ed insists. Ed sees the issue as a competition that he must win.

Each of us has some need to control and also some need to be controlled by others. But people who have a **competition** conflict management style have a win–lose philosophy. They want to win at the expense of the other person, to claim victory over their opponents. They want to control others. They are typically not other-oriented; instead, they are focused on themselves.

People who compete often resort to blaming, or seeking a scapegoat, rather than assuming responsibility for a conflict. "I didn't do it," "Don't look at me," and "He made me do it" are typical blaming statements.

If these strategies do not work, people with a competitive style may try threats and warnings. Threats refer to actions that people can actually carry out.[40] Warnings are negative prophecies they cannot actually control. The boyfriend who says, "If you don't stop calling me names, I'm going to leave you," has issued a threat; he has the power to leave. If he were to say, "Don't call your parents names, or they'll write you out of their will," that would be a warning. In reality, he has no control over his partner's parents.

Obviously, threats are more powerful than warnings in changing behavior, and then only if the other person would genuinely find the threatened actions punishing or disruptive. If a parent threatens to ground a child, the child will take the threat seriously only if he or she knows the parent will carry it out. If the parent has backed down in the past, the child will probably not pay much attention to the threat.

Is it ever appropriate to compete with others? Yes, if you believe that your position is clearly the best approach and that anything short of achieving your goal would be harmful to you and to others. In an election, someone will win and someone will lose. At the conclusion of a judicial trial, someone typically wins and someone loses. But even hard-fought elections and controversial trials have rules designed to maintain fairness for all involved in the conflict or decision. During often-emotional periods of competition, those involved nonetheless need to maintain an ethical concern for others.

Compromise

To compromise is to attempt to find a middle ground—a solution that somewhat meets the needs of all concerned. The word *somewhat* is important. Often, when people compromise, no one gets precisely what he or she wants; each has to give up a bit of what he or she had hoped to get. When trying to craft a compromise, you're really expecting to lose something and win something simultaneously; you also expect your partner to lose and win. That's why the **compromise** style is called "a lose/win–lose/win" approach to conflict. As shown in Figure 8.2, when you compromise, you have some concern for others as well as some concern for yourself.

Compromise has some advantages. It can be a good thing if a quick resolution to the conflict is needed. And it reinforces the notion that all parties involved share in

competition. Conflict management style that stresses winning a conflict at the expense of the other person involved.

compromise. Conflict management style that attempts to find the middle ground in a conflict.

equal power. Compromise can also be useful if what is needed is a temporary solution. And it has the advantage of helping everyone save face, because everyone wins at least something.

But if compromising results in each person giving in but no person feeling pleased with the compromise, then a more collaborative approach to managing the conflict may be appropriate.

Collaboration

BE OTHER-ORIENTED

To collaborate is to have a high concern for both yourself and others. People who use a **collaboration** style of conflict management are more likely to view conflict as a set of problems to be solved rather than a game in which one person wins and another loses. Collaboration, which requires other-oriented strategies that foster a win–win climate, is based on the following principles offered by Harvard researchers Roger Fisher and William Ury.[41]

Separate the people from the problem. Leave personal grievances out of the discussion, describing problems without making judgmental or evaluative statements about personalities.

Focus on shared interests. Ask questions such as "What do we both want? What do we both value? Where are we already agreeing?" to emphasize common interests, values, and goals.

Generate many options to solve the problem. People who collaborate use brainstorming and other techniques to generate alternative solutions. (You will learn more about problem-solving techniques later in this chapter.)

Base decisions on objective criteria. Try to establish standards for an acceptable solution to a problem—these standards may involve cost, timing, and other factors. Suppose, for example, that you and your neighbor are discussing possible ways to stop a nearby dog from barking throughout the night. You decide on these criteria: The solution must not harm the dog; it must be easy for the owner to implement; the owner must agree to it; it should not cost more than fifty dollars; and it must keep the dog from disturbing the sleep of others. Your neighbor says, "Maybe the dog can sleep in the owner's garage at night." This solution meets all but one of your criteria, so you call the owner, who agrees to put the dog in the garage by 10 P.M. Now everyone wins, because the solution meets a sound, well-considered set of objective criteria.

The collaboration conflict management style is best used when those on all sides of the conflict need some new, fresh ideas. Using a collaborative approach also enhances commitment to the resolution of the conflict because all are involved in shaping the outcome. Collaborative approaches to managing conflict build rapport because everyone's concerns are at least noted, if not fully addressed. Finally, collaboration considers feelings and affirms the value of the interpersonal relationship.

It may sound as though collaboration is always the best approach to managing conflict. However, there are times when its disadvantages may outweigh the advantages.[42] One of the biggest disadvantages is the time, skill, patience, and energy required to manage conflict collaboratively. If a solution is needed quickly, other approaches such as compromise may be best.

collaboration. Conflict management style that uses other-oriented strategies to achieve a positive solution for all involved.

So, which style of managing conflict is best? The short answer to this question is "It depends." It depends on the outcome you seek, the amount of time you have, the quality of the relationship you have with the other people involved, and the amount of perceived power you and others have.[43] Each style has advantages and disadvantages; no style has an inherent advantage all of the time. The competent, other-oriented communicator consciously decides whether to compete, avoid, compromise, accommodate, or collaborate. Although collaboration seems to be the style preferred by most people, it, too, may not always be appropriate. Research suggests that what most people find most uncomfortable is (1) no clear resolution to a conflict, (2) a conflict management process that is poorly managed, or (3) the avoidance of issues that they would like to discuss.[44] *There is no single conflict management style that "works" in all situations.* We do, however, strongly suggest that, when time and other factors permit, a collaborative (win–win) conflict management style is worth exploring.[45] The conflict management skills presented in the final section of this chapter are anchored in a collaborative approach to managing conflict.

Although we emphasize the value of the collaborative approach to managing conflict, your cultural background strongly influences the style of conflict management that you prefer. Communication researcher Mitchell Hammer suggests that people from highly individualistic cultures (such as the predominant U.S. culture) prefer a conflict management style that is more direct in addressing the conflict-producing issues.[46] Collectivistic cultures—those that emphasize group and team interests over individual interests—typically prefer a more indirect approach to addressing conflict. Hammer also suggests that our cultural preferences for expressing or restraining our emotions have an important influence on our preferred conflict management style.[47] People from cultures that emphasize less explicit expression of emotions (Asian cultures, for example) will find intense emotional expressions of anger and frustration distracting and unproductive in managing conflict. Your culture is a strong influence in the degree to which you are direct or indirect when you communicate with others during conflict. Your culture also influences how emotionally expressive or restrained you are when you experience interpersonal conflict.

Conflict Management Styles

	The person who uses this style . . .
Avoidance	Withdraws from conflict; tries to side-step confrontation; finds conflict uncomfortable. A lose–lose approach to conflict.
Accommodation	Easily gives in to the demands of others; typically wants to be liked by others. A lose–win approach to conflict.
Competition	Dominates the discussion and wants to accomplish the goal even at the expense of others. A win–lose approach to conflict.
Compromise	Seeks the middle ground; will give up something to get something. A lose/win–lose/win approach to conflict.
Collaboration	Views conflict as a problem to be solved; negotiates to achieve a positive solution for all involved in the conflict. A win–win approach to conflict.

Applying Theory and Research

Cultural Differences and Preferred Conflict Management Style

Can cultural differences explain why people have a preference for using a specific conflict management style? That was a question that researchers Deborah Cai and Edward Fink wanted to explore. More specifically, do people from an individualistic culture (people who prefer establishing and maintaining their individual rights) have different preferences for ways of managing conflict than people from a collectivistic culture (where the tendency to work for the good of the group is often stronger than the tendency to achieve individual goals)? The researchers also wanted to know whether there are general trends in preferences for conflict management style.

To address these two issues, the researchers gave people from more than thirty different countries a questionnaire to complete. Some questions were designed to determine whether subjects were from a primarily individualistic or primarily collectivistic culture; other questions assessed subjects' preferred style of managing conflict. The five conflict styles that Cai and Fink defined were similar to the five styles we describe in this chapter: (1) obliging (accommodating), (2) avoiding, (3) domineering (competing), (4) compromising, and (5) integrating (collaborating).

Overall, the researchers found that the integrating (collaborating) style was the preferred conflict style, regardless of cultural background, followed by obliging (accommodating), compromising, and domineering (competing). People from individualistic cultures preferred the avoiding style more than did people from collectivistic cultures. People from collectivistic cultures seemed to prefer compromising and integrating (collaborating) more than did people from individualistic cultures. Another interesting finding was that people from different cultures actually interpreted four of the five conflict styles slightly differently. In other words, people from collectivistic cultures had a different interpretation of what compromising really involved, compared to people from individualistic cultures. Dominating (competing) was the only conflict management style that was interpreted similarly by people in different cultural groups.

APPLYING the Research to Your Life

What do these results mean to you? Although one survey does not let us draw conclusions that refer to everyone, the results nonetheless suggest some trends.

- As noted above, collaboration (or integration, as it was called in this study) was the preferred conflict management style, regardless of cultural background. So, if you're uncertain of another person's cultural background, collaboration may be a good "default" approach to managing conflict.
- People from individualistic cultures (such as individuals from the United States) are more likely to avoid conflict than are people from collectivistic cultures. Although this is a preference, it doesn't mean that it's always best to avoid conflict; it just means that people from individualistic cultures tend to reach for that style first. If you're from an individualistic culture, you shouldn't be surprised if others from the same cultural background have a tendency to avoid conflict. Of course, avoidance of conflict does have its advantages, but also, as we noted on pages 235–236, its disadvantages.
- Because people from collectivistic cultures prefer compromising and integrative collaboration, styles that take time, it may be wise to not rush the conflict management process if you're interacting with someone from a collectivistic culture. In fact, taking your time in managing conflict is probably a good idea no matter whom you're interacting with, unless finding a resolution quickly is important.
- Finally, because someone from a culture other than your own may have a different understanding of what a conflict management style entails, you may think you're being collaborative, but the person from the other culture may not interpret your behavior as collaborative. The competencies and strategies for enhancing the quality of communication with people from other cultures that we presented in Chapter 4 are especially useful when managing conflict.

Source: Deborah A. Cai and Edward L Fink, "Conflict Style Differences Between Individualists and Collectivists," *Communication Monographs,* 69 (March 2002): 67–87.

Conflict Management Skills

For many people, at the heart of enhancing the quality of interpersonal relationships is learning to manage conflict.[48] Managing conflict, especially emotion-charged ego conflict, is not easy. The more stress and anxiety you feel at any given time, the more likely you are to experience conflict in your relationships with others. When you are under stress, it's more likely that conflict will become personal and degenerate into ego conflict. And just the opposite is true: When you're rested and relaxed, you're less likely to experience conflict. But even while relaxed and with a fully developed set of skills, don't expect to avoid conflict. Conflict happens. The following skills, previewed in our discussion of a collaborative approach to conflict, can help you generate options that promote understanding and provide a framework for collaboration.[49]

Manage Your Emotions

For weeks, you have been working on a brochure with a tight deadline. You turned it over to the production department with instructions two weeks ago. Today, you call to check on its progress, and you discover that it is still sitting on the production coordinator's desk. You feel your anger begin to erupt. You're tempted to march into the production coordinator's office and scream at her, or to shout at her supervisor.

Try to avoid taking action when you are in such a state. You may regret what you say, and you will probably escalate the conflict.

Often, the first sign that we are in a conflict situation is a feeling of anger, frustration, fear, or even sadness, which sweeps over us like an ocean wave. If we feel powerless to control our own emotions, we will have difficulty taking a logical or rational approach to managing the conflict. Expressing our feelings in an emotional outburst may make us feel better for the moment, but it may close the door to logical, rational negotiation.

When we are emotionally charged, we experience physical changes as well. One researcher found that

> . . . our adrenaline flows faster and our strength increases by about 20 percent. The liver, pumping sugar into the bloodstream, demands more oxygen from the heart and lungs. The veins become enlarged and the cortical centers where thinking takes place do not perform nearly as well. . . . The blood supply to the problem-solving part of the brain is severely decreased because, under stress, a greater portion of blood is diverted to the body's extremities.[50]

Such changes fuel our fight–flight responses. If we choose to stay, verbal or physical violence may erupt; if we flee from the conflict, we cannot resolve it. Until we can tone down (not eliminate) our emotions, we will find it difficult to apply other skills. Let's look at some specific strategies that you can draw on when an intense emotional response to conflict clouds your judgment and decision-making skills.[51]

Be Aware That You Are Becoming Angry and Emotionally Volatile

One characteristic of people who "lose it" is that they let their emotions get the best of them. Before they know it, they are saying and doing things that they later regret. Unbridled and uncensored emotional outbursts rarely enhance the quality of an interpersonal relationship. An emotional purge may make you feel better, but your partner is likely to reciprocate, which will only escalate the conflict spiral.

Before that happens, become aware of what is happening to you. As we described earlier, your body will start to react to your emotions with an increased heart rate. Be sensitive to what is happening to you physically.

Seek to Understand Why You Are Angry and Emotional

Understanding what's behind your anger can help you manage it. Realize that it is normal and natural to be angry. It's a feeling everyone experiences. You need not feel guilty about it. Anger is often expressed as a defense when you feel violated or when you are fearful of losing something that is important to you. Two powerful anger triggers are (1) feeling that you have not been treated fairly, and (2) feeling entitled to something that you are being denied. Think about the last time you became very angry. Often, you experience a sense of righteous indignation when you are angry. You are being denied something you feel you should have.

Make a Conscious Decision About Whether to Express Your Anger

Rather than just letting anger and frustration build and erupt out of control, make a conscious choice about whether you should express your frustration and irritation. We're not denying that there are valid reasons for you to express anger and frustration, or suggesting that you should not express your feelings. Sometimes, there is no way to let someone know how important an issue is to you other than by forcefully expressing your irritation or anger. As these lines from William Blake illustrate, sometimes the wisest strategy is to be honest with others and express how you feel.

> I was angry with my friend:
> I told my wrath, my wrath did end.
> I was angry with my foe:
> I told it not, my wrath did grow.

If you do decide to express your anger, don't lose control. Be direct and descriptive. The guidelines for listening and responding that we provided in Chapter 5 can serve you well. Keep your anger focused on issues rather than personalities.

Select a Mutually Acceptable Time and Place to Discuss a Conflict

If you are upset, or even tired, you risk becoming involved in an emotion-charged shouting match. If you ambush someone with an angry attack, don't expect him or her to be in a receptive frame of mind. Instead, give yourself time to cool off before you try to resolve a conflict. In the case of the lapsed deadline mentioned earlier, you could call both the production coordinator and her boss and schedule an appointment to meet with them later in the day. By that time, you could gain control of your feelings and also think the issue through. Of course, issues sometimes need to be discussed on the spot; you may not have the luxury of waiting. But whenever practical, make sure the other person is ready to receive you and your message.

Plan Your Message

If you are approaching someone to discuss a disagreement, take care to organize your message. Consider rehearsing what you will say. Identify your goal, and determine what outcome you would like; do not barge in and pour out your emotions.

Breathe

One of the simplest yet most effective ways to avoid overheating is to breathe. As you become aware that your emotions are starting to erupt, take a slow, deep breath. Then breathe again. This can help calm you and manage the physiological changes that

Interpersonal Communication and Emotion
Connecting Heart to Heart

Tips for Managing Anger

One of the biggest obstacles to being other-oriented during conflict is the anger we often experience when we feel we're not being listened to or our rights are being violated.[52] Anger is an emotional response to fear. Stated another way, anger is an outward response to an inward feeling of fear. And fear is often about losing something or not getting something we believe is rightfully ours. We may become angry, for example, if we fear we may lose our job or if we sense a relationship that is important to us may be dissolving or becoming less important to the other person. Anger also occurs when we feel someone is keeping us from what we want and have a right to have, someone is unjustly blaming us for something, or someone is attacking us. Some people may tell you it is a good idea to express your anger to the person who is making you angry; get your anger out—don't keep it bottled up. There are times when expressing your anger is appropriate. Being assertive in expressing what bothers you is appropriate when the other person is not aware of what is bothering you. But uncensored angry words can escalate the anger you feel and also increase others' anger.[53] One research team offers these prescriptions for managing your own anger or coping with someone else's anger during conflict.[54]

- *Be determined not to get angry yourself.* If you know you are going to face someone who is likely to tick you off, prepare yourself before you meet with him or her. Assertively express your feelings, but make a promise to yourself not to "lose it" and allow the encounter to degenerate into a shout fest.
- *Get on the same physical level as the other person.* One person should not be standing and the other sitting. Try to face each other eye-to-eye. You can also build rapport by trying to mirror the posture of the other person. We're not suggesting that you mimic your partner (this would probably make him or her more angry), but try to adopt a similar communication position.
- *Be silent.* If you are angry and afraid you might say something you'll regret, just be quiet and listen.
- *Express your concern nonverbally.* Because much of an emotional message is communicated nonverbally, use your facial expression and eyes to let the other person know you care about him or her. Your communication partner will believe what you do, more than what you say.
- *Make an appropriate empathic statement.* Saying "I would probably feel angry if I had experienced what you experienced" or "I think I can see why you are so upset" may help. But be careful not to say, "I know just how you feel" or "I know where you're coming from." For many people, those statements can seem patronizing.
- *Remind yourself that you control your own emotions.* Even though others may do and say things that can upset you, you are the only person who can control yourself and your response to others. Try to respond mindfully to others rather than just reacting emotionally to them.
- *Recognize that angry emotional outbursts rarely change someone's mind.* Exploding in an angry tirade may make you feel better for a moment by getting it "off your chest," but it usually does little to advance understanding and manage the issues at hand.

adrenaline creates. Deep breathing—the prime strategy women use to manage the pain of childbirth—can be a powerful way to restore calmness to your spirit. Focusing on your breathing is also one of the primary methods of meditation. We're not suggesting that you hyperventilate. But taking deep, slow breaths that not only fill your upper lungs but move your diaphragm—the muscle that moves as your lungs expand and contract—is an active strategy to help you regain rational control.

Monitor Nonverbal Messages

As you learned in Chapter 7, your actions play a key role in establishing the emotional climate in any relationship. Monitoring your nonverbal messages can help to de-escalate an emotion-charged situation. Speaking calmly, using direct eye contact, and maintaining a calm, nonthreatening facial expression will signal that you wish to collaborate rather than control. Your nonverbal message should also support your verbal

What strategies do these two people seem to have drawn on to manage their conflict?

response. If you say you are listening to someone, but you continue to read the paper or work on a report, you are communicating a lack of interest in the speaker and the message.

Avoid Personal Attacks, Name Calling, and Emotional Overstatement

Using threats and derogatory names can turn a simple conflict into an ego conflict. When people feel attacked, they respond by protecting themselves. Research has found that when husbands and wives feel disconfirmed during conflict because of name calling or because their partner has made nasty comments, relational satisfaction significantly decreases.[55] It's not surprising that people don't like to be called names. Although you may feel hurt and angry, try to avoid exaggerating your emotions and hurling negative, personal comments at your partner.[56] If you say you are irritated or annoyed rather than furious, you can still communicate your emotions, but you take the harsh sting out of your description. We're not advocating that you be dishonest about how you are feeling; just don't overstate your emotions for dramatic effect. It may make you feel better, but it may make matters worse.[57]

Also avoid the bad habit of **gunny-sacking**. This occurs when you dredge up old problems and issues from the past, like pulling them out of an old bag or gunny sack, to use against your partner. Keep your focus on the issues at hand, not on old hurts. Gunny-sacking usually succeeds only in increasing tension, escalating emotions, and reducing listening effectiveness.

Take Time to Establish Rapport

Evidence suggests that you'll be more successful in managing conflict if you don't immediately dive in and attempt to sort out the issues with your partner.[58] Taking time to establish a positive emotional climate can pay big dividends; this is especially important if you're not well acquainted with the person you're having the conflict with. One study compared how effectively conflict was managed in two different groups.[59] In one group, the conflict negotiators spent time face-to-face, "schmoozing" and getting to know one another, before trying to negotiate a solution to a conflict. In the other group, the negotiators exchanged information via e-mail but did not meet face-to-face. The negotiators who spent time establishing a positive relationship in person were more successful in managing the conflict to everyone's satisfaction.

Even if you know the other person well, take some time to build rapport. Chatting about such seemingly innocuous topics as the weather or local events can help break the ice and provide a basis for a more positive conversational climate. A positive emotional climate is especially important when trying to sort through vexing, conflict-producing issues.

BE OTHER-ORIENTED 

Several researchers also note how important it is to help the other person in the conflict save face—to not leave the conversation feeling demoralized and humiliated.

gunny-sacking. Dredging up old problems and issues from the past to use against your partner.

Use Self-Talk

Kosta was chairing the committee meeting when Monique accused him of falsifying the attendance numbers at the last fine arts festival. Instead of lashing back at Monique, he paused, took a slow, deep breath, and thought, "I'm tired. If I snarl back, all we will do is escalate this issue out of proportion. I'll talk with Monique later, after we have both cooled down." Perhaps you think that talking to yourself is an eccentricity. Nothing could be further from the truth. As you saw in Chapter 2, thoughts are directly linked to feelings,[60] and the messages we tell ourselves play a major role in how we feel and respond to others. Ask yourself whether an emotional tirade and an escalating conflict will produce the results you want. When Eleanor Roosevelt noted, "No one can make you feel inferior without your consent," she was acknowledging the power of self-talk to affect your emotional response to what others say and do.

As you read the discussion about managing emotions, you may wonder if it's ever useful or productive to express negative emotions, especially anger, overtly when negotiating an issue. One research study found that expressing your anger and frustration might be a productive conflict management strategy if you are negotiating with someone who simply offers no useful alternatives.[61] The research suggests that by expressing your irritation, you may motivate the other person to come up with better alternatives. In most cases, escalating emotional tension decreases the likelihood that the conflict will be managed smoothly and effectively. But sometimes, being honest in expressing your bubbling frustration may nudge things along in a productive way, especially if there are no good options to discuss.

Manage Information

Because uncertainty, misinformation, and misunderstanding are often byproducts of conflict and disagreement, skills that promote mutual understanding are an important component of cooperative conflict management. Based on the listening and responding skills discussed in Chapter 5, the following specific suggestions can help you reduce uncertainty and enhance the quality of communication during conflict.

Clearly Describe the Conflict-Producing Events

Instead of just blurting out your complaints in random order, think of delivering a brief, well-organized minispeech. Offer your perspective on what created the conflict, sequencing the events like a well-organized story. Describe the events dispassionately so that the other person shares your understanding of the problem.

When Marsha almost had a car accident, she came home and told her husband, "Last week, you said you would get the brakes fixed on the car. On Monday, when you still hadn't taken the car in, you said you would do it on Wednesday. Now it's Friday, and the brakes are in even worse shape. I had a close call this afternoon when the car almost wouldn't stop. We've got to get those brakes fixed before anyone drives that car again."

"Own" Your Statements by Using Descriptive *I* Language

"I feel upset when you post the week's volunteer schedule without first consulting with me," reveals Katrina. Her statement is an example of the ***I* language** that we have discussed several times in this book. *I* language expresses how a speaker is feeling. The use of the word *I* conveys a willingness to "own" one's feelings and statements about them.

And sometimes, to make sure your communication partner doesn't miss the subtlety of your owning your feelings by using an *I* message, it may be useful to extend your *I* message[62] by saying, for example, "I really don't want you to take this the wrong way. I really care about you. But I want you to know that when you take food from my plate, I feel uncomfortable. My sister sometimes did that when I was a kid, and I didn't like it."

If Katrina had said, "You always prepare a schedule without telling anyone first. All of us who volunteer are mad about that," her statement would have had an ac-

***I* language.** Statements that use the word *I* to express how a speaker is feeling.

cusatory sting. Beginning the statement with "you" sets the listener up for a defensive response. Also, notice that the speaker does not take responsibility for the anger; she suggests that it belongs to several unidentified people as well. If you instead narrow the issue down to a conflict between you and the other person, you put the conflict into a more manageable framework.

One final tip about using *I* messages: Monitor your ***but* messages.** What's a *but* message? It's a statement that makes it seem as though whatever you've said prior to the word *but* is not truly the way you feel. Here's an example: "I love you. I really love you. But I feel really frustrated when you leave your clothes lying on every chair." A *but* message diminishes the positive sentiment you expressed with your *I* language. We're not suggesting that you never say *but,* only that you realize how the word may create noise for the listener; it may make your entire statement seem untrue.

Use Effective Listening Skills

Managing information is a two-way process. Whether you are describing a conflict situation to someone, or that individual is bringing a conflict to your attention, good listening skills will be invaluable.

Give your full attention to the speaker and make a conscious point of tuning out your internal messages. Sometimes, the best thing to do after describing the conflict-producing events is simply to wait for a response. If you don't stop talking and give the other person a chance to respond, he or she will feel frustrated, the emotional pitch will go up a notch, and it will become more difficult to reach an understanding.

BE OTHER-ORIENTED 

Finally, remember to not only focus on the facts or details, but also analyze them so you can understand the major point the speaker is making. Try to use your understanding of the details to interpret the speaker's major ideas. Remember to stay other-oriented and to "seek to understand rather than to be understood."[63]

Check Your Understanding of What Others Say and Do

***but* message.** Statement using the word *but* that may communicate that whatever you've said prior to *but* is not really true.

Respond clearly and appropriately. Your response and that of your conflict partner will confirm that you have understood each other. Checking perceptions is vital when emotions run high.

If you are genuinely unsure about facts, issues, or major ideas addressed during a conflict, ask questions to help you sort through them instead of barging ahead with solutions. Then summarize your understanding of the information; do not parrot the speaker's words or paraphrase every statement, but check key points to ensure that you have understood the message. Note how Ted adeptly paraphrases to check his understanding:

Maggie: I don't like the conclusion you've written to the conference report. It doesn't mention anything about the ideas suggested at the symposium. I think you have also misinterpreted the CEO's key message.

Ted: So if I understand you, Maggie, you're saying the report missed some key information and may also include an inaccurate summary of the CEO's speech.

Maggie: Yes, Ted. Those are my concerns.

Be Empathic

BE OTHER-ORIENTED

Understand others not only with your head, but also with your heart. To truly understand another person, you need to do more than catch the meaning of his or her words; you need to put yourself in the person's place emotionally. Ask yourself these questions: What emotions is the other person feeling? Why is he or she experiencing these emotions? Throughout this book, we have stressed the importance of becoming other-oriented. It's especially important to be other-oriented when you disagree with another person.[64] Trying to understand what's behind your partner's emotions may give you the insight you need to reframe the conflict from your partner's point of view. And with this other-oriented perspective, you may see new possibilities for managing the conflict.

Manage Goals

As you've seen, conflict is goal-driven. Both individuals involved in an interpersonal conflict want something. And for some reason, be it competition, scarce resources, or lack of understanding, the goals appear to be in conflict. To manage conflict, you must seek an accurate understanding of these goals and identify where they overlap.

Communication researchers Sandra Lakey and Daniel Canary found clear support for the importance of being sensitive to and aware of your communication partner's goals when trying to manage conflict.[65] People who were focused on the other person's goals were perceived as much more competent than people who weren't aware of what the other person wanted to accomplish. Let's look at some specific strategies to help manage conflict by being aware of the other person's goals during conflict.

BE OTHER-ORIENTED

Identify Your Goal and Your Partner's Goal

After you describe, listen, and respond, your next task should be to identify what you would like to have happen. What is your goal? Most goal statements can be phrased in terms of wants or desires. Consider the following examples:

Problem	Goals
Your boss wants you to work overtime; you need to pick up your son from day care.	You want to leave work on time; your boss wants the work completed ASAP.
Your spouse wants to sleep with the window open; you like a warm room and sleep better with the window closed.	You want a good night's rest; your spouse wants a good night's rest.

Becoming Other-Oriented

Empathy: The Essential Other-Oriented Skill Set

Empathy is not a single skill, but a family of related skills that help you understand others not only with your head, but also with your heart. To truly understand another person, you need to do more than catch the meaning of his or her words; you need to put yourself in the person's place emotionally. In addition, being empathic is more than just *acknowledging* that someone has certain thoughts or emotions; it is thinking and feeling as another person thinks and feels. During episodes of interpersonal conflict, it's especially important to be empathically other-oriented.

Why is being empathic important during interpersonal conflict? Trying to understand what's behind your partner's emotions may give you the insight you need to reframe the conflict from your partner's point of view. And with this other-oriented perspective, you may see new possibilities for managing the conflict. You may see, for example, that the person's outburst of anger is really anchored in fear—perhaps a fear of losing something that is precious. Or maybe the other person believes he or she was entitled to something that has already been taken away. With this new insight about the thought process behind the bubbling emotion that you see in your partner, you may generate additional, creative options for addressing the real catalyst for the conflict.

How do you become empathic? You start by asking yourself these questions:

- What is the other person thinking?
- What emotions is he or she experiencing?
- Why is he or she experiencing these emotions?
- What would I be thinking and feeling if I interpreted the situation as my partner has interpreted it?

Using these questions to get started, you then apply the collection of skills that we've discussed in several previous chapters as well as this chapter. Here's a brief summary of how to be empathic:

- *Stop:* Stop making your arguments and concentrate on your partner's points. Socially decenter by taking into account the other person's thoughts, feelings, values, culture, and perspective. How is your partner "making sense" out of what has happened to him or her? Don't keep hammering at your own ideas; think about how the other person got to the conclusion he or she has arrived at.
- *Look:* Monitor your partner's emotions by observing his or her nonverbal messages. Look for emotional cues in your partner's face; listen for the tone of voice; observe posture and gestures to gauge the intensity of the feelings being expressed. Mentally summarize what emotions you think your partner is experiencing.
- *Listen:* Concentrate on what the other person is saying. Listen both for the details and for the main points the other person is making. Focus on the overall story he or she is telling. Mentally summarize the key ideas your partner is making.
- *Imagine:* Based on your understanding of what your conflict partner has experienced and is feeling, imagine how you would feel if *you* were in your partner's place. True empathy is feeling what your partner is feeling, or at least trying to imagine as best you can the emotions your partner is experiencing.
- *Question:* If you need more information about what your partner has experienced or if there is something you don't understand, gently ask appropriate questions. Don't blast your partner with accusing or negative questions. Just calmly ask for more background information if you need it.
- *Paraphrase:* To confirm your understanding of your partner's point of view, briefly summarize what you think your partner is thinking or feeling. Statements such as "You're upset with me because you believe I lied to you," "You're feeling frustrated," or "You're angry at me" are examples of paraphrasing statements.

No checklist of skills will magically melt tensions resulting from long-standing or entrenched conflict. But trying honestly to understand both a person's position and the emotion behind it is a good beginning to developing understanding. Realize that it will be difficult to stop, look, listen, imagine, question, and paraphrase if both you and your partner are emotionally agitated. In fact, it's likely you won't use a rational approach to managing conflict until emotional outbursts and intense feelings are toned down a bit. Unchecked emotions are a formidable barrier to understanding others or empathizing with another person's feelings.

Often in conflicts you will face balancing your goal against the goal of maintaining the relationship that you have with your partner. Eventually, you may decide that the latter goal is more important than the substantive conflict issue.

Research by Charles Pavitt and Bradley Kemp confirms the significant role of relationships in conflict and negotiation situations.[66] If you're negotiating with someone you like, you will expect your negotiation partner to use more supportive approaches to achieve the goal. Conversely, if you're negotiating with someone you don't like, you will expect that person to use more threats and demands and be more obstinate.

Next, it is useful to identify your partner's goal. In order to manage conflict, you need to know what the other person wants. Use effective listening and responding skills to determine what each of you wants and to verbalize your goals. Obviously, if you both keep your goals hidden, it will be difficult to manage the conflict.

Identify Where Your Goals and Your Partner's Goals Overlap

The authors of the best-selling book *Getting to Yes,* Roger Fisher and William Ury, stress the importance of focusing on shared interests when seeking to manage differences.[67] Armed with an understanding of what you want and what your partner wants, you can then determine whether the goals overlap. In the conflict over whether the window should be open or closed, the goal of both parties is the same: Each wants a good night's sleep. Framing the problem as "How can we achieve our mutual goal?" rather than arguing over whether the window should be up or down moves the discussion to a more productive level.

If you focus on shared interests (common goals) and develop objective, rather than subjective, criteria for the solution, there is hope for finding a resolution that will satisfy both parties.

Manage the Problem

If you can structure conflicts as problems to be solved rather than as battles to be won or lost, you are well on your way to finding strategies to manage the issues that confront you and your partner. Of course, as we have stressed earlier, not all conflicts can be resolved. However, approaching the core of a conflict as a problem to be managed can provide a constructive way of seeking resolution. Structuring a conflict as a problem also helps to manage the emotion and keeps the conversation focused on issues (simple conflict) rather than personalities (ego conflict). The problem-solving structure we suggest here is straightforward: Define the problem, analyze the problem's causes and effects, determine the goals you and your partner seek, generate many possible options, then select the option that best achieves both your goals and your partner's goals.

What conflict management techniques could be used instead of the in-your-face confrontation shown here?

Define the Problem

You can apply all the skills described so far to pursue a proven method for problem solving, which is shown in Table 8.1. First, *define the problem.* Most problems boil down to something you or your conflict partner want more or less of. For example, you may want more time, money, or freedom. Or you may want less interference,

TABLE 8.1 **Solving Problems: One Method of Organizing Problem-Solving Discussions**

1. Define the problem.	Determine the issue you disagree about.
2. Analyze the problem.	Determine the causes, symptoms, effects, and obstacles.
3. Determine the goals.	Determine what you want. Determine what your partner wants. How do the goals overlap?
4. Generate many solutions.	List many options, rather than debating one or two strategies for achieving the goal.
5. Select the best solution, and try it.	Eliminate options that are not mutually agreeable. If possible, take the best idea(s) among those generated to reach an amicable resolution.

control, or criticism. To help you define the problem that is producing the conflict, renew your focus on your own and the other person's goals.[68] What do you want to happen, or not to happen?

Cara and Vaughn have been going together for over a year. Lately, they have been fighting over small issues, so they decide to spend some time talking about what is wrong and trying to understand one another. At the root of their conflicts, they discover, is a basic problem: Cara wants to get married to Vaughn now. Vaughn wants to stay with Cara, but he doesn't want to get married until he feels ready. He also wants to feel financially secure before he marries.

Analyze the Problem

Next, *analyze the problem.* To analyze is to break something down into its components. With your partner, begin by describing the conflict-producing events in chronological order (see page 245). Then decide whether you're facing a pseudoconflict, a simple conflict, or an ego conflict (see pages 226–231). Attempt to ferret out symptoms, effects, and obstacles; decide whether the conflict stems from several sub-problems or from one major issue. As you proceed with your analysis, you and your partner may decide that you need more information to help clarify the issues.

After some discussion, Cara and Vaughn analyze the problem. They realize they come from different family backgrounds and have different expectations about marriage. Cara's folks were high school sweethearts and got married when they were 18. Vaughn's parents are older; they met after each of them had been divorced, and they married after a long, slow-paced relationship. Cara and Vaughn's different frames of reference help explain their feelings about the timing of marriage.

Determine the Goals

BE OTHER-ORIENTED

The next step in managing the problem is to *determine your own and your partner's goals,* following the suggestions on pages 247 and 249. Also, generate objective criteria for a solution (see page 238). The more measurable, verifiable, and objective the criteria, the greater the likelihood that you and your partner will be able to agree when the criteria have been met. Cara and Vaughn decide that, ultimately, they have the same goal: to get married. The issue boils down to timing. So they decide to seek a course of action that will make them both feel secure.

Generate Multiple Solutions

The next step is to *generate multiple solutions.* Simply understanding the issues and the causes, effects, symptoms, and history of a problem will not enable you to manage a conflict. It takes time and creativity to find mutually satisfactory solutions to most problems. It stands to reason that the more solutions you generate, the greater the probability that you can manage the conflict constructively. One way to generate options is through brainstorming. To use brainstorming, try the following suggestions:

1. Make sure the problem and the goals are clear to both of you.
2. Try to suspend judgment and evaluation temporarily; do not censor your thoughts.
3. Specify a certain time period for brainstorming.
4. Consider brainstorming ideas separately before meeting with your partner, or write ideas down before verbalizing solutions.
5. Try to develop at least one unique or far-out idea. You can always tame down wild ideas later.
6. Piggyback your ideas onto those of your partner. Encourage your partner to use or modify your ideas.
7. Write down all the ideas suggested.
8. Review all ideas, noting ways to combine, eliminate, or extend them.

If the goal is to find the best way to manage the difficulty, it may take only one good idea to help move the conflict forward to a constructive resolution.

When they brainstorm, Cara and Vaughn generate the following options: Save money for a year, and then get married; take turns going to college; take turns working to support each other while the other gets a degree; get married now, get jobs, and postpone college; get married now, and take out college loans.

Select the Best Solution

Finally, Cara and Vaughn decide to *select the best solution.* Sometimes, it may take several attempts at defining, analyzing, goal setting, and generating multiple ideas before a mutually agreeable solution emerges. It is always appropriate to recheck your understanding of the issues and goals. Cara and Vaughn decide to combine the best of several ideas. They agree to get engaged, but not to set a date. Instead, they set a financial goal of $5,000 in savings. When they hit that goal, they will set a wedding date. If they are both attending college, they will get part-time jobs so that they have income, and they will also apply for college loans.

If, after repeated attempts, you cannot arrive at a mutually acceptable solution, you may decide to keep trying. Or you may agree to take the issue to an impartial person who can help you identify conflict management strategies and solutions. At work, your immediate superior may be called in to help settle the matter. Or, occasionally, you may agree to disagree and drop it.

The goal of managing conflict is not just to solve a problem, but to help manage relational issues with your partner, especially if your partner thinks he or she has "lost" the conflict. When seeking a solution to interpersonal problems, try to find ways for your partner to "win" while you also achieve your goal. Help your partner save face. The concept of **face,** first introduced in Chapter 2, refers to the self-image or self-respect that you and your partner seek to maintain.[69] Communication researcher Stella Ting-Toomey has conducted studies that emphasize the importance of face-saving or maintaining a positive image, especially in collectivist cultures such as those in Asia, where maintaining face is especially important.[70] How do you help someone save face and avoid embarrassment? Sometimes you can offer genuine forgiveness. Or you can offer explanations that help reframe the differences, perhaps suggesting that it was really just a misunderstanding that led to the disagreement.[71] Such face-restoring comments can help mend bruised egos. Finding ways to be gracious or allow your partner to save face is an important other-oriented approach to dealing with people. After a family feud between a mother and her teenage daughter, Mom might say, "You're right, I should not get so upset. I'm sorry I lost my temper. You're a great daughter." Admitting that you're wrong and offering an affirming, positive expression of support can begin to help heal a rift and help the other person save face.[72]

BE OTHER-ORIENTED

Communicating with Prickly People

Some people just seem to rub us the wrong way. They generate both friction and heat when we're trying to negotiate with them. In his popular book *Getting Past No,* William Ury suggests we try to change face-to-face confrontation into side-by-side problem solving.[73] Here are Ury's tips for managing conflict with difficult people based on his review of negotiation literature:[74]

Go to the Balcony

Going to the balcony is a metaphor for taking a time out. Take a moment to excuse yourself to cool off when someone pushes your hot buttons. Staying on the "main stage" to keep banging out a solution may be counterproductive.

Step to the Side

Rather than continuing to debate and refute every argument, step to the side by just asking questions and listening. Change the dynamic of the relationship from a confrontation to a conversation.

Change the Frame

Rather than rejecting an idea quickly, try to see it in a different way. Reframe by trying to see more than an either/or way of managing the conflict. See it from a third, fourth, or fifth point of view. Change your overall perspective for viewing the conflict by not being you; consider how someone else may view the issue.

Build a Golden Bridge

This is Ury's metaphor for identifying ways to help the other person say yes by saving face. Find an alternative that allows the other person his or her dignity by using objective standards to find a solution.

face. Self-image or self-respect that you and your partner seek to maintain.

Make It Hard to Say No

Use information to educate rather than pummel the other person. As Ury puts it, bring them to their senses, not their knees. Help the other person understand the consequences of what he or she supports and the benefits of your alternatives.

Even though we have presented these conflict management steps as prescriptive suggestions, it is important to remember that *conflict is rarely a linear, step-by-step sequence of events.* These skills are designed to serve as a general framework for collaboratively managing differences. But if your partner does not want to collaborate, your job will be more challenging.

In reality, you don't simply manage your emotions and then move neatly on to developing greater understanding with another person. Sorting out your goals and your partner's goals is not something you do once and then put behind you. It will take time and patience to balance your immediate goal with the goal of maintaining a relationship with your partner. In fact, as you try to manage a conflict, you will more than likely bounce forward and backward from one step to another. The framework we've described gives you an overarching perspective for understanding and actively managing disagreements, but the nature of interpersonal relationships means that you and your partner will respond—sometimes in unpredictable ways—to a variety of cues (psychological, sociological, physical) when communicating. Think of the skills you have learned as options to consider, rather than as hard-and-fast rules to follow in every situation.

Summary

Interpersonal conflict is an expressed struggle that occurs when two people cannot agree on a way to meet their needs or goals. At the root of all conflicts are our individual perspectives, needs, and experiences.

Many people believe myths about conflict, such as conflict should always be avoided, conflict always occurs because of misunderstandings, conflict always occurs because of a poor interpersonal relationship, or conflict can always be resolved. But conflict in interpersonal relationships is inevitable and is not always destructive. It can actually play a constructive role by identifying areas that need attention and transformation.

Conflict can result from misunderstanding someone (pseudoconflict), or it can stem from a simple difference of opinion or viewpoint (simple conflict). Ego conflict occurs when personalities clash; the conflict becomes personal and you may feel a need to defend your self-image.

Although conflict seems to erupt suddenly, it often originates in events that occur long before the conflict manifests itself. It evolves from these prior conditions into frustration awareness, active conflict, solution, and follow-up stages. Understanding conflict as a process also involves recognizing how people seek and are given control over others.

People develop patterns or styles of managing conflict. We identified five conflict management styles in this chapter: (1) avoidance, (2) accommodation, (3) competition, (4) compromise, and (5) collaboration. A person using the avoidance style simply seeks to withdraw from conflict. The accommodation style involves easily giving in to the demands of others. To compete is to dominate the discussion in order to achieve the desired goal, typically at the expense of another person's achieving his or her goal. The compromiser seeks middle ground and is willing to give up something in order to gain something. Finally, the collaborator views conflict as a problem to be solved and seeks a solution that allows all parties to win.

We concluded the chapter by presenting a summary of conflict management skills. Specifically, we addressed how to manage emotions, manage information, manage goals, manage the problem and manage the people. It's usually best to focus on your conflict partners' needs before attempting to resolve the underlying cause of your conflict.

For Discussion and Review

Focus on Critical Thinking

1. Richard has an explosive temper. He consistently receives poor performance evaluations at work because he lashes out at those who disagree with him. What strategies might help him manage his emotional outbursts?
2. Melissa and Jake always seem to end up making personal attacks and calling each other names when they get into a disagreement. What type of conflict are they experiencing when they do this, and how can they avoid it?
3. Analyze the opening dialogue in this chapter. What are Anya and Paolo doing wrong in managing their differences? Are they doing anything right?

Focus on Ethics

4. Is it ethical to mask your true emotions in order to get along with others? Is honesty in a relationship always the best policy? Explain your response.
5. Are certain types of power more ethical to use during a conflict than others? Explain your answer, describing conditions that would justify the use of certain types of power.
6. Are there situations in which you should *not* assert your point of view? Provide an example to support your answer.

Learning with Others

1. Win as Much as You Can[75]

This activity is designed to explore the effects of trust and conflict on communication. You will be paired with a partner. There will be four partner teams working in a cluster.

4 Xs: Lose $1 each
3 Xs: Win $1 each 1 Y: Lose $3
2 Xs: Win $2 each 2 Ys: Lose $2 each
1 X: Win $3 3 Ys: Lose $1 each
4 Ys: Win $1 each

Directions: Your instructor will provide detailed instructions for playing this game. For ten successive rounds, you and your partner will choose either an X or a Y. Your instructor will tell all partner teams to reveal their choices at the same time. Each round's payoff will depend on the decision made by others in your cluster. For example, according to the scoring chart, if all four partner teams choose X for round one of this game, each partner team loses $1. You are to confer with your partner on each round to make a joint decision. Before rounds 5, 8, and 10, your instructor will permit you to confer with the other pairs in your cluster; in these three rounds, what you win or lose will be multiplied by either 3, 5, or 10. Keep track of your choices and winnings on the score sheet on page 255. When you finish the game, compare your cluster's results with those of others. Discuss the factors that affected your balances. There are three rules:

- Do not confer with the other members of your cluster unless you are given specific permission to do so. This applies to nonverbal and verbal communication.
- Each pair must agree on a single choice for each round.
- Make sure that the other members of your cluster do not know your pair's choice until you are instructed to reveal it.

Round	Time Allowed	Confer with	Choice	$ Won	$ Lost	$ Balance	
1	2 min.	Partner	_____	_____	_____	_____	
2	1 min.	Partner	_____	_____	_____	_____	
3	1 min.	Partner	_____	_____	_____	_____	
4	1 min.	Partner	_____	_____	_____	_____	
5	3 min.	Cluster					Bonus Round: Pay × 3
	1 min.	Partner	_____	_____	_____	_____	
6	1 min.	Partner	_____	_____	_____	_____	
7	1 min.	Partner	_____	_____	_____	_____	
8	3 min.	Cluster					Pay × 5
	1 min.	Partner	_____	_____	_____	_____	
9	1 min.	Partner	_____	_____	_____	_____	
10	3 min.	Cluster					Pay × 10
	1 min.	Partner	_____	_____	_____	_____	

2. Statements About Conflict

   Read each statement once, and mark whether you agree (A) or disagree (D) with it. Take five or six minutes to do this.

   _____ 1. Most people find an argument interesting and exciting.

   _____ 2. In most conflicts, someone must win and someone must lose. That's the way conflict is.

   _____ 3. The best way to handle a conflict is simply to let everyone cool off.

   _____ 4. Most people get upset at a person who disagrees with them.

   _____ 5. If people spend enough time together, they will find something to disagree about and will eventually become upset with each other.

   _____ 6. Conflicts can be solved if people just take the time to listen to one another.

   _____ 7. If you disagree with someone, it is usually better to keep quiet than to express your personal opinion.

   _____ 8. To compromise is to take the easy way out of conflict.

   _____ 9. Some people produce more conflict and tension than others. These people should be restricted from working with others.

   After you have marked the preceding statements, break into small groups and try to come to a unanimous opinion about each statement. Especially try to find reasons for differences of opinion. If your group cannot reach a unanimous opinion, you may change the wording in any statement to promote consensus. Assign one group member to observe your group interactions. After your group has attempted to reach consensus, the observer should report how effectively the group used the guidelines suggested in this chapter.

Weblinks

Go to *www.mycommunicationlab.com* (access code required) to find Web resources for your text that supplement the material in Chapter 8, including links to information on the following topics:

Conflict and anger
How to keep conflict from escalating
Arguing Style Test
Negotiation tips and techniques
Asserting yourself during conflict
Emotions and conflict

Part Three

Interpersonal Communication in Relationships

The next four chapters focus specifically on interpersonal communication within the context of relationships. In the previous chapters, you learned about some of the fundamental skills of interpersonal communication; now you will see how these skills can be used to initiate, develop, maintain, and terminate relationships with other people. Chapter 9 explores the nature of relationships, focusing on intimacy, attraction, and power and the nature of our relationships with friends, lovers, and family members. Chapter 10 presents a model of relational development, theories to explain the forces that move you through relationships, and skills and strategies specific to developing relationships. Chapter 11 examines the challenges we face in developing and sustaining relationships, some of the darker aspects of interpersonal communication, and finally, relational de-escalation and termination. Chapter 12 applies interpersonal communication principles and skills to interactions with family, in computer-mediated relationships, and with co-workers.

CHAPTER 9 Understanding Interpersonal Relationships

OBJECTIVES

1. Define an interpersonal relationship.
2. Differentiate between relationships of choice and relationships of circumstance.
3. Differentiate short-term initial attraction from long-term maintenance attraction.
4. Describe the factors that lead to both short-term initial attraction and long-term maintenance attraction.
5. Identify the principles of interpersonal power.
6. Describe the types of power and how to negotiate power in a relationship.
7. Explain how friendships change during our lifetimes.
8. Explain the triangular theory of love, and identify the six types of love.
9. Discuss differences among the relationships found in families.

OUTLINE

You can hardly make a friend in a year, but you can lose one in an hour.

Chinese Proverb

Pat:	Hi, aren't you in my communication course?
Chris:	Oh, yeah, I've seen you across the room.
Pat:	What do you think about the course so far?
Chris:	It's okay, but I feel a little intimidated by some of the class activities.
Pat:	I know what you mean. It gets kind of scary to talk about yourself in front of everyone else.
Chris:	Yeah. Plus some of the stuff you hear. I was paired up with this one student the other day who started talking about being arrested last year on a drug charge. It made me feel uncomfortable.
Pat:	Really? I bet I know who that is. I don't think you have to worry about it.
Chris:	Don't mention that I said anything.
Pat:	It's okay. I know that guy, and he just likes to act big.

This interaction between Pat and Chris illustrates the reciprocal nature of interpersonal communication and interpersonal relationships. The character and quality of interpersonal communication are affected, in turn, by the nature of the interpersonal relationship. The conversation between Pat and Chris begins with a casual acknowledgment but quickly proceeds to a higher level of intimacy. Chris confides in Pat; Pat, an other-oriented listener, offers confirmation and support; this response encourages Chris to confide even more. In this brief encounter, Pat and Chris have laid the groundwork for transforming their casual acquaintanceship into an intimate interpersonal relationship.

In this chapter, we examine the nature of interpersonal relationships, particularly in terms of intimacy, attraction, and power. In addition, we examine the various types of interpersonal relationships.

Interpersonal Relationships Defined

In Chapter 1, we defined a **relationship** as a connection you establish when you communicate with another person. So every time you engage in interpersonal communication, you are in a relationship; but it is only through ongoing, recurring interactions that you develop interpersonal relationships. An **interpersonal relationship** is a perception shared by two people of an ongoing connection that results in the development of relational expectations and varies in interpersonal intimacy. Let's consider the four elements that constitute this definition: shared perception, ongoing connection, relational expectations, and interpersonal intimacy.

Shared Perception

To be in an interpersonal relationship, both individuals must share a perception that they have an ongoing relationship. Sometimes, only one person believes there is a relationship—a belief which, at the extreme, might lead to obsessive behavior or stalking. While each partner might recognize that he or she has a relationship with the other, that doesn't mean the partners think of the relationship in the same way. One difficulty often encountered in relationships is the discrepancy that exists in how each partner sees the relationship. Such discrepancies can be a source of interpersonal conflict and can often necessitate heart-to-heart talks about what each person wants or expects in the relationship. Having a shared perception means interpersonal relationships are transactional; that is, both partners affect each other simultaneously. As a result, a change in one partner has a direct impact on the relationship and on the other person. You've probably had friends who are moody at times (or maybe you're the moody one), and when they are, it affects you and how you talk to them.

Ongoing Connection

The second component of the definition, an ongoing connection, means that the interpersonal relationship is a process. As a process, the relationship is dynamic, constantly changing and evolving. That an interpersonal relationship is a process is most apparent in relational development—the movement of a relationship through a series of stages, each representing different levels of trust, self-disclosure, and intimacy. In the next chapter, specific stages of relational development are identified. Relationships are always moving to a new level and being redefined. As you interact with a person, you share a growing history together; as such, the relationship is cumulative. That history becomes part of the relationship and affects each subsequent interaction. The *Harry Potter* books and films provide good examples of the process nature of relationships. The relationships among the three main characters—Harry, Hermione, and Ron—evolve and change as they share experiences and learn more about each other. Processes are also irreversible—once something is done, it can't be undone (unless by some wizard's magic). For example, you can't un-initiate, or take back, an argument you've had in a relationship. While you can be forgiven, the argument will always have an impact on the partners and the relationship.

relationship. Connection we establish when we communicate with another person.

interpersonal relationship. Perception shared by two people of an ongoing connection that results in the development of relational expectations and varies in interpersonal intimacy.

Relational Expectations

As you continue to interact and develop your relationships, you also form relational expectations. Any time you interact with someone, you bring a set of preformed expectations based on your socialization and experiences; but as you develop an interpersonal relationship, you and your partner establish expectations specific to that relationship. Think about the expectations you have of your friends and that they have of you. For example, you might have a friend with whom you primarily play video games; thus, you know what your time together will be like, how you'll talk, what you'll talk about, etc. These expectations are part of the relationship process and are continually developing and changing. Sometimes, the expectations are violated, which can create turmoil in the relationship (this problem is discussed further in Chapter 11).

In an intimate, trusting relationship, we can feel safe in telling our deepest secrets to another person.

Interpersonal Intimacy

Interpersonal intimacy is the degree to which relational partners mutually confirm and accept each other's sense of self. The closer the relationship, the more you depend on a partner to accept and confirm your sense of self; your partner does the same. Think about the range of interpersonal relationships you have. You should be able to classify them according to how much interpersonal intimacy (confirmation of your self) they provide. Our closest relationships play important roles in helping us confirm our value. And although we depend on them less, even casual relationships confirm our value; we look for others to implicitly (and sometimes explicitly) tell us that they like who we are. As interpersonal intimacy increases, we are more and more able to just be ourselves and still feel accepted. In the most intimate relationships, our partners know our strengths and our weaknesses but still accept us; they love us in spite of our flaws—we reach a point where we don't have to hide our flaws or fear rejection because of those flaws.

interpersonal intimacy. Degree to which relational partners mutually accept and confirm each other's sense of self.

We depend on intimate relationships to provide us with information about ourselves (as exemplified in the Johari window) and to bolster our self-confidence. The more intimate the relationship, the more we depend on others for acceptance and confirmation of our self-image.[1] During periods when we might not have very intimate relationships, it is sometimes hard to maintain a strong positive self-image. Research confirms that having strong social support networks is related to subjective well-being.[2]

Your self-image can only be confirmed when another person really knows who you are. That is one reason some theorists see self-disclosure as the most significant factor in moving people toward intimate relationships.[3] Chapter 2 discussed how self-disclosure is necessary to develop an intimate relationship. Figure 9.1 orders the types of interpersonal relationships according to their relative intimacy.

FIGURE 9.1

Continuum of Interpersonal Intimacy and Relationships

Non-Intimate

Highly Intimate

Stranger ↔ Acquaintance ↔ Casual Friend ↔ Friend ↔ Close Friend ↔ Best Friend/Spouse

Going from being strangers to being best friends involves moving through a number of relational stages that are associated with sharing information about ourselves. (Chapter 10 covers more on relationship stages.) Our communication behaviors and strategies are directly linked to the level of relational intimacy—we communicate differently depending on the level of intimacy in a relationship. Interpersonal communication scholars Denise Solomon and Leanne Knobloch hypothesize that in more intimate relationships, people exhibit direct information-seeking behavior to reduce uncertainties, while those in less intimate relationships exhibit indirect behaviors.[4] For example, if a close friend uncharacteristically began binge drinking, you would ask him or her about it. On the other hand, you would be less inclined to ask an acquaintance so directly about his or her drinking. Solomon and Knobloch also speculate that direct information seeking creates greater clarity and understanding, thus increasing the solidarity of intimate relationships.

We communicate our sense of intimacy to others both directly, through our words, and indirectly, through actions. We might tell another person how we feel about him or her and how much we value the relationship. On the other hand, being open and honest by disclosing highly personal information is an indirect way of expressing interpersonal intimacy. We also might use nonverbal cues, such as close physical proximity, eye contact, tone of voice, touch, and time spent interacting.

Genesis of Interpersonal Relationships: Attraction

Genesis is the coming into being of something. This section addresses how interpersonal relationships come into being and what sustains them. Some relationships come into being because of circumstances, while others come into being because we choose to pursue and develop them.

Relationships of circumstance form not because we choose them, but simply because our lives overlap with others' in some way. Relationships with family members, teachers, classmates, and co-workers fall into this category. In contrast, relationships that we seek out and intentionally develop are **relationships of choice.** These relationships might include those with friends, lovers, spouses, and counselors. As German poet Emmanuel Von Geibel wrote, "It is chance that makes brothers but hearts that make friends."

relationship of circumstance. Interpersonal relationship that exists because of life circumstances (who your family members are, where you work or study, and so on).

relationship of choice. Interpersonal relationship you choose to initiate, maintain, and, perhaps, terminate.

We act and communicate differently in the two types of relationships because the stakes are different. The effect of the same behavior on different relationships can be dramatic. If we act in foolish or inappropriate ways, our friends might end the relationships. If we act the same way within the confines of our family, our relatives may not like us much, but we will still remain family.

Of course, these categories are not mutually exclusive. Relationships of circumstance can also be relationships of choice: Your brother or sister can also be your best friend. You can break off contact with family members or quit your job to sever your relationships with fellow employees. In addition, the other individual can define and redefine the relationship. Your boss might fire you, a relative might cut you off, or a lover might desert you.

In some sense, all relationships begin by circumstance; through circumstance, we become aware of another person. What we learn as a result of circumstance determines if we then establish a relationship of choice and serves as

"Sometimes it's smooth sailing and sometimes they sink. That's why they're called relation*ships!*"

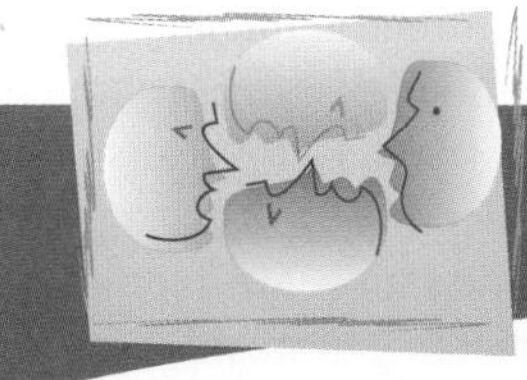

Understanding Diversity

Dating Customs Around the World

The development of relationships varies from culture to culture. The following list describes some dating behaviors from cultures throughout the world.

Afghanistan
Dating is rare because most marriages are arranged by parents, and schools are separate for boys and girls. Opportunities to meet are rare. Girls have a 7 P.M. curfew, whereas boys have an 11 P.M. curfew.

Australia
Most teens go out in large groups and don't pair off until they are 18 or 19 years old. Girls often ask boys out, and pay for the date, too. Couples often go to dinner parties, barbecues, or the beach.

Central and South America
Dating is not allowed until the age of 15. When of age, most boys and girls date in large groups, going out together to weekend dance parties. When not dancing, teens gather at local clubs to eat and talk.

Europe
Dating is usually a group event. In Finland, as many as thirty teens may attend a movie together. Slumber parties are common in Italy and Switzerland, where teens gather for parties at a home and sleep there when the party is over.

In Russian small towns, teens often meet in the streets downtown to socialize together. How does this compare with your experiences?

In Spain, teens join a *pandilla*, a club or a group of friends with the same interests, such as cycling or hiking. Dating is done one-to-one, and both girls and boys ask each other out and split the cost of the evening's entertainment.

In Russia, dates take place at dances or at clubs where teens eat or chat with friends. In small towns, teens meet in the streets downtown or gather around a fountain.

Iran
It is against the law to date. Teens are separated until they are of marrying age; then their families introduce them to each other and sometimes a courtship follows.

Japan and Korea
Most high school students don't date or go to parties, but spend their time studying instead. Dating begins in college, when only boys do the asking and pay for the dates.

Source: "Dating Customs Around the World." http://www.factmonster.com/ipka/A0767654.htm. Infoplease.com, 2003. Pearson Education: http://www.infoplease.com

the basis for our interpersonal attraction toward the other person. **Interpersonal attraction** is the degree to which you want to form or maintain an interpersonal relationship. The attraction that moves relationships of circumstance to relationships of choice differs sometimes from the type of attraction that sustains relationships once they are formed. **Short-term initial attraction** is the degree to which you sense a potential for developing an interpersonal relationship. For example, you might find one of your classmates (relationship of circumstance) to be physically attractive, but never move to introduce yourself. Despite the short-term initial attraction, you might decide

interpersonal attraction. Degree to which you want to form or maintain an interpersonal relationship.

short-term initial attraction. Degree to which you sense a potential for developing an interpersonal relationship.

there is little potential for developing a relationship. On the other hand, as you walk out of the class, you might strike up a conversation with another classmate about an upcoming concert by one of your favorite bands, which happens to be this classmate's favorite as well. You decide it would be fun to go together. Over time, you discover lots of areas of compatibility and attraction that serve as the foundation for a long-term friendship. **Long-term maintenance attraction** is the level of liking or positive feelings that motivate us to maintain or escalate a relationship. Through interpersonal communication, self-disclosure, and continued interactions, we learn information about others that either fosters or diminishes our long-term maintenance attraction to them.

Both types of attraction involve assessing and acting on the potential value of a relationship. We try to determine how promising, viable, and rewarding the relationship might be and continue to make such assessments throughout the course of the relationship. According to communication scholar Michael Sunnafrank's theory of **predicted outcome value (POV)**, we assess the potential for any given relationship to meet our need for self-image confirmation and weigh that potential against the potential costs.[5] We are attracted to others with whom a relationship may yield a high outcome value (the rewards might exceed the costs). Over time, our assessments may change. In the romantic comedy *Two Weeks' Notice*, a liberal activist attorney, played by Sandra Bullock, initially thought that working for the capitalist, played by Hugh Grant, would do little to meet either of their needs. Eventually, the two developed a working relationship that did meet some needs. At a certain point, they both thought the relationship had gone as far as it could. In the end, however, they discovered that they could have a more intimate relationship, with a high outcome value for them both.

Like these film characters, most of us begin predicting outcome values in initial interactions and continually modify our predictions as we learn more about the other person. We pursue attractions beyond the initial interaction stage if we think they can yield positive outcomes, and generally avoid or terminate relationships for which we predict negative outcomes.[6]

Of particular interest is the role interpersonal communication plays in attraction. Attraction and interpersonal communication are interdependent; that is, each affects the other. Short-term initial attraction acts as the impetus to communicate interpersonally—it prompts us to interact with others. The resulting interpersonal communication provides additional information that might contribute to long-term maintenance attraction. While several factors act to increase our likelihood of actually talking to another person, it is what occurs during those interactions that really determines whether we remain attracted to the person.[7]

Factors Leading to Short-Term Initial Attraction

You enter a room filled with people you don't know and proceed to the area where beverages are being served. As you stand there looking around the room, whom do you talk to? Whom do you approach? To whom are you attracted? Two factors particularly affect us in such situations: proximity and physical appearance.

Proximity

You are probably going to start talking to whoever is standing closest to you. As you talk, you develop an impression of your partner, and you assess the interaction's POV—the potential for continuing a pleasant and rewarding conversation. In this way, proximity can lead to the development of interpersonal relationships. For example, you are more likely to form relationships with classmates sitting on either side of you than with someone seated at the opposite end of the room. This is partly because

long-term maintenance attraction. Degree of liking or positive feelings that motivate us to maintain or escalate a relationship.

predicted outcome value (POV). Potential for a relationship to confirm our self-image compared to its potential costs.

physical **proximity** increases communication opportunities. We are more likely to talk, and therefore to feel attracted to, neighbors who live right next door than to those who live down the block. Any circumstance that increases the possibilities for interacting is also likely to increase attraction; proximity has been found to be a more important factor in initial attraction than in maintenance attraction.[8]

In impromptu surveys of students in our classes over the years, we have found that a high percentage form close friendships with dorm roommates who were randomly assigned. There is a good chance that two individuals will become good friends simply because they share living accommodations.

Physical Appearance

As you stand in the room full of people, you are also likely to approach people because of their physical appearance. **Physical appearance**, a form of nonverbal communication, provides us with information that again helps us make some decision about POV. It acts as a filter to reduce relationship possibilities.[9] If everyone in the room was of a different age, culture, or race than your own except for one person ten feet away, whom would you approach for conversation? Similarity with another person creates an attraction because we assume the other person will have values and interests similar to ours. We use physical appearance to make predictions about who is most likely to reciprocate our overtures for conversation—that is, who is most likely to have something in common with us. Whether a relationship escalates depends on what happens in the initial interaction and subsequent interactions.

You have probably found that even if you and another person are of a similar age, culture, or race, you won't continue a relationship if you don't have much else in common. That's one reason physical appearance is not a strong factor for long-term maintenance attraction.[10] However, researchers recently found positive social interactions increased our estimation of others' physical attractiveness.[11] Thus, not only can physical attractiveness lead to interpersonal attraction, it can also be the product of interpersonal attraction.

Sexual attraction also influences interest in forming relationships. At the most basic level, people might seek partners for physical affection and sexual gratification, to meet sexual needs.[12] In short-term sexual relationships, physical appearance tends to be more important than in long-term romantic relationships.[13] However, in the process of meeting sexual needs, people may develop long-term relationships. Indeed, research shows that sexual satisfaction is a significant factor in marital satisfaction.[14] However, sexual attraction by itself is unlikely to serve as a foundation on which to build successful long-term intimate relationships. Research also shows that strong communication is associated with marital satisfaction, regardless of sexual satisfaction, among married couples.[15]

Factors Leading to Both Short-Term Initial Attraction and Long-Term Maintenance Attraction

Some qualities serve both to lead us to initiate interactions and to continue to sustain attraction as the relationship develops. These qualities are generally readily visible on first meeting another person and increase as we gather more information about the other person.

Credibility, Competence, and Intelligence

Credibility, competence, and intelligence are related personal qualities that, in and of themselves, evoke attraction. Most of us are attracted to individuals who seem competent. We like those who are sure of themselves, but not full of themselves. We as-

proximity. Physical nearness to another that promotes communication and thus attraction.

physical appearance. Nonverbal cues that allow us to assess relationship potential (POV).

sume they are competent if they seem skilled, knowledgeable, and experienced. Intelligence/competence is a more important predictor of initial attraction in eventual romantic relationships than in friendships.[16] We find people credible if they display a blend of enthusiasm, trustworthiness, competence, and power.

Self-Disclosure and Reciprocation of Liking

While providing negative or intimate information about ourselves too early might have a negative impact on a developing relationship, a certain amount of openness and self-disclosure increases attraction. Similarly, an open display of attraction or liking for another person can result in a reciprocation of that attraction: We like those who like us. As relationships progress from initiation to intimacy, further openness increases attraction. In one study of newly acquainted men and women who interacted for eight minutes, participants reported favorable reactions to partners' being forthcoming about themselves, with self-disclosure being seen as communicating openness and interest.[17] Another study found that expressiveness and openness were among the most desirable qualities in a partner, regardless of the type of relationship.[18] Self-disclosure has a positive impact on liking between strangers and an even greater impact in more developed relationships.[19] In addition, our attraction to another person increases our tendency to self-disclose.[20]

Reciprocation of liking means that we like those who like us. One way to get other people to reciprocate liking, particularly in romantic relationships, is to show that we like them.[21] In a study in which participants were instructed to display liking, the frequency of their smiles, intensity of gaze, proximity during a conversation, forward leaning, and pitch variations correlated with their partners' reports of social attraction.[22] In another study, pairs of male and female college students interacting for the first time underestimated the amount of attraction that their partners felt after a brief get-acquainted conversation.[23] Perhaps we protect ourselves—"save face"—by assuming the other person doesn't like us as much; it is probably less embarrassing to find out someone likes us more than we thought than to find out we've overestimated how much they like us.

Similarities

In general, we are attracted to people on the basis of **similarity**—we like people whose personality, values, upbringing, personal experiences, attitudes, and interests are similar to ours. We seek them out through shared activities. For example, you may join a folk dance group because you know the members share your interest in dance. Within the group, you would be especially attracted to those who have a similar sense of humor, who share the same attitudes on certain issues, or who enjoy some of the other activities that you do.

Results of a study by communication scholars Leslie Baxter and Lee West indicate that the main reason for placing a positive value on similarity is because it facilitates communication.[24] Similarities give people something in common to talk about, making interactions comfortable and communication effective. Similarities are also viewed as positive because they represent sources of shared fun and pleasure as well as a basis for social and emotional support. However, people also recognize that similarities can have a downside. One of the Marx Brothers comedy team, Groucho, once quipped, "I wouldn't want to belong to any club that would accept me as a member." Besides assailing the club's criteria for membership, Groucho's comment implied he didn't want to be in a club with people like himself. Being stuck with people just like us can be boring and can lead to conflicts (imagine two people who are both assertive and dominating).

reciprocation of liking. Liking those who like us.

similarity. Having comparable personalities, values, upbringing, personal experiences, attitudes, and interests.

Are Your Needs Complementary?

Evaluate your level of interpersonal needs by putting your first initial in the appropriate spot on the rating scale.

1. How much do you like to include others in the activities you do?

   Very little 1——2——3——4——5——6——7——8——9——10 A great deal

2. How much do you like to be included by others when they are involved in activities?

   Very little 1——2——3——4——5——6——7——8——9——10 A great deal

3. How much do you like to take responsibility for decision making?

   Very little 1——2——3——4——5——6——7——8——9——10 A great deal

4. How much do you like to let others make decisions for you?

   Very little 1——2——3——4——5——6——7——8——9——10 A great deal

5. How much do you feel a need to be accepted and loved by others?

   Very little 1——2——3——4——5——6——7——8——9——10 A great deal

6. How much do you feel a need to accept others and to give love to others?

   Very little 1——2——3——4——5——6——7——8——9——10 A great deal

Now think of two close friends. Go back and place their first initials along each rating scale to indicate how much each item applies to them. Or ask your friends to initial the scale for themselves. Compare your ratings with those of your friends. Are there areas where you are similar? Complementary? Are there differences that cause difficulties in the relationship—for example, you both want to make decisions rather than accept others' decisions?

In the initial stages of a relationship, we try to emphasize positive information about ourselves to create a positive and attractive image. We reveal those aspects of ourselves that we believe we have in common with the other person, and the other person does the same.[25] You save your revelations about important attitudes and issues for a later stage in the relational development process.[26] Attitude similarity is more likely to be a source of long-term maintenance attraction than of short-term initial attraction. Similarity of interests and leisure activities appears more important in same-sex friendships than in opposite-sex relationships.[27]

Differences and Complementary Needs

"Vive la différence!" "Opposites attract." "Variety is the spice of life." Such phrases reflect a positive attitude toward differences. One reason we are drawn to people who are different from us is because we learn and grow by such exposure.[28] People who are different from us expose us to new ideas, activities, and perspectives and prompt self-assessment. Differences can also lead to points of conflict and hamper our ability to effectively communicate.[29] Numerous popular books and articles have claimed that inherent differences between men and women interfere with their ability to understand and communicate with each other.

Differences can lead to long-term maintenance attraction when we find a person whose strengths complement our weaknesses. People in a relationship have **complementary needs** when each partner contributes something to the relationship that the other partner needs. As we discussed in Chapter 2, Schutz identified three interpersonal needs that motivate us to form and maintain relationships with others: inclusion, control, and affection.[30] *Inclusion* represents the need to include others in our activities, or to be included in theirs. *Control* represents the need to make decisions and take responsibility, or the willingness to accept others' decision making. *Affection* represents the need to be loved and accepted by others, or the willingness to give love and acceptance to others.

If you have a high need to control and make decisions, and little respect for others' decision making, you will be more compatible with someone who does not have a similar need—instead, you'll be more comfortable with someone who wants others to make decisions. In essence, we can view a pair of individuals as a team in which each person complements the other. If you're not very good at keeping track of your bills and balancing your checkbook, you might pair up with someone who is good at maintaining a budget to create a strong personal finance team. In reality, there are no "perfect" matches, only degrees of compatibility relative to needs.

complementary needs. Needs that match; each partner contributes something to the relationship that the other partner needs.

Recap

Genesis of Interpersonal Relationships: Attraction

Relationship of Circumstance	Interpersonal relationship that develops because of life circumstances
Relationship of Choice	Interpersonal relationship you choose to initiate, maintain, and, perhaps, terminate
Interpersonal Attraction	Degree to which you want to form or maintain an interpersonal relationship
Short-Term Initial Attraction	Degree to which you sense a potential for developing a relationship
Long-Term Maintenance Attraction	Level of liking or positive feelings motivating us to maintain or escalate a relationship
Predicted Outcome Value (POV)	Potential for a relationship to confirm our self-image compared to its potential costs
Factors Leading to Short-Term Initial Attraction	
Proximity	Physical nearness to someone that promotes communication and thus attraction
Physical Appearance	Nonverbal cues that allow us to assess relationship potential (POV)
Factors Leading to Both Short-Term Initial Attraction and Long-Term Maintenance Attraction	
Credibility, Competence, and Intelligence	Personal qualities that, in and of themselves, evoke attraction
Self-Disclosure and Reciprocation of Liking	Openness; attraction toward a person who seems attracted to us
Similarity	Comparable personalities, values, upbringing, personal experiences, attitudes, and interests
Differences and Complementary Needs	Appreciation of diversity; matching needs

Influence in Interpersonal Relationships: Power

As relationships move toward intimacy, partners often struggle with the question of who makes the decisions or with the problem of one partner dominating the other. These are issues of power, and they play a significant role in the development, maintenance, and health of a relationship. **Interpersonal power** is a relative state that is typified by the degree to which a person is able to influence his or her relational partner. As relationships develop, interpersonal interactions reflect changes in the interpersonal power between the partners. The ability of partners to reach a mutually acceptable understanding of their interpersonal power is a determining factor in achieving and maintaining intimate relationships.

Principles of Interpersonal Power

Think about the people with whom you have interpersonal relationships: friends, co-workers, family members, classmates, and teachers. The people in each of these relationships inevitably have some power over you, and you have power over them. Most of us don't like to think that other people have power over us, but interpersonal power is a fundamental element of all our personal relationships. Understanding the following five principles will enable you to more effectively manage power in your day-to-day interactions and ongoing relationships.

1. *Power exists in all interactions and all relationships.* Influence is one of the defining qualities of interpersonal communication presented in Chapter 1. When you talk, you are attempting to exert power over other people, if for no other purpose than to get them to listen to you. Have you ever tried to talk to someone who didn't want to listen? This situation can be frustrating because you are exerting power but meeting resistance; the other person's refusal to listen is an exertion of power against you. Most of the time, our interactions flow fairly easily as the participants share power, taking turns speaking and listening. By definition, being in a relationship means letting someone have some influence on you.
2. *Power primarily derives from an individual's ability to meet another person's needs within a given relationship.* The degree to which one person can satisfy another person's interpersonal needs (for inclusion, control, and affection) and/or other needs (for food, clothing, safety, sex, money) represents the amount of power that person has. In a **dependent relationship**, one person has a greater need for the partner to satisfy his or her needs. One study of heterosexual romantic couples found that the partner with less emotional involvement in the relationship had more power, and this was generally the man.[31] Maybe you've wanted to continue a relationship that lost its value for your partner, and as a result of this power imbalance, you agreed to requests that you normally would have rejected. The more we depend on one person to satisfy our needs, the more power that person has over us. On the other hand, the more people available to meet our needs, the less power any one individual has.
3. *Both partners in an ongoing relationship have some degree of power.* In some relationships, it might appear as though one person has all the power and his or her partner is powerless. You might have felt that imbalance in your relationship with your parents as you were growing up. However, children do have power in their relationships with their parents. Parents want their children's love, they want to protect their children, they want their children to be happy. These

interpersonal power. Degree to which a person is able to influence his or her partner.

dependent relationship. Relationship in which one partner has a greater need for the other to meet his or her needs.

parental wants and needs give children some foundation for influencing their parents.

When two individuals are mutually satisfying each other's needs, they create an **interdependent relationship**; each person in the relationship has a similar amount of power over the other. The more intimate and exclusive a given relationship, the more we turn to that one person to satisfy a broader spectrum of our needs.

4. *Power is circumstantial.* Because our needs change, so does power. As you were growing up, you were very dependent on your parents and other adults. However, as you grew and developed skills, you no longer needed your parents to meet certain needs, and thus their power diminished. This change isn't always without some tension, as parents begin to realize they don't have the degree of control over their children that they used to. One of the authors vividly remembers that sending a young son to his room for "time out" was easy when the son could be carried to his room if he refused to go. However, during the teen years, when the son was as large and strong as his parent, physical power was no longer an option—circumstances had changed. Since power is linked to needs, as those needs change, so will power. Think of how no longer having certain needs resulted in changes in your relationships.

5. *Relational development involves a negotiation of each partner's power.* In developing interpersonal relationships, we decide who will have power over us and what type of power they will have. Your relational partners make similar decisions. In Chapter 10, you will read about the tension that is created in deciding to give up some of your autonomy in order to forge a more intimate relationship. Partners often negotiate which individual will have decision-making responsibility over what issues. The process often involves tension and conflict. The ability to reach a point at which both partners are content with how power is shared in the relationship is one factor that can affect relational success and satisfaction. Relational stability occurs when partners reach agreement about power in their relationship. Unfortunately, even in established relationships, men and women often approach power's impact on decision making differently. One study of such relationships found that women were more satisfied than their male partners with shared decision making because of concerns with overall relationship health; males, unlike females, expressed dissatisfaction when they felt they failed to influence decisions.[32]

interdependent relationship. Relationship in which each person has a similar amount of power over the other.

complementary relationship. Relationship in which power is divided unevenly, with one partner dominating and the other submitting.

symmetric relationship. Relationship in which both partners attempt to have the same level of power.

competitive symmetric relationship. Relationship in which both partners vie for control or dominance of the other.

Types of Power Relationships

In the discussion of attraction, you read about complementary needs; for example, one person who likes to make decisions would make a good partner with another person who likes other people to make decisions for him or her. Complementarity also characterizes relationship power. In **complementary relationships**, one partner usually dominates and the other usually submits: One likes to talk, the other to listen; one likes to lead, the other to follow. You might find such a relationship undesirable for yourself, but for many people such a relationship works to the satisfaction of both partners.

What happens when both partners want to call the shots and make the decisions? In **symmetric relationships**, both partners behave in similar ways.[33] Sometimes both partners want to dominate, and sometimes both want to be submissive. A **competitive symmetric relationship** exists when both partners are vying for control or dominance over the other person. For example, each might try to control which TV program they watch or might insist on participating in every spending decision. Such equality is likely to result in more overt attempts at control than when there is strong discrepancy in power.[34] Competition in such relationships often increases the amount of conflict and negotiation associated with decision making. In some relationships, neither partner wants to take control or make a decision, and this creates a **submissive symmetric relationship**. The following is an example of submissive symmetry (does it sound familiar to you?):

Bea: What movie do you want to rent?

Vic: Oh, I don't care. You decide.

Bea: No, you decide. I don't care either.

Most relationships, however, are neither purely complementary nor purely symmetrical; they are parallel. **Parallel relationships** involve a shifting back and forth of the power between the partners, depending on the situation. For example, if Janene knows more about computers than her husband, Justin, then he might defer to her the decision about what new computer to purchase. However, Janene might defer to her husband to plan their upcoming vacation, because of his experience planning business trips. Establishing who has power in various situations is a point of contention in developing relationships and takes time for the parties involved to resolve. Power in any relationship changes as individuals change.

Who appears to have more power in this interaction? What do you think are the sources of each person's power?

Types of Power

Why does one person in a relationship have power over the other? There are many explanations. One explanation that works well identifies five sources of power: legitimate (or position) power, referent power, expert power, reward power, and coercive power.[35]

Legitimate power is power that is based on respect for a position that a person holds. Teachers, parents, law officers, store managers, and company presidents all have power because of the position they hold relative to other people. When a police officer tells you to pull off to the side of the road, you respond to this enactment of power by obeying the officer's command.

Referent power is power that comes from our attraction to another person, or the charisma a person possesses. We let people we like influence us. We change our behavior to meet their demands or desires because we are attracted to them.

Expert power is based on a person's knowledge and experience. We grant power to those who know more than we do or have some expertise we don't possess. This expertise can even include knowledge about how to manage a relationship effectively. We grant power to partners who have more experience in relationships. In many episodes of the television series *C.S.I.*, the characters often defer to the expertise of their colleagues, depending on the nature of the issue being investigated.

Reward power is based on another person's ability to satisfy your needs. There are obvious rewards, such as money and gifts, but most rewards are more interpersonal in nature. Reward power is probably the most common form of power in interpersonal relationships. Withholding rewards is actually a form of punishment, or what is called *coercive power*.

Coercive power involves the use of sanctions or punishment to influence others. Sanctions include holding back or removing rewards. If you have a high need for physical affection, your partner might withhold that affection if you do not comply with a given request. Punishment involves imposing something on another person that he or she does not want.

submissive symmetric relationship. Relationship in which neither partner wants to take control or make decisions.

parallel relationship. Relationship in which power shifts back and forth between the partners, depending on the situation.

legitimate power. Power that is based on respect for a person's position.

referent power. Power that comes from our attraction to another person, or the charisma a person possesses.

expert power. Power based on a person's knowledge and experience.

reward power. Power based on a person's ability to satisfy our needs.

coercive power. Power based on the use of sanctions or punishments to influence others.

Compliance Gaining: Interpersonal Persuasion

How do you influence those who hold more power than you do? Suppose you don't own a car, but one of your friends does. The two of you are hanging out, and you'd like your friend to drive you to the mall for some shopping. How do you get your friend to take you? While you might have some power you could exert over your friend, you'll probably just try to talk your friend into it—that is, you'll probably use compliance gaining. **Compliance gaining** is actions we take in interpersonal relationships to gain something from our partners—to get others to comply with our goals. Compliance gaining is persuasion in an interpersonal context. We use communication to influence others by developing and applying compliance-gaining/persuasive strategies.

People's level of power affects what compliance-gaining strategies they employ. People with more power can be more efficient in gaining compliance by using simple, more direct (and sometimes inappropriate) strategies while still accomplishing their goals.[36] Those with less power need to carefully consider which strategies they can use that won't result in negative consequences. For example, telling your boss that you want Friday night off or you'll quit might result in your no longer having a job. The appropriateness of compliance gaining varies according our goals.[37] For example, persuasive strategies involving either logic or emotion were seen as more effective in face-to-face interactions than in computer-mediated ones.[38] Communication scholar Kathy Kellerman compiled a list of fifty-six strategies that people might employ in trying to gain compliance (Table 9.1). Think about the last time you sought compliance from a friend, and see if you can identify the strategy or strategies you employed.

Compliance-gaining strategies are responsive to the ongoing, transactive nature of interpersonal relationships.[39] We plot strategies that develop over a number of interactions and modify them in accordance with others' responses. For example, before you ask to borrow money from your friend, you might first do a few favors for her dur-

TABLE 9.1 Compliance-Gaining Strategies[40]

Accuse	Comment	Hint	Protest
Acknowledge	Complain	Inform	Question
Advise	Compliment	Insist	Remark
Apologize	Confess	Insult	Report
Approve	Confirm	Joke	Reprimand
Argue	Criticize	Justify	Request
Ask	Demand	Offer	Ridicule
Assert	Disagree	Order	Suggest
Assure	Disclose	Permit	Summarize
Attack	Excuse	Plead	Tell
Blame	Explain	Point out	Thank
Boast	Forbid	Praise	Threaten
Challenge	Forgive	Prohibit	Vow
Claim	Give	Promise	Warn

compliance gaining. Persuasive actions taken to get others to comply with our goals.

ing the day. Then if your friend says no, you might remind her that she owes you for all you've done for her. If she still says no, you might offer to help her over the weekend with her class project. The type of relationship you have established with the other person will affect your strategy selection. Often, because of our power, we face little resistance from our partners to our requests, so we have no need for any compliance-gaining strategy.

Negotiating Power in Interpersonal Relationships

You decide how much control another person has over you, but the decision is usually the result of weighing the costs of compliance against the costs of noncompliance. Defining who has power can be a source of conflict in interpersonal relationships, potentially bringing about the end of a relationship. When a partner abuses power, then ending the relationship may be warranted. Ideally, partners establish a mutually acceptable and rewarding power relationship.

Assess Needs and Their Fulfillment in Relationships

The first step to negotiating a satisfactory balance of power is to identify your needs and those of your partner. What are you looking for from your relationships? Remember that needs can include everything from financial rewards to confirmation of your self-concept. Your assessment should include both needs that are being satisfied and those that are unsatisfied. Your friendships could be meeting your interpersonal needs but leave unmet your desire to start a family. Unmet needs affect both the development of other relationships and the power that other people have over you. Examine how well a given relationship meets your needs and how well you meet the needs of your relationship partners. The degree to which others satisfy your needs reflects the amount of power those people have. The more needs that are met by one relationship, the more likely you are to sustain that relationship.

You also should strive to understand the needs of those with whom you have relationships. Identifying your best friends' needs helps you to understand what motivates them as well as to appreciate the basis of power that you might have over them. Changes in their needs will also change your ability to influence them.

BE OTHER-ORIENTED

Identify Need-Based Conflicts and Tensions

Examine your interpersonal conflicts for unresolved power issues. For example, in the first year of marriage, couples often argue about balancing job and family, about financial problems (including who spends money and on what), about the frequency of sexual relations, and about the division of household tasks.[41] These problems involve issues of power, control, responsibility, and decision making. Such issues exist in other relationships as well. Examine your relationships for recurring patterns of conflict, and try to determine the role that power is playing. Conflicts can result from unacceptable imbalances of power (the feeling that one or the other partner has too much), from equal amounts of power (with each partner attempting to influence the other), or as a reaction to attempts to exert control or to dominate.

Directly Discuss Power Issues

Everyday conversation helps engaged and married couples work toward equality of power and task responsibilities and ultimately affects their relational satisfaction, and this is likely true of our friendships as well.[42] In some instances, the other person might be unaware that he or she is exerting power over you in a manner you dislike. Simply pointing out this problem might be enough to remedy the situation. On the other hand, you might need to adopt a more active conflict management style. For example, describe the power problem without evaluation, describe your feelings about the power situation, solicit information from your partner in an active and open manner, and engage in a cooperative approach to negotiating power.

Recap: Influence in Interpersonal Relationships: Power

Principles of Power

1. Power exists in all interactions and all relationships.
2. Power primarily derives from an individual's ability to meet another person's needs within a given relationship.
3. Both partners in an ongoing relationship have some degree of power.
4. Power is circumstantial.
5. Relational development involves a negotiation of each partner's power.

Types of Power Relationships	
Complementary relationship	One partner dominates and the other submits
Symmetric relationship	Both partners attempt to have the same level of power
Competitive Symmetric	Both partners want power and control
Submissive Symmetric	Neither partner wants power or control
Parallel relationship	Power shifts back and forth between the partners

Types of Power	**Basis for the Power**
Legitimate power	Power based on respect for the position a person holds
Referent power	Power based on attraction to another person or his or her charisma
Expert power	Power based on a person's knowledge or experience
Reward power	Power based on a person's ability to satisfy our needs
Coercive power	Power based on the use of sanctions or punishment to influence others

Compliance Gaining: Interpersonal Persuasion

1. Actions taken in an interpersonal relationship to gain something from a partner.
2. Strategies are developed and modified in accordance with goals, circumstances, and partners' responses.

Negotiating Power in Interpersonal Relationships

1. Assess needs and need fulfillment in the relationship. What needs do you and your partner have? How well is the relationship meeting those needs?
2. Identify need-based conflicts and tensions. To what degree is power a factor in relational conflicts?
3. Directly discuss power issues. What issues about power need to be discussed?

Relationships with Friends, Lovers, and Family

Friends, lovers, and family represent the three most important types of relationships in our lives. These relationships define our social being, satisfy our interpersonal needs, and are associated with changes during our lifetimes. Friendships provide us with valuable support. In a survey of more than 100,000 men and women, single women rated friends and social life as the most important source of happiness in their lives, while single men rated friends second only to their job duties.[43]

Generally, in relationships between lovers there is a high degree of intimacy and attachment, as well as sexual activity and/or attraction.[44] Historically, marriage was considered the most intimate relationship, rooted in the goal of procreation and forming a family.[45] Today, gay and lesbian relationships also reflect a form of intimate romantic relationship with relational dynamics similar to heterosexual relationships, including marriage and child rearing.

Families include a variety of relationships: between wife and husband, between parents and children, between siblings, and among other relatives. The relationship between spouses is primarily one of choice; other family relationships are more circumstantial. Familial relationships provide nurture and support, affect the development of self-concept, exert lifetime and cross-generational influence, and in general represent complex systems of relationships.[46] In this chapter, you will read about the types of family relationships, and in Chapter 12, you will read about family communication in general.

Friends

Friendship is a relationship that exists over time between people who share a common history.[47] A friend is someone we like and who likes us. We trust our friends. We share good and bad times with them. We want to be with them, and we make time for that purpose.

Here's a list of some of the qualities of friendship identified in a variety of research studies.[48] Which ones match your idea of what makes a friend?

Self-disclosure/feeling free to express intimate information

Openness/honesty/authenticity

Compatibility/similarity

Ego-reinforcement/self-concept support

Acceptance of one's individuality

Respect

Helping behavior

Positive evaluation

Trust

Concern and empathy

We each have our own expectations of friendship that include some of the items from this list, as well as additional qualities. How well a given person meets these expectations is one factor that we use in making a choice about whether to establish a friendship. As we noted earlier, friends represent relationships of choice. Friendship develops naturally into an interdependent relationship that is different from other interpersonal relationships; we have no external constraints that keep us together, such as a job, school, or family, even though we often make friends with people in these situations. Usually, we form friendships with our equals, whereas we often form other types of relationships with people of different ages or social backgrounds.[49]

Besides helping us enjoy a healthy life, friends help us cope with stress and take care of physical needs, and even help in the development of our personality. Friends also help shape our attitudes and beliefs. Especially during periods of change and crisis in our lives, such as adolescence and retirement, friends help us cope with uncertainty and have a profound influence on our behavior.[50]

One of the most important functions that friends perform is to help us manage the mundane. Most friendships are not based on unusual activities. On the contrary, most of us seek out friends just to talk, to share a meal, or enjoy entertainment together.

How many friends do we need? Typically, people have up to five close friends, fifteen other friends, twenty or more members in a social network (which could include family members), and many more people who are simply acquaintances.[51] In all our social interactions, we are happiest when we are in the company of our friends. Perhaps the ancient Roman orator Cicero said it best: A friend multiplies our joys and divides our sorrows.

Friends also perform other functions, such as bolstering our self-esteem. Most of us need people who provide encouragement and tell us that we are decent and likable. It is confirming to have a friend become indignant on our behalf when we have experienced an injustice. Friends can help keep a stream of positive acceptance flowing to counteract the numerous nicks and bruises that our self-worth suffers in the course of daily living.

Friends also provide material help when we need it. When you are away on vacation, you might ask a friend to feed your cat and water your plants. If you run out of gas, you might call a friend to bring you some or pick you up.

Friendships at Different Stages in Life

Establishing intimacy with another person takes time, so most of us have a limited number of intimate relationships. We also have different needs for intimacy at various stages of our lives.

Psychologist Howard Markman and his colleagues found that self-disclosure, one of the most important components of friendship, did not seem to change in either depth or amount from young adulthood through age ninety-one.[52] They did report, however, that as friends get older, they engaged in more negative self-disclosure; apparently, as we age, we are more willing to tell our friends less positive things about ourselves, rather than limiting our disclosures to information that makes us "look good."

Another change that occurs as we age is the development of a more complex view of friendship. Young adults tend to lump "best friends" together, while older adults differentiate among best friends from their youth, best friends from work, best friends to do activities with, and so on.[53] Relationship scholars W. J. Dickens and D. Perlman examined the differences among friendships at four stages in life: childhood, adolescence, adulthood, and old age.[54]

Childhood Friendships At about the age of two, when we start to talk, we begin parallel play with others. As toddlers, we perceive our playmates as people who can help meet our needs. Our first friendships are usually superficial and self-centered. Childhood friendships can be categorized into five sometimes overlapping stages.[55] From ages three to seven, we have *momentary playmates*—we interact with those in our presence. From ages four to nine, our friendships involve *one-way assistance.* We still view friendships from a "take" perspective, as instruments to help meet our needs, rather than from a "give" or "give-and-take" perspective.

The third stage, ages six to twelve, is the *fair-weather friend* stage. There is more give and take in friendships, but the reciprocity occurs when things are going well; the relationship is likely to end if problems and conflicts develop. The fourth stage, ages nine to fifteen, is called *mutual intimacy.* With the closeness that develops, relationships become more possessive. The last stage (beginning at about age twelve and continuing through adulthood) allows for more *independence* in friendships, as well as deepening interdependence with friends that permits greater levels of intimacy and sharing.

Adolescent Friendships During adolescence, beginning with the onset of puberty around age twelve, we move away from relationships with parents and other adults and toward greater intimacy with our peers. During adolescence, peer relationships are the most important social influence on our behavior. We develop cliques of friends and form friendship networks. Boys are more likely to join either socially acceptable groups such as a sports or debate team, or less socially desirable groups bent on violence and destruction of property. Girls are more likely to develop intimate relationships with one or two good friends. During adolescence, boys seem to have more friends, whereas girls appear to develop closer, more intense, and more intimate relationships. Friendship relationships usually peak in late adolescence and early adulthood, before we select a mate.[56]

Among the changes we experience as we move from high school to college or to jobs are changes in our friendships. In a study of these effects, first-year college students completed a survey concerning their best friend from high school in the beginning of the fall term and again at the end of the spring term.[57] By spring, over half of the partners in these relationships were no longer classified as "best friends." The best friendships declined in satisfaction and commitment and increased in costs and investment. Compared to those who did not remain best friends, those who did had best friendships with greater self-disclosure and more interactions, used positive and supportive communication, and experienced less social loneliness. Your own experiences might parallel the findings in this study, and the evolution of your friendships will continue as you move through adulthood.

In our late teens and early twenties, we also expand our social networks not only in terms of the number of friendships we establish but also in the diversity of those relationships.[58] We turn less to parents and more to these relationships for support, though the friendships often become interrelated with our family relationships (friends become like members of the family; you invite friends to join in family activities).[59]

Adult Friendships Adult friendships are among our most valued relationships. Typically, they provide emotional support, partners for activities, and opportunities to socialize.[60] Women friends are more likely than men friends to routinely engage in the communication of sharing, supporting, and venting.[61] Often, neighbors, relatives, or co-workers become our adult friends after we leave college. These sources of friendships mean that many of them are temporary relationships. We move or take a new job and make friends with the new neighbors or new co-workers while the previous friendships usually fade away. In addition, adult friendships are affected by marriage and usually become secondary to the spousal relationship. Marriage usually lessens the likelihood of having cross-sex friendships, so most adult friendships are with people of one's own sex. Sometimes, we are fortunate enough to have special friendships that last throughout our adulthood, despite moving, marriage, or new jobs.

Elderly people may make new friends, but they usually rely most on their spouses and oldest friends to fulfill their need for companionship.

Elderly People and Friendships Although elderly people make new friends, they value old ones most. During retirement, when people have more time for socializing, friendships become increasingly important, but older adults form fewer new friendships. Instead, they tend to maintain a small, highly valued network of friends.

Recap: Friendships at Different Life Stages

Childhood Friendships	Self-focused and often superficial
Adolescent Friendships	Peers influence social behavior. Boys often associate with others in groups, whereas girls develop deep friendships with a smaller circle of friends.
Adult Friendships	Other relationships may change once a person chooses a lifelong mate.
Elderly Friendships	Old friends are valued, and friendship networks often shrink.

Intergenerational, Intercultural, Interracial, and Cross-Sex Friendships

Most of our friendships are with people who are fairly similar to us. Similarity makes it easier to communicate effectively and to reach mutual understanding. The more we differ from other people, the greater the challenges that must be overcome to maintain a relationship, as discussed in Chapter 4. However, both friendships and romantic relationships do develop between people who differ in terms of culture, age, and race. Part of the success of these relationships depends on whether the difference is more superficial than profound. For example, the impact of a ten-year age difference between you and another person is likely to be minimal if you both have the same interests in activities and similar values. However, someone forty years older might have a very different outlook on life from yours. Usually, the older people become, the less impact age differences have on them.[62] A fifteen-year-old's interactions with a thirty-year-old represent a very different kind of relationship than that of a thirty-year-old talking to a forty-five-year-old.

Think about your relationships with people older or younger than you. How do these relationships differ from relationships with people close to your age? How many close relationships do you have with anyone significantly older or younger? Developing and sustaining such relationships often requires special effort. We are probably more likely to have casual intergenerational relationships. One study compared close friendships between peers of similar age and between friends who were at least ten years different in age.[63] The sample included participants who ranged from eighteen to seventy-six. Close relationships with peers, as compared to relationships with those who were of a different age, were seen as providing more companionship, satisfaction, intimacy, and nurturance and as being more likely to continue in the future.

The qualities and expectations associated with being a friend differ among cultures, ethnic groups, and racial groups. You might engage in behavior that you think is appropriate in your friendship with a person from another culture, only to find that you have offended your friend by violating his or her culturally based expectations. In fact, one study that examined the qualities associated with friendship in various ethnic groups in the United States found that "Latinos emphasized relational support, Asian Americans emphasized a caring, positive exchange of ideas, African Americans emphasized respect and acceptance, and Anglo Americans emphasized recognizing the needs of the individual."[64] Realize, of course, that such generalities may not be valid for a particular member of an ethnic group. However, the study also found that in developing interethnic relationships, individuals seemed unaware of cultural or ethnic differences; in essence, they developed a unique relationship defined by their own relational rules rather than by cultural rules.[65] This is similar to the notion of developing a third culture, as discussed in Chapter 4.

Perhaps as you grew up, you had friends of the opposite sex. Adolescents often develop cross-sex friendships that are not romantic in nature.[66] However, the development of male–female friendships between heterosexual adults is sometimes a challenge because of underlying sexual attraction. In the movie *When Harry Met Sally*, Harry proclaims that ". . . men and women can't be friends. The sex part always gets in the way." Fortunately, research and your own experiences might indicate that Harry wasn't totally correct. We can develop cross-sex adult friendships with minimal sexual attraction or redefine romantic relationships as friendships. Heidi Reeder, a communication researcher, conducted two studies on cross-sex relationships: one in which she interviewed twenty pairs of cross-sex friends, and the other in which 231 students completed questionnaires.[67] Both studies found that romantic attraction and physical/sexual attraction diminished as the relationship progressed over time, while friendship attraction increased. While sexual attraction might indeed be an issue within cross-sex relationships, it is reduced when there is a commitment to developing and maintaining the relationship as friends.

Not all cross-sex friendships are devoid of sex; sometimes, individuals develop relationships that are colloquially referred to as "friends with benefits" (FWB). Underlying these relationships is the maintenance of a friendship in which sexual activity occurs. These relationships are distinct from hookups, one-night stands, and/romantic relationships with lovers. Surveys of college students reveal that around half of the respondents have had such a relationship.[68] Reasons for engaging in such a relationship include the avoidance of relational commitment, a desire to engage in sex with a friend, a perception that such relationships are simpler and less problematic than romantic ones, a desire to feel closer to the friend, and finally just a general desire to have a friends-with-benefits experience.[69] Participants in such relationships appear to discuss and establish specific relational maintenance rules, with the most frequent being emotional rules (not falling in love or being jealous) and communication rules (guidelines about honesty, topics, and phone calling).[70] However, the term *friends with benefits* seems to imply that friendships without sex do not have benefits, which misrepresents the values of same- and cross-sex friendships.

Cross-sex friendships can be important relationships because, as with the other relationships that have just been discussed, you can gain insights into how other people think. In this case, your friends can help you better understand the opposite sex. On the basis of interviews with 300 men and women about their cross-sex friendships, psychotherapist and author Lillian Rubin found that the men reported feeling a higher level of intimacy and friendship than their female counterparts (some women were surprised to find out they were even considered a friend).[71] Men seemed to gain more from their friendships with women than women did from men. Men valued their friendships with women for providing more nurturance and intimacy than their male friendships. Women did not feel their male friendships were as intimate or rewarding as their female friendships. However, women did enjoy the masculine interaction style, the fun activities, and learning about the male perspective.

In interacting with people, focus on working toward a mutual understanding and acceptance of what your expectations are for your friendship. There is great value in forming relationships with individuals who are different from you; not only can you learn about other people, but you can also gain a better sense of yourself. Learning how another person's age, race, ethnicity, or sex affects his or her values, thoughts, and behaviors can increase your awareness of how those factors have influenced you.

Applying Theory and Research

Expectations of Same-Sex Friends

How do you know if you have an intimate friendship? Canadian researcher Beverly Fehr has conducted a number of studies that address this question.[72] Her research demonstrates that we hold certain expectations (prototypes) of the kinds of interactions that lead to a sense of intimacy in friendships. She had students and members of the community provide lists of the ways in which a sense of intimacy is created in a friendship. The lists generated were collapsed and combined into common categories (some of which are listed below), and their reliability was demonstrated in follow-up studies. Underlying Dr. Fehr's research is the notion that we use these expected interaction patterns to let us know the level of intimacy we have reached in a relationship; we use them to evaluate the state of a relationship's intimacy. Changes in the number and intensity of our prototype interaction patterns let us know whether we are moving toward or away from intimate friendships. Both men and women respondents saw the lists of interaction patterns as more applicable to female–female friendships than to male–male friendships.

APPLYING the Research to Your Life

The following statements are adapted from the top patterns (prototypes) of relating found in Fehr's study. Think about your relationship with your closest, most intimate friend; a relationship with a more casual friend; and a relationship with a family member. Put 2 on the line if the interaction pattern strongly applies to the relationship, 1 if it sort of applies, and 0 if it doesn't apply.

	Closest Friend	Casual Friend	Family Member
If I need to talk, this person will listen.	_____	_____	_____
If I am in trouble, this person will help me.	_____	_____	_____
If I need this person, he or she will be there for me.	_____	_____	_____
If I have a problem, this person will listen.	_____	_____	_____
If someone is insulting me or saying negative things behind my back, this person will stick up for me.	_____	_____	_____
If I need food, clothing, or a place to stay, this person will provide it.	_____	_____	_____
If I need support, this person will provide it.	_____	_____	_____
No matter who I am or what I do, this person will accept me.	_____	_____	_____
If we have a fight or an argument, we will work it out.	_____	_____	_____
Even if I feel as though no one cares, I know this person does.	_____	_____	_____
If this person upsets me, I am able to let him or her know.	_____	_____	_____
If something good happens to me, this person will be happy for me.	_____	_____	_____
If I do something wrong, this person will forgive me.	_____	_____	_____
If I set a goal, this person will support and encourage me.	_____	_____	_____
If I am lonely, this person will provide companionship.	_____	_____	_____
Totals:	_____	_____	_____

Examine how your relationships differ. Your highest totals should be for your closest friend and, possibly, for the family member.

- In what ways are the relationships similar?
- In what ways are they different?
- Are there patterns of interaction listed that aren't that important to you? Why?
- What patterns of interaction not listed do you expect from your most intimate relationships?
- What patterns of interaction do you wish occurred more in your relationships?
- What can you do to develop those in your current relationships?

Source: Beverly Fehr, "Intimacy Expectations in Same-Sex Friendships: A Prototype Interaction-Pattern Model," *Journal of Personality and Social Psychology*, 86 (2004): 265–84.

Lovers: Romantic Relationships

We use the term *lovers* to describe people who are involved in a romantic relationship. Romantic relationships fill particular needs that differ from those that friendships fill. One pair of researchers suggests that love differs from friendship "in the identity of interest that the partners share. Love exists to the extent that the outcomes enjoyed or suffered by each are enjoyed or suffered by both."[73]

Another key difference between friends and lovers lies in how they talk about their relationship. Friends are less likely to talk about what attracted them to each other. Friends are also less likely to celebrate anniversaries and mark the passage of time in formal ways, such as with a card or a special dinner. Love involves an increase in a sense of "we-ness," of passionate solidarity and identification with the other.

Zick Rubin, a lawyer and social psychologist, attempted to identify differences between love and friendship by developing two scales—one to measure love and the other to measure liking.[74] He found that people do make distinctions between love and liking. Love relationships are more passionate and intimate than friendships, but interestingly, people like their lovers only slightly more than they like their friends. And women make greater distinctions between loving and liking than do men. Love has also been conceptualized as an individual's having a goal to preserve and promote the well-being of a person who is valued.[75] Think about those you love; isn't promoting their well-being an integral part of your relationship?

The closest relationship you develop with another human being will probably be a romantic one. When one research team asked a group of students, "With whom do you have the closest relationship?" 47 percent said it was with a romantic partner.[76] (Thirty-six percent said they were closest to their friends, 14 percent said they were closest to a family member, and 3 percent reported "other.")

Sexual orientation is another factor in how people think about romantic relationships. Romantic relationships can exist between opposite-sex couples as well as same-sex couples. Gay and lesbian romantic relationships share many of the same qualities as heterosexual relationships, though homosexual couples often face the added pressures of social mores, restrictive laws, and condemning attitudes. Conducting research comparing heterosexual and homosexual relationships is difficult, since homosexual couples can't legally marry, except in Massachusetts. Nonetheless, one study found that gay and lesbian couples displayed patterns similar to married heterosexual couples in terms of change in satisfaction over a five-year period.[77] However, same-sex couples were more likely than opposite-sex married couples to end their relationship within those five years, perhaps because of a lack of social acceptance.

The **triangular theory of love** identifies three dimensions that can be used to describe variations in loving relationships: intimacy, commitment, and passion.[78] In this model, intimacy includes such attributes as trust, caring, honesty, supportiveness, understanding, and openness (many of the qualities of intimacy discussed earlier). The second dimension, commitment, includes loyalty, devotion, putting the other first, and needing each other. The final dimension, passion, includes excitement, sexual interest and activity, and extreme longing. Passion has been identified as the most important dimension for developing romantic relationships.[79] Despite controversy over how valid this theory is, research has found relationship satisfaction to be related to variations among the three dimensions.[80] These dimensions provide a valuable way of thinking about how love might manifest itself in relationships. According to the triangular theory of love, the presence and strength of each of these three dimensions varies from relationship to relationship, with each combination defining a style of love.

Sociologist John Alan Lee created a similar scheme that defined six types of love found in both romantic and nonromantic relationships: eros, ludis, storge, mania, pragma, and agape.[81] As you read descriptions of these types, see which best describes the types of love you find in your relationships.

Eros is sexual love based on the pursuit of beauty and pleasure. The physical need for sex brings many couples together. Erotic lovers crave sexual intimacy and passionately seek sexual activity to satisfy their need. Sexual attraction brings special needs and emotions to a relationship, sometimes obscuring other concerns. Shakespeare described this phenomenon when he wrote, "But love is blind, and lovers cannot see the petty folly that themselves commit."

Ludis describes love as a game, something to pass the time. Ludic lovers are not seeking long-term relationships; rather, they seek immediate gratification and to win their partner's affection. Their goal is to be in love and to enjoy their partner rather than to achieve a sexual victory.

Early dating relationships are often of the ludic type. Going on a date to a junior high dance is a casual pleasure, not a prelude to a lifelong commitment. Ludis lasts as long as the couple has fun and finds the relationship mutually satisfying.

Storge is the sort of love found in most friendships and in relationships with siblings and other family members. Sexual consummation is not a factor in this sort of love, although sexual attraction may be present. A storgic relationship usually develops over a long period of time, and it is solid and more resistant to change than erotic love. Trust, caring, and compassion are high; selfishness is low.

Mania describes a love relationship that swings wildly between extreme highs and lows. A manic lover is obsessed with the relationship with the other person. Each of the lovers may have an insatiable need for attention, often fueled by a low self-concept.

Pragma is the root word for *pragmatic.* This kind of relationship works because the partners' personal requirements, personalities, backgrounds, likes, and dislikes are compatible. In some cultures, parents prearrange marriages because of pragmatic concerns, and if the couple is lucky, passion develops later on, as the relationship takes its course.

Agape love is based on a spiritual ideal of love. It involves giving of yourself and expecting nothing in return. This kind of "pure" love may characterize the relationship between a parent and a child, or the relationship between a spiritual leader and his or her followers.

triangular theory of love. Theory that suggests that all loving relationships can be described according to three dimensions: intimacy, commitment, and passion.

eros. Sexual, erotic love based on the pursuit of physical beauty and pleasure.

ludis. Game-playing love based on the enjoyment of another.

storge. Solid love found in friendships and family, based on trust and caring.

mania. Obsessive love driven by mutual needs.

pragma. Practical love based on mutual benefits.

agape. Selfless love based on giving of yourself for others.

Family Relationships

Most of you will get married at some point in your life, and many of you will become parents. Most of you had a relationship with your parents or other adult that greatly influenced your development through childhood. And many of you grew up with at least one younger or older sibling. These relationships are the most common ones that constitute family relationships. One feature you probably recognize about your own family relationships is how they have changed and continue to change. Your current relationships with your parents and siblings are considerably different than when you were a pre-adolescent. Your relationship with your spouse will also change over the course of your marriage, as will your relationships with your own children. All of our family relationships are important to us because, among other things, they affect our self-concept and sense of self-worth.

Research shows that "traditional" married couples are the most satisfied.

Husbands and Wives

You've already read about the nature of intimate and loving relationships, information that obviously applies to married couples. Formal recognition and approval by a culture through the ritual of marriage adds additional meaning and challenges to a relationship. This is one reason some gay and lesbian couples seek the right to marry and thereby gain public and legal recognition of their relationships. Most of us take the commitment of marriage very seriously. When two people enter into marriage, they spend a lot of time defining their roles and working through the trials of cohabitation. The nature of their relationship depends on a variety of factors, such as how they distribute power and make decisions (symmetric, complementary, or parallel) and what roles they each assume. Despite the variety of differences, couples can be classified according to how the partners communicate with one another.

Researcher Mary Anne Fitzpatrick identified four types of married couples found in American society: traditional, independent, separate, and mixed.[82] According to Fitzpatrick, **traditional couples** are interdependent, exhibit a lot of sharing and companionship, follow a daily routine, are not assertive, have conflicts, emphasize stability over spontaneity, and follow traditional community customs (such as the wife taking the husband's last name). **Independent couples** share and exhibit companionship but allow each other individual space; they believe the relationship should not limit their individual freedoms. They are psychologically interdependent but have a hard time matching schedules, and they also engage in conflict. **Separate couples** hold somewhat opposing values; on the one hand, they support traditional marriage and family values; on the other hand, they stress the individual over the couple. They have low interdependence and avoid conflict. This means that by maintaining their autonomy, they display less companionship and sharing than the other couple types, but they still try to keep a daily routine. In each of the preceding three types of married couples, both the wife and the husband share the same perspective about the nature of their relationship. When the husband and the wife have divergent perspectives on their roles, they are a **mixed couple** (the fourth type). There are six possible combinations of the three other types that make up the mixed category:

Husband independent and wife traditional

Husband separate and wife traditional

Husband traditional and wife independent

Husband independent and wife separate

traditional couples. Married partners who are interdependent and who exhibit a lot of sharing and companionship.

independent couples. Married partners who exhibit sharing and companionship and are psychologically interdependent but allow each other individual space.

separate couples. Married partners who support the notion of marriage and family but stress the individual over the couple.

mixed couples. Married couples in which the husband and wife each adopt a different perspective (traditional, independent, separate) on the marriage.

Husband separate and wife independent

Husband traditional and wife separate

Before you decide that the separate style sounds appealing, you should know that research shows traditional couples are the most satisfied, while separate couples are the least.[83] One explanation for this is that traditional partners are the most likely to meet each other's relational expectations.[84]

Parents and Children

A great deal of study has been done on the nature of the interaction between parents and their children. Most studies focus on identifying the most effective ways for parents to communicate with their children or describing the nature of parent–child interactions. And some studies have examined the impact of a parent's communication with the child on the development of the child's communication skills as an adult.

The way your parents interacted with you affects your behavior and attitudes, although the effect is not always straightforward. One study found a correlation between self-reports of mothers' aggressive communication style and those of their college-aged children, but did not find such a relationship between fathers' communication style and those of their children.[85] Another study found that seventh graders' responses were similar to their mothers' views on openness in sharing thoughts and feelings and to their fathers' views on conformity and authority. By the eleventh grade, however, children's views on openness matched those of their fathers, whereas their views on conformity matched those of their mothers.[86] Students' views on sex and alcohol use were not found to correlate with their parents' attitudes, but the more open the communication about sex and alcohol in the family, the more likely students were to engage in safe behavior.[87] (You've probably seen public service announcements on television that reflect this principle, encouraging parents to talk to their kids about tough issues.) The exact effects of your parents' communication style on you, and of yours on your children, are obviously unclear; however, it is clear that there are effects.

Siblings

Making generalizations about communication between siblings is difficult, because so many factors influence the nature of the relationship, most notably the sexes and ages of the siblings. Just as your relationships with your parents change over time, so do your relationships with your siblings. Family communication researcher Patricia Noller notes that warm sibling relationships help us maintain positive self-evaluations. However, differential treatment of children by their parents is likely to undermine warm, supportive sibling relationships.[88] During childhood, sibling rivalry often occurs as children vie for their parents' love or compete with one another. This rivalry can last throughout the siblings' lifetime. Sibling rivalry is only one issue that leads to conflict among children in the same family. However, there is a positive side to sibling relationships. Siblings often provide warmth and support to each other, both as children and as adults. One study found that young adults were more likely to turn to their siblings than to their parents to discuss such things as their dating experiences and life problems.[89] In addition, young adults preferred talking to a same-sex sibling about sexual matters rather than talking to any other family member.[90] The authors of this study found that such disclosures occurred because there was less fear of evoking disappointment or disapproval from a sibling than from a parent.

Often, children's first playmates are their brothers and sisters. Children gain valuable psychosocial skills through interactions with siblings that translate into how they interact with friends and peers. Some learn parenting skills when there is a large age

Becoming Other-Oriented

Intimacy and Power in Relationships

Differences in partners' perceptions of their relationship often spur conflicts. You might see your relationship as more intimate than your partner does and thus behave in a way your partner feels is inappropriate. Your partner might feel more attracted to you than you are to him or her and thus request more of your time than you are willing to give. Although partners' perceptions will always differ, one way to minimize any detrimental impact is to recognize and understand these differences. Being other-oriented can enhance your understanding of your partner's perceptions and thus your understanding of your partner's communication and behaviors.

Two important dimensions examined in this chapter are intimacy/attraction and power. See if you can identify some of the differences in your perceptions and those of some of your relational partners. For each of the two dimensions, put an X at the point on each line that you think represents a partner's perception of the relationship and an O on the line at the point that represents how you see the relationship. After marking each scale, write down one reason that you believe your perceptions differ from those of the other person.

If possible (and if you are comfortable doing so), show your responses to the three people whose perceptions you recorded. Ask them to share with you their actual perception and discuss whether you were accurate or not.

Intimacy

Friend	Very Intimate	______________________	Not at all intimate
Current/Past Romantic Partner	Very Intimate	______________________	Not at all intimate
Father or Mother	Very Intimate	______________________	Not at all intimate

Power

Friend	Partner dominates	______________________	I dominate
Current/Past Romantic Partner	Partner dominates	______________________	I dominate
Father or Mother	Partner dominates	______________________	I dominate

difference between siblings, with the older children playing nurturing roles. In *War of the Worlds*, Robbie provided comfort and protection for his little sister, Rachel. In divorced families such as theirs, the older sibling might be particularly nurturing, though the younger child tends to resent the older sibling's control.[91]

Children without siblings may be somewhat at a disadvantage in that they miss the opportunity to practice and develop certain interpersonal skills. One study of first-through sixth-graders found that only children weren't any different from those with siblings in terms of the number or quality of friends; however, only children were less well liked, more aggressive, and victimized by their peers.[92] The researchers suggest these problems reflect only children's difficulty in managing interpersonal conflict. If you have effective conflict management skills, perhaps they were nurtured as you were forced to work through sibling squabbles in your childhood. How your parents responded to sibling conflicts is also likely to have influenced your conflict management skills as well as your relationships with your siblings.

Summary

An interpersonal relationship can be viewed as a perception shared by two people of an ongoing connection resulting in the development of relational expectations and varying in interpersonal intimacy. Viewing a relationship as a shared perception and an ongoing connection acknowledges that it is constantly changing. The genesis of relationships — how our relationships begin—can be a result of either our circumstances or our choices. Relationships of circumstance occur because surrounding conditions cause you to interact with someone. In contrast, you create relationships of choice when you intentionally seek to establish a relationship you could otherwise avoid.

The degree to which you wish to form or maintain a relationship represents your interpersonal attraction. Our interest in potential relationships reflects short-term initial attraction that might lead to escalating or sustaining a relationship through the development of long-term maintenance attraction. Factors that contribute to short-term initial attraction include proximity, which increases communication, and physical appearance, including sexual attraction. Some factors contribute to both short-term and long-term attraction, including the credibility, competence, and intelligence of the other person; being open and self-disclosing, which contributes to reciprocation of liking; similarities; and differences, or complementary needs.

Your ability to influence your partner—interpersonal power—is an important factor in the development and success of relationships. Power exists in all interactions and relationships, derives from individuals' needs, is possessed by both partners, is circumstantial, and is negotiated in the relationship. The pattern of power in relationships can be complementary (one partner dominates and the other submits), symmetrical (both have the same amount of power, which is competitive when both are strong or submissive when both are weak), or parallel (changing from situation to situation).

Five specific sources of power include legitimate power (associated with a position); referent power (attraction to the other person); expert power (based on knowledge and experience); reward power (ability to satisfy needs); and coercive power (ability to punish or withhold rewards). There are also a variety of compliance-gaining strategies we can use to persuade other people. Power is negotiated by first assessing needs and how a relationship meets those needs, identifying how power affects interpersonal conflicts, and, finally, discussing power issues directly.

Relationships with friends, lovers, and family represent the most important interpersonal relationships we experience. Friends (people we like and who like us) play an important part in our lives by providing support, helping us manage the mundane and cope with stress, shaping our personality, and providing material help. Our friendships change as we move from childhood through adolescence to adulthood and then to old age. A variety of factors influence our friendships with those who differ from us in age, sex, culture, race, and ethnicity. These relationships require a special sensitivity to how the differences affect our partners and these relationships.

Romantic relationships differ from friendships because lovers expect more, talk more about the relationship, and are more passionate, more intimate, and more committed. Our relationships with lovers vary according to three dimensions (passion, intimacy, and commitment) that make up the triangular theory of love. Love can be categorized as eros, ludis, storge, mania, pragma, or agape.

Communication among family members includes interactions between husbands and wives, between parents and their children, and among siblings. Married couples can be categorized as traditional (being interdependent, sharing, and compassionate), independent (allowing for individual space but exhibiting sharing and compassion), separate (supporting marriage but putting the individual above the couple), or mixed (displaying different styles). The way parents interact with their children strongly affects the development of their children's interpersonal communication skills. As children grow up, their relationships with their parents often change a great deal. The communication skills covered in this text are as applicable to parents dealing with children as they are to any relationship. Siblings often support each other by discussing such issues as dating or negative experiences without having to worry about disapproval or disappointment (which their parents might display in discussing such matters).

For Discussion and Review

Focus on Critical Thinking

1. Imagine that you wanted to increase an acquaintance's attraction to you. Formulate strategies to accomplish this using each of the elements that contribute to attraction described in the chapter.
2. Under what circumstances is the exercise of power in a relationship appropriate? Inappropriate?
3. How do your friendships with same-age friends differ from friendships you have with anyone substantially older or younger than you?

4. What types of love are most likely to characterize the different types of relationships found in a family?

Focus on Ethics

5. Under what circumstances is it appropriate for a person to use the power he or she has over another person to satisfy personal goals?
6. Under what conditions is it ethical or unethical to seek an intimate relationship with (a) a co-worker, (b) a subordinate, or (c) a supervisor you feel attracted to?
7. What ethical responsibilities do you have toward a person you consider your best friend?

Learning with Others

1. Create two lists of names: people you regard as casual friends and those you regard as close friends. Identify what attracts you to the people on your list. Compare your ideas of what attracts you to casual friends and close friends with the ideas of other students. How does your list fit with the categories of attraction identified in the text? What's different? What's the same?
2. Write down all the qualities you can think of that you associate with someone you would call your "friend." Now write down the qualities you associate with someone you would call your "lover." Get together in groups of four or five students, and compare your lists. What qualities have you listed that nobody else has? Why do you think you included that quality in your list? What qualities did everyone in the group list? To what degree are the qualities defined by your culture? In what way are the qualities for friends the same as for lovers? In what ways are they different?
3. Some people develop relationships of choice with their family members. In groups of five or six, identify someone who has developed such a relationship with (a) a sibling, (b) a parent, and (c) another relative. Discuss why some students have developed friendships with these family members and why other students have not. Explore how these relationships are likely to change over the next ten to twenty years.

Weblinks

Go to *www.mycommunicationlab.com* (access code required) to find Web resources for your text that supplement the material in Chapter 9, including links to information on the following topics:

Soulmates
Relationship quizzes
Cultural differences in marriage practices
Love texts
Friendship test

CHAPTER 10

Developing Interpersonal Relationships

OBJECTIVES

1. Explain the stages of relational escalation.
2. Explain the stages of relational de-escalation, and define post-intimacy relationships.
3. Describe two theories that explain how relationships develop.
4. Describe the skills and strategies used primarily to initiate a relationship.
5. Describe the skills and strategies used in both initiating and escalating relationships.
6. Describe the skills and strategies used in escalating and maintaining relationships.

OUTLINE

You can't stay in your corner of the forest waiting for others to come to you. You have to go to them sometimes.

Winnie-the-Pooh

Scenario 1: Josh and Nona are strangers standing at a bus stop.

Josh: Hi. I noticed your T-shirt says Michigan Tech. Are you a student there?

Nona: Huh, oh, no, I picked this up at a T-shirt clearance sale. I just thought it looked cool—I liked the husky on it. Are you from Michigan Tech?

Josh: My family used to vacation near there, and we've visited the campus.

Nona: Where exactly is it?

Josh: It's in Houghton, Michigan, which is way up in northern Michigan. Have you ever been in northern Michigan?

Nona: No, but I've been in lower Michigan. I went skiing there once with some friends from school.

Scenario 2: Several months later:

Nona: Hey, Josh, I was thinking that maybe you'd like to go home with me over break and meet my family and friends. How about it?

Josh: Wow. It's really nice that you'd like me to meet your family and all, but I really don't think I'd be very comfortable doing that.

Nona: Oh. Okay, I guess. I just wanted them to meet you, but if you don't want to . . . .

Josh: Don't be angry. I just think it's a little early for us to be meeting each other's families. Maybe we can make the trip another time.

Scenario 3: A couple of months after that:

Josh: Nona, where do you want to go to eat?

Nona: I'm not really up for going out, but you go ahead. I'll see you tomorrow.

Josh: What's wrong?

Nona: I don't know, Josh. I'm just feeling the need to cool things in our relationship right now. I think I just need something different from a relationship.

Josh: Oh. I'm sorry if I haven't been able to give you what you want. I guess I've been feeling a little distant in our relationship too.

Nona: I do like you, Josh, and I really value your friendship. You've really become like a big brother to me.

The three scenarios that start this chapter provide a snapshot of how communication changes as relationships develop. In the first scenario, Josh and Nona are following a getting-acquainted ritual and sharing safe information as they initiate a relationship. The communication in scenario 2 is much more relaxed and personal, reflecting an interaction between two individuals who have gotten to know each other well. In the final scenario, the communication signals problems in the relationship that lead Josh and Nona to discuss a de-escalation of the relationship. These snapshots reflect some of the stages that people experience as their relationships move toward and away from intimacy. While Josh and Nona's relationship is a romantically intimate one, remember that the term *intimacy* is not used in this book to refer to sexual activity but rather to describe any close relationship in which each partner confirms the other's sense of self.

This chapter begins with a model and description of the typical stages through which interpersonal relationships progress. Next, we discuss two theories that offer explanations of why we move from one stage to another. Finally, the chapter presents three sets of skills and strategies for initiating, escalating, and maintaining interpersonal relationships.

Stages of Interpersonal Relationships

Although researchers use different terms and different numbers of stages, all agree that **relational development** does proceed in discernible stages. The stage we are in affects our interpersonal communication, and our interpersonal communication is the tool we use to move ourselves from stage to stage. Individuals in an intimate stage discuss topics and display nonverbal behaviors that do not appear in the early stages of a relationship. Outsiders usually can tell what stage a relationship is in by observing the interpersonal communication.

You can think of the stages, from first meeting to intimacy, as the floors in a high-rise building. Relational development is like an elevator that stops at every floor. As you get to each floor, you might get off and wander around for a while before taking the elevator to the next floor (see Figure 10.1). Each time you get on, you don't know how many floors up the elevator will take you, or how long you will stay at any given floor. In fact, sometimes you never get back on the elevator, electing instead to stay at a particular stage of relational development. But sometimes we move quickly from floor to floor toward intimacy. Part of the time, you share this elevator with your partner, and the two of you make decisions about how far up you will go on the elevator, how long to stay at each floor, and when and whether to ride the elevator down.

relational development. Movement of a relationship from one stage to another, either toward or away from greater intimacy.

turning point. Specific event or interaction associated with positive or negative changes in a relationship.

Just as there are lights on a panel to let you know the elevator has moved from one floor to another, markers, or turning points, signal a move from one stage to another in a relationship. **Turning points** are specific events or interactions that are associated with positive or negative changes in a relationship.[1] A first meeting, first date, first road

Types of Relationships	Escalation Stages	De-Escalation Stages
Best friend/ Lover/ Spouse	Intimacy	Turmoil or Stagnation
Close friend	Intensification	Deintensification
Friend	Exploration	Individualization
Acquaintance	Acquaintance	Separation
Stranger	Preinteraction Awareness	Postseparation Effects

FIGURE **10.1**

Model of Relational Development

trip together, first sex, saying "I love you" for the first time, meeting a partner's family, making up after a conflict, becoming roommates, providing help in a crisis, or providing a favor or gift might all be turning points that indicate a relationship is moving forward. One pair of researchers found that 55 percent of the time, these turning points inspired a discussion about the nature of the relationship.[2] Such discussion helps the partners reach mutual agreement about the definition of the relationship.

Turning points can be divided into two types. **Causal turning points** are events that directly affect the relationship. Finding out that your friend has told you a significant lie might cause you to terminate the relationship. Because the event causes a change in the relationship, it is a causal turning point. On the other hand, receiving and accepting an invitation from a friend to visit his or her family for the first time is a **reflective turning point**, because it signals that a change has occurred in the definition of the relationship. The invitation and acceptance don't cause a change, but reflect a change in how you and your friend perceive the relationship.

causal turning point. Event that brings about a change in a relationship.

reflective turning point. Event that signals that a change has occurred in the way a relationship is defined.

Relational Escalation

Relational escalation is the movement of a relationship toward greater intimacy. This movement usually goes through a series of discernible stages: preinteraction awareness, acquaintance, exploration, intensification, and intimacy. Movement from one stage to another represents an increase in the amount of intimacy between two people. Each stage is accompanied by specific communication patterns, turning points, and relational expectations.

Preinteraction Awareness

As you can see in the model in Figure 10.1, the first floor is the *preinteraction awareness stage.* At this stage, you might observe someone or even talk with others about him or her without having any direct interaction. Gaining information about others without directly interacting with them is a *passive strategy.*[3] Through your passive observations, you form an initial impression. You might not move beyond the preinteraction awareness stage if that impression is not favorable or the circumstances aren't right.

Acquaintance

On the basis of the impression you formed in the preinteraction awareness stage, you might decide to interact with the other person. Or, when circumstances lead immediately to interaction, you might not even experience the preinteraction awareness stage. In either case, the very first interaction is a turning point that begins the *acquaintance stage,* in which conversations stick to safe and superficial topics and you present a "public self" to the other person. There are actually two sub-stages in the acquaintance stage: introductions and casual banter. In the **introductions** sub-stage, we tell each other our names and share basic demographic information—where we're from, what we do, etc. In this sub-stage, the interaction typically is routine—partners usually spend the first four minutes asking each other various standard questions.[4] Except for those of us who are forgetful or who don't pay attention, we only introduce ourselves to another person once. Once we have made his or her acquaintance, we can interact without having to introduce ourselves again. There are times when attempts at introductions are declined, and the other person never joins you on the elevator to the acquaintance floor.

When you do move past introductions, you move into the sub-stage of **casual banter**, talking about impersonal topics with little or no self-disclosure. Casual banter can occur in the same interaction as the introductions sub-stage if you continue interacting long enough. You've probably experienced this in classrooms many times, as you make the acquaintance of a classmate sitting next to you and you move from introductions to talking about lots of casual topics, but sharing very limited personal information. Subsequent interactions in the acquaintance stage involve continuing casual banter—discussing the weather, current events, daily news, or some common experience (what happened in class today, how the company picnic went, etc.). Many of our relationships never move beyond this stage.

Exploration

If you decide to go to the next floor, *exploration,* you will begin to share more in-depth information about yourselves. But you will have little physical contact, maintain your social distance, and limit the amount of time you spend together. This stage can occur in conjunction with the initiation stage. During this stage, communication becomes easier, and a large amount of low-risk disclosure occurs.

Intensification

If you proceed to the *intensification stage,* you will start to depend on each other for self-confirmation and engage in more risky self-disclosure. You will spend more time

relational escalation. Movement of a relationship toward intimacy through five stages: preinteraction awareness, acquaintance, exploration, intensification, and intimacy.

introductions. Sub-stage of the acquaintance stage of relationship development, in which interaction is routine, and basic information is shared.

casual banter. Sub-stage of the acquaintance stage of relationship development, in which impersonal topics are discussed but very limited personal information is shared.

As couples proceed from exploration to intensification, they have more physical contact and begin sharing more activities and confidences.

together, increase the vari ... pt a more personal physical distance, engage in more phy ... ze your language. Also, you may discuss and redefine the re ... this stage, perhaps putting a turning-point label on yourselves, su ... going steady," "good buddies," or "best friends." Other turning points associated with this stage include decisions to date each other exclusively, to become roommates, or to spend time with each other's families.

Intimacy

The "top floor" in the relational high-rise is the *intimacy stage.* In this stage, the two partners turn to each other for confirmation and acceptance of their self-concepts. Their communication is highly personalized and synchronized. They talk about anything and everything. There is a free flow of information and intimate self-disclosure. There is a commitment to maintaining the relationship that might even be formalized through marriage or some other agreement. The partners share an understanding of each other's language and nonverbal cues and have a great deal of physical contact. They use fewer words to communicate effectively, and they have a clearer definition of their roles and of the relationship. Reaching this stage takes time—time to build trust, time to share personal information, time to observe each other in various situations, and time to build a commitment and an emotional bond.

Relational De-Escalation

Relational de-escalation is the movement that occurs when a relationship decreases in intimacy. Our model identifies five stages in this process: turmoil or stagnation, deintensification, individualization, separation, and post-separation. These stages can be observed when an intimate relationship becomes less so or comes to an end. The process of ending a relationship is not as simple as going down the same elevator you came up on: It is not a reversal of the relationship formation process. Relational de-escalation can also involve only one or two of the stages. For example, a relationship might move from being one between good friends to a more casual

relational de-escalation. Movement of a relationship away from intimacy through five stages: turmoil or stagnation, deintensification, individualization, separation, and post-separation.

Graphing Your Relationship Changes

Think of an interpersonal relationship that you have had for at least a year. On the graph at right, plot the development of that relationship from stage to stage, reflecting the relative amount of time you spent in each stage. You can also indicate whether you backed up to a previous stage at any point.

If possible, have your relational partner fill out a similar graph, and compare your perceptions of how the relationship has developed. What differences are there and why?

You also might want to share your graph with those of classmates to compare how different relationships develop. What can you tell from the graphs about the nature of their relationships?

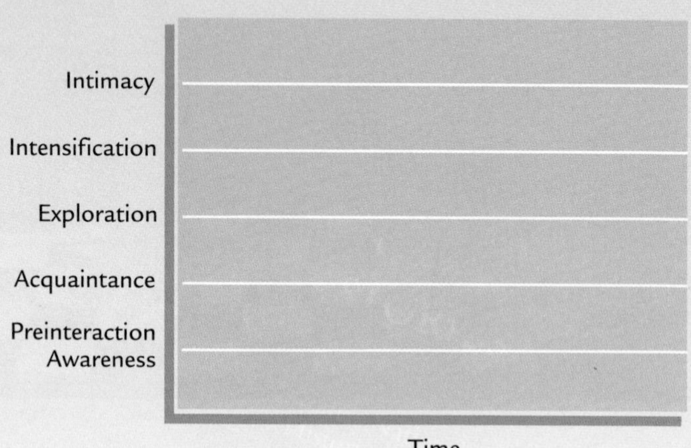

friendship.[5] A **post-intimacy relationship** occurs when partners de-escalate from the intimate stage but still maintain a relationship. A couple might decide they like each other as friends but no longer want a romantic or exclusive relationship; thus, they de-escalate and maintain the relationship at the intensification or exploratory stage.

Turmoil or Stagnation

When an intimate relationship is not going well, it usually enters the stage of either *turmoil* or *stagnation.* Turmoil involves an increase in conflict, as one or both partners tend to find more faults in the other. The definition of the relationship seems to lose its clarity, and mutual acceptance declines. The communication climate is tense, and exchanges are difficult.

Stagnation occurs when the relationship loses its vitality and the partners become complacent. Communication and physical contact between the partners decrease; they spend less time together, but do not necessarily fight. Partners in a stagnating relationship tend to go through the motions of an intimate relationship without the commitment; they simply follow their established relational routines.

As with the up elevator, individuals can stop at this point on the down elevator and decide to quit descending. The relationship can remain in turmoil or stagnate for a long time, or the individuals can repair, redefine, or revitalize the relationship and return to intimacy.

post-intimacy relationship. Formerly intimate relationship that is maintained at a less intimate stage.

Deintensification

If the turmoil or stagnation continues, however, the individuals might move to the *deintensification stage,* decreasing their interactions; increasing their physical, emotional, and psychological distance; and decreasing their dependence on the other for self-confirmation. They might discuss the definition of their relationship, question its future, and assess each partner's level of satisfaction or dissatisfaction. The relationship can be repaired and the individuals can move back to intensification and intimacy, but that is more difficult to accomplish at this stage.

Individualization

On the next floor down, the *individualization stage,* the partners tend to define their lives more as individuals and less as a couple. Neither views the other as a partner or significant other anymore. Interactions are limited. The perspective changes from "we" and "us" to "you" and "me," and property is defined in terms of "mine" or "yours" rather than "ours." Both partners turn to others for confirmation of their self-concepts.

Separation

In the *separation stage,* individuals make an intentional decision to eliminate or minimize further interpersonal interaction. If they share custody of children, attend mutual family gatherings, or work in the same office, the nature of their interactions will change. They will divide property, resources, and friends. Early interactions in this stage are often tense and difficult, especially if the relationship has been intimate. For relationships that never went beyond exploration or intensification, however, the negotiation is often relatively painless.

For former intimates, one of the awkward things about separating is their extensive personal knowledge about one another. Their talk is limited to superficial things, although they still know a lot about each other. This tends to make the interactions fairly uncomfortable. Over time, of course, each partner knows less about who the other person has become. For example, even after spending just a few years away from your high school friends, you might have difficulty interacting with them because your knowledge of one another is out of date.

Post-Separation Effects

Although interaction may cease altogether, the effect of the relationship is not over. The relational-stages high-rise is like something out of the old TV series *Twilight Zone:* Once you enter it, you can never leave it. The bottom floor on the down elevator, where you remain, is the *post-separation stage.* This floor represents the lasting effects the relationship has on your self and, therefore, on your other interactions and relationships. Noted relationship scholar Steve Duck claims that in this final stage of terminating relationships, we engage in "grave-dressing."[6] We create a public statement for people who ask why we broke up and also come to grips with losing the relationship. Sometimes, our sense of self gets battered during the final stages of a relationship, and we have to work hard to regain a healthy sense of self.

Of course, we are all aware of people who hop on an express elevator to get out of a relationship, bypassing all the normal stages of decline. One study found that of the various ways to terminate a relationship, abandoned partners most dislike the quick exit without discussion.[7]

Theories of Interpersonal Relationship Development

The model of relational stages provides a description of the stages you can expect to experience as you move through interpersonal relationships. However, it doesn't really provide an explanation of what motivates people to move from one stage to another. Think about some of your closer relationships. How did you move from being acquaintances to being close friends? The earlier description of attraction theories provides a partial answer to this question by offering explanations of what evokes your interest in another person. However, the theories don't adequately explain why you might stay at one stage, back down from a stage, or move forward to the next. Steve Duck suggests we go through a process of **filtering,** by which we reduce the number of partners at each stage of relational development by applying selection criteria that a potential close friend must meet.[8] In essence, a move from one stage to another toward intimacy means that a person has passed through another, finer screen or filter. These screens represent decision points in which we make some assessment of the relationship and decide how we want to proceed. We can choose to either escalate, maintain, or de-escalate the relationship. Two theories reflect the kind of decision making that might be taking place: social exchange theory and dialectical theory (or dialectics).

Social Exchange Theory

Social exchange theory is an economic model of human behavior, that has been used to explain how people arrive at decisions in a variety of situations. **Social exchange theory** posits that people seek the greatest amount of reward with the least amount of cost.[9] You've probably been in a difficult relationship where you have asked yourself, "Is this relationship really worth it?" What you are asking is whether the rewards you are gaining from the relationship are worth the trouble or expense necessary to sustain the relationship (the costs). Students frequently tell us about breaking up from long-distance relationships because the expense (driving time, telephone calls, missing activities where they live, and so on) ends up being greater than the rewards of the intermittent contact. For others, the rewards associated with long-distance relationships remain greater than the costs, and those relationships continue to prosper.

Immediate and Forecasted Rewards and Costs

Relationships can be evaluated in terms of immediate, forecasted, and cumulative rewards and costs.[10] **Immediate rewards and costs** occur in a relationship in the present moment. You can think about your current relationships and assess their present value. **Forecasted rewards and costs** are based on projection or prediction. We make guesses about the potential of a relationship or its future outlook (what communication scholar Michael Sunnafrank calls its *predicted outcome value*).[11] When you meet someone, you go through an initial assessment about whether a relationship with this person would be rewarding. You use forecasting to decide whether to remain in existing relationships during troubled times (when costs escalate or rewards deteriorate). However, you don't immediately abandon long-term relationships at the first sign of trouble (low immediate rewards/high immediate costs) if you believe that things will improve (forecasted rewards).

Cumulative Rewards and Costs

Another reason people remain in relationships during periods of low immediate rewards has to do with cumulative rewards and costs. **Cumulative rewards and costs** represent the total rewards and costs accrued over the duration of the relationship. Just as when you have more income than expenses, you put your extra money in savings, so you build up a relational savings account of the extra rewards. You can draw on that savings account during times when the relationship is not paying off well. You hold on to a relationship because you have invested a lot in it and have gotten a lot out of it. However, just as your savings account can run out of money, cumulative rewards can lose value, and at that point you might decide to terminate the relationship.

filtering. Process of reducing partners moving to each stage by applying selection criteria.

social exchange theory. Theory that claims people make relationship decisions by assessing and comparing the costs and rewards.

immediate rewards and costs. Rewards and costs that are associated with a relationship at the present moment.

forecasted rewards and costs. Rewards and costs that an individual assumes will occur, based on projection and prediction.

cumulative rewards and costs. Total rewards and costs accrued during a relationship.

Magnitude and Ratio

You can also consider rewards and costs in terms of their magnitude and ratio. Suppose you have two friends, Kelsey and Moira. Kelsey makes you feel good about yourself (+1) is helpful (+2) and is lots of fun (+3) (rewards) but she is very needy (−1) and demanding (−2) (costs). Moira is lots of fun (+1) and helpful (+2), but she is also needy (−1). Which friendship would you pursue more? You might be inclined to pursue the relationship with Kelsey, because she is helpful, fun, and makes you feel good, whereas Moira is only helpful and fun. The magnitude of the rewards from the relationship with Kelsey is greater than that of the rewards of the relationship with Moira. However, you might pursue a relationship with Moira because that relationship has a better ratio of rewards to costs (two rewards to one cost, compared to Kelsey's three rewards to two costs). You might think that further developing a relationship with Moira might result in increased rewards with the same costs. However, at some point relationships seem to achieve a maximum return for the investment—that is, a point where no matter how much you invest, either the reward does not increase further or the costs increase significantly. Suppose your only shared interest with Moira is movies. Once a week, you spend some very satisfying time together, seeing and talking over a new film. You decide to spend more time with her (cost) and find awkward dead spots in the conversation because there isn't really anything else of mutual interest to talk about (reward). In terms of your relationship with Moira, this means that having fun with her and getting her help is the only reward you will gain, regardless of how much you invest in the relationship. Finding that point where you maximize your rewards while minimizing costs is one challenge of relational development.

Expected Rewards and Costs

People seem to construct templates in their minds for what relationships should be like. **Expected rewards and costs** represent expectations and ideals about how rewarding a relationship should be relative to its costs. We have a mental model of the ideal friend, the ideal lover, the ideal co-worker, and so on. We use the expected costs and rewards associated with these ideals to assess current relationships. We might abandon a relationship if we don't think it matches or has the potential to match our ideal. In essence, we set standards or criteria for our relationships by which we assess the desirability of a given relationship. Like Duck's filtering process, ideal images allow you to sort through relationships and focus on those that come closest to or exceed your ideal. The major difficulty associated with such comparisons rests in setting reasonable standards or ideals. For example, some parents adopt a philosophy of never arguing in front of their children. As the children become adults, they may have an expectation that happy marriages are ones without conflicts, and thus they may evaluate their own marriages as unsuccessful because they do not achieve this ideal. If you find that you are continually unable to find relationships that measure up to your ideals, you may need to reassess your standards.

Finally, we compare our current relationships to the rewards and costs we forecast for other potential relationships. We reduce our time spent with one friend when we believe we can have a more rewarding relationship with another person. Communication researchers Gerald Miller and Malcolm Parks have proposed that we will move quickly to terminate a relationship if it falls below our expectations and we think we have an opportunity to develop a new relationship that has the potential to exceed all of our expectations.[12] We try to spend the most time with those relationships that have the best relative outcomes. All these comparisons work in concert with one another. We compare our current relationships to previous ones, to the ideal, and to potential ones.

expected rewards and costs. Expectation of how much reward we should get from a given relationship in comparison to its costs.

One research study used social exchange principles to examine whether couples maintained friendships after dissolving their romantic relationship.[13] In this study, couples who continued to provide each other with rewards and/or resources (love, status, services, information, goods, or money) continued to maintain a friendship. Those couples for which there were costs or barriers (lack of support by family or friends for a friendship, involvement in a new romance, or use of neglect to end the romance) had lower-quality friendships.

Dialectical Theory

Dialectical theory looks at the human condition in terms of sets of opposing forces. When applying dialectical theory to interpersonal relationships, we can identify forces pulling us toward intimacy and opposing forces pulling us toward independence.

Three Dialectical Tensions

Researcher Leslie Baxter has identified three dialectical tensions that have been widely used in interpersonal research.[14]

Connectedness versus Autonomy We desire to connect with others and to become interdependent at the same time we have a desire to remain autonomous and independent. In one study of married couples, the desire to be both connected and autonomous was found to be the most frequently occurring of the dialectical tensions.[15]

Predictability versus Novelty (Certainty versus Uncertainty) Knowing what to expect and being able to predict the world around us helps reduce the tension that occurs from uncertainty. At the same time, we get bored by constant repetition and routine and therefore are attracted to novelty and the unexpected. This might explain why people relish horror movies, where the unexpected jumps out at them. Fright becomes pleasurable because it meets a need for the unexpected.

dialectical theory. Theory that relational development occurs in conjunction with various tensions that exist in all relationships, particularly connectedness versus autonomy, predictability versus novelty, and openness versus closedness.

Openness versus Closedness We wish to disclose information to others and to hear those we are attracted to disclose to us. One ideal we seem to want to achieve in relationships is the ability to be totally open with our partner. However, we also value

When a couple commits to a relationship, they must find a new balance between autonomy and connectedness.

our privacy and feel a desire to hold back information. This tension was identified in the study of married couples mentioned earlier as the most important of the three tensions, although it did not occur as often as the other two tensions.[16]

Dialectical Tensions and Relational Development

According to the dialectical theory, each pair of tensions is present in every relationship, but the impact of each changes as a relationship progresses. Movement in relationships can be seen as a shift that occurs in the relative pull of one tension. For example, when you begin developing a new friendship, one issue you have to address is whether you want to give up some of your autonomy (freedom to do your own things) in order to spend time with this other person (connectedness). Notice how this is similar to social exchange theory, in that you weigh costs (giving up autonomy) against rewards (becoming connected).

Both forces of autonomy and forces of connectedness can be found even in close relationships.[17] Even though long-married couples have usually settled the issue of interdependence versus independence, dialectical theory asserts (and research supports) that tension is still present from these forces. Generally, such tension diminishes as we become more intimate; however, many an engagement has been called off at the last minute because of the inability of the bride or the groom to resolve this tension. This tension represents the challenge faced by individuals forming close relationships who are attempting to maintain their own identities while at the same time meld their identity with that of another person.

One study of married couples found that dialectical tensions existed both at the individual level (for example, the wife or the husband trying to decide whether to be open or closed) and at the relational level (partners differing in terms of desires for autonomy, openness, or novelty).[18] In addition, the study found that extreme closedness related to greater autonomy—which makes sense, since those couples who share less information may also be likely to share less time together.

Movement in relationships can be seen as occurring because some element of tension has been resolved or overcome.[19] For example, during the initial stages of a relationship, you are restrained in your self-disclosures (closedness). As long as you remain closed, the relationship can only progress so far. You are confronted with the question of whether you should share information and increase the level of intimacy in the relationship. Thus, a tension exists until you make your decision. Once you have decided, some of the tension is relieved. If you decide on more openness, the reduction in tension is accompanied by a change in the relationship—a turning point.

Still, tensions remain, and we often decide to back away from intimacy as another way of managing them. Rather than a straight, linear progression toward intimacy, the management of dialectical tensions results in relationships moving up a stage or two, then down a stage or more, and back up again as partners negotiate the tensions. One study found that over half of the friendships studied progressed through a cycle of development, deterioration, and then development again, with each change being signaled by a turning point.[20]

Strategies and Skills for Developing Interpersonal Relationships

So far, this chapter has focused on the nature of relational development. Now, the focus shifts to discussing specific strategies and skills for starting, escalating, and maintaining interpersonal relationships. The lists provided are neither fail-safe nor

Interpersonal Communication and Emotion: Connecting Heart to Heart

Emotions in Relational Development, Social Exchange Theory, and Dialectical Theory

In reading about the movement of relationships through various stages, the assessment of relational costs and rewards, and management of dialectical tensions, you might get the sense that people in relationships act in very logical and thoughtful ways. While that is partially true, you should not ignore the role of emotions in these processes. Communication scholar Sally Planalp urges a reconsideration of these three processes that recognizes the role of emotion.[21] The appraisal theory of emotion covered in Chapter 2 applies to these three processes, because it suggests that we decide on our emotional reactions by labeling what we feel. Appraisal theory of emotion explains why when two people meet for the first time, one can come away feeling like a fool, while the other is excited about the relationship potential. Their focus and interpretations differ, resulting in different emotions. Let's look at relational development, social exchange, and dialectics within an emotional context.

Emotions and Relational Development

For each of the three relational turning points, choose from the list those emotions you would most likely feel.

Turning Point

1. Meeting for the first time someone whom you find attractive and see as a potential romantic partner
2. Being invited to a party after work by one of your co-workers, whom you like but only know through work
3. Having a big fight with a close friend after several weeks of bickering; now it looks like the relationship might be over

Emotions

Fear	Anxiety
Concern	Warmth
Pleasure	Joy
Uncertainty	Anger
Liking	Gratification
Frustration	Excitement
Bashfulness	Anticipation
Worry	Optimism
Playfulness	Happiness

Your ability to identify different emotions associated with each turning point illustrates that movement through the relational stages is, in fact, marked by a succession of emotions. As you move toward and away from intimacy, you experience both positive and negative emotions (often at the same time—a dialectical tension). The emotions you selected from the list are likely to be somewhat different from other people's selections, illustrating the individuality and uniqueness of emotions. Also, you might have selected more than one term to describe your general emotional state associated with each turning point, because emotional experiences are complex and involve a combination of emotions. If you had difficulty deciding which emotions to select, perhaps the terms didn't adequately reflect your likely emotions, or perhaps imagining the emotions isn't really the same as experiencing them. In sum, relational development is very much an emotional process that influences our willingness to initiate, escalate, maintain, and terminate relationships.

Emotions and Social Exchange

The social exchange approach to relationships makes it seem as though we are all bookkeepers, tabulating our expected rewards and costs as we decide what to do in our relationships. But emotions are also part of social exchange. While rewards usually have a positive emotional value and costs often have a negative value, emotions make relational bookkeeping a bit more complex than simply calculating a bottom line. If you love someone, is that a cost to you, because it is something you are giving away? Or is it a reward, because loving someone makes you feel good? The answer to this depends on the person. There are people who are very cautious and reluctant to love others. Perhaps they've given their love in the past but the relationship ended painfully—thus creating a negative expectation regarding love.

Think about one of your closest relationships. What rewards and costs do you associate with that relationship? What emotions do you associate with each of those rewards and costs? For example, if one reward is having someone to do something with on Friday nights, the emotions might be contentment, certainty, and a feeling of belonging. If one cost you see in the relationship is sometimes having to listen to your friend drone on about personal

complete—they are offered primarily to stimulate consideration of your own thoughts and behaviors as you develop new relationships.

When you meet someone whom you initially like, how do you go about fostering a relationship? Once you have established a relationship, how do you ensure that it

problems, the emotions associated with this cost might be boredom, frustration, and even a little anger. Social exchange theory would probably predict that we stay in relationships in which we have more positive emotional experiences than negative. Does that hold true for your relationships? What exceptions to this prediction have you experienced?

Emotions also represent a contradiction or exception to the principle of social exchange. We don't just balance the positive and negative emotions; our behaviors can be altered by a single emotion that outweighs other emotions. Perhaps you've gotten so angry at a friend that you decide to end the relationship. In acting on that emotion, you reflect very little on the positive feelings you have for the person and the happiness you usually feel when together. Instead, you act on the single emotion in a way that overrides any assessment of the relative rewards and costs of the relationship. Acting on such emotion is not intrinsically bad—such impulses are part of our natural emotional survival patterns. Think about times in your life when the emotion of the moment has dictated your relational behavior. To what degree was the final outcome positive or negative? Hopefully, you have had times when acting on your emotions without concern for the cost of doing so produced a positive result—perhaps acting on your attraction toward another that resulted in a close relationship, or feeling so happy about some news you unexpectedly hugged a family member, brightening his or her day, too.

Emotions and Dialectical Theory

In some ways, emotions are a key element of dialectical theory; after all, what is tension but an emotion. Each of the dialectical tensions can be couched in terms of the emotions that they arouse, and each dialectical pole evokes both positive and negative emotions. For example, on the positive side, connectedness arouses such emotions as affection, companionship, love, a feeling of confirmation, and warmth; on the negative side, connection represents constraint, feeling smothered, fear of being hurt, fear of rejection, feeling loss of control. Autonomy can evoke such emotions as a feeling of freedom from restraint, independence, and confidence, while also evoking loneliness, a feeling of reclusiveness, a sense of unattractiveness, and insecurity. The management of dialectical tensions is an emotion-filled journey: We are constantly experiencing and shifting back and forth between positive and negative feelings as we sort out what we want from a given relationship. Think about a recent relational experience in which you were faced with managing a dialectical tension—moving toward connectedness and away from autonomy (or vice versa); being open and sharing information or withholding information by being closed; or seeking a predictable relationship over one filled with uncertainty. Now consider what emotions you experienced while dealing with the tension. The tension itself probably created some degree of angst or a feeling of carrying a burden. What else did you feel? What emotions were associated with the various options you were considering? For example, giving a key to your apartment to a romantic partner (connection–autonomy) might produce fear, anxiety, excitement, relief, love, a sense of togetherness, vulnerability, or commitment. As with social exchange theory, decisions about managing dialectical tensions can be expected to result in a more positive overall emotional state. In essence, we know we will be "happier" with a certain person if we opt for more connectedness (or more autonomy); more (or less) predictability and certainty; and more (or less) openness.

Both positive and negative emotions are experienced in all relationships and are unavoidable. So one goal we set for ourselves is to attain relationships that provide the greatest amount of positive emotions with the least amount of negative. Our movement toward intimacy is usually marked with optimism about experiencing a plethora of positive emotions—of good feelings. Our assessment of relationships includes assessing the positive feelings against the negative. We constantly negotiate the emotions associated with dialectical tensions as we manage our relationships. It's essential to recognize the role your emotions play in the attainment of satisfying and happy interpersonal relationships.

remains healthy and at the level of intimacy with which you are most comfortable? The following three sections provide strategies you can use to address these questions. The first section discusses skills and strategies used primarily in initiating interaction. The next section covers skills and strategies used in both initiating and escalating

We can learn the skills that can help us reduce the interpersonal tensions that most of us feel at the start of a relationship.

relationships. The final section focuses on skills used in either maintaining a relationship or moving it toward more intimacy once it has been established.

Skills and Strategies Used Primarily to Initiate a Relationship

In the opening scenarios, Josh used the "free" information that was available on Nona's T-shirt as a way to open a conversation with her. You can use readily available information to begin conversations and initiate relationships. In the introductions sub-stage of the acquaintance stage, people generally follow a script that helps both parties reduce their level of anxiety about interacting with a stranger. They also stick to safe topics and disclose only descriptive information about themselves as they begin to build the foundations for a potential relationship. The following sections explain some of the principles to follow as you interact with others for the first time.

Observe and Act on Approachability Cues

Subway riders in New York learn to avoid eye contact because it is a signal of approachability. Other ways we can signal approachability include turning toward another person, smiling, being animated (versus sitting very still), taking an open body posture, winking, and waving. In the absence of these cues, we generally conclude that a person wants to be left alone.

Sometimes, circumstances prevent us from exchanging approachability cues. The seating arrangements in your class, for example, might hamper the use of nonverbal cues. So instead, you may try to develop some sensitivity to the way other people respond to your greetings. Saying "Hello" lets people know that you are approachable, and it tests approachability. If the other person responds with a warm smile and a few words, such as "Have you finished today's assignment yet?" then the door might be open for further interaction. But if the person gives you a silent half-smile and hurries on, you can take this as a signal that the door is closed.

Identify and Use Conversation Starters

Like Nona in the opening scenario of this chapter, we all are sources of a certain amount of "free" information that others can easily observe. You can use that information as a starting point for a conversation. When Josh noted that Nona was wearing a Michigan Tech T-shirt, he asked her whether she was a student there. You can apply the same approach. If someone is walking a dog of the same breed as your childhood pet, you can open a conversation by offering an observation about some peculiarity of the breed. If someone is carrying a book from a class you took last semester, ask him or her how the course is going. For example, "Hi; isn't that book you're carrying the one for the dreaded Dr. Bellfinger's class? I really had to work my tail off in that class."

Follow Initiation Norms

Many of the initial interactions in a relationship are almost ritualistic, or at least scripted. In the United States, when two strangers meet for the first time, they typically follow this pattern of conversation.[22]

Greetings: Say "Hello," "Hi," or "Howdy."

Introductions: Exchange names and pleasantries.

Topic 1: Discuss the present situation or weather.

Topic 2: Discuss current or past residences (streets, dorms, hometown, and so on).

Topic 3: Determine whether they know people in common.

Topic 4: Discuss their educational backgrounds or occupations.

Topic 5: Discuss general topics such as TV shows, movies, music, family, sports, books, and/or travel.

Discuss further meeting (optional): Say something like "Let's get together sometime."

Exchange pleasantries: "Nice to meet you," "Hope to see you again," and so on.

Close conversation: Indicate the intent to end the conversation with such statements as "See you later," "Got to go to class now," or "Give me a call."

Goodbyes: Make final statements, say "Bye," and move in different directions.

Following the script provides some comfort and security because it reduces the uncertainties associated with meeting a stranger. If you deviate too much from this script, you might increase uncertainty and discourage your partner from pursuing a relationship. For example, after an initial greeting, how would you react to a stranger who deviated from the script by saying, "Nice to meet you, too. Don't you agree that television is becoming the vast wasteland of American intellect, draining the very life blood of our youth?" Most of us would be a bit leery of jumping directly into a discussion of such an issue with a person we had just met.

As you follow the script, however, you should take advantage of opportunities to expand and develop the conversation in safe ways. Listen for details about the person's background and interests that you can inquire about, and share information about your own interests.

Ask Questions

The very act of asking questions can enhance your partner's attraction to you.[23] Asking questions shows your interest in the other person in an indirect way and promotes reciprocity of liking. Asking questions can also provide you with information about the other person, helping reduce uncertainty and improving your ability to adapt to your partner. However, accomplishing these benefits requires the ability to ask questions without "interrogating" the other person, to ask open questions that invite elaboration and discussion, and to ask meaningful follow-up, or probing, questions. Starting with impersonal, specific questions, often about the circumstance or surroundings, encourages a response by reducing a person's reluctance to answer (for example, while standing in a movie line, "Have you heard any reviews of this movie?"). After the initial question, asking more open and encompassing questions helps to facilitate the conversation ("What did they have to say?").

Once you've asked an initial question, be flexible and ask follow-up questions related to the answer you get. Be open and provide information about yourself that is relevant to the questions. Usually, the other person will also ask you questions. If the other person gives short responses without any reciprocal questions, that may be a signal that he or she is not particularly interested in interacting. If so, you're probably better off not pursing the interaction any further.

You might ask a question that you believe is safe and appropriate, such as "What does your father do for a living?" to which the stranger gives an unexpected response: "I haven't heard from him since I was 5." Unknowingly, you may have evoked uncomfortable feelings and memories. Some questions should obviously be avoided because of their inappropriateness in an initial interaction; however, almost any seemingly simple question can sometimes evoke a negative reaction. Having little information about a stranger on which to base your communication decisions means you need to monitor the interaction carefully. Recognize that the experiences and feelings evoked by your questions differ from person to person. A question that is easy and comfortable for you to answer may not be for others. Be sensitive to how the other person responds to your questions, and be prepared to adapt your comments appropriately. Other-oriented communication skills can help you manage sensitive situations. Put yourself in the other person's shoes. If you hadn't seen your father since you were five, what would you most like your conversation partner to say next?

BE OTHER-ORIENTED

Don't Expect Too Much from the Initial Interaction

Initial interactions do not necessarily determine the future of a relationship. In movies, initial interactions between the hero and the heroine are often brusque and unfriendly, but after sharing traumatic experiences, they eventually find love. Although real life does not usually work this way, keep in mind that the scripted nature of an initial interaction limits the opportunity for you and your partner to achieve an in-depth understanding of each other. Relax and arrange another meeting if you feel attraction. It will probably take a few interactions before you can make a sound cost–benefit analysis of the relationship.

Initiating conversation is only one step in the process of developing an interpersonal relationship. Next, we examine ways to escalate a relationship once it gets started.

Skills and Strategies Used in Both Initiating and Escalating Relationships

"No kidding! I love chocolate-covered strawberries, too." "It's nice to be able to talk to someone else who's a fan of *Survivor.*" Statements like these emphasize commonalities in order to encourage the listener to like the speaker (this is called *affinity seeking*). We sometimes make these types of statements when we are first getting to know someone, but similar statements are also used when trying to escalate a relationship. Trying to increase someone's attraction to us is just one strategy that is common to both the initiation and the escalation of interpersonal relationships. Other skills and strategies include appropriately self-disclosing, gathering information to reduce uncertainties, monitoring your perceptions, listening actively and responding confirmingly, and socially decentering and adapting. Let's look more closely at each of these ways to initiate and escalate relationships.

Communicate and Cultivate Attraction

Communicating our attraction increases the likelihood our partners will reciprocate, thus cultivating their attraction to us. When we are attracted to people, we use both indirect and direct strategies to communicate our liking through nonverbal and verbal cues. *Nonverbal immediacy* refers to the nonverbal cues we display when we are attracted to someone. For instance, we tend to reduce the physical distance between us, increase our eye contact and use of touch, lean forward, keep an open body orientation, and smile. We also use the courtship readiness behaviors, preening behaviors, positional cues, and appeals to invitation described in Chapter 7.

We also indirectly communicate our attraction verbally. We use informal and personal language, addressing the person by his or her first name and often referring to "you and I" and "we." We ask questions to show interest, probe for details when our partner shares information, listen responsively, and refer to information shared in past interactions. All these behaviors confirm that we value what the other person is saying.

We can also directly communicate our attraction verbally. Most of us don't do this very often. But think about how you feel when a friend tells you that he or she likes you. It raises your self-esteem; you feel valued. You can make others feel that way by communicating your liking for them, although in the early stages of relational development, there are social mores against doing so. We verbally communicate liking in more subtle ways as well. We might tell someone that we like a particular trait or ability, such as the way she tells jokes, or the way he handled an irritating customer. Or we might compliment someone's outfit, hairstyle, or jewelry. Each of these messages communicates attraction for the other person and is likely to elicit a positive response from him or her.

In social situations, we learn to present ourselves in a positive way, using both nonverbal and verbal cues.

We also use **affinity-seeking strategies** to get people to like us. Table 10.1 summarizes strategies identified by the research team of Robert Bell and John Daly.[24] Deciding to display nonverbal immediacy cues or to verbally confirm the other person are not only ways we communicate our attraction toward other people, they are also ways of getting other people to like us. Other affinity-seeking strategies include establishing mutual trust, being polite, showing concern and caring, and involving people in our activities. Apparently, these strategies do work. Bell and Daly found that individuals who seemed to use many affinity-seeking strategies were perceived as likeable, socially successful, and satisfied with their lives.[25]

Be Open and Self-Disclose Appropriately

Disclosing information about yourself allows the other person to make an informed decision about whether to continue the relationship. Remember, both of you need to be in a position to make such a decision. You may have found out what you want to know and decided that you have a lot in common with the other person, but he or she may not have reached that same point. However, be careful not to violate the script or cultural expectations about what is appropriate to disclose in an initial conversation. You have probably had the experience of having someone you just met tell you his or her problems. Such disclosures usually alienate the other, rather than advancing the relationship.

In Chapter 2, we pointed out that self-disclosure is a critical element for movement toward intimacy. People cannot form truly intimate relationships without mutual self-disclosure. Restricting the amount of self-disclosure is one way to control the development of a relationship. If a relationship is moving too fast, you might choose to reduce how much you are self-disclosing as a way to slow the progression of the relationship. The level of self-disclosure needs to be appropriate to the level of development, and both partners must be sensitive to the timing of the disclosures. Failing to disclose or disclosing the wrong thing at the wrong time can damage a relationship.

Gather Information to Reduce Uncertainty

Meeting strangers and starting relationships is rarely easy. We all seem to share a fear of the unknown, which includes interactions with strangers whose behavior we cannot predict. The research team of Charles Berger, Richard Calabrese, and James Bradac developed a theory to explain relational development.[26] Their **uncertainty reduction theory** is based on one basic assumption: We like to have control and predictability in our lives; therefore, when we are faced with uncertainty, we are driven to gain information to reduce that uncertainty. Reducing uncertainty requires using a number of skills we have already covered, but primarily depends on effective perception and active listening. You need to gather as much information as you can about your partner to increase predictability and reduce anxiety.

Usually we reduce uncertainty by gathering either cognitive or behavioral information about others.[27] Cognitive information relates to thoughts, attitudes, and opinions. Behavioral information relates to reactions and remarks in various situations. As you have seen, you gather some of this information during the preinteraction awareness stage of a relationship through observations and conversations with others who know the person. Later, you can observe the other's behaviors directly in your own interactions with him or her and also ask direct questions. Usually, people gather behavioral information through observation and cognitive information through interactions.

We are particularly motivated to gain information early in a relationship when uncertainty is greatest and when we are trying to evaluate the relationship's predicted out-

affinity-seeking strategies. Strategies for getting other people to like you.

uncertainty reduction theory. Theory that claims people seek information in order to reduce uncertainty, thus providing control and predictability.

TABLE **10.1** **Affinity-Seeking Strategies**

	Strategies	Examples
1. Control	Present yourself as in control, independent, free-thinking; show that you have the ability to reward the other person.	• "I'm planning on going to grad school, and after that I'm going to Japan to teach English." • "You can borrow my notes for the class you missed if you'd like."
2. Visibility	Look and dress attractively; present yourself as an interesting, energetic, and enthusiastic person; increase your visibility to the other person.	• "Wow, that was a great show about Chinese acrobats. I do gymnastics, too. Would you like to come watch me next week in our dual meet?"
3. Mutual Trust	Present yourself as honest and reliable; display trustworthy behaviors; show that you trust the other person by self-disclosing.	• "That guy you're having problems with called me and asked about you. I told him I didn't have anything to say." • "I've never told anyone this, but I've always hoped I could find my birth parents."
4. Politeness	Follow appropriate conversational rules; let the other person assume control of the interaction.	• "I'm sorry I interrupted. I thought you were done. Please, go on." • "No, you're not boring me at all; it's very interesting. Please tell me more about it."
5. Concern and Caring	Show interest in and ask questions about the other person; listen; show support and be sensitive; help the other person accomplish something or feel good about himself or herself.	• "How is your mother doing after her operation?" • "I'd like to help out at the benefit you're chairing this weekend." • "That must have been really hard for you, growing up under those conditions."
6. Other-Involvement	Put a positive spin on activities you share; draw the other person into your activities; display nonverbal immediacy and involvement with the other person.	• "This is a great party. I'm glad you came." • "A group of us are going to get a midnight snack; how about coming along?"
7. Self-Involvement	Try to arrange for encounters and interactions; engage in behaviors that encourage the other person to form a closer relationship.	• "Oh hi! I knew your class ended at two, so I thought I'd try to catch you." • "It would really be fun to go camping together this summer; I have this favorite place."
8. Commonalities	Point out similarities between yourself and the other person; try to establish equality (balanced power); present yourself as comfortable and at ease around the other person.	• I've got that computer game, too. Don't you love the robots?" • "Let's work on the project together. We're a great team." • "It's so easy to talk to you. I really feel comfortable around you."

Source: Adapted from R. A. Bell and J. A. Daly, "The Affinity Seeking Function of Communication," *Communication Monographs,* 51 (1984): 91–115.

Applying Theory and Research

Initiation Stage: Male-Initiated versus Female-Initiated Date Requests

According to custom in the United States, men are expected to take the initiative in asking women out. While certain taboos or negative impressions have been associated with women initiating dates, more women seem to be taking this initiative. Communication scholars Paul Mongeau, Jerold Hale, Kristin Johnson, and Jacqueline Hillis examined male-initiated versus female-initiated date requests. For one part of their study, they created four written scenarios describing a male asking a female out, a male or a female initiating the date request after hints from the other, and a female asking a male out. Over four hundred student participants evaluated the females and males in these scenarios. In comparison to the woman who waited for the man to ask her out, the woman who directly asked the man out was seen as more active, flexible, truthful, and extroverted; more of a feminist; more socially liberal; and less physically attractive (though no pictures were provided). Female students perceived the female initiator as more likeable and tactful than did the males.

Applying the Research to Your Life

What is your view of a woman who asks a man out for a first date? To what degree does your view differ if the woman asks the man to (a) go to a movie, (b) come over to her apartment for dinner, or (c) go to a party with her?

(Male students should answer these questions):

Has a woman ever asked you out on a first date?

How was your attitude toward her affected by her request?

(Female students should answer these questions):

Have you ever asked a man out for a first date?

How do you think the man's attitude toward you was affected by your request?

If you haven't initiated a date with a man, how do you think a man would react if you did?

Survey five or six of your male and female friends and collect their answers to the above questions. How similar are their responses? To what degree do males and females agree or disagree?

Source: P. A. Mongeau, J. L. Hale, K. L. Johnson, and J. D. Hillis. "Who's Wooing Whom? An Investigation of Female Initiated Dating," in P. J. Kalbleisch (Ed.), *Interpersonal Communication: Evolving Interpersonal Relationships* (Hillsdale, NJ: Erlbaum, 1993), 51–68.

come value.[28] In a study on first dates, reducing uncertainty by finding out about the partner was the number-one goal, followed by trying to determine the possibility for a romantic relationship.[29]

We also are likely to seek out information if others behave in an unexpected way.[30] If your close friend who watches *South Park* every night suddenly begins reading during that time slot, you will probably ask why. Whether the friend shares with you what is going on will depend on how comfortable he or she is revealing information about himself or herself.

Finally, we experience uncertainty about the very nature and definition of our relationships and our partners' regard for us. This uncertainty can hamper the development, escalation, and maintenance of our interpersonal relationships. What does your new friend think about the relationship? How intimate a relationship does your boyfriend or girlfriend want? Why hasn't your best friend called you in the last two weeks? The most obvious approach to addressing these questions would be simply to ask the other person; however, we risk "losing face" in using such direct strategies to reduce uncertainty. There are also times where uncertainty is preferable to certainty—for example, uncertainty about your romantic partner's desire to end the relationship can be preferable to finding out for sure. Researchers Leanne Knobloch and Denise Solomon have conducted numerous studies on uncertainty in relationships. In one

Building Your Skills

Anxiety Level and Familiarity

Write down at least ten different social situations you can recall having been in, such as attending weddings, funerals, or ball games; going to your grandmother's for dinner; visiting your best friend's parents for the first time; or meeting your new roommate. Next to each one, indicate how nervous you felt in that situation. Use a scale from 1 to 10, with 1 being calm and cool and 10 being highly apprehensive. After you have rated each situation, go back and rate each one on how familiar or unfamiliar the situation was. Again use a scale of 1 to 10, with 1 being very familiar and 10 being very unfamiliar.

According to uncertainty reduction theory, there should be a strong correlation between your level of anxiety and the level of familiarity. Which situations caused the most anxiety? To what degree did your unfamiliarity with the situation affect your level of anxiety? What were you most uncertain about in each situation? In which situations were you most comfortable and why? Did you feel uncomfortable in some circumstances even though the situation was familiar? Why?

study, they found that the uncertainty hampered the ability to identify and interpret relational information while also making interactions more difficult (for example, uncertainty led partners to be overly concerned about avoiding certain topics).[31] However, these researchers also believe that the more intimate the relationship, the more likely we are to use direct approaches to reduce uncertainty, which means stronger communication and the possibility of more positive outcomes.[32] In general, our level of satisfaction in a relationship is linked to feelings of certainty,[33] probably because those relationships that are the most satisfying are also the ones in which partners have a strong mutual understanding and a shared vision of the relationship.

Monitor Your Perceptions

You need to be aware of your perceptual biases that affect your reactions to your partner. Such biases might inhibit the growth of a relationship because of an inaccurate inference. Effective perception can enhance your ability to understand and adapt to your partner as a relationship escalates. Perception checking helps you reach a more accurate understanding of your partner and thus provides you with better information about whether to continue the relationship. Directly asking your partner for explanations about things you have perceived can potentially lead to more effective relationship management. For example, suppose you are interacting with Miguel, whom you don't know very well. During the conversation, every time you start to talk about a mutual friend, Sandra, Miguel changes the subject. One interpretation of this observation is that Miguel is rude and impolite, and if you assume this is the case, you might decide to abandon the relationship. Or you might ask Miguel about your perception. The explanation might be that he and Sandra recently had a fight and he prefers not to talk about her. A hasty inference in this case might have precluded the development of a potentially satisfying relationship.

Listen Actively and Respond Confirmingly

Listening skills are also crucial for developing and maintaining relationships. Listening clues you in to others' needs, wants, and values, and it enables you to respond to them in appropriate ways. In the initial stages of a relationship, partners share a great deal of information. The amount of information tapers off in the later stages and as a relationship continues over time. This tapering off creates the illusion that you don't

Well-adjusted couples display support and affection for each other through positive nonverbal cues.

have to listen as much or as well as you did early on. But listening is a way to demonstrate ongoing interest in another person. Even in long-term relationships, you do not know everything your partner has to say. It is still important to stop, look, and listen—to put down the newspaper or turn off the radio when your close friend begins talking to you.

You also need to listen actively and provide confirming responses, as discussed in Chapter 5. Using confirming responses increases your partner's sense of self-worth and communicates the value you place on him or her. In addition, if you can develop an awareness of the biases that prevent you from responding with empathy, you can work to overcome them as you ask questions and paraphrase your partner's messages.

Socially Decenter and Adopt an Other-Oriented Perspective

The skills covered in Chapter 4 for social decentering, empathizing, and adapting to others enhance the initiation, escalation, and maintenance of relationships. Social decentering helps you better understand your partner, which provides you with a basis for choosing the most effective strategies for accomplishing your communication goals. We have been discussing the notion of "appropriateness" of your behaviors to the effective advancement and maintenance of your relationships. Determining appropriateness depends on your ability to read the situation and your partner, and then to adapt or choose the best behaviors. Essentially, you can consider either what your partner is thinking now or what he or she will think in response to your actions—put yourself in your partner's shoes. For example, suppose you recently met someone to whom you are attracted and you are trying to decide whether to tell this person about a very intimate relationship you had, which just ended. Put yourself in the other person's shoes. Would *you* want someone you just met to tell you about his or her recent breakup? What information do you have that can help you determine this person's reaction? As relationships become more intimate, you receive more and more information that can improve decentering and adaptation. This information will prove valuable in providing the comfort and social support that help maintain your close relationships.

BE OTHER-ORIENTED 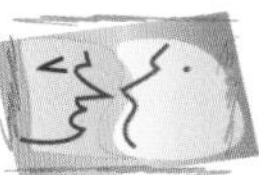

Skills and Strategies Specific to Escalating and Maintaining Relationships

Certain skills and strategies can be used to further escalate a relationship or to keep a relationship at a given stage. These include a willingness to express your emotions, provision of comfort and social support, openness to relationship talk, tolerance of your partner's flaws and failures, and the ability to manage conflict cooperatively. The use of the entire range of skills and strategies covered in these sections can help you develop and maintain strong and satisfying relationships.

Express Emotions

Expressing emotions is a particular form of self-disclosure and a skill that can be improved. Many of us are embarrassed about expressing our feelings, yet sharing feelings at the appropriate time during the development of a relationship is one way to continue its escalation. Conversely, sharing the wrong feelings at the wrong time can have a detrimental effect.

"You want me to talk about my feelings? Okay – I feel like talking about sports."

There are two ways we share feelings with our partners. The first is to disclose information about our past or current emotional states that do not relate to our partner, such as sadness about the death of a family member, or fear about what we will do after we graduate. The second way is to directly express our emotional reactions to our partner, such as feelings of attraction to, love for, or disappointment in our partner. As relationships become more intimate, we have a greater expectation that our partner will disclose emotions openly. The amount of risk associated with such emotional disclosures varies from person to person. Most of us are comfortable sharing positive emotions, such as happiness and joy, but are more reserved about sharing negative emotions, such as fear or disappointment. We may think expressing negative emotions makes us appear weak or vulnerable. However, in a study of forty-six committed, romantic couples, researchers found that the number-one problem was the inability to talk about negative feelings.[34] For example, partners often made the following types of observations: "When she gets upset, she stops talking"; "He never lets me know when he's upset with something he doesn't like"; and "He just silently pouts." We generally want to know how our partners in intimate relationships are feeling, even if those feelings are negative.

However, a constant barrage of negative expressions can also alienate a partner. Research has found that marital satisfaction rises with the number of positive feelings the partners disclose, not with the number of negative ones.[35] Happy couples tend to display their positive emotional state in their smiles, laughs, and affection, while distressed couples display agitation, anger, and coldness.[36] A balance has to be found that includes expressing both positive and negative emotions at the right time in a constructive and confirming manner.

Provide Comfort and Social Support

The abilities to provide comfort, social support, and ego support are qualities associated with being a best friend.[37] We expect to be able to turn to our friends to help us through emotionally trying events. Offering social support and comfort not only provides direct benefit for our partners, but also confirms the value of the relationship and the partner. Communication scholar Brant Burleson found that being other-oriented was a key factor in being able to offer effective comforting messages. Other-oriented comforting messages confirm and accept the other person's feelings, help him or her express and examine those feelings, and help put the feelings into a broader context.[38] One research study found three outcomes of receiving comforting messages: (1) They put the distressed person in a more positive mood, (2) they empower the person to better manage the issues, and (3) they help reduce brooding (rumination) about the problems.[39]

It can be challenging to provide social and emotional support, and sometimes our attempts even produce negative effects, making the situation worse and/or negatively affecting the other person's self-esteem.[40] For example, providing advice might be viewed as controlling and implying that the person is incompetent to make his or her own decision (plus, the advice might be wrong). Attempts to display empathic understanding by sharing your own similar experience with a distressed friend might help him or her gain some insight, or it might disconfirm the other by changing the focus

to you and your life. There is no single correct supportive behavior, but socially decentering can help you decide how to behave. Consider what you'd like to hear if you were in the other person's situation, but adapt your strategy to accommodate differences between you and the other person—what is comforting to one person can be threatening to another. The Interpersonal Communication and Emotion feature in Chapter 5 (page 144) provides a list of specific suggestions for providing comforting messages to others.

One pair of researchers, Ruth Ann Clark and Jesse Delia, studied how people wanted to be treated by their friends in response to six different distressing situations.[41] There was wide variation in how people wanted their friends to approach the six issues. Clark and Delia found that people did not have a strong desire to talk about the situations. When people were distressed, they wanted to be the ones to decide whether to bring up the issue. Clark and Delia also found that people wanted their friends to keep attempts at comforting short. There are times where the best support involves saying nothing at all but simply being with the other person or providing a hug.

Engage in Relationship Talk

Relationship talk is talk about the nature, quality, direction, or definition of a relationship. Relationship talk is generally considered inappropriate in the early stages of a relationship. A relationship might be terminated prematurely if one partner tries to talk about it too early. Willingness to talk about the relationship is one way to implicitly signal your level of interest and commitment to the relationship. One study of cross-sex friendships found that those in which both partners had an interest in becoming romantic included more relational talk than did those in which the friends wished to maintain a platonic relationship.[42] As relationships move toward greater intimacy, the amount of direct relationship talk increases. As the relationship escalates, we should be prepared to discuss our thoughts and feelings about it. In more intimate relationships, relationship talk helps the partners resolve differences in their perceptions of the relationship that might be contributing to conflict and dissatisfaction. Unwillingness to talk about the relationship in an intimate relationship can ultimately drive a partner away.

Be Tolerant and Show Restraint

The most satisfying relationships are those in which both partners refrain from continually disagreeing, criticizing, and making negative comments to each other. Both individuals learn to accept the other and do not feel compelled to continually point out flaws or failures. One study found that well-adjusted couples focus their complaints on specific behaviors, whereas maladjusted couples complain about each other's personal characteristics. Well-adjusted couples are also kinder and more positive and have more humor in their interactions. They tend to agree with each other's complaints, whereas the partners in maladjusted relationships launch counter-complaints.[43] In addition, happy couples, when compared to unhappy couples, display more affection through positive nonverbal cues, display more supportive behaviors, and make more attempts to avoid conflict.[44]

Maintaining a relationship requires tolerance. You must learn to accept your partners for who they are and put up with some things you dislike. When couples lose their tolerance, they begin focusing on and criticizing characteristics that they used to accept. Then relationships begin to deteriorate.

relationship talk. Talk about the nature, quality, direction, or definition of a relationship.

Manage Conflict Cooperatively

Conflicts are inevitable in interpersonal relationships. As relationships develop, the individuals share more personal information and spend more time together, so the likelihood for conflict increases. The key to successful relational development and maintenance is not to avoid conflict altogether, but rather to manage it effectively. As we discussed in Chapter 8, a cooperative management style can actually transform conflict into an experience that strengthens a relationship. It can clarify the definition of a relationship, increase the exchange of information, and create a cooperative atmosphere for problem solving.

Becoming Other-Oriented

Adapting Relational Strategies and Skills to Your Partner

Besides presenting a model of the stages of relational development, this chapter discusses a variety of skills and strategies you can use to initiate, escalate, and maintain interpersonal relationships. Your decisions about what strategies to implement should be adapted to the anticipated reactions of your partner. In addition, to be effective, you must understand what is appropriate for a given stage of development, and then adapt the strategy or strategies accordingly. Below is a list of some of the skills and strategies covered in this chapter, to which your partner is likely to have some reaction. Think about a friend whom you know fairly well, but who isn't your best friend. Briefly assess how comfortable and skilled you are at using each strategy, what you think your friend's reaction would be to its use, and how you can adapt the strategy to fit the level of intimacy that exists in your relationship.

Skill/Strategy	How would I feel about using this skill/strategy?	How would my friend react/feel if I used this skill/strategy?	How should the skill/strategy be adapted to be appropriate to the relationship stage?
Communicating Attraction	________	________	________
Being Open and Self-Disclosing	________	________	________
Listening Actively and Confirmingly	________	________	________
Expressing Emotions	________	________	________
Providing Comfort and Social Support	________	________	________
Talking About the Relationship	________	________	________
Being Tolerant and Showing Restraint	________	________	________
Managing Conflict Cooperatively	________	________	________

Recap

Skills and Strategies for Developing Interpersonal Relationships

Skills and Strategies Used Primarily to Initiate a Relationship

Observe and Act on Approachability Cues

Identify and Use Conversation Starters

Follow Initiation Norms

Ask Questions

Don't Expect Too Much from the Initial Interaction

Skills and Strategies Used in Both Initiating and Escalating Relationships

Communicate and Cultivate Attraction

Be Open and Self-Disclose Appropriately

Gather Information to Reduce Uncertainty

Monitor Your Perceptions

Listen Actively and Respond Confirmingly

Socially Decenter and Adopt an Other-Oriented Perspective

Skills and Strategies Specific to Escalating and Maintaining Relationships

Express Emotions

Provide Comfort and Social Support

Engage in Relationship Talk

Be Tolerant and Show Restraint

Manage Conflict Cooperatively

Summary

As relationships escalate toward intimacy or de-escalate away from it, they go through identifiable stages. Each stage is marked by turning points, differences in self-disclosure, and specific verbal and nonverbal communication patterns. Escalating relationships move through preinteraction awareness, acquaintance, exploration, intensification, and intimacy. Relationships that are becoming less intimate go through turmoil or stagnation, deintensification, individualization, separation, and post-separation effects. The de-escalation of a romantic relationship does not mean that the relationship necessarily ends; sometimes couples are able to maintain effective post-intimacy relationships.

Two theories that explain relationship development are social exchange theory and dialectical theory. Social exchange theory posits that we make decisions about becoming more or less intimate on the basis of the rewards and costs that we perceive to be associated with the relationship. Decisions are made on the basis of forecasted and cumulative rewards and costs as well as comparisons with previous, potential, and ideal relationships. Dialectical theory sees our decisions being based on resolution of competing forces in our lives, particularly connectedness versus autonomy, predictability versus novelty, and openness versus closedness. As we address these forces, we move either toward or away from intimacy in our relationships.

A variety of strategies and skills can be applied to the initiation, escalation, and maintenance of interpersonal relationships. Certain skills and strategies are used primarily during the initiation of a relationship, including observing and acting on approachability cues, identifying and using conversation starters, following initiation norms, asking questions, and controlling expectations. Another set of skills and strategies is applicable to both the initiation of a relationship and the escalation of relationships toward greater intimacy. These include communicating and cultivating attraction, being open and appropriately self-disclosing, gathering information to reduce uncertainty, monitoring perceptions, listening actively and responding confirmingly, and socially decentering and adopting an other-oriented perspective. The final set of skills and strategies covered in this section are used primarily for moving a relationship toward intimacy or for maintaining existing relationships. This set includes expressing emotions, providing comfort and social support, engaging in talk about the relationship, being tolerant and showing restraint, and managing conflict cooperatively. All of these skills and strategies can be learned and enhanced to help you more effectively manage your interpersonal relationships.

For Discussion and Review

Focus on Critical Thinking

1. Trace two of your own close relationships—one with a friend of the same sex, and one with a friend of the opposite sex—through the applicable stages of relational escalation and de-escalation. What differences and similarities do you find at each stage? How can you explain them?
2. Explain how social exchange theory relates to dialectical theory.
3. Of all the skills for developing interpersonal relationships, which three are the most important? Why? Which three are the least important? Why?

Focus on Ethics

4. If two people have agreed to maintain a relationship below the highest level in the model of relational stages (the intimacy stage), is it ethical for one of the people to nonetheless continually try to move the relationship to the intimacy stage?
5. Assuming you were very skilled and adept at using strategies for developing interpersonal relationships, how ethical would it be for you to use those skills to satisfy your interpersonal needs in a given relationship, knowing that your partner was less skilled at getting his or her own needs met?
6. You are in a romantic relationship that has become physically intimate. How ethical is it for you to say, "I love you" if you really aren't sure you do? If your partner says "I love you," should you say, "I love you, too," even if you don't mean it?

Learning with Others

1. In class, divide up into at least five pairs of students. Each pair should choose a particular stage of relational development without telling the rest of the class. Then each pair should spend two minutes role-playing a discussion of plans for the upcoming weekend in a way that communicates the stage they have chosen. The rest of the class should write down what stage they think each pair is portraying. After all the pairs have finished their dialogues, score each others' responses. Which stage was easiest to portray and identify? Which stage was most difficult? How easy is it to see differences in communication behavior at various stages?
2. In small groups, brainstorm some of the turning points that each of you has experienced in important relationships. Identify the relational stages that the turning points led to. Which stages crop up most often? Least often? What does the frequency tell you about those stages?
3. Divide into groups of four or five students. Each member of the group should describe the most successful conversation starter he or she has experienced or used. What made it successful? What did the person like about it? What was the outcome? Next, each group member should describe the worst conversation starter that he or she has experienced or used. What made it the worst? What was the outcome?

Weblinks

Go to *www.mycommunicationlab.com* (access code required) to find Web resources for your text that supplement the material in Chapter 10, including links to information on the following topics:

Marriage stages
Social exchange theory
Relational dialectics
Conversation and intimacy skills
Relationship advice for men

CHAPTER 11

Managing Relationship Challenges

OBJECTIVES

1. Describe the process by which we address and respond to violations of relational expectations and failure events.
2. Explain the impact of distance on interpersonal relationships.
3. Identify the types of relationships that challenge social norms.
4. Describe the types of deception and their impact on interpersonal relationships.
5. Explain how messages can be hurtful.
6. Describe obsessive relational intrusion and stalking.
7. Explain the impact and use of jealousy in interpersonal relationships.
8. Discuss what relational violence includes.
9. Discuss potential responses to relational problems.
10. Identify some of the causes of relational de-escalation and termination.
11. Describe a model of how relationships end.
12. Discuss strategies for ending relationships.
13. Describe steps to promote post-dissolution recovery.

OUTLINE

Love begins with a smile, grows with a kiss, and ends with a teardrop.

Anonymous

Charise: I heard you went to the new Tom Hanks movie last night.

Simon: Yeah, it was pretty good.

Charise: I thought we agreed to go see it together?

Simon: Oh, sorry. I forgot; besides, you were busy anyway.

Charise: Don't lie. You didn't forget—you just didn't want to go with me.

Simon: Hey, wait a minute. It's no big deal. It was just a movie.

Charise: Who'd you go with?

Simon: A gang of us from work went.

Charise: Who?

Simon: Just some people from work.

Charise: You're a liar! I heard it was just you and some girl.

Throughout this book you have read about various factors that can impede effective interpersonal communication: language misunderstandings, biased perceptions, incorrect interpretation of nonverbal cues, weak listening skills, destructive conflict styles, and inappropriate self-disclosures. All of these factors can have a negative effect on interpersonal relationships. The above exchange between Charise and Simon reflects another set of issues that are covered in this chapter. Simon has obviously broken a promise he made to Charise about seeing a movie together, which places a strain on the relationship. Simon compounds the problem by being deceptive, but Charise calls him on it in an aggressive manner. Unlike the specific conflicts that you read about in Chapter 8, the challenges covered in this chapter reflect larger, more systemic relational issues. Interpersonal communication also has a dark side, in that it can be used in ways that are detrimental to others. These include being deceitful, as Simon is, saying things that hurt other people's feelings, like Charise does, and being verbally aggressive or argumentative. These relationship challenges and the darker aspects of interpersonal communication can contribute to relational de-escalation and termination, which are the focus of the last section of this chapter.

Relationship Challenges

The movement toward an intimate relationship doesn't always go smoothly. You've read about a variety of potential difficulties in the previous chapters. Chapter 10 identified some of the skills and strategies that can be utilized in the day-to-day management of relationships—but what happens when you encounter the unexpected? Any relationship can be challenged by one partner's failure to meet the other's expectations (a failure event), by attempts to maintain a relationship over long distances, or by social biases against certain types of relationships. Overcoming each of these challenges requires strong resolve and commitment by the relationship partners.

Violations of Relational Expectations and Failure Events

Remember that relational expectations are part of the definition of relationships; thus, violations of expectations are an unavoidable part of relationship development. We operate from a set of general expectations about relationships that are applied to specific relationships. We enter each relationship with a set of socially based relational expectations associated with a given type of relationship, including expectations about its rewards and costs. You have sets of expectations for what a best friend should be, what a romantic partner or spouse should be like, how rewarding a relationship with an opposite-sex friend should be, and so on. Violations of these expectations arouse uncertainty and produce emotional reactions such as hurt and anger.[1] We might assess the relationship in light of our expectations and decide to de-escalate or terminate the relationship. Or, we might modify our expectations, so that what had been a violation is no longer. For example, if you held the expectation that friends lend other friends money, but your friends kept turning down your requests, you might stop seeing lending money as a quality of a friend. Finally, we might decide to discuss the violation of the expectation with the other person. How we manage relational violations affects the health of the relationship.

We also develop, in concert with our partners, sets of expectations or understandings that are specific to each relationship. These understandings can be either implicit or explicit. Implicit understandings represent an unspoken compact between the partners about the relationship and each other. Explicit understandings represent a stated compact and agreement. Violations of both types of understandings arouse uncertainty and evoke various responses. For example, your roommate agrees to clean up the apartment over the weekend (an explicit understanding) and then fails to do so. Your friend says he'll meet you at the restaurant at 7:00 (an explicit understanding) but doesn't show up until 8:00. Some very personal information that you shared with only one other person (an implicit understanding) suddenly becomes common knowledge among your other friends. Your fiancée is seen out on a date with your best friend (either an implicit or an explicit understanding). These are called **failure events**—violations of understandings that occur between people in interpersonal relationships. Effective management of a failure event can lead to a clearer understanding and greater appreciation of the relationship.

failure events. Violations of understandings between people in relationships.

Assessing the Severity of Failure Events

Failure events and other violations of expectations vary in their severity and thus in their impact on the relationship—the failure of a roommate to clean up the apartment is less severe than a spouse having an affair. Failure events can be thought of as occurring along a continuum of severity, with those that are least severe probably being ignored altogether. However, those that are most severe can have a traumatic impact on the relationship. In an intimate romantic relationship, partners often see sexual fidelity as a defining characteristic. Cheating on one's partner is a severe failure event, which often leads to the termination of the relationship.[2] People in dating relationships can view "unfaithfulness" or "transgressions" as anything from spending time with another person to breaking a promise, flirting, betraying a trust or confidence, keeping secrets from the partner, and failing to return affection.[3] Indeed, romantic partners often hold certain sexual expectations of each other, such that too much affection at the wrong time or not enough affection at another can be seen as a failure event. An unwanted sexual advance (including sexual harassment) is an example of a violation of relational expectations. Such a potential violation might arise from the different relational expectations of males and females about first dates. In two studies by Paul Mongeau and his associates, men and women reported different expectations for the type of physical intimacy that would occur on a first date; however, the presence of alcohol was found to increase the level of sexual activity expected by both.[4] Recognizing that people have different relational expectations can help you avoid failure events. Discussion of relational expectations, even early in a relationship, helps improve the relationship for both partners.

Responding to Failure Events with Discussion

The process of addressing failure events often follows the reproach-account pattern, in which a number of decisions must be made by both partners. The first decision is whether a failure event has actually occurred. Had both parties agreed to a specific rule or expectation? Did both parties understand the rule? Was the rule appropriate or acceptable? After answering these questions, both parties must decide whether to discuss the failure.[5] Many times we ignore minor failures or focus on establishing explicit rules.

The decision to complain to or reproach a partner should be motivated by a desire to clarify relational expectations or to avoid the failure event in the future by modifying the partner's behaviors.[6] If we don't care that much about the relationship, or the issue, we might opt to ignore the failure—deciding it is not worth the effort. A **reproach** is a message that a failure event has occurred. Reproaches are usually direct statements, but they can also be conveyed indirectly through hints or nonverbal messages. For example, if you are upset that a close friend forgot your birthday, you might act cold and distant. Reproaches range from *aggravating* (threatening and severe) to *mitigating* (mild). For example, if your friend forgets to return a book she borrowed, you might offer a mitigating reproach such as, "Hey, Sally, I was wondering if you were done with that book I loaned you?" On the other hand, "Remind me to never loan you a book again, Sally; you are obviously irresponsible" is an aggravating reproach. What would you say to each reproach if you were Sally? To which reproach would you be more likely to apologize? Which would you be more likely to ignore?

The nature of the reproach affects the response, or the **account**.[7] Accounts can also be self-initiated, simply because a person knows he or she has failed to live up to an expectation. Relationship scholar Frank Fincham postulated that self-initiated accounts are more likely to evoke a favorable reaction from a partner than are accounts given in response to reproaches.[8] Apologizing as you arrive late at a friend's house for dinner is more likely to appease the irritated friend than acting like you've done nothing wrong. The following are the typical types of accounts people offer:

- *Apologies* include admission that the failure event occurred, acceptance of responsibility, and expression of regret.
- *Excuses* include admission that the failure event occurred, coupled with a contention that nothing could have been done to prevent the failure; it was due to unforeseen circumstances.

reproach. Message that a failure event has occurred.

account. Response to a reproach.

Responding to Failure Events

For each of the following failure events, suggest an aggravating reproach and a mitigating reproach.

- Your best friend borrowed two of your CDs without asking and lost them.
- Your roommate has been making long-distance phone calls on your cell phone without permission.
- A person you are dating says he or she can't get together with you because he or she needs to study, but then you hear that the person was seen at a party.
- A friend is supposed to pick you up from work at 5:00 but doesn't show up.

Now suppose you are the person who caused each of the above failure events. What accounts could you give that would be the least infuriating to the other person? What accounts would be the most infuriating?

- *Justifications* involve accepting responsibility for the event but redefining the event as not a failure.
- *Denials* are statements that the failure event never took place.
- *Absence of an account,* or *silence,* involves ignoring the reproaches or refusing to address them.

In providing an account to another person, you should examine your culpability. You should adopt an other-oriented perspective by considering the reproacher's objectives, desires, and feelings so that you can understand his or her reason for the reproach. Regardless of the legitimacy of the reproach, the person's feelings and reactions are real, and you must determine the most effective manner to address them. Sometimes simply admitting your failure and making a genuine effort to correct it is the best response.

Once they receive an account, reproachers must decide whether they find the account acceptable and can consider the issue resolved. When accounts are rejected, account givers often provide another account. However, rejection of accounts can escalate the failure event into an interpersonal conflict. Management of the conflict requires the skills and strategies discussed in Chapter 8.

Responding to Failure Events with Forgiveness

Forgiveness of a violation or failure event has lots of different meanings, but respondents in one study defined it as accepting the event, moving on, coming to terms, getting over it, letting go of negative feelings and grudges, and continuing the relationship.[9] Think about the last time you experienced a failure event and felt hurt by another person's actions. Did you forgive your partner? If so, why? Respondents in the above study reported forgiving others because the relationship was important or for personal health and happiness.[10] In essence, we forgive others when it is in our own best interest to do so. Did you forgive your partner because it was in your best interest—because you wanted to continue the relationship? We are also more likely to forgive those who apologize, are remorseful, admit their violation, and/or make restitution.[11] Did that occur in your situation? One study identified five forgiveness-granting strategies: nonverbal display (not directly saying that the other is forgiven, but acting in ways that show he or she is—showing affection, resuming interactions, etc.); conditional (expressing forgiveness but with stipulations—"You're forgiven as long as you . . ."); minimizing (shrugging off the offense as not very serious); discussion (acknowledging and talking about the failure event, sharing perspectives); and explicit (a straight declaration of forgiveness, often in combination with the other types).[12] Which of those five strategies did you use to communicate forgiveness to your partner? The forgiveness-granting strategy you use probably depends on the severity of the violation and the degree to which you wish to change your partner's future behavior. Consider your goals when you are determining how to grant forgiveness. Minimizing and nonverbal display will probably not create as much change as the discussion and conditional strategies.

Responding to Failure Events with Retaliation

Instead of a reproach, failure events might be met with retaliation. Emotional reactions to a partner's failing to meet expectations can even include violence toward the transgressor.[13] Retaliation involves an attempt to hurt the partner in response to the hurt she or he has caused. One possible reason for retaliation is to "even the score," hurtwise.[14] We want our partner to feel the same amount of hurt that we felt—thus creating a sense of equity. Retaliation behaviors can include aggressive communication (yelling, accusing, and sarcasm); active distancing (giving the partner the silent treatment or withholding affection); manipulation attempts (evoking counter jealousy, guilt, or loyalty testing); and contacting a rival.[15]

Physical Separation and Distance

The mobility of today's population means that we are often moving away or being separated for a time from people with whom we have formed interpersonal relationships. In addition, more people are meeting and developing long-distance relationships through computer-mediated communication (discussed in Chapter 12). Distance creates another challenge to maintaining relationships. Long-distance relationships vary in terms of expected length of separation, length of time between face-to-face visits, and the actual distance between the partners. Even temporary separation requires adjustment and management by the partners. On the other hand, permanent physical separation produces different expectations, interactions, and relational management strategies.

How often partners are able to get together face-to-face also determines the impact of the physical distance. One study suggests that people who are in long-distance romantic relationships but who are able to get together at least once a week can maintain relationships similar to those between people who are geographically close.[16] Think about your own experience of being in a long-distance relationship: Was it the number of miles between you or the frequency of getting together that had the most impact? (Of course, usually the more miles between people, the less frequent their visits.) There are times when partners are relatively close geographically but are limited in how often they can get together. The infrequency of face-to-face interactions might have an artificially positive effect on the partners, because they might work harder to be on their good behavior when they do get together.[17] This good behavior is probably one reason partners in romantic long-distance relationships report as much satisfaction and closeness as those who are geographically close.[18] Another reason for this reported satisfaction is that it is apparently easier to maintain an idealized image of a romantic relationship when you don't spend as much time with your partner.[19] Researchers Laura

Stafford and James Reske found that couples in long-distance premarital relationships had less communication but surprisingly greater satisfaction and higher expectation for the likelihood of marriage than those in *proximal,* or geographically close, relationships.[20] Couples who are apart have fewer facts about their partners to get in their way. Long-distance partners report feeling "moral commitment"; they feel they "ought" to continue the relationship.[21]

Social exchange theory (analysis of rewards and costs) offers one way to analyze the survival of long-distance relationships.[22] Distance introduces added costs to maintaining a relationship, including actual monetary costs such as long-distance phone charges and expenses involved in commuting (for gasoline, airline tickets, food), as well as the expenditure of time spent commuting to see a partner and the disruption of normal routines (leaving less time available for other activities). These costs are weighed against the benefits or rewards of the relationship. The rewards depend on what you are seeking in the relationship. Obviously, if you are looking for a relationship that meets physical needs and need for affection, a permanent long-distance relationship would probably be unsatisfactory. On the other hand, if your need is for a confidant, and you don't require face-to-face interactions, a long-distance arrangement might be acceptable.[23]

Tensions sometimes arise when one person is trying to maintain both long-distance relationships and proximal relationships.[24] For example, the autonomy that a long-distance relationship affords provides more time for proximal relationships with others. Visits by long-distance partners can put strains on proximal partners if the two sets of friends don't get along, or if they vie for the mutual friend's time together during those visits.[25] Long-distances couples also create tensions by over-planning their time together so they don't feel they've wasted their time—planning activities, discussion topics, and even sex.[26]

Social exchange theory predicts that we maintain long-distance relationships when we feel the rewards exceed the costs; however, if we consider the costs to be too high, we are likely to end such relationships. Usually, the costs continue to escalate while the rewards diminish, causing the relationship to simply fade away. However, individuals in some long-distance relationships may perceive the costs as investments rather than losses and thus sustain their commitment to the relationship.[27] Some relationships continue for a lifetime, even with little face-to-face time, because the interactions that do occur are rewarding.

Maintaining communication is probably the most important factor in sustaining strong relationships, even over long distances. The more open and honest you can keep the communication, the more similar your long-distance relationships will be to proximal ones. However, lack of communication might also sustain a relationship, because we believe we have a close, "dormant" relationship that we can call on if needed.[28] Partners in romantic long-distance relationships should try their best to reduce the impact of idealization if they seriously want to determine the viability of the relationship and reduce potential disappointments when they are no longer physically separated.

Relationships That Challenge Social Norms

Each culture establishes certain norms about what are appropriate and inappropriate relationships, based on social values, biases, and prejudices. Among the types of relationships often discouraged are those between people of different races, religions, or ethnicity. In addition, many societies have social mores against romantic relationships between individuals who differ significantly in age or who are of the same sex. When norms are violated, partners face social pressure to conform or risk being ostracized. Fortunately, the norms can be changed, and in the United States the number of relational restrictions have decreased in the last thirty years; nonetheless, developing any of these types of relationships poses challenges.

Partners in intercultural relationships face the challenge of communicating and interacting effectively, as discussed in Chapter 4. In addition, like partners in interracial relationships, they also may confront bias against their very relationship. Movies such as *South Pacific, West Side Story, Guess Who's Coming to Dinner, Remember the Titans, Jungle Fever,* and *Snow Falling on Cedars* have explored the difficulty partners in intercultural and interracial relationships have communicating with each other, as well as the negative responses they face from those around them.

Couples who choose to establish relationships outside of a culture's norms face challenges and social pressures.

One aspect of many of these relationships is the clash between out-groups and in-groups. One's racial or ethnic group is one's **in-group;** those who are not part of this group are part of an **out-group.** People can be considered part of an in-group whenever they view themselves as such; cliques and gangs are examples of such in-groups. If you have a friend or romantic partner from a different racial or ethnic group, you must adapt your behavior to what is, to you, an out-group when you are with your partner's in-group. A white person invited home for dinner by a Hispanic friend may be seen as an "outsider" by the family. This can create discomfort and uncertainty until the outsider gains the family's acceptance by adapting his or her communication to this other group. However, the outsider who totally abandons his or her own cultural heritage in order to adapt to another group is usually viewed suspiciously. A variety of racist terms are used to label individuals who try to act as though they are members of another culture.

One model of relational development, based on interviews with romantic couples, suggests that interracial couples (and probably intercultural couples as well) go through four stages: (1) awareness of racial differences balanced against attraction between the individuals; (2) coping with their racial difference and the responses they get as a couple; (3) the emergence of their own identity as a couple (similar to the third culture concept discussed in Chapter 4; and (4) maintenance of the relationship.[29] To succeed, interracial couples need to develop communication strategies for coping with negative social reactions to their relationships.[30] In addition, interracial couples can reframe their relationship in a positive light by recognizing the value of such a unique relationship. Sometimes interracial couples may be inclined to ignore their racial difference, but (like any difference between two people in a relationship) racial and cultural differences usually need to be discussed so that the partners can genuinely understand and appreciate each other. While interracial couples might face numerous obstacles, a recent study of dating college students in a racially diverse community found no differences between interracial couples and those of the same race in reported relational conflict or relationship quality.[31]

Unlike the other relationships that we've been discussing, homosexual relationships are not relationships between two people who are different, but relationships between two people who are similar. Gay and lesbian relationships often face strong social hostility, which may be one reason gays and lesbians seek social networks that confirm their relationships and allow them to be forthright about them.[32] Many individuals hide their homosexual relationships from others for fear of the reactions and rejection they may face. Despite the social stigma that these are "abnormal" relationships, gay and lesbian couples engage in the same kinds of relational maintenance activities as heterosexual couples.[33]

in-group. One's racial or ethnic group.

out-group. A race, culture, religion, or ethnic group different from one's own.

Friends with a Difference

Think of someone you know or imagine yourself in a friendship with someone from each of the following groups: (a) someone at least ten years older than you are; (b) someone from a country where people speak a different language than you do; (c) someone of a different sexual orientation; (d) someone of a different race; (e) someone of a different religion.

1. With which of these people is communication easiest? Why?
2. With which of these people is communication hardest? Why?
3. How do your family and friends react to this relationship? Why?
4. How have your differences affected your interpersonal communication in each friendship?
5. How does this friendship compare to friendships with those who are similar to you?

Besides relationships among gays and lesbians, there are also nonsexual relationships between heterosexuals and homosexuals. Such a relationship has served as the foundation for the friendship portrayed on the TV show *Will and Grace.* An individual's sexual orientation shouldn't be a factor in whether you form a friendship, any more than a person's race, ethnicity, or age should be—but it often is. Straight people are referred to as *homophobic* when they fear interaction and friendship with gays and lesbians. While you might not find a person's sexual orientation to be a problem, one study found that heterosexual respondents reported that even if they had a lot in common with someone identified as homosexual, they were more inclined to forgo a friendship with that person and restrict themselves to relationships with heterosexuals.[34] This tendency was significantly stronger for the male respondents than for the females.

Knowing that others are likely to avoid developing friendships with them might lead gays and lesbians to hide their sexual orientation. The desire to be able to form nonsexual friendships has to be weighed against the risks of being open and self-disclosing. This scenario creates a paradox, because interactions with homosexuals positively influence the attitudes heterosexuals have toward them.[35] Regardless of your own sexual orientation, take some time to consider your attitudes and openness to forming relationships with all people, no matter how they differ from you.

Relationship Challenges

Failure Events	Violations of understandings between people in relationships.
Reproach	Message by a partner that a failure event has occurred.
Account	A response to a reproach.
Physical Separation and Distance	Add costs and challenges to the maintenance of a relationship.
Relationships That Challenge Social Norms	Include relationships between those who differ in age, race, religion, ethnicity, or sexual orientation.

The Dark Side of Interpersonal Communication and Relationships

The "dark side" of interpersonal communication is the use of interpersonal communication in damaging, unethical ways. Throughout the text, we have focused primarily on how interpersonal communication can be used for developing fulfilling relationships, for managing conflict cooperatively, for improving relationships, and for helping you meet your interpersonal needs. However, interpersonal communication can also be used to deceive and hurt people. Regrettably, the dark side of interpersonal communication and relationships is more prevalent than you might think; for example, studies focusing on deception have found that it is pervasive in interpersonal interactions.[36] There is a dark side to relationships as well, including obsessive relational intrusion, stalking, jealousy, and relational violence.

The Dark Side of Interpersonal Communication: Deception

You wake up to discover you've overslept, but because an absence would hurt your grade, you come to class late and tell the instructor that you had car trouble. Your roommate is going on a date wearing an outfit that you think is nice—but not on her; when asked what you think, you say, "I've always liked that outfit," omitting the fact that you don't think it suits her. You're involved in an intimate relationship but find you no longer have strong feelings toward your partner. Your partner asks, "Do you still love me?" and you answer, "Yes." You are developing a close physical relationship with someone but are unwilling to disclose the extent of your previous sexual relationships.

Each of these scenarios represents a situation in which there is deception, but the impact and seriousness of the deceptions differ. One way to assess the seriousness is to ask yourself, "What would happen if the other person found out I was deceitful?" Your instructor and your roommate might be upset, but deceiving them would probably not have the same impact as falsely declaring your love or not disclosing your sexual activity to a partner. Communication scholar Mark Knapp classifies lies as high stake and low stake lies.[37] The size of the stake represents how much might be gained by the deception and how much would be lost if the lie were detected. The lie to the instructor is a low stake lie, while not revealing previous sexual activity might be considered a high stake lie.

Deception by Omission (Concealment)

Deception by omission (concealment) involves intentionally holding back some of the information another person has requested or that you are expected to share. For example, your parents ask where you were last night, and you reply that you went to the movies. While that is true, you don't tell your parents that you also went to a party at a friend's house afterwards. You have not "lied," but you have been deceptive. Determining whether an omission is deceptive depends on the intention of the deceiver. What was your reason for omitting the information about the party? Were you attempting to avoid your parents' response, or did you simply forget?

We can also present information and leave out information so as to intentionally mislead the listener. For example, telling your roommate "I've always liked that outfit" is intended to create the impression that you think the outfit is attractive on her. This deception provides you some protection if you are later called to task by your

deception by omission (concealment). Intentionally holding back some of the information another person has requested or that you are expected to share.

How might the mother react if she found out her daughter's lies were lies of commission and not of omission?

roommate for not saying the outfit looked bad. You can reply, "I never said it looked good on you." Despite your claim, your roommate would know your intention was to deceive. These types of omissions are sometimes called "half-truths," because the statements themselves are truthful, but they are not the complete truth.

Another form of deception by omission demonstrates how deceptions can be failure events. You may fail to share information that you know you should provide to another person because of relational expectations. For example, knowing that your best friend's fiancée has been having an affair but not telling your friend about it is deception by omission. Your friend's discovery that you didn't share the information is likely to create a conflict, because he will no doubt believe you owed it to him to share your "secret." Deception by omission can undermine decision making; for example, not disclosing sexual history prevents one's partner from making informed decisions about the level of risk he or she might be encountering.[38] While omitting information usually is not considered as grievous as falsifying information,[39] when the omitted information is important, omission is viewed as just as deceptive as falsifying.[40]

Deception by Commission

Deception by commission is the deliberate presentation of false information[41]—lying. Among the types of deception by commission are white lies, exaggeration or embellishment, and baldfaced lies. **White lies** typically involve only a slight degree of falsification that has a minimal consequence. Calling these deceptions "white lies" seems to make us feel a little less guilty. Telling someone you were at the library studying when you really fell asleep in your room would probably be considered a white lie. Sometimes we use **exaggeration**—"stretching the truth" or embellishing the facts. Telling someone you were at the library for a couple of hours when it was only twenty minutes is an exaggeration, and a lie. Most of us have stories that we've told over and over that continue to become more embellished as we tell them. **Baldfaced lies** are outright falsifications of information intended to deceive the listener. Baldfaced lies have more impact on the behavior of those who hear them than other kinds of deception by commission. The emotional impact of such deception is related to the importance of the relationship, the importance of the information, and the importance of honesty to the people involved (see Applying Theory and Research for more details).[42] The potential impacts explain why we are less likely to lie to our best friends than we are to strangers.[43]

deception by commission. Deliberate presentation of false information.

white lie. Deception by commission involving only a slight degree of falsification that has a minimal consequence.

exaggeration. Deception by commission involving "stretching the truth" or embellishing the facts.

baldfaced lie. Deception by commission involving outright falsification of information intended to deceive the listener.

Reasons for Deception

While there are a variety of reasons people are deceptive,[44] those reasons can be placed into two general categories: altruistic and self-serving. Altruistic motivation is a common reason we lie to a close friend. Our concerns about hurting other people may lead us to lie to protect them—for example, not telling a roommate her outfit is unbecoming. On the other hand, we might deceive others because we either gain personally through the deception or avoid some undesirable consequence. Not being truthful with the instructor about why you were late to class is an attempt to avoid a negative consequence. In general, we lie more to strangers and acquaintances than to friends, and those lies are more likely to be for personal gain or exploitation, whereas relatively more of our lies to friends are altruistic or other-centered.[45] The two categories of altruistic and self-serving lies include a number of specific reasons for deception.

1. *To gain resources.* Deception might help us acquire material resources, such as money or property. We may also use deception to achieve intangible goals, such as fostering a relationship or bolstering our self-esteem.

2. *To avoid harm or loss of resources.* Deception may be used to prevent another person's negative reaction or to protect resources. For example, if an angry friend suspected you had broken her computer, you might lie if you were afraid she would damage something of yours in retaliation. Or you might avoid having to give up your free time by lying to a friend about not being able to help her move over the weekend.

3. *To protect one's self-image.* Most people attempt to present or maintain a certain image that they think others will find desirable, and people will lie if they fear their actions undermine that image. For instance, you might always be late for appointments, but you don't want people to think you are habitually late, so you lie about what made you late.

4. *For entertainment.* Teasing can be a form of deception if we tell other people things that aren't true. "I heard that Billy has a crush on you—not!" The reason for this kind of deception is to laugh at the other person's reaction.

5. *To protect another person's resources, self-image, or safety.* If we believe that certain information is harmful to another person, we might choose to keep it secret or to falsify it. In lying to protect friends from what we view as "harmful truths," we need to be honest with ourselves about whether the lies are really for their benefit. Is saying "I love you" when you don't really love someone a way to avoid hurting the person—or is it a way to avoid facing conflict and threats to your resources?

Effects of Deception

While at times deception seems to be acceptable because of the benefits it provides, deception can also cause harm, and there are also fundamental ethical questions about dishonesty. Harm can either be the direct result of the deception, or can result when deception is detected or uncovered. Here are some of the more obvious ways deception can be harmful:

1. *Leading to incorrect decisions or actions.* If false information is used in decision making, then a person may take the wrong course of action; for example, telling your roommate that he is supposed to meet his girlfriend (whom you don't like) at 8:00 in the student union, when you know she expects to meet him at 7:00, will obviously cause your friend to do the wrong thing.

2. *Harming relationships.* Obviously, lying to your roommate about when to meet his girlfriend may have a negative impact on his relationship with his girl-

Applying Theory and Research

When Lies Are Uncovered

What happens when you find out your best friend has lied to you? Do you end the relationship? Do you ignore the lie? Do you accept an apology and continue the relationship? These kinds of questions led Steve McCornack and Timothy Levine to investigate the emotional impact and the impact on the relationship of detecting a partner's deception. Student participants were asked to think of a recent situation in which they discovered their relational partner had lied. They then completed a number of scales that assessed such things as how intimate the relationship was, the respondents' inclination to be generally suspicious, the importance of the topic the person lied about, the importance attributed to the act of lying, and the level of emotional response. In addition, respondents indicated whether the relationship was a friendship or a romance and the current state of the relationship and gave an open-ended explanation of why the relationship had ended, if it had.

The level of emotional response was related to the type of relational involvement, the importance of the information, and the importance attributed to the act of lying. Examining the impact of the lying on respondents' relationships was more challenging. Only 24 percent of the respondents reported that their relationships had terminated since the lie occurred, which meant that at least when the study was conducted, students were maintaining relationships despite discovering the lie. Nonetheless, the more important the information that was lied about, the greater the likelihood that the relationship had ended. The researchers coded the open-ended explanations of the forty-six students whose relationships had terminated and found that 51.6 percent of them reported breaking up because of what was lied about, 32.3 percent because of the act of lying itself (which resulted in loss of trust), and the remaining 16.1 percent because of a combination of the two.

On one hand, this study suggests that lying about important information can have a serious impact on close relationships, even leading to their termination. On the other hand, the majority of us continue our relationships even after discovering our partner has lied.

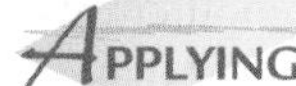

Applying the Research to Your Life

Consider your own experiences of lying. Examine the grid below and think about four times when you were caught telling a lie that fit into one of each of the four quadrants. What was the impact of the lie in each case?

	Casual Relationship	Intimate Relationship
Unimportant Lie	Impact?	Impact?
Important Lie	Impact?	Impact?

Now think about a time when you caught someone else lying to you. What impact did each lie have on you and on the relationship? To what degree do your responses match those found in McCornack and Levine's study?

Source: Steven A. McCornack and Timothy R. Levine, "When Lies Are Uncovered: Emotional and Relational Outcomes of Discovered Deception," *Communication Monographs,* 57 (June 1990): 119–38.

friend—but it could also have a negative impact on your roommate's relationship with you. Thus, another significant impact of deception is harming relationships, perhaps even leading to their termination.

3. *Loss of trust.* Part of the harm to a relationship that results from lying is the development of suspicion and the erosion of trust. Trust is a fundamental element of relationships, and once deception has been detected in a relationship, it may be hard for partners to regain trust.[46] Repeated deception and detection may lead others to label someone a liar, with the result that anything the person says is assumed to be untrue.

4. *Harming innocent bystanders.* Lies often have a ripple effect, whereby other people (innocent bystanders) are harmed by the lie. Your roommate's girlfriend will

be indirectly affected by your misreport of the time for meeting. If she lashes out angrily at your roommate for being late, she will have to apologize and defend herself to your roommate, and he may be wary of her for a while afterwards. This might also cause her to be short-tempered with other people, who then become additional unwitting victims of your deception.

What we say and how we say it can hurt other people's feelings, especially those of family members or romantic partners.

5. *Additional harm.* Among other negative consequences of deception listed by students in response to a survey by communication scholars Dan O'Hair and Michael Cody were punishment, embarrassment, guilty conscience, and a damaged reputation.[47]

The closer the relationship, the more effective people become at recognizing their partners' deceptions.[48] However, expressing suspicion can also signal inherent distrust in a partner. Interestingly, the closer the relationship, the more people know what cues their partners are suspicious of, and therefore the better equipped they are to adapt and avoid detection of their deception.[49] Deception occurs in all our relationships. We are both instigators and recipients of deception. Ethically, we should strive for honest relationships, and it would be nice to believe we could be totally honest all the time. However, we know that honesty can be harmful too, so we are faced with weighing the harms of honesty against the harms of deception. The survival of our interpersonal relationships depends upon our ability to effectively manage the challenge of deception.

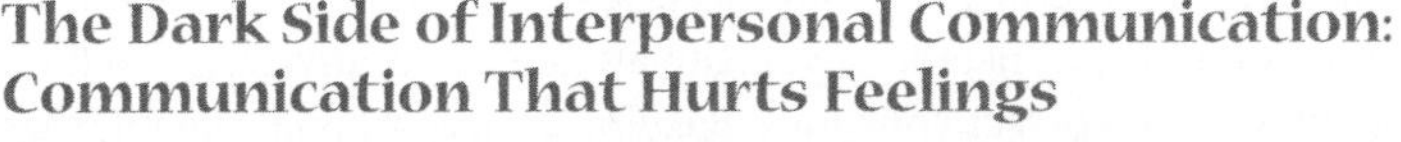

The Dark Side of Interpersonal Communication: Communication That Hurts Feelings

When people discover that they have been deceived, they usually feel betrayed, foolish, angry, and/or hurt. But deception is only one way in which we hurt people's feelings. As we discussed earlier, the truth can hurt, too. One of the more powerful aspects of language is that it can be used to cause emotional pain. Think of the last time someone said something that hurt your feelings. What hurt you about what was said? We can be hurt by insults, criticism, or teasing about our personality, intelligence, abilities, ethnicity, relationships, or sexual behavior.[50]

Disconfirming responses (discussed in Chapter 5) are one type of message that hurts listeners by undermining their sense of self-esteem, even when that is not the speaker's intention. When we receive a hurtful message, such as a disconfirming response, we try to determine the speaker's intention. The intention affects how hurt we feel.[51] A heartfelt apology can help alleviate another person's hurt when we have said something casually that has an effect that we didn't really intend: "I'm sorry, I didn't mean it like it sounded." In some instances, speakers can minimize the impact by claiming they were "just kidding." Researchers Stacy Young and Amy Bippus found that as the perceived intentionality of hurtful messages increased, so did the reported emotional pain.[52] In addition, they determined that, in general, humorously phrased hurtful messages were found to be less hurtful than non-humorously phrased comments. However, humorous messages were found to hurt more than nonhumorous messages when they were about abilities or intelligence, de-escalating the relationship, or about a person's hopes or plans. Apparently, there are some issues, like our abilities or dreams, about which kidding is more hurtful than straightforward comments.

Research by Anita Vangelisti and Linda Crumley identified three general categories of reactions to messages that hurt.[53] The first category, **active verbal responses**, includes reactive statements made by the hurt person, such as counterattacks, self-defense statements, sarcastic comments, and demands for explanations. The second category includes crying, conceding, or apologizing, which are considered **acquiescent responses**. Finally, **invulnerable responses** such as ignoring the message, laughing, or being silent are attempts to show that the message did not hurt. Of course, in addition to responding verbally, we are also reacting emotionally, such as by being angered by someone's criticism of us.[54]

Among their other findings on hurtful messages, Vangelisti and Crumley found that people are more hurt by messages from family members than from nonfamily members and that romantic relationships are more damaged by hurtful messages than either family or nonromantic, nonfamily relationships.[55] Vangelisti has found that, in general, informative messages that evoke pain ("I've been cheating on you" or "I don't love you anymore") have a more negative impact than an accusation or comment about one's abilities.[56] She speculates that people can defend themselves against accusations or point to times when they have shown ability, but it's more difficult to dismiss negative informative messages. How you convey the message also affects the impact, with harsh, abrasive messages creating greater hurt.[57]

Hurtful messages are probably unavoidable in interpersonal relationships, but how you respond to and manage the impact of those messages affects the level of satisfaction and happiness you feel in your relationships. When you are the recipient of a hurtful message, you should let the speaker know that your feelings are hurt and ask the person to clarify the reasons for making such a statement. The speaker might not realize that the message was hurtful.

BE OTHER-ORIENTED

A strong other-orientation is needed if you are to monitor the impact of your messages on other people. You might unknowingly send a message that hurts another person, but by closely monitoring responses to your messages, you will be able to tell when your messages are hurtful. In these instances, you can apologize for any pain you have caused, clarify your intent, and correct your message. On the other hand, the message might be intentional, even if the pain is not. Generally, your understanding of the other person can help you select the best strategy for presenting a potentially hurtful message and the best time to deliver the message.

The Dark Side of Relationships: Obsessive Relational Intrusion and Stalking

Fortunately, most of us accept it when a person we are attracted is no longer attracted to us—we move on. Our dependence on a partner in a close relationship might lead us to express some resistance to his or her decision to terminate the relationship, but eventually we accept the decision. Unfortunately, some individuals do not give up when another person fails to reciprocate their attraction, has no interest in a relationship, or desires to terminate a relationship. These individuals often engage in obsessive behaviors, trying to form or to continue a relationship. In some instances, such pursuit is simply annoying, but at its extreme, it arouses well-founded fears for personal safety.

active verbal responses. Reactive statements made in response to a hurtful message.

acquiescent responses. Crying, conceding, or apologizing in response to a hurtful message.

invulnerable responses. Ignoring, laughing, or being silent in response to a hurtful message.

A person who feels stalked experiences concern for her or his personal safety and fear of unwelcome intrusions.

Obsessive relational intrusion (**ORI**) was described by communication scholars William Cupach and Brian Spitzberg as those situations in which a stranger or acquaintance who desires or assumes a close relationship with another person repeatedly invades the other person's privacy.[58] In other words, someone wants a relationship with someone else who doesn't. Unlike stalking, ORI is usually annoying and frustrating but not threatening.[59] Obsessive relational intrusion is marked by such behaviors as unregulated self-disclosing; trying to get the other person to disclose; offering unwanted gifts, notes, calls, and other expressions of affection; arranging coincidental meetings; and expressing a desire for physical contact.[60]

There is a fine line between trying to hang on to or pursue a relationship and becoming obsessive. With ORI, normal relationship development behaviors become exaggerated and are pursued obsessively, making the change from non-intrusive to intrusive difficult to pinpoint.[61] Thus, it is the repeated and sustained display of these behaviors after rejection that indicates ORI. In addition, we often negotiate relationships through indirect and implicit ways, increasing the likelihood that one partner will misunderstand the other's intentions and interest. For instance, the ambiguity of nonverbal messages could cause a smile to be seen as an invitation to interact rather than as a general expression of someone's happy mood, leading someone, even a stranger, to initiate an unwanted approach and attempt to establish a relationship. Confusion about relational goals and definitions can lead one partner to think the relationship is more intimate than the other partner does. Such confusion can result in intrusions on a person's privacy. Clear discussions of each participant's goals, interests, and desires, as well as straight talk about the nature of the relationship, can help clarify these confusions.

Stalking involves repeated, unwelcome intrusions that create concern for personal safety and fear in the target.[62] It can be thought of as an extreme form of ORI, though sometimes stalking is motivated by revenge and not the pursuit of a relationship.[63] Stalking is an instance of the dark side of interpersonal communication, in which unwanted communication—in the form of phone calls, face-to-face meetings, letters, and e-mails—is used to instill fear. Stalking appears more prevalent on college campuses than among the general public, with studies showing almost 30 percent of males and females surveyed feeling they have been stalked.[64] Possible reasons for this prevalence are the lack of social and relational skills in young adults and the close proximity and sharing of space that occur on college campuses.

The response to stalking needs to be proportionate to the potential harm. Direct contact with the stalker in an attempt to end the behavior might actually reinforce the stalker's efforts—he or she is getting the chance to interact. Contact professionals or relevant organizations in your community for specific advice on how best to manage stalkers.

The advent of new technologies has made communication intrusions easier, in the form of phone calls, text messages, and e-mails. Such stalking behavior forces the targeted to get new or unlisted phone numbers or to change e-mail addresses, but these steps often only serve as temporary deterrents. The more we use the Internet, the more information about us becomes available to anyone who wishes to find it. In face-to-face interactions, we control what information we disclose to someone else, but on the Internet, information is freely available to anyone. Concern is increasing about such open accessibility to information on those who create a presence on MySpace.com or Facebook.com. But information isn't just limited to what we ourselves post online.

obsessive relational intrusion (ORI). Repeated invasion of a person's privacy by a stranger or acquaintance who desires or assumes a close relationship.

stalking. Repeated, unwelcome intrusions that create concern for personal safety and fear in the target.

Becoming Other-Oriented

What Constitutes Stalking?

What might seem like perfectly acceptable behavior to one person can be perceived as stalking by another. Understanding how your view compares to those of others can help you appreciate their reactions and fears. The items below are from a study of college student perceptions of stalking behaviors and are divided into two categories: approach behaviors (actual interactions or attempts at interaction) and surveillance behaviors (observation and information collection).[65] Look at the lists and decide which behaviors you consider stalking. Next, think of a friend of the opposite sex and decide which behaviors that person would consider stalking. Finally, think about people in general, and decide which behaviors are typically regarded as stalking.

Approach Behaviors

Someone asks for a date, even after being told "No."

Someone gives someone else flowers, even though the recipient doesn't want them.

Someone sends e-mails without signing them.

Someone calls a person just to hear his or her voice on the answering machine, but doesn't leave a message.

Someone calls a person, knowing the person doesn't want to talk.

Surveillance Behaviors

Someone follows another person around campus to see where he or she goes.

Someone goes through trash to find out things about someone else.

Someone asks another person's friend for personal information about that person.

Someone takes a class just because a particular person will be there.

Someone drives behind a person from the store to his or her home.

Someone goes to a party just because a particular person will be there.

Someone peeps into the window of someone else's home to see who is there.

Someone watches another person during a weekend without him or her knowing it.

If you get the chance, have your opposite-sex friend select the behaviors he or she sees as stalking (without seeing your responses). How accurately did you guess your friend's responses to the list items? What, if anything, caused errors? If you or your friend has ever experienced stalking, what impact did that experience have on your tendency to assess behaviors as stalking? If you feel comfortable discussing the lists with your classmates, examine the degree of similarity in your views of people in general.

Public records, newspaper archives, chat room archives, and the like are readily available online. *Cyberstalking* is essentially stalking through the use of the Internet—keeping tabs on a person, sending unsolicited e-mails including photographs, and sending viruses. Stalkers can be either strangers who connect with someone through the Internet, or acquaintances who use the Internet as a means of relational intrusion. In general, you should be cautious about what information you make available online.

The Dark Side of Relationships: Jealousy

George, the pharmacist on *Desperate Housewives,* displayed jealousy by burning the car of his girlfriend's ex and slapping her for talking to another man. His behavior demonstrates another example of the dark side of interpersonal relationships—jealousy. Even when it doesn't reach the extremes that George displayed, jealousy can cause individuals to engage in a variety of behaviors that are detrimental to the relationship and possibly to the partner. **Jealousy** is a reaction to the threat of losing a valued relationship a person believes he or she has.[66] The future of the relationship is in doubt and the part-

jealousy. A reaction to the threat of losing a valued relationship.

ner's loyalty is questioned.[67] Sometimes concern about loss of the relationship arises because of the presence of a third party, but it can also result from outside factors jeopardizing the relationship—the partner turning to others for advice, loss of influence over the partner to someone else, or a partner's spending increased time on hobbies, school, or work.[68] Jealousy presents a paradox in that, on one hand, it represents a strong display of interest and love, while on the other hand representing paranoia and lack of trust.[69] Sometimes people are flattered by another's jealousy and even seek to evoke it to confirm the value of the relationship. Other times, jealousy is seen as a statement of possessiveness and restriction. Interestingly, the two partners in a relationship usually have contrasting emotional reactions to the jealousy. For the person feeling jealous, the potential loss of a relationship creates fear, anger, and sadness.[70] The person's partner might also feel fearful and angry, but may also feel a wide variety of other possible emotions, including being amused, flattered, mistrustful, baffled, condescending, upset, and put off.

Concern over the loss of or a significant change in a relationship is neither inappropriate nor unusual. For example, the discovery (or the assumption) that a friend is spending increased time on some other interest implicitly disconfirms us—the object of the friend's attention is more important than we are. While one reaction is simply to accept the situation, another is to feel jealousy. The change in the relationship represents an expectancy violation or a failure event. A jealous partner can respond aggressively or by withdrawing from the relationship. Or, he or she can handle the situation more directly. First, since one person feels uncertainty about the relationship, there is a need for more information. Directly discussing the situation with the partner and asking for explanation tends to evoke a more positive response than spying or seeking information from a third party.[71] The jealous partner can decide whether to even raise the issue, depending on whether he or she is interested in relational repair. How the person expresses feelings of jealousy directly affects the partner's response. Calmly expressing feelings, presenting oneself in a positive manner, and expressing caring are viewed more positively than displays of violence, being insulting or threatening, or confronting a rival.[72] Expressing jealousy arouses uncertainty toward the jealous partner, particularly when the jealousy is expressed indirectly through crying or acting hurt and depressed.[73]

You can probably think of several TV shows or movies in which one character tries to make some other character jealous. You might have also attempted this or been the recipient of someone else's attempt. The reasons for evoking jealousy are primarily for relational rewards (such as testing the relationship, bolstering self-esteem, increasing rewards, or improving the relationship) or for relational revenge (teaching the partner a lesson or punishing the partner).[74] Among the tactics people use to make another person jealous are relational distancing (being too busy to get together; excluding the other from plans, activities, and other friends; or ignoring the other person); flirtation façade (sending oneself flowers, leaving out fake phone numbers and pictures of oneself with others, or expressing attraction to or sexual interest in another); relational alternatives (letting your partner know you are thinking about other relationships by talking about past relationships, present relationships, or other men or women).[75]

The use of jealousy as a tactic to improve a relationship by getting the partner to pay more attention to you or display greater commitment is risky. Predicting a partner's response becomes even more complex if the partner discovers you have intentionally evoked his or her jealousy. In general, such a discovery could have a negative impact, because, as you read in Chapter 6, manipulative behavior elicits defensiveness. Whether you feel jealousy in your relationships or a relational partner expresses jealousy to you, the way the jealousy is managed can either enhance or destroy the relationship. Use your interpersonal communication skills to address jealousy openly, honestly, and cooperatively, as a serious relational concern.

The Dark Side of Relationships: Relational Violence

A full discussion of violence and abuse in relationships is beyond the scope of this text. The following is only an overview, with particular attention to the role of interpersonal communication. Stalking, obsessive relational intrusion, and jealousy can all be precursors to violent behavior in relationships, but relational violence extends beyond these limited factors. Relational violence can occur in any relationship—with a spouse, a dating partner, children, family members, friends, or co-workers. Unlike acts of violence against unknown individuals, relational violence occurs within the context of an ongoing relationship and is sometimes a defining characteristic or dynamic of the relationship.[76] The term *violence* often connotes physical harm inflicted on another person, but we will use the term **relational violence** to refer to the full range of destructive behaviors aimed at other people, including aggressiveness, threats, violent acts, and verbal, psychological, and physical abuse. At the extreme, relational violence involves forceful acts against another person. But hitting your fist through a plaster wall in rage during an argument is certainly a violent act, even though the partner is not directly abused. The act still instills fear, and the violence it represents can escalate.

Relational violence varies in its severity, frequency, and focus. What behaviors on the part of other people raise your fears? Does being yelled at or sworn at cause you concern? Does someone smashing a dinner plate in anger evoke fear? In the midst of a heated argument, would you be frightened if the other person pushed you? Being slapped, hit, or knocked to the floor are clearly frightening acts. Each behavior mentioned above represents a form of relational violence of an increasing level of intensity.

Sociologist Michael Johnson separates partner violence into three types: first, "intimate terrorism," which is the use of violence to control or dominate a relationship; second, "violent resistance," in which control attempts are met with a violent response; and third, "situational couple violence," in response to specific relational conflicts or tensions.[77] Males are responsible for almost all intimate terrorism, females for violent resistance, and both men and women engage in situational couple violence, which is probably the most frequently occurring form of relational violence.[78] The presence of intimate terrorism will most likely lead to the abused partner's leaving the relationship, whereas incidents of situational couple violence are usually not so severe as to end the relationship.[79]

Sadly, acts of relational violence are a form of communication—the dark side of communication. Acts of relational violence communicate anger, frustration, lack of control, and disregard for a partner and the relationship while instilling fear and engendering retaliation, counterattacks, and subversion. The results of a study of males participating in a domestic violence program found that compared to nonviolent males, violent males engaged in more name calling, criticizing, blaming, swearing, ridiculing, and mutual verbal aggression with their partners.[80] Patterns of negative communication, ineffective conflict management and problem-solving skills, and lack of good argumentation skills all appear to contribute to an individual's propensity for relational violence. The appearance of relational violence provides an additional rationale for the value of a course that helps improve your interpersonal communication. Relational violence is never acceptable, nor is it the fault of the victim; do not accept relational violence as a condition of your relationships. If you find yourself either the victim or the perpetrator of relational violence, you should seek professional help. A quick search online will direct you to numerous help agencies.

relational violence. Range of destructive behaviors aimed at other people, including aggressiveness, threats, violent acts, and verbal, psychological, or physical abuse.

The Dark Side of Interpersonal Communication and Relationships

Deception	The use of communication to deceive through false or misleading information.
Deception by Omission	Holding back information so as to leave an incorrect impression with a listener.
Deception by Commission	Deliberately presenting false information in such forms as white lies, exaggeration, or baldfaced lies.
Communication That Hurts Feelings	We can cause pain to others either intentionally or unintentionally, by such means as offering unwelcome or negative information or criticizing traits or abilities.
Obsessive Relational Intrusion	Repeated invasion of a person's privacy by a stranger or an acquaintance who desires or assumes a close relationship with the other person.
Stalking	Repeated, unwelcome intrusions that create concern for personal safety and fear in the target.
Jealousy	A reaction to the threat of losing a valued relationship a person believes he or she has.
Relational Violence	A range of destructive behaviors aimed at other people that includes aggressiveness, threats, violent acts, and verbal, psychological, and physical abuse.

De-Escalation and Termination of Relationships

The inability to effectively manage relational challenges or the dark side of interpersonal communication can contribute to the de-escalation or even termination of a relationship. For example, how likely would you be to continue a relationship after discovering that your partner had deceived you? Once a deception has been uncovered, relationships are more likely to be terminated when the offender can be avoided and there is lack of overall communication.[81] When you pick up signals of relational problems, you have three choices: you can wait and see what happens, make a decision to redefine or end the relationship, or try to repair the relationship.

Signs of Relationship Problems

Part of effective relationship management is being sensitive to cues that signal relational problems or change. As Understanding Diversity: Gender and Ending Relationships indicates, women usually sense trouble in a relationship earlier than men do—but what exactly do they sense? Because each stage in a relationship has unique communication qualities, specific verbal and nonverbal cues can tip us off when a relationship begins to de-escalate.[82] There is a decrease in touching and physical contact (including less sexual activity), physical proximity, eye contact, smiling, vocal variety, and ease of interaction. In addition, there is a decrease in the amount of time spent together, an increase in time between interactions, and more separation of possessions. The interactions become less personal, and so does the language the partners use. Couples use fewer intimate terms; they use present tense less and passive language more often; they make fewer references to their future in the relationship; they use more

Understanding Diversity

Gender and Ending Relationships

Men and women differ when it comes to dating and marital breakups. Women tend to be stronger monitors of the relationship, so they usually detect trouble before men do. Women's sensitivity to the health of the relationship may be one factor that makes them more likely to initiate the termination of a relationship as well.[83] However, some men who want out of a relationship engage in behaviors that women find totally unacceptable so that their partners are then motivated to break up with them. This allows each partner to feel as if he or she was the one who initiated the breakup and therefore lets them both "save face."

Relationship-ending problems are sometimes associated with behaviors that appear early in a relationship. Marriages in which the men avoid interaction by stonewalling and responding defensively to complaints are more likely to end in divorce.[84]

In one study of divorce, men tended to see the later part of the process as more difficult, whereas the women said the period before the decision to divorce was more difficult. In addition, two-thirds of the women were likely to discuss marital problems with their children as compared to only one-fourth of the men; and men were twice as likely to say that no one helped them cope with the worst part of the process.[85]

---

qualified language ("maybe," "whatever," "we'll see"); make fewer evaluative statements; and spend less time discussing any given topic. They fight more, and they disclose less.

John Gottman, who studied couples relationships for over twenty years, identified four categories of communication behavior that indicate increasing problems in a marriage.[86] These behaviors undermine effective communication between couples and can lead to the end of the relationship. The first warning sign is criticism or attacks on someone's personality. The second sign is the display of contempt through insults and psychological abuse. The third sign is defensive behavior such as denying responsibility, making excuses, whining, and countercomplaining. The final communication behavior that undermines a marriage is stonewalling, in which the partners withdraw, quit responding to each other, and become minimally engaged in the relationship. Among the four, stonewalling is the single best predictor of divorce. If all four signs are consistently present, there is a 94 percent chance the couple will eventually divorce.[87] Most couples experience some of these behaviors, but happy couples develop effective communication patterns to overcome them.

Repair and Rejuvenation of Relationships

Repairing a relationship involves applying all the maintenance skills we talked about earlier. Some of the strategies for dealing with conflict that you learned in Chapter 8 will also help you. Underlying the success of any repair effort, however, is the degree to which both partners want to keep the relationship going. The nature of the problem, the stage of the relationship, and the commitment and motivation of the partners all affect the success of repair efforts. There is no single quick solution to relational problems because so many factors influence each one. You need to focus on the specific concerns, needs, and issues that underlie the problem; then adapt specific strategies to resolve it. Professional counseling may be an important option.

What if it is your partner who wants to end the relationship? There is no pat answer for addressing this situation. If a friend stops calling or visiting, should you just assume the relationship is over and leave it alone, or should you call and ask what's up? People lose contact for a myriad of reasons. Sometimes it is beneficial to ask someone directly if he or she is breaking off the relationship, although such direct requests place your self-concept on the line. How should you react if your friend confirms a desire to end the relationship? If possible, try to have a focused discussion on what has contributed to his or her decision. You might get information you need to repair the relationship. Or you might gain information that will help you in future relationships.

Another response to signs of relationship disintegration is to rejuvenate the relationship—to put new life back in it. The ability to rejuvenate a relationship depends on the degree to which partners recognize the reasons for relational decay and the level of their interest in rejuvenating the relationship. When only one partner wishes to rejuvenate the relationship, the first task becomes convincing the uninterested partner of the value of doing so. Sometimes, if the de-escalation is caused by specific behavioral problems of one partner, then commitment to changing those behaviors is one avenue for re-energizing the relationship. Because the problem behavior represents a failure event, the partner might have to provide an account, admit failure, and ask for forgiveness. In general, rejuvenation is usually conducted through implicit moves rather than direct discussion.[88] In other words, we change our behaviors or engage in positive behaviors that we hope our partner will recognize as an effort on our part to improve the relationship. Think about times when you have made a change or put forth extra effort for friends or family members to help reduce relational tension—cutting back on your use of swear words you know your mother dislikes, studying more, doing the dishes without being asked, washing your father's car, or baking your friend some cookies. However, another problem might arise if the partner fails to recognize that you've made such efforts. Has this happened to you? Not recognizing your effort can be another failure event: "I can't believe you didn't even say anything about my doing the dishes for you." Not all efforts are implicit; having a serious relational talk, reconnecting after separating (reconciliation), accepting or forgiving a partner's transgression, and seeking outside help are other ways people report rejuvenating their relationships.[89]

The Decision to End a Relationship

If you do choose to change the level of intimacy in a relationship, consider your goals. Do you want to continue the relationship at a less intimate level, or terminate it altogether? Do you care enough about the other person to want to preserve his or her self-esteem? Are you aware of the costs of ending the relationship? There is no one correct or best way to end a relationship. Ending relationships is also not something you can practice. But you *can* practice the effective relational management skills of decentering, empathy, and adaptation. These skills will also help you in ending relationships.

We rely on our social networks for support and self-confirmation when an intimate relationship comes to an end. Advice about how to handle the loss of a close relationship is plentiful, but basically each person must find his or her own way to compensate for the loss of intimacy and companionship. The loss of an important relationship hurts, but it need not put us out of commission if we make the most of our social support network—friends and family.

De-escalation or termination of a relationship is not inherently bad. Not all relationships are meant to endure. Ending a relationship can be a healthy move if the relationship is harmful, or if it no longer provides confirmation of the self or satisfies interpersonal needs; ending a relationship also can open the door to new ones. Sometimes we choose not to end a relationship but rather to de-escalate to a less intimate stage that offers a better balance between benefits and costs.

Breaking up an intimate relationship is hard because of the degree to which we become dependent on the other person to confirm our sense of self. When a relationship ends, we may feel as if we need to redefine who we are. The most satisfying breakups are those that confirm both partners' worth rather than degrade it. "I just can't be what you want me to be"; "I'll always love you, but . . ."; or "You're a very special person, but I need other things in life" are all examples of statements intended to protect the other person's self-esteem.

The process of ending a relationship is considerably different when only one party wants out of the relationship than it is when both parties agree to the breakup.[90] In **bilateral dissolutions**, both parties are predisposed to ending the relationship; they simply need to sort out details such as agreeing on timing, dividing possessions, and defining conditions for contact after the breakup. In a **unilateral dissolution**, when one party wants the relationship to continue, the person who wants to end the relationship must use compliance-gaining strategies to get his or her partner to agree to the dissolution. Sometimes, however, people simply walk out of a relationship.

How Relationships End

bilateral dissolution. Ending of a relationship by mutual agreement of both parties.

unilateral dissolution. Ending of a relationship by one partner, even though the other partner wants it to continue.

fading away. Ending a relationship by slowly drifting apart.

sudden death. Abrupt and unplanned ending of a relationship.

A declining relationship usually follows one of several paths. Sometimes a relationship loses energy slowly, like a dying battery. Instead of a single event causing the breakup, the relationship ends by **fading away**—the two partners just drift further and further apart. They spend less time together, let more time go by between interactions, and stop disclosing much about themselves. You've probably had a number of friendships that ended this way—perhaps long-distance relationships. Long-distance relationships require a great deal of effort to maintain, so a move can easily decrease the level of intimacy.

Some relationships end in sudden death.[91] As the name suggests, **sudden death** is the abrupt and unplanned ending of a relationship. One partner might move away or actually die; more frequently, however, a single precipitating event such as infidelity,

Partners may experience one of three types of relationship termination: fading away—where the partners drift slowly apart; sudden death—where separation is immediate; or incrementalism—where the conflicts gradually build until the couple reaches the breaking point.

Understanding Diversity

Empathy and Sexual Orientation

I once volunteered as a crisis phone counselor in a large metropolitan area. We were trained to use effective counseling skills, such as empathy, in relating to the callers' crises. One night, a call came in from a very distressed and depressed man about his breakup with his homosexual partner, with whom he had a long-term intimate relationship. At first I was uncomfortable dealing with the situation. Despite extensive training and role-playing, I wondered how I, as a heterosexual male, could empathize with or relate to this caller. However, I continued to ask questions about how he felt, what he saw as his needs, and his perception of the problems. The more we talked, the more empathic I became, because I realized that his description was very familiar. I had been divorced some four years earlier, and this caller's descriptions of his feelings matched the feelings I experienced during that time. I was able to talk about some of the feelings I had experienced, and this seemed to help him understand his own situation. I realized that though the sex of our partners was different, the overriding issue was the loss of an intimate relationship. I grew a little wiser that night.

—Mark V. Redmond

breaking a confidence, a major conflict, or some other major role violation precipitates the breakup. Sudden death is like taking an express elevator from the top floor to ground level.

In between fading away and sudden death lies incrementalism. **Incrementalism** is the systematic progression through each of the de-escalation stages. At each stage, the relationship reaches a threshold, at which point the relationship moves down to the next level. Turmoil or stagnation in an intimate relationship leads one or both partners to evaluate the relationship, and if they determine that they have reached a certain threshold of intolerance (that is, the costs exceed the rewards), the relationship moves to de-intensification. Then, if and when another threshold is reached, the relationship de-escalates to individualization, and finally to separation.

Reasons for De-Escalating and Terminating Relationships

When a relationship comes to an end, we often ask ourselves, "What happened?" "Why did the relationship come to an end?"[92] We engage in this "postmortem" regardless of who initiated the breakup. If our partner initiated the breakup and did not provide adequate explanations, we are left to wonder and guess about what happened. We may continue behaviors that undermine future relationships because we failed to understand how we contributed to the termination of the present relationship.

Researcher Michael Cody had students assess what caused their intimate heterosexual relationships to break up.[93] "Faults" were cited as the number-one cause. These are personality traits or behaviors in one partner that the other partner dislikes. The number-two cause, "unwillingness to compromise," represents a variety of failings on the part of one or both partners, including failure to put enough effort into the relationship, a decrease in effort, or failure to make concessions for the good of the relationship. The final cause, "feeling constrained," reflects one partner's desire to be free of the commitments and constraints of a relationship. But a variety of other elements can contribute to the breakup of both romantic and nonromantic relationships, including loss of interest in the other person, desire for independence, and conflicting

incrementalism. Systematic progression of a relationship through each of the de-escalation stages.

attitudes about issues affecting the relationship, such as sexual conduct, marriage, and infidelity.

Just as there are behavioral rules for making and maintaining friends, there are behaviors that, if you pursue them, will almost certainly cost you a friendship. Listed in order of offensiveness, they are as follows.[94]

1. Acting jealous or being critical of your relationship
2. Discussing with others what your friend said in confidence
3. Not volunteering help in time of need
4. Not trusting or confiding in your friend
5. Criticizing your friend in public
6. Not showing positive regard for your friend
7. Not standing up for your friend in his or her absence
8. Not being tolerant of your friend's other friends
9. Not showing emotional support
10. Nagging your friend

Friendships differ from romantic relationships in many ways, including the reasons for relational disintegration. When one researcher asked individuals to identify why their same-sex friendships ended, first on the list was physical separation.[95] Second, respondents reported that new friends replaced old friends as circumstances changed. Third, people often just grow to dislike a characteristic of the friend's behavior or personality. And finally, one friend's dating activity or romantic relationships can interfere with and contribute to the decay of a friendship. It should come as no surprise that casual friendships are more likely to end than are those between close or intimate friends. Close friendships are better able to withstand change, uncertainty, and separation.

A Model of Ending Relationships

Steve Duck developed a model to show stages in the ending of a relationship.[96] As Figure 11.1 shows, first one partner reaches some threshold of dissatisfaction that prompts him or her to consider ending the relationship. Having passed this threshold, the person enters an **intrapsychic phase**, in which he or she privately evaluates the partner's behaviors, often focusing on the reasons mentioned earlier to justify withdrawing. Social exchange theory predicts that in this phase we would assess the relationship's costs and rewards and would be inclined to terminate a relationship that was no longer "profitable."[97] We might still remain in an unprofitable relationship if there was a reservoir of profits to offset the current costs. However, as with a savings account, there is only so much we can withdraw before we have to close the account (end the relationship). We might also remain in an unprofitable relationship if we predicted that the relationship would become profitable again.

From time to time we all become frustrated with a relationship—and for some of us the frustration may become severe enough that we consider terminating, but never proceed further than this phase. However, we might "leak" our thoughts and feelings through our communication, displaying such emotions as hostility, anxiety, stress, or guilt. We might consider various strategies for ending the relationship and/or decide to confide in our other close friends or family about our dissatisfaction. Perhaps you have served as a sounding board for a friend in an unsatisfactory relationship.

intrapsychic phase. First phase in relationship termination, when an individual engages in an internal evaluation of the partner.

dyadic phase. Second phase in relationship termination, when the individual discusses termination with the partner.

At some point we might decide to move from our private internal contemplations about the relationship to confronting our partner. This is the **dyadic phase** in the model. If our partner feels challenged and intimidated by our desire to end the rela-

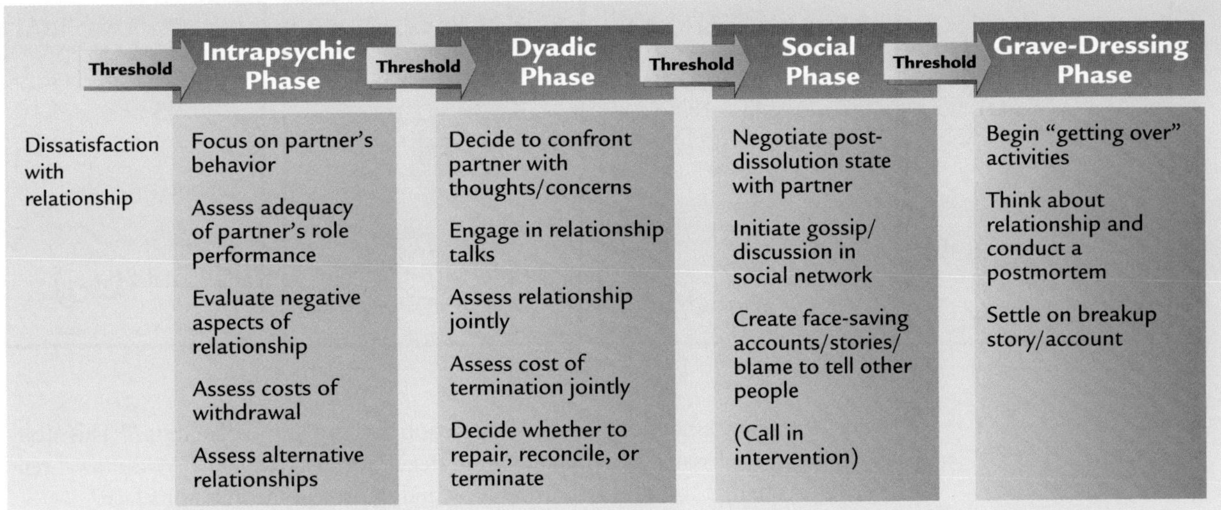

FIGURE 11.1

A Model of Ending Relationships

Source: S. Duck, "A Typography of Relationship Disengagement and Dissolution," from *Personal Relationships, 4: Dissolving Relationships,* edited by S. Duck (London: Academic Press, 1982), p. 16.

tionship, we might have to justify our thoughts and feelings. Our partner might also criticize our behavior and identify our failings.

If we decide to end the relationship, we enter the **social phase** and begin making the information public. Sometimes a person's social network will mobilize to preserve the relationship. Friends might act as mediators, encouraging reconciliation and suggesting ways to repair the relationship. Of course, friends can also reinforce a decision to separate. Rumors and stories about what happened and what is happening can fuel bad feelings and hasten the end of the relationship.

In the **grave-dressing phase**, one or both partners may attempt to "place flowers on the grave" of their relationship to cover up the hurt and pain associated with its death. They need a public story that they can share with others about what happened: "We still love each other; we just decided we needed more in our lives." Such a story often places blame on the other partner: "I knew he had his faults, but he thought he could change, and he just wasn't able to." Most importantly, we go through an internal stage in which we try to accept the end of the relationship and let go of feelings of guilt, failure, and blame.

Strategies for Ending Relationships

When the vitality in long marriages fades away over a period of years, the individuals move slowly through the de-escalation stages before finally divorcing. Relationships that haven't lasted as long are far more likely to end abruptly. As you saw in Chapter 10, the further up in the relational high-rise you go on the elevator, the longer the ride down.

But no matter what stage a relationship is in, partners use both direct and indirect strategies when they wish to end it. **Indirect termination strategies** represent attempts to break up a relationship without explicitly stating the desire to do so. **Direct termination strategies** involve explicit statements. The strategy that a person chooses will depend on the level of intimacy in the relationship, the level of desire to help the partner save face, the degree of urgency about terminating the relationship, and the person's interpersonal skills.

Indirect Termination Strategies

Relationship scholar Leslie Baxter identified three strategies that people use to indirectly disengage: withdrawal, pseudo–de-escalation, and cost escalation. *Withdrawal* involves

social phase. Third phase in relationship termination, when members of the social network around both parties are informed of and become involved in the termination process.

grave-dressing phase. Final phase in relationship termination, when the partners generate public explanations and move past the relationship.

indirect termination strategies. Attempts to break up a relationship without explicitly stating the desire to do so.

direct termination strategies. Explicit statements of a desire to break up a relationship.

reducing the amount of contact and interaction without any explanation.[98] This strategy is the most dissatisfying of the three strategies for the recipient.[99] Withdrawal represents an attempt to avoid a confrontation and to protect the initiator's face.

In *pseudo–de-escalation,* one partner claims that he or she wants to redefine the relationship at a lower level of intimacy, but in reality, he or she wants to end the relationship. Statements such as "Let's just be friends" or "I think of you as more of a sister" may be sincere, or they may reflect an unspoken desire to disengage completely. When both parties want to end the relationship, they sometimes use mutual pseudo-de-escalation and enter into a false agreement to reduce the level of intimacy as they move to disengagement.

Cost escalation is an attempt to increase the costs associated with the relationship in order to encourage the other person to terminate it. A dissatisfied partner may ask for an inordinate amount of the other person's time, pick fights, criticize the other person, or violate relational rules. As Understanding Diversity: Gender and Ending Relationships (on page 336) indicates, men apparently use this strategy more often than women do.

Direct Termination Strategies

Baxter also identified four direct strategies that people use to terminate relationships: negative identity management, justification, de-escalation, and positive tone.[100] *Negative identity management* is a direct statement of the desire to terminate the relationship. It does not take into account the other's feelings, and it may even include criticisms. "I want out of our relationship," "I just can't stand to be around you anymore," and "I'm no longer happy in this relationship and I want to date other people" are examples of negative identity management.

Justification is a clear statement of the desire to end the relationship, accompanied by an honest explanation of the reasons. Justification statements may hurt the other person's feelings: "I've found someone else that I want to spend more time with who makes me happy" and "I feel as if I've grown a great deal and need more than this relationship provides." But a person who uses justification does not fault the other person, and he or she makes some attempt to protect both parties' sense of self. One researcher found that most people on the receiving end can tolerate this strategy best.[101]

De-escalation is an honest statement of a desire to redefine the relationship at a lower level of intimacy or to move toward ending the relationship. One partner might ask for a trial separation so that both people can explore other opportunities and gain a clearer understanding of their needs.[102] "Neither of us seems to be too happy with the relationship right now, so I think we should cool it for a while and see what happens."

Positive tone is the direct strategy that is most sensitive to the other person's sense of self. This strategy can seem almost contradictory, because the initiator tries to affirm the other's personal qualities and worth while nevertheless calling a halt to the relationship. "I love you; I just can't live with you," "I'm really sorry I've got to break off the relationship," and "You really are a wonderful person, you're just not the one for me" are examples of positive tone statements.

Strategies for Ending Relationships

	Term	Explanation
How Relationships End	Fading away	The relationship dissolves slowly as intimacy declines.
	Sudden death	The relationship ends abruptly, usually in response to some precipitating event.
	Incrementalism	Systematic progression of a relationship through each of the de-escalation stages.
Indirect Termination Strategies	Withdrawal	Reducing the amount of contact, without any explanation.
	Pseudo-de-escalation	Claiming a desire for less intimacy, when you really want out.
	Cost escalation	Increasing relational costs to encourage the other to end the relationship.
Direct Termination Strategies	Negative identity management	Directly stating a desire to end the relationship, without concern for the other person's feelings.
	Justification	Directly stating a desire to end the relationship, with an explanation of the reasons.
	De-escalation	Directly stating a desire to lower the level of intimacy or move toward termination.
	Positive tone	Directly stating a desire to end the relationship, while affirming the other person's value.

Strategies for Post-Dissolution Recovery

Our identities are often tied to our relationships, and the more intimate the relationship, the more our identity is likely to be threatened if the relationship ends. Letting go of a close relationship is not easy, and the accompanying grief and pain can be debilitating. However, maintaining positive self-esteem and being able to nurture other relationships requires engaging in effective post-dissolution recovery. Relationship researcher Ann Weber created a list of strategies to help address the grief and loss of nonmarital breakups.[103] The following strategies are adapted from her list:

1. *Express your emotions.* You need to vent your feelings, if not to your "ex," then to a sympathetic listener, in a journal, or in some other forum. (There are even web sites where you can share your story.)
2. *Figure out what happened.* Understanding what occurred in the relationship is one way to get a handle on your current emotions. You need to accept the reasons for the breakup and work toward acceptance.
3. *Realize, don't idealize.* We sometimes view the end of a relationship as the death of a dream. In order to deal with a loss more realistically, Weber suggests mentally reviewing your partner's flaws.

Interpersonal Communication and Emotion
Connecting Heart to Heart

Assessing Your Emotional Responses to Relationship Challenges

This chapter could be subtitled "Experiencing Negative Emotions," because most of the issues discussed involve such negative emotions as anger, fear, sadness, jealousy, resentment, humiliation, uncertainty, disappointment, and heartbreak. However, positive feelings can arise when we successfully navigate relational challenges. Having a partner sincerely apologize for a failure event, deception, or a hurtful message can make us feel better and perhaps even increase affection for the partner. We might even feel relief and a sense of freedom when a negative relationship finally comes to an end.

A list of various topics covered in this chapter appears on page 345. Think of a particular time when you experienced each relational challenge. Our emotions are dynamic; we experience certain emotions when we are first confronted with a situation; other emotions emerge as we address the issue; and still other emotions occur after the challenge has passed. Identify the positive and negative emotions that you experienced both initially and subsequently.

Questions to Consider

- In what ways do the number and types of items you selected reflect the breadth and depth of your experiences with relational challenges?
- In what ways do the number and types of emotions you experienced reflect your general emotional responsiveness?
- Which situations produced the strongest negative emotional responses?
- What was there about the situations that caused these negative responses?
- How did you manage the negative emotional reactions?
- What could you do in the future to lessen or shorten the negative reactions?
- Which situations resulted in positive emotional responses?
- How likely do you think it is that other people would have reacted with similar positive emotions?
- During which, if any, of the twelve relational challenges did you discuss your emotional reactions with your partner?
- What impact did the discussion have on the relationship? On you? On your partner?
- During which, if any, of the twelve relational challenges did you discuss your emotional reactions with another person (perhaps a close friend or family member)?
- What impact did the discussion have on you? On the other person? On your relationship with that person?

4. *Prepare to feel better.* You might be surprised to find yourself feeling relief and joy. Finding the humor and irony in the breakup can help you cope with the grief.
5. *Expect to heal.* Some of the hardest words to accept from others are "It will get better." Although we may not want to believe it, we do recover.
6. *Talk to others.* Isolation is usually not a very healthy way to handle grief. Friends expect to provide comfort by listening to you discuss your feelings. Don't be afraid to be direct in explaining to friends what you want or need from them; they can't read your mind.
7. *Get some perspective.* This strategy involves a little bit of wallowing in your misery by reading stories, seeing movies, or listening to songs about other people's experiences in breaking up. These can help you put your own situation into perspective.

Relational Challenge	Initial Emotional Reactions	Subsequent Emotional Reactions
1. A violation of a relational expectation or a failure event on the part of a close friend	______	______
2. A violation of a relational expectation or a failure event on the part of a family member	______	______
3. Prolonged physical separation from a close friend or family member	______	______
4. Negative reactions from others to a relationship of yours that was outside social norms	______	______
5. Discovery that a friend deceived you by omission (not telling you something important)	______	______
6. Finding out that a romantic partner lied to you	______	______
7. Receiving criticism from a boss or teacher	______	______
8. Being the target of obsessive relational intrusion or stalking	______	______
9. Being the target of jealousy on the part of a friend, co-worker, or lover	______	______
10. Being the target of relational violence (either threats or actual physical violence)	______	______
11. Apparent de-escalation of a friendship	______	______
12. A romantic partner announcing he or she wants to end the relationship	______	______

8. *Be ready for further punishment, or maybe reward.* Weber suggests that once you've gone through the above strategies, it's time to explore potential relationships. Learn from your past experiences, hang on to pleasant memories, and move forward.

Facing the end of a relationship that has meant a great deal to us is one of the more difficult experiences we face in our social lives. The more intimate and involved we become, the more heartbreaking the end. But as the advice above suggests, there is life after the breakup of a relationship, and it is important to go through a recovery cycle that includes accepting the breakup, accepting the pain, realizing that you still have value and worth, and then moving on. Of course, all of this is easy to say and much more difficult to accomplish—which is one reason we should not isolate ourselves but lean on other interpersonal relationships and family members to help us cope. Regrettably, relationships do come to an end, but just as we develop skills in initiating relationships, we can develop the ability to cope effectively with their termination.

Building Your Skills

Assessing Your Past Relationships

Identify two relationships that you ended and two relationships that the other person ended. In each case, try to determine which of the indirect or direct strategies were used. What differences were there in how the relationships ended? What effects do you think the choice of strategy had on you and your partner? What strategies did you use to recover from the breakup? Which was the most helpful? Which the least? What other strategies for recovery have you used that helped?

Survey your friends to find out how they have ended close relationships and how they recovered from the termination of a close relationship. Try to identify the termination and recovery strategies they seem to have used.

Summary

The development and maintenance of an interpersonal relationship often depends on the ability to handle relationship challenges and the dark side of interpersonal communication. The inability to effectively manage these perils can mean the end of the relationship. Sometimes partners violate each other's expectations, which leads to failure events. Such violations may evoke a reproach, whereby the failure is pointed out. In response, the violator may offer an account in the form of an apology, excuse, justification, denial, or silence. Whether the account is accepted determines the likelihood of the failure event escalating into a conflict. Violations are assessed for their severity and can evoke discussion, retaliation, or forgiveness. Physical separation and distance are other challenges that many relationships face. Long-distance relationships lend themselves to the maintenance of ideal images and good behavior during face-to-face interactions, creating general relationship satisfaction. However, long-distance relationships sometimes incur greater costs, which lead to their de-escalation. Communication is a critical element in the successful maintenance of long-distance relationships. Social norms can pose a challenge to relationships between individuals who differ in race, religion, ethnicity, or age. Relationships with and between gays and lesbians also face social disapproval. Development of such relationships requires an appreciation and acceptance of people's differences and willingness to face the social pressure to conform.

The dark side of interpersonal communication refers to the ways in which communication can be harmful or detrimental. Deception varies in intent and severity and can be accomplished either by omission (leaving out information) or by commission (providing false information). Deception by commission includes white lies, exaggeration, and bald-faced lies. People lie to gain resources, avoid harm, protect their self-image, for entertainment, and to protect others. The consequences of deception include promoting incorrect decisions, causing harm to the relationship, causing loss of trust, and causing harm to others.

Messages are sometimes hurtful, either by intention or accident. We are hurt when others (particularly family members and romantic partners) make negative comments about such things as the relationship or our personality, appearance, abilities, or dreams. People respond to such messages by either defending themselves, conceding the issue, or ignoring the message. The dark side of interpersonal relationships is seen in obsessive relational intrusion, stalking, jealousy, and relational violence. People who repeatedly invade another person's privacy are engaging in obsessive relational intrusion. When such intrusions lead to concern for personal safety and fear in the target, intrusion becomes stalking. Stalkers exploit communication (whether phone calls, e-mails, or face-to-face interactions) in accomplishing their goals. Jealousy is a reaction to the threat of losing a valued relationship that a person believes he or she has. Jealousy occurs between siblings, co-workers, friends, and lovers. Creating jealousy by acting distant, creating a flirtation façade, or indicating relationship alternatives can be a tactic for strengthening a relationship. Relational violence represents a range of destructive behaviors including aggressiveness, threats, violent acts, and verbal, psychological, and physical abuse. Relational violence varies in severity, frequency, and focus. Three types of partner violence are intimate terrorism, violent resistance, and situational couple violence.

People can react to relational problems by either ignoring them, trying to address and repair them, or choosing to redefine or end the relationship. In a bilateral dissolution, both parties want to end the relationship, whereas in a unilateral dissolution, one person wants to end the relationship and the other wants to maintain it. Relationships typically end in one of three ways: by fading away, through sudden death, or incrementally.

In general, relationships seem to end when the costs exceed the rewards over some period of time. Reasons for ending a relationship fall into three categories: faults, unwillingness to compromise, and feeling constrained.

One model of how relationships end identified four phases: the intrapsychic phase, the dyadic phase, the social phase, and the grave-dressing phase. First, we internally assess the value of the relationship and consider termination; then we discuss it with our partner; we proceed by announcing the termination and interacting with friends and family; and finally, we come to grips with the consequences of separation.

Partners can use direct or indirect strategies to bring a relationship to an end. Indirect strategies to terminate a relationship include withdrawal, pseudo-de-escalation, and cost escalation. Among the direct strategies for ending a relationship are negative identity management, justification, de-escalation, and positive tone. Strategies for post-dissolution recovery include expressing emotions, figuring out what happened, talking to others, and getting some perspective.

For Discussion and Review

Focus on Critical Thinking

1. James was supposed to help clean up the apartment Saturday, but he was gone all day. His roommate reproached him when he returned. Create three accounts that James could provide that differ in terms of how likely they are to make the situation worse.
2. What factors would influence your reaction to the discovery that another person had deceived you?
3. How do you know when it is time to get out of a relationship?

Focus on Ethics

4. Jack and Jill are in an exclusive romantic relationship, but because they attend different schools, they are living 300 miles apart. Things have not been going very smoothly recently, and Jill decided to go out with a guy at school a few times without telling Jack. Is Jill's behavior ethical?
5. Under what circumstances is it okay to be deceptive?
6. Under what circumstances is it ethical for a person in an intimate relationship to use sudden death withdrawal as a strategy for ending a relationship? Under what circumstances would this behavior be unethical?

Learning with Others

1. In a group of three or four students, generate a list of failure events that you have experienced and rank them in terms of their severity. What makes some failure events more injurious than others? Discuss how violators responded to these failure events.
2. Get together with two or three other students and identify long-distance relationships that each of you have experienced, including those with friends, lovers, and family. Discuss which relationships have continued and why. Discuss which relationships have ended and why.
3. Working in groups of four or five students, use your own experiences to develop an answer to the following question: Do the reasons for breaking up a relationship change as the relationship becomes more intimate? To answer this question, start with casual relationships and identify reasons that people end those relationships. Next, talk about friendships, and discuss reasons for ending them. And finally, talk about intimate relationships and the reasons they break up. What are the similarities and differences among these different types of relationships and the reasons they break up?

Weblinks

Go to *www.mycommunicationlab.com* (access code required) to find Web resources for your text that supplement the material in Chapter 11, including links to information on the following topics:

Personal relationship blogs
Relationship issues (jealousy, distance)
Breaking up
Break-up songs
Advice on breakups
Abusive relationships

CHAPTER 12

Interpersonal Relationships at Home, through Computer-Mediated Communication, and at Work

OBJECTIVES

1. Define the term *family* and describe four types of families.
2. Briefly describe the circumplex model of family interaction.
3. Identify and describe ways of improving family communication.
4. Compare face-to-face communication with computer-mediated communication.
5. Describe principles for initiating and establishing relationships through computer-mediated communication.
6. Explain how computer-mediated communication contributes to face-to-face relationships.
7. Describe the dark side of computer-mediated communication.
8. Identify the communication skills that facilitate effective computer-mediated communication.
9. Describe the impact of workplace friendships and romances.
10. Describe principles of upward, downward, horizontal, and outward communication.

OUTLINE

People who have good relationships at home are more effective in the marketplace.

Zig Ziglar

Debbie logs on to her e-mail account and a chirpy voice says, "You've got mail!" The first message is from her dad:

> It was great seeing you this weekend. Your mom and I always appreciate it anytime you can get home during the semester. As to your changing majors, I want you to know that whatever decision you make is okay with me. I've got to get back to work. Just wanted you to know how nice it was to have you home for a couple days. Write when you get a chance, Love Dad.

Debbie clicks on the Reply button and writes her dad a quick response. Next she opens an e-mail from Tyrone, one of her co-workers:

> Man, you picked a great weekend not to work. Harry went ballistic with all the employees—he yelled his head off, accusing everyone of being lazy and good for nothing before storming out. It was quite the scene. He came back a couple hours later and apologized, but everyone still felt tense. Be prepared when you come in today. How was your visit with your folks?

Suddenly a small box appears on the screen with an Instant Message from Maria:

> *Maria:* What's up girl?
>
> *Debbie:* Not much, just got back into town.
>
> *Maria:* Whoa, I forgot. You missed a big blowup at work.
>
> *Debbie:* Yea, Tyrone e-mailed me about it.
>
> *Maria:* Tyrone? I didn't know you two were an item—coooooooooooool.
>
> *Debbie:* We're just friends, you jerk :-)

Computer-mediated communication is quickly becoming another tool to use in interacting with friends and families. The interactions just described illustrate three specific contexts that are the focus of this chapter: the family, cyberspace, and the workplace. Each of these contexts has unique characteristics and demands that involve particular forms of interpersonal communication. Family relationships and those at work are typically relationships of circumstance—relationships that are created not by choice, but because of the situation. In Chapter 9 you read about how these relationships can become relationships of choice when people become friends or develop more intimate relationships with family members or co-workers.

E-mail messages convey information about the nature of the relationships among the correspondents. The opening e-mails show that Debbie has formed friendships with at least two of her co-workers, Maria and Tyrone. Debbie's father expresses his feelings about her weekend visit and confirms his support for the decisions she's making. Tyrone's e-mail contains information about work, includes personal disclosures, and lets Debbie know he values her friendship. Maria's comments reflect an easy and relaxed interactive style typical of close friends. In each instance, computer-mediated communication supplements face-to-face relationships. It is also possible to develop and maintain relationships over the Internet without ever meeting face to face.

Interpersonal Relationships at Home

Families have changed since your parents and grandparents were children. At one time, almost two-thirds of American families consisted of a working father, stay-at-home mother, and at least two biological children. Today, according to the U.S. Bureau of the Census, less than 7 percent of all American families fit that description. Divorce, single-parent families, mothers with careers outside the home, the longer wait to start families, the move from an agrarian to an industrial society, and increasing mobility all have dramatically altered the very nature of American families. Communication within the family has changed too. The way family members interact with one another has been altered by a variety of social influences.

Like many other entities covered in this book, families are dynamic and changing. Because the members of a family get older, roles and relationships change over time. In addition, families add members and lose others. As new children are born, or as a member moves out of the home, the dynamics of the family changes. Ultimately, what is true of a family at one moment of time may not hold true later. By now you have already experienced the kinds of change that takes place in families as you have become older and gone from being very dependent on your parents to becoming more independent. As you get older, you may discover that your relationship with your parents changes still more if you begin providing care for them. As you consider your own family experiences and apply the principles we discuss in this chapter, remember above all to continually monitor your family relationships and adapt accordingly.

Family Defined

You might think that because families are basic to human existence, there's no need for a formal definition of a family—but definitions have been attempted, and there has been considerable controversy as to what constitutes a family. Which of these constitute a "family" in your mind: a single mother and her child; two brothers sharing an apartment; two gay men who live together and share a bank account; a lesbian couple raising two children; a husband and wife who have separated now that their children are grown? Traditional definitions of a family focus on the roles of husbands, wives, and children who all live together under one roof. Here is one definition written by sociologist George Murdock in 1949:

> The family is a social group characterized by common residence, economic cooperation, and reproduction. It includes adults of both sexes, at least two of whom

> maintain a socially approved sexual relationship, and one or more children, of one's own or adopted, of the sexually cohabitating adults.[1]

More recently, sociologists Gilbert Nass and Gerald McDonald defined a family as

> a social group having specified roles and statuses (e.g., husband, wife, father, mother, son, daughter) with ties of blood, marriage, or adoption who usually share a common residence and cooperate economically.[2]

Other definitions of a family deemphasize the traditional role of mother, father, and children, placing more emphasis on interpersonal relationships and personal commitment. Art Bochner's definition of a family echoes this relational emphasis. For him, the family is

> an organized, naturally occurring relational interaction system, usually occupying a common living space over an extended time period, and possessing a confluence of interpersonal images which evolve through the exchange of messages over time.[3]

Interpersonal communication scholar Mary Ann Fitzpatrick incorporates the transactional nature of interpersonal communication into her definition of family, which she defines as "groups of intimates with a history, a future, strong ties of loyalty and emotion, and a sense of identity and commitment."[4] For Fitzpatrick, communication is the key element that underlies the very existence of a family, with each of the elements in her definition rooted in and evolving from communication.

For our purposes in this chapter, we synthesize these perspectives to define the **family** as a self-defined unit made up of any number of persons who live or have lived in relationship with one another over time in a common living space, and who are usually, but not always, united by marriage and kinship.

Family Types

Virginia Satir, a well-known expert in family therapy, has identified four types of families: natural, blended, single-parent, and extended.[5] The traditional family—a mother and father and their biological children—is often considered to be the **natural family,** or nuclear family. But because changes in culture, values, economics, and other factors have rendered this family type no longer typical, the traditional family is sometimes called an *idealized natural family.*

An increasingly common family type today is the **blended family.** This family type consists of two adults and their children. But because of divorce, separation, death, or adoption, the children may be the offspring of other biological parents or of just one of the adults who is raising them.

The **single-parent family** is self-explanatory. This type of family has one parent and at least one child. Divorce, unmarried parenthood, separation, desertion, and death make single-parent families the fastest growing type of family unit in the United States today.

The **extended family** typically refers to the relatives—aunts, uncles, cousins, or grandparents—who are part of the family unit. Some extended families also include individuals who are not related by marriage or kinship but are treated like family.

In addition to Satir's categories, at least one other can encompass any of her definitions. The family in which you were raised—no matter what type it is—is your **family of origin.** It is in your family of origin that you learned the rules and skills of interpersonal communication and developed your basic assumptions about relationships. If you come from a blended family—one that was created following divorce, sep-

family. Self-defined unit made up of any number of persons who live or have lived in relationship with one another over time in a common living space and who are usually, but not always, united by marriage and kinship.

natural family. Mother, father, and their biological children.

blended family. Two adults and their children. Because of divorce, separation, death, or adoption, the children may be the offspring of other parents, or of just one of the adults who is raising them.

single-parent family. One parent raising one or more children.

extended family. Relatives such as aunts, uncles, cousins, or grandparents and/or unrelated persons who are part of a family unit.

family of origin. Family in which a person is raised.

aration, or death of a parent—you may have been reared in more than one family of origin.

Families come in all sizes and forms. A gay or lesbian couple may decide to live together and form a family and raise a child or children. At the heart of our definition of a family is the concept that it includes people who live in a relationship with one another. A family is a family if the people in it think of themselves as a family.

A Model of Family Interaction

Regardless of the type of family you have, communication plays a major role in determining the quality of family life. As shown in Figure 12.1, one research team found that over 86 percent of the families who reported family difficulty and stress said that communication was the key source of the problem.[6] Virginia Satir thinks good family communication is so important that she calls it "the largest single factor determining the kinds of relationships [we make] with others.[7] Psychologist Howard Markman found that the more positively premarital couples rated their communication with their partner, the more satisfied they were with their marriage relationships more than five years later.[8]

Another team of researchers developed a model called the **circumplex model of family interaction** to explain the dynamics of both effective function and dysfunction within family systems.[9] The model's three basic dimensions, as indicated in Figure 12.2 are adaptability, cohesion, and communication. Complete the Building Your Skills questions about family systems to find out how these dimensions apply to your family. **Adaptability,** which ranges from chaotic to rigid, is the family's ability to modify and respond to changes in its own power structure and roles. For some families, tradition, stability, and historical perspective are important to a sense of comfort and well-being. Other families that are less tradition-bound are better able to adapt to new circumstances.

circumplex model of family interaction. Model of the relationships among family adaptability, cohesion, and communication.

adaptability. Family's ability to modify and respond to changes in the family's power structure and roles.

cohesion. Emotional bonding and feelings of togetherness that families experience.

The term **cohesion** refers to the emotional bonding and feelings of togetherness that families experience. Family cohesion ranges from excessively tight, or enmeshed, to disengaged. Because family systems are dynamic, families usually move back and forth along the continuum from disengaged to enmeshed.

FIGURE 12.1

Sources of Family Difficulties

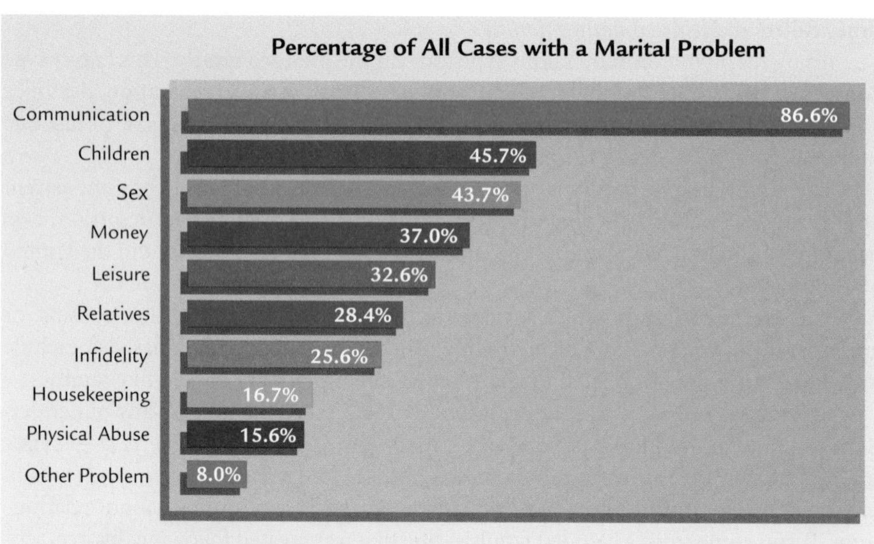

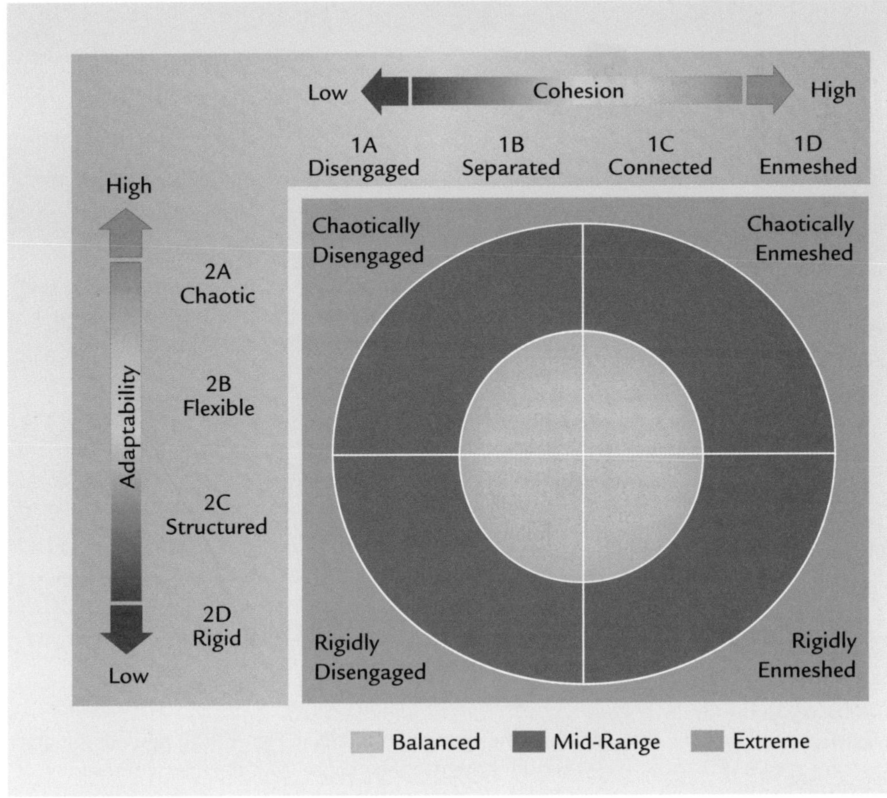

FIGURE 12.2

A Circumplex Model of Family Interaction

Source: Adapted from David H. L. Olson, Candyce S. Russell, and Douglas H. Sprenkle (Eds.), *Circumplex Model: Systemic Assessment and Treatment of Families* (New York: Haworth Press, 1989). Used by permission.

The third key element in the model—and the most critical one—is communication. It is not labeled in Figure 12.2 because *everything* in the model is influenced by communication. Through communication families can adapt to change (or not) and maintain either enmeshed or disengaged relationships or something in-between. Communication determines how cohesive and adaptable families are. Communication keeps the family operating as a system. The nature of the communication in the family has a direct impact on the development of your interpersonal communication skills. For example, one study found that the abilities to self-disclose, to offer emotional support, and to manage conflicts among friends and romantic partners were related to being raised in a family that supports learning about a diverse world and sharing opinions without fear of condemnation (a family high in flexibility and cohesion).[10] How has your family background shaped your interpersonal communication?

The circumplex model helps explain relationships among family cohesiveness, adaptability, and communication at different stages of family development. In general, families with balanced levels of cohesion and adaptability function better across the entire family life cycle than do those at the extremes of these dimensions. A balanced family has a moderate amount of cohesion and adaptability—represented by the center circle on the model. Balanced families can often adapt better to changing circumstances and manage stressful periods, such as the children's adolescence. Not surprisingly, these balanced families usually have better communication skills.

Research suggests that *there is no single best way to be a family.* At some stages of family life, the ideal of the balanced family may not apply. Older couples, for example, seem to operate more effectively when there is more rigid structure and a lower level of cohesiveness. Families with younger children seem to function well with high levels of both cohesion and adaptability. Only one thing is constant as we go through family

Identifying Your Family System

Choose the statement from each set of four that best describes the behavior typical of your family.

Level of Cohesion

1A. There is little closeness in my family. We are all pretty independent of each other. None of us have any real strong feelings of attachment to the family, and once the kids get to move out, there's not much drive to stay connected with the family.

1B. There is some closeness in my family and some interdependence, but not much—mainly we each do our own thing. The family usually gets together just for special occasions.

1C. My family is connected to each other, but we also have our independence. We get together at times besides just the holidays. There are feelings of loyalty to the family and we are pretty close to each other.

1D. My family is very close-knit and tight. We depend a lot on each other. We are always doing things together. There is nothing family members wouldn't do for each other. My family members feel a need for each other.

Level of Adaptability

2A. Family members come and go to the dinner table as they see fit. There are few rules about how to behave at the dinner table. My parents don't have a particular role at dinner.

2B. There are a few rules that govern dinner table behavior. My mom and dad are about equal in terms of who says what the kids should do, but the kids get a lot of say in what happens and how things are done. Both parents play a similar role.

2C. In my family, usually my mom [dad] makes most of the decisions, and my dad [mom] goes along with that. The kids get to have some input about what happens. We usually get together for dinner and have a set of rules to follow.

2D. Only one parent in my family makes the decisions and the other parent follows along. There are a lot of rules about how the kids should behave. At dinner, there are a number of rules that we follow and roles that we play—who clears the dishes, asking for things, etc.

Look at the circumplex model in Figure 12.2 and determine where the statement you chose from the first set fits along the Cohesion continuum; then locate your choice from the second set on the Adaptability continuum. Draw a vertical line down from the point you marked on the Cohesion continuum; draw a horizontal line to the right from the point you marked on the Adaptability continuum. Where the lines intersect gives a rough idea of what your family might be like in terms of its cohesion and adaptability. What communication behaviors might be typical for your family type? How does your family compare to the typical type?

life: Effective communication skills play an important role in helping families change their levels of cohesiveness or adaptability. These skills include active listening, problem solving, empathy, and being supportive. Dysfunctional families—those that are unable to adapt or alter their levels of cohesion—invariably display poor communication skills. Family members blame others for problems, criticize one another, and listen poorly.

Improving Family Communication

Wouldn't it be fantastic if you could learn special techniques guaranteed to enrich your family life? But, alas, there are no sure-fire prescriptions for transforming your family system into one that a TV sitcom family would envy. Instead, we can pass on some skills and principles that researchers have either observed in healthy families or applied successfully to improve dysfunctional ones.

Use what you know about the circumplex model and the cues you see in this photo to describe the relationships in this family.

Virginia Satir found that in healthy families, "the members' sense of self-worth is high; communication is direct, clear, specific, and honest; rules are flexible, humane, and subject to change; and the family's links to society are open and hopeful."[11] In such families, she notes, people listen actively; they look *at* one another, not *through* one another or at the floor; they treat children as people; they touch one another affectionately regardless of age; and they openly discuss disappointments, fears, hurts, angers, and criticism, as well as joys and achievements.[12]

In his study, John Caughlin identified ten factors that were associated with families that had good communication.[13] Those factors, in order of impact, are openness, maintenance of structural stability, expression of affection, emotional/instrumental support, mind-reading (knowing what others are thinking and feeling), politeness, discipline (clear rules and consequences), humor/sarcasm, regular routine interaction, and avoidance of personal and hurtful topics. After reviewing several research studies, family communication scholars Kathleen Galvin and Bernard Brommel identified eight qualities exhibited by functional families: interactions are patterned and understood; there is more compassion and less cruelty; problems are addressed to the person who created them—other family members are not scapegoated; there is self-restraint; boundaries about safe territories and roles are clear; life includes joy and humor; misperceptions are minimal; and positive interactions outweigh negative ones.[14] Of the qualities identified in these two studies, how many are present in your family? Which qualities do you think your family could use more of?

Not all of the qualities identified in the above lists specifically involve communication, though all are certainly affected by and affect communication. The following sections explore some of the skills and strategies you can follow to improve your family communication.

Take Time to Talk About Relationships and Feelings

Healthy families talk.[15] The quantity of communication depends on family members' needs, expectations, personalities, careers, and activities. But the talking extends beyond idle chatter to focus on issues that help the family adapt to change and maintain a sense of cohesiveness.

Often, because of the crush of everyday responsibilities and tasks, family members may lapse into talking only about the task-oriented, mundane aspects of making life work: house cleaning, grocery shopping, errand running, and other uninspiring topics. Healthy families communicate about much more: their relationships, how they are feeling, and how others are feeling. They make time to converse, no matter how busy they are. Family members have an other-orientation in these conversations, instead of focusing on themselves. In addition, they enjoy each other and don't take themselves too seriously.[16] If you haven't done so recently, try to talk to your family members about how they really are and share information about yourself.

Listen Actively and Clarify the Meaning of Messages

Because talking about relationships is important in healthy families, it is not surprising that effective listening is also important. In the often stressful context of family life, good listening skills are essential.

BE OTHER-ORIENTED

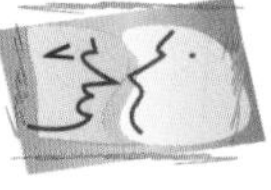

Good listening requires an other-orientation. In Chapter 5, we presented fundamental skills for listening and responding to messages. Family members will communicate with greater accuracy if they learn to stop, look, and listen. Stop: Minimize mental and outside distractions; don't try to carry on a conversation over a TV blaring, a video game bleeping, or a stereo's distracting rhythmic pulse. Look: Constantly monitor the rich meaning in nonverbal messages; remember that the face and voice are prime sources for revealing emotional meaning; body posture and gestures provide clues about the intensity of an emotion. Listen: Focus on both details and major ideas. Asking appropriate follow-up questions and reflecting content and feelings are other vital skills for clarifying the meaning of messages. And remember the importance of checking your perceptions of the meaning of nonverbal messages.

Support and Encourage One Another

A smoothly functioning family can be a supportive, encouraging sanctuary from everyday stresses. Through communication, people can let others know that they support and value them. Satir suggests that many, if not most, sources of dysfunction in families are related to feelings of low self-worth.[17] Healthy families take time to nurture one another, express confirming messages, and take a genuine interest in each person's unique contributions to the family. Researchers have found that supportive messages—those that offer praise, approval, help, and affection—can lead to higher self-esteem in children, more conformity to the wishes of the parent, higher moral standards, and less aggressive and antisocial behavior.[18] Jane Howard, who traveled extensively in search of a "good family," found that "good" families have a sense of valuing and supporting each other.[19] How can you let your family members know you value and support them?

Wise parents use support and encouragement rather than coercion as a primary strategy for shaping their children's behavior. The challenge is to find a middle ground that tempers support with appropriate control.

Use Productive Strategies for Managing Conflict, Stress, and Change

The inability to manage conflict and stress in a family may be a contributing factor to family violence. In Chapter 11 you read about relational violence, which is the extreme result of what happens when people fail to resolve conflicts in a collaborative manner. Husbands and wives must learn to manage conflict in constructive ways and to manage their conflicts with their children similarly.

John Gottman has developed a set of suggestions for handling conflict between couples, some of which apply equally well to parent–child and sibling conflicts.[20] Many of his suggestions reflect recommendations made in Chapter 8 on managing conflict. Gottman suggests picking your battles carefully, scheduling the discussion, employing a structure (build an agenda, persuade and argue, resolve), and moderating your emotions. In dealing with your partner, acknowledge his or her viewpoint before presenting your own, trust your partner, communicate nondefensively, and provide comfort and positive reinforcement. Conflict might be tempered by enhancing the romance and finding enjoyment in the relationship. He further suggests taking stock of the relationship and knowing when to seek help or to end the relationship.

No list of dos and don'ts will help you manage all differences in a family relationship. The suggestions offered here provide only a starting point. As we have emphasized, you will need to adapt these skills and suggestions to the context of your unique family system. But research consistently shows that listening skills and empathy are strong predictors of family satisfaction.

Recap: How to Improve Family Relationships

Take time to talk about relationships and feelings.

- Be other-oriented in your focus.
- Don't take yourself too seriously.

Listen and clarify the meaning of messages.

- Stop, look, and listen.
- Check your interpretation of messages.

Support and encourage one another.

- Use confirming messages.
- Be selective in disclosing your feelings.

Use productive strategies for managing conflict, stress, and change.

- Watch for communication warning signs.
- Learn to renegotiate role conflicts.

Applying Theory and Research

Family Communication Patterns

Chapter 9 includes a discussion of a typology of married couples developed by prominent communication scholar Mary Anne Fitzpatrick: traditional, independent, separate, and mixed (in which the husband and wife have different perspectives). Recognizing the importance of husbands and wives to the overall communication patterns in a family, Dr. Fitzpatrick and her colleagues combined her research on the types of couples with a typology of families. According to their research, people develop and enact their types through the use of *schemas,* which are mental structures or models used to organize knowledge. Three schemas contribute to family communication patterns: our knowledge about who we are (self-concept), our knowledge of other family members and their roles, and a set of expectations for various interaction situations (how a family "should" behave).

For their research, Fitzpatrick and her colleagues employ a family typology that is based on two dimensions (similar to the circumplex model): conformity orientation and conversation orientation. The degree to which a family pushes all members to agree to the same set of beliefs, values, and attitudes represents its conformity orientation. High conforming families tend to be very structured, with children obeying the parents and family members emphasizing harmony and agreement. Low conforming families support individuality and diverse perspectives. Strongly conversation-oriented families talk a lot about a lot of different things; they encourage open and diverse conversations. Families with a low conversation orientation don't talk much and only talk about a few things. The combination of these two orientations results in four types of families, labeled *consensual* (high conformity and high conversation), *pluralistic* (low conformity, high conversation), *protective* (high conformity, low conversation) and *laissez-faire* (low conformity, low conversation).

Traditional couples are linked to a consensual family communication pattern in which open expression is encouraged (high conversation) but there is an expectation that eventually, children will agree with the parents (high conformity). Both parents sacrifice some independence for the good of the marriage and seek a consensual relationship as part of a warm and friendly climate (high cohesion). They encourage children's interests in issues within the bounds of a traditional structure and hierarchy (low adaptability).

The pluralistic family is most closely aligned with the independent marital type, in which partners value independence and are willing to engage in conflict but strongly value their

Interpersonal Relationships and Computer-Mediated Communication (CMC)

Interactions among friends and family members have been dramatically altered by the introduction of cell phones, text messaging, PDAs, personal computers, and computer-mediated communication. **Computer-mediated communication (CMC)** was initially seen as a tool for accessing information, but it has quickly become an integral tool for human interaction. People have moved from using independent computers for word processing to using networked computers that allow them to send and receive messages and documents. As the technology has been introduced to the home, more and more families use the Internet to keep in contact. E-mail, instant messaging, and even text messaging provide useful communication tools for maintaining interpersonal relationships with friends, family members, and lovers. Chat rooms and discussion groups give people the ability to meet strangers and develop new interpersonal relationships. Thus, CMC allows you to meet two interpersonal goals: making contact with

computer-mediated communication (CMC). Communication between and among people through the medium of computers (includes e-mail, chat rooms, bulletin boards, and newsgroups).

companionship and sharing. The independent pluralistic family displays openness without a need for conformity. Communication in these families involves open expression of desires and interests and the pursuit of individual goals.

The protective family type is associated with separate couples, who are committed to the concept of marriage but avoid conflict and have limited shared interactions. Conformity is emphasized and interaction minimized. This type of family creates an image of harmony and peace by enforcing conformity.

The final family type, laissez-faire, is connected to one of the six possible mixed marital types: the type in which one spouse is independent and the other is separate. Not much ties such a couple together except a shared belief in their independence. This view carries over into the family communication pattern, in which there is little interaction and little push for conformity. Family members are free to pursue their own goals and interests without interference or guidance from other members; children are treated with indifference, neglect, and even rejection. The other five mixed marital types have not been connected to specific family types but are likely to lead to some combined family type, depending on which parent's marital type is dominant.

APPLYING the Research to Your Life

You can use the information on family communication patterns in two ways: first, to understand and appreciate your own upbringing, and second, to prepare for and make decisions regarding any family you create. In looking at your own family, you should be able to detect the type (consensual, pluralistic, protective, or laissez-faire) and your parent's related marital type. Consider the impact of your family communication pattern on your approach to relationships and to life in general. Do you value conformity? Do you foster openness in others? Do you enjoy conversation and sharing of ideas? To what degree has your family communication pattern influenced these attitudes?

One challenge you will face in forming a long-term commitment with someone is defining the nature of your relationship and consequently of your family communication pattern. The way you define your relationship will have an impact on communication in the family and on your children's development. For example, you might seek a relationship in which each partner is able to pursue his or her own interests with little interference from the other—but do you also want to create an environment in which your children feel a sense of indifference and unimportance? Any discussion of how you and your partner wish to define the relationship should include an exploration of its impact on the communication pattern that will develop when you start a family.

Sources: M. A. Fitzpatrick, "Family Communication Patterns Theory: Observations on its Development and Application," *Journal of Family Communication,* 4 (2004): 167–80. M. A. Fitzpatrick and L. D. Ritchie, "Communication Schemata within the Family: Multiple Perspectives on Family Interactions," *Human Communication Research,* 20 (2004): 275–301, A. F. Koerner and M. A. Fitzpatrick, "Toward a Theory of Family Communication," *Communication Theory,* 12 (2002): 70–91.

strangers, thus initiating and developing new relationships, and maintaining existing relationships. These two goals affect computer-mediated communication differently.

Comparing Face-to-Face (FtF) Communication and Computer-Mediated Communication (CMC)

There are advantages and disadvantages to both face-to-face (FtF) communication and computer-mediated communication (CMC). In FtF communication, people obtain a lot of information by seeing how other people behave, how they react, and how they look. However, such visual information has a down side when we have biased reactions to what we see (reacting to a person's age, sex, race, or physical size). Such attributes may not be readily apparent in CMC, and we might engage in fruitful and fulfilling chat with someone online whom we might have avoided if we had seen what he or she looked like first. Besides minimizing the use of nonverbal cues, CMC has interesting characteristics related to the importance of the written word, how much time delay there is between the interactants' messages, and the occurrence of deception.

Nonverbal Cues

Words and graphics become more important in CMC than in FtF communication because you must rely solely on them to carry nonverbal messages. There are some basic things users do to add emotion to their messages, including CAPITALIZING THE MESSAGE (which is considered "yelling"), making letters **bold,** and inserting face graphics, or emoticons (smiley faces :-), frowning faces with glasses 8-(, and so on). The ability to tease or make sarcastic remarks is limited in CMC, because there is no tone of voice in the written message, which means the author must usually write out an accompanying interpretation—for example, "Boy, am I insulted by that! (just kidding)."

CMC researchers Lisa Tidwell and Joseph Walther think that the lack of nonverbal communication cues in CMC might be one reason they found CMC partners using direct communication strategies like disclosure or asking questions to reduce their uncertainties more than partners in similar FtF interactions.[21]

The Role of the Written Word

The reliance on the written word also affects CMC interactions. One online scholar suggests that a person's typing ability and writing skills affect the quality of any relationship that is developed.[22] The ability to encode thoughts quickly and accurately into written words is not a skill everyone has. Not only do writing skills affect your ability to express yourself and manage relationships, they also affect how you are perceived by others. Your written messages provide insights to others about your personality, skills, sense of humor, and even your values. Consider the following two e-mail messages and think about the impressions you form of the two authors.

GigoloMan: "Hey, babe, whaddup? no what im thnking now we shuld do?"

GentleJim: "Hi. Boy, have I been swamped with work lately. How's your day been?"

What's your impression of the two e-mailers? What affected your impression? The first example is filled with grammar and spelling errors that might create a negative impression because the author is not particularly skilled at writing. The second author uses correct grammar and spelling, which is more likely to produce a positive impression. The user name or nickname (also called a "nick" among CMC users) that is listed for each author also affects our impression.[23] "GigoloMan" sends a clear but politically incorrect message to those who see his moniker. Our selection of words has a strong impact on the impression of us that others form.

Response Time

It takes longer to formulate a typewritten response than a spoken or nonverbal one. The amount of delay (which is similar to silence in FtF interactions) can have an impact on the interpretation of the message's meaning. When instant messaging, participants expect to see a response to their posting very quickly. This is one reason instant messages are often very short and concise. A rapid succession of short messages fosters a sense of synchronicity and interaction. By the time a long message gets written and sent, it is often no longer germane to the discussion.

E-mailing someone allows you time to compose your message and craft it more carefully than you might in an FtF interaction. You can take time to consider your message and delete it before sending if you don't feel you have worded the message the way you want. Even when instant messaging, you might finish typing a line and then decide to delete it and write something else. In FtF interactions, people can think about what they want to say; but once having spoken, they cannot take their words back. As a sender of Internet messages, you have more control over what you say and the impression you create; as the receiver of Internet messages, realize that the other person has had the chance to shape his or her message carefully for its greatest impact on you. Such deliberation is one reason you must be cautious about accepting the validity of Internet messages—deception is relatively easy.

Challenges of Computer-Mediated Communication

The use of CMC as a surrogate for face-to-face encounters creates some unique and intriguing challenges. One overriding rule that you should follow when communicating on the Internet is to follow all the rules you would normally follow in face-to-face interactions.[24] For example, in getting acquainted with someone, don't disclose too much too soon. Be a good "listener" and confirm the statements made by your Internet partners. Be other-oriented by considering how your Internet partners will react to what you have written: What is their context for interpreting your messages? What do they know about you? What do you know about them?

BE OTHER-ORIENTED

The kind of information you provide and acquire through CMC has a direct impact on impression formation and relational attraction. Even though you do not have the usual nonverbal cues that allow you to form impressions of other people (for example, their physical looks), you still form impressions about those with whom you interact. Prominent Internet researcher Joseph Walther has found that the impressions people developed about other people on the Internet became more similar to the impressions formed in face-to-face interactions the more users interacted.[25]

Initially, those in face-to-face interactions are likely to form a more detailed and comprehensive impression than those interacting through CMC; however, the impressions formed in CMC have been found to be stronger or more extreme.[26] This finding may reflect the fact that there are fewer cues in CMC on which to focus; thus, greater emphasis may be placed on those cues, resulting in more stereotyping. This might be one reason that often one of the first questions you're asked when you join a chat room is "A/S/L" for age, sex, and location. That small amount of information serves as the categorical foundation for impressions.

Computer-mediated communication has made it easy for us to have access to family, friends, co-workers, and even complete strangers. The key to success is to apply the same skills that you would in a face-to-face relationship.

Ease of Deception

A survey of 191 students at one college found that 40 percent had lied on the Internet: 15 percent about their age, 8 percent about their weight, 6 percent about appearance, 6 percent about marital status, and 3 percent about what sex they were.[27] As we've noted, the detection of deception in face-to-face encounters is aided by nonverbal cues. Online deception, by contrast, is almost as easy as typing. We say "almost," because you *can* assess the content of the written message for clues to deceit. College student respondents in another study reported the most common indicator of deception was someone's implausible statement or bragging.[28] The criteria for detecting deception apparently change as the Internet relationship becomes more intimate. As friendships develop over the Internet, to detect deception people come to depend on the personal knowledge and impressions of their partners acquired over the course of their correspondence.[29] Interestingly, this study also found that those who reported lying most were the ones most likely to suspect other users of lying.[30]

The ease with which someone can create a false persona means that you need to be cautious in forming relationships with Internet strangers.

Types of Computer-Mediated Communication

E-mail, chat rooms, instant messaging, bulletin boards, listservs, and mailing lists are among the ways we use personal computers to connect with other people. Text messaging on cell phones allows another way of connecting. Sometimes we direct our comments to a particular person (e-mail and instant messaging); at other times we simply put our ideas out for anybody to read (blogs, Internet sites such as Facebook and MySpace, bulletin boards, listservs, and chat rooms). Some forms allow us to have an active conversation with someone (chat rooms and instant messaging), while others allow us to post our ideas for others to read and respond to at a later time (e-mail and blogs). This last distinction refers to *synchronicity*—whether individuals are engaging in an interaction simultaneously or with some period of delay between the messages being sent and being read.

The more synchronous our interaction, the more similar it is to face-to-face interactions. There is always some delay in sending and receiving messages (even in FtF interactions, sound takes time to travel). The key distinction among different forms of CMC is whether we *feel* we are in a synchronous interaction. When we e-mail or text message quickly back and forth or instant-message, we can create a sense of social or psychological co-presence with our partners. **Social or psychological co-presence** occurs when we think and act as though we are in a face-to-face conversation. For example, while instant messaging, both participants create each other's "presence" in their minds and interact accordingly. When you are instant messaging with friends, do you experience this sense of co-presence? Co-present interactions, in which both participants are actively engaging in the interaction at the same time, represent **synchronous interactions.** Among the types of CMC that can be thought of as synchronous are instant messaging, chat room discussions, and any quick series of exchanges of e-mail or text messages.

Asynchronous interactions occur when messages are posted or sent without an expectation of an instant response, if any. Most e-mail falls into this category, as do bulletin board postings, most cell phone text messages, and postings on message forums, blogs, and even MySpace or Facebook. We expect replies from the specific recipients to whom we send our e-mails. In contrast, posting information about yourself on a site such as MySpace might or might not generate a response from people you know or people you don't know.

Each of the ways we have of communicating with others fulfills different needs and functions. In responding to a list of needs that might be met by various media, students indicated FtF interactions, cell phones, and instant messaging best met their need to communicate more easily.[31] E-mail, instant messaging, and cell phones best met the need to stay in touch. FtF interactions most met the need for doing something fun, followed by IMing (instant messaging) and talking on their cell phones. IMing and FtF interactions best met the need for passing the time when bored. However, computer-mediated communication still fell behind face-to-face communication when it came to satisfying the need to find out interesting things, be entertained, do something exciting, learn how to do things, meet and get to know other people, generate ideas, and learn about oneself and others.

A final quality that distinguishes types of computer-mediated communication relates to the last part of the definition of interpersonal communication—"usually for the purposes of managing interpersonal relationships." Consider the degree to which the various forms of CMC you use help you manage relationships. Obviously, instant

social or psychological co-presence. State of mind that occurs during computer-mediated interactions or text messaging, in which partners think and act as though they were face to face.

synchronous interaction. Interaction in which participants are actively engaging at the same time.

asynchronous interaction. Interaction in which participants send and receive messages from each other with delays between reception and response.

Allison Barrows/Universal Press Syndicate.

messaging or e-mailing friends and family is one of the communication tools you have for maintaining those relationships. We use these tools to self-disclose, to "listen" and respond to and confirm the other person, and to coordinate other interactions. Sending a text message to find out what time you are meeting someone allows you to manage your relationship. On the other hand, posting a blog about college life for public consumption doesn't help you manage relationships (unless your friends are regular readers), though some readers might initiate a relationship with you. Creating a site on Facebook also has little impact on managing relationships, except as you get requests from others to be listed as a friend and begin exchanging messages.

Initiating and Establishing Relationships Through CMC

Computer-mediated communication provides avenues for initiating relationships, such as chat rooms and dating services. In a 2005 survey by the Pew Internet and American Life Project, 11 percent of respondents reported having visited an online dating site; however, 66 percent viewed online dating as dangerous because it requires placing personal information online.[32] Nonetheless, of those visiting a dating site, 43 percent actually went on a date, and 17 percent developed a long-term relationship or got married.[33] Friends can also act as go-betweens, suggesting an e-mail exchange or instant messaging between individuals they think could hit it off. CMC provides the opportunity for appropriately introduced individuals to enter the acquaintance stage by sharing information and engaging in casual banter before moving to the exploration stage. While the social information processing theory discussed in Chapter 1 suggests that it takes longer to develop relationships over the Internet, CMC might also accelerate the process and lead to hyperpersonal relationships.

Hyperpersonal relationships are relationships formed primarily through CMC that become even more personal than equivalent face-to-face relationships, in part because of the absence of distracting external cues (such as physical qualities), an overdependence on smaller amounts of personal information, and idealization of the partner.[34] Hyperpersonal relationships were first identified in a study in which pairs of students who were initially strangers interacted for up to an hour in a simulated instant-messaging situation, while another group of pairs met face to face for up to 15 minutes. Those in CMC interactions skipped the typical superficial getting-acquainting questions and used more direct questioning and disclosing with their partners.[35] Online dyads engaged in more intimate probes and more responses and reached a similar level of understanding and ability to predict their partners' behaviors as those in FtF interactions. This study also reflects social information processing theory, because

hyperpersonal relationships. Relationships formed primarily through CMC that become more personal than equivalent FtF relationships.

even when the CMC pairs had up to four times as many minutes to interact, they still only generated about half as many utterances (messages) as the face-to-face pairs. This means the CMC pairs took more time, delivered half as many messages, but still exceeded the level of intimacy that occurred in initial face-to-face interactions.

Can you form intimate relationships strictly through the Internet? Assuming an open and honest exchange of information, individuals can learn as much about another person through e-mail disclosures as they might in face-to-face interactions. The main limitations to such relationships are the lack of opportunities to observe another person's behavior in a variety of non-CMC situations and the inability to engage in affectionate touch. Among the factors that have been identified as contributing to relationship satisfaction in romantic relationships formed exclusively through the Internet are trust, intimacy (perceived closeness), and communication satisfaction (measured by enjoyment of conversations, perceived ease of conversations, interest, ability to say what they wanted, and so on).[36] You can easily see why communication satisfaction is a key element of CMC-based romantic relationship satisfaction, since such relationships are so dependent on effective and satisfying communication in the absence of shared activities or direct in-depth observation of behaviors.[37] The more times online romantic couples communicate during the week, the more they appear to experience communication satisfaction, trust, intimacy, commitment, similarity, and ability to predict their partners' behaviors.[38] Couples in relationships primarily or exclusively maintained on the Internet report that they maintain their relationships by the use of openness (self-disclosing, providing and seeking advice, and talking about the relationship) and positivity (being cheerful and making the interactions pleasant).[39]

Face-to-Face Interpersonal Relationships and CMC

By far the most frequent role for computer-mediated communication in interpersonal relationships is to help escalate or maintain relationships formed face to face. People use e-mail and cell phones for maintaining contact with their close friends. One survey found that among 18- to 28-year-old computer users, 88 percent used e-mail, 66 percent instant messaged, and 60 percent engaged in text messaging.[40] Overall, 35 percent of cell phone users reported using text messaging, and an additional 13 percent would if they had it available on their cell phones.[41] Increasing services and changing technology are likely to make cell phones an even more prominent factor in maintaining relationships.

Does communicating over the Internet or by cell phone detract from quality relational time? To answer this, think about the last time you e-mailed, instant messaged, or text messaged. What would you have been doing instead? You might have been watching TV, reading, listening to music, or playing computer games. In other words, often you are not giving up relational time to engage in CMC, but you are giving up alone time—which means you are increasing the amount of communication you have with other people. (However, some individuals might indeed be forfeiting face-to-face interactions for computer-mediated ones. We will discuss this possibility later in this section.) One study found that those who send e-mail are just as likely, and in some instances more likely, than non-e-mailers to make phone calls or visit face to face with their closest friends.[42] When computer use results in an increase in communication within a relationship, that in and of itself enhances the relationship.

Nearly 30 years ago, an advertising campaign promoting long-distance telephone calling used the slogan "Reach out and touch somebody." That phrase is particularly applicable to the current use of CMC. Individuals are using CMC to touch others, creating and maintaining their social networks. Does your computer have an address book of your regular e-mail partners? If so, that address book reflects your online social network. Think of your list and decide how many of those individuals you would interact with as often as you do if you had to depend on phone calls, letters, or face-to-face meetings. There are probably some names that would drop from your list. And those that remained would probably have less contact with you than they do now. In other words, your social network is enhanced by the convenience that text messaging and e-mailing provides. A study in Japan found that e-mail tended to be used more in maintaining distant relationships than text messaging; text messaging was used more to support a network of those living close to users and with whom users had frequent fact-to-face interactions.[43] Because text messaging is mobile, it provides a convenient tool for arranging and coordinating face-to-face meetings and thus helps maintain social networks.

Look again at your e-mail address book. You might notice that you are a member of several different social "networks." That is, different subgroups on your list know and interact with each other, and by association, you are a member of networks created by others. These networks allow us to have what has been called "networked individualism"; that is, we are connected to a wide number of other people, but it is our choice whether to respond to or send e-mail. These computer-mediated communication networks have several characteristics: We can belong to many networks at the same time; the networks can be both local and distant; some help maintain strong ties (arranging FtF meetings) and some (occasional e-mails) help maintain weak ones; we can easily form and abandon these social networks; and CMC networks include more diverse members.[44] These social networks also serve as support systems.[45] Our networks provide information to help us in decision making, support and empathy in times of crisis, and encouragement and confirmation when we are troubled. Think about the times you have faced tough decisions or crises and have used e-mail or IMing to tap into your support network. You can tap into your own existing network or find other established networks devoted to specific issues.

The Dark Side of CMC: Cyberstalking and Harassment, Addiction and Compulsion

Chapter 11 introduced the notion of stalking and its electronic equivalent, cyberstalking. We easily forget that messages sent through CMC can be accessed by other people and that information you post on public Web sites is public. This means that information about you can be accessed by a stalker—which is why there is growing concern about teenagers posting information on MySpace or Facebook. Cyberstalkers use harassment as one of their tools for controlling and threatening others. We can receive harassing CMC from both anonymous senders and known associates. After ending a relationship, a person might be subjected to repeated unwanted phone calls, e-mails, or text messages from the former partner. These unwanted messages might simply be pleas for reconciliation, or they might involve relational violence (threats of abuse or retaliation). Other dark uses of CMC include circulating intimate, private, or false information (slander) about an individual (including real or manufactured images); sending viruses or hacking into and controlling other people's computers when they log on; and posing as another person on the Internet (identity theft), including sending e-mails attributed to the other person. Someone could use your name and personal information while participating in a chat room or a bulletin board and you might never know.

The best way to handle cyberstalking and harassment is to be smart about how you use CMC. Use an alias and not your real name when participating in chat rooms or posting on bulletin boards. Avoid posting personal information on Web sites, or limit what you do post. Be smart about the passwords you use; nonsense combinations are

Building Your Skills

Assessing Problematic Uses of Computer-Mediated Communication

Put a check mark by any of the following statements that apply to you. The term "communicating online" is meant to include e-mailing, IMing, and participating in chat rooms or other forums. Be as honest and as objective as you can.

_____ 1. I have gotten into arguments with others over communicating online or text messaging.

_____ 2. I have been told I spend too much time communicating online or text messaging.

_____ 3. If it has been a while since I checked my messages, I find it hard to stop thinking about what will be waiting for me when I do.

_____ 4. My work and/or school performance has deteriorated since I started communicating online or text messaging.

_____ 5. I feel guilty about the amount of time I spend communicating online or text messaging.

_____ 6. I have communicated online to make myself feel better when I was down or anxious.

_____ 7. I have attempted to spend less time communicating online or text messaging but have not been able to.

_____ 8. I have routinely cut short on sleep to spend more time communicating online or text messaging.

_____ 9. I have communicated online to talk to others when I was feeling isolated.

_____ 10. I have missed classes or work because of communicating online or text messaging.

_____ 11. I have gotten into trouble with my employer or at school because of communicating online or text messaging.

_____ 12. I have missed social engagements because I was communicating online or text messaging.

_____ 13. I have tried to hide from others how much time I actually spend online or how often I text message.

Use your responses as the basis for an objective self-evaluation of your use of computer-mediated communication. Double check any items you did not mark, to ensure that you didn't underestimate your use. For each item you marked, consider whether it is a recurring issue or just an occasional occurrence. How might you better manage any recurring behaviors so that they have less impact on other aspects of your life? Many of the items address feelings and emotions (guilt, shame, embarrassment, frustration, helplessness, loneliness, and so on). Examine the items you marked and consider the emotions you associate with them. If you feel your use of CMC is excessive, what options are available to you to help you address this behavior?

You might consider having other people you know evaluate themselves using the list and then compare your responses with theirs. Talk about how each of you interpreted the items and provide examples of the issues you have marked. Focus particularly on how your interpersonal relationships are affected.

Source: Adapted from J. Morahan-Martina and P. Schumacher, "Incidence and Correlates of Pathological Internet Use among College Students," *Computers in Human Behavior,* 16 (2000): 13–29, with permission from Elsevier.

best, since hackers have software that allows them to test long lists of actual words. Just as you are careful about who you share your phone number with, you should be careful about sharing your e-mail address (though both are often available through an assortment of directories if a person knows your name). If you are faced with CMC harassment, provide one clear statement that you do not want to be contacted, and keep copies of any messages you receive. Inform your Internet service provider, and consider changing your Internet address, cell phone number, or service provider. Since many of these harassing behaviors are illegal, it is also appropriate to report the incidents to law enforcement agencies.

"Internet addiction," "Internet abuse," "Internet compulsion," "pathological Internet use," "Internet dependency," and "problematic Internet use" are phrases used to describe another dark side of Internet use: devoting endless hours to surfing the Net, interacting in chat rooms, or gaming. Although some people consider the term "Internet addiction" overly dramatic and misrepresentative,[46] apparently there is a point at which use of the Internet becomes "abnormal." Most of us have spent an inordinate amount of time on something—watching TV, listening to music, reading, studying (okay, maybe not studying). Does this mean we are addicted to these things? Does spending a lot of time e-mailing friends, IMing, or visiting chat rooms necessarily mean you are abnormal? If you spent the same amount of time engaging in face-to-face conversations, would that be considered abnormal? We might be at a point in social evolution where our conception of human behavior and interactions has not caught up with technology. Nonetheless, there are some potential downsides to compulsive computer and Internet use.

The most obvious impact of any excessive or compulsive behavior is the amount of time it consumes—which can prevent the person from meeting his or her home, school, or work responsibilities. For example, all-night use of the Internet might cause you to fall asleep in class or at work or distract you from studying. In addition to this impact, problematic Internet use can hamper or reduce human interaction. Individuals who stay in their own room all day playing computer games or surfing the Net while passing up opportunities to socialize with others might be isolating themselves from personal relationships. Being alone is not, in and of itself, a negative or detrimental behavior. But if one is motivated by fear to avoid face-to-face human contact, then such behavior could be detrimental.

But are people really isolating themselves socially when they spend hours and hours e-mailing other people, IMing others, or participating in chat rooms or in other online forums? In essence, such individuals have created a virtual social world that might be as effective or even more effective at meeting their interpersonal needs as face-to-face interactions. Individuals who are uncomfortable or shy in FtF interactions might be quite adept and comfortable engaging in online relationships. Is this a bad thing? Are FtF relationships inherently better and more desirable than CMC relationships? The answers to such questions could be a matter of personal preference rather than a matter of mental or social health.

Nevertheless, depending primarily on online relationships for social satisfaction does reduce an individual's FtF interactions and related interpersonal skill development. People who prefer online social interactions to face-to-face interactions have been found to experience other negative characteristics, including excessive and compulsive use of the Internet, social withdrawal, mood alteration, and personal, social, and professional problems attributed to Internet use.[47] One study assessed students' compulsive use of the Internet and found that in comparison to others, pathological users were lonelier and went online to relax, to meet new people, to interact with others with similar interests, and to find support.[48] They also reported being friendlier and more open online.

Communication Skills for CMC

The abilities to talk and to express oneself nonverbally are critical in face-to-face interactions, but other skills substitute for these in CMC. In electronic communication, we depend on the ability to type (or on having agile thumbs), to incorporate shorthand codes, and to convey emotions in creative ways. Surprisingly, in one study of strangers asked to interact by describing either their commentary on a "worst-dressed" fashion show or their plan for a five-course meal of disgusting foods to serve to someone they disliked, participants in the CMC situation produced almost five times as many sarcastic comments than those interacting FtF.[49] However, those communicating by computer received considerably less indication about whether others understood their sarcasm, even though after interacting, their partners rated them higher than the FtF speakers on sense of humor. Why this happened is open to speculation. Perhaps when communicating anonymously without the expectation of meeting again, we take more risks in making sarcastic remarks, trying to use humor as a way of creating a positive impression. Rejection in CMC might be less face-threatening than the immediate rejection that might be sensed in face-to-face interactions, where others' nonverbal cues alert us to their negative reaction to our attempts at humor. When communicating online or with text messages, partners in established relationships have their knowledge of one another to use as a foundation for interpreting the messages and recognizing attempts at humor or sarcasm. Nonetheless, to ensure understanding of sarcastic or ironic remarks, online communicators need to provide cues such as emoticons, jk (for "just kidding") or a smiley :). More and more emoticons that can be attached to text to help convey emotions are becoming available.

Text-based messages require the sender to incorporate more information in the message than would be provided in an oral message delivered face to face. You often need to literally spell out your feelings, since the receiver cannot see expressions on your face, feel your hug, or hear the tone of your voice. In CMC, you have to let your partner know when you are angry, happy, amused, or confused. How comfortable are you with disclosing information about yourself, including your emotional state, in written messages? Some people have difficulty verbalizing their thoughts and feelings, and others are reluctant to do so. Such people might find face-to-face interactions preferable. For others, expressing themselves over the Internet or in text messages might be easier than doing so in FtF interactions. They appreciate that while composing an e-mail, they have the freedom to consider the best words and then to edit the message. Sending an e-mail provides some face protection and allows them to present a message without a partner interrupting, challenging, or immediately disconfirming them.

Besides the content of your messages, your "behavior" on the Internet affects the impression other people have of you. So what behavior can people observe about you? People observe your grammar, spelling errors, skill in using Internet conventions (emoticons, font stylings, images), response speed, the parts of their messages you respond to, use of humor, clarity of expression, use of slang or vulgarity, and so on. Developing sensitivity to how you might be perceived can help ensure you are conveying an accurate impression. You should also be aware of what factors in other people's e-mails or text messages affect your impression of them. Do you react negatively to a person's use of slang, misspellings, lack of capitalization, raunchy humor, or slow response?

BE OTHER-ORIENTED

Do strong writing skills provide an advantage in computer-mediated communication? In face-to-face communication we tend to be attracted to those whose communication skills are similar to our own;[50] this is probably true of CMC, too. To some degree, the way we communicate with our friends in person is probably similar to the way we communicate with them online. However, speaking and writing are not the same thing—otherwise we'd never have to study English composition. E-mail literacy includes effective writing skills. Paramount among those might be the ability to be other-oriented in the composition and adaptation of messages. E-mails to girlfriends, boyfriends, family members, and bosses are likely to differ in both content and style. Failing to adapt the message to your partner will likely undermine communication effectiveness and relational outcomes. You should also create messages (especially e-mails) with a sense of your goal. Are you trying to increase someone's attraction to you,

BE OTHER-ORIENTED

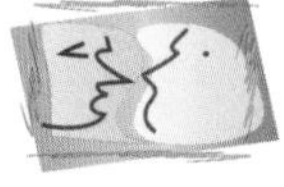

gain a favor, or simply provide an update to maintain the relationship? Try to apply the writing skills you have learned in the composition of any of your text-based messages.

Finally, remember that although computer-mediated communication may seem implicitly impersonal, we are indeed communicating interpersonally. Almost all of the skills that have been covered throughout this text can and should be applied to your computer-mediated communication. This includes listening, being other-centered, providing confirming responses, and practicing effective interpersonal perception, conflict management, and relational management. How do you "listen" effectively to computer-mediated messages? You let other people know you have "heard" them by sending confirming responses, by seeking clarification of things you don't understand, by reacting to and paraphrasing what they wrote. You can provide supportive responses that show you care about what others have communicated. Be cognizant of your perceptions and check them to ensure that they are accurate. Supportive responses convey your concern, commitment, interest, and love. You can disclose information and seek disclosure. You can use CMC to manage interpersonal conflicts, whether they arise in person or online, by using a collaborative approach, so that both parties work toward mutually acceptable goals. CMC provides a forum for relationship talk—expressing your perception of and expectations for a relationship while seeking those of your partners.

CMC can be used to terminate relationships, although it is probably more appropriate for relationships that exist exclusively on the Internet. In general, people prefer direct termination strategies. When asked, our students overwhelming supported the face-to-face approach to terminating a relationship; they felt that sending an e-mail to end a relationship leaves the recipient with too many unresolved issues.

Interpersonal Relationships and Computer-Mediated Communication (CMC)

Initiating and Establishing Relationships through CMC

- Chat rooms, dating services, and mutual friends can be avenues for initiating online relationships.
- CMC can lead to the development of hyperpersonal relationships that are more personal than face-to-face interactions.
- Romantic, intimate relationships can be developed totally though CMC.

Face-to-Face Interpersonal Relationships and CMC

- CMC is used to escalate and maintain face-to-face interpersonal relationships.
- E-mail, instant messaging, and text messaging are used extensively by 18- to 28-year-olds.
- The impact of CMC on overall relationship time and quality is not yet clear.
- CMC helps create and maintain many social and support networks.

The Dark Side of CMC

- Cyberstalking involves using CMC to harass, control, and threaten others.
- Internet use becomes problematic and may be characterized as abuse or addiction when use of CMC detracts from performance of other responsibilities.
- CMC allows users to avoid face-to-face interactions and can detract from social skills.

Communication Skills for CMC

- Those who use CMC need to compensate for the lack of nonverbal cues in these formats. More information must be conveyed in writing, including self-disclosures.
- Our CMC behavior affects the impression other people have of us.
- We are attracted to others who are similar to us in CMC skills.
- The interpersonal communication skills covered throughout the text apply to CMC.

Interpersonal Relationships at Work

Organizations look for employees who can relate effectively to other people—bosses, subordinates, peers, and clients. All the skills you have been studying throughout this text can improve your effectiveness in organizational relationships.

Your interactions in the workplace typically vary according to their degree of task versus social orientation. This variation is the source of both personal satisfaction and conflict. After you graduate, the workplace becomes a major source for developing interpersonal relationships. You make friends with the people with whom you work. You will socialize both on and off the job with various people from the organization. Conflicts arise when job-related decisions affect personal relationships, and vice versa. As a manager, you might become friends with some of your subordinates, but if the work performance of one of those subordinates falls below a satisfactory level, the friendship could interfere with your ability to address that problem. Many companies used to have policies prohibiting socializing among employees; however, such policies created strong dissatisfaction and discontent. Organizational policies that nurture relationships among employees build camaraderie and a supportive work atmosphere.[51]

Workplace Friendships

Friendships at work are like any other relationships in terms of their dimensions and development. One study, in which co-workers were extensively interviewed, identified three distinct transitions: acquaintance to friend, friend to close friend, and close friend to "almost best" friend.[52] Interestingly the researchers found respondents hesitant to refer to a co-worker as "best" friend, opting instead for "best friend at work" or "very close." The initial development of workplace friendships occurred for a variety of reasons, such as proximity, sharing tasks, sharing a similar life event, or perceiving similar interests.[53] As the relationships developed, the changes identified in this study were similar to those typically found in any developing friendship—easier and more flexible communication, increased self-disclosing, more frequent interactions, more socializing, and increased discussion of both work problems and nonwork topics.[54]

Interpersonal communication skills help in interactions with co-workers. Developing satisfying interpersonal relationships in an organization is often a rewarding part of a job.

Workplace friendships might be limited to a particular context: perhaps you have a lunch buddy, or you develop a friendship with someone working on a shared project, in which case the relationship ends when the project is completed. Outside of the workplace, friendships often find us associating with other people who are similar in age, status, and the like; however, workplace friendships often involve people who differ in age or status.[55] For example, you may find yourself becoming friends with a supervisor or subordinate who is considerably older or younger than you. Having a friend who is of the opposite sex may be more likely at work than it is outside of work, where such relationships might be expected to become romantic or might threaten existing intimate relationships. Results of one study indicated that men felt that socializing outside of the workplace was more important to their friendships with male co-workers than to friendships with female co-workers.[56] In addition, as their workplace relationships became more intimate, same-sex friends continued and expanded their relationships outside of the workplace; however, cross-sex relationships continued to be defined specifically as "workplace friendships." Workplace friendships enhance an organization's communication network by increasing the flow and openness of information. Just as outside friendships provide us with support and resources, so do workplace friendships. Workplace friends are in a position to understand and appreciate our organizational complaints and related frustrations. Friends help friends, and in an organization that can mean lending a hand, providing information, being an ally, or providing material support.

Just as with any friendship, those at work can deteriorate and end. However, unlike other friendships, we often continue in relationships of circumstance as co-workers, superiors, or subordinates. Some reasons for the deterioration of workplace friendships are personality issues, interference of one friend's personal life in work, problems created by different expectations for friend and work roles, promotion of one person to a position of authority over the other, and betrayal of trust.[57] How do you go about ending workplace friendships? Chapter 11 discussed some direct and indirect strategies for ending relationships that also apply to workplace friendships. Specific indirect strategies for the workplace include keeping all conversations focused on work topics; nonverbally distancing from the other (through the use of a condescending tone and disapproving facial expressions); escalating the cost of maintaining the friendship by being more independent or making more demands (although this strategy is less useful, given its negative impact on the continuing work relationship); and avoiding socializing outside the workplace.[58] When all else fails, some of our students have reported quitting their jobs to end a workplace relationship. The ability to redefine a friendship as only a work-based relationship requires strong relationship management skills to minimize the stress and potential resentfulness felt by a co-worker or a subordinate.

Workplace Romances

The workplace actually provides an opportune arena for the development of intimate relationships, because of the convenience and exposure to a pool of potential partners. Many people find their future spouses in the workplace. In one survey of managers and executives, 13 percent reported meeting their future spouses at work.[59] Some companies even hire married couples because they see a value in having both partners working for the same company. On the other hand, some companies have policies prohibiting dating a co-worker—but how can a policy prevent people from becoming attracted? In the workplace you interact with people in a safe and defined context that affords the opportunity to learn about others and share information about yourself. Trust evolves, similarities are discovered, attraction develops, and the interactions move toward more intimacy. In general, dating in the workplace is not particularly problematic when those involved work in different units or when there are no direct job-related power issues. Dating among members of the same unit can be a problem if it interferes with the ability of the individuals to perform their jobs. If you are involved in such a situation, your interactions with your partner at work need to remain professional. Co-workers sometimes are uncomfortable around romantic partners and may worry about inappropriate sharing of information, unequal work distribution, or other potential problems.

The most significant problems in workplace romances occur when the relationship is between a boss and his or her employee. The employee might feel coerced into the romantic relationship, which constitutes sexual harassment. Even if the superior does not threaten or show favoritism to the subordinate, the subordinate could believe that rejecting the superior's advances would be professionally detrimental. This type of sexual harassment is usually referred to as **quid pro quo,** a Latin phrase that basically means "You do something for me and I'll do something for you." A supervisor who says or implies, "Have sex with me or your job will be in jeopardy" or "If you want

quid pro quo. Latin phrase that can be used to describe a type of sexual harassment. The phrase roughly means "You do something for me and I'll do something for you."

Workplace satisfaction is related to the quality of the communication between boss and employees.

this promotion, you should have sex with me," is obviously using his or her power as a boss to gain sexual favors in exchange for something the employee wants. To avoid these situations, organizations often develop extensive policies about these types of relationships. You should learn the policies of any organization that employs you and assert your rights if you find yourself being sexually harassed.

Upward Communication: Talking with Your Boss

"Please place your suggestions in the suggestion box," announces the boss. The suggestion box is the symbol for upward communication. **Upward communication** involves the flow of communication from subordinates up to superiors. Today's organizations recognize that good communication improves quality, and thus many organizations encourage communication from lower levels to higher levels; however, effective upward communication is still far from the norm. Many employees fear that candid comments will not be well received. Others may wonder, "Why bother?" If managers offer no incentive for sharing information up the line, it is unlikely that their subordinates will make the effort. In 1952, an organizational researcher discovered that subordinates were more satisfied in their jobs when they felt their immediate supervisor had influence on decisions made at higher levels.[60] This is called the Pelz effect, after its discoverer, Donald Pelz. Subsequent research by organizational communication scholar Fred Japlin found when subordinates perceived their supervisors as supportive, the Pelz effect was particularly strong in creating a sense of openness and satisfaction.[61]

If there is little upward communication, the organization may be in a precarious situation. Those lower down in the organization are often the ones who make contact with the customer, make the product, or work most closely with the development and delivery of the product or service; they hear feedback about the product's virtues and problems. If supervisors remain unaware of these problems, productivity or quality may suffer. In addition, if employees have no opportunities to share problems and complaints with their boss, their frustration level may be dangerously high. Upward communication helps managers deal quickly with problems and gather suggestions for improving processes and procedures. One pair of researchers suggests that subordinates can "manage up" by being sensitive to the needs of supervisors.[62] If you know

upward communication. Communication that flows from subordinates to superiors.

what your boss's most important goals are, along with his or her strengths, weaknesses, and preferred working style, you will be in a good position to establish a more meaningful relationship that will benefit both of you.

If you are a manager yourself, encourage your subordinates to share both good news and bad. Be visible and cultivate their trust by developing a system that elicits feedback and comments. Use a suggestion box (paper or electronic), informal discussions, or more formal meetings and presentations. Formal meetings with structured agendas actually appear more conducive to problem solving and negotiation than informal meetings that otherwise seem less focused and task oriented.[63] Making time for these exchanges will pay off in the long run.

Downward Communication: Talking with Your Subordinates

The owner of the local movie theater tells the manager that she plans on changing the theater format to specialize in international and independent films. During a weekly meeting, the manager tells the shift supervisors of the impending change. Your supervisor then tells you and the rest of the crew working Friday nights about the new format. This sequence of interactions represents **downward communication,** the flow of information from those higher up in an organization to those of lower rank. It can happen via memo, phone call, newsletter, poster, or e-mail or, of course, face to face. Most downward communication consists of instructions about how to do a job, rationales for doing things, statements about organizational policies and procedures, feedback about job performance, and information that helps develop the mission or vision of the organization.[64] The amount and quality of the information a manager provides to subordinates determine the quality of the relationship between them and the attitude of the employees. Information that is timely, useful, and accurate results in a better relationship and fosters more satisfaction and commitment to the organization among employees.[65]

What is the best way to communicate with employees—in writing or face to face? It depends on the situation. Often it's best to communicate orally, with a written follow-up. If you need immediate employee action, face-to-face communication followed by a written reminder is the most effective (sending only a written memo is the least effective).[66] On the other hand, if you are communicating about long-term actions, a written message is the most effective. Certain situations, such as reprimanding an employee or settling a dispute, are best handled in face-to-face interactions rather than through the use of any written messages.[67] The best managers take care to develop and send ethical, other-oriented messages. Then they follow up to ensure that the receiver understood the message and that it achieved its intended effect. Managers need to be especially other-oriented when they are sharing sensitive information or broaching personal topics.

BE OTHER-ORIENTED

As mentioned earlier, behaviors by supervisors that involve using power against subordinates for sexual favors constitute sexual harassment. However, supervisors also have a responsibility to eliminate a second type of sexual harassment that represents another dark side of interpersonal communication: a hostile environment. An employee in a **hostile environment** feels his or her rights are being violated because of working conditions or offensive behavior on the part of other workers. Telling lewd or obscene stories or jokes about members of the opposite sex, using degrading terms to describe women or men, or displaying risqué photographs of nude or seminude people can contribute to a hostile working environment. A supervisor who either creates or fails to change work situations that are threatening to a subordinate is a party to sex-

downward communication. Communication that flows from superiors to subordinates.

hostile environment. Type of sexual harassment in which an employee's rights are threatened through offensive working conditions or behavior on the part of other workers.

Understanding Diversity

Male and Female Interactions in the Workplace

The following six scenarios reflect some of the general ways men and women differ in their approach to communication in the workplace. These scenarios are based on U.S. stereotypes about men and women in the workplace. As you read each one, see if the description of your sex's approach actually reflects how you behave. Also think about the degree to which you believe the stereotype presented for the opposite sex. The author of these scenarios does a good job of taking an other-oriented approach to helping improve communication, and the principles she offers apply regardless of the sex of those involved.

Power Plays

Her way: Women tend to ask lots of questions before beginning work.

His way: Men simply roll up their sleeves.

The result: Men assume women aren't up to the job. If they were competent, reason men, then women wouldn't be asking so many questions. But in fact, women typically verify and validate data before starting tasks, sometimes to improve their performance. If you're a male boss, listen to the questions women ask. Sometimes, these may add information or clarify things for everyone.

The reverse scenario is that men hate to ask for directions (big news, right?). But women assume that if men don't ask questions, they must know enough to complete a job. That's often not the case. For women bosses, it's a good idea to verify that men have enough knowledge to complete a task. Oversee the work in the early phases or offer help without being asked.

Picture Imperfect

Her way: Women frequently use anecdotes or illustrations about home or relationships.

His way: Men rely on metaphors about sports or war.

The result: Dialogue can hit a dead end. Women often do not follow the touchdown, full-court-press images, and vice versa. Don't simply gender-reverse images to communicate. Instead, consider your audience and use gender-neutral images (of nature, movies, or weather, for example). Or use images you like, but with an explanation of what you mean.

Command Conflicts

Her way: Growing up, girls tend to establish relationships.

His way: Boys usually vie for leadership.

The result: Men and women impose authority differently. "Women tend to be more collaborative in the workplace, putting relationships first," says Roz Usheroff, a business trainer and author of *Customize Your Career.* "Men routinely challenge and expect to be challenged." Each often finds the other's style ineffective or insulting. To jump the divide, borrow a bit from the other's style. Men can try a more collaborative approach. Women need to take over more often.

ual harassment. Jokes are not innocent and pictures are not "all in fun" if they make an employee feel degraded. Supervisors must adopt an other-oriented approach with respect to this issue; it is the receiver, not the sender, of the message who determines whether the behavior is hostile. Defendants have won court cases by proving that a supervisor tolerated a hostile work environment, even if the supervisor did not directly participate in the offensive behavior. Wise supervisors do not wait for a problem to occur. They take a proactive approach, offering all workers seminars on how to avoid engaging in sexually offensive behavior and explicitly discussing what workers should do if they become the victims of sexual harassment.

Horizontal Communication: Talking with Your Colleagues

You poke your head into your co-worker's office and say, "Did you hear about the possible merger between Byteware and Datamass?" Or while you are tossing pizza dough

Detailed Disputes

Her way: Women like to tell and hear stories, including stories about trials and errors, turnings and returnings.

His way: Men "cut to the chase."

The result: Each sex becomes too impatient to hear the other. "Women push for details generally for three reasons: to show concern, to vicariously participate in an experience or conversation, and to verify assumptions," says Dianna Booher, author of *Communicate with Confidence.* "Men tend to gather details just long enough to get the big-picture message and then dump them as trivial."

Again, each sex can benefit from the other's behavior. Men ought to explain their thinking and not simply jump to conclusions. Women need to get to the bottom line more quickly.

Emotional Exchanges

Her way: She tends to treat male colleagues like her husband or boyfriend.

His way: He often handles women associates like his wife or girlfriend.

The result: Subtle and tricky gender miscommunication. Typically, men and women bring into the office some version of the sexual dynamics they have at home. We also gravitate to workplace confidants, mentors, or employees who resemble the intimates in our personal lives, especially spouses. If you're in some kind of standoff or you feel like he or she "doesn't understand" you, take a break to think it through. Make sure you're not importing a personal issue into the workplace environment.

Decision Drivers

Her way: Women are generally more comfortable talking about their feelings.

His way: Men prefer to dwell on the facts and skip the feelings.

The result: Communication trouble. Every communication has both an intellectual and an emotional component; misunderstandings arise when we ignore one of the two dimensions. A man can acknowledge the emotional dimension: "I know this is a difficult conversation for you. It's difficult for me, too." A woman might dial down emotional intensity by increasing her focus on problem analysis: "I think there are three pieces to the issues we've been discussing."

The definition of a diverse work force, of course, is an environment where people accept differences rather than deny them. If we pay attention to gender differences, we just might untangle the gender communications knots—and get the job done faster, too.

Source: Written by Joanna Krotz for Microsoft Small Business Center Web page. Adapted with permission of the author and Microsoft Small Business Center, www.microsoft.com/SmallBusiness.

at the Pizza Palace, one of your fellow workers asks how much pepperoni to put on a Super Duper Supreme. Both situations illustrate horizontal communication. **Horizontal communication** refers to communication among co-workers at the same level within an organization. In larger organizations you may talk with other workers in different departments or divisions who perform similar jobs at a similar level; that, too, is horizontal communication. Most often you communicate with your colleagues to coordinate job tasks, share plans and information, solve problems, make sure you understand job procedures, manage conflict, or get a bit of emotional support on the job.[68]

Information travels through a workplace the way gossip travels through "the grapevine." And sometimes errors creep into workplace information that is spread this way. Although grapevine errors can cause problems for an organization, most continue to encourage co-worker communication because it enhances teamwork and allows the work group to develop a certain degree of independence. Some organizations even try to formalize horizontal communication by forming *quality circles,* or groups of

horizontal communication. Communication among colleagues or co-workers at the same level within an organization.

Becoming Other-Oriented

At Home, Online, and at Work

Throughout this text we have advocated taking an other-oriented approach to interpersonal communication. There are times when taking an other-oriented perspective or being empathic could be disadvantageous, if you ignore your own needs, values, or priorities. Look at the following situations and consider how being other-oriented might be counterproductive or lead to poor decisions. How can you be other-oriented and still make good decisions in each situation?

- You receive a call from the middle-school principle, who tells you that your seventh-grade son is being suspended for two days for fighting with another student. Because you are other-oriented, you understand the following about your son: He is very self-conscious about being overweight, and the other kids make fun of him for it. He has been struggling with his studies because he has a hard time concentrating and reading material. He has low self-esteem and does not feel that other kids like him.
- You have developed an online friendship with someone of the opposite sex whom you have never met. You have been exchanging e-mails and instant messaging for over a year and have become very close. You are considering flying out to meet this person. Based on information presented by your friend and your own impressions, you have concluded the following: Your cyberpal is very lonely; is an only child whose parents divorced when he or she was ten; was laid off from work two weeks ago; places a lot of importance on the relationship with you; depends on you for self-confirmation; has lots of self-doubt; and appreciates your support and kind words.
- You are a manager and one of your subordinates is increasingly late to work, is missing deadlines and appointments, and is turning in poor work. Taking an other-oriented approach, you remind yourself that this employee is facing a divorce, has a child who was recently arrested, and is suffering from panic attacks.

employees who meet together on a regular basis. These groups usually talk about such issues as how to improve the quality of services or products, reduce mistakes, lower costs, improve safety, or develop better ways of working together. This active participation in the work process encourages workers to do a better job. Moreover, the training they receive to participate in these groups—in group problem solving, decision-making skills, listening, relating, speaking, and managing conflict—applies to other areas of their work as well.

Outward Communication: Talking with Your Customers

outward communication. Communication that flows to those outside an organization (such as customers).

More and more companies are becoming service oriented; as such, one of the most important factors for success is building positive relationships with customers and clients. Company members are taught many of the lessons contained in this book about building relationships. Successful organizations are other-oriented; they focus on the needs of those they serve through **outward communication.** They train their staffs to develop more empathy, better listening skills, and more awareness of nonverbal messages from customers.

Interpersonal Communication and Emotion Connecting Heart to Heart

Emotions at Home, in Computer-Mediated Interactions, and in the Workplace

The three communication contexts covered in this chapter differ in that we experience and express emotions differently in each context. We probably express and experience more emotions within the context of our families and with our spouses than in any other interpersonal situation. In the majority of families, the feeling and expression of love—between a wife and husband, between parents and children, between siblings—is pervasive. Some emotions are present at birth, but the process of interpreting and managing those emotions is learned.[69] Our initial emotional socialization comes from observing our parents' emotional behavior, from direct instruction from our parents ("You should be happy about that" or "Don't be afraid of the dark"), from parental expectations about their children's emotional behaviors that are subtly conveyed, and from reinforcement of emotional behavior by the parents (giving a piece of candy if a child stops crying or reciprocating a child's hug).[70] Boys in the United States are often taught to be emotionally guarded, whereas girls are expected to give and receive emotional support.[71] The types of family and related family communication patterns vary in terms of openness toward emotional expression and the likelihood of positive or negative emotional expressions.

Unlike families, where people share and experience emotions together, the computer-mediated communication context often finds us experiencing emotions alone. We generally read an e-mail, a text message, or some chat room comment in seclusion, and therefore our emotional reactions are known only to us (until we respond). In addition, our responses to the communication we receive from others might be more restrained than they would be if other people were around. How often do you smile or laugh out loud when reading e-mails, compared to when listening to others in face-to-face conversations? If you watch a movie or sporting event on TV alone, are you as expressive (crying, laughing, cheering, or booing) as when other people are around? People seem to need to share their emotions with other people.[72] The more synchronous your CMC, the more opportunity there is to share and respond to each person's emotions. However, a lot of emotional display depends on nonverbal cues (facial expressions, tone of voice, body posture, and so on), which are missing in CMC. People don't observe your smile in reaction to a humorous text message and therefore can only speculate as to your emotional reaction. The desire to display and express our emotions online is probably one reason for the development of emoticons and such acronyms as LOL (laughing out loud) or ROTFL (rolling on the floor laughing). In general, we must describe in text or symbols what we are feeling when expressing emotions in computer-mediated communication.

In contrast to the open expression of emotions in the family or in CMC, we tend to hold our emotions in check in many of our workplace interactions; if we do express emotions, they are generally positive or related specifically to the interpersonal relationships we have established. In U.S. culture there is an expectation that people in organizations will act "professional," which implies emotional restraint. Unfortunately, examples of employees or customers acting in rage or anger, sometimes with devastating effects on others, are all too common. Our workplace friendships are often vital to our emotional support. Being able to discuss your frustration with a colleague who understands and shares that emotion can help you effectively cope with and manage the emotion. Most organizations are concerned with the emotions of their members, because they wish to maintain positive employee morale and create positive relationships with customers. Attempts to create a positive corporate emotional image are reflected in such slogans as "A smile in every aisle," used by some grocery-store chains, or "Fly the friendly skies of United."

Take a minute to think about your own experiences with emotions in your family, online, and in the workplace (or some other organization to which you belong). Identify a situation in each setting when you experienced and expressed a positive emotion. In what ways are the three situations similar and in what ways are they different? How did others respond to you when you expressed yourself? Now identify a situation in each setting when you experienced and expressed a negative emotion. In what ways are the three situations similar and in what ways are they different? How did others respond?

Think about emotions you experienced during a family gathering, while online, and at work that you did not express explicitly. What inhibited your expression? What did you expect the effect of expressing the emotion would be? How adept were those around you at picking up any cues about your emotional state?

Look at a couple of e-mails you've received from friends. To what degree have they conveyed your friends' emotions? Reread a couple of e-mails you sent out. To what degree did you include cues to your emotional state?

Summary

Interpersonal interactions occur in a variety of contexts. Communication principles and skills can be applied to interpersonal relationships at home, on the Internet, and at work.

A family unit is made up of any number of people who live in relationship with one another over time in a common living space and are usually, but not always, united by marriage and kinship. One model for describing families considers family cohesion and adaptability and the role of communication in affecting family members' roles and relationships. The term *cohesion* refers to the emotional bonding and the feeling of closeness that families experience. The term *family adaptability* refers to the flexibility of family members in responding to changes in family roles, rules, and relationships.

There is no one best way to be a family. However, several skills and strategies can enhance the quality of family life: Take time to talk with other family members about relationship issues; listen to others; support and encourage one another; use productive strategies for managing conflict and stress.

Another context for interpersonal relationships is cyberspace, or the Internet. You can initiate and develop new relationships totally through computer-mediated communication (CMC) or you can use the Internet as a tool for maintaining existing relationships. Compared to face-to-face (FtF) communication, CMC offers fewer nonverbal cues, requires more reliance on the written word, can be either synchronous or asynchronous, allows communicators to be deceptive, and meets different needs.

Online relationships can be initiated and established in chat rooms, through dating services, or through introductions by mutual friends. Online relationships can become hyperpersonal relationships, being even more personal than face-to-face relationships. High disclosure, trust, and commitment can lead to the development of strictly online relationships that are as intimate and satisfying as face-to-face relationships. E-mails, instant messaging, and text messaging on cell phones can all be used to escalate and maintain our face-to-face interpersonal relationships. We create extended social and support networks through the use of computer-mediated communication. We can belong to many networks, each providing various types of information and support.

Computer-mediated communication also has a dark side. Cyberstalking occurs when individuals harass others using CMC to control, interfere with, or threaten them. Cyberstalkers engage in such activities as sending computer viruses, sending unwanted e-mail or text messages, or circulating private or false information. Extensive use of CMC can be problematic if it causes a drop in performance in other aspects of your life or a reduction of or failure to develop face-to-face interpersonal communication skills. Such use has been referred to as abuse, compulsion, or even addiction.

Computer-mediated communication requires an ability to express oneself in writing; good writing skills can help offset the lack of nonverbal cues. More information must be incorporated in text messages, including self-disclosure. Sensitivity to the impressions created by your CMC behavior can help you correct false impressions and create a more accurate picture for other people. Ultimately, all the interpersonal communication skills covered throughout this text are relevant to computer-mediated communication: listening, conflict management, and being other-oriented all contribute to effective use of CMC to manage our interpersonal relationships.

Relationships at work can involve both a task and a social dimension. Forming friendships at work is one way people meet social needs and often helps produce a positive work atmosphere. The challenge of workplace interpersonal relationships is maximizing the satisfaction derived from such relationships while minimizing any negative impact on work performance. Relationships are often defined by the organization, especially in terms of power.

In most organizations, communication flows up, down, horizontally, and out to customers. Through upward communication you can share ideas and strategies for improving the work process; you can also enhance your relationship with your boss. Downward communication involves making contact with those who work for you. Decide whether you will send messages in writing, in person, or through mediated channels. Horizontal communication concerns the communication you have with colleagues on your level throughout the organization; most of the time, however, horizontal communication occurs with those who work in your immediate vicinity. Most organizations are encouraging better communication with customers and clients. Contacting those outside the organization who receive the organization's goods and services is an important way to ensure that what the organization offers is of high quality.

For Discussion and Review

Focus on Critical Thinking

1. Do you think the institution of the family is deteriorating, or is it just changing? Support your answer.
2. Despite the availability of relatively cheap interactive Web cams for Internet use, people don't seem to be turning to them as much as they are to text-only interactions. Why might this be the case? Which would you use if you had a choice? Why?
3. Jerry is president of Southwest Technical Computing. He has a sense that his managers are not tapping the wealth of ideas and suggestions that lower-level employees might have for improving productivity. What specific strategies could Jerry implement to improve upward communication?

Focus on Ethics

4. Is it ethical to withhold honest thoughts and feelings from other family members? Should family members always "tell it like it is"? Should parents encourage their children to tell everything they know and feel?
5. In chat sessions on the Internet, is it really wrong to present false information about yourself just for fun, when you know you will never meet the other people with whom you are interacting? Under what circumstances is presenting yourself over the Internet as someone of a different sex, age, race, or ethnicity ethical? When is it unethical?
6. Clayton has e-mail service at work, but not at home. His brother has e-mail service at his home. Is it ethical for Clayton to use the computer at work on company time to send and receive e-mail messages from his brother three or four times a week?

Learning with Others

Indicate whether you agree or disagree with the following statements. Then break into small groups and try to get group members to agree or disagree unanimously with each statement. Try to find reasons for differences of opinion. If your group cannot reach consensus, you may change the wording in any statement to promote unanimity.

Statements About Families

_____ 1. Most family members know how to communicate effectively; they just don't take the time to practice what they know.

_____ 2. Family conflict is a symptom rather than a cause of deteriorating family relationships.

_____ 3. Family conflict is harmful to family harmony, and all conflict should be avoided at all costs.

_____ 4. Most family conflict occurs because we don't understand the other family member; we fail to communicate effectively.

_____ 5. Families function best if there is one leader of the family.

_____ 6. Ineffective communication is the single most important cause of family conflict, divorce, and family tension.

_____ 7. Nonverbal communication (facial expression, eye contact, tone of voice, posture, and so on) is more important than verbal communication; what you do is more important than what you say.

_____ 8. It is sometimes necessary to ignore the feelings of others in order to reach a family decision.

_____ 9. The best way to love your spouse is to care more for your partner than you care for yourself.

_____ 10. Generally speaking, the quality of family life is deteriorating today.

_____ 11. There is one best approach or set of rules and principles that will ensure an effectively functioning family.

Internet Study Group

Find three or four other students in your class with whom you feel comfortable and confident. Arrange times when you can all log on to the Internet to do instant messaging, send e-mails copied to all the other group members, or create a chat room for your group. Share information with one another about assignments, examinations, or papers for this class. Discuss among yourselves through the Internet what is expected for the assignments, share any information each of you has that might help the others prepare better, and ask questions to help clarify information. If you are preparing for an exam, each of you might pose practice questions to the others, or each take a turn explaining some concept.

Workplace Interviews

Divide into teams of two or three people. Each team will interview a businessperson or supervisor in a nonprofit organization such as a hospital or school about the workplace issues covered in this chapter. Ask such questions as

- What do you do to enhance upward communication among the people you supervise?
- How do your interpersonal relationships with co-workers affect your job?

Afterward, discuss your results with other groups and see what general conclusions you can reach.

Weblinks

Go to *www.mycommunicationlab.com* (access code required) to find Web resources for your text that supplement the material in Chapter 12, including links to information on the following topics:

Your TV family
Building strong families
Reports on relationships and the Internet
Cyberspace relationships
Workplace relationships
Appropriate Workplace Behavior Test

Notes

Chapter 1

1. E. T. Klemmer and F. W. Snyder, "Measurement of Time Spent Communicating." *Journal of Communication,* 20 (June 1972): 142; also see L. Barker et al., "An Investigation of Proportional Time Spent in Various Communication Activities of College Students," *Journal of Applied Communication Research* 8 (1981): 101–09.

2. E. E. Graham and C. K. Shue, "Reflections on the Past, Directions for the Future: A Template for the Study and Instruction of Interpersonal Communication," *Communication Research Reports,* 17 (Fall 2000): 337–48.

3. F. E. X. Dance and C. Larson, *Speech Communication: Concepts and Behavior* (New York: Holt, Rinehart and Winston, 1972).

4. Dance and Larson, *Speech Communication.*

5. J. T. Masterson, S. A. Beebe, N. H. Watson, *Invitation to Effective Speech Communication* (Glenview, IL: Scott, Foresman, 1989).

6. L. M. Webb and M. E. Thompson-Hayes, "Do Popular Collegiate Textbooks in Interpersonal Communication Reflect a Common Theory Base? A Telling Content Analysis," *Communication Education,* 51 (April 2002): 210–24.

7. W. Carl and S. Duck, "How to Do Things with Relationships . . . and How Relationships Do Things with Us," *Communication Yearbook,* 28 (2004): 1–35.

8. M. Buber, *I and Thou* (New York: Scribners, 1958); also see M. Buber, *Between Man and Man* (New York: Macmillan, 1965). For a detailed discussion of perspectives on interpersonal communication and relationship development, see G. H. Stamp, "A Qualitatively Constructed Interpersonal Communication Model: A Grounded Theory Analysis," *Human Communication Research,* 25 (June 1999): 531–47; J. P. Dillard, D. H. Solomon, and M. T. Palmer, "Structuring the Concept of Relational Communication," *Communication Monographs,* 66 (March 1999): 49–65.

9. Buber, *I and Thou.*

10. D. Yankelovich, *The Magic of Dialogue: Transforming Conflict into Cooperation* (New York: Simon & Schuster, 1999); for an excellent discussion of dialogue, also see S. W. Littlejohn and K. Domenici, *Engaging Communication in Conflict: Systemic Practice* (Thousand Oaks, CA: Sage, 2001), 25–51.

11. Buber, *I and Thou.*

12. V. Satir, *Peoplemaking* (Palo Alto, CA: Science and Behavior Books, 1972); J. B. Miller and P. A. deWinstanley, "The Role of Interpersonal Competence in Memory for Conversation," *Personality and Social Psychology Bulletin,* 28 (January 2002): 78–89.

13. K. E. Davis and M. Todd, "Assessing Friendship: Prototypes, Paradigm Cases, and Relationship Description," in *Understanding Personal Relationships,* edited by S. W. Duck and D. Perlman (London: Sage, 1985); B. Wellman, "From Social Support to Social Network," in *Social Support. Theory, Research and Applications,* edited by I. G. Sarason and B. R. Sarason (Dordrecht, Netherlands: Nijhoff, 1985); R. Hopper, M. L. Knapp, and L. Scott, "Couples' Personal Idioms: Exploring Intimate Talk," *Journal of Communication,* 31 (1981): 23–33; S. Pendell, "Affection in Interpersonal Relationships: Not Just 'A Fond or Tender Feeling,'" in *Communication Yearbook 26,* edited by W. B. Gudykunst (Mahwah, NJ: Erlbaum, 2002): 71–115.

14. M. Argyle and M. Hendershot, *The Anatomy of Relationships* (London: Penguin Books, 1985), 14.

15. See J. L. Winsor, D. B. Curtis, and R. D. Stephens, "National Preferences in Business and Communication Education: A Survey Update," *Journal of the Association for Communication Administration,* 3 (September 1997), 174; *The Wall Street Journal,* September, 9, 2002: 1A.

16. K. Martell and S. Carroll, "Stress the Functional Skills When Hiring Top Managers," *HRMagazine,* 39 (1994): 85–87; E. Tanyel, M. Mitchell, and H. G. McAlum, "The Skill Set for Success of New Business School Graduates: Do Prospective Employers and University Faculty Agree?" *Journal of Education for Business,* 75 (1999): 33–37; W. J. Wardrope, "Department Chairs' Perceptions of the Importance of Business Communication Skills," *Business Communication Quarterly,* 65 (2002): 60–72.

17. M. Argyle, *The Psychology of Happiness* (London: Routledge, 1987).

18. J. J. Lynch, *The Broken Heart: The Medical Consequences of Loneliness* (New York: Basic Books, 1977).

19. R. Korbin and G. Hendershot, "Do Family Ties Reduce Mortality: Evidence from the United States 1968," *Journal of Marriage and the Family,* 39 (1977): 737–45.

20. D. P. Phillips, "Deathday and Birthday: An Unexpected Connection," in *Statistics: A Guide to the Unknown,* edited by J. M. Tanur (San Francisco: Holden Day, 1972).

21. M. Argyle, *The Psychology of Happiness* (London: Routledge, 2001).

22. For a comprehensive overview of the history of the study of interpersonal communication, see M. L. Knapp, J. A. Daly, K. F. Albada, and G. R. Miller, "Background and Current Trends in the Study of Interpersonal Communication," in *Handbook of Interpersonal Communication,* edited by M. L. Knapp and J. A. Daly (Thousand Oaks, CA: Sage, 2002), 3–20.

23. Among the first scholars to identify a link between the sender of a message and message context was Kurt Lewin in K. Lewin, *A Dynamic Theory of Personality* (New York: McGraw-Hill, 1935); Carl and Duck, "How to Do Things with Relationships."

24. See V. E. Cronen, W. B. Pearce, and L. M. Harris, "The Coordinated Management of Meaning: A Theory of Communication," in *Human Communication Theory: Comparative Essays,* edited by F. E. X. Dance (New York: Harper & Row, 1982), 61–89.

25. L. C. Tidwell and J. B. Walther, "Computer-Mediated Communication Effects on Disclosure, Impressions, and Interpersonal Evaluations: Getting to Know One Another a Bit at a Time," *Human Communication Research,* 28 (July 2002): 317–48.

26. M. J. Dutta-Bergman, "Interpersonal Communication After 9/11 Via Telephone and Internet: A Theory of Channel Complementarity," *New Media & Society,* 6 (2004): 659–73.

27. K. Campbell and K. Wright, "On-Line Support Groups: An Investigation of Relationships Among Source Credibility, Dimensions of Relational Communication, and Perceptions of Emotional Support," *Communication Research Reports,* 19 (2002): 183–93.

28. Y. Amichai-Hamburger, *The Social Net: Human Behavior in Cyberspace* (Oxford, England: Oxford University Press, 2005), v.

29. J. B. Walther and J. K. Burgoon, "Relational Communication in Computer-Mediated Interaction," *Human Communication Research,* 19 (1992): 50–88.

30. Tidwell and Walther, 2002.

31. J. B. Walther, "Computer-Mediated Communication: Impersonal, Interpersonal, and Hyperpersonal Interaction," *Communication Research,* 23 (1996): 3–43; also see Campbell and Wright, 2002.

32. R. Kraut, M. Patterson, V. Lundmark, S. Kiesler, M. Tridas, and W. Scherlis, "Internet Paradox: A Social Technology That Reduces Social Involvement and Psychological Well-Being?" *American Psychologist,* 53 (1998): 1017–31.

33. R. Kraut, S. Kiesler, B. Boneva, J. Cummings, V. Helgeson, and A. Crawford, "Internet Paradox Revisited," *Journal of Social Issues,* 58 (2002): 49–74; P. E. N. Howard, L. Raine, and S. Jones, "Days and Nights on the Internet: The Impact of a Diffusing Technology," *American Behavioral Scientist,* 45 (2001): 383–404.

34. I. Sproull and S. Kiesler, "Reducing Social Context Cues: Electronic Mail in Organizational Communication," *Management Science,* 32 (1986): 1492–1513.

35. L. K. Trevino, R. L. Draft, and R. H. Lengel, "Understanding Managers' Media Choices: A Symbolic Interactionist Perspective," in *Organizations and Communication Technology,* edited by J. Fulk and C. Steinfield (Newbury Park, CA: Sage, 1990), 71–74.

36. Tidwell and Walther, 2002.

37. J. B. Walther and L. Tidwell, "When Is Mediated Communication Not Interpersonal?" in K. Galvin and P. Cooper, *Making Connections* (Los Angeles, CA: Roxbury Press, 1996).

38. I. Reed, "The World Is Here," in *Writin' Is Fighting* (New York: Atheneum, 1988).

39. C. R. Berger and J. J. Bradac, *Language and Social Knowledge: Uncertainty in Interpersonal Relations* (London: Arnold, 1982); C. R. Berger and R. J. Calabrese, "Some Explorations in Initial Interaction and Beyond: Toward a Developmental Theory of Interpersonal Communication," *Human Communication Research,* 1 (1975): 99–112.

40. See D. Barnlund, *Interpersonal Communication: Survey and Studies* (Boston: Houghton Mifflin, 1968).

41. O. Wiio, *Wiio's Laws—and Some Others* (Espoo, Finland: WelinGoos, 1978).

42. S. B. Shimanoff, *Communication Rules: Theory and Research* (Beverly Hills: Sage, 1980).

43. M. Argyle, M. Hendershot, and A. Furnham, "The Rules of Social Relationships," *British Journal of Social Psychology,* 24 (1985): 125–39.

44. T. Watzlawick, J. Bavelas, and D. Jackson, *The Pragmatics of Human Communication* (New York: Norton, 1967).

45. B. Parkinson, A. H. Fischer, and A. S. R. Manstead, *Emotion in Social Relations: Cultural, Group, and Interpersonal Processes* (New York: Psychology Press, 2004).

46. W. Gerrod Parrott, "The Nature of Emotion," in M. B. Brewer and M. Hewston, *Emotion and Motivation* (Oxford, England: Blackwell Publishing, Ltd., 2004), 6.

47. See A. Mehrabian, *Nonverbal Communication* (Chicago: Aldine Atherton, 1972).

48. For a review of emotional response theory, see S. A. Beebe and T. Biggers, "The Relationship of Trait and State Emotion: Emotional Responses to 'The Day After.'" *World Communication Journal,* 15 (1986): 20–30; T. Biggers and J. T. Masterson, "Communication Apprehension as a Personality Trait: An Emotional Defense of a Concept." *Communication Monographs,* 52 (1984): 381–90; A. Mehrabian and J. A. Russell. *An Approach to Environmental Psychology* (Cambridge, MA: MIT Press, 1974); J. A. Russell and L. F. Barrett, "Core Affect, Prototypical Emotional Episodes, and Other Things Called Emotion: Dissecting the Elephant," *Journal of Personality and Social Psychology,* 76 (1999): 805–19; S. A. Beebe, "Emotional Response Theory: Applications to Instructional Communication Research," paper presented at the annual meeting of the National Communication Association, Chicago, IL (November 2004); T. P. Mottet and S. A. Beebe, "Relationships Between Teacher Nonverbal Immediacy, Student Emotional Response, and Perceived Student Learning," *Communication Research Reports,* 19 (2002): 77–88; Mehrabian, 1972, 108; also see J. K. Burgoon, D. B. Buller, and W. G. Woodall, *Nonverbal Communication: The Unspoken Dialogue* (New York: McGraw-Hill, 1996).

49. M. S. Clark, J. Fitness, and I. Brissette, "Understanding People's Perceptions of Relationships Is Crucial to Understanding Their Emotional Lives," in M. B. Brewer and M. Hewston, *Emotion and Motivation* (Oxford, England: Blackwell Publishing, Ltd., 2004), 21–46.

50. D. Matsumoto, J. LeRoux, C. Wilson-Cohn, J. Raroque, K. Kooken, P.

Ekman, N. Yrizarry, S. Loewinger, H. Uchida, A. Yee, L. Amo, and A. Goh, "A New Test to Measure Emotion Recognition Ability: Matsumoto and Ekman's Japanese and Caucasian Brief Affect Recognition Test (JACBART)," *Journal of Nonverbal Behavior,* 24 (Fall 2000): 179–209; F. Trompenaars and C. Hampden-Turner, *Riding the Waves of Culture* (New York: McGraw Hill, 1988); M. R. Hammer, "The Intercultural Conflict Style Inventory: A Conceptual Framework and Measure of Intercultural Conflict Resolution Approaches," *International Journal of Intercultural Relations,* 29 (2005): 675–95.

51. P. Ekman and W. Friesen, "Constants Across Cultures in the Face and Emotion," *Journal of Personality and Social Psychology,* 12 (1971): 124–29.

52. See J. C. McCroskey and M. J. Beatty, "The Communibiological Perspective: Implications for Communication in Instruction," *Communication Education,* 49 (January 2000): 1–6; M. J. Beatty and J. C. McCroskey, "Theory, Scientific Evidence, and the Communibiological Paradigm: Reflections on Misguided Criticism," *Communication Education,* 49, (January 2000): 36–44. Also see J. C. McCroskey, J. A. Daly, M. M. Martin, and M. J. Beatty (eds.), *Communication and Personality: Trait Perspectives* (Cresskil, NJ: Hampton Press, 1998); and M. J. Beatty, A. D. Heisel, A. E. Hall, T. R. Levine, and B. H. La France, "What Can We Learn from the Study of Twins about Genetic and Environmental Influences on Interpersonal Affiliation, Aggressiveness, and Social Anxiety? A Meta-Analytic Study," *Communication Monographs,* 69 (March 2002): 1–18.

53. See J. Ayres and T. S. Hopf, "The Long-Term Effect of Visualization in the Classroom: A Brief Research Report," *Communication Education,* 39 (1990): 75–78; and J. Ayres and T. S. Hopf, "Visualization: A Means of Reducing Speech Anxiety," *Communication Education,* 34 (1985): 318–23.

54. For a discussion of criticism of the communibiological approach, see C. M. Condit, "Culture and Biology in Human Communication: Toward a Multi-Causal Model," *Communication Education,* 49 (January 2000): 7–24.

55. A. Bandura, *Social Learning Theory* (Englewood Cliffs, NJ: Prentice-Hall, 1977).

56. S. R. Wilson and C. M. Sabee, "Explicating Communicative Competence as a Theoretical Term," in *Handbook of Communication and Social Interaction Skills,* edited by J. O. Greene and B. R. Burleson (Mahwah, NJ: Erlbaum, 2003), 3–50.

57. M. J. Collier, "Researching Cultural Identity: Reconciling Interpretive and Postcolonial Approaches," in *Communication and Identity Across Cultures,* edited by D. Tanno and A. Gonzalez (Thousand Oaks, CA: Sage, 1998), 142. Also see S. DeTurk, "Intercultural Empathy: Myth, Competency, or Possibility for Alliance Building?" *Communication Education,* 50 (October 2001): 374–84.

58. G. A. Hullman, "Interpersonal Communication Motives and Message Design Logic: Exploring Their Interaction on Perceptions of Competence," *Communication Monographs,* 71 (2004): 208–25.

59. Miller and deWinstanley, 2002.

60. M. Argyle, *The Psychology of Interpersonal Behavior* (London: Penguin, 1983).

61. J. Hakansson and H. Montgomery, "Empathy as an Interpersonal Phenomenon," *Journal of Social and Personal Relationships,* 20 (2003): 267–84; Y. Nakatani, "The Effects of Awareness-Raising Training on Oral Communication Strategy Use," *The Modern Language Journal,* 89 (2005): 76–91.

62. K. J. K. Asada, E. Lee, T. R. Levine, and M. H. Ferrara, "Narcissism and Empathy as Predictors of Obsessive Relational Intrusion," *Communication Research Reports,* 21 (2004): 379–90.

63. J. M. Twenge, *Generation Me: Why Today's Young Americans Are More Confident, Assertive, Entitled—and More Miserable Than Ever Before.* New York: Free Press (2006): 69.

64. Twenge, 2006.

65. M. V. Redmond, "Adaptation in Everyday Interactions," paper presented at the annual meeting of the National Communication Association (November, 1997).

66. C. H. Adams, "Prosocial Bias in Theories of Interpersonal Communication Competence: Must Good Communication Be Nice? In *Communication and Community,* edited by G. Shepherd and E. W. Rothenbuhler (Mahwah, NJ: Erlbaum, 2001), 37–52.

67. M. Argyle is widely acknowledged as the first scholar to suggest a systematic approach to apply learning theory to the development of social skills, including interpersonal communication skills. See Argyle, 1983.

Chapter 2

1. K. Horney, *Neurosis and Human Growth* (New York: Norton, 1950), 17.

2. R. A. Baron and D. Byrne, *Social Psychology* (Boston: Allyn & Bacon, 2003).

3. E. Goffman, *The Presentation of Self in Everyday Life* (Garden City, NY: Doubleday, Anchor Books, 1959). Also see E. Goffman, *Frame Analysis: An Essay on the Organization of Experience* (Cambridge, MA: Harvard University Press, 1974).

4. Goffman, *Frame Analysis,* 508.

5. W. James, *The Principles of Psychology* (New York: Holt, 1890).

6. C. H. Cooley, *Human Nature and the Social Order* (New York: Scribners, 1902).

7. G. H. Mead, *Mind, Self, and Society* (Chicago: University of Chicago Press, 1934).

8. H. S. Sullivan, *The Interpersonal Theory of Psychiatry* (New York: Norton, 1953).

9. Mead, *Mind, Self, and Society.*

10. J. T. Masterson, *Speech Communication in Traditional and Contemporary Marriages* (doctoral dissertation, University of Denver, 1977). Also see S. A. Beebe and J. T. Masterson, *Family Talk: Interpersonal Communication in the Family* (New York: Random House, 1986), 91–100.

11. D. G. Ancona, "Groups in Organizations: Extending Laboratory Models," in *Annual Review of Personality and Social Psychology: Group and Intergroup Processes,* edited by C. Hendrick (Beverly Hills, CA: Sage, 1987), 207–31. Also see D. G. Ancona and D. E. Caldwell, "Be-

yond Task and Maintenance: Defining External Functions in Groups," *Group and Organizational Studies,* 13 (1988): 468–94.

12. S. L. Bem, "The Measurement of Psychological Androgyny," *Journal of Consulting and Clinical Psychology,* 42 (1974): 155–62.

13. L. A. Lefton, *Psychology* (Boston: Allyn & Bacon, 2000).

14. J. C. McCroskey and M. J. Beatty, "The Communibiological Perspective: Implications for Communication Instruction," *Communication Education,* 49 (January 2000): 1–28.

15. C. M. Condit, "Culture and Biology in Human Communication: Toward a Multi-Causal Model," *Communication Education,* 49 (January 2000): 7–24.

16. P. Zimbardo, *Shyness: What It Is, What to Do About It* (Reading, MA: Addison-Wesley, 1977).

17. S. Booth-Butterfield, "Instructional Interventions for Situational Anxiety and Avoidance," *Communication Education,* 37 (1988): 214–23.

18. J. C. McCroskey and V. P. Richmond, *Fundamentals of Human Communication: An Interpersonal Perspective* (Prospect Heights, IL: Waveland Press, 1996).

19. Booth-Butterfield, "Instructional Interventions."

20. Zimbardo, *Shyness.*

21. W. Gerrod Parrott, "The Nature of Emotion," in M. B. Brewer and M. Hewston, *Emotion and Motivation* (Oxford, England: Blackwell Publishing, 2004), 6. Also see R. A. Baron, B. Earhard, and M. Ozier, *Psychology* (Toronto: Pearson Education, 2001).

22. See W. James, "What Is an Emotion?" *Mind,* 9 (1884): 188–205. Also see B. Parkinson, A. H. Fischer, and A. S. R. Manstead, *Emotion in Social Relations: Cultural, Group, and Interpersonal Processes* (New York: Psychology Press, 2004).

23. S. Schacter and J. E. Singer, "Cognitive, Social, and Physiological Determinants of Emotional States," *Psychological Review,* 69 (1962): 379–99.

24. E. Sahlstein and M. Allen, "Sex Differences in Self-Esteem: A Meta-Analytic Assessment," in *Interpersonal Communication Research: Advances Through Meta-Analysis,* edited by M. Allen, R. W. Preiss, B. M. Gayle, and N. A. Burrell (Mahwah, NJ: Erlbaum, 2002), 59–72; K. Dindia, "Self-Disclosure Research: Knowledge Through Meta-Analysis," in *Interpersonal Communication Research: Advances Through Meta-Analysis,* edited by M. Allen, R. W. Preiss, B. M. Gayle, and N. A. Burrell (Mahwah, NJ: Erlbaum, 2002), 169–85. G. V. Caprara and P. Steca, "Self-Efficacy Beliefs as Determinants of Prosocial Behavior Conducive to Life Satisfaction Across Ages," *Journal of Social and Clinical Psychology,* 24 (2005): 191–217.

25. E. Berne, *Games People Play* (New York: Grove Press, 1964).

26. S. Ting Toomey, J. G. Oetzel, and K. Yee-Jung, "Self-Construal Types and Conflict Management Styles," *Communication Reports,* 14 (Summer 2001): 87–104.

27. Ting Toomey, Oetzel, and Yee-Jung, "Self-Construal Types."

28. L. Armstrong, *It's Not About the Bike: My Journey Back to Life* (New York: Putnam's, 2000), 146.

29. J. L. S. Borton, L. J. Markowitz, and J. Dieterich, "Effects of Suppressing Negative Self-Referent Thoughts on Mood and Self-Esteem," *Journal of Social and Clinical Psychology,* 24 (2005): 172–90.

30. D. B. Feldman and C. R. Snyder, "Hope and the Meaningful Life: Theoretical and Empirical Associations Between Goal-Directed Thinking and Life Meaning," *Journal of Social and Clinical Psychology,* 24 (2005): 401–21.

31. J. Ayres and T. S. Hopf, "The Long-Term Effect of Visualization in the Classroom: A Brief Research Report," *Communication Education,* 39 (1990): 75–78.

32. J. W. Younger, R. L. Piferi, R. L. Jobe, and K. A. Lawler, "Dimensions of Forgiveness: The Views of Laypersons," *Journal of Social and Personal Relationships,* 21 (2004): 837–55.

33. K. Weber, A. Johnson, and M. Corrigan, "Communicating Emotional Support and Its Relationship to Feelings of Being Understood, Trust, and Self-Disclosure," *Communication Research Reports,* 21 (2004): 316–23.

34. F. E. X. Dance and C. Larson, *The Functions of Human Communication* (New York: Holt, Rinehart and Winston, 1976), 141.

35. Our discussion of decentering and the specific-other and generalized-other perspectives is from M. V. Redmond, "The Functions of Empathy (Decentering) in Human Relations," *Human Relations,* 42 (1993): 593–606. Also see M. V. Redmond, "A Multidimensional Theory and Measure of Social Decentering," *Journal of Research in Personality* (1995).

36. P. A. Siegel, J. Scillitoe, and R. Parks-Yancy, "Reducing the Tendency to Self-Handicap: The Effect of Self-Affirmation," *Journal of Experimental Social Psychology,* 41(6) (2005): 589–97.

37. G. V. Caprara and P. Steca, "Self-Efficacy Beliefs as Determinants of Prosocial Behavior Conducive to Life Satisfaction Across Ages," *Journal of Social and Clinical Psychology,* 24 (2005): 191–217.

38. H. Brody. *The Placebo Response: How You Can Release Your Body's Inner Pharmacy for Better Health* (New York: HarperCollins, 2000). Also see H. Brody, "Tapping the Power of the Placebo," *Newsweek* (August 14, 2000): 68.

39. A. A. Milne, "Pooh Does a Good Deed," in *Pooh Sleepytime Stories* (New York: Golden Press, 1979), 44.

40. *Looking Out/Looking In,* edited by R. B. Adler and N. Towne (Fort Worth, TX: Harcourt Brace Jovanovich, 1993). Also see C. R. Berger, "Self Conception and Social Information Processing," in *Personality and Interpersonal Communication,* edited by J. C. McCroskey and J. A. Daly (1986): 275–303.

41. A. A. Milne, "Owl Finds a Home," in *Pooh Sleepytime Stories* (New York: Golden Press, 1979), 28.

42. D. E. Hamachek, *Encounters with the Self* (New York: Holt, Rinehart and Winston, 1982); Berger, "Self-Conception."

43. W. C. Schutz, *FIRO: A Three-Dimensional Theory of Interpersonal Behavior* (New York: Holt, Rinehart and Winston, 1958).

44. McCroskey and Beatty, "Communibiological Perspective."

45. See McCroskey and Richmond, *Fundamentals of Human Communication.*

46. V. P. Richmond, R. S. Smith, A. D. Heisel, and J. C. McCroskey, "The Association of Physician Socio-Communicative Style with Physician Credibility and Patient Satisfaction," *Communication Research Reports,* 19 (2002): 207–15.

47. Dindia, "Self-Disclosure Research."

48. I. Altman and D. A. Taylor, *Social Penetration: The Development of Interpersonal Relationships* (New York: Holt, Rinehart and Winston, 1973).

49. W. B. Gudykunst and T. Nishida, "Social Penetration in Japanese and American Close Friendships," in *Communication Yearbook 7,* edited by R. N. Bostrom (Beverly Hills, CA: Sage, 1963), 592–611.

50. M. Kito, "Self-Disclosure in Romantic Relationships and Friendships Among American and Japanese College Students, *The Journal of Social Psychology,* 145 (2005): 127–40.

51. J. C. Korn, "Friendship Formation and Development in Two Cultures: Universal Constructs in the United States and Korea," in *Interpersonal Communication in Friend and Mate Relationships,* edited by A. M. Nicotera (Albany: State University of New York Press, 1993), 61–78.

52. J. Luft, *Group Process: An Introduction to Group Dynamics* (Palo Alto, CA: Mayfield, 1970).

53. Dindia, "Self-Disclosure Research."

54. Dindia, "Self-Disclosure Research."

55. S. Petronio, *Boundaries of Privacy: Dialectics of Disclosure* (Albany: State University of New York Press, 2000).

56. J. P. Caughlin and T. D. Afifi, "When Is Topic Avoidance Unsatisfying? Examining Moderators of the Association Between Avoidance and Dissatisfaction," *Human Communication Research,* 30 (2004): 479–513.

57. J. Powell, *Why Am I Afraid to Tell You Who I Am?* (Niles, IL: Argus Communications, 1969), 12.

58. Powell, *Why Am I Afraid.*

59. L. C. Tidwell and J. B. Walther, "Computer-Mediated Communication Effects on Disclosure, Impressions, and Interpersonal Evaluations: Getting to Know One Another a Bit at a Time," *Human Communication Research,* 28, (July 2002): 317–48.

60. B. Cornwell and D. C. Lundgren, "Love on the Internet: Involvement and Misrepresentation in Romantic Relationships in Cyberspace vs. Realspace," *Computers in Human Behavior,* 17 (2001): 197–211.

61. M. Argyle, M. Henderson, and A. Furnham, "The Rules of Social Relationships," *British Journal of Social Psychology,* 24 (1985): 125–39.

62. A. L. Vangelisti, J. P. Caughlin, and L. Timmerman, "Criteria for Revealing Family Secrets," *Communication Monographs,* 68 (March 2001): 1–27.

63. T. D. Afifi, L. N. Olson, and C. Armstrong, "The Chilling Effect and Family Secrets: Examining the Role of Self Protection, Other Protection, and Communication Efficacy," *Human Communication Research,* 31 (2005): 564–98.

64. A. P. Bochner, "On the Efficacy of Openness in Close Relationships," in *Communication Yearbook 5,* edited by M. Burgoon (New Brunswick, NJ: Transaction Books, 1982), 109–24.

Chapter 3

1. P. R. Hinton, *The Psychology of Interpersonal Perception* (New York: Routledge, 1993).

2. M. Gladwell, *Blink: The Power of Thinking Without Thinking* (New York: Little, Brown and Company, 2005).

3. J. Gottman with N. Silver, *Why Marriages Succeed or Fail* (New York: Simon and Schuster, 1994); also see J. M. Gottman and J. S. Gottman, *10 Lessons to Transform Your Marriage* (New York: Crown Publishers, 2006).

4. P. Watzlawick, J. Bevelas, and D. Jackson, *The Pragmatics of Human Communication* (New York: Norton, 1967).

5. A. L. Sillars, "Attribution and Communication: Are People Naive Scientists or Just Naive?" in *Social Cognition and Communication,* edited by M. E. Roloff and C. R. Berger (Beverly Hills: Sage, 1982), 73–106.

6. Watzlawick et al., *The Pragmatics of Human Communication.*

7. C. R. Berger and J. J. Bradac, *Language and Social Knowledge* (Baltimore: Edward Arnold, 1982).

8. S. Asch, "Forming Impressions of Personality," *Journal of Abnormal and Social Psychology,* 41 (1946): 258–90.

9. D. M. Wegner and R. R. Vallacher, *Implicit Psychology: An Introduction to Social Cognition* (New York: Oxford University Press, 1977).

10. S. Bruner and R. Tagiuri, "The Perception of People," in *Handbook of Social Psychology,* edited by G. Lindzey (Cambridge, MA: Addison-Wesley, 1954).

11. G. A. Kelly, *The Psychology of Personal Constructs* (New York: Norton, 1995).

12. A. L. Sillars, "Attributions and Communication in Roommate Conflicts," *Communication Monographs,* 47 (1980): 180–200.

13. D. A. Infante and A. S. Rancer, "Argumentativeness and Verbal Aggressiveness: A Review of Recent Theory and Research," in *Communication Yearbook 19,* edited by B. R. Burleson (Thousand Oaks, CA: Sage, 1996), 319–52.

14. D. Hample, "The Life Space of Personalized Conflicts," in *Communication Yearbook 23,* edited by M. E. Roloff (Thousand Oaks, CA: Sage, 1999), 171–208.

15. F. Heider, *The Psychology of Interpersonal Relations* (New York: Wiley, 1958). Also see E. E. Jones and K. E. Davis, "From Acts to Dispositions: The Attribution Process in Person Perception," in *Advances in Experimental Social Psychology,* vol. 2, edited by L. Berkowitz (New York: Academic Press, 1965).

16. G. A. Kelly, *The Psychology of Personal Constructs* (New York: Norton, 1955).

17. D. F. Henson and K. C. Dybvig-Pawelko, "The Effects of Loneliness on Relational Maintenance Behaviors: An Attributional Perspective," *Communication Research Reports,* 21 (2004): 411–19.

18. A. L. Vangelisti and S. L. Young, "When Words Hurt: The Effects of Perceived Intentionality on Interpersonal Relationships," *Journal of Social and Personal Relationships,* 17 (2000): 393–424.

19. G. W. F. Hegel, *Phenomenology of Mind* (Germany: Wurzburg & Bamburg, 1807).

20. R. M. Kowalski, S. Walker, R. Wilkinson, A. Queen, and B. Sharpe, "Lying, Cheating, Complaining, and Other Aversive Interpersonal Behaviors: A Narrative Examination of the Darker Side of Relationships," *Journal of Social and Personal Relationships,* 20 (2003): 472–90.

21. R. Nisbett and L. Ross, *Human Inference: Strategies and Shortcomings of Social Judgment* (Englewood Cliffs, NJ: Prentice Hall, 1980).

22. Nisbett and Ross, *Human Inference.*

23. E. E. Jones and R. Nisbett, "The Actor and the Observer: Divergent Perceptions of the Causes of Behavior," in *Attribution: Perceiving the Causes of Behavior,* edited by E. E. Jones et al. (Morristown, NJ: General Learning Press, 1972), 79–94; D. E. Kanouse and L. R. Hanson, Jr., "Negativity in Evaluations," in Jones et al., *Attribution,* 47–62.

24. F. F. Jordan-Jackson and K. A. Davis, "Men Talk: An Exploratory Study of Communication Patterns and Communication Apprehension of Black and White Males," *The Journal of Men's Studies,* 13 (2005): 347–67.

25. F. T. McAndrew, A. Akande, R. Bridgstock, L. Mealey, S. C. Gordon, J. E. Scheib, B. E. Akande-Adetoun, F. Odewale, A. Morakinyo, P. Nyahete, and G. Mubvakure, "A Multicultural Study of Stereotyping in English-Speaking Countries," *The Journal of Social Psychology,* 140 (2000): 487–502.

26. Nisbett and Ross, *Human Inference.*

27. Asch, "Forming Impressions of Personality."

28. K. Floyd, "Attributions for Nonverbal Expressions of Liking and Disliking: The Extended Self-Serving Bias," *Western Journal of Communication,* 64 (Fall 2000): 388.

29. Floyd, "Attributions for Nonverbal Expressions of Liking and Disliking."

30. P. Brown and S. C. Levinson, *Politeness: Some Universals in Language Use* (Cambridge, England: Cambridge University Press, 1987).

31. E. Goffman, *The Presentation of Self in Everyday Life* (New York: Doubleday, 1959).

32. Goffman, *The Presentation of Self in Everyday Life.*

33. Brown and Levinson, *Politeness.*

34. M. V. Redmond, "The Functions of Empathy (Decentering) in Human Relations," *Human Relations,* 42(4), (1993): 593–606.

Chapter 4

1. W. B. Gudykunst and Y. Y. Kim, *Communicating with Strangers: An Approach to Intercultural Communication.* (New York: McGraw-Hill, Inc. 1997). Also see W. B. Gudykunst, "Similarities and Differences in Perceptions of Initial Intracultural and Intercultural Encounters," *Southern Speech Communication Journal,* 49 (1983): 49–65; W. B. Gudykunst, "Theorizing in Intercultural Communication: An Introduction," in *Intercultural Communication Theory: Current Perspectives,* edited by W. B. Gudykunst (Beverly Hills, CA: Sage, 1983), 13–20; W. B. Gudykunst, "A Model of Uncertainty Reduction in Intercultural Encounters," *Journal of Language and Social Psychology,* 4 (1985): 79–97; W. B. Gudykunst, E. Chua, and A. Gray, "Cultural Dissimilarities and Uncertainty Reduction Processes," in *Communication Yearbook 10,* edited by M. L. McLaughlin (Beverly Hills, Sage, 1987), 456–69; W. B. Gudykunst and T. Nishida, "Individual and Cultural Influences on Uncertainty Reduction," *Communication Monographs,* 51 (1984): 23–36; W. B. Gudykunst, S.-M. Yang, and T. Nishida, "Cultural Differences in Self-Consciousness and Self-Monitoring," *Communication Monographs,* 14 (1987): 7–14; J. R. Baldwin and S. K. Hunt, "Information-Seeking Behavior in Intercultural and Intergroup Communication," *Human Communication Research,* 28 (April 2002): 272–86.

2. Gudykunst and Kim, *Communicating with Strangers: An Approach to Intercultural Communication,* 20.

3. T. Friedman, *The World Is Flat: A Brief History of the Twenty-First Century* (New York: Farrar, Straus and Giroux, 2005).

4. M. E. Ryan, "Another Way to Teach Migrant Students," *Los Angeles Times,* March 31, 1991, B20, as cited by M. W. Lustig and J. Koester, *Intercultural Competence: Interpersonal Communication Across Cultures* (Boston: Allyn & Bacon, 2003), 11.

5. Lustig and Koester, *Intercultural Competence,* 8.

6. G. Chen and W. J. Starosta, "A Review of the Concept of Intercultural Sensitivity," *Human Communication,* 1, (1997): 7.

7. Lustig and Koester, *Intercultural Competence,* 10.

8. *Newsweek,* July 12, 1999, 51.

9. U.S. Bureau of the Census, *Statistical Abstract of the United States: 1996,* 116th ed. (Washington, DC: 1996), as cited by Lustig and Koester, *Intercultural Competence,* 8.

10. U.S. Bureau of the Census, *Report 1999,* A20.

11. "One Nation, One Language?" *U.S. News & World Report,* September 25, 1995, 40, as cited by Lustig and Koester, *Intercultural Competence,* 10.

12. United States Census Bureau. Retrieved December 10, 2002 from http://www.prb.org/AmeristatTemplate.

13. S. Roberts, *Who We Are Now: The Changing Face of America in the Twenty-First Century* (New York: Henry Holt, 2004), 122.

14. Roberts, *Who We Are Now,* 122.

15. Roberts, *Who We Are Now,* 126.

16. We acknowledge and appreciate the contributions in this section of D. Ivy, from her work in D. K. Ivy and P. Backlund, *GenderSpeak: Personal Effectiveness in Gender Communication* (New York: McGraw-Hill, 2004); S. A. Beebe, S. J. Beebe, and D. K. Ivy, *Communication: Principles for a Lifetime* (Boston: Allyn & Bacon, 2007).

17. J. Gray. *Men Are from Mars, Women Are from Venus* (New York: HarperCollins, 1992).

18. J. T. Wood, "A Critical Response to John Gray's Mars and Venus Portrayals of Men and Women," *The Southern Communication Journal,* 67 (2002): 201–11.

19. D. Tannen, *You Just Don't Understand* (New York: William Morrow, 1990).

20. Tannen, *You Just Don't Understand.*

21. P. Gibson, "Gay Male and Lesbian Youth Suicide," *Report of the Secretary's Task Force on Youth Suicide*, ed. Marcia R. Feinleib (Washington, DC: U.S. Department of Health and Human Services, January 1989).

22. T. Mottet, "The Role of Sexual Orientation in Predicting Outcome Value and Anticipated Communication Behaviors," *Communication Quarterly*, 43 (Summer 2000): 223–39.

23. G. M. Herek, "Heterosexuals' Attitudes Toward Lesbian and Gay Men: Correlates and Gender Differences," *The Journal of Sex Research*, 25 (1988): 451–77.

24. G. M. Herek, "Heterosexuals' Attitudes Toward Lesbian and Gay Men"; M. S. Weinberg and C. J. Williams, *Male Homosexuals: Their Problems and Adaptations* (New York: The Free Press, 1974); T. Mottet, "The Role of Sexual Orientation in Predicting Outcome Value and Anticipated Communication Behaviors."

25. APA Style.org, "Removing Bias in Language: Sexuality." Retrieved March 2006 from www.apastyle.org/sexuality.html.

26. *Random House Webster's Unabridged Dictionary* (New York: Random House, 1998), 1590.

27. R. Lewontin, "The Apportionment of Human Diversity," *Evolutionary Biology*, 6 (1973): 381–97.

28. D. Matsumoto and L. Juang, *Culture and Psychology* (Belmont, California: Wadsworth/Thomson, 2004), 16; also see H. A. Yee, H. H. Fairchild, F. Weizmann, and E. G. Wyatt. "Addressing Psychology's Problems with Race," *American Psychologist*, 48 (1994): 1132–40.

29. B. J. Allen, *Differences Matter: Communicating Social Identity* (Long Grove, Illinois: Waveland Press, Inc., 2004), 68.

30. Allen, *Differences Matter: Communicating Social Identity.*

31. Matsumoto and Juang, *Culture and Psychology*, 80–81.

32. A. Williams and P. Garrett, "Communication Evaluations Across the Life Span: From Adolescent Storm and Stress to Elder Aches and Pains," *Journal of Language and Social Psychology*, 21 (June 2002): 101–126; also see D. Cai, H. Giles, and K. Noels, "Elderly Perceptions of Communication with Older and Younger Adults in China: Implications for Mental Health," *Journal of Applied Communication Research*, 26 (1998): 32–51.

33. J. Montepare, E. Koff, D. Zaitchik, and M. Albert, "The Use of Body Movements and Gestures as Cues to Emotions in Younger and Older Adults," *Journal of Nonverbal Behavior*, 23 (Summer 1999): 133–52.

34. J. Harwood, E. B. Ryan, H. Giles, and S. Tysoski, "Evaluations of Patronizing Speech and Three Response Styles in a Non-Service-Providing Context," *Journal of Applied Communication Research*, 25 (1997): 170–95.

35. C. Segrin, "Age Moderates the Relationship Between Social Support and Psychosocial Problems," paper presented at the International Communication Association, San Diego, California (2003).

36. N. Howe and W. Strauss, *Millennials Rising: The Next Great Generation* (New York: Vintage Books, 2000).

37. Howe and Strauss, *Millennials Rising: The Next Great Generation.*

38. Our discussion of generational differences and communication is also based on J. Smith, "The Millennials Are Coming," workshop presented at Texas State University, San Marcos, TX (2006).

39. Howe and Strauss, *Millennials Rising: The Next Great Generation.*

40. H. Karp, C. Fuller, and D. Sirias, *Bridging the Boomer Exer Gap: Creating Authentic Teams for High Performance at Work.* (Palo Alto, California: Davies-Black Publishing, 2002).

41. Howe and Strauss, *Millennials Rising: The Next Great Generation.*

42. M. Argyle, *The Psychology of Social Class* (London: Routledge, 1994).

43. B. J. Allen, *Differences Matter: Communicating Social Identity.* (Long Grove, Illinois: Waveland Press, Inc. 2004), 113.

44. P. Henry, "Modes of Thought That Vary Systematically with Both Social Class and Age," *Psychology & Marketing*, 17 (2000): 421–40.

45. Argyle, *The Psychology of Social Class*, 62.

46. Allen, *Differences Matter: Communicating Social Identity*, 100.

47. G. Hofstede, *Culture's Consequences: International Differences in Work-Related Values* (Beverly Hills, CA: Sage, 1980).

48. P. Cateora and J. Hess, *International Marketing* (Homewood, IL: Irwin, 1979), 89; as discussed by L. A. Samovar and R. E. Porter, *Communication Between Cultures* (Belmont, CA: Wadsworth, 2001), 52.

49. Hofstede, *Culture's Consequences.*

50. For an extensive summary and critique of Hofstede's research, see Lustig and Koester, *Intercultural Competence,* 111.

51. Hofstede, *Culture's Consequences;* also see G. Hofstede, "Cultural Dimensions in Management and Planning," *Asia Pacific Journal of Management* (January 1984): 81–98.

52. For an extensive review of communication gender differences see L. H. Turner, K. Dindia, and J. C. Pearson, "An Investigation of Female/Male Verbal Behaviors in Same-Sex and Mixed-Sex Conversations," *Communication Reports,* 8 (Summer 1995): 86–96.

53. C. R. Berger and R. J. Calabrese, "Some Explorations in Initial Interactions and Beyond: Toward a Developmental Theory of Interpersonal Communication," *Human Communication Research,* 1 (1975): 99–112.

54. For an excellent comprehensive discussion of uncertainty reduction theory, see R. West and L. H. Turner, *Introducing Communication Theory: Analysis and Application* (Mountain View, CA: Mayfield, 2000), 132–46.

55. G. Hofstede, *Cultures and Organizations: Software of the Mind* (London: McGraw-Hill, 1997).

56. Hofstede, "Cultural Dimensions in Management and Planning."

57. Hofstede, *Culture's Consequences.*

58. W. B. Gudykunst, *Bridging Differences: Effective Intergroup Communication* (Newbury Park, CA: Sage, 1998), 45.

59. Gudykunst, *Bridging Differences.*

60. E. T. Hall, *Beyond Culture* (Garden City, NY: Doubleday, 1976).

61. Samovar and Porter, *Communication Between Cultures,* 234.

62. J. L. Allen, K. M. Long, J. O'Mara, and B. B. Judd, "Verbal and Nonverbal Orientations Toward Communication and the Development of Intracultural and Intercultural Relationships," *Journal of Intercultural Communication Research,* 32 (2003): 129–60.

63. M. V. Redmond and J. M. Bunyi, "The Relationship of Intercultural Communication Competence with Stress and the Handling of Stress as Reported by International Students," *International Journal of Intercultural Relations,* 17 (1993): 235–54; R. Brislen, *Cross-Cultural Encounters: Face-to-Face Interaction* (New York: Pergamon Press, 1981).

64. W. G. Sumner, *Folkways* (Boston: Ginn, 1906), as cited by James W. Neuliep, *Intercultural Communication: A Contextual Approach* (Boston: Houghton Mifflin, 2000), 160.

65. Lustig and Koester, *Intercultural Competence.*

66. J. W. Neuliep and J. C. McCroskey, "The Development of a U.S. and Generalized Ethnocentrism Scale," *Communication Research Reports,* 14 (1997): 385–98.

67. R. K. Dillon and N. J. McKenzie, "The Influence of Ethnicity on Listening, Communication Competence, Approach, and Avoidance," *International Journal of Listening,* 12 (1998): 106–21.

68. R. E. Axtell, *Do's and Taboos of Hosting International Visitors* (New York: John Wiley & Sons, 1989), 118.

69. F. T. McAndrew, A. Akande, R. Bridgstock, L. Mealey, S. C. Gordon, J. E. Scheib, B. E. Akande-Adetoun, F. Odewale, A. Morakinyo, P. Nyahete, and G. Mubvakure, "A Multicultural Study of Stereotyping in English-Speaking Countries," *The Journal of Social Psychology,* 140 (2000): 487–502.

70. J. A. Richeson and J. N. Shelton, "Brief Report: Thin Slices of Racial Bias," *Journal of Nonverbal Behavior,* 29 (2005): 75–85.

71. C. Kluckhohn and H. A. Murry, 1953 as quoted by J. S. Caputo, H. C. Hazel, and C. McMahon, *Interpersonal Communication* (Boston: Allyn & Bacon, 1994), 304.

72. L. Mae and D. E. Carlston, "Hoist on Your Own Petard: When Prejudiced Remarks are Recognized and Backfire on Speakers," *Journal of Experimental Social Psychology,* 41 (2005): 240–55.

73. S. Kamekar, M. B. Kolsawalla, and T. Mazareth, "Occupational Prestige as a Function of Occupant's Gender," *Journal of Applied Social Psychology,* 19 (1988): 681–88.

74. F. F. Jordan-Jackson and K. A. Davis, "Men Talk: An Exploratory Study of Communication Patterns and Communication Apprehension of Black and White Males," *Journal of Men's Studies,* 13 (2005): 347–67.

75. D. E. Brown, "Human Universals and Their Implications," in N. Roughley (ed.), *Being Humans: Anthropological Universality and Particularity in Transdisciplinary Perspectives* (New York: Walter de Gruyter, 2000). For an applied discussion of these universals, see Steven Pinker, *The Blank Slate: The Modern Denial of Human Nature* (London: Penguin Books, 2002).

76. D. W. Kale, "Ethics in Intercultural Communication," in *Intercultural Communication: A Reader,* 6th ed., edited by L. A. Samovar and R. E. Porter (Belmont, CA: Wadsworth, 1991).

77. L. A. Samovar and R. E. Porter, *Communication Between Cultures* (Stamford, CT: Wadsworth and Thomson Learning, 2001), 29.

78. M. Obernauer, "Lessons on Values to Go Beyond Schools," *Austin-American Statesman* (March 30, 2005): B1, B5.

79. Eleanor Roosevelt, as cited by Lustig and Koester, *Intercultural Competence.*

80. M. R. Hammer, M. J. Bennett, and R. Wiseman, "Measuring Intercultural Sensitivity: The Intercultural Development Inventory," *International Journal of Intercultural Relations* 27 (2003): 422.

81. R. Plutchick, *Emotion: A Psychoevolutionary Synthesis* (New York: Harper & Row, 1980).

82. See, for example, M. Biehl, D. Matsumoto, P. Ekman, V. Hearn, K. Heider, T. Kudoh, and V. Ton, "Matsumoto and Ekman's Japanese and Caucasian Facial Expressions of Emotion (JACFEE): Reliability Data and Cross-National Differences," *Journal of Nonverbal Behavior,* 21 (1997): 3–21; J. D. Boucher and G. E. Carlson, "Recognition of Facial Expressions in Three Cultures," *Journal of Cross-Cultural Psychology,* 11 (1980): 263–80; D. Keltner and J. Haidt, "Social Functions of Emotions at Four Levels of Analysis," *Cognition and Emotion,* 13 (1999): 505–21.

83. C. Darwin and P. Ekman, *The Expression of the Emotions in Man and Animals,* 3rd ed. (London: Oxford University Press, 1998), 391.

84. J. A. Russell, "Is There Universal Recognition of Emotion from Facial Expressions?: A Review of the Cross-Cultural Studies," *Psychological Bulletin,* 115 (1994): 102–41.

85. E. Suh, E. Diener, S. Oishi, and H. C. Triandis, "The Shifting Basis of Life Satisfaction Judgments Across Cultures: Emotions versus Norms," *Journal of Personality and Social Psychology,* 74 (1998): 482–93.

86. See B. Parkinson, A. H. Fischer, and A. S. R. Manstead, *Emotion in Social Relations: Cultural, Group, and Interpersonal Processes* (New York: Psychology Press, 2004).

87. Parkinson, Fischer, and Manstead, *Emotion in Social Relations,* 63.

88. B. H. Spitzberg and W. R. Cupach, "Interpersonal Skills," in *Handbook of Interpersonal Communication,* edited by M. L. Knapp and J. A. Daly (Thousand Oaks, CA: Sage, 2002), 564–611.

89. S. A. Myers and R. L. Knox, "The Relationship Between College Student Information Seeking Behaviors and Perceived Instructor Verbal Responses," *Communication Education,* 50 (2001): 343–56; Baldwin and Hunt, "Information-Seeking Behavior."

90. For an excellent discussion of world view and the implications for intercultural communication, see C. H. Dodd, *Dynamics of Intercultural Communication* (New York: McGraw-Hill, 1998).

91. Dodd, *Dynamics,* 75.

92. R. Berger and R. J. Calabrese, "Some Explorations in Initial Interactions and Beyond," *Human Communication Research,* 1 (1975): 99–125.

93. B. J. Broome, "Building Shared Meaning: Implications of a Relational Approach to Empathy for Teaching Intercultural Communication," *Communication Education,* 40 (1991): 235–49.

94. F. L. Casmir, "Foundations for the Study of Intercultural Communication Based on a Third-Culture Building Model," *International Journal of Intercultural Relations,* 23 (1999): 91–116; also see S. DeTurk, "Intercultural Empathy: Myth, Competency, or Possibility for Alliance Building?" *Communication Education,* 50 (October 2001): 374–84.

95. F. L. Casmir and N. C. Asuncion-Lande, "Intercultural Communication Revisited: Conceptualization, Paradigm Building, and Methodological Approaches," in *Communication Yearbook,* vol. 12, edited by J. A. Anderson (Newbury Park, CA: Sage, 1989), 278–309.

96. Broome, "Building Shared Meaning."

97. Gudykunst and Kim, *Communicating with Strangers;* Gudykunst, *Bridging Differences.*

98. L. B. Szalay and G. H. Fisher, "Communication Overseas," in *Toward Internationalism: Readings in Cross-Cultural Communication,* edited by E. C. Smith and L. E Luce (Rowley, MA: Newbury House, 1979); also see Paul E. King and Chris R. Sawyer, "Mindfulness, Mindlessness and Communication Instruction," *Communication Education,* 47 (October 1998): 326–36.

99. P. Brown and S. Levinson, *Politeness: Some Universals in Language Usage* (Cambridge, England: Cambridge University Press, 1987).

100. C. S. Lewis, *The Abolition of Man* (New York: Macmillan Publishing Company, 1947).

101. DeTurk, "Intercultural Empathy."

102. M. V. Redmond, "The Functions of Empathy (Decentering) in Human Relations," *Human Relations,* 42 (1993): 593–606; also see M. V. Redmond, "A Multidimensional Theory and Measure of Social Decentering," *Journal of Research in Personality,* 29 (1995): 35–58. For an excellent discussion of the role of emotions in establishing empathy, see D. Goleman, *Emotional Intelligence* (New York: Bantam, 1995).

103. D. F. Barone, P. S. Hutchings, H. J. Kimmel, H. L. Traub, J. T. Cooper, and C. M. Marshall, "Increasing Empathic Accuracy Through Practice and Feedback in a Clinical Interviewing Course," *Journal of Social and Clinical Psychology,* 24 (2005): 156–71.

104. See H. Giles, A. Mulack, J. J. Bradac, and P. Johnson, "Speech Accommodation Theory: The First Decade and Beyond," in *Communication Yearbook,* vol. 10, edited by M. L. McLaughlin (Newbury Park, CA: Sage, 1987), 13–48. For an excellent summary and application of accommodation theory, see R. West and L. H. Turner, *Introducing Communication Theory: Analysis and Application* (Mountain View, CA: Mayfield, 2000).

105. M. J. Bennett, "Overcoming the Golden Rule: Sympathy and Empathy," in *Communication Yearbook 3,* edited by D. Nimmo (Beverly Hills, CA: Sage, 1979), 407–22.

106. Bennett, "Overcoming the Golden Rule."

107. L. J. Carrell, "Diversity in the Communication Curriculum: Impact on Student Empathy," *Communication Education,* 46 (October 1997): 234–44.

Chapter 5

1. H. J. M. Nouwen, *Bread for the Journey* (San Francisco: HarperCollins, 1997), entry for March 11.

2. Nouwen, *Bread for the Journey,* March 11.

3. "The Most Valued Workplace Skills," *The Wall Street Journal,* September 9, 2002: 1A.

4. R. W. Young and C. M. Cates, "Emotional and Directive Listening in Peer Mentoring," *International Journal of Listening,* 18 (2004): 21–33; also see D. A. Romig, *Side by Side Leadership* (Marietta, GA: Bard, 2001).

5. L. Barker et al., "An Investigation of Proportional Time Spent in Various Communication Activities of College Students," *Journal of Applied Communication Research,* 8 (1981): 101–09.

6. A. D. Wovin and C. G. Coakley, "Listening Education in the 21st Century," *International Journal of Listening,* 14 (2001): 143–52.

7. S. C. Bentley, "Listening in the 21st Century," *International Journal of Listening,* 14 (2000): 129–42; also see A. D. Wovin and C. G. Coakley, "Listening Education in the 21st Century."

8. D. A. Schwartz, "Review Essay Listening Out of the Box: New Perspectives for the Workplace," *International Journal of Listening,* 18 (2004): 47–55.

9. Adapted from the International Listening Association's definition of *listening,* which may be found on their Web site at http://www.listen.org

10. W. G. Powers and G. D. Bodie, "Listening Fidelity: Seeking Congruence Between Cognitions of the Listener and the Sender," *International Journal of Listening,* 17 (2003): 20–31.

11. L. A. Januskik, "Listening and Cognitive Processing: Is There a Difference?" paper presented at the annual conference of the National Communication Association (November 2002), New Orleans, LA. Januskik suggests that it's important to include a behavioral component, such as responding to a message, in any definition of listening.

12. K. W. Watson, L. L. Barker, and J. B. Weaver, *The Listener Style Inventory* (New Orleans: SPECTRA, 1995).

13. For support of the validity and reliability of the Listening Styles Profile, see D. L. Worthington, "Exploring the Relationship Between Listening Style Preference and Personality," *International Journal of Listening,* 17 (2003): 68–87; also see J. B. Weaver, K. W. Watson, and L. L. Barker, "Individual Differences in Listening Styles: Do You Hear What I Hear?" *Personality and Individual Differences,* 20 (1996): 381–87; S. Sargent, J. B. Weaver, and C. Kiewitz, "Correlates Between Communication Apprehension and Listening Style Preferences," *Communication Research Reports,* 14 (1997): 74–78; M. K. Johnston, J. B. Weaver, K. W. Watson, and L. B. Barker, "Listening Styles: Biological or Psychological Differences?" *International Journal of Listening,* 14 (2000): 32–46.

14. R. K. Dillon and N. J. McKenzie, "The Influence of Ethnicity on Listen-

ing, Communication Competence, Approach, and Avoidance," *International Journal of Listening,* 12 (1998): 106–21.

15. Sargent and Weaver, "Correlates Between Communication Apprehension and Listening Style Preferences"; G. D. Bodie and W. A. Villaume, "Aspects of Receiving Information: The Relationship Between Listening Preferences, Communication Apprehension, Receiver Apprehension, and Communicator Style," *International Journal of Listening,* 17 (2003): 48–67.

16. Worthington, "Exploring the Relationship Between Listening Style Preference and Personality."

17. D. L. Worthington, "Exploring Juror's Listening Processes: The Effect of Listening Style Preference on Juror Decision Making," *International Journal of Listening,* 15 (2001): 20–37.

18. M. D. Kirtley and J. M. Honeycutt, "Listening Styles and Their Correspondence with Second Guessing," *Communication Research Reports,* 13 (1996): 174–82.

19. Sargent and Weaver, "Correlates Between Communication Apprehension and Listening Style Preferences."

20. Bodie and Villaume, "Aspects of Receiving Information."

21. L. L. Barker and K. W. Watson, *Listen Up* (New York: St. Martin's Press: 2000); also see M. Imhof, "Who Are We as We Listen? Individual Listening Profiles in Varying Contexts," *International Journal of Listening,* 18 (2004): 36–45.

22. W. Winter, A. J. Ferreira, and N. Bowers, "Decision-Making in Married and Unrelated Couples," *Family Process,* 12 (1973): 83–94.

23. J. Stauffer, R. Frost, and W. Rybolt, "The Attention Factor in Recalling Network News," *Journal of Communication,* 33(1), (1983): 29–37.

24. O. E. Rankis, "The Effects of Message Structure, Sexual Gender, and Verbal Organizing Ability upon Learning Message Information," doctoral dissertation, Ohio University, 1981; C. H. Weaver, *Human Listening. Process and Behavior* (New York: Bobbs-Merrill, 1972); R. D. Halley, "Distractibility of Males and Females in Competing Aural Message Situations: A Research Note," *Human Communication Research,* 2 (1975): 79–82. Our discussion of gender-based differences and listening is also based on a discussion by S. A. Beebe and J. T. Masterson, *Family Talk: Interpersonal Communication in the Family* (New York: Random House, 1986); J. Lurito, "Listening and Gender," paper presented to the Radiological Society of North America, Chicago (2000), as cited by L. Tanner, "Listening Study Finds Difference in the Sexes," *Austin-American Statesman,* November 29, 2000: A11.

25. S. L. Sargent and J. B. Weaver III, "Listening Styles: Sex Differences in Perceptions of Self and Others," *International Journal of Listening,* 17 (2003): 5–18.

26. J. T. Wood, "A Critical Response to John Gray's Mars and Venus Portrayals of Men and Women," *The Southern Communication Journal,* 67 (2002): 201–11.

27. This discussion is based on A. Vangelisti, M. Knapp, and J. Daly, "Conversational Narcissism," *Communication Monographs,* 57 (1990): 251–74.

28. R. Montgomery, *Listening Made Easy* (New York: Amacon, 1981); O. Hargie, C. Sanders, and D. Dickson, *Social Skills in Interpersonal Communication* (London: Routledge, 1994); O. Hargie (Ed.), *The Handbook of Communication Skills* (London: Routledge, 1997). Also see S. W. Littlejohn and K. Domenici, *Engaging Communication in Conflict: Systemic Practice* (Thousand Oaks, CA: Sage, 2001), 105–08.

29. R. G. Owens, "Handling Strong Emotions," in *A Handbook of Communication Skills,* edited by O. Hargie (London: Croom Helm/New York University Press, 1986).

30. K. B. Staples, "Black Men and Public Space," in *Literature for Composition,* 3rd ed., edited by S. Barnet et al. (Glenview, IL: Scott, Foresman, 1992), 73.

31. R. G. Nichols, "Factors in Listening Comprehension," *Speech Monographs,* 15 (1948): 154–63; G. M. Goldhaber and C. H. Weaver, "Listener Comprehension of Compressed Speech When the Difficulty, Rate of Presentation, and Sex of the Listener Are Varied," *Speech Monographs,* 35 (1968): 20–25.

32. ABC News, *20/20,* January 12, 1998, featuring the research of communication researcher Kittie Watson.

33. M. V. Redmond, "The Functions of Empathy (Decentering) in Human Relations," *Human Relations,* 42 (1993): 593–606.

34. M. Fitch-Hauser, L. A. Barker, and A. Hughes, "Receiver Apprehension and Listening Comprehension: A Linear or Curvilinear Relationship?" *Southern Communication Journal* (1988): 62–71; P. Schrodt and L. R. Wheeless, "Aggressive Communication and Informational Reception Apprehension: The Influence of Listening Anxiety and Intellectual Inflexibility on Trait Argumentativeness and Verbal Aggressiveness," *Communication Quarterly,* 49 (Winter 2001): 53–69.

35. A. Mulanx and W. G. Powers, "Listening Fidelity Development and Relationship to Receiver Apprehension and Locus of Control," *International Journal of Listening,* 17 (2003): 69–78.

36. D. Carnegie, *How to Win Friends and Influence People* (New York: Holiday House, 1937).

37. K. K. Halone and L. L. Pecchioni, "Relational Listening: A Grounded Theoretical Model," *Communication Reports,* 14 (2001): 59–71.

38. Halone and Pecchioni, "Relational Listening."

39. K. Ruyter and M. G. M. Wetzels, "The Impact of Perceived Listening Behavior in Voice-to-Voice Service Encounters," *Journal of Service Research,* 2 (February 2000): 276–84.

40. J. Harrigan, "Listeners' Body Movements and Speaking Turns," *Communication Research,* 12 (1985): 233–50.

41. S. Strong et al., "Nonverbal Behavior and Perceived Counselor Characteristics," *Journal of Counseling Psychology,* 18 (1971): 554–61.

42. Halone and Pecchioni, "Relational Listening."

43. M. Imhof, "How to Listen More Efficiently: Self-Monitoring Strategies in Listening," *International Journal of Listening,* 17 (2003): 2–19.

44. See R. G. Nichols and L. A. Stevens, "Listening to People," *Harvard Business Review,* 35 (September–October 1957): 85–92.

45. C. W. Ellison and I. J. Fireston, "Development of Interpersonal Trust as a Function of Self-Esteem, Target Status and Target Style," *Journal of Personality and Social Psychology,* 29 (1974): 655–63.

46. R. Bommelje, J. M. Houston, and R. Smither, "Personality Characteristics of Effective Listeners: A Five Factor Perspective," *International Journal of Listening,* 17 (2003): 32–46.

47. J. Hakansson and H. Montomery, "Empathy as an Interpersonal Phenomenon," *Journal of Social and Personal Relationships,* 20 (2003): 267–84.

48. D. Goleman, *Emotional Intelligence* (New York: Bantam, 1995).

49. Goleman, *Emotional Intelligence.*

50. O. Hargie, C. Sanders, and D. Dickson, *Social Skills in Interpersonal Communication* (London: Routledge, 1994); Hargie (Ed.), *The Handbook of Communication Skills.*

51. J. B. Weaver and M. B. Kirtley, "Listening Styles and Empathy," *The Southern Communication Journal,* 60 (1995): 131–40.

52. C. Rogers, *Client-Centered Therapy* (Boston: Houghton Mifflin, 1951).

53. R. Lemieux and M. R. Tighe, "Attachment Styles and the Evaluation of Comforting Responses: A Receiver Perspective," *Communication Research Reports,* 21 (2004): 144–53; also see W. Samter, "How Gender and Cognitive Complexity Influence the Provision of Emotional Support: A Study of Indirect Effects," *Communication Reports,* 15 (2002): 5–16.

54. Our discussion of the appropriate and inappropriate social support responses is taken from B. D. Burleson, "Emotional Support Skill," in *Handbook of Communication and Social Interaction Skills,* edited by J. O. Greene and B. R. Burleson (Mahwah, NJ: Erlbaum, 2003), 566–68.

55. J. Gottman and J. DeClaire, *The Relationship Cure* (New York: Crown, 2001), 198–201.

56. Hargie, Sanders, and Dickson, *Social Skills;* R. Boulton, *People Skills* (New York: Simon & Schuster, 1981).

57. E. Sieburg and C. Larson, "Dimensions of Interpersonal Response," paper delivered at the annual conference of the International Communication Association, Phoenix, Arizona, April 1971; K. Ellis, "Perceived Teacher Confirmation: The Development and Validation of an Instrument and Two Studies of the Relationship to Cognitive and Affective Learning," *Human Communication Research,* 26 (2000): 264–91.

58. S. DeTurk, "Intercultural Empathy: Myth, Competency, or Possibility for Alliance Building?" *Communication Education,* 50 (October 2001): 374–84.

59. Boulton, *People Skills.* We also acknowledge others who have presented excellent applications of listening and responding skills in interpersonal and group contexts: D. A. Romig and L. J. Romig, *Structured Teamwork Guide* (Austin, TX: Performance Resources, 1990); S. Deep and L. Sussman, *Smart Moves* (Reading: MA. Addison-Wesley, 1990); P. R. Scholtes, *The Team Handbook* (Madison, WI: Joiner Associates, 1992); Hargie, Sanders, and Dickson, *Social Skills;* Littlejohn and Domenici, *Engaging Communication in Conflict.*

60. R. Lemieux and M. R. Tighe, "Attachment Styles and the Evaluation of Comforting Responses: A Receiver Perspective," *Communication Research Reports,* 21 (2004): 144–53; also see J. M. Gottman and J. S. Gottman, *10 Lessons to Transform Your Marriage* (New York: Crown Publishers, 2006).

61. S. Gilbert, "Self-Disclosure, Intimacy, and Communication in Families," *Family Coordinator,* 25 (1976).

Chapter 6

1. B. Spitzberg and J. P. Dillard, "Social Skills and Communication," in *Interpersonal Communication Research: Advances Through Meta-Analysis,* edited by M. Allen, R. W. Preiss, B. M. Gayle, and N. Burrell (Mahwah, NJ: Erlbaum, 2002), 89–107.

2. K. Kellermann and N. A. Palomares, "Topical Profiling: Emergent, Co-Occurring, and Relationally Defining Topics in Talk," *Journal of Language and Social Psychology,* 23 (2004): 308–37.

3. C. K. Ogden and I. A. Richards, *The Meaning of Meaning* (London: Kegan, Paul Trench, Trubner, 1923).

4. C. F. Hockett, *A Course in Modern Linguistics* (New York: Macmillan, 1958).

5. C. S. Lewis, *Studies in Words* (Cambridge, England: Cambridge University Press, 1960).

6. See G. H. Mead, *Mind, Self and Society* (Chicago: University of Chicago Press, 1934); H. Blumer, *Symbolic Interactionism: Perspective and Method* (Englewood Cliffs, NJ: Prentice Hall, 1969).

7. D. Tannen, *You Just Don't Understand: Women and Men in Conversations* (New York: Morrow, 1990).

8. R. Edwards, "The Effects of Gender, Gender Role, and Values on the Interpretation of Messages," *Journal of Language and Social Psychology,* 17 (1998): 52–71.

9. *The American Heritage Dictionary of the English Language* (Boston: Houghton Mifflin, 1969), 1162.

10. A. Korzybski, *Science and Sanity* (Lancaster, PA: Science Press, 1941).

11. G. Gusdorff, *Speaking* (Evanston, IL: Northwestern University Press, 1965), 9.

12. A. Ellis, *A New Guide to Rational Living* (North Hollywood, CA: Wilshire Books, 1977); also see W. Glaser, *Choice Theory* (New York: HarperCollins, 1998).

13. R. C. Martin and E. R. Dahlen, "Irrational Beliefs and the Experience and Expression of Anger," *Journal of Rational-Emotive & Cognitive-Behavior Therapy,* 22 (2004): 3–20.

14. C. Peterson, M. E. P. Seligman, and G. E. Vaillant, "Pessimistic Explanatory Style Is a Risk Factor for Physical Illness: A 35-Year Longitudinal Study," *Journal of Personality and Social Psychology,* 55 (1988): 23–27.

15. E. K. Heussenstaunn, "Bumper Stickers and Cops," *Transaction,* 35 (1971): 32–33.

16. C. S. Areni and J. R. Sparks, "Language Power and Persuasion," *Psychology & Marketing,* 22 (2005): 507–25.

17. W. M. O'Barr. *Linguistic Evidence* (New York: Academic Press, 1982).

18. B. L. Whorf, "Science and Linguistics," in *Language, Thought and Reality,* edited by J. B. Carroll (Cambridge, MA: MIT Press, 1956), 207. This discussion of the Sapir–Whorf hypothesis is based on D. Crystal, *The Cambridge Encyclopedia of Language* (Cambridge, Eng-

land: Cambridge University Press, 1997).

19. We thank one of our anonymous reviewers for this example.

20. W. Johnson, *People in Quandaries* (New York: Harper & Row).

21. A fascinating article, "The Melting of a Mighty Myth" in *Newsweek* (July 22, 1991) explores the topic of Eskimos' words for snow.

22. J. Coupland, "Small Talk: Social Function," *Research on Language and Social Interaction,* 36 (2003): 1–6; M. M. Step and M. O. Finucane, "Interpersonal Communication Motives in Everyday Interactions," *Communication Quarterly,* 50 (2002): 93–100.

23. M. McCarthy, "Talking Back: 'Small' Interactional Response Tokens in Everyday Conversation," *Research on Language and Social Interaction,* 36 (2003): 33–63.

24. S. Duck, "Talking Relationships into Being," *Journal of Social and Personal Relationships.*" 12 (1995): 535–40.

25. J. K. Alberts, C. G. Yoshimura, M. Rabby, and R. Loschiavo, "Mapping the Topography of Couples' Daily Conversation," *Journal of Social and Personal Relationships,* 22 (2005): 299–322.

26. R. L. Howe, *The Miracle of Dialogue* (New York: The Seabury Press, 1963), 23–24.

27. C. C. Kopecky and W. G. Powers, "Relational Development and Self-Image Communication Accuracy," *Communication Research Reports,* 19 (2002): 283–90.

28. S. Emling, "NuSrvc2 OffrGr8 Litr8tr On YrFon," *Austin American-Statesman* (November 26, 2005): A1, A6.

29. T. M. Karelitz and D. V. Budescu, "You Say 'Probable' and I Say 'Likely': Improving Interpersonal Communication with Verbal Probability Phrases," *Journal of Experimental Psychology,* 10 (2004): 25–41.

30. H. S. O'Donnell, "Sexism in Language," *Elementary English,* 50 (1973): 1067–72.

31. See D. K. Ivy and P. Backlund, *Exploring Genderspeak* (New York: McGraw-Hill, 2004).

32. *Newsweek,* November 20, 1995, 81.

33. We acknowledge and appreciate D. K. Ivy's contribution to this section on biased language. For an expanded discussion on this topic, see Ivy and Backlund, *Genderspeak.*

34. J. S. Seiter, J. Larsen, and J. Skinner, "'Handicapped' or 'Handi-capable'? The Effects of Language About Persons with Disabilities on Perceptions of Source Credibility and Persuasiveness," *Communication Reports,* 11(1) (1998): 21–31.

35. D. O. Braithwaite and C. A. Braithwaite, "Understanding Communication of Persons with Disabilities as Cultural Communication," in *Intercultural Communication: A Reader,* 8th ed., edited by L. A. Samovar and R. E. Porter (Belmont, CA: Wadsworth, 1997): 154–64.

36. D. Yankelovich, *The Magic of Dialogue: Transforming Conflict into Cooperation* (New York: Simon & Schuster, 1999).

37. J. R. Gibb, "Defensive Communication," *Journal of Communication,* 11 (1961): 141–48. Also see R. Boulton, *People Skills* (New York: Simon & Schuster, 1979), 14–26; O. Hargie, C. Sanders, and D. Dickson, *Social Skills in Interpersonal Communication* (London: Routledge, 1994); O. Hargie (Ed.), *The Handbook of Communication Skills* (London: Routledge, 1997); S. W. Littlejohn and K. Domenici, *Engaging Communication in Conflict* (Thousand Oaks, CA: Sage, 2001).

38. S. M. Yoshimura, "Emotional and Behavioral Responses to Romantic Jealousy Expressions," *Communication Reports,* 17 (2004): 85–101.

39. K. K. Sereno, M. Welch, and D. Braaten, "Interpersonal Conflict: Effects of Variations in Manner of Expressing Anger and Justifications for Anger upon Perceptions of Appropriateness, Competence, and Satisfaction," *Journal of Applied Communication Research,* 15 (1987): 128–43; J. Gottman, *A Couples Guide to Communication* (Champaign, IL; Research Press, 1976); E. S. Kubany, G. B. Bauer, M. E. Pangilinan, M. Y. Muraoka, and V. G. Enriquez, "Impact of Labeled Anger and Blame in Intimate Relationships: Cross-Cultural Extension of Findings," *Journal of Cross-Cultural Psychology,* 26 (1995): 65–83; E. S. Kubany, G. B. Bauer, M. Muraoka, D. C. Richard, and P. Read, "Impact of Labeled Anger and Blame in Intimate Relationships," *Journal of Social and Clinical Psychology,* 14 (1995): 53–60; M. R. Leary, C. Springer, L. Negel, E. Ansell, and K. Evans, "The Causes, Phenomenology, and Consequences of Hurt.Feelings," *Journal of Personality and Social Psychology,* 74 (1998): 1225–37.

40. A. M. Bippus and S. L. Young, "Owning Your Emotions: Reactions to Expressions of Self- versus Other-Attributed Positive and Negative Emotions," *Journal of Applied Communication Research,* 33 (2005): 26–45.

41. C. Rogers, *On Becoming a Person: A Therapist's View of Psychotherapy* (Boston: Houghton Mifflin, 1961); C. Rogers, *A Way of Being* (Boston: Houghton Mifflin, 1980); C. Rogers, "Comments on the Issue of Equality in Psychotherapy," *Journal of Humanistic Psychology,* 27 (1987): 38–39.

42. A. M. Bippus, "Recipients' Criteria for Evaluating the Skillfulness of Comforting Communication and the Outcomes of Comforting Interactions," *Communication Monographs,* 68 (2001): 301–13.

43. K. Floyd and M. T. Morman, "Affectionate Communication in Nonromantic Relationships: Influences of Communicator, Relational, and Contextual Factors," *Western Journal of Communication,* 61 (1997): 279–98; K. Floyd and M. Voloudakis, "Affectionate Behavior in Adult Platonic Friendships: Interpreting and Evaluating Expectancy Violations," *Human Communication Research,* 25 (1999): 341–69.

44. B. R. Burleson, "Comforting Messages: Features, Functions, and Outcomes," in *Strategic Interpersonal Communication,* edited by J. A. Daly and J. M. Wiemann (Hillsdale, NJ: Erlbaum, 1994), 135–61.

45. B. M. Gayle and R. W. Preiss, "An Overview of Interactional Processes in Interpersonal Communication," in *Interpersonal Communication Research: Advances Through Meta-Analysis,* edited by M. Allen, R. W. Preiss, B. M. Gayle, and N. Burrell (Mahwah, NJ: Erlbaum, 2002), 213–26.

46. M. Allen, "A Synthesis and Extension of Constructivist Comforting Research," in *Interpersonal Communication Research,* 237–45.

47. D. J. Dolin and M. Booth-Butterfield, "Reach Out and Touch Someone: Analysis of Nonverbal Comforting Responses," *Communication Quarterly,* 41 (1993): 383–93.

48. A. M. Bippus, "Human Usages in Comforting Episodes: Factors Predicting Outcomes," *Western Journal of Communication,* 54 (Fall 2000): 359–84; A. M. Bippus, "Recipients' Criteria for Evaluating the Skillfulness of Comforting Communication and the Outcomes of Comforting Interactions," *Communication Monographs,* 68 (September 2001): 301–13; A. M. Bippus, "Humor Motives, Qualities, and Reactions in Recalled Conflict Episodes," *Western Journal of Communication,* 67 (2003): 413–26.

49. K. Ohbuchi, M. Kameda, and N. Agarie, "Apology as Aggression Control: Its Role in Mediating Appraisal of and Response to Harm," *Journal of Personality and Social Psychology,* 56 (1989): 219–27.

50. M. McCollough, K. Rachal, J. Steven, E. Worthington, S. Brown, and T. Hight. "Interpersonal Forgiving in Close Relationships II: Theoretical Elaboration and Measurement," *Journal of Personality and Social Psychology,* 75 (1998): 1586–1603.

51. J. R. Meyer and K. Rothenberg, "Repairing Regretted Messages: Effects of Emotional State, Relationship Type, and Seriousness of Offense," *Communication Research Reports,* 21 (2005): 348–56.

52. B. W. Darby and B. R. Schlenker, "Children's Reactions to Transgressions: Effects of the Actor's Apology, Reputation and Remorse," *British Journal of Social Psychology,* 28 (1989): 353–64.

53. S. J. Scher and J. M. Darley, "How Effective Are the Things People Say to Apologize? Effects of the Realization of the Apology Speech Act," *Journal of Psycholinguistic Research,* 26 (1997): 127–40.

54. C. McPherson Frantz and C. Bennigson, "Better Late Than Early: The Influence of Timing on Apology Effectiveness," *Journal of Experimental Social Psychology,* 41 (2005): 201–07.

55. Our prescriptions for assertiveness are based on a discussion by R. Boulton, *People Skills.* Also see J. S. St. Lawrence, "Situational Context: Effects on Perceptions of Assertive and Unassertive Behavior," *Behavior Therapy,* 16 (1985): 51–62; D. Borisoff and D. A. Victor, *Conflict Management: A Communication Skills Approach* (Boston: Allyn & Bacon, 1999).

56. D. Cloven and M. E. Roloff, "The Chilling Effect of Aggressive Potential on the Expression of Complaints in Intimate Relationships," *Communication Monographs,* 60 (1993): 199–219.

Chapter 7

1. J. Kabat-Zinn, *Wherever You Go, There You Are: Mindfulness Meditation in Everyday Life* (New York: Hyperion Books, 1994).

2. J. V. Cordova, C. B. Gee, and L. Z. Warren, "Emotional Skillfulness in Marriage: Intimacy as a Mediator of the Relationship Between Emotional Skillfulness and Marital Satisfaction," *Journal of Social and Clinical Psychology,* 24 (2005): 218–35.

3. A. Mehrabian, *Nonverbal Communication* (Chicago: Aldine Atherton, 1972), 108.

4. D. Lapakko, "Three Cheers for Language: A Closer Examination of a Widely Cited Study of Nonverbal Communication," *Communication Education,* 46 (1997): 63–67.

5. D. Matsumoto, J. LeRoux, C. Wilson-Cohn, J. Raroque, K. Kooken, P. Ekman, N. Yrizarry, S. Loewinger, H. Uchida, A. Yee, L. Amo, and A. Goh, "A New Test to Measure Emotion Recognition Ability: Matsumoto and Ekman's Japanese and Caucasian Brief Affect Recognition Test (JACBART)," *Journal of Nonverbal Behavior,* 24 (Fall 2000): 179–209; J. K. Burgoon and A. E. Bacue, "Nonverbal Communication Skills," in *Handbook of Communication and Social Interaction Skills,* edited by J. O. Greene and B. R. Burleson (Mahwah, NJ: Erlbaum, 2003), 179–219; B. H. LaFrance, A. D. Heisel, and M. J. Beatty, "Is There Empirical Evidence for a Nonverbal Profile of Extraversion?" A Meta-Analysis and Critique of the Literature," *Communication Monographs,* 71 (2004): 28–48.

6. M. Zuckerman, D. DePaulo, and R. Rosenthal, "Verbal and Nonverbal Communication of Deception," *Advances in Experimental Social Psychology,* 14 (1981): 1–59.

7. P. Ekman and W. V. Friesen, "The Repertoire of Nonverbal Behavior: Categories, Origins, Usage and Coding," *Semiotica,* 1 (1969): 49–98.

8. E. Hess, *The Tell-Tale Eye* (New York: Van Nostrand Reinhold, 1975).

9. P. Ekman, "Communication Through Nonverbal Behavior: A Source of Information About an Interpersonal Relationship," in *Affect Cognition and Personality,* edited by S. S. Tomkins and C. E. Izard (New York: Springer, 1965).

10. J. K. Burgoon, J. A. Bonito, A. Ramirez Jr., N. E. Dunbar, K. Kam, and J. Fischer, "Testing the Interactivity Principle: Effects of Mediation, Propinquity, and Verbal and Nonverbal Modalities in Interpersonal Interaction," *Journal of Communication,* 52(3) (2002): 657–77.

11. J. K. Burgoon, L. A. Stern, and L. Dillman, *Interpersonal Adaptation: Dyadic Interaction Patterns* (Cambridge, England: Cambridge University Press, 1995).

12. A. S. E. Hubbard, "Interpersonal Coordination in Interactions: Evaluations and Social Skills," *Communication Research Reports,* 17 (Winter 2000): 95–104.

13. R. L. Birdwhistell, *Kinesics and Context* (Philadelphia: University of Pennsylvania Press, 1970).

14. J. M. Gottman, J. Coan, S. Carrere, and C. Swanson, "Predicting Marital Happiness and Stability from Newlywed Interactions," *Journal of Marriage and the Family,* 60 (1998): 5–22.

15. P. Noller, "Nonverbal Communication in Marriage," in *Applications of Nonverbal Behavioral Theories,* edited by R. S. Feldman (Hillsdale, NJ: Erlbaum, 1992), 31–59.

16. N. Zunin and M. Zunin, *Contact: The First Four Minutes* (New York: Signet, 1976).

17. J. H. Bert and K. Piner, "Social Relationships and the Lack of Social Relations," in *Personal Relationships and Social Support,* edited by S. W. Duck with R. C. Silver (London: Sage, 1989).

18. S. M. Jones and L. K. Guerrero, "The Effects of Nonverbal Immediacy and Verbal Person Centeredness in the Emotional Support Process," *Human Communication Research,* 27 (October 2001): 567–96.

19. Koerner and Fitzpatrick, "Nonverbal Communication and Marital Adjustment and Satisfaction."

20. Cordova, Gee, and Warren, "Emotional Skillfulness in Marriage."

21. Burgoon and Bacue, "Nonverbal Communication Skills."

22. B. M. DePaulo and H. S. Friedman, "Nonverbal Communication," in *The Handbook of Social Psychology,* edited by D. T. Gilbert, S. T. Fiske, and G. Lindzey (New York: McGraw-Hill, 1998).

23. P. Ekman and W. V Friesen, "Constants Across Cultures in the Face and Emotion," *Journal of Personality and Social Psychology,* 17 (1971): 124–29; M. Argyle, *Bodily Communication* (New York: Methuen, 1988), 157; I. Eibl-Eibesfeldt, "Similarities and Differences Between Cultures in Expressive Movements," in *Nonverbal Communication,* edited by R. A. Hinde (Cambridge, England: Royal Society & Cambridge University Press, 1972); P. Collett, "History and Study of Expressive Action," in *Historical Social Psychology,* edited by K. Gergen and M. Gergen (Hillsdale, NJ: Erlbaum, 1984); E. T. Hall, *The Silent Language* (Garden City, NY: Doubleday, 1959); R. Shuter, "Gaze Behavior in Interracial and Intraracial Interaction," *International and Intercultural Communication Annual,* 5 (1979): 48–55; R. Shuter, "Proxemics and Tactility in Latin America," *Journal of Communication,* 26 (1976): 46–52; E. T. Hall, *The Hidden Dimension* (New York: Doubleday, 1966). For an excellent discussion of world view and the implications for intercultural communication, see C. H. Dodd, *Dynamics of Intercultural Communication* (Dubuque, IA: Brown & Benchmark, 1995); G. W. Beattie, *Talk: An Analysis of Speech and Non-Verbal Behavior in Conversation* (Milton Keynes: Open University Press, 1983); O. Hargie, C. Sanders, and D. Dickson, *Social Skills in Interpersonal Communication* (London: Routledge, 1994); O. Hargie (Ed.), *The Handbook of Communication Skills* (London: Routledge, 1997).

24. Several studies offer evidence of the universality of facial expressions. See P. Ekman, "Strong Evidence for Universals in Facial Expressions: A Reply to Russell's Mistaken Critique," *Psychological Bulletin,* 115 (1994): 268–87; P. Ekman and W. Friesen, "Constants Across Culture in the Face and Emotion," *Journal of Personality and Social Psychology,* 17 (1971): 124–29; P. Ekman and W. Friesen, *Facial Action Coding System: Investigator's Guide* (Palo Alto, CA: Consulting Psychologists Press, 1978); P. Ekman and W. Friesen, "A New Pan-Cultural Facial Expression of Emotion," *Motivation & Emotion,* 10 (1986): 159–68; P. Ekman, E. R. Sorenson, and W. Friesen, "Pancultural Elements in Facial Displays of Emotion," *Science,* 164 (1969): 86–88; D. Matsumoto, "Scalar Ratings of Contempt Expressions," *Journal of Nonverbal Behavior,* 29 (2005): 91–104.

25. Argyle, *Bodily Communication.*

26. W. G. Woodal and J. K. Burgoon, "The Effects of Nonverbal Synchrony on Message Comprehension and Persuasiveness," *Journal of Nonverbal Behavior,* 5 (1981): 207–23.

27. Argyle, *Bodily Communication.*

28. K. N. Blurton-Jones and G. M. Leach, "Behavior of Children and Their Mothers at Separation and Parting," in *Ethological Studies of Child Behavior,* edited by N. Blurton-Jones (Cambridge, England: Cambridge University Press, 1972).

29. This example originally appeared in Collett, "History and Study of Expressive Action."

30. Birdwhistell, *Kinesics and Context.* Also see D. G. Leathers, *Successful Nonverbal Communications and Applications* (Boston: Allyn & Bacon, 1998).

31. A. E. Scheflen, "Quasi-Courtship Behavior in Psychotherapy," *Psychiatry,* 28 (1965): 245–57.

32. M. Moore, "Interpreting Nonverbal Messages," *Journal of Ethology and Sociology* (Summer 1994); also see D. Knox and K. Wilson, "Dating Behaviors of University Students," *Family Relations,* 30 (1981): 255–58.

33. M. Reece and R. Whitman, "Expressive Movements, Warmth, and Verbal Reinforcement," *Journal of Abnormal and Social Psychology,* 64 (1962): 234–36.

34. A. Mehrabian, *Silent Messages* (Belmont, CA: Wadsworth, 1972), 108.

35. Ekman and Friesen, "The Repertoire of Nonverbal Behavior."

36. A. T. Dittman, "The Body Movement–Speech Rhythm Relationship as a Cue to Speech Encoding," in *Studies in Dyadic Communication,* edited by A. W. Siegman and B. Pope (New York: Pergamon, 1972).

37. A. A. Cohen and R. P. Harrison, "Intentionality in the Use of Hand Illustrators in Face-to-Face Communication Situations," *Journal of Personality and Social Psychology,* 28 (1973): 276–79.

38. C. Darwin, *The Expression of the Emotions in Man and Animals* (Chicago: University of Chicago Press, 1965). Originally published 1872.

39. A. Mehrabian and M. Williams, "Nonverbal Concomitants of Perceived and Intended Persuasiveness," *Journal of Personality and Social Psychology,* 13 (1969): 37–58.

40. M. Argyle, E. Alkema, and R. Gilmour, "The Communication of Friendly and Hostile Attitudes by Verbal and Nonverbal Signals," *European Journal of Social Psychology,* 1 (1972): 385–402.

41. D. Morris, *People Watching* (London: Vantage Press, 2002), 104.

42. A. Kendon, "Some Functions of Gaze-Direction in Social Interaction," *Acta Psychologica,* 26 (1967): 22–63.

43. M. Knapp and J. A. Hall, *Nonverbal Communication in Human Interaction* (Fort Worth, TX: Harcourt Brace, 1997), 313.

44. P. Ekman, W. V. Friesen, and S. S. Tomkins, "Facial Affect Scoring Technique: A First Validity Study," *Semiotica,* 3 (1971): 37–58; P. Ekman and W. V. Friesen, *Unmasking the Face* (Englewood Cliffs, NJ: Prentice Hall, 1975).

45. Associated Press, "Frowning Outlawed in Meeting Code of Conduct," Retrieved May 7, 2003 from www.Boston.com.

46. Ekman and Friesen, *Unmasking the Face;* Ekman, Friesen, and Tomkins, "Facial Affect Scoring Technique."

47. Ekman and Friesen, *Unmasking the Face;* Ekman, Friesen, and Tomkins, "Facial Affect Scoring Technique."

48. A. Buck, R. E. Miller, and C. F. William, "Sex, Personality, and Physiological Variables in the Communication of Affect via Facial Expression," *Journal of Personality and Social Psychology,* 30 (1974): 587–89

49. Ekman and Friesen, *Unmasking the Face.*

50. J. Schwartz, "NASA Official Says He Held Out Hope in Final Moments," *The New York Times,* February 15, 2003: A14.

51. Ekman and Friesen, *Unmasking the Face.*

52. G. J. McHugo, "Emotional Reactions to a Political Leader's Expressive Displays," *Journal of Personality and Social Psychology,* 49 (1985): 513–29.

53. D. LaPlante and N. Ambady, "Multiple Messages: Facial Recognition Advantage for Compound Expressions," *Journal of Nonverbal Behavior,* 24 (Fall 2000): 211–25.

54. E. Krumhuber and A. Kappas, "Moving Smiles: The Role of Dynamic Components for the Perception of the Genuineness of Smiles," *Journal of Nonverbal Behavior,* 29 (2005): 3–24.

55. J. Elliott, "If You're Happy and You Know It, You're a Buddhist," *The Sunday Times* [London], May 25, 2003: 1.14.

56. J. K. Burgoon, D. B. Buller, and W. G. Woodall, *Nonverbal Communication: The Unspoken Dialogue* (New York: McGraw-Hill, 1996).

57. B. Le Poire, C. Shepard, A. Duggan, and J. Burgoon, "Relational Messages Associated with Nonverbal Involvement, Pleasantness, and Expressiveness in Romantic Couples," *Communication Research Reports,* 19 (2002).

58. R. Davitz, *The Communication of Emotional Meaning* (New York: McGraw-Hill, 1964).

59. M. J. Owren and J. Bachorowski, "Reconsidering the Evolution of Nonlinguistic Communication: The Case of Laughter," *Journal of Nonverbal Behavior,* 27 (2003): 183–200.

60. K. K. Sereno and G. J. Hawkins, "The Effect of Variations in Speakers' Nonfluency upon Audience Ratings of Attitude Toward the Speech Topic and Speakers' Credibility," *Speech Monographs,* 34 (1967): 58–74; G. R. Miller and M. A. Hewgill, "The Effect of Variations in Nonfluency on Audience Ratings of Source Credibility," *Quarterly Journal of Speech,* 50 (1964): 36–44; Mehrabian and Williams, "Nonverbal Concomitants of Perceived and Intended Persuasiveness."

61. R. L. Street, R. M. Brady, and W. B. Putman, "The Influence of Speech Rate Stereotypes and Rate Similarity on Listeners' Evaluations of Speakers," *Journal of Language and Social Psychology,* 2 (1983): 37–56.

62. T . Bruneau, "Communicative Silences: Forms and Functions," *Journal of Communication,* 23 (1973): 17–46.

63. S. J. Baker, "The Theory of Silence," *Journal of General Psychology,* 53 (1955): 145–67.

64. Our discussion of how to accurately interpret emotions in others is adapted from an excellent distillation of the research conducted by Burgoon and Bacue, "Nonverbal Communication Skills."

65. Burgoon, Buller and Woodall, *Nonverbal Communication.*

66. N. Horatcsu and B. Ekinci, "Children's Reliance on Situational and Vocal Expression of Emotions: Consistent and Conflicting Cues," *Journal of Nonverbal Behavior,* 16 (1992): 231–47.

67. R. Banse and K. R. Schere, "Acoustic Profiles in Vocal Emotion Expression," *Journal of Personality and Social Psychology,* 70 (1996): 614–36.

68. N. Ambady, "Cross-Cultural Perspectives on Social Judgments and Behavior," paper presented at the annual meeting of the Society of Experimental Social Psychology, St. Louis, MO (1999), as cited by Burgoon and Bacue, "Nonverbal Communication Skills."

69. J. M. Montepare and J. S. Tucker, "Aging and Nonverbal Behavior: Current Perspectives and Future Directions," *Journal of Nonverbal Behavior,* 23 (1999): 105–10.

70. R. E. Riggio, B. Throckmorton, and S. DePaola, "Social Skills and Self-Esteem," *Personality and Social Psychology Bulletin,* 13 (1990): 568–77.

71. Burgoon and Bacue, "Nonverbal Communication Skills."

72. E. T. Hall, *The Hidden Dimension* (Garden City, NY: Doubleday, 1966).

73. R. Sommer, "Studies in Personal Space," *Sociometry,* 22 (1959): 247–60.

74. Sommer, "Studies in Personal Space."

75. See B. Stenzor, "The Spatial Factor in Face-to-Face Discussion Groups," *Journal of Abnormal and Social Psychology,* 45 (1950): 552–55.

76. A. Montague, *Touching: The Human Significance of the Skin* (New York: Harper & Row, 1978).

77. Montague, *Touching.*

78. N. M. Henley, *Body Politics: Power, Sex, and Nonverbal Communication* (Englewood Cliffs, NJ: Prentice Hall, 1977).

79. L. K. Guerrero and P. A. Andersen, "Patterns of Matching and Initiation: Touch Behavior and Touch Avoidance Across Romantic Relationship Stages," *Journal of Nonverbal Behavior,* 18 (1994): 137–53; M. M. Martin and C. M. Anderson, "Psychological and Biological Differences in Touch Avoidance," *Communication Research Report,* 10 (1993): 141–47.

80. J. Kelly, "Dress as Non-Verbal Communication," paper presented to the annual conference of the American Association for Public Opinion Research, May 1969.

81. J. C. Valentine, V. Blankenship, H. Cooper, and E. S. Sullins, "Interpersonal Expectancy Effects and the Preference for Consistency," *Representative Research in Social Psychology,* 25 (2001): 26–33.

82. J. Lefkowitz, R. Blake, and J. Mouton, "Status Factors in Pedestrian Violation of Traffic Signals," *Journal of Abnormal and Social Psychology,* 51 (1970): 4–6.

83. J. T. Molloy, *Dress for Success* (New York: Warner Books, 1975); J. T. Molloy, *The Woman's Dress for Success Book* (Chicago: Follett, 1977).

84. Mehrabian, *Nonverbal Communication.*

85. L. Hinkle, "Nonverbal Immediacy Communication Behaviors and Liking in Marital Relationships," *Communication Research Reports,* 16(1), (1999): 81–90.

86. J. K. Burgoon and B. A. Le Poire, "Nonverbal Cues and Interpersonal Judgments: Participant and Observer Perceptions of Intimacy, Dominance, Composure, and Formality," *Communication Monographs,* 66 (1999): 105–24.

87. Jones and Guerrero, "The Effects of Nonverbal Immediacy"; also see D. J. Dolin and M. Booth-Butterfield, "Reach Out and Touch Someone: Analysis of Nonverbal Comforting Responses," *Communication Quarterly,* 41 (1993): 383–93.

88. Argyle, *Bodily Communication.*

89. For an excellent review of gender and nonverbal cues, see J. Pearson, L. Turner, and W. Todd-Mancillas, *Gender and Communication* (Dubuque, IA: William C. Brown, 1991); D. K. Ivy and P. Backlund, *Exploring GenderSpeak: Personal Effectiveness in Gender Communication* (New York: McGraw-Hill, 1994). Also see D. G. Leathers, *Successful Nonverbal Communication: Principles and Applications* (Boston: Allyn & Bacon, 1997).

90. K. J. Tusing and J. P. Dillard, "The Sounds of Dominance: Vocal Precursors of Perceived Dominance During Interpersonal Influence," *Human Communication Research,* 26 (January 2000): 148–71; N. E. Dunbar and J. K. Burgoon, "Perceptions of Power and Interactional Dominance in Interpersonal Relationships," *Journal of Social and Personal Relationships,* 22 (2005): 207–33.

91. Mehrabian, *Nonverbal Communication.*

92. A. Pease and B. Pease, *The Definitive Book of Body Language* (London: Orion, 2005): 42.

93. P. Collett, *The Book of Tells* (London: Doubleday, 2003).

94. J. A. Hall, J. C. Rosip, L. Smith LeBeau, T. G. Horgan, and J. D. Carter, "Attributing the Sources of Accuracy in Unequal-Power Dyadic Communication: Who Is Better and Why?" *Journal of Experimental Social Psychology,* 41 (2005): 1–10.

95. D. A. Carney, J. A. Hall, and L. Smith LeBeau, "Beliefs About the Nonverbal Expression of Social Power," *Journal of Nonverbal Behavior,* 29 (2005): 105–23.

96. Argyle, *Bodily Communication.*

97. Burgoon, Stern, and Dillman, *Interpersonal Adaptation.*

98. B. A. Le Poire and S. M. Yoshimura, "The Effects of Expectancies and Actual Communication on Nonverbal Adaptation and Communication Outcomes: A Test of Interaction Adaptation Theory," *Communication Monographs,* 66 (1999): 1–30.

99. Burgoon and Bacue, "Nonverbal Communication Skills."

100. See Birdwhistell, *Kinesics and Context.*

101. E. Hatfield, J. T. Cacioppo, and R. L. Rapson, *Emotional Contagion* (New York: Cambridge University Press, 1994).

102. Hubbard, "Interpersonal Coordination in Interactions."

103. For an excellent summary of deception and nonverbal communication, see Leathers, *Successful Nonverbal Communication,* 253–74. Also see P. Ekman, M. O' Sullivan, W. V. Friesen, and K. R. Scherer, "Invited Article: Face, Voice, and Body in Detecting Deceit," *Journal of Nonverbal Behavior,* 15 (1991): 125–35; P. Ekman and W. Friesen, "Detecting Deception from the Body and Face," *Journal of Personality and Social Psychology,* 29 (1974): 288–98; M. Millar and K. Millar, "Detection of Deception in Familiar and Unfamiliar Persons: The Effects of Information Restriction," *Journal of Nonverbal Behavior,* 19 (1995): 69–84; D. B. Buller, J. K. Burgoon, A. Buslig, and J. F. Roiger, "Interpersonal Deception: VIII. Further Analysis of the Nonverbal Correlates of Equivocation from the Bavelas et al. (1990) Research," *Journal of Language & Social Psychology,* 13 (1994): 396–417.

104. Adapted from Leathers, *Successful Nonverbal Communication,* with supporting research from Ekman and Friesen, "Detecting Deception from the Face and Body"; M. Zuckerman, B. M. DePaulo, and R. Rosenthal, "Verbal and Nonverbal Communication of Deception," in *Advances in Experimental Social Psychology,* vol. 14, edited by L. Berkowitz (New York: Academic Press, 1981), 1–60.

105. A. Vrij, K. Edward, K. P. Roberts, and R. Bull, "Detecting Deceit Via Analysis of Verbal and Nonverbal Behavior," *Journal of Nonverbal Communication,* 24 (Winter 2000): 239–63; also see Burgoon and Bacue, "Nonverbal Communication Skills."

106. H. S. Park, T. R. Levine, S. A. McCornack, K. Morrison, and M. Ferrara, "How People Really Detect Lies," *Communication Monographs,* 69 (June 2002): 144–57.

Chapter 8

1. S. A. Lloyd, "Conflict in Premarital Relationships: Differential Perceptions of Males and Females," *Family Relations,* 36 (1987): 290–94.

2. H. B. Braiker and H. H. Kelley, "Conflict in the Development of Close Relationships," in *Social Exchange in Developing Relationships,* edited by R. L. Burgess and T. L. Huston (New York: Academic Press, 1979), 135–68.

3. Our definition of conflict is adapted from W. Wilmot and J. Hocker, *Interpersonal Conflict* (New York: McGraw-Hill, 2007).

4. D. Cramer, "Relationship Satisfaction and Conflict Style in Romantic Relationships," *Journal of Psychology,* 134 (2000): 337–41.

5. For a review of literature about violence in relationships, see L. N. Olson and T. D. Golish, "Topics of Conflict and Patterns of Aggression in Romantic Relationships," *Southern Communication Journal,* 67 (Winter 2002): 180–200.

6. D. J. Canary, W. R. Cupach, and R. T. Serpe, "A Competence-Based Approach to Examining Interpersonal Conflict: Test of a Longitudinal Model," *Communication Research,* 29 (February 2001): 79–104; also see L. N. Olson and D. O. Braithwaite, " 'If You Hit Me Again, I'll Hit You Back:' Conflict Management Strategies of Individuals Experiencing Aggression During Conflicts," *Communication Studies,* 55 (2004) 271–85; L. L. Marshall, "Physical and Psychological Abuse," in *The Dark Side of Interpersonal Communication,* edited by W.

R. Cupach and B. H. Spitzberg (Hillsdale, NJ: Erlbaum, 1994): 281–311; Olson and Golish, "Topics of Conflict and Patterns of Aggression in Romantic Relationships."

7. J. W. Keltner, *Mediation: Toward a Civilized System of Dispute Resolution* (Annandale, VA: Speech Communication Association, 1987); also see Wilmot and Hocker, *Interpersonal Conflict.*

8. R. Dumlao and R. A. Botta, "Family Communication Patterns and the Conflict Styles Young Adults Use with Their Fathers," *Communication Quarterly,* 48 (Spring 2000): 174–89; also see W. Aquilino, "From Adolescent to Young Adult: A Prospective Study of Parent-Child Relations During the Transition to Adulthood," *Journal of Marriage and the Family,* 59 (1997): 670–86.

9. R. J. Doolittle, *Orientations of Communication and Conflict* (Chicago: Science Research Associates, 1976), 7–9.

10. Canary, Cupach and Serpe, "A Competence-Based Approach to Examining Interpersonal Conflict."

11. D. H. Solomon, L. K. Knoblock, and M. A. Fitzpatrick, "Relational Power, Marital Schema, and Decisions to Withhold Complaints: An Investigation of the Chilling Effect of Confrontation in Marriage," *Communication Studies,* 55 (2004): 146–67.

12. D. Canary, W. Cupach, and S. Messman, *Relationship Conflict* (Thousand Oaks, CA: Sage, 1995); J. Gottman, *What Predicts Divorce? The Relationship Between Marital Process and Marital Outcomes* (Hillsdale, NJ: Erlbaum, 1994).

13. Lloyd, "Conflict in Premarital Relationships."

14. E. H. Mudd, H. E. Mitchell, and J. W. Bullard, "Areas of Marital Conflict in Successfully Functioning and Unsuccessfully Functioning Families," *Journal of Health and Human Behavior,* 3 (1962): 88–93; N. R. Vines, "Adult Unfolding and Marital Conflict," *Journal of Marital and Family Therapy,* 5 (1979): 5–14.

15. B. A. Fisher, "Decision Emergence: Phases in Group Decision Making," *Speech Monographs,* 37 (1970): 60.

16. G. R. Miller and M. Steinberg, *Between People: A New Analysis of Interpersonal Communication* (Chicago: Science Research Associates, 1975), 264.

17. C. M. Hoppe, "Interpersonal Aggression as a Function of Subject's Sex Role Identification, Opponent's Sex, and Degree of Provocation," *Journal of Personality,* 47 (1979): 317–29.

18. Wilmot and Hocker, *Interpersonal Conflict;* also see S. W. Littlejohn and K. Domenici, *Engaging Communication in Conflict: Systemic Practice* (Thousand Oaks, CA: Sage, 2001).

19. J. M. Olsen, *The Process of Social Organization* (New York: Holt, Rinehart and Winston, 1978).

20. B. M. Gayle, R. W. Preiss, and M. Allen, "A Meta-Analytic Interpretation of Intimate and Nonintimate Interpersonal Conflict," in *Interpersonal Communication Research: Advances Through Meta-Analysis,* edited by M. Allen, R. W. Preiss, B. M. Gayle, and N. Burrell (Mahwah, NJ: Erlbaum, 2002), 345–70.

21. Olsen, *The Process of Social Organization.*

22. S. Ting-Toomey, "A Face Negotiation Theory," in *Theories in Intercultural Communication,* edited by Y. Kim and W. Gudykunst (Newbury Park, CA: Sage, 1988).

23. Ting-Toomey, "A Face Negotiation Theory."

24. Y. B. Zhang, J. Harwood, and M. L. Hummert, "Perceptions on Conflict Management Styles in Chinese Intergenerational Dyads," *Communication Monographs,* 72 (2005): 71–91.

25. Wilmot and Hocker, *Interpersonal Conflict,* 15–16.

26. S. L. Young, "Factors That Influence Recipients' Appraisals of Hurtful Communication," *Journal of Social and Personal Relationships,* 21 (2004): 291–303; S. L. Young, T. L. Kubicka, C. E. Tucker, D. Chavez-Appel, and J. S. Rex, "Communicative Responses to Hurtful Messages in Families," *The Journal of Family Communication,* 5 (2005): 123–40.

27. For an excellent review of the literature on flaming, see A. N. Joinson, *Understanding the Psychology of Internet Behavior: Virtual Worlds, Real Lives* (Houndsmill, England: Palgrave Macmillan, 2003), 64–77.

28. A. C. Filley, *Interpersonal Conflict Resolution* (Glenview, IL: Scott Foresman, 1975); R. H. Turner, "Conflict and Harmony," *Family Interaction* (New York: Wiley, 1970); K. Galvin and B. J. Brommel, *Family Communication: Cohesion and Change* (New York: Addison Wesley Longman, 2000).

29. Olson and Golish, "Topics of Conflict and Patterns of Aggression in Romantic Relationships."

30. Wilmot and Hocker, *Interpersonal Conflict,* 10.

31. Canary, Cupach, and Serpe, "A Competence-Based Approach to Examining Interpersonal Conflict."

32. Adapted from D. W. Johnson, *Reaching Out: Interpersonal Effectiveness and Self-Actualization* (Boston: Allyn & Bacon, 2000), 314.

33. M. Deutsch, *The Resolution of Conflict* (New Haven, CT: Yale University Press, 1973).

34. V. Satir, *Peoplemaking* (Palo Alto: Science and Behavior Books, 1972).

35. A. F. Koerner and M. A. Fitzpatrick, "You Never Leave Your Family in a Fight: The Impact of Family of Origin on Conflict Behavior in Romantic Relationships," *Communication Studies,* 53 (2002): 234–51.

36. R. Kilmann and K. Thomas, "Interpersonal Conflict-Handling Behavior as Reflections of Jungian Personality Dimensions," *Psychological Reports,* 37 (1975): 971–80; K. W. Thomas and R. H. Kilmann, *Thomas-Kilmann Conflict Mode Instrument* (Tuxedo, NY: XICOM, 1974).

37. A. Buysse. A. De Clercq, L. Verhofstadt, E. Heene, H. Roeyers, and P. Van Oost, "Dealing with Relational Conflict: A Picture in Milliseconds," *Journal of Social and Personal Relationships,* 17 (2000): 574–79.

38. J. P. Caughlin and R. S. Malis, "Demand/Withdraw Communication Between Parents and Adolescents as a Correlate of Relational Satisfaction," *Communication Reports,* 17 (2004): 59–71.

39. R. Bello and R. Edwards, "Interpretations of Messages: The Influence of

Various Forms of Equivocation, Face Concerns, and Sex Differences," *Journal of Language and Social Psychology,* 24 (2005): 160–81.

40. J. T. Tedeschi, "Threats and Promises," in *The Structure of Conflict,* edited by R. Swingle (New York: Academic Press, 1970).

41. R. Fisher and W. Ury, *Getting to Yes: Negotiating Agreement Without Giving In* (Boston: Houghton Mifflin, 1988); also see D. Yankelovich, *The Magic of Dialogue: Transforming Conflict into Cooperation* (New York: Simon & Schuster, 1999).

42. Our discussion of the advantages and disadvantages of using different conflict management styles is based on material in Wilmot and Hocker, *Interpersonal Conflict.*

43. L. Powell and M. Hickson, "Power Imbalance and Anticipation of Conflict Resolution: Positive and Negative Attributes of Perceptual Recall," *Communication Research Reports,* 17 (Spring 2000): 181–90.

44. D. Cramer, "Linking Conflict Management Behaviors and Relational Satisfaction: The Intervening Role of Conflict Outcome Satisfaction," *Journal of Social and Personal Relationships,* 19 (2000): 425–32.

45. D. A. Cai and E. L. Fink, "Conflict Style Differences Between Individualists and Collectivists," *Communication Monographs,* 69 (March 2002): 67–87.

46. M. R. Hammer, "The Intercultural Conflict Style Inventory: A Conceptual Framework and Measure of Intercultural Conflict Resolution Approaches," *International Journal of Intercultural Relations,* 29 (2005): 675–95.

47. Hammer, "The Intercultural Conflict Style Inventory."

48. Canary, Cupach, and Serpe, "A Competence-Based Approach to Examining Interpersonal Conflict."

49. Our discussion of conflict management skills is based on several excellent discussions of conflict management prescriptions. We acknowledge Fisher and Ury, *Getting to Yes;* R. Boulton, *People Skills* (New York: Simon & Schuster, 1979); D. A. Romig and L. J. Romig, *Structured Teamwork® Guide* (Austin, TX: Performance Resources, 1990); O. Hargie, C. Saunders, and D. Dickson, *Social Skills in Interpersonal Communication* (London: Routledge, 1994); S. Deep and L. Sussman, *Smart Moves* (Reading, MA: Addison-Wesley, 1990); Wilmot and Hocker, *Interpersonal Conflict;* M. D. Davis, E. L. Eshelman, and M. McKay, *The Relaxation and Stress Reduction Workbook* (Oakland, CA: New Harbinger Publications, 1982); W. A. Donohue and R. Kolt, *Managing Interpersonal Conflict* (Newbury Park: CA: Sage, 1992); O. Hargie (Ed.), *The Handbook of Communication Skills* (London: Routledge, 1997); Littlejohn and Domenici, *Engaging Communication in Conflict;* and M. W. Isenhart and M. Spangle, *Collaborative Approaches to Resolving Conflict* (Thousand Oaks, CA: Sage, 2000).

50. Boulton, *People Skills,* 217.

51. For additional strategies on managing emotion, see J. Gottman, *Why Marriages Succeed and Fail: And How You Can Make Yours Last* (New York: Simon & Schuster, 1994); J. Gottman, *The Seven Principles for Making Marriage Work* (New York: Crown, 1999). Also see Johnson, *Reaching Out.*

52. A. Ellis, *A New Guide to Rational Living* (North Hollywood, CA: Wilshire Books, 1977).

53. Fisher and Ury, *Getting to Yes;* Boulton, *People Skills;* Romig and Romig, *Structured Teamwork® Guide;* T. Gordon, *Leader Effectiveness Training (L.E.T): The No-Lose Way to Release the Productive Potential of People* (New York: Wyden Books, 1977).

54. Deep and Susman, *Smart Moves.*

55. J. A. Feeney, "Hurt Feelings in Couple Relationships: Towards Integrative Models of the Negative Effects of Hurtful Events," *Journal of Social and Personal Relationships,* 21 (2004): 487–508.

56. Young, "Factors That Influence Recipients' Appraisals of Hurtful Communication."

57. H. Weger Jr., "Disconfirming Communication and Self-Verification in Marriage: Associations Among the Demand/Withdraw Interaction Pattern, Feeling Understood, and Marital Satisfaction," *Journal of Social and Personal Relationships,* 22 (2005): 19–31.

58. J. Gottman, *What Predicts Divorce? The Relationship Between Marital Process and Marital Outcomes* (Hillsdale, NJ: Erlbaum, 1994).

59. M. Morris, J. Nadler, T. Kurtzberg, and L. Thompson, "Schmooze or Lose: Social Friction and Lubrication in E-Mail Negotiations," *Group Dynamics: Theory, Research and Practice,* 6 (2002): 89–100.

60. Ellis, *A New Guide to Rational Living.*

61. M. Sinaceau and L. Z. Tiedens, "Get Mad and Get More Than Even: When and Why Anger Expression Is Effective in Negotiations," *Journal of Experimental Social Psychology,* 20 (2005): 1–9.

62. A. M. Bippus and S. L. Young, "Owning Your Emotions: Reactions to Expressions of Self- versus Other-Attributed Positive and Negative Emotions," *Journal of Applied Communication Research,* 33 (2005): 26–45.

63. S. R. Covey, *The Seven Habits of Highly Effective People* (New York: Simon & Schuster, 1989), 235.

64. S. G. Lakey and D. J. Canary, "Actor Goal Achievement and Sensitivity to Partner as Critical Factors in Understanding Interpersonal Communication Competence and Conflict Strategies," *Communication Monographs,* 69 (2002): 217–35.

65. Lakey and Canary, "Actor Goal Achievement and Sensitivity to Partner as Critical Factors in Understanding Interpersonal Communication Competence and Conflict Strategies."

66. C. Pavitt and B. Kemp, "Contextual and Relational Factors in Interpersonal Negotiation Strategy Choice," *Communication Quarterly,* 47(2), (1999): 133–50.

67. Fisher and Ury, *Getting to Yes.*

68. Lakey and Canary, "Actor Goal Achievement and Sensitivity to Partner as Critical Factors in Understanding Interpersonal Communication Competence and Conflict Strategies."

69. E. Goffman, *Interaction Rituals: Essays on Face-to-Face Interaction* (Garden City, NY: Doubleday, 1967).

70. S. Ting-Toomey, "Face and Facework: An Introduction," in *The Challenge of Facework,* edited by S.

Ting-Toomey (Albany, NY: SUNY Press, 1994), 1–14; S. Ting-Toomey, "Managing Intercultural Conflicts Effectively," in *Intercultural Communication: A Reader,* edited by L. A. Samovar and R. E. Porter (Belmont, CA: Wadsworth, 1994), 360–72; also see S. Ting-Toomey and L. Chung, "Cross-Cultural Interpersonal Communication: Theoretical Trends and Research Directions," in *Communication in Personal Relationships Across Cultures,* edited by W. B. Gudykunst, S. Ting-Toomey, and T. Nishida (Thousand Oaks, CA: Sage, 1996), 237–61; Isenhart and Spangle, *Collaborative Approaches to Resolving Conflict,* 19–20.

71. V. Manusov, J. K. Kellas, and A. R. Trees, "Do Unto Others? Conversational Moves and Perceptions of Attentiveness Toward Other Face in Accounting Sequences Between Friends," *Human Communication Research,* 30 (2004): 514–39.

72. M. L. McLaughlin, M. J. Cody, and H. D. O'Hair, "The Management of Failure Events: Some Contextual Determinants of Accounting Behavior," *Human Communication Research,* 9 (1983): 102–25; Manusov, Kellas, and Trees, "Do Unto Others?"

73. W. Ury, *Getting Past No* (New York: Bantam Books, 1993); also see S. Hackley, "When Life Gives You Lemons: How to Deal with Difficult People," *Harvard Business School Publishing Corporation* (2004): 3–5.

74. For an excellent review and analysis of collaborative, side-by-side leadership research, see D. Romig, *Side by Side Leadership: Achieving Outstanding Results Together* (Marietta, GA: Bard Press, 2001).

75. J. W. Pfeiffer and J. E. Jones (Eds.), *A Handbook of Structured Experiences for Human Relations Training,* vol. 2 (La Jolla, CA: University Associates, 1974), 62–76.

Chapter 9

1. F. E. Millar and L. E. Rogers, "A Relational Approach to Interpersonal Communication," in *Explorations in Interpersonal Communication,* edited by G. R. Miller (Newbury Park, CA: Sage, 1976), 87–103.

2. K. Chow, "Social Support and Subjective Well-Being Among Hong Kong Chinese Young Adults," *Journal of Genetic Psychology,* 160 (September 1999): 319–31.

3. I. Altman and D. Taylor, *Social Penetration: The Development of Interpersonal Relationships* (New York: Holt, Rinehart, and Winston, 1973).

4. L. K. Knobloch and D. H. Solomon, "Information Seeking Beyond Initial Interaction: Negotiating Relational Uncertainty Within Close Relationships," *Human Communication Research,* 28 (April 2002): 243–57.

5. M. Sunnafrank, "Predicted Outcome Value During Initial Interaction: A Reformulation of Uncertainty Reduction Theory," *Human Communication Research,* 13 (1986): 3–33.

6. Sunnafrank, "Predicted Outcome Value During Initial Interaction."

7. M. Sunnafrank, "Interpersonal Attraction and Attitude Similarity: A Communication Based Assessment," in *Communication Yearbook, 14,* edited by J. A. Anderson (Newbury Park, CA: Sage, 1991), 451–83.

8. S. Sprecher, "Insiders' Perspectives on Reasons for Attraction to a Close Other," *Social Psychology Quarterly,* 61 (1998): 287–300.

9. S. W. Duck, *Personal Relationships and Personal Constructs: A Study of Friendship Formation* (New York: Wiley, 1993).

10. Sprecher, "Insiders' Perspectives."

11. K. F. Albada, M. L. Knapp, and K. E. Theune, "Interaction Appearance Theory: Changing Perceptions of Physical Attractiveness Through Social Interaction," *Communication Theory,* 12 (2002): 8–40.

12. P. A. Mongeau and K. L. Johnson, "Predicting Cross-Sex First-Date Sexual Expectations and Involvement: Contextual and Individual Difference Factors," *Personal Relationships,* 2 (1995): 301–12.

13. P. C. Regan, L. Levin, S. Sprecher, F. S. Christopher, and R. Cate, "Partner Preferences: What Characteristics Do Men and Women Desire in Their Short-Term Sexual and Long-Term Romantic Partners?" *Journal of Psychology and Human Sexuality,* 12 (2000): 1–21.

14. S. Litzinger and K. Gordon, "Exploring Relationships Among Communication, Sexual Satisfaction, and Marital Satisfaction," *Journal of Sex and Marital Therapy,* 31 (2005): 409–24; S. Sprecher, F. S. Christopher, and R. Cate, "Sexuality in Close Relationships," in *The Cambridge Handbook of Personal Relationships,* edited by A. L. Vangelisti and D. Perlman (New York: Cambridge University Press, 2006), 463–84.

15. Litzinger and Gordon, "Exploring Relationships Among Communication, Sexual Satisfaction, and Marital Satisfaction."

16. Sprecher, "Insiders' Perspectives."

17. R. A. Clark, M. Dockum, H. Hazeu, M. Huang, N. Luo, J. Ramsey, and A. Spyrou, "Initial Encounters of Young Men and Women: Impressions and Disclosure Estimates," *Sex Roles,* 50 (2004): 699–709.

18. S. Sprecher and P. C. Regan, "Liking Some Things (in Some People) More Than Others: Partner Preferences in Romantic Relationships and Friendships," *Journal of Social and Personal Relationships,* 19 (2002): 463–81.

19. N. L. Collins and L. C. Miller, "Self-Disclosure and Liking: A Meta-Analytic Review," *Psychological Bulletin,* 116 (1994): 457–75.

20. Collins and Miller, "Self-Disclosure and Liking."

21. Sprecher, "Insiders' Perspectives."

22. G. B. Ray and K. Floyd, "Nonverbal Expressions of Liking and Disliking in Initial Interaction: Encoding and Decoding Perspectives," *Southern Communication Journal,* 71 (2006): 45–65.

23. M. V. Redmond and D. A. Vrchota, "The Effects of Varying Lengths of Initial Interaction on Attraction and Uncertainty Reduction," paper presented at the annual meeting of the National Communication Association, New Orleans (1994).

24. L. A. Baxter and L. West, "Couple Perceptions of Their Similarities and Differences: A Dialectical Perspective," *Journal of Social and Personal Relationships,* 20 (2003): 491–514.

25. Sunnafrank, "Interpersonal Attraction and Attitude Similarity."

26. Sunnafrank, "Interpersonal Attraction and Attitude Similarity."

27. Sprecher, "Insiders' Perspectives."

28. Baxter and West, "Couple Perceptions of Their Similarities and Differences."

29. Baxter and West, "Couple Perceptions of Their Similarities and Differences."

30. W. Schutz, *Interpersonal Underworld* (Palo Alto, CA: Science and Behavior Books, 1966).

31. S. Sprecher and D. Felmlee, "The Balance of Power in Romantic Heterosexual Couples over Time from 'His' and 'Her' Perspectives," *Sex Roles,* 37 (1997): 361–79.

32. R. J. Fisher and Y. Grégoire, "Gender Differences in Decision Satisfaction Within Established Dyads: Effects of Competitive and Cooperative Behaviors," *Psychology and Marketing,* 23 (2006): 313–33.

33. F. E. Millar and L. E. Rogers, "Relational Dimensions of Interpersonal Dynamics," in *Interpersonal Processes: New Directions in Communication Research,* edited by M. E. Roloff and G. R. Miller (Newbury Park, CA: Sage, 1987), 117–39.

34. N. E. Dunbar and J. K. Burgoon, "Perceptions of Power and Interactional Dominance in Interpersonal Relationships," *Journal of Social and Personal Relationships,* 22 (2005): 207–33.

35. J. R. P. French and B. H. Raven, "The Bases of Social Power," in *Group Dynamics,* edited by J. D. Cartwright and A. Zander (Evanston, IL: Row, Peterson, 1962), 607–22.

36. K. Kellerman, "A Goal-Directed Approach to Gaining Compliance: Relating Differences Among Goals to Differences in Behaviors," *Communication Research,* 31 (2004): 397–445.

37. K. Kellerman, "A Goal-Directed Approach to Gaining Compliance."

38. E. V. Wilson, "Perceived Effectiveness of Interpersonal Persuasion Strategies in Computer-Mediated Communication," *Computers in Human Behavior,* 19 (2003): 537–52.

39. G. R. Miller and F. Boster, "Persuasion in Personal Relationship," in *A Handbook of Personal Relationships,* edited by S. Duck (New York: Wiley, 1988): 275–88; M. G. Garko, "Perspectives and Conceptualizations of Compliance and Compliance Gaining," *Communication Quarterly,* 38, no. 2 (1990): 138–57.

40. K. Kellerman, "A Goal-Directed Approach to Gaining Compliance."

41. M. G. Lawler and G. S. Risch, "Time, Sex and Money: The First Five Years of Marriage," *America,* 184 (2001): 16–20.

42. J. M. Honeycutt and J. M. Wiemann, "Analysis of Functions of Talk and Reports of Imagined Interactions (IIs) During Engagement and Marriage," *Human Communication Research,* 25 (1999): 399–419.

43. For an excellent review of the nature of friendship, see M. Argyle, *The Psychology of Interpersonal Behavior* (London: Penguin, 1983).

44. A. M. Nicotera, "The Importance of Communication in Interpersonal Relationships," in *Interpersonal Communication in Friend and Mate Relationships,* edited by A. M. Nicotera and Associates (Albany: State University of New York Press, 1993), 3–12.

45. Nicotera, "The Importance of Communication in Interpersonal Relationships."

46. J. Yerby, N. Buerkel-Rothfuss, and A. P. Bochner, *Understanding Family Communication* (Needham Heights, MA: Allyn & Bacon, 1998).

47. M. Argyle, *The Social Psychology of Everyday Life* (London: Routledge, 1991).

48. Nicotera, "The Importance of Communication in Interpersonal Relationships."

49. Argyle, *The Social Psychology of Everyday Life.*

50. Argyle, *The Social Psychology of Everyday Life,* 49.

51. P. Marsh, *Eye to Eye: How People Interact* (Topfield, MA: Salem House, 1988).

52. H. J. Markman, F. Floyd, and F. Dickson, "Towards a Model for the Prediction of Primary Prevention of Marital and Family Distress and Dissolution," in *Personal Relationships, 4: Dissolving Personal Relationships,* edited by S. W. Duck and R. Gilmour (London: Academic Press, 1982).

53. J. F. Nussbaum, L. L. Pecchinoni, D. K. Baringer, and A. L. Kundrat, "Lifespan Communication," in *Communication Yearbook 26,* edited by W. B. Gudykunst (Mahwah, NJ: Erlbaum, 2002), 366–89.

54. W. J. Dickens and D. Perlman, "Friendship over the Life-Cycle," in *Personal Relationships, 2: Developing Personal Relationships,* edited by S. W. Duck and R. Gilmour (London: Academic Press, 1981).

55. R. L. Selman, "Toward a Structural Analysis of Developing Interpersonal Relations Concepts: Research with Normal and Disturbed Preadolescent Boys," in *Minnesota Symposia on Child Psychology,* vol. 10, edited by A. D. Pick (Minneapolis: University of Minnesota Press, 1976).

56. Dickens and Perlman, "Friendship over the Life-Cycle."

57. D. L. Oswald and E. M. Clark, "Best Friends Forever? High School Best Friendships and the Transition to College," *Personal Relationships,* 10 (2003): 187–96.

58. W. A. Collins and S. D. Madsen, "Personal Relationships in Adolescence and Early Adulthood," in *The Cambridge Handbook of Personal Relationships,* edited by A. L. Vangelisti and D. Perlman (New York: Cambridge University Press, 2006), 191–210.

59. Collins and Madsen, "Personal Relationships in Adolescence and Early Adulthood."

60. M. Dainton, E. Zelley, and E. Langan, "Maintaining Friendships Throughout the Lifespan," in *Maintaining Relationships Through Communication,* edited by D. J. Canary and M. Dainton (Mahwah, NJ: Erlbaum, 2003), 79–102.

61. C. Buress and J. Pearson, "Interpersonal Rituals in Marriage and Adult Friendship," *Communication Monographs,* 64 (1997): 25–46.

62. S. H. Mathews, *Friendships Through the Life Course: Oral Biographies in Old Age* (Beverly Hills, CA: Sage, 1986).

63. S. J. Holladay and K. S. Kerns, "Do Age Differences Matter in Close

and Casual Relationships? A Comparison of Age Discrepant and Age Peer Friendships," *Communication Reports,* 12 (1999): 101–14.

64. M. J. Collier, "Communication Competence Problematics in Ethnic Relationships," *Communication Monographs,* 63 (1996): 314–35.

65. Collier, "Communication Competence."

66. Collins and Madsen, "Personal Relationships in Adolescence and Early Adulthood."

67. H. M. Reeder, "'I Like You . . . as a Friend': The Role of Attraction in Cross-Sex Friendship," *Journal of Social and Personal Relationships,* 17 (2000): 329–48.

68. M. Hughes, K. Morrison, and K. J. K. Asada, "What's Love Got to Do with It? Exploring the Impact of Maintenance Rules, Love Attitudes, and Network Support on Friends with Benefits Relationships," *Western Journal of Communication,* 69 (2005): 49–66.

69. Hughes, Morrison, and Asada, "What's Love Got to Do with It?"

70. Hughes, Morrison, and Asada, "What's Love Got to Do with It?"

71. L. Rubin, *Just Friends: The Role of Friendship in Our Lives* (New York: Harper & Row, 1985).

72. B. Fehr, "Intimacy Expectations in Same-Sex Friendships: A Prototype Interaction-Pattern Model," *Journal of Personality and Social Psychology,* 86 (2004): 265–84.

73. J. D. Cunningham and J. K. Antill, "Love in Developing Romantic Relationships," in *Personal Relationships, 2: Developing Personal Relationships,* edited by S. W. Duck and R. Gilmour (London: Academic Press, 1981).

74. Z. Rubin, *Liking and Loving: An Invitation to Social Psychology* (New York: Holt, Rinehart and Winston, 1973).

75. J. K. Rempel and C. T. Burris, "Let Me Count the Ways: An Integrative Theory of Love and Hate," *Personal Relationships,* 12 (2005): 297–313.

76. A. Aron and E. N. Aron, "Love," in *Perspectives on Close Relationships,* edited by A. Weber and J. Harvey (Boston: Allyn & Bacon, 1994).

77. L. A. Kurdek, "Relationship Outcomes and Their Predictors: Longitudinal Evidence from Heterosexual Married, Gay Cohabiting, and Lesbian Cohabiting Couples," *Journal of Marriage and Family,* 60 (1998): 553–68.

78. R. J. Sternberg, "A Triangular Theory of Love," *Psychological Review,* 93 (1986): 119–35.

79. C. Hendrick and S. S. Hendrick, "Research on Love: Does It Measure Up?" *Journal of Personality and Social Psychology,* 56 (1989): 784–94.

80. R. Lemieux and J. L. Hale, "Intimacy, Passion, and Commitment in Young Romantic Relationships: Successfully Measuring the Triangular Theory of Love," *Psychological Reports,* 85 (1999): 497–504.

81. J. A. Lee, "A Typology of Styles of Loving," *Personality and Social Psychology,* Bulletin 3 (1977): 173–82.

82. M. A. Fitzpatrick, *Between Husbands and Wives: Communication in Marriage* (Newbury Park, CA: Sage, 1988).

83. D. L. Kelly, "Relational Expectancy Fulfillment as an Explanatory Variable in Distinguishing Couple Types," *Human Communication Research,* 25 (1999): 420–42.

84. Kelly, "Relational Expectancy Fulfillment."

85. M. M. Martin and C. M. Andersen, "Aggressive Communication Traits: How Similar Are Young Adults and Their Parents in Argumentiveness, Assertiveness, and Verbal Aggressiveness?" *Western Journal of Communication,* 61 (1997): 299–314.

86. L. D. Ritchie and M. A. Fitzpatrick, "Family Communication Patterns: Measuring Intrapersonal Perceptions of Interpersonal Relationships," *Communication Research,* 17 (1990): 523–44.

87. M. Booth-Butterfield and R. Sidelinger, "The Influence of Family Communication on the College-Aged Child: Openness, Attitudes and Actions About Sex and Alcohol," *Communication Quarterly,* 46 (1998): 295–308.

88. P. Noller, "Sibling Relationships in Adolescence: Learning and Growing Together," *Personal Relationships,* 12 (2005): 1–22.

89. L. K. Guerrero and W. A. Afifi, "Some Things Are Better Left Unsaid: Topic Avoidance in Family Relationships," *Communication Quarterly,* 43 (1995): 276–96.

90. Guerrero and Afifi, "Some Things Are Better Left Unsaid."

91. Noller, "Sibling Relationships in Adolescence."

92. K. Kitzmann, R. Cohen, and R. L. Lockwood, "Are Only Children Missing Out? Comparison of the Peer-Related Social Competence of Only Children and Siblings," *Journal of Social and Personal Relationships,* 19 (2002): 299–316.

Chapter 10

1. L. A. Baxter and C. Bullis, "Turning Points in Developing Romantic Relationships," *Communication Research,* 12 (1986): 469–93.

2. Baxter and Bullis, "Turning Points."

3. C. R. Berger and J. J. Bradac, *Language and Social Knowledge: Uncertainty and Interpersonal Relations* (Baltimore: Edward Arnold, 1982).

4. W. Douglas, "Question Asking in Same and Opposite Sex Initial Interactions: The Effects of Anticipated Future Interactions," *Human Communication Research,* 14 (1987): 230–45.

5. S. W. Duck, "A Topography of Relationship Disengagement and Dissolution," in *Personal Relationships 4: Dissolving Personal Relationships,* edited by S. W. Duck (London: Academic Press, 1982), 1–29.

6. Duck, "A Topography of Relationship Disengagement and Dissolution."

7. D. DeStephen, "Integrating Relational Termination into a General Model of Communication Competence," paper presented at the annual meeting of the National Communication Association, Denver (1985).

8. S. Duck, "Interpersonal Communication in Developing Relationships," in *Explorations in Interpersonal Communication,* edited by G. R. Miller (Newbury Park, CA: Sage, 1976), 127–47.

9. J. W. Thibaut and H. H. Kelley, *The Social Psychology of Groups* (New York: Wiley, 1959).

10. I. Atlman and D. A. Taylor, *Social Penetration: The Development of*

Interpersonal Relationships (New York: Holt, Rinehart and Winston, 1973).

11. M. Sunnafrank, "Predicted Outcome Value During Initial Interactions," *Human Communication Research,* 13 (1986): 3–33.

12. G. R. Miller and M. R. Parks, "Communicating in Dissolving Relationships," in *Personal Relationships 4: Dissolving Personal Relationships,* edited by S. W. Duck (London: Academic Press, 1982), 127–54.

13. A. L. Busboom, D. M. Collins, M. D. Givertz, and L. A. Levin, "Can We Still Be Friends? Resources and Barriers to Friendship Quality after Romantic Relationship Dissolution," *Personal Relationships,* 9 (2002): 215–23.

14. L. A. Baxter, "Dialectical Contradictions in Relationship Development," in *Handbook of Personal Relationships,* edited by S. W. Duck (Chichester, England: Wiley, 1988), 257–73; L. A. Baxter and B. M. Montomery, "Rethinking Communication in Personal Relationships from a Dialectical Perspective," in *Handbook of Personal Relationships,* 2nd ed., edited by S. W. Duck (Chichester, England: Wiley, 1997), 325–49.

15. D. R. Pawlowski, "Dialectical Tensions in Marital Partners' Accounts of Their Relationships," *Communication Quarterly,* 46 (1998): 396–416.

16. Pawlowski, "Dialectical Tensions."

17. L. A. Baxter, "Interpersonal Communication as Dialogue: A Response to the 'Social Approaches' Forum," *Communication Theory,* 2 (1992): 330–38.

18. A. Hoppe-Nagao and S. Ting-Toomey, "Relational Dialectics and Management Strategies in Marital Couples," *Southern Communication Journal,* 67 (Winter 2002): 142–59.

19. Baxter, "Interpersonal Communication as Dialogue."

20. A. J. Johnson, E. Wittenberg, M. M. Villagran, M. Mazur, and P. Villagran,"Relational Progression as a Dialectic: Examining Turning Points in Communication Among Friends," *Communication Monographs,* 70 (2003): 230–49.

21. S. Planalp, "The Unacknowledged Role of Emotion in Theories of Close Relationships: How Do Theories Feel?" *Communication Theory,* 13 (2003): 78–99.

22. Adapted from K. Kellerman et al., "The Conversation MOP: Scenes in the Stream of Discourse," *Discourse Processes,* 12 (1989): 27–61.

23. A. E. Lindsey and W. R. Zahaki, "Perceptions of Men and Women Departing from Conversational Sex Role Stereotypes During Initial Interaction," in *Sex Differences and Similarities in Communication,* edited by D. J. Canary and K. Dindia (Mahwah, NJ: Erlbaum, 1998): 393–412.

24. R. A. Bell and J. A. Daly, "The Affinity Seeking Function of Communication," *Communication Monographs,* 51 (1984): 91–115.

25. Bell and Daly, "The Affinity Seeking Function of Communication."

26. C. R. Berger and R. J. Calabrese, "Some Explorations in Initial Interaction and Beyond: Toward a Developmental Theory of Interpersonal Communication," *Human Communication Research,* 1 (1975): 99–112; C. R. Berger and J. J. Bradac, *Language and Social Knowledge: Uncertainty in Interpersonal Relations* (Baltimore: Edward Arnold, 1982).

27. Berger and Bradac, *Language and Social Knowledge.*

28. Sunnafrank, "Predicted Outcome Value During Initial Interactions," and "Interpersonal Attraction and Attitude Similarity," in *Communication Yearbook 14,* edited by J. A. Anderson (Newbury Park, CA: Sage, 1991), 451–83.

29. P. A. Mongeau, M. C. M. Serewicz, and L. F. Therrien, "Goals for Cross-Sex First Dates: Identification, Measurement, and the Influence of Contextual Factors," *Communication Monographs,* 71 (2004): 121–47.

30. Berger and Bradac, *Language and Social Knowledge.*

31. L. K. Knobloch and D. H. Solomon, "Relational Uncertainty and Relational Information Processing: Questions Without Answers?" *Communication Research,* 32 (2005): 349–88.

32. L. K. Knobloch and D. H. Solomon, "Information Seeking Beyond Initial Interaction: Negotiating Relational Uncertainty Within Close Relationships," *Human Communication Research,* 28 (2002): 243–57.

33. M. Dainton, "Equity and Uncertainty in Relational Maintenance," *Western Journal of Communication,* 67 (2003): 164–86.

34. A. L. Vangelisti, "Communication Problems in Committed Relationships: An Attributional Analysis," in *Attributions, Accounts, and Close Relationships,* edited by J. H. Harvey, T. L. Orbuch, and A. L. Weber (New York: Springer Verlag, 1992), 144–64.

35. G. Levinger, and D. J. Senn, "Disclosure of Feelings in Marriage," *Merrill-Palmer Quarterly* 12, (1967): 237–49; A. Bochner, "On the Efficacy of Openness in Close Relationships," in *Communication Yearbook 5,* edited by M. Burgoon (New Brunswick, NJ: Transaction Books, 1982), 109–24.

36. A. B. Kelly, F. D. Fincham, and S. R. H. Beach, "Communication Skills in Couples: A Review and Discussion of Emerging Perspectives," in *Handbook of Communication and Social Interaction Skills,* edited by J. O. Greene and B. R. Burleson (Mahwah, NJ: Erlbaum, 2003), 723–51.

37. S. A. Westmyer and S. A. Myers, "Communication Skills and Social Support Messages Across Friendship Levels," *Communication Research Reports,* 13 (1996): 191–97.

38. B. R. Burleson and S. R. Mortenson, "Explaining Cultural Differences in Evaluations of Emotional Support Behaviors," *Communication Research,* 30 (2003):113–46; B. R. Burleson, "Comforting Messages: Features, Functions, and Outcomes," in *Strategic Interpersonal Communication,* edited by J. A. Daly and J. M. Weimann (Hillsdale, NJ: Erlbaum, 1994), 135–61.

39. A. M. Bippus, "Recipients' Criteria for Evaluating the Skillfulness of Comforting Communication and the Outcomes of Comforting Interactions," *Communication Monographs,* 68 (2001): 301–13.

40. B. R. Sarason and I. G. Sarason, "Close Relationships and Social Support: Implications for the Measurement of Social Support," in *The Cambridge*

Handbook of Personal Relationships, edited by A. L. Vangelisti and D. Perlman (NY: Cambridge University Press, 2006), 429–43.

41. R. A. Clark and J. G. Delia, "Individuals' Preferences for Friends' Approaches to Providing Support in Distressing Situations," *Communication Reports,* 10 (1997): 115–21.

42. L. K. Guerrero and A. M. Chavez, "Relational Maintenance in Cross-Sex Friendships Characterized by Different Types of Romantic Intent: An Exploratory Study," *Western Journal of Communication,* 69 (2005): 339–58.

43. J. K. Alberts, "An Analysis of Couples' Conversational Complaints," *Communication Monographs,* 55 (1988): 184–97.

44. M. A. Fitzpatrick and D. M. Badzinski, "All in the Family: Interpersonal Communication in Kin Relationships," in *Handbook of Interpersonal Communication,* edited by M. L. Knapp and G. R. Miller (Beverly Hills, CA: Sage, 1985), 687–736.

Chapter 11

1. P. Noller, "Bringing It All Together: A Theoretical Approach," in *The Cambridge Handbook of Personal Relationships,* edited by A. L. Vangelisti and D. Perlman (New York: Cambridge University Press, 2006): 769–89.

2. A. P. Buunk and P. Dijkstra, "Temptation and Threat: Extradyadic Relations and Jealousy," in *The Cambridge Handbook of Personal Relationships,* 533–56.

3. S. Metts, "Relational Transgressions," in *The Dark Side of Interpersonal Communication,* edited by W. R. Cupach and B. H. Spitzberg (Hillsdale, NJ: Erlbaum, 1994), 217–39.

4. P. A. Mongeau and K. L. Johnson, "Predicting Cross-Sex First-Date Sexual Expectations and Involvement: Contextual and Individual Difference Factors," *Personal Relationships,* 2 (1995): 301–12, M. C. Morr and P. A. Mongeau, "First-Date Expectations: The Impact of Sex of Initiator, Alcohol Consumption, and Relationship Type," *Communication Research,* 31 (2004): 3–35.

5. F. D. Fincham, "The Account Episode in Close Relationships," in *Explaining One's Self to Others: Reason-Giving in a Social Context,* edited by M. L. McClaughlin, M. J. Cody, and S. J Read (Hillsdale, NJ: Erlbaum, 1992), 167–82.

6. G. Makoul and M. E. Roloff, "The Role of Efficacy and Outcome Expectations in the Decision to Withhold Relational Complaints," *Communication Research,* 25 (1998): 25–30.

7. M. L. McLaughlin, M. J. Cody, and H. D. O'Hair, "The Management of Failure Events: Some Contextual Determinants of Accounting Behavior," *Human Communication Research,* 9 (1983): 208–24.

8. Fincham, "The Account Episode in Close Relationships."

9. J. W. Younger, R. L. Piferi, R. L. Jobe, and K. A. Lawler, "Dimensions of Forgiveness: The Views of Laypersons," *Journal of Social and Personal Relationships,* 21 (2004): 837–55.

10. Younger, Piferi, Jobe, and Lawler, "Dimensions of Forgiveness."

11. Younger, Piferi, Jobe, and Lawler, "Dimensions of Forgiveness."

12. V. R. Waldron and D. L. Kelley, "Forgiving Communication as a Response to Relational Transgressions," *Journal of Social and Personal Relationships,* 22 (2005): 723–42.

13. Noller, "Bringing It All Together."

14. L. K. Guerrero and W. A. Afifi, "Toward a Goal-Oriented Approach for Understanding Communicative Responses to Jealousy," *Western Journal of Communication,* 63 (1999): 216–48.

15. Guerrero and Afifi, "Toward a Goal-Oriented Approach."

16. M. Dainton and B. Aylor, "A Relational Uncertainty Analysis of Jealousy, Trust, and Maintenance in Long-Distance Versus Geographically Close Relationships," *Communication Quarterly,* 49 (Spring 2001), 172–88.

17. Dainton and Aylor, "A Relational Uncertainty Analysis."

18. G. T. Guldner and C . H. Swensen, "Time Spent Together and Relationship Quality: Long-Distance Relationships as a Test Case," *Journal of Social and Personal Relationships,* 12 (1995): 313–20; A. J. Johnson, "Examining the Maintenance of Friendships: Are There Differences Between Geographically Close and Long-Distance Friends?" *Communication Quarterly,* 49 (Fall 2001): 424–35.

19. L. Stafford and J. R. Reske, "Idealization and Communication in Long-Distance Premarital Relationships," *Family Relations,* 39 (July, 1990): 274–79.

20. Stafford and Reske, "Idealization and Communication in Long-Distance Premarital Relationships."

21. J. Lyndon, T. Pierce, and S. O'Regan, "Coping with Moral Commitment to Long-Distance Dating Relationships," *Journal of Personality and Social Psychology,* 73 (1997): 104–13.

22. L. Stafford, *Maintaining Long-Distance and Cross-Residential Relationships* (Mahwah, NJ: Erlbaum, 2005).

23. B. Le and C. R. Agnew, "Need Fulfillment and Emotional Experience in Interdependent Romantic Relationships," *Journal of Social and Personal Relationships,* 18 (2001): 423–40.

24. E. M. Sahlstein and T. Truong, "Proximal and Long-Distance Relations: A Web of Contradictions," paper presented at the annual meeting of the National Communication Association (2002).

25. Sahlstein and Truong, "Proximal and Long-Distance Relations."

26. E. M. Sahlstein, "Making Plans: Praxis Strategies for Negotiating Uncertainty-Certainty in Long-Distance Relationships," *Western Journal of Communication,* 70 (2006): 147–65.

27. Lyndon, Pierce, and O'Regan, "Coping with Moral Commitment to Long-Distance Dating Relationships."

28. Stafford, *Maintaining Long-Distance and Cross-Residential Relationships.*

29. A. Foeman and T. Nance, "Building New Cultures, Reframing Old Images: Success Strategies of Interracial Couples," *The Howard Journal of Communications,* 13 (2002): 237–49.

30. Foeman and Nance, "Building New Cultures, Reframing Old Images."

31. A. B. Troy, J. Lewis-Smith, and J. Laurenceau, "Interracial and Intraracial Romantic Relationships: The Search for Differences in Satisfaction, Conflict, and Attachment Style," *Journal of Social and Personal Relationships,* 23 (2006): 65–80.

32. S. M. Haas and L. Stafford, "An Initial Examination of Maintenance Behaviors in Gay and Lesbian Relationships," *Journal of Social and Personal Relationships,* 15 (1998): 846–55.

33. Haas and Stafford, "An Initial Examination of Maintenance Behaviors in Gay and Lesbian Relationships."

34. T. P. Mottet, "The Role of Sexual Orientation in Predicting Outcome Value and Anticipated Communication Behaviors," *Communication Quarterly,* 48 (Summer 2000): 223–39.

35. Mottet, "The Role of Sexual Orientation in Predicting Outcome Value and Anticipated Communication Behaviors."

36. D. O'Hair and W. Cody, "Deception," in *The Dark Side of Interpersonal Communication,* edited by W. R. Cupach and B. H. Spitzberg (Hillsdale, NJ: Erlbaum, 1994), 181–213.

37. M. Knapp, "Lying and Deception in Close Relationships," in *The Cambridge Handbook of Personal Relationships,* edited by A. L. Vangelisti and D. Perlman (New York: Cambridge University Press, 2006), 517–32.

38. A. E. Lucchetti, "Deception in Disclosing One's Sexual History: Safe-Sex Avoidance or Ignorance?" *Communication Quarterly,* 47 (1999): 300–14.

39. O'Hair and Cody, "Deception."

40. T. R. Levine, K. J. K Asada, and L. L. Massi Lindsey, "The Relative Impact of Violation Type and Lie Severity on Judgments of Message Deceitfulness," paper presented at the annual meeting of the National Communication Association (2002).

41. M. V. Redmond, *Human Communication: Theories and Applications* (Boston, MA: Houghton Mifflin, 2000).

42. S. A. McCornack and T. R. Levine, "When Lies Are Uncovered: Emotional and Relational Outcomes of Discovered Deception," *Communication Monographs,* 57 (1990): 119–38.

43. D. A. DePaulo and B. M. Kashy, "Everyday Lies in Close and Casual Relationships," *Journal of Personality and Social Psychology,* 74 (1998): 63–80.

44. D. B. Buller and J. K. Burgoon, "Deception: Strategic and Nonstrategic Communication," in *Strategic Interpersonal Communication,* edited by J. A. Daly and J. M. Wiemann (Hillsdale, NJ: Erlbaum, 1994), 191–223; O'Hair and Cody, "Deception."

45. DePaulo and Kashy, "Everyday Lies in Close and Casual Relationships."

46. O'Hair and Cody, "Deception."

47. O'Hair and Cody, "Deception."

48. Knapp, "Lying and Deception in Close Relationships."

49. Knapp, "Lying and Deception in Close Relationships."

50. A. L. Vangelisti, "Messages That Hurt," in *The Dark Side of Interpersonal Communication,* edited by W. R. Cupach and B. H. Spitzberg (Hillsdale, NJ: Erlbaum, 1994), 181–213.

51. Vangelisti, "Messages That Hurt."

52. S. L. Young and A. M. Bippus, "Does It Make a Difference If They Hurt You in a Funny Way? Humorously and Non-Humorously Phrased Hurtful Messages in Personal Relationships," *Communication Quarterly,* 49 (Winter 2001): 35–52.

53. A. L. Vangelisti and L. P. Crumley, "Reactions to Messages That Hurt: The Influence of Relational Contexts," *Communication Monographs,* 65 (1998): 173–96.

54. J. A. Feeney, "Hurt Feelings in Couple Relationships: Towards Integrative Models of the Negative Effects of Hurtful Events," *Journal of Social and Personal Relationships,* 21 (2004): 487–508.

55. Vangelisti and Crumley, "Reactions to Messages That Hurt."

56. Vangelisti, "Messages That Hurt."

57. S. L. Young, "Factors that Influence Recipients' Appraisals of Hurtful Communication," *Journal of Social and Personal Relationships,* 21 (2004): 291–303.

58. W. R. Cupach and B. H. Spitzberg, "Obsessive Relational Intrusion and Stalking," in *The Dark Side of Close Relationships,* edited by B. H. Spitzberg and W. R. Cupach (Mahwah, NJ: Erlbaum, 1998): 233–64.

59. W. R. Cupach and B. H. Spitzberg, *The Dark Side of Relationship Pursuit: From Attraction to Obsession and Stalking* (Mahwah, NJ: Erlbaum, 2004).

60. Cupach and Spitzberg, *The Dark Side of Relationship Pursuit.*

61. B. H. Spitzberg and W. R. Cupach, "The Inappropriateness of Relational Intrusion," in *Inappropriate Relationships: The Unconventional, the Disapproved, and the Forbidden,* edited by R. Goodwin and D. Cramer (Mahwah, NJ: Erlbaum, 2002), 191–220.

62. Cupach and Spitzberg, "Obsessive Relational Intrusion and Stalking."

63. Cupach and Spitzberg, *The Dark Side of Relationship Pursuit.*

64. V. Ravensberg and C. Miller, "Stalking among Young Adults: A Review of the Preliminary Research," *Aggression and Violent Behavior,* 8 (2003): 455–69; B. H. Spitzberg, A. M. Nicastro, and A. V. Cousins, "Exploring the Interactional Phenomenon of Stalking and Obsessive Relational Intrusion," *Communication Reports,* 11 (1998): 33–48.

65. K. L. Yanowitz, "Influence of Gender and Experience on College Students' Stalking Schemas," *Violence and Victims,* 21 (2006): 91–100.

66. L. K. Guerrero and P. A. Anderson, "Jealousy and Envy," in *The Dark Side of Close Relationships,* 33–70.

67. L. K. Knobloch, "Evaluating a Contextual Model of Responses to Relational Uncertainty-Increasing Events: The Role of Intimacy, Appraisals, and Emotions," *Human Communication Research,* 31 (2005): 60–101.

68. J. L. Bevan and W. Samter, "Toward a Broader Conceptualization of Jealousy in Close Relationships: Two Exploratory Studies," *Communication Studies,* 55 (2004): 14–28.

69. Guerrero and Anderson, "Jealousy and Envy."

70. Guerrero and Anderson, "Jealousy and Envy."

71. S. M. Yoshimura, "Emotional and Behavioral Responses in Romantic Jealousy Expressions," *Communication Reports,* 17 (2004): 85–102.

72. Yoshimura, "Emotional and Behavioral Responses."

73. J. L. Bevan, "General Partner and Relational Uncertainty as Consequences of Another Jealousy Expression," *Western Journal of Communication,* 68 (2004): 195–218.

74. A. A. Fleishmann, B. H. Spitzberg, P. A. Anderson, and S. C. Roesch, "Tickling the Green Monster: Jealousy Induction in Relationships," *Journal of Social and Personal Relationships,* 22 (2005): 49–73.

75. Fleishmann, Spitzberg, Anderson, and Roesch, "Tickling the Green Monster."

76. M. P. Johnson, "Violence and Abuse in Personal Relationships: Conflict, Terror, and Resistance in Intimate Partnerships," in *The Cambridge Handbook of Personal Relationships,* edited by A. L. Vangelisti and D. Perlman (New York: Cambridge University Press, 2006), 557–76.

77. Johnson, "Violence and Abuse in Personal Relationships."

78. Johnson, "Violence and Abuse in Personal Relationships."

79. Johnson, "Violence and Abuse in Personal Relationships."

80. C. M. Feldman and C. A. Ridley, "The Role of Conflict-Based Communication Responses and Outcomes in Male Domestic Violence toward Female Partners," *Journal of Social and Personal Relationships,* 17 (2000): 552–73.

81. S. A. Jang, S. W. Smith, and T. R. Levine, "To Stay or to Leave? The Role of Attachment Styles in Communication Patterns and Potential Termination of Romantic Relationships Following Discovery of Deception," *Communication Monographs,* 69 (2002): 236–52.

82. G. R. Miller and M. R. Parks, "Communication in Dissolving Relationships," in *Personal Relationships 4: Dissolving Personal Relationships,* edited by S. W. Duck (London: Academic Press, 1982), 127–54.

83. S. W. Duck, *Understanding Relationships* (New York: Guilford Press, 1991).

84. J. M. Gottman and S. Carrere, "Why Can't Men and Women Get Along? Developmental Roots and Marital Inequities," in *Communication and Relational Maintenance,* edited by D. J. Canary and L. Stafford (San Diego: Academic Press, 1991): 203–29.

85. G. O. Hagestad and M. A. Smyer, "Dissolving Long-Term Relationships: Patterns of Divorcing in Middle Age," in *Personal Relationships 4: Dissolving Personal Relationships,* edited by S. W. Duck (London: Academic Press, 1982), 155–88.

86. J. Gottman with N. Silver, *Why Marriages Succeed or Fail* (New York: Simon and Schuster, 1994).

87. Gottman and Silver, *Why Marriages Succeed or Fail.*

88. W. W. Wilmot, "Relationship Rejuvenation," in *Communication and Relational Maintenance,* edited by D. J. Canary and L. Stafford (San Diego, CA: Elsevier, 1994), 255–74.

89. W. W. Wilmot and D. C. Stevens, "Relationship Rejuvenation: Arresting Decline in Personal Relationships," in *Uses of "Structure" in Communication Studies,* edited by R. L. Conville (Westport, CT: Praeger, 1994), 103–24.

90. Miller and Parks, "Communication in Dissolving Relationships."

91. S. W. Duck, "A Topography of Relationship Disengagement and Dissolution," in *Personal Relationships 4: Dissolving Personal Relationships,* edited by S. W. Duck (London: Academic Press, 1982), 1–29.

92. A. Weber, "Loving, Leaving, and Letting Go: Coping with Nonmarital Breakups," in *The Dark Side of Close Relationships,* edited by B. H. Spitzberg and W. R. Cupach (Mahwah, NJ: Erlbaum, 1998), 267–306.

93. M. J. Cody, "A Typology of Disengagement Strategies and an Examination of the Role Intimacy, Reactions to Inequity and Relational Problems Play in Strategy Selection," *Communication Monographs,* 49 (1982): 148–70.

94. M. Argyle and M. Henderson, *The Anatomy of Relationships* (New York: Guilford Press, 1991).

95. Duck, *Understanding Relationships.*

96. Duck, "A Typography of Relationship Disengagement and Dissolution."

97. Miller and Parks, "Communication in Dissolving Relationships."

98. L. A. Baxter, "Accomplishing Relationship Disengagement," in *Understanding Personal Relationships: An Interdisciplinary Approach,* edited by S. Duck and D. Perlman (Beverly Hills, CA: Sage, 1984): 243–65.

99. D. DeStephen, "Integrating Relational Termination into a General Model of Communication Competence," paper presented at the annual meeting of the Speech Communication Association, Denver (1985).

100. Baxter, "Accomplishing Relationship Disengagement."

101. DeStephen, "Integrating Relational Termination."

102. Cody, "A Typology of Disengagement Strategies."

103. A. Weber, "Loving, Leaving, and Letting Go."

Chapter 12

1. G. P. Murdock, *Social Structure* (New York: Free Press, 1965). Originally published 1949.

2. G. D. Nass and G. W. McDonald, *Marriage and the Family* (New York: Random House, 1982), 5.

3. A. P. Bochner, "Conceptual Frontiers in the Study of Communication in Families: An Introduction to the Literature," *Human Communication Research,* 2 (Summer 1976): 382.

4. M. A. Fitzpatrick, "Family Communication Patterns Theory: Observations on its Development and Application," *Journal of Family Communication,* 4 (2004): 167–80.

5. V. Satir, *Peoplemaking* (Palo Alto, CA: Science and Behavior Books, 1972).

6. D. E. Beck and M. A. Jones, *Progress on Family Problems: A Nationwide Study of Clients' and Counselors' Views on Family Agency Services* (New York: Family Service Association of America, 1973).

7. Satir, *Peoplemaking.*

8. H. J. Markman, "Prediction of Mental Distress: A 5-Year Follow-Up," *Journal of Consulting and Clinical Psychology,* 49 (1981): 760–62.

9. D. H. L. Olson, H. L. McCubbin, H. L. Barnes, A. S. Larsen, M. J. Muxem, and M. A. Wilson, *Families: What Makes Them Work* (Beverly Hills, CA: Sage, 1983).

10. J. Koesten, "Family Communication Patterns, Sex of Subject, and Communication Competence," *Communication Monographs,* 71 (2004): 226–44.

11. V. Satir, *The New Peoplemaking* (Mountain View, CA: Science and Behavior Books, 1988), 4.

12. Satir, *Peoplemaking,* 13–14.

13. J. P. Caughlin, "Family Communication Standards: What Counts as Excellent Family Communication and How Are Such Standards Associated with Family Satisfaction?" *Human Communication Research,* 29 (January 2003): 5–40.

14. K . M. Galvin and B. J. Brommel, *Family Communication: Cohesion and Change,* 5th ed. (New York: Longman, 2000).

15. J. Stachowiak, "Functional and Dysfunctional Families," in *Helping Families to Change,* edited by V. Satir, J. Stachowiak, and H. A. Taschman (New York: Jason Aronson, 1975).

16. A. Bockner and E. Eisenberg, "Family Process: Systems in Perspectives," in *Handbook of Communication Science,* edited by C. Berger and S. Chaffee (Beverly Hills: Sage, 1987).

17. Satir, *The New Peoplemaking.*

18. P. Noller and M. A. Fitzpatrick, *Communication in Family Relationships* (Englewood Cliff, NJ: Prentice Hall, 1993), 202.

19. J. Howard, *Families* (New York: Simon & Schuster, 1978), 286–91.

20. J. Gottman with N. Silver, *Why Marriages Succeed or Fail* (New York: Simon and Schuster, 1994).

21. L. C. Tidwell and J. B. Walther, "Computer-Mediated Communication Effects on Disclosure, Impressions, and Interpersonal Evaluations, *Human Communication Research,* 28 (July 2002): 317–48.

22. J. Shuler, "E-Mail Communication and Relationships," in *The Psychology of Cyberspace,* www.rider.edu/users/suler/psycyber/psycyber.html (August 1998).

23. P. Wallace, *The Psychology of the Internet* (New York: Cambridge University Press, 1999).

24. N. L. Buerkel-Rothfuss, "Rule-Breaking in Cyberspace Relationships: Netiquette Vs. Interpersonal Competence," paper presented at the annual meeting of the National Communication Association, Chicago (November, 1999).

25. J. B. Walther, "Impression Formation in Computer-Mediated Interaction," *Western Journal of Communication,* 57 (1993): 381–98.

26. J. T. Hancock and P. J. Dunham, "Impression Formation in Computer-Mediated Communication Revisited," *Communication Research,* 28 (June 2001): 325–47.

27. D. Knox, V. Daniels, L. Sturdivant, and M. E. Zusman, "College Student Use of the Internet for Mate Selection," *College Student Journal,* 35 (March 2001): 158.

28. K. M. Cornetto, "Suspicion in Cyberspace: Deception and Detection in the Context of Internet Relay Chat Rooms," paper presented at the annual meeting of the National Communication Association, Chicago (November, 1999).

29. Cornetto, "Suspicion in Cyberspace."

30. Cornetto, "Suspicion in Cyberspace."

31. A. J. Flanagan, "IM Online: Instant Messaging Use Among College Students," *Communication Research Reports,* 22 (2005): 175–87.

32. September 2005 Daily Tracking Survey/Online Dating Extension, Pew Internet & American Life Project, http://www.pewinternet.org/pdfs/Online_Dating_Questions.pdf

33. September 2005 Daily Tracking Survey/Online Dating Extension.

34. J. B. Walther, "Computer-Mediated Communication: Impersonal, Interpersonal, and Hyperpersonal Interaction," *Communication Research,* 23 (1996): 3–43. J. B. Walther, C. L. Slovacek, and L. C. Tidwell, "Is a Picture Worth a Thousand Words? Photographic Images in Long-Term and Short-Term Computer-Mediated Communication," *Communication Research,* 28 (2001): 105–34.

35. L. C. Tidwell and J. B. Walther, "Computer-Mediated Communication Effects on Disclosure, Impressions, and Interpersonal Evaluations: Getting to Know One Another a Bit at a Time," *Human Communication Research,* 28 (2002): 317–48.

36. T. L. Anderson and T. M. Emmers-Sommer, "Predictors of Relationship Satisfaction in Online Romantic Relationships," *Communication Studies,* 57 (2006): 153–72.

37. Anderson and Emmers-Sommer, "Predictors of Relationship Satisfaction."

38. Anderson and Emmers-Sommer, "Predictors of Relationship Satisfaction."

39. K. B. Wright, "On-Line Relational Maintenance Strategies and Perceptions of Partners within Exclusively Internet-Based and Primarily Internet-Based Relationships," *Communication Studies,* 55 (2004): 239–53.

40. S. Fox and M. Madden, "Generations Online," Pew Internet & American Life Project, December 2005, http://www.pewinternet.org/pdfs/PIP_Generations_Memo.pdf

41. L. Rainie and S. Keeter, "Cell Phone Use," Pew Internet & American Life Project, April 2006, http://www.pewinternet.org/pdfs/PIP_Cell_phone_study.pdf

42. J. Boase, J. B. Horrigan, B. Wellman, and L. Rainie, "The Strength of Internet Ties," Pew Internet & American Life Project, January 25, 2006, http://www.pewinternet.org/pdfs/PIP_Internet_ties.pdf

43. K. Ishii, "Implications of Mobility: The Uses of Personal Communication Media in Everyday Life," *Journal of Communication,* 56 (2006): 346–65.

44. J. Boase and B. Wellman, "Personal Relationships: On and Off the Internet," in *The Cambridge Handbook of Personal Relationships,* edited by A. L. Vangelisti and D. Perlman (New York: Cambridge University Press, 2006), 709–23.

45. Boase, Horrigan, Wellman, and Rainie, "The Strength of Internet Ties."

46. J. Morahan-Martin, "Internet Abuse: Addiction? Disorder? Symptom? Alternative Explanations?" *Social Science Computer Review,* 23 (2005): 39–48.

47. S. E. Caplan, "Preference for Online Social Interaction: A Theory of Problematic Internet Use and Psychosocial Well-Being," *Communication Research,* 30 (2003): 625–48; S. E. Caplan, "A Social Skill Account of Problematic Internet Use," *Journal of Communication,* 55 (2005): 721–36.

48. J. Morahan-Martina and P. Schumacher, "Incidence and Correlates of Pathological Internet Use among College Students," *Computers in Human Behavior,* 16 (2000): 13–29.

49. J. T. Hancock, "Verbal Irony Use in Face-to-Face and Computer-Mediated Conversations," *Journal of Language and Social Psychology,* 23 (2004): 447–63.

50. B. R. Burleson and W. Samter, "Similarity in the Communication Skills of Young Adults: Foundations of Attraction, Friendship, and Relationship Satisfaction," *Communication Reports,* 9 (1996): 127–39.

51. See reviews in C. Conrad, *Strategic Organizational Communication: Toward the Twenty-First Century,* 3d ed. (Fort Worth, TX: Harcourt Brace, 1994); and T. D. Daniels, B. K. Spicer, and M. J. Papa, *Perspectives on Organizational Communication,* 4th ed. (Dubuque, IA: Brown & Benchmark, 1997).

52. P. M. Sias and D. J. Cahill, "From Coworkers to Friends: The Development of Peer Friendships in the Workplace," *Western Journal of Communication,* 62 (1998): 273–99.

53. Sias and Cahill, "From Coworkers to Friends."

54. Sias and Cahill, "From Coworkers to Friends."

55. E. M. Berman, J. P. West, and M. N. Richter, Jr., "Workplace Relations: Friendship Patterns and Consequences (According to Managers)," *Public Administration Review,* 62 (2002): 217–30.

56. P. Sias, G. Smith, and T. Avdeyeva, "Sex and Sex-Composition Differences and Similarities in Peer Workplace Friendship Development," *Communication Studies,* 54 (Fall 2003): 322–40.

57. P. M. Sias, R. G. Heath, T. Perry, D. Silva, and B. Fix, "Narratives of Workplace Friendship Deterioration," *Journal of Social and Personal Relationships,* 21(2004): 321–40.

58. Sias et al., "Narratives of Workplace Friendship Deterioration."

59. American Management Association, "Workplace Dating" [AMA online news release], February, 2003. Retrieved July, 2004 from http://www.amanet.org/press/amanews/workplace_dating.htm

60. F. Japlin, "Superior's Upward Influence, Satisfaction, and Openness in Superior-Subordinate Communication: A Reexamination of the 'Pelz Effect'," *Human Communication Research,* 6 (1980): 210–20.

61. Japlin, "Superior's Upward Influence."

62. J. Gabarro and J. Kotter, "Managing Your Boss," *Harvard Business Review,* 58 (1980): 92–100.

63. E. B. Meiners and V. D. Miller, "The Effect of Formality and Relational Tone on Supervisor/Subordinate Negotiation Episodes," *Western Journal of Communication,* 68 (2004): 302–21.

64. D. Katz and R. Kahn, *The Social Psychology of Organizations* (New York: Wiley, 1966).

65. P. M. Sias, "Workplace Relationship Quality and Employee Information Experiences," *Communication Studies,* 56 (2005): 375–96.

66. D. A. Level, Jr., "Communication Effectiveness: Methods and Situation," *Journal of Business Communication,* 10 (Fall 1972): 19–25.

67. Level, "Communication Effectiveness: Methods and Situation."

68. R. W. Pace and D. F. Faules, *Organizational Communication* (Englewood Cliffs, NJ: Prentice Hall, 1994).

69. P. A. Anderson and L. K. Guerrero, "Principles of Communication and Emotion in Social Interaction," in *Handbook of Communication and Emotion,* edited by P. A. Anderson and L. K. Guerrero (San Diego, CA: Academic Press, 1998), 49–96.

70. Anderson and Guerrero, "Principles of Communication and Emotion."

71. L. K. Guerrero, S. M. Jones, and R. R. Boburka, "Sex Differences in Emotional Communication," in *Sex Differences and Similarities in Communication,* 2nd ed., edited by K. Dindia and D. J. Canary (Mahwah, NJ: Erlbaum, 2006), 241–62.

72. Anderson and Guerrero, "Principles of Communication and Emotion."

Photo Credits

Page 1, Henri Matisse, *Conversation,* © 2006 Succession H. Matisse, Paris/Artists Rights Society (ARS), New York; p. 6, © Bob Daemmrich/Stock Boston; p. 7, © Al Bello/Getty Images; p. 20, © Ian Shaw/Getty Images; p. 23, © Catherine Barnow/ Woodfin Camp & Associates; p. 26, © LWA-Dann Tardif/CORBIS; p. 36, Peter Blake, "Self-Portrait with Badges," © 1961. Tate Gallery, London/Art Resource, NY. © 2006 Artists Rights Society (ARS), New York; p. 41, © Tom McCarthy/PhotoEdit; p. 45, © William Stevens; p. 51, © Jim Craigmyle/CORBIS; p. 60, Sandra Rice; p. 67, *The Runaway,* Norman Rockwell. Printed by permission of the Norman Rockwell Family Agency. Copyright © 2006 The Norman Rockwell Family Entities; p. 74, © Peter Hvizdak/The Image Works; p. 75, © Brigid Alliq; p. 79, © Michael Newman/ PhotoEdit; p. 84, © Jon Feingersh/CORBIS; p. 89, © Bob Mahoney/The Image Works; p. 100, © Ilyas Dean/The Image Works; p. 103, © Hideo Haga/HAGA/The Image Works; p. 112, © Gina Minielli/CORBIS; p. 116, © Jerry Lampen/Reuters/ CORBIS; p. 122, Diana Ong, *Parts Equal the Whole I,* © Diana Ong/SuperStock; p. 127, © Dorothy Littell Greco/The Image Works; p. 136, © White Packert/Getty Images; p. 138, © Blend Images/Getty Images; p. 153, © Rachel Epstein/PhotoEdit; p. 155, © Jeff Greenberg/PhotoEdit; p. 164, © Bob Daemmrich/The Image Works; p. 165, © Zac Macaulay/Getty Images; p. 171, © R. Sidney/The Image Works; p. 175, © Walter Hodges/Getty Images; p. 193, © Scala/Art Resource, NY; p. 199, *The Soda Jerk,* Norman Rockwell. Printed by permission of the Norman Rockwell Family Agency. Copyright © 2006 The Norman Rockwell Family Entities; p. 209, © Eyebyte/ Alamy; p. 210, © Nancy Kaszerman/ZUMA/CORBIS; p. 216 bottom, © Bonnie Kamin/PhotoEdit; p. 224, Shooting Star, © All rights reserved; p. 227, © Michael Newman/PhotoEdit; p. 234, © Richard Paley/Stock Boston; p. 244, © James Marshall/ The Image Works; p. 249, © Jeff Smith/Getty Images; p. 256, © Giraudon/Art Resource, NY. © Jean Francois Debord; p. 261, © Tom McCarthy/PhotoEdit; p. 262 left, © Daly & Newton/Getty Images; p. 262 right, © Erik Dreyer/Getty Images; p. 263, © Jeff Greenberg/PhotoEdit; p. 271, © Alvaro Leiva/age fotostock; p. 277, Sandra Rice; p. 283, © Spencer Grant/PhotoEdit; p. 293, Sandra Rice; p. 298, © Don Smetzer/Getty Images; p. 302, © Bob Daemmrich/The Image Works; p. 305, © Image Source/Alamy; p. 310, © PhotoDisc; p. 323, © Robert W. Ginn/PhotoEdit; p. 326, © Myrleen Ferguson Cate/PhotoEdit; p. 329, © Gary Conner/PhotoEdit; p. 331, © Brand X/SuperStock; p. 338, © Donna Day/Getty Images; p. 355, © Bob Daemmrich/The Image Works; p. 357, © John Lei, Jr./Stock Boston; p. 361, *Power Book Girl,* © Christian Pierre/SuperStock; p. 370, © BananaStock/Alamy; p. 372, © Frank Siteman/PhotoEdit.

Glossary

A

accommodation. Conflict management style that involves giving in to the demands of others.

account. Response to a reproach.

acculturation. Process through which an individual acquires new approaches, beliefs, and values by coming into contact with other cultures.

acquiescent responses. Crying, conceding, or apologizing in response to a hurtful message.

action-oriented listener. Listener who prefers information that is well-organized, brief, and error-free.

active listening. Interactive process of responding mentally, verbally, and nonverbally to a speaker's message.

active perception. Perception that occurs because you seek out specific information through intentional observation and questioning.

active verbal responses. Reactive statements made in response to a hurtful message.

adapt. To adjust one's behavior in accord with what someone else does. We can adapt based on the individual, the relationship, and the situation.

adapt predictively. To modify or change behavior in anticipation of an event.

adapt reactively. To modify or change behavior after an event.

adaptability. Family's ability to modify and respond to changes in the family's power structure and roles.

adaptors. Nonverbal behaviors that satisfy a personal need and help a person adapt or respond to the immediate situation.

affect display. Nonverbal behavior that communicates emotions.

affinity-seeking strategies. Strategies for getting other people to like you.

agape. Selfless love based on giving of yourself for others.

aggressive. Expressing one's interests while denying the rights of others by blaming, judging, and evaluating other people.

allness. Tendency to use language to make unqualified, often untrue generalizations.

ambush listener. Person who is overly critical and judgmental when listening to others.

androgynous role. Gender role that includes both masculine and feminine qualities.

apology. Explicit admission of an error, along with a request for forgiveness.

arousal. Feelings of interest and excitement communicated by such nonverbal cues as vocal expression, facial expressions, and gestures.

assertive. Able to pursue one's own best interests without denying a partner's rights.

assertiveness. Tendency to make requests, ask for information, and generally pursue your own rights and best interests.

asynchronous interaction. Process in which messages are not necessarily read, heard, or seen at the time you send them; there may be a time delay between when you send a message and when it is received.

asynchronous listening. Listening to someone's recorded message (on an answering machine, via voicemail, or on a cell phone) without the person being present.

attending. Process of focusing on a particular sound or message.

attitude. Learned predisposition to respond to a person, object, or idea in a favorable or unfavorable way.

attribution theory. Theory that explains how you generate explanations for people's behaviors.

avoidance. Conflict management style that involves backing off and trying to side-step conflict.

B

backchannel cues. Vocal cues that signal your wish to speak or not to speak.

baldfaced lie. Deception by commission involving outright falsification of information intended to deceive the listener.

belief. Way in which you structure your understanding of reality—what is true and what is false for you.

bilateral dissolution. Ending of a relationship by mutual agreement of both parties.

blended family. Two adults and their children. Because of divorce, separation, death, or adoption, the children may be the offspring of other parents, or of just one of the adults who is raising them.

***but* message.** Statement using the word *but* that may communicate that whatever you've said prior to *but* is not really true.

bypassing. Confusion caused by the same words' meaning different things to different people.

C

casual banter. Sub-stage of the acquaintance stage of relationship development, in which impersonal topics are discussed but very limited personal information is shared.

causal attribution theory. Theory of attribution that identifies the cause of a person's actions as circumstance, a stimulus, or the person himself or herself.

causal turning point. Event that brings about a change in a relationship.

channel. Pathway through which messages are sent.

circumplex model of family interaction. Model of the relationships among family adaptability, cohesion, and communication.

closure. Process of filling in missing information or gaps in what we perceive.

coercive power. Power based on the use of sanctions or punishments to influence others.

cohesion. Emotional bonding and feelings of togetherness that families experience.

collaboration. Conflict management style that uses other-oriented strategies to achieve a positive solution for all involved.

communibiological approach. Theoretical perspective that suggests communication behavior can be predicted based on personal traits and characteristics that result from people's genetic or biological background.

communication. Process of acting on information.

communication accommodation theory. Theory that all people adapt their behavior to others to some extent.

communication apprehension. Fear or anxiety associated with either real or anticipated communication with other people.

communication privacy management theory. Theory that suggests that we each manage our own degree of privacy by means of personal boundaries and rules for sharing information.

communication style. Style that is identifiable by habitual ways in which you communicate with other people.

competition. Conflict management style that stresses winning a conflict at the expense of the other person involved.

competitive symmetric relationship. Relationship in which both partners vie for control or dominance of the other.

complementary needs. Needs that match; each partner contributes something to the relationship that the other partner needs.

complementary relationship. Relationship in which power is divided unevenly, with one partner dominating and the other submitting.

compliance gaining. Persuasive actions taken to get others to comply with our goals.

compromise. Conflict management style that attempts to find the middle ground in a conflict.

computer-mediated communication (CMC). Communication between and among people through the medium of computers (includes e-mail, chat rooms, bulletin boards, and newsgroups).

confirming response. Statement that causes another person to value himself or herself more.

conflict style. Consistent pattern or approach you use to manage disagreement with others.

connotative meaning. Personal and subjective meaning of a word.

construct. Bipolar quality used to classify people.

constructive conflict. Conflict that helps build new insights and establishes new patterns in a relationship.

content. Information, ideas, or suggested actions that a speaker wishes to share.

content-oriented listener. Listener who is more comfortable listening to complex, detailed information than are those with other listening styles.

context. Physical and psychological environment for communication.

conversational narcissism. Focus on personal agendas and self-absorption rather than a focus on the needs and ideas of others.

critical listening. Listening to evaluate and assess the quality, appropriateness, value, or importance of information.

cues-filtered-out theory. Theory that suggests that communication of emotions is restricted when people send messages to others via e-mail because nonverbal cues such as facial expression and tone of voice are filtered out.

cultural context. Information not explicitly communicated through language but through environmental or nonverbal cues.

cultural elements. Categories of things and ideas that identify the most profound aspects of cultural influence (such as schools, governments, music, theater, language).

cultural values. What a given group of people values or appreciates.

culture. Learned system of knowledge, behavior, attitudes, beliefs, values, and norms that is shared by a group of people.

culture shock. Feelings of stress and anxiety a person experiences when encountering a culture different from his or her own.

cumulative rewards and costs. Total rewards and costs accrued during a relationship.

D

deception by commission. Deliberate presentation of false information.

deception by omission (concealment). Intentionally holding back some of the information another person has requested or that you are expected to share.

decode. To interpret ideas, feelings, and thoughts that have been translated into a code.

demand-withdrawal pattern of conflict management. Pattern in which one person makes a demand and the other person avoids conflict by changing the subject or walking away.

denotative meaning. Restrictive or literal meaning of a word.

dependent relationship. Relationship in which one partner has a greater need for the other to meet his or her needs.

destructive conflict. Conflict that dismantles rather than strengthens relationships.

dialectical theory. Theory that relational development occurs in conjunction with various tensions that exist in all relationships, particularly connectedness versus autonomy, predictability versus novelty, and openness versus closedness.

direct perception checking. Asking for confirmation from the observed person of an interpretation or a perception about him or her.

direct termination strategies. Explicit statements of a desire to break up a relationship.

disconfirming response. Statement that causes another person to value himself or herself less.

discrimination. Unfair or inappropriate treatment of people based on their group membership.

dominance. Power, status, and control communicated by such nonverbal cues as a relaxed posture, greater personal space, and protected personal space.

downward communication. Communication that flows from superiors to subordinates.

dyadic effect. The reciprocal nature of self-disclosure: "You disclose to me, and I'll disclose to you."

dyadic phase. Second phase in relationship termination, when the individual discusses termination with the partner.

E

ego conflict. Conflict in which the original issue is ignored as partners attack each other's self-esteem.

egocentric communicator. Person who creates messages without giving much thought to the person who is listening; a communicator who is self-focused and self-absorbed.

elaborated code. Conversation that uses many words and various ways of describing an idea or concept to communicate its meaning.

emblems. Nonverbal cues that have specific, generally understood meanings in a given culture and may substitute for a word or phrase.

emotional contagion theory. Theory that emotional expression is contagious; people can "catch" emotions just by observing others' emotional expressions.

emotional noise. Form of communication interference caused by emotional arousal.

emotional response theory. Theory that suggests any human emotion experienced can be interpreted along three dimensions: (1) pleasure–displeasure, (2) arousal–nonarousal, and (3) dominance–submissiveness. Our emotional response to what we experience helps determine whether we ultimately approach or avoid what we are experiencing.

empathy. Emotional reaction that is similar to the reaction being experienced by another person; empathizing is feeling what another person is feeling.

encode. To translate ideas, feelings, and thoughts into a code.

enculturation. Process of communicating a group's culture from generation to generation.

episode. Sequence of interactions between individuals, during which the message of one person influences the message of another.

eros. Sexual, erotic love based on the pursuit of physical beauty and pleasure.

ethics. Beliefs, values, and moral principles by which people determine what is right or wrong.

ethnicity. Social classification based on nationality, religion, language, and ancestral heritage, shared by a group of people who also share a common geographical origin.

ethnocentrism. Belief that your cultural traditions and assumptions are superior to those of others.

exaggeration. Deception by commission involving "stretching the truth" or embellishing the facts.

expectancy violation theory. Theory that you interpret the messages of others based on how you expect others to behave.

expected rewards and costs. Expectation of how much reward we should get from a given relationship in comparison to its costs.

expert power. Power based on a person's knowledge and experience.

expressive conflict. Conflict that focuses on issues about the quality of the relationship and managing interpersonal tension and hostility.

extended family. Relatives such as aunts, uncles, cousins, or grandparents and/or unrelated persons who are part of a family unit.

extended *I* language. Brief preface to a feedback statement, intended to communicate that you don't want your listener to take your message in an overly critical way.

F

face. Person's positive perception of himself or herself that he or she seeks to maintain through communication with others.

facework. Using communication to maintain your own positive self-perception (self-face) or to support, reinforce, or challenge someone else's self-perception (other-face).

fact. Something that has been directly observed to be true and thus has been proven to be true.

fading away. Ending a relationship by slowly drifting apart.

failure events. Violations of understandings between people in relationships.

family. Self-defined unit made up of any number of persons who live or have lived in relationship with one another over time in a common living space and who are usually, but not always, united by marriage and kinship.

family of origin. Family in which a person is raised.

feedback. Response to a message.

feminine culture. Culture that emphasizes relationships, caring for the less fortunate, and overall quality of life.

filtering. Process of reducing partners moving to each stage by applying selection criteria.

flaming. Sending an overly negative online message that personally attacks another person.

forecasted rewards and costs. Rewards and costs that an individual assumes will occur, based on projection and prediction.

fundamental attribution error. Error that arises from attributing another person's behavior to internal, controllable causes rather than to external, uncontrollable causes.

G

gender. Socially learned and reinforced characteristics that include one's biological sex and psychological characteristics (femininity, masculinity, androgyny).

generalized-other perspective. Perspective that uses observed or imagined information about many people, or people in general, to predict a person's behavior.

globalization. The integration of economics and technology that is contributing to a worldwide, interconnected business environment.

grave-dressing phase. Final phase in relationship termination, when the partners generate public explanations and move past the relationship.

gunny-sacking. Dredging up old problems and issues from the past to use against your partner.

H

halo effect. Attributing a variety of positive qualities to those you like.

hearing. Physiological process of decoding sounds.

high-context culture. Culture that derives much information from nonverbal and environmental cues.

horizontal communication. Communication among colleagues or co-workers at the same level within an organization.

horn effect. Attributing a variety of negative qualities to those you dislike.

hostile environment. Type of sexual harassment in which an employee's rights are threatened through offensive working conditions or behavior on the part of other workers.

human communication. Process of making sense out of the world and sharing that sense with others by creating meaning through the use of verbal and nonverbal messages.

hyperpersonal communication. A certain type of interpersonal communication that is facilitated by using a computer to establish relationships with others.

hyperpersonal relationships. Relationships formed primarily through CMC that became more personal than equivalent FtF relationships.

I

***I* language.** Statements that begin with the word *I* to express how a speaker is feeling.

illustrators. Nonverbal behaviors that accompany a verbal message and either contradict, accent, or complement it.

immediacy. Feelings of liking, pleasure, and closeness communicated by such nonverbal cues as increased eye contact, forward lean, touch, and open body orientation.

immediate rewards and costs. Rewards and costs that are associated with a relationship at the present moment.

impersonal communication. Process that occurs when we treat others as objects or respond to their roles rather than to who they are as unique persons.

implicit personality theory. Your unique set of beliefs and hypotheses about what people are like.

impression. Collection of perceptions about others that you maintain and use to interpret their behaviors.

impression formation theory. Theory that explains how you develop perceptions about people and how you maintain and use those perceptions to interpret their behaviors.

incrementalism. Systematic progression of a relationship through each of the de-escalation stages.

independent couples. Married partners who exhibit sharing and companionship and are psychologically interdependent but allow each other individual space.

indexing. Avoiding generalizations by using statements that separate one situation, person, or example from another.

indirect perception checking. Seeking additional information to confirm or refute interpretations you are making through passive perception such as observing and listening.

indirect termination strategies. Attempts to break up a relationship without explicitly stating the desire to do so.

inference. Conclusion based on speculation.

information triage. Process of evaluating information to sort good information from less useful or valid information.

in-group. One's racial or ethnic group.

instrumental conflict. Conflict that centers on achieving a particular goal or task and less on relational issues.

interaction adaptation theory. Theory suggesting that people interact with others by adapting to their communication behaviors.

interactional synchrony. Mirroring of each other's nonverbal behavior by communication partners.

intercultural communication. Communication between or among people who have different cultural traditions.

intercultural communication competence. Ability to adapt one's behavior toward another in ways that are appropriate to the other person's culture.

interdependent. Dependent on each other; one person's actions affect the other person.

interdependent relationship. Relationship in which each person has a similar amount of power over the other.

interpersonal attraction. Degree to which you want to form or maintain an interpersonal relationship.

interpersonal communication. A distinctive, transactional form of human communication involving mutual influence, usually for the purpose of managing relationships.

interpersonal conflict. Expressed struggle that occurs when people cannot agree on a way to meet their needs or goals.

interpersonal intimacy. Degree to which relational partners mutually accept and confirm each other's sense of self.

interpersonal perception. Process of selecting, organizing, and interpreting your observations of other people.

interpersonal power. Degree to which a person is able to influence his or her partner.

interpersonal relationship. Perception shared by two people of an ongoing connection that results in the development of relational expectations and varies in interpersonal intimacy.

intimate space. Zone of space most often used for very personal or intimate interactions, ranging from 0 to 1½ feet from the individual.

intrapersonal communication. Communication with yourself; thinking or self-talk.

intrapsychic phase. First phase in relationship termination, when an individual engages in an internal evaluation of the partner.

introductions. Sub-stage of the acquaintance stage of relationship development, in which interaction is routine, and basic information is shared.

invulnerable responses. Ignoring, laughing, or being silent in response to a hurtful message.

J

jargon. Another name for restricted code; specialized terms or abbreviations whose meanings are known only to members of a specific group.

jealousy. A reaction to the threat of losing a valued relationship.

Johari Window model. Model of self-disclosure that summarizes how self-awareness is influenced by self-disclosure and information about yourself from others.

K

kinesics. Study of human movement and gesture.

L

legitimate power. Power that is based on respect for a person's position.

life position. Feelings of regard for yourself and others, as reflected in your sense of worth and self-esteem.

linguistic determinism. Theory that describes how use of language determines or influences thoughts and perceptions.

linguistic relativity. Theory that each language includes some unique features that are not found in other languages.

listening. Process of selecting, attending to, creating meaning from, remembering, and responding to verbal and nonverbal messages.

listening style. Preferred way of making sense out of spoken messages.

long-term maintenance attraction. Degree of liking or positive feelings that motivate us to maintain or escalate a relationship.

looking-glass self. Concept that suggests you learn who you are based on your interactions with others, who reflect your self back to you.

low-context culture. Culture that derives much information from the words of a message and less information from nonverbal and environmental cues.

ludis. Game-playing love based on the enjoyment of another.

M

malapropism. Confusion of one word or phrase for another that sounds similar to it.

mania. Obsessive love driven by mutual needs.

masculine culture. Culture that emphasizes achievement, assertiveness, heroism, and material wealth.

mass communication. Process that occurs when one person issues the same message to many people at once; the creator of the message is usually not physically present, and there is virtually no opportunity for listeners to respond immediately to the speaker.

material self. Concept of self as reflected in a total of all the tangible things you own.

media richness theory. Theory that identifies the richness of a communication medium based on the amount of information, including emotional expression, it communicates.

mediated interpersonal communication. Communication with others established or maintained through media (such as e-mail, telephones, or faxes) rather than through face-to-face encounters.

message. Written, spoken, and unspoken elements of communication to which people assign meaning.

metacommunication. Verbal or nonverbal communication about communication.

meta-message. A message about a message; the message a person is expressing via nonverbal means (such as by facial expression, eye contact, and posture) about the message articulated with words.

mindful. Conscious of what you are doing, thinking, and sensing at any given moment; aware of cultural differences and the connection between thoughts and deeds in one's interactions with someone from a background different from one's own.

mixed couples. Married couples in which the husband and wife each adopt a different perspective (traditional, independent, separate) on the marriage.

motivation. Internal state of readiness to respond to something.

N

natural family. Mother, father, and their biological children.

need for affection. Interpersonal need to give and receive love, support, warmth, and intimacy.

need for control. Interpersonal need for some degree of influence in our relationships, as well as the need to be controlled.

need for inclusion. Interpersonal need to be included and to include others in social activities.

noise. Anything literal or psychological that interferes with accurate reception of a message.

nonverbal communication. Behavior other than written or spoken language that creates meaning for someone.

O

objective self-awareness. Ability to be the object of one's own thoughts and attention—to be aware of one's state of mind and that one is thinking.

obsessive relational intrusion (ORI). Repeated invasion of a person's privacy by a stranger or acquaintance who desires or assumes a close relationship.

other-oriented communicator. One who considers the thoughts, feelings, and perspectives of communication partners while maintaining his or her own integrity.

out-group. A race, culture, religion, or ethnic group different from one's own.

outward communication. Communication that flows to those outside an organization (such as customers).

P

parallel relationship. Relationship in which power shifts back and forth between the partners, depending on the situation.

paraphrase. Verbal summary of the key ideas of your partner's message that helps you check the accuracy of your understanding.

passive perception. Perception that occurs without conscious effort, but simply because your senses are in operation.

people-oriented listener. Listener who is comfortable with and skilled at listening to people's feelings and emotions.

perception. Process of experiencing the world and making sense out of what you experience.

perception checking. Asking someone whether your interpretation of his or her nonverbal behavior is accurate.

personal space. Zone of space most often used for conversations with family and friends, ranging from 1½ to 4 feet from the individual.

personality. Set of enduring internal predispositions and behavioral characteristics that describe how people react to their environment.

physical appearance. Nonverbal cues that allow us to assess relationship potential (POV).

polarization. Description and evaluation of what you observe in terms of extremes such as good or bad, old or new, beautiful or ugly.

post-intimacy relationship. Formerly intimate relationship that is maintained at a less intimate stage.

pragma. Practical love based on mutual benefits.

predicted outcome value (POV). Potential for a relationship to confirm our self-image compared to its potential costs.

prejudice. A judgment or opinion of someone formed before you know all of the facts or the background of that person.

primacy effect. Tendency to attend to the first pieces of information observed about another person in order to form an impression.

proxemics. Study of how close or far away from people and objects people position themselves.

proximity. Physical nearness to another that promotes communication and thus attraction.

pseudoconflict. Conflict triggered by a lack of understanding and miscommunication.

psychology. Study of how thinking influences behavior.

public communication. Process that occurs when a speaker addresses an audience in person.

public space. Zone of space most often used by public speakers or anyone speaking to many people, ranging beyond 12 feet from the individual.

punctuation. Process of making sense out of stimuli by grouping, dividing, organizing, separating, and categorizing information.

Q

quid pro quo. Latin phrase that can be used to describe a type of sexual harassment. The phrase roughly means "You do something for me and I'll do something for you."

R

race. Genetically transmitted physical characteristics of a group of people.

receiver. Person who decodes a message and attempts to make sense of what the source has encoded.

recency effect. Tendency to attend to the most recent information observed about another person in order to form or modify an impression.

reciprocation of liking. Liking those who like us.

referent. Thing that a symbol represents.

referent power. Power that comes from our attraction to another person, or the charisma a person possesses.

reflective turning point. Event that signals that a change has occurred in the way a relationship is defined.

reframing. Process of redefining events and experiences from a different point of view.

regulators. Nonverbal messages that help to control the interaction or flow of communication between two people.

relational de-escalation. Movement of a relationship away from intimacy through five stages: turmoil or stagnation, deintensification, individualization, separation, and post-separation.

relational development. Movement of a relationship from one stage to another, either toward or away from greater intimacy.

relational empathy. Essence of a relationship that permits varying degrees of understanding, rather than requiring complete comprehension of another's culture or emotions.

relational escalation. Movement of a relationship toward intimacy through five stages: preinteraction awareness, acquaintance, exploration, intensification, and intimacy.

relational violence. Range of destructive behaviors aimed at other people, including aggressiveness, threats, violent acts, and verbal, psychological, or physical abuse.

relationship. Connection established with another person through communication.

relationship dimension. The implied aspect of a communication message, which conveys information about emotions, attitudes, power, and control.

relationship of choice. Interpersonal relationship you choose to initiate, maintain, and, perhaps, terminate.

relationship of circumstance. Interpersonal relationship that exists because of life circumstances (who your family members are, where you work or study, and so on).

relationship talk. Talk about the nature, quality, direction, or definition of a relationship.

remembering. Process of recalling information.

reproach. Message that a failure event has occurred.

responding. Process of confirming your understanding of a message.

responsiveness. Tendency to be sensitive to the needs of others, including being sympathetic to others' feelings and placing the feelings of others above your own feelings.

restricted code. Set of words that have particular meaning to a person, group, or culture.

reward power. Power based on a person's ability to satisfy our needs.

rule. Followable prescription that indicates what behavior is obligated, preferred, or prohibited in certain contexts.

S

Sapir–Whorf hypothesis. Based on the principles of linguistic determinism and linguistic relativity, the hypothesis that language shapes our thoughts and culture, and our culture and thoughts affect the language we use to describe our world.

second-guessing. Questioning the ideas and assumptions underlying a message; assessing whether the message is true or false.

selecting. Process of choosing one sound while sorting through various sounds competing for your attention.

selective attention. Process of focusing on specific stimuli, locking on to some things in the environment and ignoring others.

selective exposure. Tendency to put ourselves in situations that reinforce our attitudes, beliefs, values, or behaviors.

selective perception. Process of seeing, hearing, or making sense of the world around us based on such factors as our personality, beliefs, attitudes, hopes, fears, and culture, as well as what we like and don't like.

selective recall. Process that occurs when we remember things we want to remember and forget or repress things that are unpleasant, uncomfortable, or unimportant to us.

self. Sum total of who a person is; a person's central inner force.

self-awareness. Person's conscious understanding of who he or she is.

self-concept. Person's subjective description of who he or she is.

self-disclosure. Purposefully providing information about yourself to others that they would not learn if you did not tell them.

self-fulfilling prophecy. Prediction about future actions that is likely to come true because the person believes that it will come true.

self-reflexiveness. Ability to think about what you are doing while you are doing it.

self-serving bias. Tendency to perceive our own behavior as more positive than others' behavior.

self-worth (self-esteem). Your evaluation of your worth or value based on your perception of such things as your skills, abilities, talents, and appearance.

separate couples. Married partners who support the notion of marriage and family but stress the individual over the couple.

short-term initial attraction. Degree to which you sense a potential for developing an interpersonal relationship.

shyness. Behavioral tendency not to talk or interact with other people.

similarity. Having comparable personalities, values, upbringing, personal experiences, attitudes, and interests.

simple conflict. Conflict that stems from different ideas, definitions, perceptions, or goals.

single-parent family. One parent raising one or more children.

skill. Behavior that improves the effectiveness or quality of communication with others.

small group communication. Process that occurs when a group of from three to fifteen people meet to interact with a common purpose and mutually influence one another.

social comparison. Process of comparing yourself to others who are similar to you to measure your worth and value.

social decentering. Cognitive process in which you take into account another person's thoughts, feelings, values, background, and perspective.

social exchange theory. Theory that claims people make relationship decisions by assessing and comparing the costs and rewards.

social information-processing theory. Theory that suggests people can communicate relational and emotional messages via the Internet, although such messages take longer to express without nonverbal cues.

social learning theory. Theory of human behavior that suggests we can learn how to adapt and adjust our behavior toward others; how we behave is not solely dependent on our genetic or biological makeup.

social penetration model. Model of self-disclosure and relational development that reflects both depth and breadth of shared information.

social phase. Third phase in relationship termination, when members of the social network around both parties are informed of and become involved in the termination process.

social or psychological co-presence. State of mind that occurs during computer-mediated interactions or text messaging, in which partners think and act as though they were face to face.

social self. Concept of self as reflected in social interactions with others.

social space. Zone of space most often used for group interactions, ranging from 4 to 12 feet from the individual.

social support. Expression of empathy and concern for others that is communicated while listening to them and offering positive, sincere, supportive messages, both verbal and nonverbal.

source. Originator of a thought or emotion, who puts it into a code that can be understood by a receiver.

specific-other perspective. Perspective that uses information that one can observe or imagine about another person to predict that person's behavior.

spiritual self. Concept of self based on thoughts and introspections about personal values, moral standards, and beliefs.

stalking. Repeated, unwelcome intrusions that create concern for personal safety and fear in the target.

standpoint theory. Theory that a person's social position, power, or cultural background influences how the person perceives the behavior of others.

static evaluation. Pronouncement that does not take the possibility of change into consideration.

stereotype. To attribute a set of qualities to a person because of the person's membership in some category; to place a person or group of persons into an inflexible, all-encompassing category.

storge. Solid love found in friendships and family, based on trust and caring.

sub-culture. A microculture; a distinct culture within a larger culture (such as the gay and lesbian sub-culture).

subjective self-awareness. Ability to differentiate the self from the social and physical environment.

submissive symmetric relationship. Relationship in which neither partner wants to take control or make decisions.

sudden death. Abrupt and unplanned ending of a relationship.

superimpose. To place a familiar structure on information you select.

symbol. Word, sound, or visual image that represents something else, such as a thought, concept, or object.

symbolic interaction theory. Theory that people make sense of the world on the basis of their interactions with other people and that members of a society are bound together through common use of symbols.

symbolic self-awareness. Uniquely human ability to think about oneself and use language (symbols) to represent oneself to others.

symmetric relationship. Relationship in which both partners attempt to have the same level of power.

sympathy. Acknowledgment that someone may be feeling bad; compassion toward someone or offer of support.

synchronous interaction. Interaction in which participants are actively engaging at the same time.

systems theory. Theory that describes the interconnected elements of a system in which a change in one element affects all of the other elements.

T

talk therapy. Technique in which a person describes his or her problems and concerns to a skilled listener in order to better understand the emotions and issues that are creating the problems.

territorial markers. Tangible objects that are used to signify that someone has claimed an area or space.

territoriality. Study of how animals and humans use space and objects to communicate occupancy or ownership of space.

thin slicing. Observing a small sample of someone's behavior and then making a generalization about what the person is like, based on the sample.

third culture. Common ground established when people from separate cultures create a third, "new," more comprehensive and inclusive culture.

thought. Mental process of creating an image, sound, concept, or experience triggered by a referent or symbol.

time-oriented listener. Listener who likes messages delivered succinctly.

traditional couples. Married partners who are interdependent and who exhibit a lot of sharing and companionship.

triangular theory of love. Theory that suggests that all loving relationships can be described according to three dimensions: intimacy, commitment, and passion.

turning point. Specific event or interaction associated with positive or negative changes in a relationship.

U

uncertainty reduction theory. Theory that claims people seek information in order to reduce uncertainty, thus providing control and predictability.

understanding. Process of assigning meaning to sounds.

unilateral dissolution. Ending of a relationship by one partner, even though the other partner wants it to continue.

upward communication. Communication that flows from subordinates to superiors.

V

value. Enduring concept of good and bad, right and wrong.

visualization. Technique of imagining that you are performing a particular task in a certain way; positive visualization can enhance self-esteem.

W

white lie. Deception by commission involving only a slight degree of falsification that has a minimal consequence.

willingness to communicate. General term for the likelihood that an individual will communicate with others in certain situations.

word picture. Short statement or story that illustrates or describes an emotion; word pictures often use a simile (a comparison using the word *like* or *as*) to clarify the image.

world view. Individual perceptions or perceptions by a culture or group of people about key beliefs and issues, such as death, God, and the meaning of life, which influence interaction with others; culturally acquired perspective for interpreting experiences.

Index